—————— >>> <<< ——————

READINGS
IN
ARGUMENT

Jeanne Fahnestock
University of Maryland

Marie Secor
Pennsylvania State University

RANDOM HOUSE   NEW YORK

—————— >>> <<< ——————

Library of Congress Cataloging in Publication Data
Main entry under title:

Readings in argument.

1. College readers.   2. English language—Rhetoric.
I. Fahnestock, Jeanne, 1945–   II. Secor, Marie,
1939–   III. Title.
PE1417.R424 1985   808'.0427   85-11843
ISBN 0-394-33155-9

Manufactured in the United States of America

Cover credit: *Metaphor and Movement* by Robert Motherwell, 1974. Albright-Knox Art Gallery, Buffalo, New York; George B. and Jenny R. Mathews Fund, 1977.

PERMISSIONS ACKNOWLEDGMENTS

JAY AMBERG, "The SAT." Reprinted from *The American Scholar*, Volume 51, Number 4, Autumn, 1982. Copyright © 1982 by the United Chapters of Phi Beta Kappa. By permission of the publishers.

ARISTIDES, "What Is Vulgar?" Reprinted from *The American Scholar*, Volume 51, Number 1, Winter, 1981–82. Copyright © 1981 by the United Chapters of Phi Beta Kappa. By permission of the publishers.

DOUG BANDOW, "A Draft Isn't Needed." Copyright © 1982 by The New York Times Company. Reprinted by permission.

EDWARD C. BANFIELD, excerpt from *The Democratic Muse: Visual Arts and the Public Interest*, a Twentieth Century Fund Essay, © 1984, Twentieth Century Fund, New York. Reprinted by permission.

ROBERT K. BASTIAN and JAY BENFORADO, "Waste Treatment: Doing What Comes Naturally." From *Technology Review*, February/March 1983. Reprinted by permission of *Technology Review*, copyright 1983.

CAMILLA PERSSON BENBOW and JULIAN STANLEY, "Sex Differences in Mathematical Ability: Fact or Artifact?" From *Science*, Volume 210, December 12, 1980, pp.

PREFACE

We offer this book in the hope that it will help restore the study of argument to the teaching of writing at all levels. It contains essays ranging in time from the eighteenth to the twentieth century, in author from the immediately recognizable to the unknown, in subject from the familiar to the exotic, and in style from the popular to the technical. But no matter their diversity, the essays have been grouped to correspond to the types of argument explained in our earlier text, *A Rhetoric of Argument* (Random House, 1982) and have been selected to represent different fields of study. We have also tried to make *Readings in Argument* a complete and independent book by prefacing each section with detailed explanations of the type of argument illustrated. And we have still focused, as in our rhetoric, on the construction rather than the criticism of arguments by pointing out the tactics that actual arguers have used, and by following each piece with very specific suggestions for writing. Thus by itself, this reader could shape a course in argument. Teamed with a rhetoric, whether our own or another, the essays we have chosen illustrate the centrality of argument to all disciplines.

We took great pleasure and learned a great deal in gathering the selections for this book. We are therefore pleased to acknowledge those who encouraged us to create the kind of reader we envisioned. In particular we wish to thank Richard L. Larson of Herbert H. Lehman College, City University of New York; Lester Faigley of the University of Texas at Austin; Karen Burke LeFevre of Rensselaer Polytechnic Institute; Jeanette P. Morgan of the University of Houston; William E. Smith of Utah State University; Thomas H. Miles of West Virginia University; and Carol J. Singley from Brown University.

The intricate task of preparing such an anthology has been handled with their usual professionalism by the staff at Random House. We wish to express our special gratitude to Anna Marie Muskelly, our project editor, Elisa Turner, development editor, and Cynthia Ward and Steve Pensinger, whose editorial support and guidance we have depended on. And as usual we would like to thank our families for their patience, especially for putting up with our arguing over arguments and our scavenging and mutilating every periodical that came within our grasp.

CONTENTS

PART I ARGUMENTS ABOUT THE NATURE OF
THINGS 1

"Panthers Wanted—Alive, Back East Where They Belong,"– by Michael
Frome– (Science and Technology) 7
"To Get a Story, 'I Flimflammed a Dead Man's Mother,' "– by Bob
Teague– (Social Science) 15
"The Blow that Hurts,"– by Gene Tunney– (Social Science) 22
"Birds Do It, Bats Do It, But the Issue Is, Who Does It Better?"– by
Mark Zieman– (Business) 28
"Longfellow vs. Shortfellow,"– by Robert Schadewald– (Humanities and
Science and Technology) 33
"The Strange Death of Silas Deane,"– by James West Davidson and Mark
Hamilton Lytle– (History and Politics) 38
"Genesis vs. Geology,"– by Stephen Jay Gould– (Science and Technology)
55
"The Rage to Know,"– by Horace Freeland Judson– (Science and
Technology and Humanities) 65
"What Is Vulgar?"– by Aristides– (Humanities) 77
"The Route to Normal Science,"– by Thomas S. Kuhn– (Science and
Technology) 89
"Kratylus Automates his Urnworks,"– by Tolly Kizilos–
(Business) 101

PART II ARGUMENTS ABOUT CAUSES 115

"Johnny Wants to Read,"– by Bruno Bettelheim– (Social Science) 123
"Can the Japanese Keep It Up?"– by Richard D. Robinson– (Business)
130
"Identical Twins Reared Apart,"– by Constance Holden– (Science and
Technology) 142
"Outbreak" and "August 1: Berlin,"– by Barbara Tuchman– (History and
Politics) 152
"Parkinson's Law,"– by C. Northcote Parkinson– (Business) 165
"Politics and the English Language,"– by George Orwell– (History and
Politics) 173
"Iridium Provides Clue to Dinosaurs' Extinction,"– by Rebecca Rawls–
(Science and Technology) 187
"How Women's Diets Reflect Fear of Power,"– by Kim Chernin– (Social
Science) 195

"The Prognosis for this Patient Is Horrible,"– by Berton Roueché–
(Science and Technology)   206

"Why We Live in the Musical Past,"– by Edward Rothstein–
(Humanities)   220

"The Politics of Crime,"– by Richard Neely– (History and Politics; Social
Science)   229

"Dreams of the Death of Persons of Whom the Dreamer Is Fond,"– by
Sigmund Freud– (Science and Technology; Social Science)   240

PART III   ARGUMENTS THAT EVALUATE   259

"The Greatness of Albert Einstein,"– by Bertrand Russell– (Science and
Technology)   265

"The Injustice of the Death Penalty,"– by Neal Devins and Roy Brasfield
Herron– (History and Politics; Social Science)   270

"A Draft Isn't Needed,"– by Doug Bandow– (History and
Politics)   274

"Minor Art Offers Special Pleasure,"– by Eva Hoffman– (Humanities)
278

"A Plea for a Corporate Conscience"– by Judge Miles W. Lord–
(Business)   284

"Above All the Man had Character,"– by Hugh Sidey– (History and
Politics)   289

"The Wisdom of Common Sense,"– by Mary Giegengack Jureller– (Social
Science)   296

"One for the Books,"– by Thomas Bender– (Social Science)   302

"The Truth About Girl Scouts,"– by Rachel Flick– (Social
Science)   306

"Is Eakins Our Greatest Painter?"– by John Russell–
(Humanities)   320

"Good Managers Don't Make Policy Decisions,"– by H. Edward Wrapp–
(Business)   325

"From Bauhaus to Our House,"– by Tom Wolfe–
(Humanities)   341

"The Last Bears of Yellowstone,"– by Alston Chase– (History and Politics;
Social Science)   350

"Paternalistic Lies,"– by Sisela Bok– (Social Science)   371

PART IV   ARGUMENTS THAT PROPOSE ACTION   385

"A Proposal to Abolish Grading,"– by Paul Goodman– (Social Science)
390

"The One-Term Presidency,"– by Edward Morris– (History and Politics)
395

"How to Fix the Premedical Curriculum,"– by Lewis Thomas– (Social
Science; Science and Technology)   401

"Trauma in Detroit,"– by Harley Shaiken– (Business and Economics)
405

"Letter to a Store President,"– by Marilyn Gordner– (Social Science;
Business and Economics)   411

"Rest in Pieces,"– by David Owen– (Social Science)   416

"Art versus Collectibles: Why Museums Should Be Filled With Fakes,"–
by Edward C. Banfield– (Humanities)   428

"Beyond the Wasteland: What American TV Can Learn From The
BBC,"– by Martin Esslin– (Humanities; Social
Science)   440

"Waste Treatment: Doing What Comes Naturally,"– by Robert K.
Bastian and Jay Benforado– (Science and Technology)   450

"A Modest Proposal,"– by Jonathan Swift– (History and Politics)   464

"Computer Literacy,"– by John Kemeny– (Science and
Technology)   473

"Habit,"– by William James– (Social Science)   494

PART V   ARGUMENTS AND REFUTATIONS   505

"Why the West Should Let Japanese Eat Whale,"– by Osamu Nakashima
512

"On Eating Whale,"– Responses to Osamu Nakashima   513

"In Defense of Pac-Man,"– by Dennis Meacham   519

"Et in Arcadia Video,"– by Margaret Logan   521

"The SAT,"– by Jay Amberg   525

"1983: The Last Days of the ETS,"– by David Owen   538

"Math and Sex: Are Girls Born With Less Ability?"– by Gina Bari Kolata
574

"Sex Differences in Mathematical Ability: Fact or Artifact?"– by Camilla
Persson Benbow and Julian C. Stanley   577

"Mathematical Ability: Is Sex a Factor?"– Letters responding to
Benbow, Stanley, and Kolata and a rebuttal from Benbow and Stanley
583

"Public Statement by Eight Alabama Clergymen: April 12, 1963,"– by
C.C.J. Carpenter et al.   595

"Letter from Birmingham Jail,"– by Martin Luther King, Jr.   597

"I Refute It Thus,"– by Samuel Florman   614

"A Close Look at the Unicorn,"– by John Ciardi   632

"The Reviewer's Duty to Damn: Letter to an Avalanche,"– by John Ciardi
637

"The Declaration of Independence,"– by Thomas Jefferson   646

"Declaration of Sentiments and Resolutions: Seneca Falls Convention, 1848,"– by Elizabeth Cady Stanton   649

——————————— →» «← ———————————

CONTENTS ACCORDING TO SUBJECT

ARGUMENTS ABOUT SCIENCE AND TECHNOLOGY

"Panthers Wanted—Alive, Back East Where They Belong,"– by Michael Frome   7
"Longfellow vs. Shortfellow,"– by Robert Schadewald   33
"Genesis vs. Geology,"– by Stephen Jay Gould   55
"The Rage to Know,"– by Horace Freeland Judson   65
"The Route to Normal Science,"– by Thomas S. Kuhn   89
"Identical Twins Reared Apart,"– by Constance Holden   142
"Iridium Provides Clue to Dinosaurs' Extinction,"– by Rebecca Rawls   187
"The Prognosis for this Patient is Horrible,"– by Berton Roueché   206
"Dreams of the Death of Persons of Whom the Dreamer Is Fond,"– by Sigmund Freud   240
"The Greatness of Albert Einstein,"– by Bertrand Russell   265
"How to Fix the Premedical Curriculum,"– by Lewis Thomas   401
"Waste Treatment: Doing What Comes Naturally,"– by Robert K. Bastian and Jay Benforado   450
"Computer Literacy,"– by John Kemeny   473
"In Defense of Pac-Man,"– by Dennis Meacham   519
"Et in Arcadia Video,"– by Margaret Logan
"Math and Sex: Are Girls Born with Less Ability?"– by Gina Bari Kolata   574
"Sex Differences in Mathematical Ability: Fact or Artifact?"– by Camilla Persson Benbow and Julian C. Stanley   577
"Mathematical Ability: Is Sex a Factor?"– responses to Benbow and Stanley   583
"I Refute It Thus,"– by Samuel Florman   614

ARGUMENTS ABOUT HISTORY AND POLITICS

"The Strange Death of Silas Deane,"– by James West Davidson and Mark Hamilton Lytle   38
"Outbreak" and "August 1: Berlin,"– by Barbara Tuchman   152
"Politics and the English Language,"– by George Orwell   173
"The Politics of Crime,"– by Richard Neely   229

"The Injustice of the Death Penalty,"– by Neal Devins and Roy Brasfield   270

"A Draft Isn't Needed,"– by Doug Bandow   274

"Above All the Man Had Character,"– by Hugh Sidey   289

"One for the Books,"– by Thomas Bender   302

"The Last Bears of Yellowstone,"– by Alston Chase   350

"The One-Term Presidency,"– by Edward Morris   395

"A Modest Proposal,"– by Jonathan Swift   464

"Public Statement by Eight Alabama Clergymen:– April 12, 1963"   595

"Letter from Birmingham Jail,"– by Martin Luther King, Jr.   597

"The Declaration of Independence,"– by Thomas Jefferson   646

"Declaration of Sentiments and Resolutions: Seneca Falls Convention, 1848,"
– by Elizabeth Cady Stanton   649

ARGUMENTS ABOUT EDUCATION AND THE SOCIAL SCIENCES

"To Get a Story, 'I Flimflammed a Dead Man's Mother,' "– by Bob Teague   15

"The Blow that Hurts,"– by Gene Tunney   22

"Johnny Wants to Read,"– by Bruno Bettelheim   123

"How Women's Diets Reflect Fear of Power,"– by Kim Chernin   195

"The Politics of Crime,"– by Richard Neely   229

"Dreams of the Death of Persons of Whom the Dreamer Is Fond,"– by Sigmund Freud   240

"The Injustice of the Death Penalty,"– by Neal Devins and Roy Brasfield   270

"The Wisdom of Common Sense,"– by Mary Giegengack Jureller   296

"One for the Books,"– by Thomas Bender   302

"The Truth About Girl Scouts,"– by Rachel Flick   306

"The Last Bears of Yellowstone,"– by Alston Chase   350

"Paternalistic Lies,"– by Sissela Bok   371

"A Proposal to Abolish Grading,"– by Paul Goodman   390

"How to Fix the Premedical Curriculum,"– by Lewis Thomas   401

"Letter to a Store President,"– by Marilyn Gardner   411

"Rest in Pieces,"– by David Owen   416

"Beyond the Wasteland,"– by Martin Esslin   440

"Habit,"– by William James   494

"Why the West Should Let Japanese Eat Whale,"– by Osamu Nakashima   512

"On Eating Whale,"– responses to Osamu Nakashima   513

"In Defense of Pac-Man,"– by R.L. Mead   519

"Et in Arcadia Video,"– by Margaret Logan   521

"The SAT,"– by Jay Amberg   525

"1983: The Last Days of the ETS,"– by David Owen   538

"Math and Sex: Are Girls Born With Less Ability?"– by Gina Bari Kolata   574

"Sex Differences in Mathematical Ability: Fact or Artifact?"– by Camilla Persson Benbow and Julian C. Stanley   577

"Mathematical Ability: Is Sex a Factor?"– Letters responding to Benbow, Stanley, and Kolata and a rebuttal from Benbow and Stanley   583

ARGUMENTS ABOUT THE HUMANITIES

"Longfellow vs. Shortfellow,"– by Robert Schadewald   33

"The Rage to Know,"– by Horace Freeland Judson   65

"What is Vulgar?"– by Aristides   77

"Johnny Wants to Read,"– by Bruno Bettelheim   123

"Politics and the English Language,"– by George Orwell   173

"Why We Live in the Musical Past,"– by Edward Rothstein   220

"Minor Art Offers Special Pleasures,"– by Eva Hoffman   278

"Is Eakins Our Greatest Painter,"– by John Russell   320

"From Bauhaus to Our House,"– by Tom Wolfe   341

"Art versus Collectibles,"– by Edward C. Banfield   428

"Beyond the Wasteland: What American TV Can Learn from the BBC,"– by Martin Esslin   440

"A Close Look at the Unicorn,"– by John Ciardi   632

"The Reviewer's Duty to Damn: Letter to an Avalanche,"– by John Ciardi   637

ARGUMENTS ABOUT BUSINESS

"To Get a Story, 'I Flimflammed a Dead Man's Mother,' "– by Bob Teague   15

"Birds Do It, Bats Do It, But the Issue Is, Who Does It Better?"– by Mark Zieman   28

"Kratylus Automates his Urnworks,"– by Tolly Kizilos   101

"Can the Japanese Keep It Up?"– by Richard D. Robinson   130

"Parkinson's Law,"– by C. Northcote Parkinson   165

"A Plea for a Corporate Conscience,"– by Judge Miles W. Lord   284

"Good Managers Don't Make Policy Decisions,"– by H. Edward Wrapp   325

"Trauma in Detroit,"– by Harley Shaiken   405

"Letter to a Store President,"– by Marilyn Gardner   411

---- →>> «<- ----

INSTRUCTOR'S
INTRODUCTION

Perhaps you are teaching a course that at some time asks students to develop essays with a point—in other words, arguments. It takes sustained application for student writers to reach the level of maturity and competence required to convince others to share their points of view. As instructors we are also challenged by this aim. We have to find methods of teaching students how to construct responsible arguments. It is not enough to show them how to recognize fallacies in the abstract, or how to manipulate syllogisms, or even how to criticize the arguments others have made. Rather, we need to help them realize that arguments are all around them, that they come in various types with identifiable components, and that a knowledge of these types assists writers in the invention of their own arguments.

There is much direct teaching we can do to convey the principles by which arguments are constructed, and we can support such instruction with illustrative readings. Still, the place of readings in a writing course remains somewhat problematic. The reading component of a writing course can be like a camel in a tent, gradually nosing all other rightful occupants out into the sand. Too often the readings are not models for what the writing students are asked to do, or they draw the class into protracted and ultimately irrelevant analysis, or they back both students and teachers into opposing corners as they defend competing assumptions and values. But we offer this collection of essays out of the conviction that reading does have an important role to play in a writing course.

What is the place of reading in a writing course, especially one that emphasizes argument? We see it as having three functions. First, essays can suggest the subject matter for writing. Rhetoric itself, as we know, has no subject matter; the corollary is that it takes in all subjects. Writers, however, do not need all subjects but only a specific one to write about, and their reading in this collection can jog invention by suggesting subjects for further investigation. None of the essays here presents the final word on its subject, but all are competent, responsible arguments. We expect that students will be moved to explore, extend, and refute the arguments presented here, adding their own knowledge and the results of their further research when they write on the same subjects.

A second function of readings in a writing course is to serve as stylistic models (or occasionally antimodels). As we gathered essays for this collection, we were impressed by the stylistic liveliness of much contemporary writing. Both large- and small-scale stylistic effects can be identified and explored in these essays, from the rich metaphors of Martin Luther King to the deadpan narration of Berton Roueché, from the high seriousness of Horace Freeland Judson to the edged humor of David Owen. All the techniques of teaching style can be practiced on the prose here by looking at paragraph coherence and sentence types, length, and variety; by identifying tropes and schemes; by practicing sentence combining and decombining; as well as by imitating any of the effects

xiii

admired. The essays offer the added advantage of being professional rather than amateur models. We present this anthology with the expectation that students will learn to "hear voices," to appreciate stylistic individuality, variety, and excellence in the arguments they read.

The third and perhaps most important function of readings in a writing course is the one most often neglected. Readings can serve as rhetorical models for student writing. By devoting our selection to argumentative literature (including what are sometimes called expository essays but excluding mimetic literature like the short story), we offer not only models of subject treatment and style but also examples of writers responding to particular occasions and audiences. Naturally, the professional models are often longer and more complex than the essays students write, but it is important for student writers to notice in them the same rhetorical techniques, the same principles of invention and arrangement of structural units, that they produce themselves on a smaller scale. By reading other writers rhetorically, students become aware of them as having made choices, just as they make choices in their own writing. To identify rhetorical models is to see other writers as having generated certain kinds of arguments for certain audiences and purposes. Thus these arguments are sources of imitation on a larger scale than the stylistic; they offer structural models.

The essays in this collection naturally fall into several broad categories of subject matter: science and technology, education and the social sciences, the humanities, business, and history and politics. Within each of these categories further disciplinary divisions are possible. Thus some of the business essays have to do with economics, some of the humanities essays with art, and so on. And although the essays and the subjects they treat can be classified according to precisely defined disciplines, all the essays in each category share both general characteristics that make them arguments and other characteristics related to the subjects they treat.

None of the essays, however, is addressed to an expert audience of professionals within a discipline. Such readings would be inaccessible to most college students. Articles from the *Journal of Bacteriology* or *PMLA* or *Research in the Teaching of English*, for instance, may be read by researchers and professionals in their fields, but the difficulties they present to uninitiated readers would distract students from noticing their rhetorical techniques. Therefore we have chosen instead articles whose audiences range from educated lay readers to knowledgeable but not expert readers. Writers assume that lay readers have no background in a particular field and that their interest must be attracted and secured; more knowledgeable readers have some familiarity with a subject and its key terms but may still need extensive explanation. And many other articles are aimed at some place between these two poles of lay and knowledgeable audiences. But no matter what the degree of expertise held by the audience, all the arguments we include here accommodate their readers.

Even though the essays in this collection are not aimed at professionals, many of them are written by expert authors, eminent authorities in their fields. Writers like Stephen Jay Gould, Bertrand Russell, and Sissela Bok speak with both the authority of their academic disciplines and with respect for their nonspecialist audiences. Their essays demonstrate how intellectual rigor can be combined with accessibility.

Because the essays are not intended for expert readers, they are drawn from an enormous variety of sources aimed at different segments of the reading public —from the checkout-counter availability of *TV Guide* to the journal *Science*, which is aimed at members of the American Association for the Advancement of Science; from a popular book like Tom Wolfe's *From Bauhaus to Our House* to a philosophically influential one like Thomas Kuhn's *The Structures of Scientific Revolutions*. The authors represented also range from the famous and soon-to-be famous to the unknown whose writing is the by-product of one occasion. Such variety is perhaps the most important feature of this reader because it makes rhetorical comparison possible. Only when we see how different authors have handled similar subjects for different audiences and from different perspectives can we begin to appreciate the tactics of accommodation skillful writers employ: how they create or efface their voices, how they position their telling points for maximum effect, how they raise or lower the threshhold of background information their ideal readers must possess.

Although the essays represent a variety of sources, subjects, authors, and audiences, they all share one essential characteristic: They are all arguments. That is, they all attempt to work on their intended readers to convince them of, or bring them around to, or simply nudge them toward their authors' points of view. This aim may be subtly indirect or glaringly overt, but it is always present. Whenever the intent to argue is present, it is also possible to identify the issue at stake: thus issues provide the organizing principle of this book and of our approach to understanding and teaching argument. The final purpose of this reader is to teach the principles of constructing effective arguments, not merely to provide the occasion for taking poor ones apart. Thus we have prefaced each section with an introduction that constructively explains the issue-bound type of argument under consideration.

STUDENT'S
INTRODUCTION

In a face-to-face discussion, it is not usually difficult to come up with reasons to back your points. If, for example, you and your friend were coming out of a movie, you would have no trouble justifying off the top of your head why you hated it: The story was incredible, the characters unattractive, the pace too slow. But if you had to review that movie for a film course, you probably would not trust your first thoughts. You would then be arguing for a critical audience, one demanding a more rigorous analysis than your immediate reaction could provide. First, you would probably try to apply the criteria you had learned in class to frame your criticism. Second, you would want to do more than assert, for example, that the plot was implausible; you would have to cite instances in the movie to support that claim, and you might even have to back up further and defend your expectation of plausibility.

The point is that when something is at stake in an argument, such as a grade in a film course, we take care in constructing it. What is at stake can be much more than a grade. For centuries the quality of arguments has affected whether leaders are praised or blamed, whether defendents are found guilty or innocent, whether nations are at war or peace. Given these weighty consequences, it is not surprising that a discipline has arisen to advise speakers and writers how to put arguments together. That discipline is rhetoric, and it offers, among other things, a two-thousand-year-old tradition of tactics for invention, the systematic discovery of arguments.

One of the methods of invention used by ancient rhetoricians like Cicero and Quintilian was to determine the kind of issue, or *stasis* being debated in a particular argumentative situation. "What," the arguer asks, "is the issue or point here?" Once the *stasis* was determined, then the arguer could go on to develop relevant arguments about it. This system for identifying issues and the arguments supporting them originated in the law courts of ancient Greece and Rome and was used to train students in the legal skills they might need in their lives as citizens. Although citizens no longer plead their own cases in the courtroom today, the ancient *stases*, with some modification, can help us identify issues and argue effectively for them.

What are the kinds of issues that can be argued? First, we argue about the nature of things. We debate whether or not they exist, what we should call them, what their attributes and characteristics are. Does Bigfoot exist? Is a particular crime burglary or theft? Is a certain political leader better described as a statesman or an opportunist? To answer these questions the arguer must support claims like the following with the best available evidence: Bigfoot probably exists; this crime was definitely theft; our leader is more an opportunist than a statesman. Though these statements convey different degrees of certainty, the arguments supporting them will all depend on definition. We must know what a Bigfoot is before we can decide if we have evidence of its existence, understand the legal distinction between burglary and theft before we can categorize a particular crime, and define the attributes of opportunism and statesmanship before we can label the actions of an individual.

Once we have grasped the nature of things, we can ask how and why they got that way. Now we are asking questions about causes and effects. Why did the dinosaurs disappear from the face of the earth? What are the reasons for Japan's industrial power? What are the long-term effects of dieting on women's mental health? Arguments that try to answer such questions will make claims about influences, converging factors, motives, conditions, precipitating causes, and even the absence of blocking causes. And just as arguments about the nature of things hinge on definitions, so arguments about causes and effects depend on another kind of assumption, on beliefs about what can cause what.

Third, we can move to the question of value. Here we are not only concerned with what things are and how they got that way, but we go on to pass judgment on them, claiming that they are beautiful or ugly, moral or immoral, beneficial or disastrous. We dispute, for instance, the merits of functional modern architecture, the fairness of the death penalty, and the wisdom of environmental policies. Certainly such arguments depend on criteria of value, on what we think an ideal architecture or justice system or environmental policy should be or do. These criteria may or may not be articulated or defended in the course of a particular argument, but they are essential to arguments about value.

In our society a negative value judgment usually leads to the next step in our hierarchy of issues, a proposal to correct the situation. When things are wrong, we want to set them right. To convince people to make changes we move into another kind of issue and thus another kind of argument. This time the arguer must persuade the audience that they are the right group to act or move others to act, that they have the time, money, personnel, and power to act. Further, arguments over policy incorporate all the issues mentioned so far—definitions, causes, and value judgments. Thus someone who proposes a one-term, six-year presidency must define this new system, show the bad effects of the current practice and the superiority of the proposed one, and finally argue that the audience addressed can bring about the desired change.

Once you know what issue you want to argue and you know the characteristics of arguments in each issue, you have made an important step toward the systematic invention of arguments. Each section of this reader collects arguments on one of the four different issues: definition, cause, evaluation, and proposal. The introduction to each of these sections explains in more detail the constituents of each type of argument, and the readings themselves illustrate how each issue comes alive when a particular arguer addresses a specific audience. You will learn a great deal about analyzing and creating your own arguments both from the introductions and from the live models of the readings.

But no matter what the issue of an argument—definition, cause, evaluation, or proposal—all arguers must consider actual or potential resistance to their positions. Part of learning how to argue *for* is learning how to argue *against.* Therefore we have included in this reader a fifth section of arguments supporting opposite sides on the same issue. These arguments directly refute each other or develop contrary positions, but you should also notice how refutation is an integral part of the arguments in earlier sections. Only by thoroughly understanding and being able to express the position opposing yours will you be able to argue effectively for your own.

In addition to the types of issues, another principle of organization informs the selection of essays in this reader. You will notice that the arguments in every part represent varied areas of learning and public concern. There are readings covering business, science, technology, the social sciences, the humanities, and education. None are addressed to specialist audiences, and although many are written by specialists, all interested general readers will find them intelligible. You are probably beginning to identify yourself as a student of one of these fields; the essays in this reader will show you how writers from that field address segments of the public on matters of common interest and concern.

As important as the determination of issue is in the invention of arguments, you will also notice in the readings that an effective argument is more than a logical outline. The arguments you read here have distinctive voices, and they work on their audiences both to inform them and to form them into receptivity. You will notice in particular that the language of these essays is a powerful means of affecting an audience. Some essays persuade because they are sober, others because they are humorous. Some authors intrude their personalities in personal pronouns; others efface them into objectivity. Some have an eloquent style befitting subject and occasion, others a plain one. Only by closely examining particular arguments will you be able to determine how these effects are achieved through language.

In addition to content and style, you should also notice how arguers arrange their material, select, and organize it. You may have heard that all arguments have a thesis, but as you read you will notice that not all arguers announce it in the last sentence of the first paragraph. Some postpone the thesis in order to give background, some start with one thesis and qualify it into another, some wait to the end to disclose the thesis, and a few even suppress it altogether, counting on their readers to supply it.

Real arguments also vary in how they manage an opening gambit, how much preliminary or supplementary information they include, how much refutation they incorporate, how straightforwardly they march toward a conclusion, or how much they digress. Finally, and again in response to real audiences, arguments differ greatly in the amount of evidence or verification they provide. Some authors sense that their readers need backing and corroboration for each point; others rely on their readers to accept some claims without explicit support. In all these ways, style and arrangement clothe the bare reasoning of an argument. Only in the shower can anyone argue without paying attention to language and disposition.

One

ARGUMENTS ABOUT THE NATURE OF THINGS

Every day, newspapers, magazines, and television fill our eyes and ears with reports about the world: The unemployment rate is down four-tenths of a percent; another candidate has declared her intention to run; the space shuttle completes a successful mission; guerrillas claim responsibility for an attack on a refugee settlement. We rarely question such information; instead, we accord it the status of fact by making two crucial assumptions: that such stories could be verified if we wanted to check into them and that the sources who deliver them have no intent to deceive us.

Yet behind the simplest news story lie definitions, perceptions, and categories that could become sources of different views by equally competent hearers and observers, that could, in other words, spawn arguments maintaining different views of reality. We can make this point more clearly by looking at our sample news items cited above. The unemployment rate, for example, is an extremely complex indicator; reporting procedures can and do change such a figure. If, for instance, only those actively looking for work are counted among the unemployed, then the figure will not indicate those who have despaired of finding work and those who have never tried. Those who are working part time and wish to be working full time also may not be included. Thus the "fact" of an increase or decrease in the rate of unemployment may not be such a fact after all; much depends on a definition of the "unemployed."

Whether a candidate has declared an intention to run for office certainly seems to fall safely into the category of fact. But such a declaration may mask a variety of motives, all short of the candidate's having any hope of winning, though most of us would regard "hope of winning" as a necessary attribute of intending to run. Yet many candidates put themselves in the running to popularize a certain issue or to position themselves for the future. Here the only "fact" may be the creation of the news story itself. Similarly, and more obviously, whether the space shuttle has had a successful mission may be a judgment rather than a fact, even if we define "successful" in the simplest way as having met the flight's stated objectives. Many apparent statements of fact, then, could very easily become subjects of argument if equally competent observers and thinkers have different definitions of key terms.

Before we talk more specifically about arguments that hinge on definition, however, we have to back up and look at what it means to argue at all. When we use the word *argument* in this book, we do not mean by it a hostile conflict of personalities looking for any excuse to disagree. Disagreement is not even a necessity for argument as we define it. Rather, we mean by argument something less personal but no less common. An argument is an attempt to convince an audience to agree with a point or a statement. We can call that statement by a name you are probably familiar with: *thesis.* When writing teachers in the past have insisted that you have a thesis statement for your essays, they were in effect asking that you argue for a point. We can also call this statement or thesis a proposition. It can be expressed in a sentence that makes a claim: "Americans have lost interest in health spas," or "Judges who fine prostitutes and then send them back on the street to work are really pimps."

An argument, then, is an attempt to support a certain proposition or point. To do that, two more elements are necessary. First, we need reasons or supporting material; no argument can simply repeat its own thesis over and over again. Though saying the same thing repeatedly may have a certain force for some people, they are not responding to an argument. Second, in order to have an actual argument in the sense we mean here, an audience is also necessary, some person or group to be brought around to the writer's point of view. (It is of course possible to argue with oneself, but only if we imagine splitting the self into an arguer and an audience.) The agreement aimed at does not have to be a state of wholehearted conviction beyond doubt. It can be merely a warming up to the thesis, an inclination to doubt it less or to acknowledge it as one a reasonable person could hold. Thus an arguer has to bring together a thesis and supporting material, fitted to some audience that has to be drawn into some state of acceptance.

When we define argument in this way we can immediately exclude some propositions as subjects for arguments. Some statements will have the status of facts, and facts are not something we need to argue about, though we may certainly set them before our readers and use them in arguments. However, not every proposition that a particular audience would agree to is a fact. A fact must also be the kind of proposition we can say yes or no to, and the kind we can reach certainty about if we have the means of verification. Thus, statements such as "John F. Kennedy was President of the United States" and "John F. Kennedy was assassinated" are facts, but statements such as "John F. Kennedy was an effective president" or "John F. Kennedy was responsible for the war in Vietnam" are not. To the first two propositions the only plausible responses would be yes or no (yes would be correct in both cases, of course). The second two, however, could also arouse responses like perhaps, probably, not likely, to some extent, and so on, responses that show degrees of adherence on the part of the audience. Consider again the first two propositions about Kennedy. Even if we did not initially know whether to say yes or no to them, we could find a source, such as a reference book or an authority that we trust, to supply the right answer, to confirm or deny the fact. If both arguer and audience agree on the means of verifying a yes-or-no proposition, then that proposition becomes a fact for them. It is not something they will argue about.

Your everyday experience of argument, however, will tell you that "facts" can easily slip out of their privileged category and become subjects of argument when arguer and audience no longer agree about the means of saying yes or no to them. When we do not know how to verify a proposition or disagree about the way to do it, that proposition becomes a matter of argument. It ought to be or not be a fact that our solar system has a tenth planet or that Napoleon was poisoned by arsenic, but since we disagree about or simply lack the evidence necessary to confirm or deny these propositions, they become matters of argument.

The problem of verifying a statement so that we can say a straightforward yes or no to it also depends critically on definition. As the opening examples show, the arguer and the audience must agree on what they mean by key terms (like *unemployment rate* or *successful mission*) before they can even begin to verify a statement as a fact. How, to use another example, can an increase or decrease in the crime rate be verified if the reporting procedures, which depend on definition, vary from place to place and time to time? The problem here is less one of compiling statistics than of creating clear definitions of what they represent. Thus arguer and audience must agree about both definition and verification before accepting a statement as fact.

Needless to say, with both definition and verification debatable, the territory for argument is enormous. No field of knowledge, no human endeavor, no moment in time escapes the scrutiny of argument. But if the possible subjects of argument are limitless, how can we come to understand how arguments are made or learn to make them ourselves? We have to order the diversity into system. There is a way to classify the issues of argument by looking first not at the actual propositions argued for but at the kinds of questions that these propositions try to answer. Some arguable propositions probe the nature and existence of things, some consider their causes, others debate their value, and still others recommend possible courses of action. What is it? How did it get that way? Is it good or bad? What should we do about it? Any arguable proposition can fall into one of these four categories, and each of these four categories requires its own kind of argument. (For further discussion, see the students' introduction.)

In this first group of readings, we want to focus on arguments about the nature of things. The question "What is it?" often takes in the question "Is it?" Does something—a thing, a state of affairs, a trend—exist or not? Does a living descendant of the giant sauropods still exist in the remote jungles of the Congo basin? Is there a growing antinuclear movement in East Germany? Do most Americans now regard labor unions as detrimental? (The question in this last example is not whether the unions are detrimental—a question of value—but whether or not a substantial portion of our population holds that opinion of them— a question about the existence of a state of affairs.) Of course, these are the kinds of questions that we would like to answer with a yes or no and so put them beyond argument. But these questions are matters of argument precisely because they cannot be answered with certainty. What would be convincing evidence of a modern-day dinosaur? How could we have access to a popular movement in East Germany or know with certainty it was an antinuclear movement, let alone a growing one? And how, even with the best sampling techniques, can we be sure about the state of public opinion on so volatile a topic as labor unions? The first reading in the section that follows gives you a chance to see an argument for the existence of its subject. Does the mountain lion still roam the forests of the eastern United States?

Any statement about the existence or nature of something will be a special type of proposition. We can call it a *categorical proposition*, or CP for short. It places its subject in a certain category (e.g., "Lions are predators"), or asserts its existence ("There are rings around Uranus"), or identifies its attributes ("The monasteries in Greece are thriving"). You will notice that some of these statements are facts: For most audiences, "predator" is a clear category in the animal kingdom, and lions are unambiguously recognizable. Until Voyager II our second example about Uranus was not a fact; only now, thanks to the wonders of computer imaging, do we have visible verification of the rings. The third example, however, is arguable because the term *thriving* is subject to various definitions, even though the set of monasteries in Greece might be easily identified.

How do we go about supporting one of these arguable categorical propositions? First it helps to look carefully at the form of the statement. A CP falls apart into subject and predicate: Something is claimed, or predicated, about something else. We need to adjust a definition of the predicate, what is being claimed, to evidence about the subject. An example will help here. Summarizing research reported in the *Journal of the American Medical Association,* a news report claimed, "Male physicians are sexist in their responses to medical complaints from patients." Supporting this CP, this report about a state of affairs, required adjusting a definition of sexism in medical practice to actual evidence of male physicians' behavior. Sexism, never an easy word to define, was in this case stipulated to mean a tendency to call for more elaborate workups (X-rays, lab tests, and so on) of male patients than female patients. By restricting the definition in this way, the researchers were able to observe and quantify specific behavior on the part of their subjects. But how did they verify that male physicians actually took the complaints of their male patients more seriously? They could not observe all visits of all patients to all doctors. In order to verify, they chose a sample of nine West Coast physicians and looked at the records of 181 office visits of fifty-two married couples about five common medical complaints. With this carefully limited definition and sample size, they certainly could not claim as a universal fact that male physicians are sexist, but they could support the possible application of that label. If they wanted to make a firmer claim, they could have chosen a larger and more typical sampling of physicians and extended their definition of sexism to include other behavior, but to the extent that definition and verification are debatable, this CP and any like it will remain arguable.

In the example we just discussed, the CP is easy to identify, the subject and what is predicated about it easy to distinguish. But arguing in support of a CP is not just a matter of making a logical adjustment between two parts of a proposition. As we said above, audience enters every argument. Audience will determine how overtly the thesis is stated, how explicitly or fully the predicate is defined, and how much evidence and verification are needed to link predicate and subject. An arguer who assumes the audience will readily accept the definitions of key terms may not state the definitions explicitly, let alone try to back them up. Different audiences require different degrees of evidence and verification.

If the proposition is one with which the audience tends to agree, fewer examples and less attention to sources will be used. Or if the evidence cited about the subject is accepted as typical, less of it is essential. Even the degree to which the clear statement of the thesis is necessary depends to a large extent on audience and situation.

The readings in this section reveal how great this kind of variety can be in actual arguments addressed to real audiences in particular contexts. Some arguments, like the one by Bob Teague, rely heavily on examples and dismiss easily grasped definitions, a practice understandable in the informal context of a *TV Guide* article. At the opposite extreme is "What is Vulgar?" It consists largely of expanded and elaborate definition illustrated by convenient examples. Definition is also particularly critical in Horace Freeland Judson's article, a serious argument about the nature of science, but less critical in the pieces on boxing and poetry, which have the air of the informal essay. Finally, in essays like "Genesis vs. Geology" and "The Strange Death of Silas Deane," meticulous attention to evidence is inextricably joined to precise definition. Knowing both the logical requirements of the CP argument and the actual rhetorical choices made by real writers will help you in constructing your own arguments of this type.

———————— →» «←- ————————

Panthers Wanted—Alive, Back East Where They Belong

MICHAEL FROME

The following article on panthers is unique among the CP arguments in this section because it argues not about what a thing is, but whether it is. What we have here is an existence argument claiming that there is evidence that the eastern mountain lion has survived. The author, Michael Frome, is a self-proclaimed aficionado of the Smoky Mountains who has written a book on them, Strangers in High Places. Frome is no sensationalist asserting that he has sighted marvels; he is careful to qualify his claims and assess his evidence, though his convictions and his attitude about the survival of the mountain lion come through.

"Panthers Wanted" first appeared in the Smithsonian, *a wide-circulation magazine published by the Smithsonian Institute in Washington, whose readers tend to be more urban than rural. As you read this essay, think what you would have to do to convince people that you had seen a creature no one believes in.*

On a July evening in 1975, five Great Smoky Mountains National Park maintenance workers were lounging on their bunkhouse porch watching a doe and two yearlings. Suddenly the deer fled into the forest and a large, grayish cat with a long tail emerged from the woods and bounded after them. The five men followed quickly, but found nothing more than tracks along a creek. They were convinced, however, that they had seen a panther hunting its traditional prey.

The report they filed in late September 1975 triggered a new sense of awareness of the largest, rarest and most secretive of the wild American cats. The Eastern panther was thought long ago to have followed the trail into oblivion of the great auk, Labrador duck, heath hen, passenger pigeon and sea mink. Recent sightings by some professional biologists, wildlife personnel, and forest and park rangers show this may not be the case. The Eastern panther may be coming back from the brink of extinction for a second chance.

For me the news was especially exciting. For years I've been an aficionado of the Great Smokies, the half-million-acre mountain sanctuary astride the North Carolina-Tennessee border. More than 15 years ago I had asked the then park naturalist about reintroducing the panther into the Smokies. After all, national parks are supposed to be wildlife sanctuaries and I can't think of any better suited for such a role than the Great Smoky Mountains. Fifty years ago, or less, it was not uncommon for mountaineers to catch sight of the sleek panther (or "painter" in the vernacular) three or four times a year, or to hear its shrill song pierce the wilderness night, and the animal's hams and shoulders were the source of "painter bacon." Even now Panther Creek, Panther Mountain, Cat Run, Painter Branch and Painter Creek are familiar place names in the Smokies and neighboring Nantahalas across the Little Tennessee River.

The biologist to whom I had posed the question responded flatly that the big cat requires too much room even to be considered for reintroduction, and that its day in these mountains was definitely done.

Now we know better. "It appears that nature has succeeded where the National Park Service feared to tread," Boyd Evison, who was the park superintendent (and who has personally seen panther tracks), conceded quite willingly when I was last in the park. "There seems no reasonable doubt that there *are* cougars in the park; and it seems likely that they have been here for some time. Very little seems to be known about their habits and needs in this kind of country, but the park, if kept free of excessive development, offers the best sanctuary for cougars north of the Everglades and east of the Rockies."

The 1975 observation in the park and concurrent reports of panthers along the Blue Ridge Parkway in North Carolina stimulated me to investigate the whereabouts of the big cat, one of the least known of North American mammals today, not only in the Southern mountains but throughout its range. I found these lonely wanderers of our mountains and forests far more widespread than I could possibly have dreamed. The numbers of animals must be dangerously low, but they apparently are breeding and the long thread of life, though tenuous, remains unbroken.

Felis concolor, "cat all of the same color," varies from light brown or gray to soft reddish brown, or tawny, possibly changing with the season. In the United States and Canada there are 15 subspecies, all essentially the same animal. Many names have been given, including catamount (for cat of the mountain) in the Northeast, cougar in Canada, panther in the Southeast, mountain lion in the West, "el león" in the Southwest (to contrast with "el tigre," the jaguar), puma in South America, as well as red tiger, silver lion, mountain devil, mountain screamer, deer killer and king cat. Now it is known mostly as panther, puma, cougar, mountain lion or long-tail cat.

That unmistakable tail is as long as an African lion's, though the panther is only half the size of the king of cats. The average male weighs about 150 pounds, the female about 100, though a large animal may weigh 200 pounds and measure eight feet in length. Our American lion is lean and lithe, endowed with tough skin, sharp claws and sharp teeth.

Though panthers are expert hunters, worthy of a sportsman's admiration, sport hunters long despised them as competitors for deer and played a key role in doing them in. "For the sake of deer supply," argued *Forest and Stream Magazine* in 1885, "the panthers should be systematically pursued and destroyed, and the bounty should be such as to encourage this." Likewise, when the nation's leading sportsman, Theodore Roosevelt, became President, he denounced the panther as "the big horse-killing cat, the destroyer of the deer, the lord of stealthy murder, facing his doom with a heart both craven and cruel."

Though deer are the main prey, a panther will eat almost anything. It does humans a good turn by devouring rabbits and rodents, but earns the wrath of stockmen by taking an occasional sheep or calf. Its diet includes porcupine, fox, skunk, badger, frogs, slugs, grasshoppers and even its little cousin, the wildcat.

In the late 1940s a Canadian biologist, Dr. Bruce S. Wright, equated the relationship between panther and deer and came up with a surprisingly hopeful forecast. Wright had observed new forests and abandoned farms developing into first-class deer habitat and hunters encouraging the increase in deer. He predicted that panthers would follow the deer back into new habitats in the East.

The Eastern panther in 1972, according to Wright, had passed the immediate danger of extinction, but only by "the merest fraction." He estimated the total number surviving in eastern North America, exclusive of Florida, at not more than 100 (with the largest number, 25 to 50, in New Brunswick) and possibly fewer, yet he foresaw the animal making a slow comeback in both the Southeast and North, from Florida to the Laurentians, providing it was given protection.

Despite reports of sightings up and down the Eastern seaboard during the 1960s, many government agencies and scientists remained dubious. Reports of panthers often turned out to be cats, dogs or spooks in the night. Even today some biologists concede only that the panther *may* exist and refuse to grant anything further in the absence of an acceptable photograph of the animal in the wild, a freshly killed specimen or a confirmed sighting by a scientifically trained observer. Ten years ago the official view of the National Park Service was simply stated: "There are no panthers in the Great Smoky Mountains." Anyone suggesting otherwise was subject to ridicule. Pranksters made things worse here and there by dropping the remains of a panther that had died in captivity, or by creating a trail with a dismembered limb. One or two footprints may be faked realistically, but not a whole trail complete with natural signs, . . . and a competent tracker can spot a fraud in a short time. But the pranks made the whole idea of living panthers seem like a fraud or joke.

Until recently, seeing one was a little like seeing the Loch Ness monster, a vision best kept to oneself. But not any longer. Reports of sightings are solicited rather than ridiculed. And instead of being a despised predator, the panther is increasingly viewed as a prized species that must be rescued from extinction.

Field Biologist Robert L. Downing has begun a five-year project, funded jointly by the Forest Service and Fish and Wildlife Service, to search for panthers and panther signs in the Southern mountains. From his headquarters at Clemson University, South Carolina, Downing has established a network of contacts among state and federal resource agencies to help screen, and validate, sighting reports.

One of the first submitted to him, a photograph of a panther track, came from West Virginia early this year. "It's the first I've seen personally and I'm pretty positive it's authentic," he told me.

The three national park units in the Appalachians—Great Smokies, Shenandoah and the Blue Ridge Parkway—are cooperating with Downing in the search for cats, tracks and scats. A young Virginia outdoorsman and expert tracker, Champlin Carney, has been hired to search Shenandoah for tracks and to attempt to obtain photographs using a self-tripping camera.

So goes the search in southern Appalachia, but it's not the only area of interest and activity. New Hampshire officials are cautious believers: "Although none has been authenticated, enough sightings have been reported by people of good judgment that our department now considers there is a distinct possibility that the mountain lion is making a comeback in our state," says a spokesman for the New Hampshire department of game management.

Reports have been made continually in Massachusetts. West Virginia has stronger evidence. In April 1976 a young 100-pound male was shot by a farmer near Droop Mountain State Park after he saw it attacking his sheep. Though several sightings have been reported in the rugged high forests of Pocahontas County, this was believed to be the first panther killed in West Virginia in at least 50 years. One week later a second mountain lion was located on another Pocahontas County farm. The cats may have been wild or released by someone; yet sightings in relatively undeveloped areas, particularly in national forests, argue against the oft-expressed idea that all such animals must be "escapees from captivity." Besides, there aren't that many zoos or keepers of pet panthers in the Appalachians.

Blue Ridge Parkway rangers reported seeing a mother panther and two cubs near the Pisgah campground on at least two occasions as recently as 1977, a single panther near Frying Pan Tower Lookout, one of the wildest sections of the Blue Ridge, and another single panther at Gales Mine Falls, at the edge of the Asheville watershed.

In the Great Smokies, Ray DeHart, a retired trails foreman of the national park, within the past five years has seen three panthers on hiking trails—including one chasing a wild boar along the Appalachian Trail.

Lions clearly have learned to avoid men. They are shy but inquisitive about humans and sometimes like to be around them, sometimes seen, sometimes unseen, like phantoms. The panther seems to be a puzzling combination of what humans call courage and cowardice. Smaller cousins, the wildcat and lynx, are much more ferocious when cornered or trapped. The panther might attack a bear one day and run from a small dog the next. Complaints of depredation are surprisingly few, and so are unprovoked attacks.

At present the Eastern panther either survives, or may possibly survive, in south central Canada and northern Maine, the White Mountains, isolated areas in Massachusetts, the Adirondacks, the Appalachian Mountains from western Pennsylvania down through Alabama, lowlands of South Carolina and Georgia, southern and central Florida, hardwood bottomlands of northern Louisiana, and the Ozarks of southern Missouri, Arkansas and eastern Oklahoma.

Firm, conclusive data are very difficult to come by. The Eastern panther has been photographed alive only in Florida, with one possible exception. While tramping in the Adirondacks in 1972, Alex McKay, a New Yorker, saw a huge cat stalking silently about 20 feet ahead of him. The cat, seeming to sense him simultaneously, crouched low in the grass and stared with yellow-almond eyes. McKay raised his camera, snapped the shutter . . . and looked down briefly to wind the film. When he looked up again the big cat had vanished.

The single picture he had taken revealed only a feline head with dark cheek patches, a clear muzzle, those glaring almond eyes, and the faint outline of the body crouched in the grass. The State Museum in Albany advised him that a photo is not acceptable documentary evidence; only the fresh skin of a specimen could be considered authentication of the animal's occurrence—yet it's against the law to collect the skin of an endangered species.

. . .

Many biologists and wildlife officials shun discussion of the Eastern panther. They seem to fear that recognizing the animal's existence would encourage hunting, regardless of its status as an endangered and protected species. They could be right. "The greatest danger to the panthers today," wrote Bruce Wright, "is from the 'shoot it to prove I saw it' philosophy." And Aldo Leopold's first response 30 years ago on learning that panthers survived in New Brunswick was: "We must not tell anybody."

In a recent study undertaken for the United States Forest Service, biologist George Lowman urged complete protection as "the most necessary step" for management of the panther in the East.

National forests in the White Mountains, Green Mountains, Southern Appalachians, Florida and the Ozarks all are designed to serve many purposes, including wildlife preservation. In places national forests border national parks, including Shenandoah, the Blue Ridge Parkway and Great Smoky Mountains, and are like extensions of them.

"As much of each national forest as possible should be maintained in unbroken undisturbed tracts," urged Dr. Lowman. "Certainly any type of habitat reduction should be avoided."

Among the states, North Carolina has moved with particular zeal. In 1971 it granted complete protection. Two years later Dr. Frederick S. Barkalow jr., professor of zoology at North Carolina State University, began to solicit photographs or casts of tracks. Most recently the North Carolina State Museum of Natural History issued 1,000 posters . . . as part of the first statewide effort to obtain reports.

With passage of the Endangered Species Act of 1973, federal agencies are obligated to give priority to saving the panther and its habitat. The Blue Ridge Parkway and Great Smokies National Park top the list because evidence of the panthers' presence there is so strong.

As Boyd Evison, who is now Assistant Director of Operations for the National Park Service, puts it: "The cats' only real enemy is Man and we will do what we can both to prevent poaching and minimize 'people activities.' You and I may not see one of these lions, but knowing they are there means a lot to us."

QUESTIONS FOR DISCUSSION

1. The thesis of this article is not difficult to find. But why is it so carefully qualified with a "maybe"? Why doesn't the author just boldly proclaim that the eastern mountain lion exists?
2. What attitude toward the preservation of panthers does the article assume on the part of its audience? Can you imagine an audience that would not share that attitude?

3. How many different kinds of signs of the panther did the author collect? What kind of evidence would convince a skeptical biologist that the animal had returned to its original habitat? Can you order the signs according to their reliability? What makes some signs more or less reliable than others?
4. Why was the photograph of a large cat taken in the Adirondacks not accepted as documentary evidence by the state museum in Albany, New York?
5. What kind of evidence would be required to convince doubters that not just isolated escapees from zoos but a good number of the species *felis concolor* had reestablished itself? Would the evidence have to be different in kind or amount?
6. This article gives a great deal of background information, which is nevertheless relevant to the argument. How do accounts of the panther's prevalence in the past (as evidenced in place names) and the clear definition of the panther's physical characteristics work in the argument?
7. Imagine how difficult this existence argument would be without a clear definition of *felis concolor* obtained from earlier times and other habitats. How would interpreters otherwise know what the evidence was supposed to represent? Is the absence of definition the problem with arguments for the existence of the Loch Ness Monster, Bigfoot, and the Chesapeake Bay Monster?

SUGGESTIONS FOR WRITING

1. Find a magazine or newspaper like *The National Enquirer,* the *Globe,* or *Star* that contains an article claiming that something or someone really exists: that Elvis Presley is alive, that flying saucers buzz the earth routinely, that Hitler is in hiding. Write a critique of the evidence offered in support and speculate on why there seems to be a tendency for some audiences to believe such claims. You could address your argument to the readers of the original piece and try to convince them not to believe such stories. Or you might try to convince people who dismiss such arguments to take them more seriously.
2. Assess the evidence that has been amassed for the existence of a creature like Bigfoot, or the Loch Ness Monster, or alligators in the sewers of New York. How qualified a CP about the existence of such creatures does the evidence seem to support? Very unlikely? Slight possibility? Good probability? What role will the absence of evidence play in your argument?
3. Do a study of the prevalence of a species in a small area, perhaps in conjunction with a course in ecology or environmental studies. Find a categorization that characterizes that species' distribution (e.g., rare, threatened, endangered, extinct) and argue for its applicability. Or argue that a species once considered endangered is so no longer (e.g., the alligator in Florida).
4. Compare the essay on panthers with "The Last Bears of Yellowstone," in

Part Three, Arguments that Evaluate. That article also debates the prevalence of a large mammal in a wilderness area. But in Yellowstone, the official opinion is that bears abound; in the Smokies the park service maintains there are no panthers. Explain how these different prevailing conceptions affect the acceptance of evidence in the two locales.

5. Existence arguments need not be about things that we can see, hear, and touch. We also argue for the existence of trends and attitudes. For example, our current concern for the welfare of some species only came into existence within the last few decades. Write a CP argument characterizing the ecological awareness of a group you can identify and survey, such as your fellow writing classmates.

6. Can you argue for the existence of a backlash against the environmental movement? Is there currently a trend away from active measures to preserve species and maintain wilderness areas?

→≫ ≪←

To Get a Story, "I Flimflammed a Dead Man's Mother"

BOB TEAGUE

Bob Teague is a twenty-year veteran news reporter for WNBC-TV New York. The following article originally appeared in his book, Live and Off-Color: News Biz, *and was excerpted for millions of readers and viewers in* TV Guide. *It may shock you. It may make you suspect that the news you see on TV is not exactly the news there is. It will also illustrate for you one of the liveliest techniques of CP argument, the use of personal and reported examples that read like stories.*

Teague's article moves from descriptive characterization of his experiences to evaluation, and you will find yourself judging the morality or immorality of the practices you read about. You may or may not agree with Teague's conclusions, but the point to notice here is whether you are convinced that the situation Teague reports on really exists.

Working the street as a local TV reporter often makes it necessary to grow a callus on your heart. When covering a murder, for example, you have to delve into the gruesome details of the bloodletting. If at all possible, you must also show the victim's friends or family, preferably in a rage or in tears. If you are covering a political campaign, you must goad the candidates into spitting obscenities at each other. Like: "He said you're incompetent and unqualified. What's your reaction to that?"

Even when you feel that you are doing something disgusting, or merely in bad taste—displaying insensitivity to the point of being inhuman—you have to hang tough and follow through; like sticking a mike under the nose of a weeping old woman whose grandson has been stabbed to death in a New York gang rumble. I did all that and worse. It came with the territory. If I failed to do it for dear old Ch. 4, some other streetwalker made of sterner stuff would certainly do it for dear old Ch. 2, Ch. 5 or Ch. 7. And if my masters saw that kind of pathos on a competing station—they all had a shelf full of TV monitors in their offices—they would ask me, "Where were you when Channel Blank was getting the good stuff?" No one has yet devised a satisfactory answer to that one.

My friend Gloria Rojas of Ch. 7 says that's exactly what happened to her in covering the aftermath of a plane crash. While other members of the *Eyewitness News* team blanketed the crash site, Gloria was sent to the nearest hospital. "What a scene," she told me. "Chaos all over the place. I just walked into the emergency section with my crew, and nobody tried to stop us. We took pictures of the injured, some of them barely conscious, struggling to live. I didn't want to bother any of them. Just being in there meant that we were increasing their chances of infection. So we just took pictures, talked with one of the surgeons, then packed up to leave. That's when a reporter from Channel 11 showed up with his crew and started interviewing some of the victims, including a guy who was obviously dying. I said to myself: This is an abomination. I am not going to stoop to anything so gross. I'm going to leave.

"Back at the station," Gloria went on, "our executive producer saw Channel 11's exclusive on the 10 o'clock news. He wanted to know whether I'd interviewed the same guy or even somebody else in critical condition. When I said I had decided not to do it as a matter of decency, he damn near had a fit. He said I should have done it, too. So what finally happened was, our station called Channel 11 and begged a copy of their tape. We ran the interview on our program at 11 with a credit line that said, 'Courtesy of WPIX.' I was so mad I couldn't even cry."

The fact is, you never know which of the many damned-if-you-do, damned-if-you-don't choices you will have to make on a given day.

Once upon a time in the Bronx, police discovered several tons of toxic chemicals illegally dumped on scattered vacant lots—a menace to neighborhood youngsters. An enterprising Ch. 2 reporter, poking through an isolated pile of glass and cardboard containers being collected by sanitation trucks, found a ledger. It gave away the manufacturer's name and address, with a catalogue of the lethal compounds in that load.

"After doing my stand-upper with the ledger," the WCBS man said later, "I planned to turn it over to the cops. Then a Channel 7 reporter showed up with his crew. I decided to share the ledger with him. You know, like some day I'll be the guy playing catch-up and maybe he will give me a clue.

"You won't believe this, but he put the ledger back in the pile, hiding it under some boxes. Then, with his camera rolling, he starts prowling through the stuff. All of a sudden he picks it up, turns to the camera and says, 'Look what I've found.'

"I was so mad I could have killed him. No point in trying to talk him out of it. I knew that. So after giving the ledger to the cops, I called his boss [then news director Ron Tindiglia] at Channel 7. Tindiglia thanked me. 'I'll take care of it,' he said. Tindiglia is a gentleman. That crummy bit with the ledger never got on the air."

The line between creative coverage and faking the news is a thin one indeed. The WABC reporter, however, had clearly gone too far.

Conflicts between local newspeople rarely involve questions of that magnitude. A typical hassle developed between Heather Bernard of Ch. 4 and Arnold Diaz of Ch. 2 on the hottest story in New Jersey at that time. The family of Karen Anne Quinlan was in a legal battle with the state for the right to disconnect the life-support apparatus that prevented their comatose daughter from "dying with dignity." When Heather reached the home of the Quinlan family, several competing camera teams were standing in line at the front door awaiting their turns to shoot.

"Arnold Diaz was next in line ahead of me," Heather recalled with rancor. "The other crews ahead of us took only 15 or 20 minutes each. Arnold was in there for over an hour. I was furious. Finally, I went inside to see what the heck was taking so long. I couldn't believe it. His crew was all packed up. He was sitting at the table with the Quinlans, having lunch.

"OK. The family had to eat anyway. No harm done. Then as they finished lunch—Arnold and his crew were starting to leave—I noticed a stack of letters on a table in the corner. I made the mistake of asking Mrs. Quinlan about all that mail. She said it was the letters and cards they had received in recent weeks expressing sympathy for their daughter and the family. Arnold had missed that angle completely. Now he tells his crew to unpack their gear. He wants to do another sound bite and shoot the letters. I grab him by the arm and say, 'Arnold, come on. Enough is enough.'

"We had such a big argument about it that Mrs. Quinlan butted in. 'Now, children. No fighting in this house.' Arnold backed off and I did my piece first.

"The next day he called NBC and told [then news director] Earl Ubell that Heather Bernard had been bitchy and obnoxious, very unprofessional on the Quinlan story. When I saw Arnold again a day later, I thanked him. I said: 'NBC had been threatening to fire me because they said I'm not aggressive enough in the field. You've saved my job'."

If your zeal propels you into conflict with another reporter, you can huff and puff with reckless abandon. You know the other guy does not want to risk damage to his money-in-the-bank profile or risk a multimillion-dollar lawsuit for damaging yours.

From Square One of my career in the news biz, I had bent my personal rules of good conduct, decency and integrity again and again to get news stories on the tube. Sure, I worried about it some, but I kept on doing it. One particular incident in the field, though, left me with a churning knot of self-loathing. In Coney Island, covering the suicide leap of a 23-year-old man from the roof of a 21-story apartment building, I flim-flammed the dead man's mother into giving me the exclusive sound bite I needed to flesh out my scenario. My excuse was: Who knows what Ch. 2 or Ch. 7 might have filmed before I reached the scene some three hours later?

After picking the brains of neighbors who had known the victim, I still had no idea why he did it. There was no suicide note. My cameraman suggested that somebody in the family might be able to fill in the blank, and added that they also might have a picture of the guy that we could put on film.

I didn't hesitate. Nothing seemed more important than getting those elements.

The man's mother, a middle-aged, red-eyed widow in a blue-and-white flower-print kimono, cracked the door only an inch or so when I rang her bell. She did not want to go on television. "Go away," she sobbed. "I'm in mourning."

In my best phony sympathetic manner I advised her that neighbors were saying that her son had killed himself because he was heavily into hard drugs. "They're claiming he started selling it, then got hooked on scag himself. I'd hate to put that on the air if it's not true. I'm sure your son was a decent guy. Unless I get the real story from you, I'll have no choice." The truth is, only one person, speculating off-camera, had suggested any such thing. Nevertheless, it worked.

While the camera rolled, the woman launched into an anguished tirade against people who will say anything to get on TV. Then she told me that her son had been depressed for several days. His 19-year-old girl friend had been devastated by his confession that he also liked to have sex with men occasionally; she had broadcast his shame to their friends.

That interview—plus an exclusive snapshot of the dead man— boosted my stock in the trade but not with my girl friend at the time. As the two of us watched that story on the TV set in my pad, she accused me with her eyes and with the question: "Wouldn't it have been better to let the reason for his suicide remain a mystery; to spare his mother that kind of useless humiliation?"

I didn't know the answer at that point. I was trying to come to grips with the problem.

A willingness to defy authorities is one of several personality traits you have to develop to be effective as a streetwalker. In many instances, the story you're out to cover is not just lying there for the taking. It is hidden by vested interests and protected by protocols. To circumvent them and get the story, you may, for example, imply to a stubborn, tight-lipped district attorney that you already know more than he has told you—to draw him out at least far enough to confirm your hunches. You may ignore "No Trespassing" signs and sneak into a mental hospital where you have reason to believe that the patients are being mistreated. You may walk into someone's home or office with a concealed micro-phone and a camera that appears to be inactive, to catch the person off guard.

Deceitful? Yes, but morally correct in my judgment. Long before my time, society gave journalists the right to play by a slightly different set of rules. We are not, of course, above the law. On the other hand, some white lies and deceits can be justified if perpetrated solely for the purpose of digging up the truth and airing it, but not for the purpose of sensation-mongering as I did with the poor woman whose son committed suicide. Realizing that, belatedly, I never again went that far.

Witnesses on Bleecker Street in Greenwich Village reported that one building superintendent shot his next-door counterpart to death—the bloody climax of a long-running feud over who had been putting garbage in front of whose building on the sly. The dead man left a wife and two preteen-age children.

On this story, I vowed in advance, I was not going to be insensitive for a change. Instead, I would show compassion by leaving the bereaved survivors alone. I would use only sound bites of neighbors and homicide detectives on the case. Which was exactly how I did it at first. I could afford to on this particular outing; no other newsreel was present to coerce me into typical gaucheries.

My crew were packing their gear in the trunk, ready to leave Bleecker Street, when two urchins with dirty faces tugged my elbow. "Put us on TV, mister. We saw the whole thing."

I explained that I already had interviewed witnesses. I didn't need them.

"But it was our father who got killed," one of the boys pleaded.

My professional instincts got the better of me. Since they had volunteered, I could put them on-camera with a relatively clear conscience. And great God in the foothills, what terrific sound bites they gave me! In simple, dramatic sentences, they took turns telling what they heard, what they saw. They could have been talking about the death of an alien from Mars. "And pow. He shot my father in the eye."

Again, my crew and I started to leave. An old guy wearing shabby and shapeless clothes tugged my elbow. "She's waiting for you," he announced. He pointed toward a frail young Puerto Rican woman in tears. She was wearing what had to be the prettiest dress she owned.

"The victim's wife?" I inquired.

The old man in the baggy suit nodded. "Yes, my granddaughter. She's waiting for you."

Reluctantly, I shoved the microphone under her quivering, freshly painted lips. She wailed about the loss of her husband; wept without embarrassment. Great TV. Some of her tears fell on my hand. That's when I got the message: she, as well as her kids, wanted the whole damn world to share their grief.

Experiences in that vein allowed me to feel more comfortable in my television role. There was a quid pro quo that mitigated my indiscretions to some degree. Just as I used people to suit my purposes, they used me. Why not? Television belonged to everybody.

QUESTIONS FOR DISCUSSION

1. This argument offers its reader five powerful extended examples of the state of news reporting practiced by TV journalists. What CP, either from the article or of your own devising, best characterizes these reporting methods?
2. How typical do you believe these examples are? What in the article either makes you believe or makes you doubt that they represent the common practices of most TV reporters?
3. Teague is interested in more than simply characterizing a state of affairs in TV journalism. Can you find the place where he turns to moral judgment about the practices revealed in the essay? Although we have not yet discussed the tactics of evaluation argument, how convincing do you find his justification?
4. Why does Teague tell two detailed stories about the activities of other reporters before he tells his own stories? What effect do these two narrations have on your sense of his character?
5. One of the problems of using detailed examples is that the very details can obscure the point of similarity among the examples that support the CP. Do the examples of the crash victims, the ledger, the Quinlan family, and the dead man's mother illustrate slightly different practices? What do they all have in common? Does their common attribute support either of Teague's statements, "Working the street as a local TV reporter often makes it necessary to grow a callus on your heart," or "The line between creative coverage and faking the news is a thin one indeed"?
6. How does Teague convince you that the examples he uses from other reporters are accurate?
7. Compare the view of the news you can gain from Teague's article with the definition of history given in "The Strange Death of Silas Deane," by James Davidson and Mark Lytle.

SUGGESTIONS FOR WRITING

1. This article illustrates an effective combination of personal experience with the reported experience of others. Write an argument for an uninitiated audience characterizing the practices in a job or profession, using your own testimony and/or that of participants gathered in interviews. How, for example, do auto mechanics really inspect cars? How do sales clerks flatter customers into buying clothes? How do professors make up exams? Your argument may stop at characterization or move on to evaluation.
2. From a viewer's point of view, compare the interviewing techniques of local newscasters with those of national ones. You will have to watch both local and national news programs several times before coming to a conclusion.
3. Observe the work of a particular reporter—news, sports, or feature—over a

period of time. Characterize his or her practices. For example, you might conclude that the sports reporter on Channel *X* favors baseball over football, or that some reporter is particularly self-effacing or self-promoting. How are you going to convince readers of your argument that your evidence is accurate?

4. Find coverage of the same news story in three different newspapers. Compare and contrast their citation of sources, their use of details, their inclusion and exclusion of material. Come to some conclusion about which seems to be the most accurate and the least slanted. (Caution: Do not compare the same wire service news story as it is run in three different newspapers.)

5. Interview journalism professors and active journalists for newspapers, radio, or television. What standards of accuracy do they profess and practice? Do practicing journalists in different media have different standards and do these standards tend to differ from those professed by journalism academics?

6. Investigate the so-called "happy news" format that has developed on some stations in recent years. Try to find out how television news coverage has changed since ten years ago, twenty years ago. You may go on to speculate on causes for the changes.

---------------- →≫ ≪← ----------------

The Blow that Hurts

GENE TUNNEY

Gene Tunney (1897–1978), one of the legendary figures of boxing, was heavyweight champion in a different era, defeating Jack Dempsey for the title in 1926. The following essay first appeared in The Atlantic Monthly *in 1939, long after Tunney retired from boxing, and it has since been frequently reprinted. It offers an excellent example of how the character, or ethos, of an arguer can account for much of an argument's persuasiveness. As you read, try to imagine how the same argument might be made by someone without Tunney's inside knowledge of boxing and his appealing stance as a gentleman of the sport. Notice too how the supporting examples are given with much circumstantial detail to enhance the pleasure of the reader.*

A punch in the nose might seem to be an intensely personal thing— much more so, for example, than pushing the queen's rook's pawn on a board of checkered squares. Yet I have been astonished to hear of enmities and feuds in the game of chess, that epitome of abstract combat. The queen's rook's pawn seems to have occasioned a surprising lot of rancor and fury. I find it difficult to understand, but then I have been merely a boxer, a devotee of one of the most noted of all physical-contest sports.

Some years ago a great international chess tournament was staged in New York, with an imposing array of the grand masters of the game. Newspaper files will reveal that this tournament made the front pages in a spectacular way, though chess is hardly of headline popularity. The tournament was ornamented by the presence not only of Capablanca, then at the height of his genius, but also of Dr. Emanuel Lasker, the venerated adept who for so many years was the champion. Dr. Lasker had a peculiarity—he loved strong black cigars and smoked them always. Other grand masters charged that when they played him he would blow clouds of acrid and noxious smoke across the board and into their faces, thereby disconcerting them and throwing them off their game. Foul play, they roared. This state of affairs was only exacerbated by the popularity and honored regard that the almost legendary chess master enjoyed in New York. His admirers, knowing his love for strong black cigars, sent him many gifts of them—the strongest and the blackest. In consequence, the Doctor had an abundance of acrid and noxious smoke to blow into the faces of his opponents. The more deeply he became absorbed in profound combinations at the chessboard, the harder he would puff away and the more wrathfully other chess masters would protest to the officials. As for the merits of the case, I surely am not one to adjudicate at this late day, but I'd suppose that where there's smoke there's fire—or at any rate some heat.

By way of contrast, take prize fighting. Few human beings have fought each other more savagely or more often than Harry Greb and I. We punched and cut and bruised each other in a series of bouts, five of them. In the first Greb gave me a ferocious beating, closed both eyes, broke my nose, chipped my teeth, and cut my lips to pieces. He did everything but knock me out. In our last fight I beat him about as badly, so badly that he was helpless in the latter rounds. He seemed like a dead-game fighter, wanting to be spared the indignity of being knocked out. Pain meant nothing—he didn't want the folks back home to read of his being knocked out. From the beginning of our first to the end of our last bout, Greb and I went through the ferocious gamut of giving and taking, hitting and being hit. We were always the best of friends; never any ill will or anger. You see, we were not chess players.

Harry was bitter about one fight, our fourth. I won the decision, and this enraged him. He was sure he had beaten me, felt to the depths of his soul that he was the victor. It was one of those newspaper-decision affairs of the period, sports writers giving the verdict in their stories. Cleveland was the place; and Regis Welsh of the *Pittsburgh Post,* one of Greb's best friends, in his newspaper story the day after the fight gave the decision to me, putting my photo on the front page with the caption "Too Much for Our Boy." Greb never spoke to him again. They were enemies ever after. All the bitterness the battle had stirred in Greb was directed, not against me, not against the antagonist who had been in there hitting him, but against his newspaper friend who had merely tapped a few keys on a typewriter. He didn't resent the physical pain of being murdered, he resented losing—losing unjustly, as he thought.

It isn't physical pain that hurts so much, it's the blow to one's vanity. But what is vanity? What are we most proud of? A whole lot of things, among which physical prowess in a fight is by no means the most important. Intellectual pride, as any theologian will tell you, is the most damning; and the vanity of artists is famous in the literature of history and comedy alike. As a boxer I should say that it's in the realm of the intellectual and artistic that a blow is the most painful, where feelings are hurt the most. For example, I think the man I hit the hardest in my whole boxing career was onetime heavyweight champion of Europe, Erminio Spalla, but I never hurt Spalla's feelings. Yet I might have— I'm sure I could have turned him into a rancorous enemy, but he remains an excellent friend. I knocked him out in a bout at the Polo Grounds back in 1924. He was no boxing master; he was crude, but he could hit. I didn't want him to lay that powerful right of his on my chin—it might be uncomfortable, and so it was when it eventually landed. After being hit I boxed him carefully, waiting for a decisive opening, and then hit him with every ounce of strength I had. I knocked him out with what I imagine was the hardest blow I ever struck. But, as I have remarked, I never hurt his feelings.

One day last fall I was having dinner in New York at Christ Cella's place of unceremonious hospitality, and heard a couple of Italian waiters chattering about Spalla. He had been Italy's pride, and my presence made them recall him. But they were by no means talking about boxing —their topic was opera, the newest operatic star in Italy. They were discussing what they had read in their Mulberry Street newspapers— that prize fighter Spalla, former champion of Italy and all Europe, had just made a resounding success in his debut at La Scala in Milan singing "Amonasro" in Verdi's *Aida.* This did not surprise me a bit, because the very point on which I remembered I had never hurt Spalla's feelings was his singing.

Several years before I fought him, he and I had trained together with other boxers in the same quarters in New Jersey—and he was always singing. He told me he was studying baritone, and when we were not sparring in training bouts he was caroling operatic arias. He had a rich and beautiful voice, and I used to ask him to sing for me, which he did with a lusty good will—*Pagliacci* and *Trovatore*. After we fought and the knockout brought Spalla's pugilistic career to an end, he went back to Italy. Later on he wrote to me, and told me that with the money he had earned in the prize ring he was pursuing his studies for an operatic career. I suspect he was grateful because that hardest punch I ever hit finished him in pugilism. We corresponded on and off, and he kept me informed how he was getting along with the arias and the high notes. Then came a letter in which he told me that he was soon to make his debut at La Scala—which he did with first-rate success.

Just a few days ago I had a letter from my old prize-ring antagonist. It's worth quoting: "Dear Gene: Following the hostiliti between America and Italy in the cinema world I was urgently called by the La Scalla Film Company to play the role in many of their films. And so to quote the old proverb—'It is an ill wind that blows, etc. etc.' I am enclosing my autographed fotograph, and I trust you will send me yours, as I always want to see you in the best of health. My wife has had another son and so I am the father of five. And how is your family progressing?" Quite nicely, Erminio, quite nicely.

What I am quite sure of is this—if, instead of hitting Spalla so hard, I had made disparaging comments about his singing, he would have hated me. Remarks about faulty production, vibrato and flatting on the top notes—that's the sort of thing which creates those embittered vendettas in opera companies. I liked Spalla's singing, but even if I hadn't I should never have told him so. I would have punched him in the nose instead, for I don't like to make enemies.

Among people who have no contact with the boxing tradition of the English-speaking world, a blow in the face is a deadly insult—while a wound with a sword may be taken with equanimity. Our boxing tradition has ameliorated the innate combativeness of man, has taken much of the homicide out of fight and physical clash. The fistic exchange has become conventionalized. It's not good sportsmanship to resent with abiding rancor a punch in a fight. So a prize fight, being the epitome of the boxing tradition, is decidedly impersonal—a thing of abstraction.

I recall a scene the morning after my first fight with Jack Dempsey as one of the strangest I ever experienced. It had me disconcerted, as well as considerably embarrassed.

After that bout in the rain in Philadelphia it seemed to me proper to go and pay my respects to Jack. He had been severely punished, and must feel pretty blue after losing the championship. The next afternoon I went to his hotel. He had a suite of rooms, and when I got there Jack was in an inside bedroom. In the outer room were gathered the Dempsey entourage of manager, handlers, trainers, and disappointed followers. They greeted me with an instant bristling of hostility. I was the focus of scowls and angry, sullen glances. Gene Normile was in tears. Jerry the Greek came to me, shook his fist, and mumbled hoarsely, "You can't licka the 'Chump,' you can't licka the 'Chump.' " Jack Dempsey always inspired loyalty, and this was it. They bitterly resented my defeating him.

I had the nervous feeling of being in the camp of the enemy, surrounded by smouldering hatred. I had only one impulse—to get in there to Jack. I found him sitting on a bed, and then I realized how badly he had been battered in that downpour the night before. He put out his hand, and said, "Hello, Gene." It was as if we were visiting casually, in the course of commonplace acquaintance. Before that Jack and I had never been friends particularly. In fact, I think he rather resented me as a challenger. But after we had fought and I had defeated him for the championship—Jack was the only friend I had in the camp of the enemy.

Of all the sports, it is my opinion that boxing, though the most physically injurious, is the most impersonal. I indulge in golf, tennis, squash rackets, and shooting, and can conscientiously say that my resentment in defeat in any of them is far greater than anything I ever felt or experienced in a long career of boxing. There is a subconscious mutuality of respect engendered by the give-and-take of the prize fight that has a certain spiritual quality to it which leaves no room for rancor, resentment, or jealousy. It is true that prize fighting seems sheerly physical and elemental, but what other sport or art has as little bitterness or envy among its devotees? Could the answer be that the more elemental we become in sport and art, the closer to the spiritual we get?

QUESTIONS FOR DISCUSSION

1. What proposition about the nature of boxing is being maintained in this essay? Where does it appear and why does it appear there?

2. Tunney defines boxing on page 25 as a conventionalized exchange that "has ameliorated the innate combativeness of man." The idea of conventionality in this definition allows the link with impersonality in the predicate of the essay's governing CP. But the definition of boxing is not argued for; Tunney relies on his audience's accepting it. Would you agree that his definition still fits boxing?

3. What sense of Tunney's personality comes through in this essay? To what extent does this argument convince because of Tunney's character, or *ethos?*

4. Why does Tunney begin with evidence from chess rather than from a sport closer to boxing, such as football? If you are convinced by the chess example that rancor exists where you least expect it, are you more likely to believe that it does not exist where you most expect it?

5. All Tunney's anecdotal examples are drawn from personal experience. Does that weaken his argument?

6. Tunney argues that he could not really hurt Spalla's feelings by beating him in the ring since Spalla's pride was really invested in his singing. What if all Spalla could do was fight? Do we have a possible wedge for refutation here?

SUGGESTIONS FOR WRITING

1. Write a CP argument convincingly characterizing the posing or boasting practices of such modern boxers as Muhammad Ali, Sugar Ray Leonard, Hector "Macho" Comacho, Gerry Cooney, and Larry Holmes. Do their activities repeal or support Tunney's thesis that boxing is impersonal? (If you were aiming this argument at a general audience, could you rely on widespread familiarity with the careers of these boxers?)

2. Characterize a sport for its code of manners, the typical behavior of its players on or off the field. Are tennis professionals noted for their politeness or hockey players for their shyness? Aim your argument at the readers of *Sports Illustrated.*

3. Compare two similar sports that differ in some particular aspect, such as the behavior of bench sitters during the game or the rituals expected from winners and losers. Your argument may be written for those who know the sport but haven't noticed what you have.

4. Argue for your choice of the most humiliating thing that can happen in a particular sport. What kind of mistake makes a player look the worst or lets down teammates the most?

5. Define for uninitiated readers the code of honor, either spoken or unspoken, in a sport or game. You should write this argument about a sport you have played, since your experience will give you access to evidence unavailable to spectators.

6. Compare boxing to wrestling from the viewpoint of Tunney's characterization. Is wrestling also impersonal, conventionalized combat?

———————— →>> <<← ————————

Birds Do It, Bats Do It, but the Issue Is, Who Does It Better?

MARK ZIEMAN

Most readers of the Wall Street Journal *look to it for news about trade, industrial development, the stock market, and legislation affecting business. But the newspaper also spots trends in business and brings them to the attention of its readers. Some of those trends are unusual, such as the one reported in this article on the booming market in bat and bird guano. To make this unfamiliar subject attractive to his readers, Zieman uses many techniques: He brings facts to our attention, presents flamboyant characters, reveals the rivalry between guano merchants, and speculates about the future of the guano market. Although this article includes causal and evaluative elements, we include it among the categorical propositions because its primary purpose is to convince us that a trend exists.*

BRACKEN CAVE, TEXAS—Every night, 20 million bats flap up from here in a chirping brown tornado and gulp down enough bugs to fill six tanker trucks. By day, in a somewhat less picturesque performance, the bats turn the bugs into guano and drop about 450 pounds of it onto the cave floor.

For three generations, Paul Vordenbaum's family has shoveled that guano, bagged it, and sold it as organic fertilizer. In the Roaring '20s, Bracken's bat guano covered Florida citrus fields. "They'd sweep the rocks clean to get every ounce," he brags, perched on a bag of droppings near a shaft in the cave roof. But soon came cheap and abundant chemical fertilizers, and the guano market disappeared.

Until now, that is. Riding on the shovels and trowels of the organic craze and a boom in home gardening, guano is undergoing a stunning revival. Two bands of entrepreneurs—one supplied by bats and the other backed by Peruvian seabirds—are battling over a big share of the thriving market, each side claiming its product is better. "Peruvian guano is the Rolls-Royce of fertilizers," boasts Roberto Risso, a Peruvian-turned-Texan who is importing guano into the U.S. from Peru, the first time anyone has done so in 15 years. Counters Eric Thompson of New Mexico, who markets bat guano from Bracken and other caves: "I think it's time bat guano took its rightful place as the king of organic fertilizers."

True, some fertilizer experts debunk guano's mystical powers. "I guarantee you the price of guano is four or five times its fertilizer value," asserts Donald McCune of the International Fertilizer Development Center. "But," he adds sheepishly, "my wife buys silly stuff like that. She's willing to pay the price."

COLORFUL HISTORY

Whether guano is magical or mediocre, it has a colorful history. Over the centuries, it has been used both as a potent fertilizer and as a source for bombs, since it is rich in nitrogen, phosphate and potash. The ancient Incas murdered folks who bothered their guano birds, and Peru once counted on guano exports for 80% of its gross national product.

In the early to mid-19th century, guano created an agricultural revolution around the globe. By the 1850s, it became such a success that President Millard Fillmore implored Congress to "employ all the means properly in its power" to import the powdery dung into the U.S. So in 1856, Congress passed the Guano Act, giving the U.S. claim to any guano islands discovered by Americans. During the Civil War, bat guano (some of which came from Mr. Vordenbaum's caves) was mined by Confederate troops to use for their explosives.

More recently, guano achieved a certain renown as the smelly killer of Doctor No, the arch enemy of Ian Fleming's James Bond. It was Bond who commandeered a crane and dumped 20 feet of the stuff on that evil pseudo-guano merchant, thinking "the stinking tomb" would make an appropriate resting place.

Today, the growing legions of "all organic" growers sparking guano's comeback include some of the fussiest gardeners of them all—the marijuana growers of Northern California. "The growers want the best-quality product they can grow, and guano gives it to them," says Tom Alexander, who started an Oregon supply store and a marijuana magazine, Sinsemilla Tips, after being busted in 1979 for growing pot. Guano distributers estimate that at least a third of the guano trade today is with the marijuana growers.

PRAIRIE FIRE

Guano "is sweeping the cannabis world like a prairie fire," observes Simeon Murren, a distributor of Mr. Risso's bird guano and a writer for

Sinsemilla Tips. In a feature called "Guano Notes" for that magazine, he wrote: "Guano cannot be beat when it comes to the taste of the buds grown with it."

Predictably, the two captains of the guano trade belittle their large marijuana market, emphasizing instead guano's potential in other areas. "If guano works on marijuana, then why in the world couldn't it work on tomatoes?" asks Mr. Thompson, the bat man. Mr. Risso, the bird man, agrees. "I don't know how many hippies use it," he says. "Guano works well on anything."

So far, it seems, the bats have an edge on their Peruvian rivals. Mr. Thompson, the owner of both an insurance agency and a hamburger drive-in in Carlsbad, N.M., began cornering the bat-guano market months ago when he and a partner bought the mining rights to an area cave. Those rights and his contracts with Mr. Vordenbaum's Bracken and Frio caves give him control of probably the three largest bat caves in the country. "I have enough guano to last my lifetime and yours," he says cheerfully.

Mr. Thompson claims his U-Bar Cave Products Inc. sold $50,000 of guano during the first three months of this year and has contracts for about $500,000 more. He sells his guano in buckets for about $1 a pound under a variety of names, including "Carlsbad Bat Guano" and "Reginald the Aristobat." Mr. Risso's Peruvian guano, which he calls, "Plantjoy," goes from $2.50 to $5 a pound, also in colorful jars and buckets.

Mr. Risso in the past has sold everything from cheesecakes to bidets to oil-field equipment, but his $80,000 of Peruvian bird dung sold last year lagged behind his competitors. That hasn't diminished his confidence, however. "If I can get every rich girl with a rose garden to use guano, that's it!" he bubbles.

That won't be easy. The bat people are swirling in for a frontal attack, with bumper stickers, free samples and brochures. Mr. Thompson has even sponsored two scientific testings of the droppings by New Mexico State University; the results haven't been released. Mr. Risso, a natural promoter, is fighting back. He has his own free samples, plus stickers, brochures, T-shirts and a videotape display of his birds doing their stuff.

An owner of a Houston health-food store calls the video promo "a little far-fetched," but Mr. Risso's guano has won admiration from dozens of gardeners. "Let's face it, he's kind of strange, but the stuff does work," admits Howard Walters, past president of the American

Rose Society. "A new user will see a greening up and a general increase in vigor at five to six weeks at the outside." Another fan swears that guano has improved his social life. "Now when I go to cocktail parties, women seek me out. They say, 'Bird guano! I lo-ve that name! I've got to get some!' "

And so the guano wars go on, with each side gearing up for the final onslaught. A recent Commerce Department report warned that rising natural-gas prices are increasing the price of chemical fertilizers; guano merchants respond that streamlined operations will lower their price. Mr. Thompson's New Mexico cave already is mined by an aerial tramway, and Mr. Vordenbaum of Bracken Cave says he is "trying to figure out some way of doing it pneumatically." This month, the good ship Kero pulls in from Peru, with a 40-ton load of guano for Mr. Risso.

And others are also awaiting their chance, like Leo Whalen of Whistling Wings Duck Farm in Hanover, Ill. Mr. Whalen's mallards leave him 100,000 pounds of guano a year, which he is happy to sell. "We'll shovel it out, we'll get a tractor with buckets and we'll bucket it out," he says.

But the question remains: Can Mr. Thompson, Mr. Risso or any others emerge victorious from the guano wars? Ask J. Peter Grace, the chairman and chief executive officer of W.R. Grace & Co., the international conglomerate. In 1854, Mr. Grace's grandfather started the company by chartering vessels to haul guano; and in 1983 chemical fertilizers still made up 8%, or $22.4 million, of the company's operating income. "I'm sure guano will do well," he says, only half-smiling. "Maybe we should have our people look into it again."

But they had better hurry. Today's guano market is "potentially in the millions," proclaims Mr. Thompson, who is certain he will get his share. So is Mr. Risso, who says he just might become another W.R. Grace. "Everybody has a place where he hits the barrier of his limitations," he adds modestly.

Mr. Risso's enthusiasm knows no bounds. He has already composed what may be the best—and worst—guano poem. It begins:

> On the islands of Peru
> Seabird droppings fall for you
> And when brought to the U.S.A.
> They cause a big hallaballo.

QUESTIONS FOR DISCUSSION

1. How does Zieman convince his readers that there really is a boom in guano sales? What kind of evidence does he present?
2. To establish the existence of a trend, an arguer must often back up into causal argument and explain what has brought about such a development. What, according to Zieman, accounts for the rise in guano sales?
3. This article seems to take on the issue of the relative superiority of bat and bird guano. Does it answer the question?
4. What do you think is the aim of this article? To persuade people to buy guano? To suggest that we should invest in guano companies? To inform us of a phenomenon? To account for the rise in guano sales? To examine the comparative merits of various fertilizers? If you decide the article has one main purpose, how do these other elements serve that purpose?
5. Does the author reveal any of his own attitude toward his subject? Point out particular word choices that suggest what he thinks of this trend.
6. What is the point of including two paragraphs on the popularity of guano as a fertilizer for marijuana? What do you think Zieman's readers in the *Wall Street Journal* will think of that?

SUGGESTIONS FOR WRITING

1. Do some research on a small scale in your local area to find out what kinds of businesses have recently been thriving or suffering. Write an article for your local paper to call attention to this trend, which readers may not have noticed.
2. If you were a guano merchant, what kind of advertising campaign would you mount? Write some promotional material for guano: brochures for direct mailing, newspaper or magazine ads, sales letters, radio and television commercials.
3. How would you go about convincing someone to buy guano, even though it is more expensive than chemical or other organic fertilizer?
4. Take the opposing stance and convince someone who buys imported guano that an ordinary domestic chemical fertilizer, even though it is cheaper, is just as good.
5. This article presents two guano entrepreneurs who have made successes out of unlikely small businesses. Find a person, either someone you know or someone you have read about, who you think deserves to be characterized as an entrepreneur. Write an article describing this person's career for readers curious about the secrets of business success.
6. Think of a product that was once popular but that people no longer seem to buy or one that is not obviously appealing (like prunes). How could you convince people to buy this product? Write a letter to its manufacturer or distributor offering some new marketing strategies.

—— ⇶ ⇷ ——

Longfellow vs. Shortfellow

ROBERT SCHADEWALD

This article combines two subjects that few people would associate with one another: computers and poetry. Yet computer programmers have long been interested in the capacity of their machines to generate art and mimic the creative potential of the human mind. "Longfellow vs. Shortfellow" tells of attempts to program a computer for the invention of poetry. It first appeared in Technology Illustrated, *a magazine that popularized technology for interested lay readers. Robert Schadewald's credentials to write on this subject are explained in the course of the piece. As you read the article, ask yourself how much background knowledge of poetry and of computers it assumes on the part of its readers. Does it assume too much? What is the thesis of the argument and, more important, at what point do you first discover that the article is an argument? Whether computers can write poetry depends entirely on the working definition of poetry, so be alert to definition as you read.*

> An icy flower
> The shade struggles near dry hills
> Autumn sunset

Haiku such as this, obscure and enigmatic, were once in vogue. It is gauche, of course, to ask poets what such poems mean. In this case, it would also be pointless, for the poem was written by my computer.

Or was it? Actually, I gave the computer lists of words and phrases and simple rules for selecting and combining items from the lists. The output seems to make vague sense. But *can* it make sense? If it has no meaning but is indistinguishable from poems written by humans (poems that supposedly *have* meaning), where are we?

Most poets scoff at the thought that someone might confuse their creations with the regurgitations of a computer. Such confidence is misplaced. Can you tell which of the following two poems was composed by a computer?

> Margaret, are you saddening
> Above the windy jumbles of the tide.
>
> Wave to me in the peace of the night.
> Jealousy is not all: It is not refreshment nor water.

Return to me in the pause of the shade,
Darling, because my spirit can chime.

Above the early flounces of the stream
Margaret, are you saddening?[1]

She's mending the rain with her hair.
She's turning the darkness on.
    Glue/switch!
That's all I have to report.[2]

Computer poetry flourished briefly during the 1960s, partly as something bored computer programmers did while the boss was at lunch and partly as a minor step toward artificial intelligence. Serious artificial-intelligence researchers quickly tired of computer verse and moved on. Goldbricking programmers found more profitable diversions (games and graphics), leaving the field dominated by hobbyists who crank out verse on their home computers.

A few serious poets and scholars have used computers to investigate the nature of poetry. Marie Borroff, a Yale English professor, has produced a set of "Five Poems from the Chinese" in this vein:

Gracious is money
And avuncular are the buttonholes of its bed;
But it is among the berries, and there only,
That the graciousness of money may guard us
And the buttonholes of its bed may be judged.[3]

When you read the other four poems, such as the one beginning "Transparent is flesh/And ancient are the shadows of its spittle," it becomes clear that she provided the structure and that the computer selected the words and plugged them into blanks. In a sense, the computer was following a respectable precedent: Dylan Thomas also used a fill-in-the-blanks approach to create some of his poetry.

[1]"Margaret" produced by Louis T. Milic's computer program ERATO. Reprinted by permission of the author and Richard W. Bailey, editor of *Computer Poems*, Potagannissing Press, Michigan, 1973.

[2]"November 24" from *The Pill Versus the Springhill Mine Disaster* by Richard Brautigan. Copyright 1968 by Richard Brautigan. Reprinted by permission of Delacorte Press/ Seymour Lawrence.

[3]Reprinted by permission of the author and Richard W. Bailey, editor of *Computer Poems*, Potagannissing Press, Michigan, 1973.

Computer poetry programs vary widely in technique and sophistication, from simple fill-in-the-blanks programs to ones that choose their own line structure, pick rhyming words for the ends of lines, consider meter in selecting words, and even impose an element of "sense" on their poems. My own program, SHORTFELLOW, is sophisticated enough to substitute the article *an* for *a* when the next word begins with a vowel, to form plural nouns and several verb cases, and to repeat previously used words or lines. Given the sequence article/adjective/noun, article/noun/verb/preposition/adjective/plural noun, adjective/noun, it concocted the ersatz Haiku that opens this article. Even that modest effort exaggerates its poetic abilities, for the following is far more typical:

A throbbing leg
A cloud murmurs near still births
Wild knee

Presumably no one would confuse "A Throbbing Leg" with genuine poetry. Still, a computer blindly choosing words from lists can hardly avoid generating some interesting idioms. The "morbid dance," "parched violets," and "broken fire" that my computer once generated in three consecutive lines compare on their own merits with the "laughing fish," "long-tailed lightning," and "drinking wings" Dylan Thomas used in three verses of his "Ballad of the Long-legged Bait." But if Thomas created any of these images by filling in blanks with words from his black book, he did *not* use just any word. He considered and rejected several before making his selection.

Published computer poetry depends upon selection of a different kind. If my computer spits out 100 pseudo Haiku, most of them will make even less sense than "A Throbbing Leg." But if I scan the output and publish one semirespectable example, it might appear that my machine can turn out decent Haiku.

SHORTFELLOW has never produced a good poem, and I say that with some regret, for I am ultimately responsible for SHORTFELLOW's shortcomings. Wading through hundreds of SHORTFELLOW's attempts, I find a powerful image here and a good line there, but the lack of reason, feeling, and intentional humor always betrays the mechanical hand. I've also examined numerous anthologies of modern poetry, some very avant-garde, and found just about every kind of poetical curiosity imaginable. Yet in every poem running more than a few lines, I could detect some sort of reason, some trace of emotion, some echo of a human voice.

Computers are logic machines. But creativity and feeling, the twin essences of poetry, are not logical, nor are they random. Thus the logic machine with its random number generator comes up short, and computer poetry cannot fairly be called poetry.

But if it isn't poetry, what is it? Perhaps SHORTFELLOW can explain:

> Computer poetry is a damp kiss
> Quietly betraying
> Never obeying
> It wanders on cold bones
>
> But yet it drifts waves
> Swiftly running
> Easily betraying
> Pursuing its black gypsy.

QUESTIONS FOR DISCUSSION

1. Schadewald disperses the definition of *poem* and *poetry* so critical to the success of his argument. Find all the attributes of *poem* or *poetry* that distinguish it from computer verse. (You may wish to write them up in a connected, isolated definition.) Would the argument have served its audience better had an isolated definition—that is, a definition given all at once —been used?

2. According to Schadewald, true poems supposedly have meaning; fake ones do not. But the meaning of the critical term *meaning* is left unspecified. How would you construct a definition of *meaning* to argue that computers do write poetry—and one to argue that they do not?

3. What tactics of definition did Schadewald use in his incremental definition of poetry? (Hint: He uses the example of Dylan Thomas's technique for one.)

4. Find some examples of real haiku such as those written by Ezra Pound. Is the opening haiku really indistinguishable from your genuine examples as Schadewald suggests in paragraph two? (What would it mean for the haiku to be indistinguishable when the words must be entirely different?) Or find a formal definition of haiku. How does the opening computer-generated example fit? Why doesn't the second example ("A throbbing leg . . .") fit?

5. Is the poem created by the computer program or by the computer programmer who selects the output? What would be the result if a bona fide poet selected from the computer's output? In other words, how could the practice of the computer program and of Dylan Thomas be reconciled by a suitably inclusive definition of the activity of creating poetry?

6. What does Schadewald tell about himself? Does the character or ethos he reveals make his argument stronger or weaker for its intended audience?

7. Why, given the intended audience, purpose, and occasion for this piece, does the actual statement of the CP thesis ("computer poetry cannot fairly be called poetry") come last?

SUGGESTIONS FOR WRITING

1. Argue that the Brautigan poem quoted fulfills or does not fulfill Schadewald's definition, or that the computer examples he selected actually do fulfill some part of his definition. That is, can you find in them "some sort of reason, some trace of emotion, some echo of a human voice" or "creativity and feeling, the twin essences of poetry"? Your audience could be Schadewald himself.
2. Select a poem (either from a current publication or a standard anthology) and argue that it does or does not fit Schadewald's definition of poetry.
3. Find another definition of poetry, perhaps in a dictionary of literary terms or in a statement by some famous writer, and compare it to Schadewald's. Then test a particular poem against both definitions. Think of your audience as the teacher of a course in which you have studied poetry.
4. Examine a collection of current poetry and construct a definition of poetry from the examples for fellow students of poetry. Let your definition be a characterization that grows as much as possible out of the material at which you are looking.
5. Find a copy of Stanley Fish's *Is There a Text in This Class?* (Cambridge, Mass.: Harvard University Press, 1980) and read the chapter titled "How to Recognize a Poem When You See One." Fish comes up with a radical redefinition of poetry as something readers do to texts and not texts to readers. Reassess Schadewald's examples of computer poetry with this new definition, which locates poetry in the reader's actions. Direct your argument to people convinced by Schadewald.
6. Write a refutation of Schadewald's thesis and a defense of the computer's ability to create poetry when a suitable program is provided.

—>>> <<<—

The Strange Death of
Silas Deane

JAMES WEST DAVIDSON AND
MARK HAMILTON LYTLE

"The Strange Death of Silas Deane" makes up the prologue of After the
Fact, *a book whose purpose is to communicate the fascination of historical
research to readers unfamiliar with what historians actually do. The two
authors, James Davidson and Mark Lytle, are concerned that most people do
not know what history really is, thinking it merely a collection of facts. Their
purpose is to correct that misbelief, and they begin by showing how doing
history can be exciting sleuthing into the past. They do their work so
convincingly that you will forget you are reading an argument about the
nature of history and lose yourself in the puzzling fate of Silas Deane. And
in the process you will become an historian yourself.*

The writing of history is one of the most familiar ways of organizing
human knowledge. And yet, if familiarity has not always bred contempt,
it has at least encouraged a good deal of misunderstanding. All of us
meet history long before we have heard of any of the social science
disciplines, at a tender age when tales of the past easily blend with heroic
myths of the culture. In Golden Books, Abe Lincoln looms every bit as
large as Paul Bunyan, while George Washington's cherry tree gets
chopped down yearly with almost as much ritual as St. Nick's Christmas
tree goes up. Despite this long familiarity, or perhaps because of it, most
students absorb the required facts about the past without any real conception of what history is. Even worse, most think they do know and
never get around to discovering what they missed.

"History is what happened in the past." That is the everyday view
of the matter. It supposes that historians must return to the past through
the surviving records and bring it back to the present to display as "what
really happened." The everyday view recognizes that this task is often
difficult. But historians are said to succeed if they bring back the facts
without distorting them or forcing a new perspective on them. In effect,
historians are seen as couriers between the past and present. Like all
good couriers, they are expected simply to deliver messages without
adding to them.

This everyday view of history is profoundly misleading. In order to demonstrate how it is misleading, we would like to examine in detail an event that "happened in the past"—the death of Silas Deane. Deane does not appear in most American history texts, and rightly so. He served as a distinctly second-rate diplomat for the United States during the years of the American Revolution. Yet the story of Deane's death is an excellent example of an event that cannot be understood merely by transporting it, courier-like, to the present. In short, it illustrates the important difference between "what happened in the past" and what history really is.

AN UNTIMELY DEATH

Silas Deane's career began with one of those rags-to-riches stories so much appreciated in American folklore. In fact, Deane might have made a lasting place for himself in the history texts, except that his career ended with an equally dramatic riches-to-rags story.

He began life as the son of a humble blacksmith in Groton, Connecticut. The blacksmith had aspirations for his boy and sent him to Yale College, where Silas was quick to take advantage of his opportunities. After studying law, Deane opened a practice near Hartford; then continued his climb up the social ladder by marrying a well-to-do widow, whose inheritance included the business of her late husband, a merchant. Conveniently, Deane became a merchant. After his first wife died, he married the granddaughter of a former governor of Connecticut.

Not content to remain a prospering businessman, Deane entered politics. He served on Connecticut's Committee of Correspondence and later as a delegate to the first and second Continental Congresses, where he attracted the attention of prominent leaders, including Benjamin Franklin, Robert Morris, and John Jay. In 1776 Congress sent Deane to France as the first American to represent the united colonies abroad. His mission was to purchase badly needed military supplies for the Revolutionary cause. A few months later Benjamin Franklin and Arthur Lee joined him in an attempt to arrange a formal treaty of alliance with France. The American commissioners concluded the alliance in March 1778.

Deane worked hard to progress from the son of a blacksmith all the way to Minister Plenipotentiary from the United States to the Court of France. Most observers described him as ambitious: someone who thoroughly enjoyed fame, honor, and wealth. "You know his ambition —" wrote John Adams to one correspondent, "his desire of making a Fortune. . . . You also know his Art and Enterprise. Such Characters are often useful, altho always to be carefully watched and contracted, specially in such a government as ours." One man in particular suspected Deane enough to watch him: Arthur Lee, the third member of the American mission. Lee accused Deane of taking unfair advantage of his official position to make a private fortune—as much as fifty thousand pounds, some said. Deane stoutly denied the accusations and Congress engaged in a heated debate over his conduct. In 1778 it voted to recall its Minister Plenipotentiary, although none of the charges had been conclusively proved.

Deane embroiled himself in further controversy in 1781, having written friends to recommend that America sue for peace and patch up the quarrel with England. His letters were intercepted, and copies of them turned up in a New York Tory newspaper just after Cornwallis surrendered to Washington at Yorktown. For Deane, the timing could not have been worse. With American victory complete, anyone advocating that the United States rejoin Britain was considered as much a traitor as Benedict Arnold. So Deane suddenly found himself adrift. He could not return to America, for no one would have him. Nor could he go to England without confirming his reputation as a traitor. And he could not stay in France, where he had injudiciously accused Louis XVI of aiding the Americans for purely selfish reasons. Rejected on all sides, Deane took refuge in Flanders.

The next few years of his life were spent unhappily. Without friends and with little money, he continued in Flanders until 1783, when the controversy had died down enough for him to move to England. There he lived in obscurity, took to drink, and wound up boarding at the house of an unsavory prostitute. The only friend who remained faithful to him was Edward Bancroft, another Connecticut Yankee who, as a boy, had been Deane's pupil and later his personal secretary during the Paris negotiations for the alliance. Although Bancroft's position as a secretary seemed innocent enough, members of the Continental Congress knew that Bancroft was also acting as a spy for the Americans, using his connections in England to secure information about the British ministry's war plans. With the war concluded, Bancroft was back in London. Out of kindness, he provided Deane with living money from time to time.

Finally, Deane decided he could no longer live in London and in

1789 booked passage on a ship sailing for the United States. When Thomas Jefferson heard the news, he wrote his friend James Madison: "Silas Deane is coming over to finish his days in America, not having one *sou* to subsist on elsewhere. He is a wretched monument of the consequences of a departure from right."

The rest of the sad story could be gotten from the obituaries. Deane boarded the *Boston Packet* in mid-September, and it sailed out of London down the estuary of the Thames. A storm came up, however, and on September 19 the ship lost both its anchors and beat a course for safer shelter, where it could wait out the storm. On September 22, while walking the quarter deck with the ship's captain, Deane suddenly "complain'd of a dizziness in his head, and an oppression at his stomach." The captain immediately put him to bed. Deane's condition worsened; twice he tried to say something, but no one was able to make out his words. A "drowsiness and insensibility continually incroached upon his faculties," and only four hours after the first signs of illness he breathed his last.

Such, in outline, was the rise and fall of the ambitious Silas Deane. The story itself seems pretty clear, although certainly people might interpret it in different ways. Thomas Jefferson thought Deane's unhappy career demonstrated "the consequences of a departure from right," whereas one English newspaper more sympathetically attributed his downfall to the mistake of "placing confidence in his [American] Compatriots, and doing them service before he had got his compensation, of which no well-bred Politician was before him ever guilty." Yet either way, the basic story remains the same—the same, that is, until the historian begins putting together a more complete account of Deane's life. Then some of the basic facts become clouded.

For example, a researcher familiar with the correspondence of Americans in Europe during 1789 would realize that a rumor had been making its way around London in the weeks following Deane's death. According to certain people, Deane had become depressed by his poverty, ill-health, and low reputation, and consequently had committed suicide. John Cutting, a New England merchant and friend of Jefferson, wrote of the rumor that Deane "had predetermin'd to take a sufficient quantity of Laudanum [a form of opium] to ensure his dissolution" before the boat could sail for America. John Quincy Adams heard that "every probability" of the situation suggested Deane's death was "voluntary and self-administered." And Tom Paine, the famous pamphleteer, also reported the gossip: "Cutting told me he took poison."

At this point we face a substantial problem. Obviously, historians cannot rest content with the facts that come most easily to hand. They must search the odd corners of libraries and letter collections in order to put together a complete story. But how do historians know when their research is "complete?" How do they know to search one collection of letters rather than another? These questions point up the misconception at the heart of the everyday view of history. History is not "what happened in the past;" rather, it is *the act of selecting, analyzing, and writing about the past.* It is something that is done, that is constructed, rather than an inert body of data that lies scattered through the archives.

The distinction is important. It allows us to recognize the confusion in the question of whether a history of something is "complete." If history were merely "what happened in the past," there would never be a "complete" history of Silas Deane—or even a complete history of the last day of his life. The past holds an infinite number of facts about those last days, and they could never all be included in a historical account.

The truth is, no historian would *want* to include all the facts. Here, for example, is a list of items from the past which might form part of a history of Silas Deane. Which ones should be included?

Deane is sent to Paris to help conclude a treaty of alliance.
Arthur Lee accuses him of cheating his country to make a private profit.
Deane writes letters which make him unpopular in America.
He goes into exile and nearly starves.
Helped out by a gentleman friend, he buys passage on a ship for America as his last chance to redeem himself.
He takes ill and dies before the ship can leave; rumors suggest he may have committed suicide.

Ben Franklin and Arthur Lee are members of the delegation to Paris.
Edward Bancroft is Deane's private secretary and an American spy.
Men who know Deane say he is talented but ambitious, and ought to be watched.

Before Deane leaves, he visits an American artist, John Trumbull.
The *Boston Packet* is delayed for several days by a storm.
On the last day of his life, Deane gets out of bed in the morning.
He puts on his clothes and buckles his shoes.
He eats breakfast.
When he takes ill, he tries to speak twice.
He is buried several days later.

Even this short list of facts demonstrates the impossibility of including all of them. For behind each one lie hundreds more. You might mention that Deane put on his clothes and ate breakfast, but consider also: What color were his clothes? When did he get up that morning? What did he have for breakfast? When did he leave the table? All these things "happened in the past," but only a comparatively small number of them can appear in a history of Silas Deane.

It may be objected that we are placing too much emphasis on this process of selection. Surely, a certain amount of good judgment will suggest which facts are important. Who needs to know what color Deane's clothes were or when he got up from the breakfast table?

Admittedly this objection has some merit, as the list of facts about Deane demonstrates. The list is divided into three groups, roughly according to the way common sense might rank them in importance. The first group contains facts which every historian would be likely to include. The second group contains less important information, which could either be included or left out. (It might be useful, for instance, to know who Arthur Lee and Edward Bancroft were, but not essential.) The last group contains information that appears either too detailed or else unnecessary. Deane may have visited John Trumbull, but then, he surely visited other people as well—why include any of that? Knowing that the *Boston Packet* was delayed by a storm reveals little about Silas Deane. And readers will assume without being told that Deane rose in the morning, put on his clothes, and had breakfast.

But if common sense helps to select evidence, it also produces a good deal of pedestrian history. The fact is, the straightforward account of Silas Deane we have just presented has actually managed to miss the most fascinating parts of the story.

Fortunately, one enterprising historian named Julian Boyd was not satisfied with the traditional account of the matter. He examined the known facts of Deane's career and put them together in ways common sense had not suggested. Take, for example, two items on our list: (1) Deane was down on his luck and left in desperation for America; and (2) he visited John Trumbull. One fact is from the "important" items on the list and the other from items that seem incidental. How do they fit together?

To answer that, we have to know the source of information about the visit to Trumbull's, which is the letter from John Cutting informing Jefferson of Deane's rumored suicide.

A subscription had been made here chiefly by Americans to defray the expense of getting [Deane] out of this country. . . . Dr. Bancroft with great humanity and equal discretion undertook the management of the *man* and his *business*. Accordingly his passage was engaged, comfortable cloaths and stores for his voyage were laid in, and apparently without much reluctance he embarked. . . . I happen'd to see him a few days since at the lodging of Mr. Trumbull and thought I had never seen him look better.

We are now in a better position to see how our two items fit together. And as Julian Boyd has pointed out, they don't fit. According to the first, Deane was depressed, dejected, almost starving. According to the second, he had "never looked better." An alert historian begins to get nervous when he sees contradictions like that, so he hunts around a little more. And finds, among the collection of papers published by the Connecticut and New York historical societies, that Deane had been writing letters of his own.

One went to his brother-in-law in America, who had agreed to help pay Deane's transportation over and to receive him when he arrived—something that nobody had been willing to do for years. Other letters reveal that Deane had plans for what he would do when he finally returned home. He had seen models in England of the new steam engines, which he hoped might operate gristmills in America. He had talked to friends about getting a canal built from Lake Champlain in New York to the St. Lawrence River, in order to promote trade. These were not offhand dreams. As early as 1785, Deane had been at work drumming up support for his canal project. He had even laboriously calculated the cost of the canal's construction. ("Suppose a labourer to dig and remove six feet deep and eight feet square in one day. . . . 2,933 days of labour will dig one mile in length, twenty feet wide and eight feet deep. . . .") Obviously, Deane looked forward to a promising future.

Lastly, Deane appeared to believe that the controversy surrounding his French mission had finally abated. As he wrote an American friend,

It is now almost ten years since I have solicited for an impartial inquiry [into the dispute over my conduct]. . . . that justice might be done to my fortune and my character. . . . You can sufficiently imagine, without my attempting to describe, what I must have suffered on every account during so long a period of anxiety and distress. I hope that it is now drawing to a close.

Other letters went to George Washington and John Jay, reiterating Deane's innocence.

All this makes the two items on our list even more puzzling. If Deane was depressed and discouraged, why was he so enthusiastic about coming back to build canals and gristmills? If he really believed that his time of "anxiety and distress" was "drawing to a close," why did he commit suicide? Of course, Deane might have been subject to dramatic shifts in mood. Perhaps hope for the future alternated with despair about his chances for success. Perhaps a sudden fit of depression caused him to take his life.

But another piece of "unimportant" information, way down on our third list, makes this hypothesis difficult to accept. After Deane's ship left London, it was delayed offshore for more than a week. Suppose Deane did decide to commit suicide by taking an overdose of laudanum. Where did he get the drug? Surely not by walking up to the ship's surgeon and asking for it. He must have purchased it in London, before he left. Yet he remained on shipboard for more than a week. If Deane bought the laudanum during a temporary "fit" of depression, why did he wait a week before taking it? And if his depression was not just a sudden fit, how do we explain the optimistic letters to America?

This close look at three apparently unrelated facts indicates that perhaps Deane's story has more to it than meets the eye. It would be well, then, to reserve judgment about our first reconstruction of Silas Deane's career, and try to find as much information about the man as possible—regardless of whether it seems relevant at first. That means investigating not only Deane himself but also his friends and associates, like Ben Franklin, Arthur Lee, and Edward Bancroft. Since it is impossible in this prologue to look closely at all of Deane's acquaintances, for purpose of example we will take only one: his friend Bancroft.

SILAS DEANE'S FRIEND

Edward Bancroft was born in Westfield, Massachusetts, where his stepfather presided over a respectable tavern, the *Bunch of Grapes*. Bancroft was a clever fellow, and his father soon apprenticed him to a physician. Like many boys before him, Edward did not fancy his position and so ran away to sea. Unlike many boys, he managed to make the most of his situation. His ship landed in the Barbadoes, and there Bancroft signed on as the surgeon for a plantation in Surinam. The plantation owner, Paul Wentworth, liked the young man and let him use his private library for study. In addition, Bancroft met another doctor who taught him much about the area's exotic tropical plants and animals. When Bancroft returned to New England in 1766 and continued on to London the following year, he knew enough about Surinam's wildlife to publish a book entitled *An Essay on the Natural History of Guiana in South America.* It was well received by knowledgeable scholars and, among other things, established that an electric eel's shock was actually caused by electricity, a fact not previously recognized.

A young American bright enough to publish a book at age twenty-five and to experiment with electric eels attracted the attention of another electrical experimenter then in London, Ben Franklin. Franklin befriended Bancroft and introduced him to many influential colleagues, not only learned philosophers but also the politicians with whom Franklin worked as colonial agent for Pennsylvania. A second trip to Surinam produced more research on plants used in making color dyes; research so successful that Bancroft soon found himself elected to the prestigious Royal Society of Medicine. At the same time, Franklin led Bancroft into the political arena, both public and private. On the public side, Bancroft published a favorable review of Thomas Jefferson's pamphlet, *A Summary View of the Rights of British America;* privately, he joined Franklin and other investors in an attempt to gain a charter for land along the banks of the Ohio River.

Up to this point it has been possible to sketch Bancroft's career without once mentioning the name of Silas Deane. Common sense would suggest that the information about Bancroft's early travels, his scientific studies, his friends in Surinam, tell us little about Deane, and that the story ought to begin with a certain letter Bancroft received from Deane in June 1776. (Common sense is again wrong, but we must wait a little to discover why.)

The letter, which came to Bancroft in 1776, informed him that his old friend Silas Deane was coming to France as a merchant engaged in private business. Would Bancroft be interested in crossing over from England to meet Deane at Calais to catch up on news for old time's sake? An invitation like that would very likely have attracted Bancroft's curiosity. He did know Deane, who had been his teacher in 1758, but not very well. Why would Deane now write and suggest a meeting? Bancroft may have guessed the rest, or he may have known it from other contacts; in any case, he wrote his "old friend" that he would make all possible haste for Calais.

The truth of the matter, as we know, was that Deane had come to France to secure military supplies for the colonies. Franklin, who was back in Philadelphia, had suggested to Congress's Committee of Secret Correspondence that Deane contact Bancroft as a good source of information about British war plans. Bancroft could easily continue his friendship with English officials, because he did not have the reputation of being a hot-headed American patriot. So Deane met Bancroft at Calais in July and the two concluded their arrangements. Bancroft would be Deane's "private secretary" when needed in Paris and a spy for the Americans when in England.

It turned out that Deane's arrangement worked well—perhaps a little too well. Legally, Deane was permitted to collect a commission on all the supplies he purchased for Congress, but he went beyond that. He and Bancroft used their official connections in France to conduct a highly profitable private trade of their own. Deane, for instance, sometimes sent ships from France without declaring whether they were loaded with private or public goods. Then if the ships arrived safely, he would declare that the cargo was private, his own. But if the English navy captured the goods on the high seas, he labelled it government merchandise and the public absorbed the loss.

Deane used Bancroft to take advantage of his official position in other ways. Both men speculated in the London insurance markets, which were the eighteenth-century equivalent of gambling parlors. Anyone who wished could take out "insurance" against a particular event which might happen in the future. An insurer, for example, might quote odds on the chances of France going to war with England within the year. The insured would pay whatever premium he wished, say £1,000, and if France did go to war, and the odds had been five-to-one against it, the insured would receive £5,000. Wagers were made on almost any public event: which armies would win which battles, which politicians would fall from power, and even on whether a particular lord would die before the year was out.

Obviously, someone who had access to inside information—someone who knew in advance, for instance, that France was going to war with England—could win a fortune. That was exactly what Bancroft and Deane decided to do. Deane was in charge of concluding the French alliance, and he knew that if he succeeded Britain would be forced to declare war on France. Bancroft hurried across to London as soon as the treaty had been concluded and took out the proper insurance before the news went public. The profits shared by the two men from this and other similar ventures amounted to approximately ten thousand pounds. Like most gamblers, however, Deane also lost wagers. In the end, he netted little for his troubles.

Historians know these facts because they now have access to the papers of Deane, Bancroft, and others. Acquaintances of the two men lacked this advantage, but they suspected shady dealings anyway. Arthur Lee publicly accused Deane and Bancroft of playing the London insurance game. (Deane shot back that Lee was doing the same thing.) And the moralistic John Adams found Bancroft's conduct distasteful. Bancroft, according to Adams, was

> a meddler in stocks as well as reviews, and frequently went into the alley, and into the deepest and darkest retirements and recesses of the brokers and jobbers . . . and found amusement as well, perhaps, as profit, by listening to all the news and anecdotes, true or false, that were there whispered or more boldly pronounced. . . . This man had with him in France, a woman with whom he lives, and who by the French was called La Femme de Monsieur Bancroft. At tables he would season his foods with such enormous quantities of cayenne pepper which assisted by generous burgundy would set his tongue a running in the most licentious way both at table and after dinner. . . .

Yet for all Bancroft's dubious habits, and for all the suspicions of men like Lee and Adams, there was one thing that almost no one at the time suspected, and that not even historians discovered until the records of certain British officials were opened to the public more than a century later. Edward Bancroft was a double agent.

At the end of July 1776, after he had arranged to be Deane's secretary, Bancroft returned to England and met with Paul Wentworth, his friend from Surinam, who was then working in London for Britain's intelligence organization. Immediately Wentworth realized how valuable Bancroft would be as a spy and introduced him to two Secretaries of State. They in turn persuaded Bancroft to submit reports on the American negotiations in France. For his services, he received a lifetime pension of £200 a year—a figure the British were only too happy to pay for such good information. So quick was Bancroft's reporting that the Secretaries of State knew about the American mission to France even before the United States Congress could confirm that Deane had arrived safely!

Eventually, Bancroft discovered that he could pass his information directly to the British ambassador at the French court. To do so, he wrote innocent letters on the subject of "gallantry" and signed them "B. Edwards." On the same paper would go another note written in invisible ink, to appear only when the letter was dipped in a special developer held by Lord Stormont, the British ambassador. Bancroft left his letters every Tuesday morning in a sealed bottle in a hole near the trunk of a tree on the south terrace of the Tuileries, the royal palace. Lord Stormont's secretary would put any return information near another tree on the same terrace. With this system in operation Stormont could receive intelligence without having to wait for it to filter back from England.

Did any Americans suspect Bancroft of double dealing? Arthur Lee once claimed he had evidence to charge Bancroft with treason, but he never produced it. In any case, Lee had a reputation for suspecting everybody of everything. Franklin, for his part, shared lodgings with Deane and Bancroft during their stays in Paris. He had reason to guess that someone close to the American mission was leaking secrets—especially when Lord Stormont and the British newspapers made embarrassingly accurate accusations about French aid. The French wished to keep their assistance secret in order to avoid war with England as long as possible, but of course Franklin knew America would fare better with France fighting, so he did little to stop the leaks. "If I was sure," he remarked, "that my *valet de place* was a spy, as he probably is, I think I should not discharge him for that, if in other respects I liked him." So the French would tell Franklin he *really* ought to guard his papers more closely, and Franklin would say yes, yes, he really would have to do something about that; and the secrets continued to leak. Perhaps Franklin suspected Deane and Bancroft of playing the London insurance markets, but there is no evidence that he knew Bancroft was a double agent.

What about Deane, who was closer to Bancroft than anyone else? We have no proof that he shared the double agent's secret, but his alliance with Bancroft in other intrigues tells against him. Furthermore, one published leak pointed to a source so close to the American commissioners that Franklin began to investigate. As Julian Boyd has pointed out, Deane immediately directed suspicion toward a man he knew perfectly well was not a spy. We can only conclude he did so to help throw suspicion away from Bancroft. Very likely, if Bancroft was willing to help Deane play his games with the London insurers, Deane was willing to assist Bancroft in his game with British intelligence.

Of the two, Bancroft seems to have made out better. While Deane suffered reproach and exile for his conduct, Bancroft returned to England still respected by both the Americans and the British. Not that he had been without narrow escapes. Some of the British ministry (the king especially) did not trust him, and he once came close to being hung for treason when his superiors rightly suspected that he had associated with John the Painter, a notorious incendiarist who tried to set England's navy ablaze. But Bancroft left for Paris at the first opportunity, waited until the storm blew over, and returned to London at the end of the war with his lifetime pension raised to £1,000 a year. At the time of Deane's death, he was doing more of his scientific experiments, in hopes that Parliament would grant him a profitable monopoly on a new process for making dyes.

DEANE'S DEATH: A SECOND LOOK

So we finally arrive, the long way around, back where the story began: September 1789 and Deane's death. But now we have at hand a much larger store of information out of which to construct a narrative. Since writing history involves the acts of analyzing and selecting, let us review the results of our investigation.

We know that Deane was indeed engaged in dubious private ventures; ventures Congress would have condemned as unethical. We also have reason to suspect that Deane knew Bancroft was a spy for the British. Combining that evidence with what we already know about Deane's death, we might theorize that Deane committed suicide because, underneath all his claims to innocence, he knew he was guilty as Congress charged. The additional evidence, in other words, reveals a possible new motive for Deane's suicide.

Yet this theory presents definite problems. In the first place, Deane never admitted any wrongdoing to anyone—not in all the letters he wrote, not in any of his surviving papers. That does not mean he was innocent, nor even that he believed himself innocent. But often it is easier for a person to lie to himself than to his friends. Perhaps Deane actually convinced himself that he was blameless; that he had a right to make a little extra money from his influential position; that he did no more than anyone would in his situation. Certainly his personal papers point to that conclusion. And if Deane believed himself innocent—correctly or not—would he have any obvious motive for suicide? Furthermore, the theory does not explain the puzzle that started this investigation. If Deane felt guilty enough about his conduct to commit suicide, why did that guilt increase ten years after the fact? If he did feel suddenly guilty, why wait a week aboard ship before taking the fatal dose of laudanum? For that matter, why go up and chat with the captain when death was about to strike?

No, things still do not set quite right, so we must question the theory. What proof do we have that Deane committed suicide? Rumors about London. Tom Paine heard it from Cutting, the merchant. And Cutting reports in his letter to Jefferson that Deane's suicide was "the suspicion of Dr. Bancroft." How do we know the circumstances of Deane's death? The captain made a report, but for some reason it was not preserved. The one account that did survive was written by Bancroft, at the request of a friend. Then there were the anonymous obituaries in the newspapers. Who wrote them? Very likely Bancroft composed at least one; certainly, he was known as Silas Deane's closest friend and would have been consulted by any interested parties. There are a lot of strings here, which, when pulled hard enough, all run back to the affable Dr. Bancroft. What do we know about *his* situation in 1789?

We know Bancroft is dependent upon a pension of £1,000 a year, given him for his faithful service as a British spy. We know he is hoping Parliament will grant him a monopoly for making color dyes. Suddenly his old associate Deane, who has been leading a dissolute life in London, decides to return to America, vindicate himself to his former friends, and start a new life. Put yourself in Bancroft's place. Would you be just a little nervous about that idea? Here is a man down on his luck, now picking up and going to America to clear his reputation. What would Deane do to clear it? Tell everything he knew about his life in Paris? Submit his record books to Congress, as he had been asked to do so many years before? If Deane knew Bancroft was a double agent, would he say so? And if Deane's records mentioned the affair of John the Painter (as indeed they did), what would happen if knowledge of Bancroft's role in the plot reached England? Ten years earlier, Bancroft would have been hung. True, memories had faded, but even if he were spared death, would Parliament grant a monopoly on color dyes to a known traitor? Would Parliament continue the £1,000 pension? It was one thing to have Deane living in London, where Bancroft could watch him; it would be quite another to have him all the way across the Atlantic Ocean, ready to tell—who knows what?

Admit it: if you were Bancroft, wouldn't you be just a little nervous? We are forced to consider, however reluctantly, that Deane was not expecting to die as he walked the deck of the *Boston Packet.* Yet if Bancroft did murder Deane, how? He was not aboard ship when death came and had not seen Deane for more than a week. That is a good alibi, but then, Bancroft was a clever man. We know (once again from the letters of John Cutting) that Bancroft was the person who "with great humanity and equal discretion undertook the management of the *man* and the *business*" of getting Deane ready to leave for America. Bancroft himself wrote Jefferson that he had been visiting Deane often "to assist him with advice, medicins, and money for his subsistence." If Deane were a laudanum addict, as Bancroft hinted to Cutting, might not the good doctor who helped with "medicins" also have procured the laudanum? And having done that, might he not easily slip some other deadly chemical into the mixture, knowing full well that Deane would not use it until he was on shipboard and safely off to America? That is only conjecture. We have no direct evidence to suggest this is what happened.

But there is one other fact we do know for sure; and in light of our latest theory, it is an interesting one. Undeniably, Edward Bancroft was an expert on poisons.

He did not advertise that knowledge, of course; few people in London at the time of Deane's death would have been likely to remember the fact. But twenty years earlier, the historian may recall, Bancroft wrote a book on the natural history of Guiana. At that time, he not only investigated electric eels and color dyes, but also the poisons of the area, particularly curare (or "Woowara" as Bancroft called it). He investigated it so well, in fact, that when he returned to England he brought samples of curare with him which (he announced in the book) he had deposited with the publishers so that any gentleman of "unimpeachable" character might use the samples for scientific study.*

Furthermore, Bancroft seemed to be a remarkably good observer not only of the poisons but also of those who used them. His book described in ample detail the natives' ability to prepare poisons

which, given in the smallest quantities, produce a very slow but inevitable death, particularly a composition which resembles wheat-flour,

---

*As the Author has brought a confiderable quantity of this Poifon to *England,* any Gentleman, whofe genius may incline him to profecute thefe experiments, and whofe character will warrant us to confide in his hands a preparation, capable of perpetrating the moft fecret and fatal villainy, may be supplied with a fufficient quantity of the *Woorara,* by applying to Mr. *Becket,* in the *Strand.* —from *An Essay on the Natural History of Guiana in South America,* by Edward Bancroft which they sometimes use to revenge past injuries, that have been long neglected, and are thought forgotten. On these occasions they always feign an insensibility of the injury which they intend to revenge, and even repay it with services and acts of friendship, until they have destroyed all distrust and apprehension of danger in the destined victim of the vengeance. When this is effected, they meet at some festival, and engage him to drink with them, drinking first themselves to obviate suspicion, and afterwards secretly dropping the poison, ready concealed under their nails, which are usually long, into the drink.

Twenty years later Bancroft was busy at work with the color dyes he had brought back from Surinam. Had he, by any chance, also held onto any of those poisons?

Unless new evidence comes to light, we will probably never know for sure. Historians are generally forced to deal with probabilities, not certainties, and we leave you to draw your own conclusions about the death of Silas Deane.

What does seem certain is that whatever "really happened" to Deane 200 years ago cannot be determined today without the active participation of the historian. Being courier to the past is not enough. For better or worse, historians inescapably leave an imprint as they go about their business: asking interesting questions about apparently dull facts, seeing connections between subjects that had not seemed related before, shifting and rearranging evidence until it assumes a coherent pattern. The past is not history; only the raw material of it.

QUESTIONS FOR DISCUSSION

1. Why, if their intended reader presumably has a mistaken notion about the nature of history, do Davidson and Lytle never address the reader directly? Examine the first three paragraphs to see what they do instead. What would the effect have been if they had written, "You probably have a mistaken notion of what history is"?
2. If history is not simply "what happened in the past," what is it? Where do Davidson and Lytle place the correct definition of what history is and why is that definition postponed?
3. Davidson and Lytle use only one extended example in this chapter to support and illustrate their corrected definition of history. Aren't they taking a chance by using only one example and that one about an obscure and unfamiliar figure? What do they hope to gain by this tactic?
4. If the general story of Silas Deane were merely being used as a supporting

example, it could be given as a brief summary of the work of the original historian, Julian Boyd. How does the elaborate form given the story of Deane amount in itself to support for Davidson and Lytle's CP characterizing history?

5. The elements of the story of Silas Deane illustrate the tactics of CP argument, the process of fitting appropriate characterizations over a body of evidence. When the evidence yields contradictory CPs, historians know their search is unfinished. At what points did contradictions in the story of Deane drive historians to further research?

6. The final version of the story of Deane claims that he was murdered by Bancroft. The authors qualify this conclusion with a "probably." Why is this probable thesis preferable to the explanation that Deane committed suicide? Can you think of any other explanations of the death of Silas Deane?

7. Davidson and Lytle are good storytellers as well as arguers; they arouse suspense and postpone the "solution" to the end of their tale. How does their narrative skill serve their argumentative purpose? Compare the use of narrative in this essay with that in "The Prognosis for this Patient Is Horrible" by Berton Roueché on pages 206–219 of Part Two.

SUGGESTIONS FOR WRITING

1. If you have an inside view of the workings of a discipline (such as your major) that many people misunderstand, write a redefinition of it for outsiders, illustrating its method on the model of Davidson and Lytle.

2. Construct a CP characterizing a person or event and try to support it with a single, extended, narrative example. You might retell a famous event in history or the life of an historical figure you have investigated in such a way that it supports a single interpretive categorization. (For example, the Battle of Gettysburg could be recounted in a way that illustrates the point that the battle was a series of miscalculations by both sides.) This kind of argument might legitimately be addressed to a historian.

3. Davidson and Lytle use the technique of elimination (important in causal argument), trying out successive characterizations and discarding them when some evidence proves contradictory. This is a useful rhetorical tactic to imitate. Try it out on the subject chosen in response to suggestion 2.

4. The research of Julian Boyd revised the prevailing interpretation of an event and a character. If you are currently taking a history course, you might persuasively recount a similar revision of a view once held. Direct your account to readers who still hold the earlier view.

5. How is history taught in your school? What working definition of history seems to be implicit in the methods of teaching history that are practiced? Write and support a CP characterizing your discovery for your classmates: "History as it is taught here is . . ."

6. How could the study and teaching of history be improved, whether at the elementary, high school, or college level? Write an appeal either to students or teachers at one level advocating that history be taught in a way that conveys Davidson and Lytle's definition of it.

———————— ≫≫ ≪≪ ————————

Genesis vs. Geology

STEPHEN JAY GOULD

Stephen Jay Gould seems in some ways to be a nineteenth-century scientist living in the twentieth century. He refuses to admit that the audience for scientific argument should be anything less than the whole educated public. As a well-known paleontologist and historian of science, he has carried out this belief in several award-winning books and collections of essays, among them Ever Since Darwin, The Panda's Thumb, *and* The Mismeasure of Man. *As a well-known spokesperson for Darwinian evolution, Gould was called upon to testify at the 1981 trial in Arkansas over "equal time" ordinances for creation science. That event spurred Gould to write on creationism for the nonscientific readers of* The Atlantic Monthly. *Whether you agree with him or not, notice how Gould combines rigorous reasoning and a careful use of evidence with the ability to capture the interest of his audience.*

G.K. Chesterton once mused over Noah's dinnertime conversations during those long nights on a vast and tempestuous sea:

> And Noah he often said to his wife
>   when he sat down to dine,
> "I don't care where the water goes if
>   it doesn't get into the wine."

Noah's insouciance has not been matched by defenders of his famous flood. For centuries, fundamentalists have tried very hard to find a place for the subsiding torrents. They have struggled even more valiantly to devise a source for all that water. Our modern oceans, extensive as they are, will not override Mt. Everest. One seventeenth-century searcher said: "I can as soon believe that a man would be drowned in his own spittle as that the world should be deluged by the water in it."

With the advent of creationism, a solution to this old dilemma has been put forward. In *The Genesis Flood* (1961), the founding document of the creationist movement, John Whitcomb and Henry Morris seek guidance from Genesis 1:6–7, which states that God created the firmament and then slid it into place amidst the waters, thus dividing "the waters which were under the firmament from the waters which were above the firmament: and it was so." The waters under the firmament include seas and interior fluid that may rise in volcanic eruptions. But what are the waters above the firmament? Whitcomb and Morris reason that Moses cannot refer here to transient rain clouds, because he also tells us (Genesis 2:5) that "the Lord God had not caused it to rain upon the earth." The authors therefore imagine that the earth, in those palmy days, was surrounded by a gigantic canopy of water vapor (which, being invisible, did not obscure the light of Genesis 1:3). "These upper waters," Whitcomb and Morris write, "were therefore placed in that position by divine creativity, not by the normal processes of the hydrological cycle of the present day." Upwelling from the depths together with the liquefaction, puncturing, and descent of the celestial canopy produced more than enough water for Noah's worldwide flood.

Fanciful solutions often generate a cascade of additional difficulties. In this case, Morris, a hydraulic engineer by training, and Whitcomb invoke a divine assist to gather the waters into their canopy, but then can't find a natural way to get them down. So they invoke a miracle: God put the water there in the first place; let him then release it.

> The simple fact of the matter is that one cannot have *any* kind of a Genesis Flood without acknowledging the presence of supernatural elements. . . . It is obvious that the opening of the "windows of heaven" in order to allow "the waters which were above the firmament" to fall upon the earth, and the breaking up of "all the fountains of the great deep" were supernatural acts of God.

Since we usually define science, at least in part, as a system of explanation that relies upon invariant natural laws, this charmingly direct invocation of miracles (suspensions of natural law) would seem to negate the central claims of the modern creationist movement—that creationism is not religion but a scientific alternative to evolution; that creationism has been disregarded by scientists because they are a fanatical and dogmatic lot who cannot appreciate new advances; and that creationists must therefore seek legislative redress in their attempts to force a "balanced treatment" for both creationism and evolution in the science classrooms of our public schools.

Legislative history has driven creationists to this strategy of claiming scientific status for their religious view. The older laws, which banned the teaching of evolution outright and led to John Scopes's conviction in 1925, were overturned by the Supreme Court in 1968, but not before they had exerted a chilling effect upon teaching for forty years. (Evolution is the indispensable organizing principle of the life sciences, but I did not hear the word in my 1956 high school biology class. New York City, to be sure, suffered no restrictive ordinances, but publishers, following the principle of the "least common denominator" as a sales strategy, tailored the national editions of their textbooks to the few states that considered it criminal to place an ape on the family escutcheon.) A second attempt to mandate equal time for frankly religious views of life's history passed the Tennessee state legislature in the 1970s but failed a constitutional challenge in the court. This judicial blocking left only one legislative path open—the claim that creationism is a science.

The third strategy had some initial success, and "balanced treatment" acts to equate "evolution science" and "creation science" in classrooms passed the Arkansas and Louisiana legislatures in 1981. The ACLU has sued for a federal-court ruling on the Louisiana law's constitutionality, and a trial is likely this year. The Arkansas law was challenged by the ACLU in 1981, on behalf of local plaintiffs (including twelve practicing theologians who felt more threatened by the bill than many scientists did). Federal Judge William R. Overton heard the Arkansas case in Little Rock last December. I spent the better part of a day on the stand, a witness for the prosecution, testifying primarily about how the fossil record refutes "flood geology" and supports evolution.

On January 5, Judge Overton delivered his eloquent opinion, declaring the Arkansas act unconstitutional because so-called "creation science" is only a version of Genesis read literally—a partisan (and narrowly sectarian) religious view, barred from public-school classrooms by the First Amendment. Legal language is often incomprehensible, but sometimes it is charming, and I enjoyed the wording of Overton's decision: ". . . judgment is hereby entered in favor of the plaintiffs and against the defendants. The relief prayed for is granted."

Support for Overton's equation of "creation science" with strident and sectarian fundamentalism comes from two sources. First, the leading creationists themselves released some frank private documents in response to plaintiffs' subpoenas. Overton's long list of citations seems to brand the claim for scientific creationism as simple hypocrisy. For example, Paul Ellwanger, the tireless advocate and drafter of the "model bill" that became Arkansas Act 590 of 1981, the law challenged by the ACLU, says in a letter to a state legislator that "I view this whole battle as one between God and anti-God forces, though I know there are a large number of evolutionists who believe in God. . . . it behooves Satan to do all he can to thwart our efforts . . ." In another letter, he refers to "the idea of killing evolution instead of playing these debating games that we've been playing for nigh over a decade already"—a reasonably clear statement of the creationists' ultimate aims, and an identification of their appeals for "equal time," "the American way of fairness," and "presenting them both and letting the kids decide" as just so much rhetoric.

The second source of evidence of the bill's unconstitutionality lies in the logic and character of creationist arguments themselves. The flood story is central to all creationist systems. It also has elicited the only specific and testable theory the creationists have offered; for the rest, they have only railed against evolutionary claims. The flood story was explicitly cited as one of the six defining characteristics of "creation science" in Arkansas Act 590: "explanation of the earth's geology by catastrophism, including the occurrence of a world wide flood."

Creationism reveals its nonscientific character in two ways: its central tenets cannot be tested and its peripheral claims, which can be tested, have been proven false. At its core, the creationist account rests on "singularities"—that is to say, on miracles. The creationist God is not the noble clock-winder of Newton and Boyle, who set the laws of nature properly at the beginning of time and then released direct control in full confidence that his initial decisions would require no revision. He is, instead, a constant presence, who suspends his own laws when necessary to make the new or destroy the old. Since science can treat only natural phenomena occurring in a context of invariant natural law, the constant invocation of miracles places creationism in another realm.

We have already seen how Whitcomb and Morris remove a divine finger from the dike of heaven to flood the earth from their vapor canopy. But the miracles surrounding Noah's flood do not stop there; two other supernatural assists are required. First, God acted "to gather the animals into the Ark." (The Bible tells us [Genesis 6:20] that they found their own way.) Second, God intervened to keep the animals "under control during the year of the Flood." Whitcomb and Morris provide a long disquisition on hibernation and suspect that some divinely ordained state of suspended animation relieved Noah's small and aged crew of most responsibility for feeding and cleaning (poor Noah himself was 600 years old at the time).

In candid moments, leading creationists will admit that the miraculous character of origin and destruction precludes a scientific understanding. Morris writes (and Judge Overton quotes): "God was there when it happened. We were not there. . . . Therefore, we are completely limited to what God has seen fit to tell us, and this information is in His written Word." Duane Gish, the leading creationist author, says: "We do not know how the Creator created, what processes He used, for He used processes which are not now operating anywhere in the natural universe. . . . We cannot discover by scientific investigation anything about the creative processes used by God." When pressed about these quotes, creationists tend to admit that they are purveying religion after all, but then claim that evolution is equally religious. Gish also says: "Creationists have repeatedly stated that neither creation nor evolution is a scientific theory (and each is equally religious)." But as Judge Overton reasoned, if creationists are merely complaining that evolution is religion, then they should be trying to eliminate it from the schools, not struggling to get their own brand of religion into science classrooms as well. And if, instead, they are asserting the validity of their own version of natural history, they must be able to prove, according to the demands of science, that creationism is scientific.

Scientific claims must be testable; we must, in principle, be able to envision a set of observations that would render them false. Miracles cannot be judged by this criterion, as Whitcomb and Morris have admitted. But is all creationist writing merely about untestable singularities? Are arguments never made in proper scientific form? Creationists do offer some testable statements, and these are amenable to scientific analysis. Why, then, do I continue to claim that creationism isn't science? Simply because these relatively few statements have been tested and conclusively refuted. Dogmatic assent to disproved claims is not scientific behavior. Scientists are as stubborn as the rest of us, but they must be able to change their minds.

In "flood geology," we find our richest source of testable creationist claims. Creationists have been forced into this uncharacteristically vulnerable stance by a troubling fact too well known to be denied: namely, that the geological record of fossils follows a single, invariant order throughout the world. The oldest rocks contain only single-celled creatures; invertebrates dominate later strata, followed by the first fishes, then dinosaurs, and finally large mammals. One might be tempted to take a "liberal," or allegorical, view of Scripture and identify this sequence with the order of creation in Genesis 1, allowing millions or billions of years for the "days" of Moses. But creationists will admit no such reconciliation. Their fundamentalism is absolute and uncompromising. If Moses said "days," he meant periods of twenty-four hours, to the second. (Creationist literature is often less charitable to liberal theology than to evolution. As a subject for wrath, nothing matches the enemy within.)

Since God created with such alacrity, all creatures once must have lived simultaneously on the earth. How, then, did their fossil remains get sorted into an invariable order in the earth's strata? To resolve this particularly knotty dilemma, creationists invoke Noah's flood: all creatures were churned together in the great flood and their fossilized succession reflects the order of their settling as the waters receded. But what natural processes would produce such a predictable order from a singular chaos? The testable proposals of "flood geology" have been advanced to explain the causes of this sorting.

Whitcomb and Morris offer three suggestions. The first—hydrological—holds that denser and more streamlined objects would have descended more rapidly and should populate the bottom strata (in conventional geology, the oldest strata). The second—ecological—envisions a sorting responsive to environment. Denizens of the ocean bottom were overcome by the flood waters first, and should lie in the lower strata; inhabitants of mountaintops postponed their inevitable demise, and now adorn our upper strata. The third—anatomical or functional—argues that certain animals, by their high intelligence or superior mobility, might have struggled successfully for a time, and ended up at the top.

All three proposals have been proven false. The lower strata abound in delicate, floating creatures, as well as spherical globs. Many oceanic creatures—whales and teleost fishes in particular—appear only in upper strata, well above hordes of terrestrial forms. Clumsy sloths (not to mention hundreds of species of marine invertebrates) are restricted to strata lying well above others that serve as exclusive homes for scores of lithe and nimble small dinosaurs and pterosaurs.

The very invariance of the universal fossil sequence is the strongest argument against its production in a single gulp. Could exceptionless order possibly arise from a contemporaneous mixture by such dubious processes of sorting? Surely, somewhere, at least one courageous trilobite would have paddled on valiantly (as its colleagues succumbed) and won a place in the upper strata. Surely, on some primordial beach, a man would have suffered a heart attack and been washed into the lower strata before intelligence had a chance to plot temporary escape. But if the strata represent vast stretches of sequential time, then invariant order is an expectation, not a problem. No trilobite lies in the upper strata because they all perished 225 million years ago. No man keeps lithified company with a dinosaur, because we were still 60 million years in the future when the last dinosaur perished.

True science and religion are not in conflict. The history of approaches to Noah's flood by scientists who were also professional theologians provides an excellent example of this important truth—and also illustrates just how long ago "flood geology" was conclusively laid to rest by religious scientists. I have argued that direct invocation of miracles and unwillingness to abandon a false doctrine deprive modern creationists of their self-proclaimed status as scientists. When we examine how the great scientist-theologians of past centuries treated the flood, we note that their work is distinguished by both a conscious refusal to admit miraculous events into their explanatory schemes and a willingness to abandon preferred hypotheses in the face of geological evidence. They were scientists *and* religious leaders—and they show us why modern creationists are not scientists.

On the subject of miracles, the Reverend Thomas Burnet published his century's most famous geological treatise in the 1680s, *Telluris theoria sacra (The Sacred Theory of the Earth)*. Burnet accepted the Bible's truth, and set out to construct a geological history that would be in accord with the events of Genesis. But he believed something else even more strongly: that, as a scientist, he must follow natural law and scrupulously avoid miracles. His story is fanciful by modern standards: the earth originally was devoid of topography, but was drying and cracking; the cracks served as escape vents for internal fluids, but rain sealed the cracks, and the earth, transformed into a gigantic pressure cooker, ruptured its surface skin; surging internal waters inundated the earth, producing Noah's flood. Bizarre, to be sure, but bizarre precisely because Burnet would not abandon natural law. It is not easy to force a preconceived story into the strictures of physical causality. Over and over again, Burnet acknowledges that his task would be much simpler if only he could invoke a miracle. Why weave such a complex tale to find water for the flood in a physically acceptable manner, when God might simply have made new water for his cataclysmic purification? Many of Burnet's colleagues urged such a course, but he rejected it as inconsistent with the methods of "natural philosophy" (the word "science" had not yet entered English usage):

> They say in short that God Almighty created waters on purpose to make the Deluge . . . And this, in a few words, is the whole account of the business. This is to cut the knot when we cannot loose it.

Burnet's God, like the deity of Newton and Boyle, was a clock-winder, not a bungler who continually perturbed his own system with later corrections.

> We think him a better Artist that makes a Clock that strikes regularly at every hour from the Springs and Wheels which he puts in the work, than he that hath so made his Clock that he must put his finger to it every hour to make it strike: And if one should contrive a piece of Clockwork so that it should beat all the hours, and make all its motions regularly for such a time, and that time being come, upon a signal given, or a Spring toucht, it should of its own accord fall all to pieces; would not this be look'd upon as a piece of greater Art, than if the Workman came at that time prefixt, and with a great Hammer beat it into pieces?

Flood geology was considered and tested by early-nineteenth-century geologists. They never believed that a single flood had produced all fossil-bearing strata, but they did accept and then disprove a claim that the uppermost strata contained evidence for a single, catastrophic, worldwide inundation. The science of geology arose in nations that were glaciated during the great ice ages, and glacial deposits are similar to the products of floods. During the 1820s, British geologists carried out an extensive empirical program to test whether these deposits represented the action of a single flood. The work was led by two ministers, the Reverend Adam Sedgwick (who taught Darwin his geology) and the Reverend William Buckland. Buckland initially decided that all the "superficial gravels" (as these deposits were called) represented a single event, and he published his *Reliquiae diluvianae (Relics of the Flood)* in 1824. However, Buckland's subsequent field work proved that the superficial gravels were not contemporaneous but represented several different events (multiple ice ages, as we now know). Geology proclaimed no worldwide flood but rather a long sequence of local events. In one of the great statements in the history of science, Sedgwick, who was Buckland's close colleague in both science and theology, publicly abandoned flood geology—and upheld empirical science—in his presidential address to the Geological Society of London in 1831.

> Having been myself a believer, and, to the best of my power, a propagator of what I now regard as a philosophic heresy, and having more than once been quoted for opinions I do not now maintain, I think it right, as one of my last acts before I quit this Chair, thus publicly to read my recantation . . .
>
> There is, I think, one great negative conclusion now incontestably established—that the vast masses of diluvial gravel, scattered almost over the surface of the earth, do not belong to one violent and transitory period . . .
>
> We ought, indeed, to have paused before we first adopted the diluvian theory, and referred all our old superficial gravel to the action of the Mosaic flood . . . In classing together distant unknown formations under one name; in giving them a simultaneous origin, and in determining their date, not by the organic remains we had discovered, but by those we expected hypothetically hereafter to discover, in them; we have given one more example of the passion with which the mind fastens upon general conclusions, and of the readiness with which it leaves the consideration of unconnected truths.

As I prepared to leave Little Rock last December, I went to my hotel room to gather my belongings and found a man sitting backward on my commode, pulling it apart with a plumber's wrench. He explained to me that a leak in the room below had caused part of the ceiling to collapse and he was seeking the source of the water. My commode, located just above, was the obvious candidate, but his hypothesis had failed, for my equipment was working perfectly. The plumber then proceeded to give me a fascinating disquisition on how a professional traces the pathways of water through hotel pipes and walls. The account was perfectly logical and mechanistic; it can come only from here, here, or there, flow this way or that way, and end up there, there, or here. I then asked him what he thought of the trial across the street, and he confessed his staunch creationism, including his firm belief in the miracle of Noah's flood.

As a professional, this man never doubted that water has a physical source and a mechanically constrained path of motion—and that he could use the principles of his trade to identify causes. It would be a poor (and unemployed) plumber indeed who suspected that the laws of engineering had been suspended whenever a puddle and cracked plaster bewildered him. Why should we approach the physical history of our earth any differently?

QUESTIONS FOR DISCUSSION

1. What attitude toward creationism does Gould assume on the part of his audience? Is he writing to fundamentalists? Could he convince them with such an argument?

2. Unlike most of the CP arguments in this section, Gould's essay supports a negative proposition, one that excludes something from a set. What is being excluded from what category? Unlike many CP arguments that simply aim at their audience's mental assent, this one has political, social, and educational consequences. What are they?

3. Gould adopts the unusual strategy of summarizing his entire argument in the first five paragraphs. He then goes over his case in much greater detail. Why does he risk disclosing his conclusion before his evidence is fully presented? Does the format that Gould adopts here resemble that of a scientific article?

4. Gould's argument works by identifying an essential attribute of creationism that is rejected by science. What is that attribute? How does he show that creationism has it and science does not?

5. How does Gould support the necessary part of his argument that science refuses miraculous explanations? His use of historical evidence is a somewhat surprising tactic. What effect does he achieve by it?

6. Gould uses a particularly strong form of evidence to support his contention that creationism invokes miracles and is therefore not science. Find the places where he uses quotations from the creationists.

7. How does Gould affect his ethos by claiming that "true science and religion are not in conflict"?

SUGGESTIONS FOR WRITING

1. Many pursuits and "isms" and "ologies" claim these days to be scientific. Write a refutation of the scientific claims of a phenomenon like parapsychology or biorhythms or astrology using Gould's definition of science or scientific behavior. Your argument could be addressed to two possible audiences: the easier one of the uncommitted or the harder one of those who believe in these mysticisms.

2. Do the opposite of Suggestion 1 and support the claims of some new study to scientific status, again by relying on Gould's distinctions.
3. Arkansas Judge Overton suggested a strategy for creationists when he maintained that "if creationists are merely complaining that evolution is religion they should be trying to eliminate it from the schools." Can you argue for a categorization of evolution as a religious belief? Of science itself as a religious system?
4. If you disagree with Gould's arguments, refute them. Address your refutation to Gould himself or to readers of *The Atlantic Monthly* who favor his position.
5. Support in detail Gould's contention that true religion and science are never in contention. Address your argument either to someone who believes only in science or someone who believes only in religion.

-»» ««-

The Rage to Know

HORACE FREELAND JUDSON

Horace Freeland Judson's credentials are in journalism, but he has spent many years and earned an impressive reputation writing about science for lay audiences. His best known work is The Eighth Day of Creation, *an authoritative history of molecular biology. In "The Rage to Know," excerpted from his book* The Search for Solutions, *Judson draws on his considerable familiarity with science and scientists to redefine the pursuit of science and make some surprising analogies with art and religion.*

Reading this article will impart a valuable lesson in one of the tactics of the CP argument, for "The Rage to Know" abounds with examples that make for good stories while they support the thesis.

Certain moments of the mind have a special quality of well-being. A mathematician friend of mine remarked the other day that his daughter, aged eight, had just stumbled without his teaching onto the fact that some numbers are prime numbers—those, like 11 or 19 or 83 or 1023, that cannot be divided by any other integer (except, trivially, by 1). "She called them 'unfair' numbers," he said. "And when I asked her why they were unfair, she told me, 'Because there's no way to share them out evenly.'" What delighted him most was not her charming turn of phrase nor her equitable turn of mind (seventeen peppermints to give to her friends?) but—as a mathematician—the knowledge that the child had experienced a moment of pure scientific perception. She had discovered for herself something of the way things are.

The satisfaction of such a moment at its most intense—and this is what ought to be meant, after all, by the tarnished phrase "the moment of truth"—is not easy to describe. It partakes at once of exhilaration and tranquillity. It is luminously clear. It is beautiful. The clarity of the moment of discovery, the beauty of what in that moment is seen to be true about the world, is the fundamental attraction that draws scientists on.

Science is enormously disparate—easily the most varied and diverse of human pursuits. The scientific endeavor ranges from the study of animal behavior all the way to particle physics, and from the purest of mathematics back again to the most practical problems of shelter and hunger, sickness and war. Nobody has succeeded in catching all this in one net. And yet the conviction persists—scientists themselves believe, at heart—that behind the diversity lies a unity. In those luminous moments of discovery, in the various approaches and the painful tension required to arrive at them, and then in the community of science, organized worldwide to doubt and criticize, test and exploit discoveries —somewhere in that constellation, to begin with, there are surely constants. Deeper is the lure that in the bewildering variety of the world as it is there may be found some astonishing simplicities.

Philosophers, and some of the greatest among them, have offered descriptions of what they claim is the method of science. These make most scientists acutely uncomfortable. The descriptions don't seem to fit what goes on in the doing of science. They seem at once too abstract and too limited. Scientists don't believe that they think in ways that are wildly different from the way most people think at least in some areas of their lives. "We'd be in real trouble—we could get nowhere—if ordinary methods of inference did not apply," Philip Morrison said in a conversation a while ago. (Morrison is a theoretical physicist at the Massachusetts Institute of Technology.) The wild difference, he went on to say, is that scientists apply these everyday methods to areas that most people never think about seriously and carefully. The philosophers' descriptions don't prepare one for either this ordinariness or this extreme diversity of the scientific enterprise—the variety of things to think about, the variety of obstacles and traps to understanding, the variety of approaches to solutions. They hardly acknowledge the fact that a scientist ought often to find himself stretching to the tiptoe of available technique and apparatus, out beyond the frontier of the art, attempting to do something whose difficulty is measured most significantly by the fact that it has never been done before. Science is carried on—this, too, is obvious—in the field, in the observatory, in the laboratory. But historians leave out the arts of the chef and the watchmaker, the development at the bench of a new procedure or a new instrument. "And *making it work,*" Morrison said. "This is terribly important." Indeed, biochemists talk about "the cookbook." Many a Nobel Prize has been awarded, not for a discovery, as such, but for a new technique or a new tool that opened up a whole field of discovery. "I am a theoretician," Morrison said. "And yet the most important problem for me is to be in touch with the people who are making new instruments or finding new ways of observing, and to try to get them to do the right experiments." And then, in a burst of annoyance, "I feel very reluctant to give any support to descriptions of 'scientific method.' The scientific enterprise is very difficult to model. You have to look at what scientists of all kinds *actually do.*"

It's true that by contrast philosophers and historians seem book-bound—or paper-blindered, depending chiefly on what has been published as scientific research for their understanding of the process of discovery. In this century, anyway, published papers are no guide to the way scientists get the results they report. We have testimony of the highest authenticity for that. Sir Peter Medawar has both done fine science and written well about how it is done: he won his Nobel Prize for investigations of immunological tolerance, which explained, among other things, why foreign tissue, like a kidney or a heart, is rejected by the body into which it is transplanted, and he has described the methods of science in essays of grace and distinction. A while ago, Medawar wrote, "What scientists *do* has never been the subject of a scientific . . . inquiry. It is no use looking to scientific 'papers,' for they not merely conceal but actively misrepresent the reasoning that goes into the work they describe." The observation has become famous, its truth acknowledged by other scientists. Medawar wrote further, "Scientists are building explanatory structures, *telling stories* which are scrupulously tested to see if they are stories about real life."

Scientists do science for a variety of reasons, of course, and most of them are familiar to the sculptor, or to the surgeon or the athlete or the builder of bridges: the professional's pride in skill; the swelling gratification that comes with recognition accorded by colleagues and peers; perhaps the competitor's fierce appetite; perhaps ambition for a kind of fame more durable than most. At the beginning is curiosity, and with curiosity the delight in mastery—the joy of figuring it out that is the birthright of every child. I once asked Murray Gell-Mann, a theoretical physicist, how he got started in science. His answer was to point to the summer sky: "When I was a boy, I used to ask all sorts of simple questions—like, 'What holds the clouds up?' " Rosalind Franklin, the crystallographer whose early death deprived her of a share in the Nobel Prize for the discovery of the structure of DNA, one day was helping a young collaborator draft an application for research money, when she looked up at him and said, "What we can't tell them is that it's so much *fun!*" He still remembers her glint of mischief. The play of the mind, in an almost childlike innocence, is a pleasure that appears again and again in scientists' reflections on their work. The geneticist Barbara McClintock, as a woman in American science in the 1930s, had no chance at the academic posts open to her male colleagues, but that hardly mattered to her. "I did it because it was *fun!*" she said forty years later. "I couldn't wait to get up in the morning! I never thought of it as 'science.' "

The exuberant innocence can be poignant. François Jacob, who won his share of a Nobel Prize as one of the small group of molecular biologists in the fifties who brought sense and order into the interactions by which bacteria regulate their life processes, recently read an account I had written of that work, and said to me with surprise and an evident pang of regret, "We were like children playing!" He meant the fun of it—but also the simplicity of the problems they had encountered and the innocence of mind they had brought to them. Two hundred and fifty years before—although Jacob did not consciously intend the parallel— Isaac Newton, shortly before his death, said:

> I do not know what I may appear to the world, but to myself I seem to have been only like a boy playing on the sea shore, and diverting myself in now and then finding a smoother pebble or a prettier shell than ordinary, whilst the great ocean of truth lay all undiscovered before me.

For some, curiosity and the delight of putting the world together deepen into a life's passion. Sheldon Glashow, a fundamental-particle physicist at Harvard, also got started in science by asking simple questions. "In eighth grade, we were learning about how the earth goes around the sun, and the moon around the earth, and so on," he said. "And I thought about that, and realized that the Man in the Moon is always looking at us"—that the moon as it circles always turns the same face to the earth. "And I asked the teacher, 'Why is the Man in the Moon always looking at us?' She was pleased with the question—but said it was hard to answer. And it turns out that it's not until you're in college-level physics courses that one really learns the answers," Glashow said. "But the *difference* is that most people would look at the moon and wonder for a moment and say, 'That's interesting'—and then forget it. But some people can't let go."

Curiosity is not enough. The word is too mild by far, a word for infants. Passion is indispensable for creation, no less in the sciences than in the arts. Medawar once described it in a talk addressed to young scientists. "You must feel in yourself an exploratory impulsion—an *acute discomfort* at incomprehension." This is the rage to know. The other side of the fun of science, as of art, is pain. A problem worth solving will surely require weeks and months of lack of progress, whipsawed between hope and the blackest sense of despair. The marathon runner or the young swimmer who would be a champion knows at least that the pain may be a symptom of progress. But here the artist and the scientist part company with the athlete—to join the mystic for a while. The pain of creation, though not of the body, is in one way worse. It must be not only endured but reflected back on itself to increase the agility, variety, inventiveness of the play of the mind. Some problems in science have demanded such devotion, such willingness to bear repeated rebuffs, not just for years but for decades. There are times in the practice of the arts, we're told, of abysmal self-doubt. There are like passages in the doing of science.

Albert Einstein took eleven years of unremitting concentration to produce the general theory of relativity; long afterward, he wrote, "In the light of knowledge attained, the happy achievement seems almost a matter of course, and any intelligent student can grasp it without too much trouble. But the years of anxious searching in the dark, with their intense longing, their alternations of confidence and exhaustion, and the final emergence into the light—only those who have experienced it can understand it." Einstein confronting Einstein's problems: the achievement, to be sure, is matched only by Newton's and perhaps Darwin's —but the experience is not rare. It is all but inseparable from high accomplishment. In the black cave of unknowing, when one is groping for the contours of the rock and the slope of the floor, tossing a pebble and listening for its fall, brushing away false clues as insistent as cobwebs, a touch of fresh air on the cheek can make hope leap up, an unexpected scurrying whisper can induce the mood of the brink of terror. "Afterward it can be told—trivialized—like a *roman policier*, a detective story," François Jacob once said. "While you're there, it is the sound and the fury." But it was the poet and adept of mysticism St. John of the Cross who gave to this passionate wrestling with bafflement the name by which, ever since, it has been known: "the dark night of the soul."

Enlightenment may not appear, or not in time; the mystic at least need not fear forestalling. Enlightenment may dawn in ways as varied as the individual approaches of scientists at work—and, in defiance of stereotypes, the sciences far outrun the arts in variety of personal styles and in the crucial influence of style on the creative process. During a conversation with a co-worker—and he just as baffled—a fact quietly shifts from the insignificant background to the foreground; a trivial anomaly becomes a central piece of evidence, the entire pattern swims into focus, and at last one sees. "How obvious! We knew it all along!" Or a rival may publish first but yet be wrong—and in the crashing wave of fear that he's got it right, followed and engulfed by the wave of realization that it must be wrong, the whole view of the problem skews, the tension of one's concentration twists abruptly higher, and at last one sees. "Not that way, *this* way!"

One path to enlightenment, though, has been reported so widely, by writers and artists, by scientists, and especially by mathematicians, that it has become established as a discipline for courting inspiration. The first stage, the reports agree, is prolonged contemplation of the problem, days of saturation in the data, weeks of incessant struggle— the torment of the unknown. The aim is to set in motion the unconscious processes of the mind, to prepare for the intuitive leap. William Lipscomb, a physical chemist at Harvard who won a Nobel Prize for finding the unexpected structures of some unusual molecules, the boranes, said recently that, for him, "The unconscious mind pieces together random impressions into a continuous story. If I really want to work on a problem, I do a good deal of the work at night—because then I worry about it as I go to sleep." The worry must be about the problem intensely and exclusively. Thought must be free of distraction or competing anxieties. Identification with the problem grows so intimate that the scientist has the experience of the detective who begins to think like the terrorist, of the hunter who feels, as though directly, the silken ripple of the tiger's instincts. One great physical chemist was credited by his peers, who watched him awestruck, with the ability to think about chemical structures directly in quantum terms—so that if a proposed molecular model was too tightly packed he felt uncomfortable, as though his shoes pinched. Joshua Lederberg, president of the Rockefeller University, who won his Nobel for discoveries that established the genetics of microorganisms, said recently, "One needs the ability to strip to the essential attributes of some actor in a process, the ability to imagine oneself *inside* a biological situation; I literally had to be able to think, for example, 'What would it be like if I were one of the chemical pieces in a bacterial chromosome?'—and to try to understand what my environment was, try to know *where* I was, try to know when I was supposed to function in a certain way, and so forth." Total preoccupation to the point of absent-mindedness is no eccentricity—just as the monstrous egoism and contentiousness of some scientists, like that of some artists, are the overflow of the strength and reserves of sureness they must find how they can.

Sometimes out of that saturation the answer arises, spontaneous and entire, as though of its own volition. In a famous story, Friedrich Kekulé, a German chemist of the mid-nineteenth century, described how a series of discoveries came to him in the course of hypnagogic reveries—waking dreams. His account, though far from typical, is charming. Kekulé was immersed in one of the most perplexing problems of his day, to find the structural basis of organic chemistry—that is, of the chemistry of compounds that contain carbon atoms. Enormous numbers of such compounds were coming to be known, but their makeup—from atoms of carbon, hydrogen, oxygen, and a few other elements—seemed to follow no rules. Kekulé had dwelt on the compounds' behavior so intensely that the atoms on occasion seemed to appear to him and dance. In the dusk of a summer evening, he was going home by horse-drawn omnibus, sitting outside and alone. "I fell into a reverie, and lo! The atoms were gamboling before my eyes," he later wrote. "I saw how, frequently, two smaller atoms united to form a pair; how a larger one embraced two smaller ones; how still larger ones kept hold of three or even four of the smaller; whilst the whole kept whirling in a giddy dance. I saw how the larger ones formed a chain." He spent hours that night sketching the forms he had envisioned. Another time, when Kekulé was nodding in his chair before the fire, the atoms danced for him again—but only the larger ones, this time, in long rows, "all twining and twisting in snakelike motion. But look! What was that? One of the snakes had seized hold of its own tail, and the form whirled mockingly before my eyes." The chains and rings that carbon atoms form with each other are indeed the fundamental structures of organic chemistry.

Several other scientists have told me that the fringes of sleep set the problem-sodden mind free to make uninhibited, bizarre, even random connections that may throw up the unexpected answer. One said that the technical trick that led to one of his most admired discoveries—it was about the fundamental molecular nature of genetic mutations—had sprung to mind while he was lying insomniac at three in the morning. Another said he was startled from a deep sleep one night by the fully worked-out answer to a puzzle that had blocked him for weeks—though at breakfast he was no longer able to remember any detail except the jubilant certainty. So the next night he went to sleep with paper and pencil on the bedside table; and when, once again, he awoke with the answer, he was able to seize it.

More usually, however, in the classic strategy for achieving enlightenment the weeks of saturation must be followed by a second stage that begins when the problem is deliberately set aside. After several days of silence, the solution wells up. The mathematician Henri Poincaré was unusually introspective about the process of discovery. (He also came nearer than anyone else to beating Einstein to the theory of relativity, except that in that case, though he had the pieces of the problem, inspiration did not strike.) In 1908, Poincaré gave a lecture, before the Psychological Society of Paris, about the psychology of mathematical invention, and there he described how he made some of his youthful discoveries. He reassured his audience, few of them mathematical: "I will tell you that I found the proof of a certain theorem in certain circumstances. The theorem will have a barbarous name, which many of you will never have heard of. But that's of no importance, for what is interesting to the psychologist is not the theorem—it's the circumstances."

The youthful discovery was about a class of mathematical functions which he named in honor of another mathematician, Lazarus Fuchs— but, as he said, the mathematical content is not important here. The young Poincaré believed, and for fifteen days he strove to prove, that no functions of the type he was pondering could exist in mathematics. He struggled with the disproof for hours every day. One evening, he happened to drink some black coffee, and couldn't sleep. Like Kekulé with his carbon atoms, Poincaré found mathematical expressions arising before him in crowds, combining and recombining. By the next morning, he had established a class of the functions that he had begun by denying. Then, a short time later, he left town to go on a geological excursion for several days. "The changes of travel made me forget my mathematical work." One day during the excursion, though, he was carrying on a conversation as he was about to board a bus. "At the moment when I put my foot on the step, the idea came to me, without anything in my former thoughts seeming to have paved the way for it, that the transformations I had used to define the Fuchsian functions were identical with those of non-Euclidian geometry." He did not try to prove the idea, but went right on with his conversation. "But I felt a perfect certainty," he wrote. When he got home, "for conscience's sake I verified the result at my leisure."

The quality of such moments of the mind has not often been described successfully; Charles P. Snow was a scientist as well as a novelist, and whenever his experience of science comes together with his writer's imagination his witness is authentic. In *The Search*, a novel about scientists at work, the protagonist makes a discovery for which he had long been striving.

> Then I was carried beyond pleasure. . . . My own triumph and delight and success were there, but they seemed insignificant beside this tranquil ecstasy. It was as though I had looked for a truth outside myself, and finding it had become for a moment a part of the truth I sought; as though all the world, the atoms and the stars, were wonderfully clear and close to me, and I to them, so that we were part of a lucidity more tremendous than any mystery.
>
> I had never known that such a moment could exist. . . . Since then I have never quite regained it. But one effect will stay with me as long as I live; once, when I was young, I used to sneer at the mystics who have described the experience of being at one with God and part of the unity of things. After that afternoon, I did not want to laugh again; for though I should have interpreted the experience differently, I thought I knew what they meant.

This experience beyond pleasure, like the dark night of the soul, has a name: the novelist Romain Rolland, in a letter to Sigmund Freud, called it "the oceanic sense of well-being."

Science is our century's art. Nearly 400 years ago, when modern science was just beginning, Francis Bacon wrote that "knowledge is power." Yet

Bacon was not a scientist. He wrote as a bureaucrat in retirement. His slogan was actually the first clear statement of the promise by which, ever since, bureaucrats justify to each other and to king or taxpayer the spending of money on science. Knowledge is power: today we would say, less grandly, that science is essential to technology. Bacon's promise has been fulfilled abundantly, magnificently. The rage to know has been matched by the rage to make. Therefore—with the proviso, abundantly demonstrated, that it's rarely possible to predict which program of fundamental research will produce just what technology and when—the promise has brought scientists in the Western world unprecedented freedom of inquiry. Nonetheless, Bacon's promise hardly penetrates to the thing that moves most scientists. Science has several rewards, but the greatest is that it is the most interesting, difficult, pitiless, exciting, and beautiful pursuit that we have yet found. Science is our century's art.

The takeover can be dated more precisely than the beginning of most eras: Friday, June 30, 1905, will do, the day when Albert Einstein, a clerk in the Swiss patent office in Bern, submitted a thirty-one-page paper, "On the Electrodynamics of Moving Bodies," to the journal *Annalen der Physik.* No poem, no play, no piece of music written since then comes near the theory of relativity in its power, as one strains to apprehend it, to make the mind tremble with delight. Whereas fifty years ago it was often said that hardly two score people understood the theory of relativity, today its essential vision, as Einstein himself said, is within reach of any reasonably bright high school student—and that, too, is characteristic of the speed of assimilation of the new in the arts.

Consider also the molecular structure of that stuff of the gene, the celebrated double helix of deoxyribonucleic acid. This is two repetitive strands, one winding up, the other down, but hooked together, across the tube of space between them, by a sequence of pairs of chemical entities—just four sorts of these entities, making just two kinds of pairs, with exactly ten pairs to a full turn of the helix. It's a piece of sculpture. But observe how form and function are one. That sequence possesses a unique duality: one way, it allows the strands to part and each to assemble on itself, by the pairing rules, a duplicate of the complementary strand; the other way, the sequence enciphers, in a four-letter alphabet, the entire specification for the substance of the organism. The structure thus encompasses both heredity and embryological growth, the passing-on of potential and its expression. The structure's elucidation, in March of 1953, was an event of such surpassing explanatory power that it will reverberate through whatever time mankind has remaining. The structure is also perfectly economical and splendidly elegant. There is no sculpture made in this century that is so entrancing.

If to compare science to art seems—in the last quarter of this century—to undervalue what science does, that must be, at least partly, because we now expect art to do so little. Before our century, everyone naturally supposed that the artist imitates nature. Aristotle had said so; the idea was obvious, it had flourished and evolved for 2000 years; those who thought about it added that the artist imitates not just nature as it accidentally happens but as it has to be. Yet today that describes the scientist. "Scientific reasoning," Medawar also said, "is a constant interplay or interaction between hypotheses and the logical expectations they give rise to: there is a restless to-and-fro motion of thought, the formulation and reformulation of hypotheses, until we arrive at a hypothesis which, to the best of our prevailing knowledge, will satisfactorily meet the case." Thus far, change only the term "hypothesis" and Medawar described well the experience the painter or the poet has of his own work. "Scientific reasoning is a kind of dialogue between the possible and the actual, between what might be and what is in fact the case," he went on—and there the difference lies. The scientist enjoys the harsher discipline of what is and is not the case. It is he, rather than the painter or the poet in this century, who pursues in its stringent form the imitation of nature.

Many scientists—mathematicians and physicists especially—hold that beauty in a theory is itself almost a form of proof. They speak, for example, of "elegance." Paul Dirac predicted the existence of antimatter (what would science fiction be without him?) several years before any form of it was observed. He won a share in the Nobel Prize in physics in 1933 for the work that included that prediction. "It is more important to have beauty in one's equations than to have them fit experiments," Dirac wrote many years later. "It seems that if one is working from the point of view of getting beauty in one's equations, and if one has really a sound insight, one is on a sure line of progress."

Here the scientist parts company with the artist. The insight must be sound. The dialogue is between what might be and what is in fact the case. The scientist is trying to get the thing right. The world is there.

And so are other scientists. The social system of science begins with the apprenticeship of the graduate student with a group of his peers and elders in the laboratory of a senior scientist; it continues to collaboration at the bench or the blackboard, and on to formal publication—which is a formal invitation to criticism. The most fundamental function of the social system of science is to enlarge the interplay between imagination and judgment from a private into a public activity. The oceanic feeling of well-being, the true touchstone of the artist, is for the scientist, even the most fortunate and gifted, only the midpoint of the process of doing science.

QUESTIONS FOR DISCUSSION

1. How many small-scale CP arguments characterizing science can you find in this essay? Do they all nest within one overriding proposition?
2. Judson's primary form of evidence is testimony from scientists about the nature of their activities. What are the different sources of this testimony? Given what Judson wants to argue for, would any other source of evidence have been possible?
3. How does Judson work to establish the authority of the scientists he quotes? How does his awareness of audience affect his introduction of each scientist?
4. In his characterization of science, does Judson seem to be reinforcing a belief his audience already holds or correcting a misconception? Why does Judson spend so much time defining *science* and so little time defining *art*? Why is the thesis "Science is our century's art" left to the end?
5. In his argument Judson takes up considerable space describing the "pathway to inspiration," the unconscious sources of creativity. Is this discussion just a pleasant and entertaining digression or does it serve his culminating thesis?
6. Judson describes scientists as experiencing an oceanic sense of well-being or a dark night of the soul. Do these religious terms undercut his argument that science is art?
7. What is wrong in the second sentence of the first paragraph? What effect does this error have on your perception of the author's ethos (though it is only fair to say it may not be his fault)?

SUGGESTIONS FOR WRITING

1. If you have had experience "doing" science, you might feel inclined to write a partial or complete refutation of one or more of Judson's characterizations of science, perhaps by maintaining the opposite (i.e., "Science is the antithesis of art"). Your intended audience might be Judson himself. Remember that if you are relying on your own and your lab partner's experiences, you can produce only a very qualified thesis. If science for you is carrying out preplanned lab experiments, you may be working with a different definition of science.

2. You may want to make an argument like Judson's for another activity, demonstrating for the uninitiated that such pursuits as music, athletics, or reading poetry also involve fun, play, curiosity, passion, and pain.

3. You may want to turn Judson's rhetorical situation inside out and write a characterization of "doing" art for an audience of the scientifically and technologically adept.

4. An eminent mathematician, Jacob Bronowski, has also argued for the similarity between scientific and artistic endeavour in his work, *Science and Human Values*. Read Chapter 1, "The Creative Mind," in Bronowski's book and write a comparison between his argumentative tactics and Judson's.

5. Tell the story of one scientific discovery or breakthrough in such a way that it either supports Judson's "artistic" view of science or suggests that the process leading up to the insight was uniquely scientific. (Hint: Use words that suggest your interpretation in your description.)

6. If, as Judson claims, "Science is our century's art," what has happened to our century's typical arts, its painting, sculpture, literature? Can you characterize any branch of twentieth-century art as scientific? Direct your essay at artists who would be surprised by such a characterization.

-->>> <<<--

What is Vulgar?

ARISTIDES

"What is Vulgar?" is the only essay in this section that explores the many meanings of a single word rather than fixing on one meaning for the purposes of argument. Yet the extensive attempt to capture the meaning of the single word vulgar *still uses the techniques of CP argument. The word itself becomes the subject of CPs with various synonyms or attributes in the predicate: "Vulgarity is pretentiousness," "To be vulgar is not to be uncouth," "Vulgarity is the inability to make distinctions."*

This essay first appeared in The American Scholar, *a journal addressed to the members of the Phi Beta Kappa society. Its author, Aristides, is really Joseph Epstein, editor of* The American Scholar *since 1974 and an accomplished practitioner of the familiar essay, which takes on, in Joseph Wood Krutch's definition, "subjects neither obviously momentous nor merely silly." As you read "What is Vulgar?" you will enjoy the lively examples and appreciate the fine distinctions that Aristides, who must be anything but vulgar, can make. Notice too that Aristides' academic exercise at extended*

*definition can work on its readers as an evaluation argument that judges a
number of targets quite harshly.*

What's vulgar? Some people might say that the contraction of the words
what and *is* itself is vulgar. On the other hand, I remember being called
a stuffed shirt by a reviewer of a book of mine because I used almost
no contractions. I have forgotten the reviewer's name but I have remembered the criticism. Not being of that category of writers who never
forget a compliment, I also remember being called a racist by another
reviewer for observing that failure to insist on table manners in children
was to risk dining with apaches. The larger criticisms I forget, but, oddly,
these goofy little criticisms stick in the teeth like sesame seeds. Yet that
last trope—is it, too, vulgar? Ought I really to be picking my teeth in
public, even metaphorically?

What, to return to the question in uncontractioned form, is vulgar?
Illustrations, obviously, are wanted. Consider a relative of mine, long
deceased, my father's Uncle Jake and hence my granduncle. I don't wish
to brag about bloodlines, but my Uncle Jake was a bootlegger during
Prohibition who afterward went into the scrap-iron—that is to say, the
junk—business. Think of the archetypal sensitive Jewish intellectual
faces: of Spinoza, of Freud, of Einstein, of Oppenheimer. In my uncle's
face you would not have found the least trace of any of them. He was
completely bald, weighed in at around two hundred fifty pounds, and
had a complexion of clear vermilion. I loved him, yet even as a child I
knew there was about him something a bit—how shall I put it?—
outsized, and I refer not merely to his personal tonnage. When he
visited our home he generally greeted me by pressing a ten- or twenty-
dollar bill into my hand—an amount of money quite impossible, of
course, for a boy of nine or ten, when what was wanted was a quarter
or fifty-cent piece. A widower, he would usually bring a lady-friend
along; here his tastes ran to Hungarian women in their fifties with
operatic bosoms. These women wore large diamond rings, possibly the
same rings, which my uncle passed from woman to woman. A big
spender and a high roller, my uncle was an immigrant version of the
sport, a kind of Diamond Chaim Brodsky.

But to see Uncle Jake in action you had to see him at table. He drank
whiskey with his meal, the bottle before him on the table along with
another of seltzer water, both of which he supplied himself. He ate and
drank like a character out of Rabelais. My mother served him his soup
course, not in a regular bowl, but in a vessel more on the order of a

tureen. He would eat hot soup and drink whiskey and sweat—my Uncle Jake did not, decidedly, do anything so delicate as perspire—and sometimes it seemed that the sweat rolled from his face right into his soup dish, so that, toward the end, he may well have been engaged in an act of liquid auto-cannibalism, consuming his own body fluids with a whiskey chaser.

He was crude, certainly, my Uncle Jake; he was coarse, of course; gross, it goes without saying; uncouth, beyond question. But was he vulgar? I don't think he was. For one thing, he was good-hearted, and it somehow seems wrong to call anyone vulgar who is good-hearted. But more to the point, I don't think that if you had accused him of being vulgar, he would have known what the devil you were talking about. To be vulgar requires at least a modicum of pretension, and this Uncle Jake sorely lacked. "Wulgar," he might have responded to the accusation that he was vulgar, "so vat's dis wulgar?"

To go from persons to things, and from lack of pretension to a mountain of it, let me tell you about a house I passed one night, in a neighborhood not far from my own, that so filled me with disbelief that I took a hard right turn at the next corner and drove round the block to make certain I had actually seen what I thought I had. I had, but it was no house—it was a bloody edifice!

The edifice in question totally fills its rather modest lot, leaving no backyard at all. It is constructed of a white stone, sanded and perhaps even painted, with so much gray-colored mortar that, even though it may be real, the stone looks fake. The roof is red. It has two chimneys, neither of which, I would wager, functions. My confidence here derives from the fact that nothing much else in the structure of the house seems to function. There is, for example, a balcony over a portico—a portico held up by columns—onto which the only possible mode of entry is by pole vault. There is, similarly, over the attached garage, a sun deck whose only access appears to be through a bathroom window. The house seems to have been built on the aesthetic formula of functionlessness follows formlessness.

But it is in its details that the true spirit of the house emerges. These details are not minuscule, and neither are they subtle. For starters, outside the house under the portico, there is a chandelier. There are also two torch-shaped lamps on either side of the front door, which is carved in a scallop pattern, giving it the effect of seeming the back door to a much larger house. Along the short walk leading up to this front door stand, on short pillars, two plaster of paris lions—gilded. On each pillar, in gold and black, appears the owner's name. A white chain fence, strung along poles whose tops are painted gold, spans the front of the property; it is the kind of fence that would be more appropriate around, say, the tomb of Lenin. At the curb are two large cars, sheets of plastic covering their grills; there is also a trailer; and, in the summer months, a boat sits in the short driveway leading up to the garage. The lawn disappoints by being not Astroturf but, alas, real grass. However, closer inspection reveals two animals, a skunk and a rabbit, both of plastic, in petrified play upon the lawn—a nice, you might say a finishing, touch. Sometimes, on long drives or when unable to sleep at night, I have pondered upon the possible decor of this extraordinary house's den and upon the ways of man which are various beyond imagining.

You want vulgar, I am inclined to exclaim, I'll show you vulgar: the house I have just described is vulgar, patently, palpably, pluperfectly. Forced to live in it for more than three hours, certain figures of refined sensibility—Edith Wharton or Harold Acton or Wallace Stevens—might have ended as suicides. Yet as I described that house, I noted two contradictory feelings in myself: how pleasant it is to point out someone else's vulgarity, and yet the fear that calling someone else vulgar may itself be slightly vulgar. After all, the family that lives in this house no doubt loves it; most probably they feel that they have a real showplace. Their house, I assume, gives them a large measure of happiness. Yet why does my calling their home vulgar also give me such a measure of happiness? I suppose it is because vulgarity can be so amusing—other people's vulgarity, that is.

. . .

The Oxford English Dictionary, which provides more than two pages on the word, is rather better at telling us what vulgar was than what it is. Its definitions run from "1. The common or usual language of a country; the vernacular. *Obs.*" to "13. Having a common and offensively mean character; coarsely commonplace; lacking in refinement or good taste; uncultured, ill-bred." Historically, the word vulgar was used in fairly neutral description up to the last quarter of the seventeenth century to mean and describe the common people. Vulgar was common but not yet contemned. I noted such a neutral usage as late as a William Hazlitt essay of 1818, "On the Ignorance of the Learned," in which Hazlitt writes: "The vulgar are in the right when they judge for themselves; they are wrong when they trust to their blind guides." Yet, according to the OED, in 1797 the *Monthly Magazine* remarked: "So the word *vulgar* now implies something base and groveling in actions."

From the early nineteenth century on, then, vulgar has been purely pejorative, a key term in the lexicon of insult and invective. Its currency as a term of abuse rose with the rise of the middle class; its spread was tied to the spread of capitalism and democracy. Until the rise of the middle class, until the spread of capitalism and democracy, people perhaps hadn't the occasion or the need to call one another vulgar. The rise of the middle class, the spread of capitalism and democracy, opened all sorts of social doors; social classes commingled as never before; plutocracy made possible almost daily strides from stratum to stratum. Still, some people had to be placed outside the pale, some doors had to be locked—and the cry of vulgarity, properly intoned, became a most effective Close Sesame.

Such seems to me roughly the social history of the word vulgar. But the history of vulgarity, the thing itself even before it had a name, is much longer. According to the French art historian Albert Dasnoy, aesthetic vulgarity taints Greek art of the fourth and third centuries B.C. "An exhibition of Roman portraits," Dasnoy writes, "shows that, between the Etruscan style of the earliest and the Byzantine style of the latest, vulgarity made its first full-blooded appearance in the academic realism of imperial Rome." Vulgarity, in Dasnoy's view, comes of the shock of philosophic rationalism, when humankind divests itself of belief in the sacred. "Vulgarity seems to be the price of man's liberation," he writes, "one might even say, of his evolution. It is unquestionably the price of the freeing of the individual personality." Certainly it is true that one would never think to call a savage vulgar; a respectable level of civilization has to have been reached to qualify for the dubious distinction of being called vulgar.

"You have surely noticed the curious fact," writes Valéry, "that a certain *word*, which is perfectly clear when you hear or use it in *everyday* speech, and which presents no difficulty when caught up in the rapidity of an ordinary sentence, becomes mysteriously cumbersome, offers a strange resistance, defeats all efforts at definition, the moment you withdraw it from circulation for separate study and try to find its meaning after taking away its temporary function." Vulgar presents special difficulties, though: while vulgarity has been often enough on display—may even be a part of the human soul that only the fortunate and the saintly are able to root out—every age has its own notion of what constitutes the vulgar. Riding a bicycle at Oxford in the 1890s, Max Beerbohm reports, "was the earmark of vulgarity." Working further backward, we find that Matthew Arnold frequently links the word *vulgar* with the word *hideous* and hopes that culture "saves the future, as one may hope, from being vulgarised, even if it cannot save the present." Hazlitt found vulgarity in false feeling among "the herd of pretenders to what they do not feel and to what is not natural to them, whether in high or low life."

Vulgarity, it begins to appear, is often in the eye of the beholder. What is more, it comes in so many forms. It is so complex and so multiple—so multiplex. There are vulgarities of taste, of manner, of mind, of spirit. There are whole vulgar ages—the Gilded Age in the United States, for one, at least to hear Mark Twain and Henry Adams tell it. (Is our own age another?) To compound the complication there is even likeable vulgarity. This is vulgarity of the kind that Cyril Connolly must have had in mind when he wrote, "Vulgarity is the garlic in the salad of life." In the realm of winning vulgarity are the novels of Balzac, the paintings of Frans Hals, some of the music of Tchaikovsky (excluding the cannon fire in the 1812 Overture, which is vulgarity of the unwinning kind).

Rightly used, profanity, normally deemed the epitome of vulgar manners, can be charming. I recently moved to a new apartment, and the person I dealt with at the moving company we employed, a woman whose voice had an almost strident matter-of-factness, instructed me to call back with an inventory of our furniture. When I did, our conversation, starting with my inventory of our living room, began:

"One couch."
"One couch."
"Two lamp tables, a coffee table, a small gateleg table."
"Four tables."
"Two wing chairs and an occasional chair."
"Three chairs."
"One box of bric-a-brac."
"One box of shit."

Heavy garlic of course is not to every taste; but then again some people do not much care for endive. I attended city schools, where garlic was never in short supply and where profanity, in proper hands, could be a useful craft turned up to the power of fine art. I have since met people so well-mannered, so icily, elegantly correct, that with a mere glance across the table or a word to a waiter they could put a chill on the wine and indeed on the entire evening. Some people have more, some less, in the way of polish, but polish doesn't necessarily cover vulgarity. As there can be diamonds in the rough, so can there be sludge in the smooth.

It would be helpful in drawing a definitional bead on the word vulgar if one could determine its antonym. But I am not sure that it has an antonym. Refined? I think not. Sophisticated? Not really. Elegant? Nope. Charming? Close, but I can think of charming vulgarians—M. Rabelais, please come forth and take a bow. Besides, charm is nearly as difficult to define as vulgarity. Perhaps the only safe thing to be said about charm is that if you think you have it, you can be fairly certain that you don't.

. . .

Coming at things from a different angle, I imagine myself in session with a psychologist, playing the word association game. "Vulgar," he says, "quick, name ten items you associate with the word vulgar." "Okay," I say, "here goes:

1. Publicity
2. The Oscar awards
3. The Aspen Institute for Humanistic Studies
4. Talk shows
5. Pulitzer Prizes
6. Barbara Walters
7. Interviews with writers
8. Lauren Bacall
9. Dialogue, as an ideal
10. Psychology."

This would not, I suspect, be everyone's list. Looking it over, I see that, of the ten items, several are linked with one another. But let me inquire into what made me choose the items I did.

Ladies first. Barbara Walters seems to me vulgar because for a great many years now she has been paid to ask all the vulgar questions, and she seems to do it with such cheerfulness, such competence, such amiable insincerity. "What did you think when you first heard your husband had been killed?" she will ask, just the right hush in her voice. "What went on in your mind when you learned that you had cancer, now for the third time?" The questions that people with imagination do not need to ask, the questions that people with good hearts know they have no right to ask, these questions and others Barbara Walters can be depended upon to ask. "Tell me, Holy Father, have you never regretted not having children of your own?"

Lauren Bacall has only recently graduated to vulgarity, or at least she has only in the past few years revealed herself vulgar. Hers is a double vulgarity: the vulgarity of false candor—the woman who, presumably, tells it straight—and the vulgarity provided by someone who has decided to cash in her chips. In her autobiography, Miss Bacall has supposedly told all her secrets; when interviewed on television—by, for example, Barbara Walters—the tack she takes is that of the ringwise babe over whose eyes no one, kiddo, is going to pull the cashmere. Yet turn the channel or page, and there is Miss Bacall in a commercial or advertisement doing her best to pull the cashmere over ours. Vulgar stuff. Give her, I say, the hook.

Talk shows are vulgar for the same reason that Pulitzer Prizes and the Aspen Institute for Humanistic Studies are vulgar. All three fail to live up to their pretensions, which are extravagant: talk shows to being serious, Pulitzer Prizes to rewarding true merit, the Aspen Institute to promoting "dialogue" (see item 9), "the bridging of cultures," "the interdisciplinary approach," and nearly every other phony shibboleth that has cropped up in American intellectual life over the past three decades.

Publicity is vulgar because those who seek it—and even those who are sought by it—tend almost without exception to be divested of their dignity. You have to sell yourself, the sales manuals used to advise, in order to sell your product. With publicity, though, one is selling only oneself, which is different. Which is a bit vulgar, really.

The Oscar awards ceremony is the single item on my list least in need of explanation, for it seems vulgar prima facie. It is the air of self-congratulation—of, a step beyond, self-adulation—that is so splendidly vulgar about the Oscar awards ceremony. Self-congratulation, even on good grounds, is best concealed; on no grounds whatever, it is embarrassing. But then, for vulgarity, there's no business like show business.

Unless it be literary business. The only thing worse than false modesty is no modesty at all, and no modesty at all is what interviews with writers generally bring out. "That most vulgar of all crowds the literary," wrote Keats presciently—that is, before the incontestable evidence came in with the advent and subsequent popularity of what is by now that staple of the book review and little magazine and talk show, the interview with the great author. What these interviews generally come down to is an invitation to writers to pontificate upon things for which it is either unseemly for them to speak (the quality of their own work) or upon which they are unfit to judge (the state of the cosmos). Roughly a decade ago I watched Isaac Bashevis Singer, when asked on a television talk show what he thought of the Vietnam War, answer, "I am a writer, and that doesn't mean I have to have an opinion on everything. I'd rather discuss literature." Still, how tempting it is, with an interviewer chirping away at your feet, handing you your own horn and your own drum, to blow it and beat it. As someone who has been interviewed a time or two, I can attest that never have I shifted spiritual gears so quickly from self-importance to self-loathing as during and after an interview. What I felt was, well, vulgar.

Psychology seems to me vulgar because it is too often overbearing in its confidence. Instead of saying, "I don't know," it readily says, "unresolved Oedipus complex" or "manic-depressive syndrome" or "identity crisis." As with other intellectual discoveries before (Marxism) and since (structuralism), psychology acts as if it is holding all the theoretical keys, but then in practice reveals that it doesn't even know where the doors are. As an old *Punch* cartoon once put it, "It's worse than wicked, my dear, it's vulgar."

Reviewing my list and attempting to account for the reasons why I have chosen the items on it, I feel I have a firmer sense of what I think vulgar. Exhibitionism, obviousness, pretentiousness, self-congratulation, self-importance, hypocrisy, overconfidence—these seem to me qualities at the heart of vulgarity in our day. It does, though, leave out common sense, a quality which, like clarity, one might have thought one could never have in overabundance. (On the philosophy table in my local bookstore, a book appeared with the title *Clarity Is Not Enough;* I could never pass it without thinking, "Ah, but it's a start.") Yet too great reliance on common sense can narrow the mind, make meager the imagination. Strict common sense abhors mystery, seldom allows for the attraction of tradition, is intolerant of questions that haven't any answers. The problem that common sense presents is knowing the limits of common sense. The too commonsensical man or woman grows angry at anything that falls outside his or her common sense, and this anger seems to me vulgar.

Vulgarity is not necessarily stupid but it is always insensitive. Its insensitivity invariably extends to itself: the vulgar person seldom knows that he is vulgar, as in the old joke about the young woman whose fiancé reports to her that his parents found her vulgar, and who, enraged, responds, "What's this vulgar crap?" Such obvious vulgarity can be comical, like a nouveau riche man bringing opera glasses to a porno film, or the Chicago politician who, while escorting the then ruling British monarch through City Hall, supposedly introduced him to the assembled aldermen by saying, "King, meet the boys." But such things are contretemps merely, not vulgarity of the insidious kind.

In our age vulgarity does not consist in failing to recognize the fish knife or to know the wine list but in the inability to make distinctions. Not long ago I heard a lecture by a Harvard philosophy professor on a Howard Hawks movie, and thought, as one high reference after another was made in connection with this low subject, "Oh, Santayana, 'tis better you are not alive to see this." A vulgar performance, clearly, yet few people in the audience of professors and graduate students seemed to take notice.

A great many people did notice, however, when, in an act of singular moral vulgarity, a publisher, an editor, and a novelist recently sponsored a convicted murderer for parole, and the man, not long after being paroled, murdered again. The reason for these men speaking out on behalf of the convict's parole, they said, was his ability as a writer; his work appeared in the editor's journal; he was to have a book published by the publisher's firm; the novelist had encouraged him from the outset. Distinctions—crucial distinctions—were not made: first, that the man was not a very good writer, but a crudely Marxist one, filled with hatreds and half-truths; second, and more important, that, having killed before, he might kill again—might just be a pathological killer. Not to have made these distinctions is vulgarity at its most vile. But to adopt a distinction new to our day, the publisher, the editor, and the novelist took responsibility for what they had done—responsibility but no real blame.

Can an entire culture grow vulgar? Matthew Arnold feared such might happen in "the mechanical and material civilisation" of the England of his day. Vladimir Nabokov felt it already had happened in the Soviet Union, a country, as he described it, "of moral imbeciles, of smiling slaves and poker-faced bullies," without, as in the old days, "a Gogol, a Tolstoy, a Chekhov in quest of that simplicity of truth [who] easily distinguished the vulgar side of things as well as the trashy systems of pseudo-thought." Moral imbeciles, smiling slaves, poker-faced bullies —the curl of a sneer in those Nabokovian phrases is a sharp reminder of the force that the charge of "vulgar" can have as an insult—as well as a reminder of how deep and pervasive vulgarity can become.

But American vulgarity, if I may put it so, is rather more refined. It is also more piecemeal than pervasive, and more insidious. Creeping vulgarity is how I think of it, the way Taft Republicans used to think of creeping socialism. The insertion of a science fiction course in a major university curriculum, a television commercial by a once-serious actor for a cheap wine, an increased interest in gossip and trivia that is placed under the rubric Style in our most important newspapers: so the vulgar creeps along, while everywhere the third- and fourth-rate—in art, in literature, in intellectual life—is considered good enough, or at any rate highly interesting.

Yet being refined—or at least sophisticated—American vulgarity is vulnerable to the charge of being called vulgar. "As long as war is regarded as wicked," said Oscar Wilde, "it will always have its fascination. When it is looked upon as vulgar, it will cease to be popular." There may be something to this, if not for war then at least for designer jeans, French literary criticism, and other fashions. The one thing the vulgar of our day do not like to be called is vulgar. So crook your little finger, purse your lips, distend your nostrils slightly as you lift your nose in the air the better to look down it, and repeat after me: *Vulgar! Vulgar! Vulgar!* The word might save us all.

QUESTIONS FOR DISCUSSION

1. One of the techniques of definition used by Aristides is the synonym. He tries out many synonyms for *vulgar*, rejecting some, accepting others. Which synonym is the best equivalent for *vulgar*? Why does he discard some, and is the process of throwing out the rejects wasted effort toward the goal of defining *vulgar*?

2. Look again at the first two examples of Uncle Jake and the house. Why is one considered vulgar and the other not? Does Aristides intend to surprise his readers with his conclusion about Uncle Jake?

3. Why does Joseph Epstein choose the pen name Aristides?

4. What does Aristides gain from his research into the history of the word *vulgar* both in the *Oxford English Dictionary* and in quotations from certain writers?

5. Aristides tries but fails to find an antonym for *vulgar*. What does the attempt nevertheless yield?

6. To try to define a word like *vulgar* puts great strain on the author's ethos.

Does Aristides succeed in fending off a charge of "overfastidiousness" against himself, or does he seem pretentious and snobbish?

7. The essay starts off lightheartedly and then changes tone. What stance toward his subject does Aristides seem to take by the end?

8. "What is Vulgar?" is especially rich in examples from many domains of experience. What is the need for or effect of so many examples?

SUGGESTIONS FOR WRITING

1. Have your classmates take the association test that Aristides gave himself and list ten things they consider vulgar. Analyze the lists to find whether you can distill from them the essential attributes of the word. With this evidence, write an extended definition on Aristides' model. Instead of *vulgar*, you may use any currently popular term of praise or insult. Remember that you are not evaluating what the term applies to but arguing for the best characterization of its meaning.

2. Take any one of the extended examples that Aristides gives (e.g., talk shows, Lauren Bacall) and argue with Aristides to what extent it coincides with his definition of *vulgar*.

3. Find a phenomenon overlooked by Aristides that you believe fits his definition of *vulgar* perfectly. Argue for the CP using your candidate as the subject and *vulgar* as the predicate. Direct your essay to Aristides himself, suggesting he add your candidate to his list.

4. Try your hand at a definition argument of a large and vague abstraction like *vulgar*. Try to use the same techniques Aristides did: examples, both positive and negative; antonyms and synonyms; the *Oxford English Dictionary* entry, or entries from other dictionaries such as the *Dictionary of American Slang*. But also add any other techniques you consider appropriate in order to make your definition convincing to readers who have never before considered this term so carefully.

5. Construct a definition argument of a word with multiple meanings and nuances by writing a series of CPs, each of which has to be supported independently with examples. In your conclusion either summarize your definitions or try, if possible, to distill an essential definition from all your partial ones.

6. What did Aristides mean when he claimed in his last line that the word *vulgar* "might save us all"?

———————— ⇉》 《⇇ ————————

The Route to Normal Science

THOMAS S. KUHN

The following piece comes from Thomas S. Kuhn's The Structure of
Scientific Revolutions, *a watershed book in the history and philosophy of
science. In it Kuhn, a historian of science, propounds his theory of how
scientific progress operates. According to Kuhn, one view of a phenomenon
like electricity or light will come to dominate and win the assent of most
researchers in a field. Such a unified view is called a* paradigm. *United by a
shared paradigm, researchers can then go on to more advanced studies in a
field. When a paradigm can no longer explain significant data that
researchers have uncovered, it must be dislodged and replaced by another.*

*Kuhn's ideas and terms have excited much interest and have been
borrowed extensively by thinkers in nonscientific disciplines. He has
established, in other words, the paradigm of paradigms. What he has to say
here will be doubly interesting to students of argument, for Kuhn explains the
genesis and perpetuation of the expert audience and its preferred mode of
publication, the scientific or scholarly article. Despite his scholarly subject
matter, Kuhn must use all the standard tools of the arguer for a CP. Notice
how he carefully stipulates definitions and carries through one extended
example, which he must explicitly claim as typical.*

In this essay, 'normal science' means research firmly based upon one or
more past scientific achievements, achievements that some particular
scientific community acknowledges for a time as supplying the foundation for its further practice. Today such achievements are recounted,
though seldom in their original form, by science textbooks, elementary
and advanced. These textbooks expound the body of accepted theory,
illustrate many or all of its successful applications, and compare these
applications with exemplary observations and experiments. Before such
books became popular early in the nineteenth century (and until even
more recently in the newly matured sciences), many of the famous
classics of science fulfilled a similar function. Aristotle's *Physica*, Ptol-
emy's *Almagest*, Newton's *Principia* and *Opticks*, Franklin's *Electricity*, Lavoisier's *Chemistry*, and Lyell's *Geology*—these and many
other works served for a time implicitly to define the legitimate problems
and methods of a research field for succeeding generations of practitioners. They were able to do so because they shared two essential character-

istics. Their achievement was sufficiently unprecedented to attract an enduring group of adherents away from competing modes of scientific activity. Simultaneously, it was sufficiently open-ended to leave all sorts of problems for the redefined group of practitioners to resolve.

Achievements that share these two characteristics I shall henceforth refer to as 'paradigms,' a term that relates closely to 'normal science.' By choosing it, I mean to suggest that some accepted examples of actual scientific practice—examples which include law, theory, application, and instrumentation together—provide models from which spring particular coherent traditions of scientific research. These are the traditions which the historian describes under such rubrics as 'Ptolemaic astronomy' (or 'Copernican'), 'Aristotelian dynamics' (or 'Newtonian'), 'corpuscular optics' (or 'wave optics'), and so on. The study of paradigms, including many that are far more specialized than those named illustratively above, is what mainly prepares the student for membership in the particular scientific community with which he will later practice. Because he there joins men who learned the bases of their field from the same concrete models, his subsequent practice will seldom evoke overt disagreement over fundamentals. Men whose research is based on shared paradigms are committed to the same rules and standards for scientific practice. That commitment and the apparent consensus it produces are prerequisites for normal science, i.e., for the genesis and continuation of a particular research tradition.

Because in this essay the concept of a paradigm will often substitute for a variety of familiar notions, more will need to be said about the reasons for its introduction. Why is the concrete scientific achievement, as a locus of professional commitment, prior to the various concepts, laws, theories, and points of view that may be abstracted from it? In what sense is the shared paradigm a fundamental unit for the student of scientific development, a unit that cannot be fully reduced to logically atomic components which might function in its stead? When we encounter them in Section V, answers to these questions and to others like them will prove basic to an understanding both of normal science and of the associated concept of paradigms. That more abstract discussion will depend, however, upon a previous exposure to examples of normal science or of paradigms in operation. In particular, both these related concepts will be clarified by noting that there can be a sort of scientific research without paradigms, or at least without any so unequivocal and so binding as the ones named above. Acquisition of a paradigm and of the more esoteric type of research it permits is a sign of maturity in the development of any given scientific field.

If the historian traces the scientific knowledge of any selected group of related phenomena backward in time, he is likely to encounter some minor variant of a pattern here illustrated from the history of physical optics. Today's physics textbooks tell the student that light is photons, i.e., quantum-mechanical entities that exhibit some characteristics of waves and some of particles. Research proceeds accordingly, or rather according to the more elaborate and mathematical characterization from which this usual verbalization is derived. That characterization of light is, however, scarcely half a century old. Before it was developed by Planck, Einstein, and others early in this century, physics texts taught that light was transverse wave motion, a conception rooted in a paradigm that derived ultimately from the optical writings of Young and Fresnel in the early nineteenth century. Nor was the wave theory the first to be embraced by almost all practitioners of optical science. During the eighteenth century the paradigm for this field was provided by Newton's *Opticks*, which taught that light was material corpuscles. At that time physicists sought evidence, as the early wave theorists had not, of the pressure exerted by light particles impinging on solid bodies.[1]

These transformations of the paradigms of physical optics are scientific revolutions, and the successive transition from one paradigm to another via revolution is the usual developmental pattern of mature science. It is not, however, the pattern characteristic of the period before Newton's work, and that is the contrast that concerns us here. No period between remote antiquity and the end of the seventeenth century exhibited a single generally accepted view about the nature of light. Instead there were a number of competing schools and subschools, most of them espousing one variant or another of Epicurean, Aristotelian, or Platonic theory. One group took light to be particles emanating from material bodies; for another it was a modification of the medium that intervened between the body and the eye; still another explained light in terms of an interaction of the medium with an emanation from the eye; and there were other combinations and modifications besides. Each of the corresponding schools derived strength from its relation to some particular metaphysic, and each emphasized, as paradigmatic observations, the particular cluster of optical phenomena that its own theory could do most to explain. Other observations were dealt with by *ad hoc* elaborations, or they remained as outstanding problems for further research.[2]

---

[1] Joseph Priestley, *The History and Present State of Discoveries Relating to Vision, Light, and Colours* (London, 1772), pp. 385–90.

[2] Vasco Ronchi, *Histoire de la lumière*, trans. Jean Taton (Paris, 1956), chaps. i–iv.

At various times all these schools made significant contributions to the body of concepts, phenomena, and techniques from which Newton drew the first nearly uniformly accepted paradigm for physical optics. Any definition of the scientist that excludes at least the more creative members of these various schools will exclude their modern successors as well. Those men were scientists. Yet anyone examining a survey of physical optics before Newton may well conclude that, though the field's practitioners were scientists, the net result of their activity was something less than science. Being able to take no common body of belief for granted, each writer on physical optics felt forced to build his field anew from its foundations. In doing so, his choice of supporting observation and experiment was relatively free, for there was no standard set of methods or of phenomena that every optical writer felt forced to employ and explain. Under these circumstances, the dialogue of the resulting books was often directed as much to the members of other schools as it was to nature. That pattern is not unfamiliar in a number of creative fields today, nor is it incompatible with significant discovery and invention. It is not, however, the pattern of development that physical optics acquired after Newton and that other natural sciences make familiar today.

The history of electrical research in the first half of the eighteenth century provides a more concrete and better known example of the way a science develops before it acquires its first universally received paradigm. During that period there were almost as many views about the nature of electricity as there were important electrical experimenters, men like Hauksbee, Gray, Desaguliers, Du Fay, Nollett, Watson, Franklin, and others. All their numerous concepts of electricity had something in common—they were partially derived from one or another version of the mechanico-corpuscular philosophy that guided all scientific research of the day. In addition, all were components of real scientific theories, of theories that had been drawn in part from experiment and observation and that partially determined the choice and interpretation of additional problems undertaken in research. Yet though all the experiments were electrical and though most of the experimenters read each other's works, their theories had no more than a family resemblance.[3]

[3]Duane Roller and Duane H. D. Roller, *The Development of the Concept of Electric Charge: Electricity from the Greeks to Coulomb* ("Harvard Case Histories in Experimental Science," Case 8; Cambridge, Mass., 1954); and I. B. Cohen, *Franklin and Newton: An Inquiry into Speculative Newtonian Experimental Science and Franklin's Work in Electric-*

One early group of theories, following seventeenth-century practice, regarded attraction and frictional generation as the fundamental electrical phenomena. This group tended to treat repulsion as a secondary effect due to some sort of mechanical rebounding and also to postpone for as long as possible both discussion and systematic research on Gray's newly discovered effect, electrical conduction. Other "electricians" (the term is their own) took attraction and repulsion to be equally elementary manifestations of electricity and modified their theories and research accordingly. (Actually, this group is remarkably small—even Franklin's theory never quite accounted for the mutual repulsion of two negatively charged bodies.) But they had as much difficulty as the first group in accounting simultaneously for any but the simplest conduction effects. Those effects, however, provided the starting point for still a third group, one which tended to speak of electricity as a "fluid" that could run through conductors rather than as an "effluvium" that emanated from non-conductors. This group, in its turn, had difficulty reconciling its theory with a number of attractive and repulsive effects. Only through the work of Franklin and his immediate successors did a theory arise that could account with something like equal facility for very nearly all these effects and that therefore could and did provide a subsequent generation of "electricians" with a common paradigm for its research.

Excluding those fields, like mathematics and astronomy, in which the first firm paradigms date from prehistory and also those, like biochemistry, that arose by division and recombination of specialties already matured, the situations outlined above are historically typical. Though it involves my continuing to employ the unfortunate simplification that tags an extended historical episode with a single and somewhat arbitrarily chosen name (e.g., Newton or Franklin), I suggest that similar fundamental disagreements characterized, for example, the study of motion before Aristotle and of statics before Archimedes, the study of heat before Black, of chemistry before Boyle and Boerhaave, and of historical geology before Hutton. In parts of biology—the study of

---

ity as an Example Thereof (Philadelphia, 1956), chaps. vii–xii. For some of the analytic detail in the paragraph that follows in the text, I am indebted to a still unpublished paper by my student John L. Heilbron. Pending its publication, a somewhat more extended and more precise account of the emergence of Franklin's paradigm is included in T. S. Kuhn, "The Function of Dogma in Scientific Research," in A. C. Crombie (ed.), "Symposium on the History of Science, University of Oxford, July 9–15, 1961," to be published by Heinemann Educational Books, Ltd.

heredity, for example—the first universally received paradigms are still more recent; and it remains an open question what parts of social science have yet acquired such paradigms at all. History suggests that the road to a firm research consensus is extraordinarily arduous.

History also suggests, however, some reasons for the difficulties encountered on that road. In the absence of a paradigm or some candidate for paradigm, all of the facts that could possibly pertain to the development of a given science are likely to seem equally relevant. As a result, early fact-gathering is a far more nearly random activity than the one that subsequent scientific development makes familiar. Furthermore, in the absence of a reason for seeking some particular form of more recondite information, early fact-gathering is usually restricted to the wealth of data that lie ready to hand. The resulting pool of facts contains those accessible to casual observation and experiment together with some of the more esoteric data retrievable from established crafts like medicine, calendar making, and metallurgy. Because the crafts are one readily accessible source of facts that could not have been casually discovered, technology has often played a vital role in the emergence of new sciences.

But though this sort of fact-collecting has been essential to the origin of many significant sciences, anyone who examines, for example, Pliny's encyclopedic writings or the Baconian natural histories of the seventeenth century will discover that it produces a morass. One somehow hesitates to call the literature that results scientific. The Baconian "histories" of heat, color, wind, mining, and so on, are filled with information, some of it recondite. But they juxtapose facts that will later prove revealing (e.g., heating by mixture) with others (e.g., the warmth of dung heaps) that will for some time remain too complex to be integrated with theory at all.[4] In addition, since any description must be partial, the typical natural history often omits from its immensely circumstantial accounts just those details that later scientists will find sources of important illumination. Almost none of the early "histories" of electricity, for example, mention that chaff, attracted to a rubbed glass rod, bounces off again. That effect seemed mechanical, not electrical.[5] Moreover,

---

[4] Compare the sketch for a natural history of heat in Bacon's *Novum Organum*, Vol. VIII of *The Works of Francis Bacon*, ed. J. Spedding, R. L. Ellis, and D. D. Heath (New York, 1869), pp. 179–203.

[5] Roller and Roller, *op. cit.*, pp. 14, 22, 28, 43. Only after the work recorded in the last of these citations do repulsive effects gain general recognition as unequivocally electrical.

since the casual fact-gatherer seldom possesses the time or the tools to be critical, the natural histories often juxtapose descriptions like the above with others, say, heating by antiperistasis (or by cooling), that we are now quite unable to confirm.[6] Only very occasionally, as in the cases of ancient statics, dynamics, and geometrical optics, do facts collected with so little guidance from pre-established theory speak with sufficient clarity to permit the emergence of a first paradigm.

This is the situation that creates the schools characteristic of the early stages of a science's development. No natural history can be interpreted in the absence of at least some implicit body of intertwined theoretical and methodological belief that permits selection, evaluation, and criticism. If that body of belief is not already implicit in the collection of facts—in which case more than "mere facts" are at hand—it must be externally supplied, perhaps by a current metaphysic, by another science, or by personal and historical accident. No wonder, then, that in the early stages of the development of any science different men confronting the same range of phenomena, but not usually all the same particular phenomena, describe and interpret them in different ways. What is surprising, and perhaps also unique in its degree to the fields we call science, is that such initial divergences should ever largely disappear.

For they do disappear to a very considerable extent and then apparently once and for all. Furthermore, their disappearance is usually caused by the triumph of one of the pre-paradigm schools, which, because of its own characteristic beliefs and preconceptions, emphasized only some special part of the too sizable and inchoate pool of information. Those electricians who thought electricity a fluid and therefore gave particular emphasis to conduction provide an excellent case in point. Led by this belief, which could scarcely cope with the known multiplicity of attractive and repulsive effects, several of them conceived the idea of bottling the electrical fluid. The immediate fruit of their efforts was the Leyden jar, a device which might never have been discovered by a man exploring nature casually or at random, but which was in fact independently developed by at least two investigators in the early 1740's.[7] Almost from the start of his electrical researches, Franklin was particularly concerned

---

[6]Bacon, op. cit., pp. 235, 337, says, "Water slightly warm is more easily frozen than quite cold." For a partial account of the earlier history of this strange observation, see Marshall Clagett, Giovanni Marliani and Late Medieval Physics (New York, 1941), chap. iv.

[7]Roller and Roller, op. cit., pp. 51–54.

to explain that strange and, in the event, particularly revealing piece of special apparatus. His success in doing so provided the most effective of the arguments that made his theory a paradigm, though one that was still unable to account for quite all the known cases of electrical repulsion.[8] To be accepted as a paradigm, a theory must seem better than its competitors, but it need not, and in fact never does, explain all the facts with which it can be confronted.

What the fluid theory of electricity did for the subgroup that held it, the Franklinian paradigm later did for the entire group of electricians. It suggested which experiments would be worth performing and which, because directed to secondary or to overly complex manifestations of electricity, would not. Only the paradigm did the job far more effectively, partly because the end of interschool debate ended the constant reiteration of fundamentals and partly because the confidence that they were on the right track encouraged scientists to undertake more precise, esoteric, and consuming sorts of work.[9] Freed from the concern with any and all electrical phenomena, the united group of electricians could pursue selected phenomena in far more detail, designing much special equipment for the task and employing it more stubbornly and systematically than electricians had ever done before. Both fact collection and theory articulation became highly directed activities. The effectiveness and efficiency of electrical research increased accordingly, providing evidence for a societal version of Francis Bacon's acute methodological dictum: "Truth emerges more readily from error than from confusion."[10]

We shall be examining the nature of this highly directed or paradigm-based research in the next section, but must first note briefly how the emergence of a paradigm affects the structure of the group that practices the field. When, in the development of a natural science, an

[8]The troublesome case was the mutual repulsion of negatively charged bodies, for which see Cohen, *op. cit.*, pp. 491–94, 531–43.

[9]It should be noted that the acceptance of Franklin's theory did not end quite all debate. In 1759 Robert Symmer proposed a two-fluid version of that theory, and for many years thereafter electricians were divided about whether electricity was a single fluid or two. But the debates on this subject only confirm what has been said above about the manner in which a universally recognized achievement unites the profession. Electricians, though they continued divided on this point, rapidly concluded that no experimental tests could distinguish the two versions of the theory and that they were therefore equivalent. After that, both schools could and did exploit all the benefits that the Franklinian theory provided (*ibid.*, pp. 543–46, 548–54).

[10]Bacon, *op. cit.*, p. 210.

individual or group first produces a synthesis able to attract most of the next generation's practitioners, the older schools gradually disappear. In part their disappearance is caused by their members' conversion to the new paradigm. But there are always some men who cling to one or another of the older views, and they are simply read out of the profession, which thereafter ignores their work. The new paradigm implies a new and more rigid definition of the field. Those unwilling or unable to accommodate their work to it must proceed in isolation or attach themselves to some other group.[11] Historically, they have often simply stayed in the departments of philosophy from which so many of the special sciences have been spawned. As these indications hint, it is sometimes just its reception of a paradigm that transforms a group previously interested merely in the study of nature into a profession or, at least, a discipline. In the sciences (though not in fields like medicine, technology, and law, of which the principal *raison d'être* is an external social need), the formation of specialized journals, the foundation of specialists' societies, and the claim for a special place in the curriculum have usually been associated with a group's first reception of a single paradigm. At least this was the case between the time, a century and a half ago, when the institutional pattern of scientific specialization first developed and the very recent time when the paraphernalia of specialization acquired a prestige of their own.

The more rigid definition of the scientific group has other consequences. When the individual scientist can take a paradigm for granted, he need no longer, in his major works, attempt to build his field anew, starting from first principles and justifying the use of each concept introduced. That can be left to the writer of textbooks. Given a textbook, however, the creative scientist can begin his research where it

---

[11] The history of electricity provides an excellent example which could be duplicated from the careers of Priestley, Kelvin, and others. Franklin reports that Nollet, who at mid-century was the most influential of the Continental electricians, "lived to see himself the last of his Sect, except Mr. B.—his Eleve and immediate Disciple" (Max Farrand [ed.], *Benjamin Franklin's Memoirs* [Berkeley, Calif., 1949], pp. 384–86). More interesting, however, is the endurance of whole schools in increasing isolation from professional science. Consider, for example, the case of astrology, which was once an integral part of astronomy. Or consider the continuation in the late eighteenth and early nineteenth centuries of a previously respected tradition of "romantic" chemistry. This is the tradition discussed by Charles C. Gillispie in "The *Encyclopédie* and the Jacobin Philosophy of Science: A Study in Ideas and Consequences," *Critical Problems in the History of Science*, ed. Marshall Clagett (Madison, Wis., 1959), pp. 255–89; and "The Formation of Lamarck's Evolutionary Theory," *Archives internationales d'histoire des sciences*, XXXVII (1956), 323–38.

leaves off and thus concentrate exclusively upon the subtlest and most esoteric aspects of the natural phenomena that concerns his group. And as he does this, his research communiqués will begin to change in ways whose evolution has been too little studied but whose modern end products are obvious to all and oppressive to many. No longer will his researches usually be embodied in books addressed, like Franklin's *Experiments . . . on Electricity* or Darwin's *Origin of Species,* to anyone who might be interested in the subject matter of the field. Instead they will usually appear as brief articles addressed only to professional colleagues, the men whose knowledge of a shared paradigm can be assumed and who prove to be the only ones able to read the papers addressed to them.

Today in the sciences, books are usually either texts or retrospective reflections upon one aspect or another of the scientific life. The scientist who writes one is more likely to find his professional reputation impaired than enhanced. Only in the earlier, pre-paradigm, stages of the development of the various sciences did the book ordinarily possess the same relation to professional achievement that it still retains in other creative fields. And only in those fields that still retain the book, with or without the article, as a vehicle for research communication are the lines of professionalization still so loosely drawn that the layman may hope to follow progress by reading the practitioners' original reports. Both in mathematics and astronomy, research reports had ceased already in antiquity to be intelligible to a generally educated audience. In dynamics, research became similarly esoteric in the later Middle Ages, and it recaptured general intelligibility only briefly during the early seventeenth century when a new paradigm replaced the one that had guided medieval research. Electrical research began to require translation for the layman before the end of the eighteenth century, and most other fields of physical science ceased to be generally accessible in the nineteenth. During the same two centuries similar transitions can be isolated in the various parts of the biological sciences. In parts of the social sciences they may well be occurring today. Although it has become customary, and is surely proper, to deplore the widening gulf that separates the professional scientist from his colleagues in other fields, too little attention is paid to the essential relationship between that gulf and the mechanisms intrinsic to scientific advance.

Ever since prehistoric antiquity one field of study after another has crossed the divide between what the historian might call its prehistory as a science and its history proper. These transitions to maturity have seldom been so sudden or so unequivocal as my necessarily schematic discussion may have implied. But neither have they been historically gradual, coextensive, that is to say, with the entire development of the fields within which they occurred. Writers on electricity during the first four decades of the eighteenth century possessed far more information about electrical phenomena than had their sixteenth-century predecessors. During the half-century after 1740, few new sorts of electrical phenomena were added to their lists. Nevertheless, in important respects, the electrical writings of Cavendish, Coulomb, and Volta in the last third of the eighteenth century seem further removed from those of Gray, Du Fay, and even Franklin than are the writings of these early eighteenth-century electrical discoverers from those of the sixteenth century.[12] Sometime between 1740 and 1780, electricians were for the first time enabled to take the foundations of their field for granted. From that point they pushed on to more concrete and recondite problems, and increasingly they then reported their results in articles addressed to other electricians rather than in books addressed to the learned world at large. As a group they achieved what had been gained by astronomers in antiquity and by students of motion in the Middle Ages, of physical optics in the late seventeenth century, and of historical geology in the early nineteenth. They had, that is, achieved a paradigm that proved able to guide the whole group's research. Except with the advantage of hindsight, it is hard to find another criterion that so clearly proclaims a field a science.

QUESTIONS FOR DISCUSSION

1. Kuhn must stipulate and defend the definitions of several key terms in this CP argument. What are these terms and how do their definitions nest together?

2. On p. 93 Kuhn claims that his examples are "historically typical." What if they were not? What happens to a CP argument when a refuter can come

[12]The post-Franklinian developments include an immense increase in the sensitivity of charge detectors, the first reliable and generally diffused techniques for measuring charge, the evolution of the concept of capacity and its relation to a newly refined notion of electric tension, and the quantification of electrostatic force. On all of these see Roller and Roller, *op. cit.*, pp. 66–81; W. C. Walker, "The Detection and Estimation of Electric Charges in the Eighteenth Century," *Annals of Science*, I (1936), 66–100; and Edmund Hoppe, *Geschichte der Elektrizität* (Leipzig, 1884), Part I, chaps. iii–iv.

along with significant exceptions and challenge typicality? How does Kuhn work to prevent that in the same sentence claiming typicality?

3. Kuhn says a theory becomes a paradigm when it "seems better" than its competitors. What can it mean to "seem better"?

4. What extended examples support Kuhn's theory? How do these examples function in the argument? How do they work if the reader is not familiar with the history of science? How do they work if the reader is? Which sort of reader did Kuhn have in mind?

5. According to Kuhn, a paradigm selects among the available facts but never explains them all. How is that possible?

6. In some ways Kuhn's chapter is about arguments and how they function with special audiences and how they lead to different types of writing. What makes a textbook or a "classic" in science possible? Why are "pre-paradigmatic" works in science accessible to general readers? Why are scientific articles not?

SUGGESTIONS FOR WRITING

1. Choose an area of science that you are familiar with, and write a history for the uninformed of the various conceptions that have been advanced about a particular phenomenon. What, for example, have been the various views on the causes of infectious diseases, the nature of combustion, the function of the brain, the nature of the atom, the nature of genetic mutation and recombination?

2. Using the same topic you would have chosen for suggestion 1, characterize a particular change in Kuhn's terms as a paradigm shift. Imagine that you are writing to an audience unfamiliar with Kuhn's ideas, so you must include careful, convincing definitions of his key terms.

3. Kuhn's ideas have not gone without criticism. Find original reviews of the book and some of the extensive published commentary on his ideas, and assemble a partial or sweeping refutation of Kuhn's notion of the paradigm and "normal" science. You might also interview research scientists to see if they agree with Kuhn's view of their methods.

4. Try to apply the notion of paradigms and paradigm shifts to fields other than science. Can you characterize a change in educational theory, political science, literary criticism, history, or psychology in the same way? Write the resulting CP argument for students in that field.

5. What do Kuhn's ideas about expert audiences imply for the popularization of scientific ideas? Find the same scientific subject written up in at least three publications addressed to audiences with different levels of background knowledge (i.e., articles on cholesterol and heart disease in the *Journal of the American Medical Association*, *Scientific American*, *Science Digest*, and

Time). Characterize the different treatments of the subject. Do paradigmatic concepts have to be explained for general readers? Do the popular accounts simplify to the point of falsifying? –

6. All of us are experts, or are becoming experts, in some field, whether an academic one like biochemistry or art history or an informal one like car engines, needlepoint, or cycling. Find an article in your area of expertise addressed to knowledgeable readers, people who do not need the special vocabulary of the field defined. "Translate" this article for general readers. Be sure you test out your simplified version on naive readers. It is very easy to overestimate what other people know about a topic very familiar to you.

Kratylus Automates His Urnworks

TOLLY KIZILOS

This unusual piece was not written by Plato in the fifth century B.C. *It appeared in a modern business journal, the* Harvard Business Review, *but it takes the ancient form of the dialogue, which can be described as a philosophical discussion, presented like a drama with several speakers, each of whom represents a different point of view toward the specific issue under discussion. Plato used the dialogue form to convey his philosophy; here the participants use it to arrive at a definition of* productivity. *The participants are Nikias, a potter who lost his job at Kratylus's urnworks when Kratylus purchased foot-operated potters' wheels; Kallias, a politician and member of the assembly; Ipponikos, a rich landowner; and Socrates, the philosopher. The author, Tolly Kizilos, is director of organizational development at the Systems and Research Center of Aerospace and Defense, Honeywell, Inc. His work at Honeywell is concerned with the way participative management policies bring about organizational change.*

KALLIAS: Here comes Nikias, troubled as usual about some social injustice or other.

SOCRATES: Good morning, Nikias. Isn't it a bit early in the day to be looking so troubled?

NIKIAS: Good morning, my friends, if you can call good a morning on which you lose your job.

IPPONIKOS: Sit down, Nikias, and tell us what happened. Remember what Socrates always says: "Nothing bad in this world is uncontaminated by good."

NIKIAS: I know what Socrates says, but it doesn't make sense to me just now. I don't know what will happen. I showed up for work at Kratylus's urnworks this morning, as I've done for three years, and he told me and seven others that we were no longer needed. He's installed some new foot-operated potter's wheels with pulleys, so he doesn't need as many people to do the work. Just like that, I'm unemployed.

KALLIAS: It wasn't all that sudden, though, was it, Nikias? I heard Kratylus almost a month ago talking openly at the agora about the new wheels he was buying from Corinth. It was no secret that he was going to install them to raise productivity. He had to do it, he told me, or he'd go out of business. I realize that you and a few others will suffer for a while, but he has to increase the productivity of his business or everyone working for him could end up without a job. And if he and others don't become more productive, Athens itself will take a backseat to Corinth and other cities, and all its citizens will suffer the consequences.

NIKIAS: We knew about it, all right, but we were hoping there would be other jobs we could do. Is it more productive to have people out of work, doing nothing, than to have them gainfully employed? How can the city's productivity grow if a lot of people are out of work? As far as I'm concerned, that kind of narrow-minded productivity increase helps no one but Kratylus; it just feeds his greed.

KALLIAS: Come now, Nikias; you can't possibly mean that! Productivity gains, no matter where, benefit everyone in the long run. You'll find another job soon, or Kratylus's business will expand and he'll need more workers to operate the faster wheels.

SOCRATES: Is productivity then both good and evil? Is it both the requirement for the workers' prosperity and the cause of their misfortunes?

IPPONIKOS: Ah, Socrates, how cleverly you always pose your questions—so pregnant with answers of your choosing! Why don't you go on and say that this is impossible, therefore productivity is either good or evil and, consequently, only one of our friends here can be right?

SOCRATES: Because, my dear Ipponikos, there is always a chance that a pregnant question will deliver a revealing answer. I find that I always discover new things as I grow older.

KALLIAS: Well, I'm always suspicious about ambiguous concepts. Productivity is either good or evil, and only one of us is right. Otherwise the concept is meaningless.

IPPONIKOS: People can always stretch the meaning of words enough to understand and agree with each other. All it takes is a common culture and goodwill.

KALLIAS: You aren't so bad at clever arguments yourself, Ipponikos. You imply that if we can't understand and agree with each other, it doesn't mean that some of us are wrong but that some are barbarians or rascals, or both. But perhaps you didn't mean that?

NIKIAS: If this is going to be a battle of wits, count me out.

SOCRATES: Nikias is right. Let's abandon generalities, which make philosophy irrelevant, and search for the meaning of productivity. Perhaps productivity is such an elusive concept that we can reach only a partial understanding of it, which, however, is acceptable to all of us. Let us be hopeful.

IPPONIKOS: With an ideologue like Kallias in the discussion, I'm afraid it'll be a waste of time.

NIKIAS: So is what we're doing right now. Let's discuss the issue instead of arguing over trivia.

KALLIAS: I'll tell you what productivity is, Socrates, or at least what it means to me—take it as you like. It's not such a difficult concept. It's simply the ratio of useful work output for a given valuable input. The higher the output for the same input, the higher the productivity is.

Take, for example, Kratylus's urnworks. I know something about his business because occasionally he asks for my opinion. Kratylus produces about 200 urns a day and used to employ about 20 workers. If he can produce the same number of urns with half the work force, then he doubles his shop's productivity. It's as simple as that.

IPPONIKOS: It's so simple, it's idiotic. Whose productivity has he increased? Nikias isn't productive anymore. He worked hard and still got laid off. Kratylus's productivity gain is Nikias's productivity loss.

NIKIAS: More productivity for Kratylus means more satisfaction of his greed.

KALLIAS: I don't understand what's happening to us. If we are here to denigrate Kratylus, I want no part of it.

SOCRATES: The path to the truth is often obscured by thorny bushes, Kallias.

KALLIAS: I know it's hard to be objective right now, but the facts are irrefutable. When you were working for Kratylus—I'm sure very hard— you weren't very productive because you were using a slow wheel to shape the urns. You were paid wages to produce something that cost so much it couldn't be sold easily. Activity isn't productivity, Nikias.

What's needed is more output for a given input; what's needed is more drachmas from the sale of urns per drachma of wages. Now you produce nothing, but your wages are also nothing; so, it makes no sense to talk about your productivity. Only when you get paid to produce something of value, that is, when there's an input and an output, can we talk meaningfully about productivity.

IPPONIKOS: This input-output stuff may be useful when talking about machines or oxen, but it makes no sense when we're discussing human beings. Productivity means productive activity. Human beings can be very productive even when they're supported by handouts. Why, only two weeks ago I heard that the geometer Diomedes, a pauper, mind you, if there ever was one, invented an instrument for measuring angles he calls a theodolite. I heard Telemachus say it will save thousands of workdays for his surveying crew when they're setting the boundaries of farmers' fields all around Attica. Diomedes received no wages—no input, as you would say, Kallias—but does that mean we can't talk about his productivity? He *is* productive, very productive.

KALLIAS: Of course he is, my dear Ipponikos. Your example of Diomedes is precisely what I've been looking for to make my point. Maximum output with minimum possible input yields the highest productivity.

NIKIAS: So, productivity according to you is using up people. Humanity subordinated to the goddess of productivity. Perhaps you'd like to add another goddess to the 12 Olympians? It wouldn't surprise me.

KALLIAS: I said minimum *possible* input, not minimum input. Possible is the essential. . . .

IPPONIKOS: I don't understand why you keep using inputs and outputs when you talk about human beings, Kallias. We could never define such things for humans, capable of an infinite variety and an infinite number of possible inputs and outputs, none of them exactly predictable. No man can be bound by defining him in terms of input and output. "Man is the measure of all things," as Protagoras said—he cannot himself be measured.

NIKIAS: But to Kratylus and others who own shops, Ipponikos, there's little difference among men, beasts, or machines. A person at work is told exactly what input he'll have (that is, what wages he'll be paid), exactly what he has to do, and what he's expected to produce. That's what happens when you work for someone else; you're dehumanized.

KALLIAS: You're too angry to contribute to this discussion, Nikias.

IPPONIKOS: Since when has anger been proven to be an obstacle in the search for truth?

SOCRATES: Nikias agrees with you, Ipponikos, that man is fundamentally different from the machine, and one of the reasons is that only machines have finite and measurable inputs and outputs by design.

IPPONIKOS: It's even more fundamental than that: Kallias talks about wages as inputs, but that's so narrow-minded it's absurd. People can get more than wages for doing their jobs; they can get satisfaction, learning, enjoyment; they can be frightened or encouraged by what happens around them; they can be made to feel stronger or weaker by the actions of others. Their productive activity is often the result of all these impressions, shaped by thinking, feeling, and judgment. And as for their output, sometimes it's so unpredictable as to instill awe, admiration, and delight.

KALLIAS: I'm really surprised by your views, Ipponikos. It seems that Protagoras and the other sophists have clouded your thoughts.

IPPONIKOS: I can do without your sarcasm, Kallias. Do me the courtesy of treating me like a person who can think for himself. If you have something to say about my views, say it without insinuations.

KALLIAS: I will, my friend, I most certainly will. You are espousing a very irresponsible view and I couldn't possibly avoid commenting on it. According to you, a workshop owner should hire workers and pay them wages, but demand nothing specific of them. Some of them may want to loaf; others may decide to take up playwriting or singing instead of making urns, and some of them may even choose to work and produce urns once in a while. Now and then, perhaps, a worker will invent a new tool that improves the quality of urns or the productivity of the shop, but there will be no guarantees. And the wages have to keep coming steadily, guaranteed.

Is this a responsible way to run a business? Could the workshop owner entrust his future to the whims of his workers? The workers have no stake in the business and, if the shop went broke, they could leave at a moment's notice to take jobs elsewhere. And, what about those who really work hard to produce urns and urns alone? Wouldn't this irresponsible approach be unfair to them?

IPPONIKOS: You talk as if the workers want to loaf and behave irresponsibly toward the owner and their fellow workers. You don't trust them.

KALLIAS: Not everyone is responsible and trustworthy.

IPPONIKOS: Perhaps not. But if the owner trusts his people and rewards them fairly, I believe that the workers would strive to do their best for the business. Some will be less productive than others, but the productivity of the whole place will be higher when people feel free to use all their talents and skills. As for fairness, the workers themselves will set standards and require that everyone pull his weight.

SOCRATES: I hear a lot of views being expressed, but no conclusions. If this were a workshop, its productivity would be very low, and some of us, I fear, would have to be replaced by more productive philosophers, probably from Sparta. Can't we first agree on what productivity means?

KALLIAS: It's apparent to me, Socrates, that this isn't possible with Ipponikos and Nikias present. If you and I were alone, we could be more productive than the whole city of Sparta discussing the issue.

SOCRATES: You and I, Kallias, might come up with conclusions very fast, but the quality of our conclusions might not be as high as it can be with our friends here contributing their ideas.

KALLIAS: Sooner or later, I suppose, we'll have to talk about effectiveness and efficiency. I believe that productivity is high only when both efficiency and effectiveness are high.

SOCRATES: All right, let's see what you mean. Suppose you hire me for a drachma a day to pick olives fallen from your olive trees in Eleusis. While I'm working, I notice that the fence protecting your property from the wild pigs is down. Pigs can get into your fields and devour the ripe olives that have fallen on the ground. Because I think this is more urgent and because I'm much better at repairing fences than gathering olives, I decide to fix your fence instead.

I work hard all day long and by sunset I'm done and I'm sitting on a rock admiring the good work I did. You return from your day's debates at the Assembly and find me in this contemplative pose. You see that I have picked no olives but have fixed your fence. The question is, will you pay me as we agreed or not?

KALLIAS: Of course not. You changed our contract arbitrarily. I could suffer losses because of that. You shouldn't have changed the output.

NIKIAS: He means he didn't want you to think; do only what you were told. Be a machine or a mindless ox.

SOCRATES: But a contract is a contract, Nikias. What if he was counting on me to pick the olives so he could deliver them to someone who had a contract with him to buy them that same evening? I was productive, all right, but not productive doing what we agreed on. In that, my productivity was zero. So isn't it true that productivity has meaning only when there's an agreement on the inputs or wages, and the outputs or the goals?

KALLIAS: Of course it is.

IPPONIKOS: And if someone produces something very valuable without any agreement?

SOCRATES: It appears that it doesn't make sense to talk about productivity when there's no agreement, explicit or implicit.

KALLIAS: Exactly. Productivity pertains to work toward a goal. There must be expectation of output and fulfillment of that expectation.

SOCRATES: I'm glad you agree with what I said. But I have some difficulty with it, and you may be able to help me. It has to do with something that happened when they were building the mound commemorating the glorious dead who fell at the battle of Marathon.

KALLIAS: I can't for the life of me imagine what Marathon has to do with productivity. Are you serious?

IPPONIKOS: Perhaps you've hit on your problem, Kallias—lack of imagination.

SOCRATES: Please, allow me to continue. Everything is related to everything else, say some philosophers, and I'll be happy to explain what I mean if you let me.

NIKIAS: You are the last person on earth I would want to stop, Socrates. You're usually able to deliver what you promise, but even if you weren't, you're too stubborn to be stopped.

SOCRATES: I'll take that as praise, Nikias, and go on. After Pericles gave his marvelous funeral oration on that hallowed ground, he left behind General Meno from Orchomenos in charge of 100 slaves and ordered him to build the mound in 30 days. Meno was determined to obey the order even though he estimated that the project would take twice that time. It is said that General Meno became a tyrant with the slaves, driving them ruthlessly to work.

One day, during an inspection of the project, he discovered a slave who sat on the nearby edge of the marsh in blissful repose. Furious, he ordered his lieutenants to flog him until he was hardly alive. General Meno wanted to make this laggard an example for the other slaves, demonstrating to them that because the slave didn't produce, he made everyone else work harder. "He is a weight upon the earth!" he shouted for all to hear, using Homer's words.

KALLIAS: I still don't see. . . .

SOCRATES: Then one of the most productive slaves stepped forward and asked to speak. General Meno could hardly hold back his anger, but because he valued this slave greatly he allowed him to say his piece. "This man, sir," the slave said, pointing to his doomed comrade, "is one of the most productive slaves you have. It is true that he neither sweats nor strains his back digging and shoveling earth, but he contributes to the building of the mound more than anyone else."

"And how does he do this? Gazing at his belly button while you and the others break your backs?" the general demanded.

"You see, General," the slave said with conviction, "he is a storyteller, not a digger. If he was shoveling dirt with all his might, he couldn't do in a day more than I do in an hour. But after work, when we all return to camp, dog-tired, miserable, and hopeless—for what can we expect from the future but more bondage and more misery?—when we are gathered around the campfire at night, this man spins tales of hope for us and makes our lot bearable. We listen to him and dream of a better life after we end this project. He makes our burdens lighter, and we can fall asleep with dreams of freedom in our heads. Next day we are ready for work, believing that if our work pleases you and the Athenians, we may some day gain our freedom."

KALLIAS: I think I'm beginning. . . .

SOCRATES: Please let me finish. "So," the slave went on, "this man does his part. If you beat him senseless, or cripple him, or—worst of fates!—kill him, who will keep us hoping, dreaming, and working? If hope vanishes, punishment and death hold no fear, General. We may not be able to build your mound. Think of that, sir, and allow this man to go on producing what he is best able to produce: tales of hope. You need him as much as, if not more than, we do."

So spoke the valued slave, and General Meno listened. He ordered his lieutenants to release the man, who went on to tell tales until the project was finished—exactly on time. The question, dear Kallias, is this: Was the storytelling slave productive or not?

KALLIAS: Of course he was productive, probably the most productive of all. He contributed to the achievement of the goal, didn't he? Whether he knew it or not, he worked toward the same goal as all the other slaves.

SOCRATES: So, you say, productivity is work toward a goal. You wouldn't pay me for fixing your fence because you had set the goal as gathering fallen olives. What about here? Here, the goal was to build a mound, just as Kratylus's goal is to produce urns, and ours is to come up with the truth. But this slave wasn't building the mound, I wasn't gathering olives, and some workers at Kratylus's urnworks may not be producing as many urns as their fellows.

Yet you just told us that this slave was probably the most productive slave working on the mound. Could I have been more productive to you by fixing your fence? Could Nikias, who wasn't producing as much with his old wheel, and I, bumbling now on my way to the truth, be more productive than others who achieve stated goals? Could it be, Kallias, that Nikias, now that he is searching for the truth with us, is more productive to our city (and of course to Kratylus) than when he was making urns?

KALLIAS: I thought you would twist things sooner or later, Socrates, and I've been alert to it.

IPPONIKOS: It won't help you much, Kallias. You're too efficient to be effective. If you're sure you know the truth and you're sitting here searching for it, you are obviously wasting your time, and your productivity has to be nil.

KALLIAS: Leave your sophistry for later, Ipponikos, and let me respond to Socrates. It seems to me, Socrates, that you are mixing two kinds of productivity. Yes, Nikias is more productive to our city when he's searching for the truth with us than he would be if he were doing nothing. To the extent that Kratylus is a citizen of Athens, he benefits from Nikias's philosophizing as does every other citizen. But Nikias is not productive to Kratylus because he simply isn't making urns any more.

SOCRATES: But if our city is more productive, doesn't Kratylus have a better chance to sell his wares? And if that is so, isn't it fair to say that Kratylus, as the owner of the workshop, is benefiting from Nikias's philosophizing?

KALLIAS: Productivity loses all meaning if you put it that way. Humanity benefits from anything productive anyone does. But I still say that productivity is a useful concept only when it's limited to specific goals achieved by specific persons.

IPPONIKOS: Come on, Kallias, use your imagination! Think of all the ways the workers, even at Kratylus's workshop, can contribute to the production and sale of urns even when they're not actually making or selling urns. No one can say whether a person is productive by just looking at him or by measuring only specific inputs and outputs.

KALLIAS: Use your reason, Ipponikos.

SOCRATES: But Kallias, how can you tell when a person is doing something or nothing? And how can you say that a person can be productive to the city but not to Kratylus's workshop, which is, after all, a part of the city? And how can you tell if a person is productive when the goals set for that person are different from the goals toward which a person works? One can still contribute to the goals if one interprets goals more broadly.

KALLIAS: All I know is that somehow or other using a new wheel makes Kratylus's workshop more productive because he can lay off Nikias and some other workers and still produce the same number of urns. Then Nikias, as Kratylus had thought, finds something else to do— philosophize, in this case—and he becomes productive again to the city and to Kratylus, because he is also a citizen.

SOCRATES: That's well put, Kallias. But if Nikias is now productive to the city, he must be paid for his productivity. Yet I haven't heard of anyone willing to put philosophers on the public payroll. Would you propose that the Assembly pass a law to do that? It certainly would help us all, Nikias and me in particular, since we are not influential politicians like you or wealthy landowners like Ipponikos.

IPPONIKOS: It's not only philosophers who are productive and should be compensated but also geometers, poets, musicians, and all kinds of other people who work with their minds.

KALLIAS: Everyone would become a freeloader.

NIKIAS: Are you saying that all thinkers are freeloaders?

KALLIAS: Don't be absurd, Nikias. I'm saying that people with no talent for geometry or music or bent for philosophical search would claim to be geometers, musicians, and philosophers in order to collect money from the city and avoid sweating in workshops and fields. Since there is no way to measure their output, no one could tell whether Socrates was more productive than the man who sweeps the steps leading up to the Parthenon. The sweeper could claim, for example, that gazing at the blue sky was helpful in proving the Pythagorean theorem in a new way.

SOCRATES: And so we have arrived at a point where we must make distinctions: there is productivity and there is productivity, and unless we sort these out we will never come to any conclusions. There is productivity of persons who perform manual work with a physical output; productivity of persons whose output is thoughts, poems, songs, inventions, proofs, and so on; and productivity of groups, such as ours, organizations or institutions, such as Kratylus's workshop or our beloved city of Athens. These are the entities to which we have attached potential for productivity.

NIKIAS: I'll start by defining the productivity of manual workers.

KALLIAS: Their productivity depends simply on their output, be it urns made, olives picked, marble slabs quarried, or what have you, divided by the cost of production, which is mostly wages.

NIKIAS: You may think it's that simple, but I don't. Even a manual worker has a mind that he can use when he does his work. His productivity can be defined your way only if you rob him of his mind. If one does that by rigidly defining the input and the output, that is, if one dehumanizes him, then one can define his productivity accurately—so many urns per drachma of wages, so much earth moved to build a mound per loaf of bread, so many olives gathered per day's wage.

One can go even further and define the productivity of those workers who work with their intellect that way—so many plays written, or songs composed, or theorems proved, or philosophical conclusions reached per drachma. But remember, the only way this can be done is if you set rigid, unalterable inputs and outputs. If a philosopher wrote a poem and an urnmaker proved a theorem of geometry, their productivity would be nothing.

IPPONIKOS: In other words, Kallias, you have to choose between having a precise definition of productivity and missing a lot of good work, or having at best a sloppy definition and allowing other, unanticipated but valuable work to be encouraged.

KALLIAS: I can't believe this! You argue with the same cunning as some unscrupulous colleagues of mine in the Assembly. I will give you a precise definition that at the same time encourages all valuable work to proceed: set outputs that are to be met unless more valuable outputs are produced. General Meno set goals, but when a slave produced stories that helped the goal indirectly, the general recognized that his output was more valuable than his manual output would have been in furthering the goal directly.

This way the worker whose output is supposed to be the production of urns will be rewarded when he produces urns or something else, a new potter's wheel or a great poem perhaps, which the person who set the goals and must pay for their accomplishment finds equally valuable or even more valuable than the production of urns. This is my position, and I challenge you to find fault with it!

SOCRATES: It is indeed an excellent position, Kallias. You have said that productivity for an individual worker is his valuable output per given input. It is a good definition, but you haven't told us how the value of the output is determined or whether the person who evaluated it is competent to do so.

IPPONIKOS: I would hate to have Kratylus decide the relative value of ten urns versus Sophocles' *Antigone.*

KALLIAS: Again, your way of arguing is to ridicule. I'm getting annoyed with you, Ipponikos, and unless you change your ways I will have to bid you farewell and seek a more congenial discussion elsewhere.

IPPONIKOS: I apologize for my sarcasm, Kallias. But please, do respond to Socrates.

KALLIAS: I don't believe that shop owners are any less competent to evaluate the relative worth of urns and plays than anyone else. Judgment, after all, is one of the most important attributes one must have to succeed in business.

SOCRATES: Wouldn't it perhaps be better if the employer and the wage earner could discuss the value of the work or the productivity of the wage earner and agree on it? After all, the person who produces something may be the only one who can explain the purpose for which he produced that thing and judge its value from his perspective.

KALLIAS: That process might work in Socrates' ideal state, but I don't think it has a chance in Athens. The wage earner can discuss all you like him to discuss, but when the time comes to decide how productive he is, when it comes to making a decision on how much he should be paid, the one who has the power, who pays the wages, will have the final word.

IPPONIKOS: You say that those who have the power set the standards and you accuse *me* of arguing like the sophists? Why, what you just said is exactly what Thrasymachus teaches.

KALLIAS: Then I have to admit that even a sophist can be right, once.

NIKIAS: I've had enough of the sophists. I want to hear Socrates on what workers have to say about the value of their work.

SOCRATES: Even if we assume that power is what one needs to set standards, what I said still stands. The wage earner also has power because the employer needs him to be as productive as possible, not be a mere machine executing set goals. If the employer doesn't evaluate him correctly, the wage earner will cease coming up with new products, new methods, or new ideas, and the productivity of the organization will suffer. Since the employer cannot *make* the wage earner be creative or take the initiative, or modify goals to suit changed situations, he must ensure that the wage earner stays motivated. And the best way for the employer to achieve that is not to be arbitrary or authoritarian but to share his power of evaluation with him.

I see you're shaking your head, Kallias. When you reflect on these thoughts you may become less skeptical. In any case, it is an alternative way of settling the issue we were discussing. Productivity increases come not only from getting faster wheels in the workshops but also from workers such as Nikias who feel in a way like owners of the workshop. Isn't it then correct to say that productivity is defined by whatever reasonable input and output both wage earner and employer agree on?

KALLIAS: Though I don't believe that this process will work, I agree that it is worth an experiment to find out. But I don't think we have really defined productivity.

NIKIAS: If we have arrived at a conclusion. . . .

SOCRATES: Definitions can get us only so far. It's the dialogue between well-meaning people that gains our ends. This is the process, it seems to me, that will also determine the productivity of organizations such as Kratylus's workshop or our beloved city of Athens. Plato may not agree entirely with me on this, but I believe that the productivity of Athens is great because we all partake in making the decisions that govern our lives. Democracy is a form of participation, and it's surprising that it hasn't been applied to our workshops in some appropriate form.

KALLIAS: Well, I have always felt that productivity was of great concern to both politics and business. If we set goals and compile a list of all the services our city provides for its citizens, then measure them. . . .

SOCRATES: I doubt that it would be either possible or meaningful, Kallias. The evaluation of our city's productivity is in the hands of future generations. Whether we sink to oblivion or history remembers us is not predictable or determined by a list of services or the Assembly's definition of goals. Athens and other cities and states will live on if they encourage their citizens to excel in what they do best.

NIKIAS: Before you go any further with an encomium to our city, Socrates, I would like to know if anyone here intends to inform Kratylus of my contributions to our discourse and ask him whether he would reconsider his decision to lay me off. If this isn't anyone's intention, I'd like to move on and look for another job before my family has to beg for food.

KALLIAS: I can certainly talk to him about it. But would you be willing to moderate your demands on wages? At least until his workshop begins to make profits again?

NIKIAS: I'll do anything reasonable to keep my job, of course. But if the job could be a little more satisfying than what I used to do, or if I have some say on what I do and how I am evaluated, then I'll bear the load more comfortably and I may even turn out more urns than ever before.

SOCRATES: I'm sure, Nikias, that you're speaking the truth.

KALLIAS: Can anyone venture a guess as to our productivity in this discussion?

SOCRATES: We've done our best, and I believe we've reached some agreements. If we didn't answer all the questions and didn't solve all the problems, it isn't because we were unproductive but because some problems are beyond our reach. Sisyphus, who rolls his stone up the mountain only to have it roll back down, is not unproductive; he works as hard as he possibly can, doing everything a human being can do. If he isn't as productive as he could be, it's because the gods have chosen it to be that way. So with us; we have done as well as we can. The gods may allow others in the future to do better.

NIKIAS: If one could only eat the truth he produces. . . .

IPPONIKOS: Of course one can, Nikias. All one has to do is make the truth wanted by many.

KALLIAS: Next time I'll ask Kratylus to join us. We should have more businessmen-philosophers around.

SOCRATES: It would be a wonderful thing to do. I pray for your success.

QUESTIONS FOR DISCUSSION

1. Given the fact that this article appeared in a journal directed at businesspeople, what is the point of setting the dialogue in ancient Greece? Are there any advantages to discussing productivity in the manufacture of urns rather than microchips or robots or automobiles?

2. In what ways does the dialogue form make the argument easier for the reader to follow? Are there any ways in which it makes understanding more difficult?

3. Characterize the four participants in the dialogue. Are they distinct from each other? Are they consistent in their points of view?

4. What value judgments or attitudes are conveyed by the term *productivity?* Do different characters convey different attitudes? What conclusion can we reach about the value of productivity by the end of the dialogue?

5. What do you think is the author's final definition of *productivity?* What definitions does he reject? Is there any reason to include in the dialogue all the rejected definitions?

6. What is the point of Socrates' anecdote of the tale-spinning slave? How is Socrates' story related to the notion of productivity?

SUGGESTIONS FOR WRITING

1. Try extracting a conventional essay from the dialogue form. Using the information presented in this article, rewrite it as a straightforward argument defining productivity. Use twentieth-century examples for illustration.

2. Write a dialogue yourself. Use the form, with at least three speakers, to define a specialized term in a field of study you are familiar with. You might,

for example, explore the meanings of such terms as evolution, macroeconomics, readability, cardiovascular fitness, or neurosis for an audience of curious nonspecialists.

3. Construct a definition of *productivity* in a situation you have experienced. That is, if you have held a job, what would you consider a fair definition of productivity for that job? Or consider productivity in another kind of situation, outside of business. How would you define a productive week for a student?

4. Put yourself in Nikias's sandals and follow up on the discussion he just completed. Write a letter to Kratylus convincing him that it will be to his advantage as well as yours if he rehires you.

5. What kind of action should follow from the discussion in this article? Draw up two plans for implementing the conclusion that employers and wage earners should both participate in setting reasonable goals for productivity. Direct one report at employers, the other at wage earners. You can either do this generally, or you can address the employer and employees at a specific place of work.

6. Kallias concludes that "we should have more businessmen-philosophers." What does he mean, and how might that goal be achieved? Write your recommendation to the administrator of a business school.

Two

ARGUMENTS ABOUT CAUSES

The natural sequel to knowing what is wondering why. Suppose you read that monarch butterfly populations are declining, that celebrity body-building books are the latest publishing success, that China is once more allowing scholars to travel abroad. All such new phenomena provoke curiosity about causes: We wonder what new events or circumstances made them happen. We also pause and ponder when the familiar turns strange, when a friend starts acting coldly, when the championship team starts losing all its games, when a senator begins to vote against the interests of constituents. Any such change or disturbance in the usual sends us to investigate causes. An answer to the question "Why?" is a causal proposition requiring a causal argument. It is also one of the most common kinds of argument we engage in, but we can learn a great deal about it by carefully scrutinizing its special tactics.

To begin with, causal arguments are fundamentally different from CP arguments. The CP argument depends on assumed or argued definition, which becomes the medium of exchange between arguer and audience. But a causal argument uses a different currency. It relies on assumed or argued *agency*, which we can define as a shared belief about what can cause what. Although we rarely articulate such beliefs, they are fundamental to much of our thinking, absorbed almost unconsciously from our culture. If someone tells us that a research project failed because the investigators ran out of funding, or that a murder was committed out of jealousy, or that a fire started because of faulty wiring, we would have no trouble believing these causal assertions. The causes they identify are all plausible; they all depend on believable agencies.

The art of supporting causal arguments is the art of finding agencies that arguer and audience can share a belief in and that also fit the evidence. Even a cause that sounds convincing may not be supported by the facts of the case. It may, for instance, sound very plausible to say that robbers commit murders, but if the victim in a particular case was not robbed, the investigators must look for another cause. Every case, every event or set of circumstances whose causes we wonder about suggests and limits the agencies we can employ in argument. In understanding and constructing causal arguments it helps to know that a variety of causes is at our disposal so that we can find a fit between agency and evidence.

In order to understand this variety, we can draw on our natural vocabulary for describing causes. For instance, in the social sciences in particular, we often speak of the influences, factors, or conditions that underlie large-scale phenomena. We can define *factors* as causes that come together to produce an effect, *conditions* as background circumstances that make effects possible, and *influences* as causes that speed up or intensify an effect. An extended example will show how these kinds of causes structure our thinking. Suppose you have evidence that the number of private schools is increasing, that you have, in other words, supported a CP argument for the existence of such a trend; your next step is to look for causes. This search will not be a random process. Your sense of what you and your audience will find plausible directs you to the kinds of influences, factors, or conditions that could bring about a social trend. The conditions behind an increasing recourse to private schools might, you speculate, include dissatisfaction with public schools, an anxious awareness of the importance of education, and sufficient affluence. When all these conditions come together to produce an effect, we call them contributing factors. An influence, like the prospect of a tuition tax credit, would intensify the effect.

All of these causes could be linked to their effect by plausible agency; we tend to believe that human beings act to correct situations that distress them, and that if they believe that private schools are better than public schools, they will change allegiance where possible. But even such plausible causes and agencies still have to be supported by evidence from the real world. If the causal arguer sampled parents of private school students and found that they were not dissatisfied with available public schools, that in fact they had almost no experience or knowledge of them, he or she would have to look elsewhere for a plausible cause, perhaps to the prestige appeal of private schooling. As this example shows, building causal arguments requires constant adjustment between the arguer's hypothesizing and the evidence of the case.

We can call this adjustment "causal model building," and the variety of causes we use to carry it out is to some extent determined by the discipline we are working in. In history, for instance, factors, influences, and conditions are very much the stuff of causal reasoning, but since historians (and really anyone dealing with particular events) must be acutely aware of the dimension of time, they often build a linear model employing the notion of *remote* and *proximate* causes. These are causes distinguished from each other only by their distance in time from the effect under consideration. Remote causes are further away, proximate causes closer, but both are ordered into a sequence leading up to the effect. When we examine the causes of events that can be as different as the outbreak of a war, a train derailment, the marketing success of a new product, or the completion of a project such as a new civic center, we will tend to marshal our possible causes into a linear array according to time, from the distant to the immediate, the remote to the proximate. The resulting causal argument will be like a narrative, a story with the effect or the cause as its conclusion. In the readings that follow, notice how carefully Berton Rouché reconstructs a sequence of events in order to track down a deadly cause.

In our time-ordered thinking about causes we may also pay particular attention to the kind of cause that immediately precedes an effect and seems to force it to happen. We call this the *precipitating cause*, and it operates on background conditions and factors the way an extra salt crystal operates on a super-saturated solution, by suddenly producing a dramatic result or setting off a chain reaction leading to a final effect. Again, nothing inherent in the cause makes it precipitating; we know it only by the effects that follow. The assassination of an Austrian archduke may have precipitated World War I, but the assassination of President James Garfield did not produce such immediate, dramatic results. Precipitating causes can also figure in scientific model building, which explains natural events, and in the article by Rebecca Rawls you will read about the argument being made for a very large precipitating cause of the extinction of the dinosaurs.

But in the experimental sciences, where causal models are constructed so that they can be tested, two other types of causes figure prominently, the *necessary* and *sufficient*. Necessary causes, as the term reveals, must be in place for an effect to occur. A virus is the necessary cause of the common cold, fuel the necessary cause of a car's movement, the consumption of alcohol the necessary cause of a drunken stupor. But none of these necessary causes by themselves can produce the effects associated with them. A virus can be present in the nasal passages and yet a cold may not develop, all the fuel in the world will not start a car with a dead battery, and big bodies can consume more alcohol than little ones without getting drunk. Still, in all of these cases, if the necessary cause were removed, the effect would not occur.

That cause in whose presence the effect *must* occur is called the sufficient cause. It may be one cause or the conjunction of several. In the case of the cold, a virus must come together with a vulnerable body for the effect to be produced. We can illustrate the difference between necessary and sufficient cause by looking at what it takes to pass a writing course. Students and teachers will agree that the necessary requisite is writing papers. But they will diverge after that in what they acknowledge as sufficient cause: Some will insist that all papers earn passing grades; others will allow one or two incomplete or failed papers, so long as the average grade is passing. After that, instructors may add other conditions for sufficiency such as class attendance, quizzes, revisions, participation, and other homework assignments.

We have distinguished between necessary and sufficient

causes, but some causes are both. They are both sufficient to bring about the effect, and their absence would prevent it from occurring. The search for causes that are both necessary and sufficient poses the greatest challenge to the arguer, but when our long-range purpose is to prevent something or to bring it about, we have to identify the cause in whose absence nothing could happen and whose presence ensures a result. If the American business community, for example, wants to emulate the success of the Japanese, it naturally looks for the necessary and sufficient cause of Japanese industrial dominance. (See the article, "Can the Japanese Keep it Up?")

A related notion often quite useful in causal argument is that of the *blocking,* or *impeding, cause.* This is a cause whose presence is sufficient to prevent an effect and in whose absence the effect will go forward. Sometimes in causal model building, the most interesting things are those that did not happen. We often ask, for example, what might or should have happened to prevent a terrorist attack, an embassy takeover, the downing of an airliner. Or, to turn the situation around, when we are planning or predicting, we often try to anticipate possible blocking causes. An economist, for instance, predicting the rate of growth for the next six months in an industry, will acknowledge the contingencies that might interfere, such as currency instability or unforeseen political catastrophes. Among the readings that follow, Richard Neely's "The Politics of Crime" focuses on ideological and financial causes blocking the effective reduction of violent crime.

Blocking or impeding causes can operate in both the natural and social worlds, but one kind of cause impinges only when human actions are concerned: *responsibility.* When people are involved, we look for the person in charge, the one who designed the plan, who started the action, who could have made a different choice, who might have prevented any disastrous results. In some sense, we identify people who act as causes, with motives, intentions, and domains of responsibility that make them causal agents, liable to praise or blame. The pilot of an airplane, for instance, is responsible for its safe operation, so we consider "pilot error" when something goes wrong. Or when a new toothpaste succeeds on the market, we give credit to the marketing team who designed the promotion; they are the cause of its brisk sales. When you read Barbara Tuchman's causal analysis of the outbreak of World War I, ask yourself how the actions and mistaken judgments of individuals can lead to international catastrophe.

All the kinds of causes we have identified imply a linear progression from cause to effect. But in some circumstances a model that depicts a direct movement from cause to effect is too simplistic. For effects can become causes too. They can operate on the causes that feed them, in turn amplifying or re-creating each other. George Orwell has given us perhaps the most famous illustration of *reciprocal causality* in his essay "Politics and the English Language." There he points out that though confused thought produces corrupt language, corrupt language can also confuse thought. We should be aware of the possibility of reciprocal causality when we deal with causes and effects that cannot be easily separated in time.

Building a causal model is only part of the arguer's task. Along with it comes consideration of what will actually convince an intended audience. Readers sometimes need to be shown how a particular cause can be connected to an effect, especially since arguments work in the realm of probability rather than easily demonstrated fact. To establish the plausibility of a causal connection we can turn to certain tactics of causal argument, ways of presenting relationships among the causes in the model we have constructed.

Among the most effective of these tactics are the four methods of causal inquiry so cogently articulated by the nineteenth-century British philosopher John Stuart Mill. These were conceived of as ways of discovering causes in the first place, but they work equally well as methods of marshaling support for causal arguments. The first of these is called the *common factor method*. Here the arguer finds several instances of the same effect and looks for antecedents in common. If the successful computer manufacturers all stayed out of the software business and allowed independent suppliers to create and market software compatible to their machines, then perhaps this strategy was a cause of their success.

The case could be made even stronger by using the second of Mill's tactics, the *single difference method*. Now the arguer looks for parallel cases, one in which the effect occurs, another in which it does not. If the unsuccessful microcomputer companies tried to control both hardware and software manufacturing and the successful ones did not, it seems even more likely that a crucial cause of success or failure in the highly competitive microcomputer market is the software marketing strategy. In the essay "Identical Twins Reared Apart," you will see both the common factor and single difference methods at work.

A third persuasive tactic is Mill's *elimination method.* Here the arguer starts with a set of possible causes, sufficient but not individually necessary, and proceeds not to support the favored one but to eliminate the others. This is a method used in everyday reasoning. Suppose you have an allergic reaction after breakfast one morning, but you do not know what food caused it. It could be the eggs, the mangoes, the bacon, the milk. So on each of four successive mornings you eliminate one of these foods from your breakfast menu; on the morning that no allergic reaction occurs, you will have found your cause. "The Prognosis for this Patient Is Horrible" shows you this method of elimination in action.

Mill's final tactic is the *method of concomitant variation.* This method works best when the arguer deals with persisting situations, such as trends that fluctuate over time. If the arguer can establish a pattern of relationship between two trends—that one seems to increase when the other decreases or that both increase or decrease together—then there is evidence of causal connection between them. Evidence, not proof. After all, trends may coincide accidentally. What is needed in arguments using concomitant variation is a strong assumption of agency, of the causal link between the two variables. How else could we establish a causal connection between increasing unemployment in the Scottish highlands and the growing consumption of wine in the United States? We need to trace the link between more wine consumed and less Scotch imported. Among the readings, notice how the essay "Parkinson's Law" relies on concomitant variation.

Four more tactics are available to the causal arguer, and the first of these is one of the most useful: the *chain of causes.* If an audience's first response to a pairing of cause and effect is likely to be a gasp of disbelief, one of the ways of bridging that gasp is by a carefully constructed linear chain of causes. The connection between the temperature of the Pacific Ocean and the state of your bank account may sound farfetched at first, but this remote cause and its effect can be linked by a chain. The warming of the ocean affects the pattern of winds and thus of weather coming across the North American continent. The weather affects the crops. When crops fail, supplies of certain foods are reduced, and if demand is consistent, prices go up. When prices go up, your bank account suffers. You will notice a condensed chain-of-causes argument in the article "Iridium Provides Clue to Dinosaurs' Extinction."

Causes can also be argued into place by appeal to *analogy,* a comparison between two similar cases. Readers are more likely to accept a causal connection if it can be shown to resemble a more familiar one they already believe in. If we accept the operation of Gresham's Law, that bad currency tends to drive the good out of circulation, then the application of that law to another field may prove convincing. We often see it argued that bad television programs drive out the good, that cheap clothing drives out the well-made, that pulp fiction drives out the less frivolous. Such analogies are never proof, of course; they are only as convincing as the audience's faith in the term of comparison. Look for the causal analogy in Edward Rothstein's "Why We Live in the Musical Past."

Like CP arguments, causal arguments can also use *examples* for support. We tend to believe a cause is operating if many apparently unambiguous examples of it are set before us. Many articles in this section use this technique, but notice that it appears only when the article supports a causal generalization rather than the nomination of a single cause to account for a single effect. When C. Northcote Parkinson compiled his famous law, he claims to have used "vast masses of statistical evidence," but to convince his readers he detailed one typical example of the growth of officialdom in the British navy. Kim Chernin uses another form of this technique, offering an extended personal example of her own obsessive dieting.

A simple but sometimes an effective way of associating cause and effect is to cite their *order in time.* Though we all know that it is a fallacy to claim priority in time as proof of causal relationship, we still assume that causes precede their effects. Therefore, establishing time order can help cement an already plausible causal relationship. Like all the other tactics, this appeal relies on an assumption of agency.

What does an arguer do when it is impossible to share assumed agency with an audience, when they will not believe the arguer's assumption about what can cause what? This was the problem Sigmund Freud faced in his ground-breaking study of dreams and the unconscious. His thesis that dreams of the death of loved ones could represent the wishes of the dreamer was both unfamiliar to its original audience and likely to arouse their hostility. In order to argue for it, Freud had to propound an entire theory about the nature of children's egoistic hatreds and loves. In other words, he had to argue for agency, the connecting link, itself. To do so is the work of a major theorist; fortunately for most of us, causal argument is a matter of appealing to the known agencies of natural and human behavior.

Johnny Wants *to Read*

BRUNO BETTELHEIM

The author of this essay, Bruno Bettelheim, is a distinguished psychoanalyst and author; he was, for thirty years, director of the Orthogenic School for Disturbed Children at the University of Chicago. He is perhaps best known for his book, The Uses of the Imagination, *which argues for the liberating effects of fairy tales and fantasies on the mental health of children. As this essay reveals, Bettelheim is a scholar with a keen sense of social responsibility who applies his insights to practical problems.*

In "Johnny Wants to Read," Bettelheim offers causes for several related phenomena: why some children do not learn to read, why some are poor readers, and what motivates others to learn despite obstacles. Notice how many of the different kinds of causes covered in the introduction to this section he considers: reciprocal causality, responsibility as cause, and blocking causes.

This article appeared in Family Weekly, *a Sunday newspaper supplement. It is thus aimed at a very large, average readership, one with no special knowledge of psychology or reading research but with a common concern for what affects children.*

Anybody who writes down to children is simply wasting his time. You have to write up, not down. Children are demanding. They are the most attentive, curious, eager, observant, sensitive, quick and generally congenial readers on earth. They accept, almost without question, anything you present them with, as long as it is presented honestly, fearlessly and clearly.
—E.B. White

Reading is the basis not only for all academic work, but also for much of the work we do to make a living. Even driving a car demands the ability to read street signs and road maps, for example. In our society today, the nonreader who does well in life has become a rare exception, and the national decline in reading achievement has become possibly the most serious educational problem confronting us today.

Failure to learn to read does not in itself necessarily make for social maladjustment, yet the connection that exists between emotional disturbance, asocial behavior and reading difficulties is widely known. There seems to be little doubt that school failure makes a child discouraged with himself, with school, society and ultimately with his life. Moreover, it's been found that who will do well in school and who will do poorly is largely determined by the end of the third grade. Thus, reading instruction during the first three grades is crucial.

There are as many different reasons that children refuse to learn to read as there are children. Fortunately, the number who actually suffer from neurological disorders that make it difficult for them to learn to read is quite small. But regrettably, reading difficulties of many perfectly normal children are ascribed to neurological causes, although no valid indications are found that such causes exist.

Many children, for example, are diagnosed as suffering from a learning disability called dyslexia, or "word blindness." But as one famous specialist explained the widespread application of this scientific-sounding diagnosis, "It calms parents, floors teachers and covers my own incompetence."

Oftentimes, such a child may respond once given a learning situation that meets his psychological needs. For instance, my colleagues and I helped one problem boy who had been moved from foster home to foster home. By the fourth grade, he still could not read. Gradually a good relationship developed between him and his teacher, who induced him to look at the pictures in the book and make up his own stories about them, most of which were still of a violent nature.

One day, the teacher observed that the boy seemed to have an emotional reaction when he overheard other children reading stories in primers about the lovely times parents and children have together—stories obviously alien to his traumatic background. So the teacher began to blot out the words "father" and "mother" with a heavy black marker whenever they appeared. Eventually the child joined her. This supposedly "word-blind" child then proceeded to blot out—with no errors —those two words on the nearly 40 remaining pages of the book. When he next tried to read the book, he did so with hardly any mistakes and was very pleased with himself. Within a few weeks, he was reading up to grade level and enjoying it.

One cannot expect that many nonreaders can be cured so dramatically. Not infrequently, learning in school means growing up to the child, and there are children who are so determined not to grow up—either because growing up seems to be dangerous, or because it means giving up infantile satisfactions they desperately crave—that they refuse to make any moves toward it. Other children feel pressured by their parents not only to grow up, but also to achieve academically. If for this or other reasons the child feels rejected by his parents, he may in turn want to reject them. Refusing to learn to read seems an easy way to hurt parents where they feel it most.

There are many more children who simply are poor readers, and these form the great bulk who suffer from reading difficulties. Poor readers are not born as such, they are made—many by the way they are taught reading in school.

The books from which children are taught reading constitute an insult to their intelligence. Children come to school with a well-developed vocabulary of, on the average, about 4,000 words, some of them quite difficult ones. Even the least verbal of first graders has mastered over 2,000 words. And then they are taught from primers containing a vocabulary of not more than 150 different words, out of which it is impossible to construct a meaningful story. Some 40 years ago, comparable U.S. primers contained over 650 different words, and children learned to read from them at least as well, and probably considerably better, than they do today. Children respond to this paucity of interesting material by becoming utterly disgusted with these texts. They conclude that if this is what reading is all about, it isn't worth the effort.

When I asked first graders about their primers, even the good readers loudly declared that on their own they would never read such "junk." Angrily, they told me how it infuriates them that they are supposed to be so stupid as to believe real people could behave the ways characters do in these terribly repetitive books. According to the children I spoke with, the people in primers are all made out of plastic. "They aren't shy! They aren't afraid! They aren't angry! They aren't upset!" As one child summed up, "They aren't anything!"

Any adult reading these primers cannot help agreeing. Nobody would want to read if this were all that reading is about. The books simply do not relate to children's lives. For instance, in examining the books of several publishers, from first pre-primer up to and including third-grade readers, we found that none contain any stories about the arrival of a new baby in a family, though this is a common occurrence and causes complex and ambivalent feelings in a child, with which he needs help in dealing.

The reason given for these boring primers is that one should make it easy for children to read by giving them only simple words at a very slow pace, although the evidence belies this. When I asked children what words they would like to learn, I never encountered a single one who wanted to learn to read Dick and Jane, or Janet and Mark, unless these happened to be their own names. Not a one wanted to learn to read "look," or "see," or "Here I come" or "Here I go," the words endlessly repeated in the primers.

On their own, children want to learn difficult words that fascinate them for some reason. And they learn these with great delight. Learning difficult, meaningful words is a real achievement to the child. Such a feeling of pride is particularly necessary to motivate a child who originally was not interested in learning to read; it induces him to make further efforts to develop his reading skills.

But the excitement of being able to read some words soon fades when the texts the child must read force him to reread the same word endlessly. Word recognition deteriorates quickly into empty rote learning when it does not lead directly to the reading of meaningful content. A child who has to read: "Nan had a pad. Nan had a tan pad. Dan ran. Dan ran to the pad . . ." and worse nonsense does not get the impression he is being guided toward becoming literate, because what he is being made to read is obviously not literature.

And as primers become simpler, children, because they are bored, read them with less and less facility. The publishers, in response, make the books even simpler and, thus, even less effective.

The mean score on the verbal section of the Scholastic Aptitude Test (S.A.T.) has been declining for the past 10 years. Although it is difficult to establish a cause-and-effect relationship between the declining verbal ability of college-bound students and the decline in primer vocabulary over the past decades, there can be no doubt that the score reflects a diminishing regard for the written word.

Textbook writers and publishers know their books are uninteresting and so have tried to make them more attractive by adding colorful illustrations. But the trouble with pictures is that the printed text then becomes even less appealing in comparison. What's worse, able to guess from the pictures what the text is about, a child reluctant to read now sees no reason to struggle with words.

Why do publishers continue putting out such dull primers? The reason is that neither children nor teachers buy textbooks—school boards and superintendents do. And their first concern is that nobody complain about their choices. For instance, one publisher came up with a story in which children bring a balloon home from a fair, whereupon a cat leaps on it and it bursts. Seems harmless enough, but when the book was tested in an Illinois school system, cat lovers were outraged, saying the story had maligned their pets. The local school superintendent—who was coming up for re-election—withdrew the book, and the publisher, afraid of similar complaints elsewhere, dropped the story.

It doesn't have to be this way. Primers used throughout Europe are far more difficult than those used in the U.S. The stories don't talk down to the readers. No words are avoided because they might be too difficult —as is done here—because the child who uses them in everyday conversation already knows what they mean and is thus eager to master any technical obstacles they present.

Perhaps it's not surprising then that at the end of the first grade, the average European child has a larger reading vocabulary than the average American child. In addition, reading retardation is much less common among European children.

Fortunately, there are many children who manage to become literate despite the way in which they are taught reading. They do so because they are highly motivated by their home environment or because of an attachment to their teacher. Studies show that nothing correlates more highly with a child's future academic success than the academic achievement of his parents. The reason for this is not just that the parents are committed to the merit of reading, a commitment which they pass on to their children, but also that from an early age the child can observe how important reading is to his parents and how much they enjoy it. Additionally, parents who are avid readers are more likely to read often—and with enjoyment—to their children. So the child becomes convinced that reading is important and enjoyable long before he is confronted for the first time with a primer in school. And he is then able to distance himself from the stupidity of the primers, since he knows not all books are like those. Still, many years later, that child will remember how disgusted he was with the books he had to read in early grades.

In our search for causes, we must not be deflected by the child's claim that he cannot learn to read, that it is impossible for him. The typical child learns early in his life that his parents tend to pay little attention if he states that he does not want to learn or do something they want him to—they simply insist that he must. But children also learn that the outcome is very different when they steadfastly assert that they would like to do what their parents want but simply cannot. Many parents just insist no further and show compassion with their children's apparent inability. The same parent who would not accept for a moment his child's assertion that he cannot put his toys away lets himself be baffled by the child's statement that he cannot learn to read, failing to see that this may be only a camouflage for his not wanting to read. This does not mean it is wise to simply continue to apply pressure on the child to learn to read; learning should never be permitted to become a battleground on which parents and children meet as enemies.

We believe that learning, particularly learning to read, must give the child the feeling that, through it, new worlds will be opened to his mind and imagination. And this would not prove difficult if we taught reading differently. Seeing how a child is lost to the world and forgets all his worries when reading a story that fascinates him, how he lives in the fantasy world of this story even long after he has finished reading it, makes one realize how easily young children can be captivated by books, provided they are the right ones.

I do not know how many children still claim that they can't stomach spinach, but I do know that hardly a child claims that he can't eat ice cream. The reason is that they enjoy eating it. The secret, then, is to make reading seem as enjoyable and tasty, as rewarding and as attractive, as we can make it. Our reaction to a child's refusal to read should be to do everything in our power to remove what caused the child's reluctance to become literate, and to read with him in ways that make reading appear to be one of the most enjoyable experiences in the world—as it surely is.

QUESTIONS FOR DISCUSSION

1. This article begins with an epigraph in praise of children as readers. What authority does E. B. White have to testify on that subject?
2. The first two paragraphs do not seem to advance Bettelheim's argument directly. What is their function? What assumptions does he appeal to or invoke in them?
3. Bettelheim must eliminate or at least downplay some causes popularly believed to prevent children from reading. What are these causes and how does he reduce their force?
4. What does Bettelheim identify as the main cause for children's poor reading? How much evidence does he present for the operation of this cause? Is he assuming a resistant or accepting audience?
5. Reread the introduction to this section on causal argument and see how many different kinds of causes you can identify in this essay.
6. At many points in this essay Bettelheim appeals, as he must, to certain universal human tendencies as causal agencies. What assumptions about the way people behave, for instance, link poor reading materials with poor readers?

SUGGESTIONS FOR WRITING

1. Sample the reading material in a local elementary school, both primers and textbooks, used in the first three grades, which Bettelheim says are so critical. Do you agree with Bettelheim that they insult the intelligence of children? Write a response to Bettelheim, either corroborating or disputing his characterization of books aimed at children.
2. Bettelheim evidently surveyed young readers to find out what they actually enjoy reading. Conduct a similar survey of readers of any age and argue into place a causal explanation for your findings. Direct your essay at publishers who will be interested in your conclusions.
3. Select and sample readers from any grade level that contain selections about children. Characterize (CP form) the image of children portrayed in the books.
4. With the same or a similar sample of school texts, consider what kinds of stories or characters or experiences are missing from children's reading. What might be the effects of these omissions? Write to the school board, pointing out what is missing and suggesting what kinds of material should be included.
5. Investigate how textbooks and readers are chosen in a particular school system. (You might focus on the selection of one book.) Who is responsible and what factors influenced the decision? Write a newspaper article whose purpose is to arouse public interest.

6. Write an editorial for your local newspaper in which you encourage parents to lobby for better texts in the schools. Or recommend a course of action that they could take to supplement the deficiencies of the school curriculum.

————————— →>> <<‹— —————————

Can the Japanese Keep It Up?

RICHARD D. ROBINSON

Richard D. Robinson is a professor specializing in international business and technology transfer at MIT's Sloan School of Management. As his essay reveals, he draws on considerable consulting experience as well as his academic experience in presenting his analysis of Japanese business success. His essay here is a causal argument in two senses. He both explains the causes of an existing condition and predicts the chances for its continuing success.

Robinson's Technology Review *readers are Americans who would make certain comparisons between the Japanese business methods they read about and the American business methods they already know about. Therefore, as you read this essay, try continually to supply the missing half of the comparison just as the intended audience would have done.*

Evidence for the high productivity of Japanese workers and the effectiveness of Japanese industry is everywhere. Without any windfalls in raw materials, Japan has maintained a healthy trade surplus for many years while making a demonstrable improvement in its people's general standard of living. This is a remarkable achievement; clearly Japan's productivity has been increasing more rapidly than that of many, if not most, of its major trading partners.

Japan uses about 2.6 times less energy per capita than the United States, and it is far behind most other industrialized countries in measures such as housing, sewerage, parks, and percentage of paved roads. But the standard of material well-being in Japan is approaching that of Europe and North America, and Japan's wealth may be more evenly distributed than in many countries. Though social investment has fallen far behind, savings have been maintained at unusually high levels (probably three times those of the United States), and the per capita tax burden in Japan is 20 percent compared with 30 percent in the U.S.

Average Japanese life expectancy at birth was the longest in the world in 1981—73.5 years for men and 78.9 years for women, compared with 68.7 and 76.5 years, respectively, in the United States. Crime rates are very low. On a per capita basis, Japan has about one-seventh as much litigation and one-sixteenth as many lawyers as the U.S. Life in Japan is comfortable and apparently satisfying—the Japanese live elsewhere reluctantly.

GOOD PLANNING OR HARD WORK?

Some of the extraordinary success of Japanese industry and agriculture can surely be attributed to three unusual circumstances. Over the past 20 years Japan has spent but 1 percent of its gross national product on the military—about $1 trillion less than the United States in the same period. Japan has no antitrust laws that effectively restrict combinations of manufacturing companies, banks, and trading companies. And the Japanese tend to follow a much-publicized—but little understood—system of management that in some respects is very different from U.S. practice.

But there is no simple explanation for the prodigious growth of Japanese industry in the last three decades, and one is tempted to attribute this success to cultural or even racial traits: Can it be that the Japanese simply work harder? (No doubt many Japanese work long hours, but why do they? And do long hours equate with high productivity?) Or are the Japanese more ingenious and creative? (But that also begs a question: Why? For they were not always that way.)

Permit me to offer my own explanation of the remarkable productivity increases characteristic of modern Japan, and to list my reasons for suspecting that this improvement is unlikely to continue at anything like the present pace. I have visited Japan repeatedly since the end of World War II, including especially the summer of 1981, when I interviewed approximately 80 Japanese executives and professors of economics, law, and management. In addition, from 1981 to 1982, ten of my students studied a sample of firms in the United States taken over or established by Japanese corporations. They sought to discover the extent to which Japanese management philosophy and practice has been applied, and with what effect. (The most recent tally of such enterprises was 213 at the end of 1980, plus 12 others in which the Japanese held a minority interest of at least 10 percent. These 225 companies operated 314 plants in the United States, representing about $6.5 billion of direct Japanese investment as of the end of 1981.) The point is, of course, that if Japanese-owned firms here do better than their U.S. counterparts, then the impact of Japanese management may be significant, and the demonstrably higher Japanese productivity may not be due entirely to environmental advantages.

A SENSE OF PERSONAL INVOLVEMENT

Unbridled praise in the popular literature for Japanese productivity and enthusiasm for the management system that allegedly makes it possible does the United States a grave disservice on three counts. Many of the more salient aspects of the Japanese experience are rarely mentioned, the serious problems now surfacing in Japan are discussed inadequately if at all, and the authors often naively project the trends of the recent past into the future.

The Japanese "management system" is said to be based on traditions and policies that confer on Japanese corporations a kind of social welfare role, including life-time employment, consensus decision making, seniority-based promotion and reward, strong company loyalty, company unions, and quality-control circles. Japanese companies are said to enjoy an atmosphere of harmony among government, business, and labor and to be characterized by high ratios of debt to equity in their financing, extensive subcontracting that restrains vertical integration, and resistance to diversification. All these characteristics are present to a degree, but a simple listing says little about what makes the system work. In fact, there is much variation from firm to firm—one can make only a few generalizations.

EVERYONE PUTS IN SOME TIME

In Japan virtually no one expects to obtain an entry-level managerial position at a relatively high salary immediately after receiving a master's degree in business administration. There is, in fact, only one MBA program in all of Japan, and in 1981 it had a total of only 50 students —47 men, 3 women. When Japanese corporations hire new employees, they hire individuals—not technical specialists. Almost all new employees start in menial jobs, and all have a shot at management. University graduates, particularly those from the prestigious schools, do constitute something of an elite—the old-college-tie connection does help—but apparently it is important only for those who demonstrate competence and even then only after a decade or more. Few become managers with less than 15 to 20 years of employment.

Between 10 and 25 percent of all top Japanese executives—the percentage varies with the size of the firm—were once labor-union officials, most often in their own corporate unions. Between 20 and 60 percent of all industrial firms, again depending on size, report the promotion of at least one former union official to top management. Virtually everyone—even engineering graduates—seems to have had blue-collar experience. This means that most technical specialists and managers have a personal identity with the ordinary factory worker and clerk—they have put in their time.

Salary and wage differentials are relatively narrow. In company after company, I am told that the ratio of a top manager's salary to that of an entry-level blue-collar employee is only 5 or 6 to 1. It is almost unthinkable for management to reward itself with higher salaries without providing similar increases to all employees. Management leads the way in reducing its own salaries when wages of employees must be reduced or in the unlikely event (it does happen) that workers have to be laid off.

Promotion is almost always from within. Outsiders are rarely brought in to assume authority over those with greater seniority, and new personnel are selected with great care through multiple interviews and examinations. In the case of university graduates, even in a large corporation, the president himself may be directly involved.

It is characteristic of Japanese enterprise that all employees are valued and their opinions solicited on matters within their competence, and when their activities will be affected by a change in company policy or procedures. No engineer or manager would urge changes in products or processes without close consultation with workers on the factory floor. For example, the management of a large textile firm that faced a long-term decline in the market took five years to lay off redundant labor. During that time the company conducted extended negotiations with the union, including candid discussion of the financial situation, and in the end made intensive efforts, including individual counseling, to encourage early retirement or find positions elsewhere for laid-off employees. One of the first steps was to reduce management salaries. Any Japanese corporation that behaved differently would be perceived as performing in an unacceptable manner.

It is precisely this kind of long-term commitment and concern on the part of both labor and management that builds the identity, loyalty, and unusual level of trust and confidence typical of the Japanese firm. The common experience, the relatively narrow financial and social distance between the top and bottom, and the sense of security together make possible a system of consensus and group decision making in which the opinions of all employees are actively sought, acted upon, and rewarded. Virtually everyone at every level seems to have a sense of personal involvement and identity with work, group, corporate community, and nation.

THE WHOLE IS GREATER THAN ITS PARTS

Many observers propose that the Japanese are relatively risk-averse, and this is consistent with the finding in our U.S. study: Japanese managers do not make decisions until all the relevant data have been assembled and analyzed, almost regardless of how much time this requires. Indeed, Japanese managers do not feel they are under time pressure as do many U.S. managers, who must respond to the demands of stockholders for progress in each quarterly and annual financial report. Owners of Japanese corporations are principally other corporations—banks, clients, customers, contractors, suppliers, trading companies. These owners' interests are in long-term success—the profitable business that comes their way—not in the short-term flow of dividends. Under these conditions, management has time to make decisions carefully.

Japanese decision makers delve into every aspect of a proposal, including human resources. For this reason, decision making becomes a highly participative process; in the end, decision and implementation become almost simultaneous. Indeed, I am told that the Japanese do not deliberately install participatory decision-making systems in U.S. operations; they simply insist on having so much data and analysis—including problems of implementation—that all employees become involved. As technology becomes more complex, consultation at this level becomes more important: essential knowledge and skills are increasingly difficult for individual managers to capture and integrate themselves.

This highly consultative process means that less authority resides in top management; the importance of the president and the directors is reduced because they do not make unilateral decisions. Everyone is important, and communication is open in both directions. The very layout of Japanese offices reflects this difference. There is also less internal competition than in U.S. companies and more communication among peers. Skill in maintaining harmony and open communication is rewarded more than sheer technical competence.

An important result of this decision-making style is that Japanese corporations, though risk-averse, may in fact be able to accept larger risks than their non-Japanese competitors. Their decisions are better because the analysis is more complete and implementation is more rapid.

THE MANAGER IS A WORKER, TOO

I believe that the demands of employees everywhere—whether of private, state, or socialist enterprises—for greater control of their work lives and the strategies of their respective enterprises is now irrepressible. As levels of longevity, education, social enlightenment, skills, and affluence rise, people everywhere expect an ever-greater role in decision making and reduced socioeconomic differences. Differentials of hundreds of thousands of dollars in annual incomes between managers and workers tear at the social fabric, leading to alienation, mistrust, anger, and conflict.

What the Japanese seem to have learned is that a manager is merely another employee. Indeed, there seems to be no clear distinction between a manager and a nonmanager; there is no common generic term for "manager." One whose function has a higher managerial content than another is not necessarily considered more valuable to the enterprise, or to society.

I was struck by a recent statement attributed to Soichiro Honda in reference to U.S. automobile plants he had seen: "The working environment was bad. Decent people don't want to work at such places, and as a result the quality of labor at those workshops is poor."

A self-educated mechanic who started from the bottom, Honda is described as believing that the workplace should be "a place where everybody finds joy in working and earning a living. . . . An organization that enforces monotonous labor and deprives workers of the right to think may work well for a while, but it is bound to decay in the long run. . . . It is wrong for executives to act like feudal lords and not know what is going on below them. What is most important in the process of democratization is for the upper people to come down. And that is where the sense of equality is found."

But there is another side to this argument, made clear by Yaichi

Ayukawa, president of Techno-Venture, speaking in Boston last winter. There is no such thing as a true venture capitalist in Japan, he said. "A genius's genius can be quickly smothered by a climate controlled by a group of average men striving for harmony." Mr. Ayukawa suggested that the highly structured nature of Japanese business and society and the reverence for consensus and team effort "are good characteristics for maintaining an existing system. But they are not good for new, diverse businesses." He noted the absence of an over-the-counter securities market in Japan, the low rate of capital accumulation and high debt of most Japanese industries, the high (40 to 50 percent) capital-gains tax in Japan, and the tendency of Japanese firms to hire generalists.

Yet the Japanese are doing something right, and the explanation seems very clear: with the reduced pressure for short-term financial return, even large corporations can become venture capitalists.

A TURNING POINT

Can the Japanese economy continue to grow at the extraordinary pace of the past 20 years? There are many reasons to be cautious about the nation's future:

> Productivity in Japanese agriculture is unlikely to continue to improve. Japan has been virtually self-sufficient in many agricultural products during the past 20 years. But population and per capita consumption are growing, and the intensity and productivity of agriculture may well have peaked. Japan will probably be forced to import a larger share of its food in the future.
>
> Japanese research and development expenditures are increasing to match those of the United States. The Japanese now recognize that they cannot continue to simply license or purchase foreign technology for modest fees or do "reverse engineering." They are on the technological frontier or virtually so in some areas, and Japan appears to be close to becoming a net seller of technology. New generations of technology are likely to be costly.
>
> The Japanese population is growing older. Because Japanese salaries and wages are linked to seniority, this translates into higher labor costs. Governmental social security payments are already beginning to increase, and this has the double effect of pushing up the tax burden and reducing the importance of the welfare function of private corporations. Eventually, layoffs—even if disguised with

incentives for early retirement—will become inevitable. Will company loyalty and the company union structure survive?

Increasingly, Japanese women are *not* leaving their jobs upon marriage or the birth of their first children. Some Japanese women are now candidates for managerial positions because of their seniority. Meanwhile, the percentage of women entering higher education has doubled in the last ten years, and the proportion of female university graduates is climbing. Can the Japanese system cope with female executives? Eventually it will have to, for Japan cannot maintain its rate of growth without fully exploiting the skills and intelligence of 50 percent of its population. But Japan will lose a source of cheap labor as pressure for equal opportunity for women grows.

Services rather than goods represent an increasing part of Japanese gross national product. Indeed, the service sector now accounts for close to 60 percent of Japan's GNP, up from 30 percent in 1950. The rapidly increasing age of the Japanese population and the growing number of retired persons will be responsible for a further increase in the service sector, with the result that productivity growth is likely to be slowed.

The increasing technical complexity of many Japanese products may make impractical the common corporate policy of employing generalists who are rotated among various areas while receiving on-the-job or company-sponsored education. Corporations are likely to require more specialized entry-level people at all ranks, thereby undermining the seniority and decision-making systems.

The internationalization of Japanese business is well underway. Direct Japanese foreign investment has increased from $4 billion in 1970 to some $40 billion today, an annual capital outflow that is between 10 and 15 percent of the world's total. Some 445,000 Japanese are now living overseas, mostly as employees of private corporations. Will today's high productivity be maintained as this flow diverts investment capital and skills from Japan? Can a Japanese corporation investing abroad recruit and hold competent local managers when it is well known that no foreign manager can aspire to a top position in the parent company?

There is statistical evidence that the average age of production facilities in Japan and the United States has been converging. In 1978, the Japanese average stood at eight years, the United States at about nine and one-half years—a spread of only one and one-half years. In the early 1970s, the difference was four years. The reason, one suspects, is the increasing pressure for social investments—housing, sewers, water systems, roads, and pollution controls—at the expense of investment in direct production.

Various indicators of social change in Japan—the incidence of crime, divorce, and drug use, for examples—although still very low by U.S. standards, are beginning to move up. This may herald some social disintegration that could translate into higher costs.

According to many recent surveys, Japanese youth are not as committed to long work days, shortened or foregone vacations, and intensive corporate responsibility as their elders. Those born in the last half of the 1940s, at the end of World War II, are now entering middle management in significant numbers; they are the first generation of Japanese managers brought up in affluence, never really having known deprivation and poverty. Have they been sufficiently indoctrinated into the corporate culture to accept the notion that corporate welfare comes first and personal and family welfare second? There is some reason to be skeptical. There is much criticism in Japan of the younger generation on this score, but I cannot be certain whether this reflects a normal generation gap or has greater social significance.

Japan's goal of catching up with its World War II victor, the United States, has been virtually achieved. To the extent that this objective fueled the country's national effort through the 1960s and 1970s, that incentive will now be lacking as the per capita level of material well-being nears that of the United States. One senses a tendency to let down, and there has been much discussion in Japan to this effect.

Japan is perhaps the one major power in history, with the possible exception of Germany, that has not developed military power commensurate with its economic power. As the international competition for raw materials increases and Japan feels its supply lines jeopardized, the nation may well decide to become more independent of the U.S. umbrella by developing its own military strength.

The growing density of population, industry, and traffic in Japan is generating problems and increasing costs. Consider these figures: The population per square mile in Japan is twice that of Indonesia and 22 times that of the United States. The cost of choice urban office sites ranges from $1,500 to $3,000 per square foot in Tokyo. And the ratio of wholesale transactions per retail sale is 4 in Japan, 1.8 in the U.S. The high cost of land and pollution controls has been joined by inefficiencies in distribution as major incentives for industry to invest abroad.

REDEFINING THE FREEDOM IN FREE ENTERPRISE

Despite all of these problems and more, the consumer price index in Japan advanced only 2.1 percent in 1980 and 3.3 percent in 1981. The average interest rates on loans and discounts of all banks remains in the range of 7 to 8 percent. Unemployment is between 2 and 3 percent, and real gross national product rose by 5.4 percent in 1981.

How do the Japanese do it?

I have already suggested one answer: the effective, full involvement of the workforce—at least the male workers. Queried as to the best English work describing Japanese management, one Japanese executive told me, "Douglas McGregor's *The Human Side of Enterprise*—the only difference is that we believe it." This was, of course, a reference to the late Professor McGregor's Theory Y: the idea that commitment and creativity stem primarily from sources within each of us, and that management's chief responsibility is to provide conditions under which these attitudes are unconstrained.

Another reason for the success of Japanese industry is the extraordinary cooperation between labor and management and between government and business. Here are some of the devices by which government has supported Japanese business to create what some critics have termed "Japan, Inc." which purportedly engages in "unfair competition":

The use of public funds to aid private corporations for training, founding new enterprises, and locating new jobs for surplus workers.

Public support for research and development and the commercialization of promising new areas of technology. Current national priorities include engineering ceramics, super-function polymers, new metallic and composite materials, biotechnology, new types of semiconductors, robots, optical fibers, alternative energy sources, fifth-generation computers, genetic technology to create self-fertilizing crops, and microbiology.

A series of incentives, including a robot-leasing company, to encourage investment in automatic machinery. By mid-1981, Japan was producing three times as many industrial robots as the United States, and 57,000 units were in use in Japanese factories.

The use of public funds for loans from private banks to stimulate investment by private business.

A plan to permit companies to set aside reserves from pretax earnings against which losses from overseas investments can be written off.

Government sponsorship of two nationally owned, nonprofit associations to market Japanese technology abroad. The services of these enterprises are promoted through Japan's largest general trading companies.

Exemption from Japanese taxation of 70 percent of a company's income from the export of technology or on property rights paid for in foreign currency.

In more than 80 recent interviews with Japanese executives and scholars, I heard not one word of real criticism of the Japanese government; there was simply no sense of the "we-or-they" relationship that is part of virtually every conversation with U.S. executives. The conflict relationships throughout American businesses that maintain economic and social distance—between producers and managers and among firms, unions, government, consumers, owners, and financial institutions—are virtually absent in Japan. The contrast is startling.

The principal lesson for the United States is that it can no longer tolerate the higher costs of its adversarial relationships. In the final analysis, achieving high national productivity may depend more on efficient, harmonious organization than on efficient technology. We are all in this international competition together, and the most socially efficient nations are very likely to be the winners.

QUESTIONS FOR DISCUSSION

1. The title of this article is a question. What answer does the argument suggest?
2. How do the opening three paragraphs serve as the basis of a causal argument? What do the miscellaneous statistics given here define? Do they all add up to the same thing?
3. What characterizations of American business practices do Robinson's descriptions of Japanese methods imply? In other words, what does the American reader understand when Robinson points out that there are few MBAs in Japan, a smaller pay differential between workers and management, and harmonious relations between them? What is gained by not making these comparisons explicit?
4. Robinson points out how "risk averse" Japanese companies are, compared to American ones. Read over that section carefully and try to articulate what definition of *risk taking* he must have in mind.
5. In the prediction part of his argument, Robinson notes many areas of Japa-

nese life that are changing. As a reader who understands American life, what pattern do you see in these changes? If the prediction is convincing, what makes it so?

6. Take a section of the argument and notice how the author uses statistics to back up his observations. What other tactics of support might he have used? Would these tactics have worked if he were writing for a less well-informed audience? How could he have made his points more dramatic?

SUGGESTIONS FOR WRITING

1. As a large-scale writing project, select two companies, a Japanese and an American one in the same industry, such as two auto or steel manufacturers, two biotechnology firms, two computer companies. Compare them in aspects that you suspect would contribute to their relative success or failure. Robinson's essay will suggest some possibilities, such as management structure and wage differential.

2. In the prediction section of his argument, Robinson lists several developing trends that may retard Japan's prosperity. Select any one of these trends and refute it as a possible cause of the Americanization of Japanese industry. Would, for instance, more women in the work force demanding better wages necessarily disrupt industrial progress? Address your argument to Robinson's *Technology Review* readers.

3. Select a successful American business and argue for the causes of its success for reasons other than those that fuel the Japanese successes. Think of your argument as a response to Robinson.

4. Develop the implied side of Robinson's comparison into an argument for the causes of the relatively uneven state of American business. Can you, in other words, argue that practices such as hiring MBAs directly into upper-level positions, giving executives very high salaries, and having antagonistic relations between unions, management, and government are detrimental to business?

5. Robinson claims that managers are not a distinct class in Japan. Can you argue (in CP form) that they are a distinct class in the United States? Address your argument to those unaware of the existence of this managerial elite.

6. Robinson quotes Soichiro Honda's observations that decent people do not want to work in unattractive working environments and that the quality of labor declines if working conditions are poor. Examine a particular working environment that you are familiar with and speculate to what extent it affects productivity. Direct your essay to the person responsible for the quality of the working environment.

————————— →>> <<← —————————

Identical Twins Reared Apart
CONSTANCE HOLDEN

This piece is not directly argumentative. The author does not have a stake in persuading her readers to a particular position. Rather, the essay reports the preliminary evidence and tentative conclusions of a large-scale research project being conducted at the University of Minnesota. However, the essay does offer the data and some of the causal reasoning used to take on one of the biggest of all causal questions: "Which is the stronger influence in shaping the individual, heredity or environment?"

Audience always influences discourse, and in this case the reader of this essay in Science *would demand a detailed, impersonal account of the complexities of the evidence and the difficulties of drawing certain conclusions from it.*

As you read the interesting accounts of astonishing similarities between long-separated twins, stop and ask yourself which resemblances seem really surprising and which potentially explainable by social rather than hereditary factors. As an active reader, think of as many alternative explanations of similarities and differences as you can.

Bridget and Dorothy are 39-year-old British housewives, identical twins raised apart who first met each other a little over a year ago. When they met, to take part in Thomas Bouchard's twin study at the University of Minnesota, the manicured hands of each bore seven rings. Each also wore two bracelets on one wrist and a watch and a bracelet on the other. Investigators in Bouchard's study, the most extensive investigation ever made of identical twins reared apart, are still bewitched by the seven rings. Was it coincidence, the result of similar influences, or is this small sign of affinity a true, even inevitable, manifestation of the mysterious and infinitely complex interaction of the genes the two women have in common?

Investigators have been bemused and occasionally astonished at similarities between long-separated twins, similarities that prevailing dogma about human behavior would ordinarily attribute to common environmental influences. How is it, for example, that two men with significantly different upbringings came to have the same authoritarian personality? Or another pair to have similar histories of endogenous depression? Or still another pair to have virtually identical patterns of headaches? These are only bits and pieces from a vast amount of data, none of it yet analyzed, being collected by the University of Minnesota twin study that began last March. So provocative have been some of the cases that the study has already received much attention in the press, and it is bound to get a lot more. The investigation is extremely controversial, aimed, as it is, directly at the heart of the age-old debate about heredity versus environment. Identical twins reared apart have been objects of scrutiny in the past, notably in three studies conducted in England, Denmark, and the United States. An indication of the sensitivity of this subject is the fact that the last one in this country was completed more than 40 years ago,* although the rarity of cases has also made this type of research rather exotic. The Minnesota investigators, however, have been able to locate more twin pairs than they expected. So far they have processed nine pairs of identical or monozygotic twins (as well as several pairs of fraternal or dizygotic twins used as controls) and, owing to the publicity given the project, have managed to locate 11 additional pairs to take part in the study.

The Minnesota study is unprecedented in its scope, using a team of psychologists, psychiatrists, and medical doctors to probe and analyze every conceivable aspect of the twins' life histories, medical histories and physiology, tastes, psychological inclinations, abilities, and intelligence. It began when Bouchard, a psychologist who specializes in investigating individual differences, heard of a pair of twins separated from birth, both coincidentally named Jim by their adoptive families, who were reunited at the age of 39. Bouchard did not have to look far to set up his study team, as Minnesota is a hotbed of twin research. There, ready to go to work, were Irving Gottesman, a behavioral geneticist who has spent his career studying twins and whose particular interest is the etiology of schizophrenia; psychologist David Lykken, who has been looking at the brain waves of twins for 10 years; psychologist Auke Tellegen, who recently completed a new personality questionnaire that is being used on the twins; and psychiatrist Leonard Heston, who has studied heritability of mental disorders with adopted children.

Bouchard has taken an eclectic approach in developing the battery of exercises through which the twins are run. Each pair goes through

---

*A. H. Newman, F. N. Freeman, and K. J. Holzinger wrote up their study of 19 twin pairs in a 1937 book, "Twins: A Study of Heredity and Environment."

6 days of intensive testing. In addition to detailed medical histories including diet, smoking, and exercise, the twins are given electrocardiograms, chest x-rays, heart stress tests, and pulmonary exams. They are injected with a variety of substances to determine allergies. They are wired to electroencephalographs to measure their brain wave responses to stimuli in the form of tones of varying intensity, and given other psychophysiological tests to measure such responses as reaction times. Several handedness tests are given to ascertain laterality.

The physiological probes are interspersed with several dozen pencil-and-paper tests, which over the week add up to about 15,000 questions; these cover family and childhood environment, fears and phobias, personal interests, vocational interests, values, reading and TV viewing habits, musical interests, aesthetic judgement tests, and color preferences. They are put through three comprehensive psychological inventories. Then there is a slew of ability tests: the Wechsler Adult Intelligence Scale (the main adult IQ test) and numerous others that reveal skills in information processing, vocabulary, spatial abilities, numerical processing, mechanical ability, memory, and so forth. Throughout the 6 days there is much overlap and repetition in the content of questions, the intent being to "measure the same underlying factor at different times," says Bouchard. Mindful of charges of investigator bias in the administration of IQ tests in past twin studies, Bouchard has contracted with outside professionals to come in just for the purpose of administering and scoring the Wechsler intelligence test.

And the upshot of all this probing? Although the data have not yet been interpreted, there have already been some real surprises. Bouchard told *Science:* "I frankly expected far more differences [between twins] than we have found so far. I'm a psychologist, not a geneticist. I want to find out how the environment works to shape psychological traits." But the most provocative morsels that have so far become available are those that seem to reveal genetic influences at work.

Take the "Jim twins," as they have come to be known. Jim Springer and Jim Lewis were adopted as infants into working-class Ohio families. Both liked math and did not like spelling in school. Both had law enforcement training and worked part-time as deputy sheriffs. Both vacationed in Florida, both drove Chevrolets. Much has been made of the fact that their lives are marked by a trail of similar names. Both had dogs named Toy. Both married and divorced women named Linda and had second marriages with women named Betty. They named their sons James Allan and James Alan, respectively. Both like mechanical drawing and carpentry. They have almost identical drinking and smoking patterns. Both chew their fingernails down to the nubs.

But what investigators thought "astounding" was their similar medical histories. In addition to having hemorrhoids and identical pulse and blood pressure and sleep patterns, both had inexplicably put on 10 pounds at the same time in their lives. What really gets the researchers is that both suffer from "mixed headache syndrome"—a combination tension headache and migraine. The onset occurred in both at the age of 18. They have these late-afternoon headaches with the same frequency and same degree of disability, and the two used the same terms to describe the pain.

The twins also have their differences. One wears his hair over his forehead, the other has it slicked back with sideburns. One expresses himself better orally, the other in writing. But although the emotional environments in which they were brought up were different, the profiles on their psychological inventories were much alike.

Another much-publicized pair are 47-year-old Oskar Stöhr and Jack Yufe. These two have the most dramatically different backgrounds of all the twins studied. Born in Trinidad of a Jewish father and a German mother, they were separated shortly after birth. The mother took Oskar back to Germany, where he was raised as a Catholic and a Nazi youth by his grandmother. Jack was raised in the Caribbean, as a Jew, by his father, and spent part of his youth on an Israeli kibbutz. The two men now lead markedly different lives: Oskar is an industrial supervisor in Germany, married, a devoted union man, a skier. Jack runs a retail clothing store in San Diego, is separated, and describes himself as a workaholic.

But similarities started cropping up as soon as Oskar arrived at the airport. Both were wearing wire-rimmed glasses and mustaches, both sported two-pocket shirts with epaulets. They share idiosyncrasies galore: they like spicy foods and sweet liqueurs, are absentminded, have a habit of falling asleep in front of the television, think it's funny to sneeze in a crowd of strangers, flush the toilet before using it, store rubber bands on their wrists, read magazines from back to front, dip buttered toast in their coffee. Oskar is domineering toward women and yells at his wife, which Jack did before he was separated. Oskar did not take all the tests because he speaks only German (some are scheduled to be administered to him in German), but the two had very similar profiles on the Minnesota Multiphasic Personality Inventory (the MMPI was already available in German). Although the two were raised in different cultures and speak different languages, investigator Bouchard professed himself struck by the similarities in their mannerisms, the questions they asked, their "temperament, tempo, the way they do things"—which are, granted, relatively intangible when it comes to measuring them. Bouchard also thinks the two supply "devastating" evidence against the feminist contention that children's personalities are shaped differently according to the sex of those who rear them, since Oskar was raised by women and Jack by men.

Other well-publicized twin pairs are Bridget and Dorothy, the British housewives with the seven rings, and Barbara and Daphne, another pair of British housewives. Both sets are now in their late 30's and were separated during World War II. Bridget and Dorothy are of considerable interest because they were raised in quite different socioeconomic settings—the class difference turns out mainly to be reflected in the fact that the one raised in modest circumstances has bad teeth. Otherwise, say the investigators, they share "striking similarities in all areas," including another case of coincidence in naming children. They named their sons Richard Andrew and Andrew Richard, respectively, and their daughters Catherine Louise and Karen Louise. (Bouchard is struck by this, as the likelihood of such a coincidence would seem to be lessened by the fact that names are a joint decision of husband and wife.) On ability and IQ tests the scores of the sisters were similar, although the one raised in the lower class setting had a slightly higher score.

The other British twins, Daphne and Barbara, are fondly remembered by the investigators as the "giggle sisters." Both were great gigglers, particularly together, when they were always setting each other off. Asked if there were any gigglers in their adoptive families, both replied in the negative. The sisters also shared identical coping mechanisms in the face of stress: they ignored it, managed to "read out" such stimuli. In keeping with this, both flatly avoided conflict and controversy—neither, for example, had any interest in politics. Such avoidance of conflict is "classically regarded as learned behavior," says Bouchard. Although the adoptive families of the two women were not terribly different, "we see more differences within families than between these two."

Only fragmentary information is available so far from the rest of the nine sets of twins, but it supplies abundant food for new lines of inquiry. Two 57-year-old women, for example, developed adult-onset diabetes at the same time in their lives. One of a pair of twins suffers from a rare neurological disease that has always been thought to be genetic in origin. Another area where identical twins differ is in their allergies.

Psychiatrically, according to Heston, who conducts personal interviews with all the twins, there has been remarkable agreement. "Twins brought up together have very high concordance in psychiatric histories," he says. (For example, if one identical twin has schizophrenia, the other one stands a 45 percent chance of developing it.) But what is surprising is that "what we see [with the twins in the study] is pretty much the same as in twins brought up together." By and large, he says, they share very similar phobias, and he has noted more than one case where both twins had histories of endogenous depression. In one case, twins who had been brought up in different emotional environments— one was raised in a strict disciplinarian household; the other had a warm, tolerant, loving mother—showed very similar neurotic and hypochondriacal traits. Says Heston, "things that I would never have thought of —mild depressions, phobias—as being in particular genetically mediated . . . now, at least, there are grounds for a very live hypothesis" on the role of genes not only in major mental illnesses, where chemistry clearly plays a part, but in lesser emotional disturbances.

Other odds and ends:

Two men brought up in radically different environments—one an uneducated manual laborer, the other highly educated and cosmopolitan—turned out to be great raconteurs. (They did, however, have very different IQ scores. The numbers are confidential but the difference was close to the largest difference on record for identical twins, 24 points.)

One of the greatest areas of discordance for twins was smoking. Of the nine pairs, there were four in which one twin smoked and the other did not. No one has an explanation for this. But, surprisingly, in at least one case a lifelong heavy smoker came out just as well on the pulmonary exam and heart stress test as did the nonsmoker.

In a couple of cases, one of a twin pair wore glasses and the other did not. But when their eyes were checked, it was found that both members of each pair required the same correction.

In the fascinating tidbit category: One pair of female twins was brought together briefly as children. Each wore her favorite dress for the occasion. The dresses were identical.

What is to be made of all this? As Tellegen warns, any conclusions at this point are "just gossip." The similarities are somehow more fascinating than the differences, and it could well be that the subjective impression they make on the investigators is heavier than is justified.

Nonetheless, even the subjective impressions offer fertile grounds for speculation. Bouchard, for example, thinks that the team may discover that identical twins have a built-in penchant for a certain level of physical exertion. The latest pair to visit the laboratory, for example—23-year-old males—both eschew exercise (although both are thin as rails).

Lykken, who does the tests on the twins' central nervous systems, uses the case of the seven rings as an example for one of his tentative ideas. Fondness for rings is obviously not hereditary, but groups of unrelated genes on different chromosomes, producing pretty hands and other characteristics, may combine to result in beringedness. These traits, called idiographic—meaning particular to an individual rather than shared across a population—may not be as much a result of chance as has been thought. "There are probably other traits that are idiographic that may be almost inevitable given the [gene] combination. . . . More of these unique characteristics than we previously thought may be determined by a particular combination of genes." Lykken adds, "people get so upset when you suggest that the wiring diagram can influence the mind." But to believe otherwise "requires a naïve dualism . . . an assumption that mental events occur independent of the physical substrate."

Such talk begins to sound pretty deterministic, but Lykken insists that when the mass of data has been ordered "there will be material that will make environmentalists very happy and material that will make hereditarians very happy." One thing that will not make the environmentalists happy is the fact that IQ seems to have a high degree of heritability, as indicated by the fact that of all the tests administered to identical twins separately reared, IQ shows the highest concordance. It is even higher than the introversion-extroversion personality trait, a venerable measure in psychological testing that shows higher concordance than other conventional categories such as sense of well-being, responsibility, dominance, and ego strength.

As several investigators mentioned to *Science,* the scores of identical twins on many psychological and ability tests are closer than would be expected for the same person taking the same test twice. Lykken also found this to be true of brain wave tracings, which is probably the most direct evidence that identical twins are almost identically wired. Several researchers also felt that there is something to the idea that identical twins reared apart may be even more similar in some respects than those reared together. The explanation is simple: competition between the two is inevitable; hence if the stronger or taller of the two excels at sports, the other twin, even if equal in inclination and ability, will avoid sports altogether in order not to be overshadowed. Or one twin will choose to be a retiring type in order not to compete with his extroverted sibling. In short, many twins, in the interest of establishing their individuality, tend to exaggerate their differences.

Although the tentativeness of the findings so far must be repeatedly emphasized, at least one of the Minnesota researchers believes it may be safe to hypothesize that only extreme differences in environment result in significant differences between identical twins. Lykken says, after observing so many similarities, that it is tempting to conclude that "native ability will show itself over a broad range" of backgrounds. So either a seriously impoverished or a greatly enriched environment is required "to significantly alter its expression."

Such an idea, if it gained broad acceptance, would have major impacts on social policies. But Bouchard wants to keep his study separate from politics, emphasizing instead that the research is "very much exploratory."

The data, once assembled and analyzed, should provide a gold mine of new hypotheses. If a great many pairs of twins are collected, says Bouchard, they may be able to present the findings quantitatively; otherwise, the findings will be in the form of case histories. Tellegen, however, whose main interest is the methodology, says "we want to invent methods for analyzing traits in an objective manner, so we can get statistically cogent conclusions from a single case." He points out that psychoanalytic theory was developed from intensive study of small numbers of people and that behavioral psychologist B. F. Skinner similarly was able to develop his theories by studying small numbers of animals. Take the twins with the identical headache syndromes: with just one pair of twins the door is opened to a new field of research.

The twin study may also make it clear that estimating the relative contribution of heredity and environment to mental and psychological traits can never be boiled down to percentages. Some people, for example, may have authoritarian personalities no matter what their upbringing; the authoritarianism of others may be directly traceable to their environment. Similarly, with intelligence, some people may be smart or dumb regardless of outside influences, whereas the intelligence of others may be extremely malleable. Theoretically, variations from individual to individual in malleability and susceptibility may be so great that any attempt to make a generalization about the relative contribution of "innate" characteristics to a certain trait across a population would have no meaning.

Twin studies have been regarded with suspicion in some quarters because, according to Gottesman, the behavioral geneticist who worked with James Shields in England, they were "originally used to prove a genetic point of view." The most notorious of these were the studies of Cyril Burt on intelligence of twins reared separately, which were subsequently discredited. But, says Gottesman, "this study is a continuation of the efforts of Shields and Nielsen [Niels Juel-Nielsen, a psychiatrist at the University of Odense in Denmark] to challenge received wisdom about the roles of genes and environment." Everyone, observes Gottesman, "seems to have made up their minds one way or the other." With such a dearth of data of the kind that can only be obtained by studying persons with identical genes raised in different environments, people have been free to be as dogmatic as they please.

Bouchard had a devil of a time getting funding for his study. Various probes at the National Institutes of Health were discouraged on the grounds that the study was too multidisciplinary for any institute to embrace it. He finally got some money from the National Science Foundation.

Although the ultimate conclusions of the study may well be susceptible to sensationalizing, Gordon Allen of the National Institute of Mental Health, head of the International Twin Society, does not believe it will find any "new and unique answers." The sample will not be large enough for that, and besides, too few of the twin pairs were reared in environments so radically different as to bring genetically based behavioral similarities into stark relief.

The most solid and unequivocal evidence will be that supplied by the physiological findings. Although the similarities are the most titillating to most observers, it is the discordances that will be the most informative. For any difference between a pair of identical twins is "absolute proof that that is not completely controlled by heredity."

At this point, no one can make any generalizations beyond that made by James Shields, who died last year. Shields wrote that the evidence so far showed that "MZ [monozygotic] twins do not have to be brought up in the same subtly similar family environment for them to be alike." He concluded, "I doubt if MZ's will ever be numerous and representative enough to provide the main evidence about environment, or about genetics, but . . . they can give unique real-life illustrations of some of the many possible pathways from genes to human behavior—and so will always be of human and scientific interest."

QUESTIONS FOR DISCUSSION

1. If the researchers' main objective is to determine the comparative influence of heredity versus environment, why do they choose to study identical twins reared apart? Which of Mill's four methods is involved?
2. The author seems to suggest cautiously that genetic factors predominate over upbringing as causes of similarities. Which traits that the twins had in common easily suggest genetic agency and which do not? Go through the similarities, from seven finger rings to migraine headaches, and sort them into the plausible and implausible.
3. The researchers chose dizygotic twins (presumably raised apart?) as a control group. Why did they not choose pairs of individuals randomly selected except for age and sex, or any siblings raised apart? In constructing a causal argument, what is the function of a control group?
4. Since the Minnesota researchers want to support claims about human nature in general, how can they justify conclusions drawn from a sample of only nine pairs of twins?
5. The author of this article uses many questions. Find them and characterize their various uses. Which are rhetorical, which represent genuine unknowns, and which are used to guide the reader through the essay?
6. Height and weight are easy to calculate and compare, but how can an authoritarian personality be measured? How many potentially loose terms like *authoritarian* are used to point up similarities and differences? How do psychologists in general try to get around this problem?

SUGGESTIONS FOR WRITING

1. Select a pair of unrelated interviewees of the same sex, age, and general physical appearance. Question them in detail about their habits, backgrounds, and preferences. How many surprising similarities do you find? To what do you attribute the likenesses? Write up your findings in an essay whose purpose is to convince readers that the similarities are the product of either chance or similar lifestyles.
2. If you know a pair of identical twins who were reared together, interview them to test the hypothesis mentioned in the article that twins often exaggerate their differences. What psychological agency explains this? Address your response to the Minnesota researchers.
3. Comb through the sets of similarities mentioned in the article and try to classify them into the merely coincidental (e.g., names), the physical (onset of diabetes), and the potentially social (vacationing in Florida). Does any category predominate? How much remains unexplained? Write up your findings as a scientific report analyzing a body of data.
4. Investigate the case of British psychologist Cyril Burt and his forged data on

the heredity-versus-environment question. Explain the social and political consequences of Burt's findings.

5. Social and educational planners must operate on assumptions about human malleability and predetermination. Select a particular institution (school, prison, the army, professional basketball) and argue which assumptions dominate its procedures and practices.

6. As genetic screening becomes a more highly refined tool, what social consequences might it have? What might a genetic counselor tell a couple who is likely to have a child with an authoritarian personality, migraine headaches, and a fondness for wearing many finger rings?

—≫≫ ≪≪—

"Outbreak" and "August 1: Berlin"

BARBARA TUCHMAN

Barbara Tuchman is a Pulitzer-Prize-winning historian who has had great success in writing detailed historical accounts for popular audiences. The excerpt below is a chapter from her best-selling Guns of August, *which describes the chain of causes that precipitated World War I. Rather than presenting dry analysis of converging factors, Tuchman tells a story. Her history reads like a novel, complete with thickening plot and character development.*

Everyone knows of the enormous death and destruction wrought by the "Great War." That historical knowledge must affect our reading of the blunders, misinterpretations, and interplay of personal animosities that marked the critical first days of the war and made it impossible for the leaders involved to turn back. Knowing the outcome, we can read this narrative as a causal argument, sifting the tangle of events for that one element that could have changed everything.

OUTBREAK

"Some damned foolish thing in the Balkans," Bismarck had predicted, would ignite the next war. The assassination of the Austrian heir apparent, Archduke Franz Ferdinand, by Serbian nationalists on June 28,

1914, satisfied his condition. Austria-Hungary, with the bellicose frivolity of senile empires, determined to use the occasion to absorb Serbia as she had absorbed Bosnia and Herzegovina in 1909. Russia on that occasion, weakened by the war with Japan, had been forced to acquiesce by a German ultimatum followed by the Kaiser's appearance in "shining armor," as he put it, at the side of his ally, Austria. To avenge that humiliation and for the sake of her prestige as the major Slav power, Russia was now prepared to put on the shining armor herself. On July 5 Germany assured Austria that she could count on Germany's "faithful support" if whatever punitive action she took against Serbia brought her into conflict with Russia. This was the signal that let loose the irresistible onrush of events. On July 23 Austria delivered an ultimatum to Serbia, on July 26 rejected the Serbian reply (although the Kaiser, now nervous, admitted that it "dissipates every reason for war"), on July 28 declared war on Serbia, on July 29 bombarded Belgrade. On that day Russia mobilized along her Austrian frontier and on July 30 both Austria and Russia ordered general mobilization. On July 31 Germany issued an ultimatum to Russia to demobilize within twelve hours and "make us a distinct declaration to that effect."

War pressed against every frontier. Suddenly dismayed, governments struggled and twisted to fend it off. It was no use. Agents at frontiers were reporting every cavalry patrol as a deployment to beat the mobilization gun. General staffs, goaded by their relentless timetables, were pounding the table for the signal to move lest their opponents gain an hour's head start. Appalled upon the brink, the chiefs of state who would be ultimately responsible for their country's fate attempted to back away but the pull of military schedules dragged them forward.

AUGUST 1: BERLIN

At noon on Saturday, August 1, the German ultimatum to Russia expired without a Russian reply. Within an hour a telegram went out to the German ambassador in St. Petersburg instructing him to declare war by five o'clock that afternoon. At five o'clock the Kaiser decreed general mobilization, some preliminaries having already got off to a head start under the declaration of *Kriegesgefahr* (Danger of War) the day before. At five-thirty Chancellor Bethmann-Hollweg, absorbed in a document he was holding in his hand and accompanied by little Jagow, the Foreign Minister, hurried down the steps of the Foreign Office, hailed an ordinary taxi, and sped off to the palace. Shortly afterward General von Moltke, the gloomy Chief of the General Staff, was pulled up short as he was driving back to his office with the mobilization order signed by the Kaiser in his pocket. A messenger in another car overtook him with an urgent summons from the palace. He returned to hear a last-minute, desperate proposal from the Kaiser that reduced Moltke to tears and could have changed the history of the twentieth century.

Now that the moment had come, the Kaiser suffered at the necessary risk to East Prussia, in spite of the six weeks' leeway his Staff promised before the Russians could fully mobilize. "I hate the Slavs," he confessed to an Austrian officer. "I know it is a sin to do so. We ought not to hate anyone. But I can't help hating them." He had taken comfort, however, in the news, reminiscent of 1905, of strikes and riots in St. Petersburg, of mobs smashing windows, and "violent street fights between revolutionaries and police." Count Pourtalès, his aged ambassador, who had been seven years in Russia, concluded, and repeatedly assured his government, that Russia would not fight for fear of revolution. Captain von Eggeling, the German military attaché, kept repeating the credo about 1916, and when Russia nevertheless mobilized, he reported she planned "no tenacious offensive but a slow retreat as in 1812." In the affinity for error of German diplomats, these judgments established a record. They gave heart to the Kaiser, who as late as July 31 composed a missive for the "guidance" of his Staff, rejoicing in the "mood of a sick Tom-cat" that, on the evidence of his envoys, he said prevailed in the Russian court and army.

In Berlin on August 1, the crowds milling in the streets and massed in thousands in front of the palace were tense and heavy with anxiety. Socialism, which most of Berlin's workers professed, did not run so deep as their instinctive fear and hatred of the Slavic hordes. Although they had been told by the Kaiser, in his speech from the balcony announcing *Kriegesgefahr* the evening before, that the "sword has been forced into our hand," they still waited in the ultimate dim hope of a Russian reply. The hour of the ultimatum passed. A journalist in the crowd felt the air "electric with rumor. People told each other Russia had asked for an extension of time. The Bourse writhed in panic. The afternoon passed in almost insufferable anxiety." Bethmann-Hollweg issued a statement ending, "If the iron dice roll, may God help us." At five o'clock a policeman appeared at the palace gate and announced mobilization to the crowd, which obediently struck up the national hymn, "Now thank we all our God." Cars raced down Unter den Linden with officers standing up in them, waving handkerchiefs and shouting, "Mobilization!" Instantly converted from Marx to Mars, people cheered wildly and rushed off to vent their feelings on suspected Russian spies, several of whom were pummeled or trampled to death in the course of the next few days.

Once the mobilization button was pushed, the whole vast machinery for calling up, equipping, and transporting two million men began turning automatically. Reservists went to their designated depots, were issued uniforms, equipment, and arms, formed into companies and companies into battalions, were joined by cavalry, cyclists, artillery, medical units, cook wagons, blacksmith wagons, even postal wagons, moved according to prepared railway timetables to concentration points near the frontier where they would be formed into divisions, divisions into corps, and corps into armies ready to advance and fight. One army corps alone—out of the total of 40 in the German forces—required 170 railway cars for officers, 965 for infantry, 2,960 for cavalry, 1,915 for artillery and supply wagons, 6,010 in all, grouped in 140 trains and an equal number again for their supplies. From the moment the order was given, everything was to move at fixed times according to a schedule precise down to the number of train axles that would pass over a given bridge within a given time.

Confident in his magnificent system, Deputy Chief of Staff General Waldersee had not even returned to Berlin at the beginning of the crisis but had written to Jagow: "I shall remain here ready to jump; we are all prepared at the General Staff; in the meantime there is nothing for us to do." It was a proud tradition inherited from the elder, or "great," Moltke who on mobilization day in 1870 was found lying on a sofa reading *Lady Audley's Secret.*

His enviable calm was not present today in the palace. Face to face no longer with specter but the reality of a two-front war, the Kaiser was as close to the "sick Tom-cat" mood as he thought the Russians were. More cosmopolitan and more timid than the archetype Prussian, he had never actually wanted a general war. He wanted greater power, greater prestige, above all more authority in the world's affairs for Germany but he preferred to obtain them by frightening rather than by fighting other nations. He wanted the gladiator's rewards without the battle, and whenever the prospect of battle came too close, as at Algeciras and Agadir, he shrank.

As the final crisis boiled, his marginalia on telegrams grew more and more agitated: "Aha! the common cheat," "Rot!" "He lies!" "Mr. Grey is a false dog," "Twaddle!" "The rascal is crazy or an idiot!" When Russia mobilized he burst into a tirade of passionate foreboding, not against the Slav traitors but against the unforgettable figure of the wicked uncle: "The world will be engulfed in the most terrible of wars, the ultimate aim of which is the ruin of Germany. England, France and Russia have conspired for our annihilation . . . that is the naked truth of the situation which was slowly but surely created by Edward VII. . . . The encirclement of Germany is at last an accomplished fact. We have run our heads into the noose. . . . The dead Edward is stronger than the living I!"

Conscious of the shadow of the dead Edward, the Kaiser would have welcomed any way out of the commitment to fight both Russia and France and, behind France, the looming figure of still-undeclared England.

At the last moment one was offered. A colleague of Bethmann's came to beg him to do anything he could to save Germany from a two-front war and suggested a means. For years a possible solution for Alsace had been discussed in terms of autonomy as a Federal State within the German Empire. If offered and accepted by the Alsatians, this solution would have deprived France of any reason to liberate the lost provinces. As recently as July 16, the French Socialist Congress had gone on record in favor of it. But the German military had always insisted that the provinces must remain garrisoned and their political rights subordinated to "military necessity." Until 1911 no constitution had ever been granted and autonomy never. Bethmann's colleague now urged him to make an immediate, public, and official offer for a conference on autonomy for Alsace. This could be allowed to drag on without result, while its moral effect would force France to refrain from attack while at least considering the offer. Time would be gained for Germany to turn her forces against Russia while remaining stationary in the West, thus keeping England out.

The author of this proposal remains anonymous, and it may be apocryphal. It does not matter. The opportunity was there, and the Chancellor could have thought of it for himself. But to seize it required boldness, and Bethmann, behind his distinguished facade of great height, somber eyes, and well-trimmed imperial, was a man, as Theodore Roosevelt said of Taft, "who means well feebly." Instead of offering France an inducement to stay neutral, the German government sent her an ultimatum at the same time as the ultimatum to Russia. They asked France to reply within eighteen hours whether she would stay neutral in a Russo-German war, and added that if she did Germany would "demand as guarantee of neutrality the handing over to us of the fortresses of Toul and Verdun which we shall occupy and restore after the war is over"—in other words, the handing over of the key to the French door.

Baron von Schoen, German ambassador in Paris, could not bring himself to pass on this "brutal" demand at a moment when, it seemed to him, French neutrality would have been such a supreme advantage to Germany that his government might well have offered to pay a price for it rather than exact a penalty. He presented the request for a statement of neutrality without the demand for the fortresses, but the French, who had intercepted and decoded his instructions, knew of it anyway. When Schoen, at 11:00 A.M. on August 1, asked for France's reply he was answered that France "would act in accordance with her interests."

In Berlin just after five o'clock a telephone rang in the Foreign Office. Under-Secretary Zimmermann, who answered it, turned to the editor of the *Berliner Tageblatt* sitting by his desk and said, "Moltke wants to know whether things can start." At that moment a telegram from London, just decoded, broke in upon the planned proceedings. It offered hope that if the movement against France could be instantly stopped Germany might safely fight a one-front war after all. Carrying it with them, Bethmann and Jagow dashed off on their taxi trip to the palace.

The telegram, from Prince Lichnowsky, ambassador in London, reported an English offer, as Lichnowsky understood it, "that in case we did not attack France, England would remain neutral and would guarantee France's neutrality."

The ambassador belonged to that class of Germans who spoke English and copied English manners, sports, and dress, in a strenuous endeavor to become the very pattern of an English gentleman. His fellow noblemen, the Prince of Pless, Prince Blücher, and Prince Münster were all married to English wives. At a dinner in Berlin in 1911, in honor of a British general, the guest of honor was astonished to find that all forty German guests, including Bethmann-Hollweg and Admiral Tirpitz, spoke English fluently. Lichnowsky differed from his class in that he was not only in manner but in heart an earnest Anglophile. He had come to London determined to make himself and his country liked. English society had been lavish with country weekends. To the ambassador no tragedy could be greater than war between the country of his birth and the country of his heart, and he was grasping at any handle to avert it.

When the Foreign Secretary, Sir Edward Grey, telephoned him that morning, in the interval of a Cabinet meeting, Lichnowsky, out of his own anxiety, interpreted what Grey said to him as an offer by England to stay neutral and to keep France neutral in a Russo-German war, if, in return, Germany would promise not to attack France.

Actually, Grey had not said quite that. What, in his elliptical way, he offered was a promise to keep France neutral if Germany would promise to stay neutral as against France *and* Russia, in other words, not go to war against either, pending the result of efforts to settle the Serbian affair. After eight years as Foreign Secretary in a period of chronic "Bosnias," as Bülow called them, Grey had perfected a manner of speaking designed to convey as little meaning as possible; his avoidance of the point-blank, said a colleague, almost amounted to method. Over the telephone, Lichnowsky, himself dazed by the coming tragedy, would have had no difficulty misunderstanding him.

The Kaiser clutched at Lichnowsky's passport to a one-front war. Minutes counted. Already mobilization was rolling inexorably toward the French frontier. The first hostile act, seizure of a railway junction in Luxembourg, whose neutrality the five Great Powers, including Germany, had guaranteed, was scheduled within an hour. It must be stopped, stopped at once. But how? Where was Moltke? Moltke had left the palace. An aide was sent off, with siren screaming, to intercept him. He was brought back.

The Kaiser was himself again, the All-Highest, the War Lord, blazing with a new idea, planning, proposing, disposing. He read Moltke the telegram and said in triumph: "Now we can go to war against Russia only. We simply march the whole of our Army to the East!"

Aghast at the thought of his marvelous machinery of mobilization wrenched into reverse, Moltke refused point-blank. For the past ten years, first as assistant to Schlieffen, then as his successor, Moltke's job had been planning for this day, The Day, *Der Tag,* for which all Germany's energies were gathered, on which the march to final mastery of Europe would begin. It weighed upon him with an oppressive, almost unbearable responsibility.

Tall, heavy, bald, and sixty-six years old, Moltke habitually wore an expression of profound distress which led the Kaiser to call him *der traurige Julius* (or what might be rendered "Gloomy Gus"; in fact, his name was Helmuth). Poor health, for which he took an annual cure at

Carlsbad, and the shadow of a great uncle were perhaps cause for gloom. From his window in the red brick General Staff building on the König-platz where he lived as well as worked, he looked out every day on the equestrian statue of his namesake, the hero of 1870 and, together with Bismarck, the architect of the German Empire. The nephew was a poor horseman with a habit of falling off on staff rides and, worse, a follower of Christian Science with a side interest in anthroposophism and other cults. For this unbecoming weakness in a Prussian officer he was consid-ered "soft"; what is more, he painted, played the cello, carried Goethe's *Faust* in his pocket, and had begun a translation of Maeterlinck's *Pelléas et Mélisande.*

Introspective and a doubter by nature, he had said to the Kaiser upon his appointment in 1906: "I do not know how I shall get on in the event of a campaign. I am very critical of myself." Yet he was neither person-ally nor politically timid. In 1911, disgusted by Germany's retreat in the Agadir crisis, he wrote to Conrad von Hotzendorff that if things got worse he would resign, propose to disband the army and "place ourselves under the protection of Japan; then we can make money undisturbed and turn into imbeciles." He did not hesitate to talk back to the Kaiser, but told him "quite brutally" in 1900 that his Peking expedition was a "crazy adventure," and when offered the appointment as Chief of Staff, asked the Kaiser if he expected "to win the big prize twice in the same lottery"—a thought that had certainly influenced William's choice. He refused to take the post unless the Kaiser stopped his habit of winning all the war games which was making nonsense of maneuvers. Surpris-ingly, the Kaiser meekly obeyed.

Now, on the climactic night of August 1, Moltke was in no mood for any more of the Kaiser's meddling with serious military matters, or with meddling of any kind with the fixed arrangements. To turn around the deployment of a million men from west to east at the very moment of departure would have taken a more iron nerve than Moltke disposed of. He saw a vision of the deployment crumbling apart in confusion, supplies here, soldiers there, ammunition lost in the middle, companies without officers, divisions without staffs, and those 11,000 trains, each exquisitely scheduled to click over specified tracks at specified intervals of ten minutes, tangled in a grotesque ruin of the most perfectly planned military movement in history.

"Your Majesty," Moltke said to him now, "it cannot be done. The deployment of millions cannot be improvised. If Your Majesty insists on leading the whole army to the East it will not be an army ready for battle but a disorganized mob of armed men with no arrangements for supply. Those arrangements took a whole year of intricate labor to complete" —and Moltke closed upon that rigid phrase, the basis for every major German mistake, the phrase that launched the invasion of Belgium and the submarine war against the United States, the inevitable phrase when military plans dictate policy—"and once settled, it cannot be altered."

In fact it could have been altered. The German General Staff, though committed since 1905 to a plan of attack upon France first, had in their files, revised each year until 1913, an alternative plan against Russia with all the trains running eastward.

"Build no more fortresses, build railways," ordered the elder Moltke who had laid out his strategy on a railway map and bequeathed the dogma that railways are the key to war. In Germany the railway system was under military control with a staff officer assigned to every line; no track could be laid or changed without permission of the General Staff. Annual mobilization war games kept railway officials in constant practice and tested their ability to improvise and divert traffic by telegrams reporting lines cut and bridges destroyed. The best brains produced by the War College, it was said, went into the railway section and ended up in lunatic asylums.

When Moltke's "It cannot be done" was revealed after the war in his memoirs, General von Staab, Chief of the Railway Division, was so incensed by what he considered a reproach upon his bureau that he wrote a book to prove it could have been done. In pages of charts and graphs he demonstrated how, given notice on August 1, he could have deployed four out of the seven armies to the Eastern Front by August 15, leaving three to defend the West. Matthias Erzberger, the Reichstag deputy and leader of the Catholic Centrist Party, has left another testimony. He says that Moltke himself, within six months of the event, admitted to him that the assault on France at the beginning was a mistake and instead, "the larger part of our army ought first to have been sent East to smash the Russian steam roller, limiting operations in the West to beating off the enemy's attack on our frontier."

On the night of August 1, Moltke, clinging to the fixed plan, lacked the necessary nerve. "Your uncle would have given me a different answer," the Kaiser said to him bitterly. The reproach "wounded me deeply" Moltke wrote afterward; "I never pretended to be the equal of the old Field Marshal." Nevertheless he continued to refuse. "My protest that it would be impossible to maintain peace between France and Germany while both countries were mobilized made no impression. Everybody got more and more excited and I was alone in my opinion."

Finally, when Moltke convinced the Kaiser that the mobilization plan could not be changed, the group which included Bethmann and Jagow drafted a telegram to England regretting that Germany's advance movements toward the French border "can no longer be altered," but offering a guarantee not to cross the border before August 3 at 7:00 P.M., which cost them nothing as no crossing was scheduled before that time. Jagow rushed off a telegram to his ambassador in Paris, where mobilization had already been decreed at four o'clock, instructing him helpfully to "please keep France quiet for the time being." The Kaiser added a personal telegram to King George, telling him that for "technical reasons" mobilization could not be countermanded at this late hour, but "If France offers me neutrality which must be guaranteed by the British fleet and army, I shall of course refrain from attacking France and employ my troops elsewhere. I hope France will not become nervous."

It was now minutes before seven o'clock, the hour when the 16th Division was scheduled to move into Luxembourg. Bethmann excitedly insisted that Luxembourg must not be entered under any circumstances while waiting for the British answer. Instantly the Kaiser, without asking Moltke, ordered his aide-de-camp to telephone and telegraph 16th Division Headquarters at Trier to cancel the movement. Moltke saw ruin again. Luxembourg's railways were essential for the offensive through Belgium against France. "At that moment," his memoirs say, "I thought my heart would break."

Despite all his pleading, the Kaiser refused to budge. Instead, he added a closing sentence to his telegram to King George, "The troops on my frontier are in the act of being stopped by telephone and telegraph from crossing into France," a slight if vital twist of the truth, for the Kaiser could not acknowledge to England that what he had intended and what was being stopped was the violation of a neutral country. It would have implied his intention also to violate Belgium, which would have been *casus belli* in England, and England's mind was not yet made up.

"Crushed," Moltke says of himself, on what should have been the culminating day of his career, he returned to the General Staff and "burst into bitter tears of abject despair." When his aide brought him for his signature the written order canceling the Luxembourg movement, "I threw my pen down on the table and refused to sign." To have signed as the first order after mobilization one that would have annulled all the careful preparations would have been taken, he knew, as evidence of "hesitancy and irresolution." "Do what you want with this telegram," he said to his aide; "I will not sign it."

He was still brooding at eleven o'clock when another summons came from the palace. Moltke found the Kaiser in his bedroom, characteristically dressed for the occasion, with a military overcoat over his nightshirt. A telegram had come from Lichnowsky, who, in a further talk with Grey, had discovered his error and now wired sadly, "A positive proposal by England is, on the whole, not in prospect."

"Now you can do what you like," said the Kaiser, and went back to bed. Moltke, the Commander in Chief who had now to direct a campaign that would decide the fate of Germany, was left permanently shaken. "That was my first experience of the war," he wrote afterward. "I never recovered from the shock of this incident. Something in me broke and I was never the same thereafter."

Neither was the world, he might have added. The Kaiser's telephone order to Trier had not arrived in time. At seven o'clock, as scheduled, the first frontier of the war was crossed, the distinction going to an infantry company of the 69th Regiment under command of a certain Lieutenant Feldmann. Just inside the Luxembourg border, on the slopes of the Ardennes about twelve miles from Bastogne in Belgium, stood a little town known to the Germans as Ulflingen. Around it cows grazed on the hillside pastures; on its steep, cobblestone streets not a stray wisp of hay, even in August harvest time, was allowed to offend the strict laws governing municipal cleanliness in the Grand Duchy. At the foot of the town was a railroad station and telegraph office where the lines from Germany and Belgium crossed. This was the German objective which Lieutenant Feldmann's company, arriving in automobiles, duly seized.

With their relentless talent for the tactless, the Germans chose to violate Luxembourg at a place whose native and official name was Trois Vierges. The three virgins in fact represented faith, hope, and charity, but History with her apposite touch arranged for the occasion that they should stand in the public mind for Luxembourg, Belgium, and France.

At 7:30 a second detachment in automobiles arrived (presumably in response to the Kaiser's message) and ordered off the first group, saying "a mistake had been made." In the interval Luxembourg's Minister of State Eyschen had already telegraphed the news to London, Paris, and Brussels and a protest to Berlin. The three virgins had made their point. By midnight Moltke had rectified the reversal, and by the end of the next day, August 2, M-1 on the German schedule, the entire Grand Duchy was occupied.

A question has haunted the annals of history ever since: What Ifs might have followed if the Germans had gone east in 1914 while remaining on the defensive against France? General von Staab showed that to have turned against Russia was technically possible. But whether it would have been temperamentally possible for the Germans to have refrained from attacking France when *Der Tag* came is another matter.

At seven o'clock in St. Petersburg, at the same hour when the Germans entered Luxembourg, Ambassador Pourtalès, his watery blue eyes red-rimmed, his white goatee quivering, presented Germany's declaration of war with shaking hand to Sazonov, the Russian Foreign Minister.

"The curses of the nations will be upon you!" Sazonov exclaimed.

"We are defending our honor," the German ambassador replied.

"Your honor was not involved. But there is a divine justice."

"That's true," and muttering, "a divine justice, a divine justice," Pourtalès staggered to the window, leaned against it, and burst into tears. "So this is the end of my mission," he said when he could speak. Sazonov patted him on the shoulder, they embraced, and Pourtalès stumbled to the door, which he could hardly open with a trembling hand, and went out, murmuring, "Goodbye, goodbye."

This affecting scene comes down to us as recorded by Sazonov with artistic additions by the French ambassador Paléologue, presumably from what Sazonov told him. Pourtalès reported only that he asked three times for a reply to the ultimatum and after Sazonov answered negatively three times, "I handed over the note as instructed."

Why did it have to be handed over at all? Admiral von Tirpitz, the Naval Minister, had plaintively asked the night before when the declaration of war was being drafted. Speaking, he says, "more from instinct than from reason," he wanted to know why, if Germany did not plan to invade Russia, was it necessary to declare war and assume the odium of the attacking party? His question was particularly pertinent because Germany's object was to saddle Russia with war guilt in order to convince the German people that they were fighting in self-defense and especially in order to keep Italy tied to her engagements under the Triple Alliance.

Italy was obliged to join her allies only in a defensive war and, already shaky in her allegiance, was widely expected to sidle out through any loophole that opened up. Bethmann was harassed by this problem. If Austria persisted in refusing any or all Serbian concessions, he warned, "it will scarcely be possible to place the guilt of a European conflagration on Russia" and would "place us in the eyes of our own people, in an untenable position." He was hardly heard. When mobilization day came, German protocol required that war be properly declared. Jurists of the Foreign Office, according to Tirpitz, insisted it was legally the correct thing to do. "Outside Germany," he says pathetically, "there is no appreciation of such ideas."

In France appreciation was keener than he knew.

QUESTIONS FOR DISCUSSION

1. What is the function of the short preliminary section called "Outbreak"? Why is it presented in such staccato, news-dispatch fashion?
2. What role did individual responsibility play in the outbreak of the war? What human motives operated? Could it be maintained that the personalities of Moltke or the Kaiser were significant causes?
3. How significant an element was chance?
4. At times Tuchman attributes thoughts, motives, and even specific words to historical characters. What is her authority for doing so? In general, how does she make herself believable without the apparatus of documentation that a scholarly history would have?
5. A reader could easily build a causal model from this piece that looks like a time line. But would that model be the most accurate representation of the interplay of causes? Which elements on the time line seem most significant?
6. How important was the absence of blocking causes? How many points were there where something could have happened but did not?

SUGGESTIONS FOR WRITING

1. Using Tuchman's narrative as a basis, create a causal argument, organized not as a story but as an analysis, in which you argue for the most important cause of Germany's entry into World War I. Address Tuchman's general readership.
2. One of Tuchman's morals seems to be that military preparedness can itself be a cause of war. Was that a factor in the start of World War II? The Vietnam War? Is military preparedness currently a threat? Write your essay as a comparison between World War I and another situation.
3. Write a causal narrative in Tuchman's style on a limited event such as a diplomatic crisis (e.g., the Cuban Missile Crisis) or a limited war (e.g., the conflict over the Falkland Islands). How do accidents, personal actions, miscalculations, and institutional inertia contribute to history? Imagine yourself writing for *Time* or *Newsweek*.
4. Take a skeptical view of Tuchman's account, questioning any point at which

her evidence for motives or her sense of the importance of an event might be vulnerable. Could you, for instance, argue that all the small maneuvers she reports really are insignificant in the face of large-scale historical and cultural forces?

5. Find an instance in history of a war that might have happened but did not. Write a causal explanation, perhaps in narrative style like Tuchman's, in which you identify the causes that prevented it. Your audience might be your fellow students in a history class.

---->>> <<<---

Parkinson's Law

C. *NORTHCOTE PARKINSON*

C. Northcote Parkinson manages to speak simultaneously to two audiences, with at least two levels of intention, in two different styles in this amazing excerpt from the first chapter of his book, Parkinson's Law *(1957). While a Professor of History at the University of Malaya, Parkinson did research on the growth of the British government. His work led him to the formulation of the famous law which, without a twinge of humility, he named after himself. His explication of his own discovery has both the force of inspired common sense—it is so self-evidently true of human nature and its many institutions— and the bite of a satirical debunking of its own methodology. In short, Parkinson seems capable of achieving opposite rhetorical effects at the same time. No one doubts that he is having fun at the expense of the social scientists, yet no one doubts the validity of his insight either.*

PARKINSON'S LAW OR THE RISING PYRAMID

Work expands so as to fill the time available for its completion. General recognition of this fact is shown in the proverbial phrase "It is the busiest man who has time to spare." Thus, an elderly lady of leisure can spend the entire day in writing and dispatching a postcard to her niece at Bognor Regis. An hour will be spent in finding the postcard, another in hunting for spectacles, half an hour in a search for the address, an hour and a quarter in composition, and twenty minutes in deciding whether or not to take an umbrella when going to the mailbox in the next street. The total effort that would occupy a busy man for three minutes all told may in this fashion leave another person prostrate after a day of doubt, anxiety, and toil.

Granted that work (and especially paperwork) is thus elastic in its demands on time, it is manifest that there need be little or no relationship between the work to be done and the size of the staff to which it may be assigned. A lack of real activity does not, of necessity, result in leisure. A lack of occupation is not necessarily revealed by a manifest idleness. The thing to be done swells in importance and complexity in a direct ratio with the time to be spent. This fact is widely recognized, but less attention has been paid to its wider implications, more especially in the field of public administration. Politicians and taxpayers have assumed (with occasional phases of doubt) that a rising total in the number of civil servants must reflect a growing volume of work to be done. Cynics, in questioning this belief, have imagined that the multiplication of officials must have left some of them idle or all of them able to work for shorter hours. But this is a matter in which faith and doubt seem equally misplaced. The fact is that the number of the officials and the quantity of the work are not related to each other at all. The rise in the total of those employed is governed by Parkinson's Law and would be much the same whether the volume of the work were to increase, diminish, or even disappear. The importance of Parkinson's Law lies in the fact that it is a law of growth based upon an analysis of the factors by which that growth is controlled.

The validity of this recently discovered law must rest mainly on statistical proofs, which will follow. Of more interest to the general reader is the explanation of the factors underlying the general tendency to which this law gives definition. Omitting technicalities (which are numerous) we may distinguish at the outset two motive forces. They can be represented for the present purpose by two almost axiomatic statements, thus: (1) "An official wants to multiply subordinates, not rivals" and (2) "Officials make work for each other."

To comprehend Factor 1, we must picture a civil servant, called A, who finds himself overworked. Whether this overwork is real or imaginary is immaterial, but we should observe, in passing, that A's sensation (or illusion) might easily result from his own decreasing energy: a normal symptom of middle age. For this real or imagined overwork there are, broadly speaking, three possible remedies. He may resign; he may ask to halve the work with a colleague called B; he may demand the assistance of two subordinates, to be called C and D. There is probably no instance in history, however, of A choosing any but the third alternative. By resignation he would lose his pension rights. By having B appointed, on his own level in the hierarchy, he would merely bring in a rival for promotion to W's vacancy when W (at long last) retires. So A would rather have C and D, junior men, below him. They will add to his consequence and, by dividing the work into two categories, as between C and D, he will have the merit of being the only man who comprehends them both. It is essential to realize at this point that C and D are, as it were, inseparable. To appoint C alone would have been impossible. Why? Because C, if by himself, would divide the work with A and so assume almost the equal status that has been refused in the first instance to B; a status the more emphasized if C is A's only possible successor. Subordinates must thus number two or more, each being thus kept in order by fear of the other's promotion. When C complains in turn of being overworked (as he certainly will) A will, with the concurrence of C, advise the appointment of two assistants to help C. But he can then avert internal friction only by advising the appointment of two more assistants to help D, whose position is much the same. With this recruitment of E, F, G, and H the promotion of A is now practically certain.

Seven officials are now doing what one did before. This is where Factor 2 comes into operation. For these seven make so much work for each other that all are fully occupied and A is actually working harder than ever. An incoming document may well come before each of them in turn. Official E decides that it falls within the province of F, who places a draft reply before C, who amends it drastically before consulting D, who asks G to deal with it. But G goes on leave at this point, handing the file over to H, who drafts a minute that is signed by D and returned to C, who revises his draft accordingly and lays the new version before A.

What does A do? He would have every excuse for signing the thing unread, for he has many other matters on his mind. Knowing now that he is to succeed W next year, he has to decide whether C or D should succeed to his own office. He had to agree to G's going on leave even if not yet strictly entitled to it. He is worried whether H should not have gone instead, for reasons of health. He has looked pale recently—partly but not solely because of his domestic troubles. Then there is the business of F's special increment of salary for the period of the conference and E's application for transfer to the Ministry of Pensions. A has heard that D is in love with a married typist and that G and F are no longer on speaking terms—no one seems to know why. So A might be tempted to sign C's draft and have done with it. But A is a conscientious man. Beset as he is with problems created by his colleagues for themselves and for him—created by the mere fact of these officials' existence —he is not the man to shirk his duty. He reads through the draft with care, deletes the fussy paragraphs added by C and H, and restores the thing back to the form preferred in the first instance by the able (if quarrelsome) F. He corrects the English—none of these young men can write grammatically—and finally produces the same reply he would have written if officials C to H had never been born. Far more people have taken far longer to produce the same result. No one has been idle. All have done their best. And it is late in the evening before A finally quits his office and begins the return journey to Ealing. The last of the office lights are being turned off in the gathering dusk that marks the end of another day's administrative toil. Among the last to leave, A reflects with bowed shoulders and a wry smile that late hours, like gray hairs, are among the penalties of success.

From this description of the factors at work the student of political science will recognize that administrators are more or less bound to multiply. Nothing has yet been said, however, about the period of time likely to elapse between the date of A's appointment and the date from which we can calculate the pensionable service of H. Vast masses of statistical evidence have been collected and it is from a study of this data that Parkinson's Law has been deduced. Space will not allow of detailed analysis but the reader will be interested to know that research began in the British Navy Estimates. These were chosen because the Admiralty's responsibilities are more easily measurable than those of, say, the Board of Trade. The question is merely one of numbers and tonnage. Here are some typical figures. The strength of the Navy in 1914 could be shown as 146,000 officers and men, 3249 dockyard officials and clerks, and 57,000 dockyard workmen. By 1928 there were only 100,000 officers and men and only 62,439 workmen, but the dockyard officials and clerks by then numbered 4558. As for warships, the strength in 1928 was a mere fraction of what it had been in 1914—fewer than 20 capital ships in commission as compared with 62. Over the same period the Admiralty officials had increased in number from 2000 to 3569, providing (as was remarked) "a magnificent navy on land." These figures are more clearly set forth in tabular form.

Admiralty Statistics

YEAR	CAPITAL SHIPS IN COMMISSION	OFFICERS AND MEN IN R.N.	DOCKYARD WORKERS	DOCKYARD OFFICIALS AND CLERKS	ADMIRALTY OFFICIALS
1914	62	146,000	57,000	3249	2000
1928	20	100,000	62,439	4558	3569
Increase or Decrease	−67.74%	−31.5%	+9.54%	+40.28%	+78.45%

The criticism voiced at the time centered on the ratio between the numbers of those available for fighting and those available only for administration. But that comparison is not to the present purpose. What we have to note is that the 2000 officials of 1914 had become the 3569 of 1928; and that this growth was unrelated to any possible increase in their work. The Navy during that period had diminished, in point of fact, by a third in men and two-thirds in ships. Nor, from 1922 onward, was its strength even expected to increase; for its total of ships (unlike its total of officials) was limited by the Washington Naval Agreement of that year. Here we have then a 78 percent increase over a period of fourteen years; an average of 5.6 per cent increase a year on the earlier total. In fact, as we shall see, the rate of increase was not as regular as that. All we have to consider, at this stage, is the percentage rise over a given period.

Can this rise in the total number of civil servants be accounted for except on the assumption that such a total must always rise by a law governing its growth? It might be urged at this point that the period under discussion was one of rapid development in naval technique. The use of the flying machine was no longer confined to the eccentric. Electrical devices were being multiplied and elaborated. Submarines were tolerated if not approved. Engineer officers were beginning to be regarded as almost human. In so revolutionary an age we might expect that storekeepers would have more elaborate inventories to compile. We might not wonder to see more draughtsmen on the payroll, more designers, more technicians and scientists. But these, the dockyard officials, increased only by 40 per cent in number when the men of Whitehall increased their total by nearly 80 per cent. For every new foreman or electrical engineer at Portsmouth there had to be two more clerks at Charing Cross. From this we might be tempted to conclude, provisionally, that the rate of increase in administrative staff is likely to be double that of the technical staff at a time when the actually useful strength (in this case, of seamen) is being reduced by 31.5 per cent. It has been proved statistically, however, that this last percentage is irrelevant. The officials would have multiplied at the same rate had there been no actual seamen at all.

It would be interesting to follow the further progress by which the 8118 Admiralty staff of 1935 came to number 33,788 by 1954. But the staff of the Colonial Office affords a better field of study during a period of imperial decline. Admiralty statistics are complicated by factors (like the Fleet Air Arm) that make comparison difficult as between one year and the next. The Colonial Office growth is more significant in that it is more purely administrative. Here the relevant statistics are as follows:

1935	1939	1943	1947	1954
372	450	817	1139	1661

Before showing what the rate of increase is, we must observe that the extent of this department's responsibilities was far from constant during these twenty years. The colonial territories were not much altered in area or population between 1935 and 1939. They were considerably diminished by 1943, certain areas being in enemy hands. They were increased again in 1947, but have since then shrunk steadily from year to year as successive colonies achieve self-government. It would be rational to suppose that these changes in the scope of Empire would be reflected in the size of its central administration. But a glance at the figures is enough to convince us that the staff totals represent nothing but so many stages in an inevitable increase. And this increase, although related to that observed in other departments, has nothing to do with the size—or even the existence—of the Empire. What are the percentages of increase? We must ignore, for this purpose, the rapid increase in staff which accompanied the diminution of responsibility during World War II. We should note rather, the peacetime rates of increase: over 5.24 per cent between 1935 and 1939, and 6.55 per cent between 1947 and 1954. This gives an average increase of 5.89 per cent each year, a percentage markedly similar to that already found in the Admiralty staff increase between 1914 and 1928.

Further and detailed statistical analysis of departmental staffs would be inappropriate in such a work as this. It is hoped, however, to reach a tentative conclusion regarding the time likely to elapse between a given official's first appointment and the later appointment of his two or more assistants.

Dealing with the problem of pure staff accumulation, all our researches so far completed point to an average increase of 5.75 per cent per year. This fact established, it now becomes possible to state Parkinson's Law in mathematical form: In any public administrative department not actually at war, the staff increase may be expected to follow this formula—

$$x = \frac{2k^m + l}{n}$$

k is the number of staff seeking promotion through the appointment of subordinates; l represents the difference between the ages of appointment and retirement; m is the number of man-hours devoted to answering minutes within the department; and n is the number of effective units being administered. x will be the number of new staff required each year. Mathematicians will realize, of course, that to find the percentage increase they must multiply x by 100 and divide by the total of the previous year, thus:

$$\frac{100\,(2k^m + l)}{yn}\%$$

where y represents the total original staff. This figure will invariably prove to be between 5.17 per cent and 6.56 per cent, irrespective of any variation in the amount of work (if any) to be done.

The discovery of this formula and of the general principles upon which it is based has, of course, no political value. No attempt has been made to inquire whether departments ought to grow in size. Those who hold that this growth is essential to gain full employment are fully entitled to their opinion. Those who doubt the stability of an economy based upon reading each other's minutes are equally entitled to theirs. It would probably be premature to attempt at this stage any inquiry into the quantitative ratio that should exist between the administrators and the administered. Granted, however, that a maximum ratio exists, it should soon be possible to ascertain by formula how many years will elapse before that ratio, in any given community, will be reached. The forecasting of such a result will again have no political value. Nor can it be sufficiently emphasized that Parkinson's Law is a purely scientific discovery, inapplicable except in theory to the politics of the day. It is not the business of the botanist to eradicate the weeds. Enough for him if he can tell us just how fast they grow.

QUESTIONS FOR DISCUSSION

1. What other laws like Parkinson's do you know? What is the attraction in formulating observations about human nature as laws?
2. Parkinson begins with an extended example of a dotty old lady sending a postcard. What tone does this example set? Why does he use such an opening strategy?
3. Take a section of this essay and examine its mixture of styles. Which sentences sound as if they were written by a social scientist, which by a humorist?
4. Look closely at the extended example of A hiring B and C. How is this example both generalized and particularized? How does it work as illustration and yet support the law?
5. Parkinson includes two impressive-looking mathematical statements of his observations. Are they serious? What other target might Parkinson have?
6. Why does Parkinson insist so forcefully that his observations are inapplicable, that they suggest no policy and have no political implications?

SUGGESTIONS FOR WRITING

1. Use Parkinson's Law as a generalization and support it with examples and observations from your own experience. Address classmates who are unfamiliar with Parkinson's Law.
2. Try defending an institution you are familiar with by showing how its increase in size results from an increase in the amount of work it does. Or take the opposite position: Examine an institution and show how Parkinson was precisely right. Both of these essays could be aimed at the institution's critics.
3. Parkinson's explanation of his law could be regarded as a satire on the techniques of social scientists. Try your hand at parodying for your classmates the methods of an academic discipline you are familiar with, perhaps using a particularly loathed textbook as a model.
4. For the campus newspaper, formulate your own law describing the way human nature usually works: of how camping trips turn out, how parties are planned, how studying gets done.
5. Take on Parkinson's conclusion and recommend what should be done to reverse Parkinson's Law and the growth of bureaucracies. Aim your argument not at the source of the problem but at those who could be pressured for change.

———————— -≫> ≪<- ————————

Politics and the English Language

GEORGE ORWELL

George Orwell's essay, "Politics and the English Language," has become a classic of modern prose, as have his two widely read novels, 1984 and Animal Farm. In both the essay and his fiction, Orwell takes to task governments that use deceptive language to hide tactics of manipulation and suppression. "Politics and the English Language" makes a powerful and original argument for reciprocal causality: Political and economic forces shape our language, and our attitude toward language affects our political destiny. Behind this argument lies the assumption that as a free people we can and must intervene in the causal process to improve both our language and our political institutions.

Most people who bother with the matter at all would admit that the English language is in a bad way, but it is generally assumed that we cannot by conscious action do anything about it. Our civilisation is decadent, and our language—so the argument runs—must inevitably share in the general collapse. It follows that any struggle against the abuse of language is a sentimental archaism, like preferring candles to electric light or hansom cabs to aeroplanes. Underneath this lies the half-conscious belief that language is a natural growth and not an instrument which we shape for our own purposes.

Now, it is clear that the decline of a language must ultimately have political and economic causes: it is not due simply to the bad influence of this or that individual writer. But an effect can become a cause, reinforcing the original cause and producing the same effect in an intensified form, and so on indefinitely. A man may take to drink because he feels himself to be a failure, and then fail all the more completely because he drinks. It is rather the same thing that is happening to the English language. It becomes ugly and inaccurate because our thoughts are foolish, but the slovenliness of our language makes it easier for us to have foolish thoughts. The point is that the process is reversible. Modern English, especially written English, is full of bad habits which spread by imitation and which can be avoided if one is willing to take the necessary trouble. If one gets rid of these habits one can think more clearly, and to think clearly is a necessary first step towards political regeneration: so that the fight against bad English is not frivolous and is not the exclusive concern of professional writers. I will come back to this presently, and I hope that by that time the meaning of what I have said here will have become clearer. Meanwhile, here are five specimens of the English language as it is now habitually written.

These five passages have not been picked out because they are especially bad—I could have quoted far worse if I had chosen—but because they illustrate various of the mental vices from which we now suffer. They are a little below the average, but are fairly representative samples. I number them so that I can refer back to them when necessary:

> 1. I am not, indeed, sure whether it is not true to say that the Milton who once seemed not unlike a seventeenth-century Shelley had not become, out of an experience ever more bitter in each year, more alien (sic) to the founder of that Jesuit sect which nothing could induce him to tolerate.
>
> Professor Harold Laski (Essay in *Freedom of Expression*).

> 2. Above all, we cannot play ducks and drakes with a native battery of idioms which prescribes such egregious collocations of vocables as the Basic *put up with* for *tolerate* or *put at a loss* for *bewilder*.
>
> Professor Lancelot Hogben (*Interglossa*).

> 3. On the one side we have the free personality: by definition it is not neurotic, for it has neither conflict nor dream. Its desires, such as they are, are transparent, for they are just what institutional approval keeps in the forefront of consciousness; another institutional pattern would alter their number and intensity; there is little in them that is natural, irreducible, or culturally dangerous. But *on the other side*, the social bond itself is nothing but the mutual reflection of these self-secure integrities. Recall the definition of love. Is not this the very picture of a small academic? Where is there a place in this hall of mirrors for either personality or fraternity?
>
> Essay on psychology in *Politics* (New York).

> 4. All the "best people" from the gentlemen's clubs, and all the frantic Fascist captains, united in common hatred of Socialism and bestial horror of the rising tide of the mass revolutionary movement, have turned to acts of provocation, to foul incendiarism, to medieval

legends of poisoned wells, to legalise their own destruction to proletarian organisations, and rouse the agitated petty-bourgeoisie to chauvinistic fervour on behalf of the fight against the revolutionary way out of the crisis.

Communist pamphlet.

5. If a new spirit *is* to be infused into this old country, there is one thorny and contentious reform which must be tackled, and that is the humanisation and galvanisation of the BBC. Timidity here will bespeak canker and atrophy of the soul. The heart of Britain may be sound and of strong beat, for instance, but the British lion's roar at present is like that of Bottom in Shakespeare's *Midsummer Night's Dream*—as gentle as any sucking dove. A virile new Britain cannot continue indefinitely to be traduced in the eyes, or rather ears, of the world by the effete languors of Langham Place, brazenly masquerading as "standard English". When the Voice of Britain is heard at nine o'clock, better far and infinitely less ludicrous to hear aitches honestly dropped than the present priggish, inflated, inhibited, school-ma'amish arch braying of blameless bashful mewing maidens!

Letter in *Tribune*.

Each of these passages has faults of its own, but, quite apart from avoidable ugliness, two qualities are common to all of them. The first is staleness of imagery: the other is lack of precision. The writer either has a meaning and cannot express it, or he inadvertently says something else, or he is almost indifferent as to whether his words mean anything or not. This mixture of vagueness and sheer incompetence is the most marked characteristic of modern English prose, and especially of any kind of political writing. As soon as certain topics are raised, the concrete melts into the abstract and no one seems able to think of turns of speech that are not hackneyed: prose consists less and less of *words* chosen for the sake of their meaning, and more of *phrases* tacked together like the sections of a prefabricated hen-house. I list below, with notes and examples, various of the tricks by means of which the work of prose construction is habitually dodged:

DYING METAPHORS

A newly invented metaphor assists thought by evoking a visual image, while on the other hand a metaphor which is technically "dead" (e.g. *iron resolution*) has in effect reverted to being an ordinary word and can generally be used without loss of vividness. But in between these two classes there is a huge dump of worn-out metaphors which have lost all evocative power and are merely used because they save people the trouble of inventing phrases for themselves. Examples are: *Ring the changes on, take up the cudgels for, toe the line, ride roughshod over, stand shoulder to shoulder with, play into the hands of, no axe to grind, grist to the mill, fishing in troubled waters, rift within the lute, on the order of the day, Achilles' heel, swan song, hotbed.* Many of these are used without knowledge of their meaning (what is a "rift", for instance?), and incompatible metaphors are frequently mixed, a sure sign that the writer is not interested in what he is saying. Some metaphors now current have been twisted out of their original meaning without those who use them even being aware of the fact. For example, *toe the line* is sometimes written *tow the line.* Another example is *the hammer and the anvil,* now always used with the implication that the anvil gets the worst of it. In real life it is always the anvil that breaks the hammer, never the other way about: a writer who stopped to think what he was saying would be aware of this, and would avoid perverting the original phrase.

OPERATORS, OR VERBAL FALSE LIMBS

These save the trouble of picking out appropriate verbs and nouns, and at the same time pad each sentence with extra syllables which give it an appearance of symmetry. Characteristic phrases are: *render inoperative, militate against, prove unacceptable, make contact with, be subjected to, give rise to, give grounds for, have the effect of, play a leading part (rôle) in, make itself felt, take effect, exhibit a tendency to, serve the purpose of,* etc etc. The keynote is the elimination of simple verbs. Instead of being a single word, such as *break, stop, spoil, mend, kill,* a verb becomes a *phrase,* made up of a noun or adjective tacked on to some general-purposes verb such as *prove, serve, form, play, render.* In addition, the passive voice is wherever possible used in preference to the active, and noun constructions are used instead of gerunds (*by examination of* instead of *by examining*). The range of verbs is further cut down by means of the *-ise* and *de-* formations, and banal statements are given an appearance of profundity by means of the *not un-* formation. Simple conjunctions and prepositions are replaced by such phrases as *with respect to, having regard to, the fact that, by dint of, in view of, in the interests of, on the hypothesis that;* and the ends of sentences are saved from anticlimax by such resounding common-

places as *greatly to be desired, cannot be left out of account, a develop-*
ment to be expected in the near future, deserving of serious considera-
tion, brought to a satisfactory conclusion, and so on and so forth.

PRETENTIOUS DICTION

Words like *phenomenon, element, individual* (as noun), *objective, cate-*
gorical, effective, virtual, basic, primary, promote, constitute, exhibit,
exploit, utilise, eliminate, liquidate, are used to dress up simple statements and give an air of scientific impartiality to biassed judgements.
Adjectives like *epoch-making, epic, historic, unforgettable, triumphant,*
age-old, inevitable, inexorable, veritable, are used to dignify the sordid
processes of international politics, while writing that aims at glorifying
war usually takes on an archaic colour, its characteristic words being:
realm, throne, chariot, mailed fist, trident, sword, shield, buckler, ban-
ner, jackboot, clarion. Foreign words and expressions such as *cul de*
sac, ancien régime, deus ex machina, mutatis mutandis, status quo,
Gleichschaltung, Weltanschauung, are used to give an air of culture
and elegance. Except for the useful abbreviations *i.e., e.g.,* and *etc,*
there is no real need for any of the hundreds of foreign phrases now
current in English. Bad writers, and especially scientific, political and
sociological writers, are nearly always haunted by the notion that Latin
or Greek words are grander than Saxon ones, and unnecessary words
like *expedite, ameliorate, predict, extraneous, deracinated, clandestine,*
sub-aqueous and hundreds of others constantly gain ground from their
Anglo-Saxon opposite numbers.[1] The jargon peculiar to Marxist writing
(*hyena, hangman, cannibal, petty bourgeois, these gentry, lacquey,*
flunkey, mad dog, White Guard, etc) consists largely of words and phrases
translated from Russian, German or French; but the normal way of
coining a new word is to use a Latin or Greek root with the appropriate
affix and, where necessary, the *-ise* formation. It is often easier to make up
words of this kind (*deregionalise, impermissible, extramarital, non-frag-*
mentatory and so forth) than to think up the English words that will cover
one's meaning. The result, in general, is an increase in slovenliness and
vagueness.

---

[1]An interesting illustration of this is the way in which the English flower names which
were in use till very recently are being ousted by Greek ones, *snapdragon* becoming
antirrhinum, forget-me-not becoming *myosotis,* etc. It is hard to see any practical reason
for this change of fashion: it is probably due to an instinctive turning-away from the more
homely word and a vague feeling that the Greek word is scientific. [Author's footnote.]

MEANINGLESS WORDS

In certain kinds of writing, particularly in art criticism and literary criticism, it is normal to come across long passages which are almost completely lacking in meaning.[2] Words like *romantic, plastic, values, human, dead, sentimental, natural, vitality,* as used in art criticism, are strictly meaningless, in the sense that they not only do not point to any discoverable object, but are hardly even expected to do so by the reader. When one critic writes, "The outstanding feature of Mr X's work is its living quality", while another writes, "The immediately striking thing about Mr X's work is its peculiar deadness", the reader accepts this as a simple difference of opinion. If words like *black* and *white* were involved, instead of the jargon words *dead* and *living,* he would see at once that language was being used in an improper way. Many political words are similarly abused. The word *Fascism* has now no meaning except in so far as it signifies "something not desirable". The words *democracy, socialism, freedom, patriotic, realistic, justice,* have each of them several different meanings which cannot be reconciled with one another. In the case of a word like *democracy,* not only is there no agreed definition, but the attempt to make one is resisted from all sides. It is almost universally felt that when we call a country democratic we are praising it: consequently the defenders of every kind of régime claim that it is a democracy, and fear that they might have to stop using the word if it were tied down to any one meaning. Words of this kind are often used in a consciously dishonest way. That is, the person who uses them has his own private definition, but allows his hearer to think he means something quite different. Statements like *Marshal Pétain was a true patriot, The Soviet press is the freest in the world, The Catholic Church is opposed to persecution,* are almost always made with intent to deceive. Other words used in variable meanings, in most cases more or less dishonestly, are: *class, totalitarian, science, progressive, reactionary, bourgeois, equality.*

Now that I have made this catalogue of swindles and perversions, let me give another example of the kind of writing that they lead to. This

---

[2]Example: "Comfort's catholicity of perception and image, strangely Whitmanesque in range, almost the exact opposite in aesthetic compulsion, continues to evoke that trembling atmospheric accumulative hinting at a cruel, an inexorably serene timelessness . . . Wrey Gardiner scores by aiming at simple bullseyes with precision. Only they are not so simple, and through this contented sadness runs more than the surface bitter-sweet of resignation." *(Poetry Quarterly.)* [Author's footnote.]

time it must of its nature be an imaginary one. I am going to translate a passage of good English into modern English of the worst sort. Here is a well-known verse from *Ecclesiastes:*

> I returned, and saw under the sun, that the race is not to the swift, nor the battle to the strong, neither yet bread to the wise, nor yet riches to men of understanding, nor yet favour to men of skill; but time and chance happeneth to them all.

Here it is in modern English:

> Objective consideration of contemporary phenomena compels the conclusion that success or failure in competitive activities exhibits no tendency to be commensurate with innate capacity, but that a considerable element of the unpredictable must invariably be taken into account.

This is a parody, but not a very gross one. Exhibit 3, above, for instance, contains several patches of the same kind of English. It will be seen that I have not made a full translation. The beginning and ending of the sentence follow the original meaning fairly closely, but in the middle the concrete illustrations—race, battle, bread—dissolve into the vague phrase "success or failure in competitive activities". This had to be so, because no modern writer of the kind I am discussing—no one capable of using phrases like "objective consideration of contemporary phenomena"—would ever tabulate his thoughts in that precise and detailed way. The whole tendency of modern prose is away from concreteness. Now analyse these two sentences a little more closely. The first contains 49 words but only 60 syllables, and all its words are those of everyday life. The second contains 38 words of 90 syllables: 18 of its words are from Latin roots, and one from Greek. The first sentence contains six vivid images, and only one phrase ("time and chance") that could be called vague. The second contains not a single fresh, arresting phrase, and in spite of its 90 syllables it gives only a shortened version of the meaning contained in the first. Yet without a doubt it is the second kind of sentence that is gaining ground in modern English. I do not want to exaggerate. This kind of writing is not yet universal, and outcrops of simplicity will occur here and there in the worst-written page. Still, if you or I were told to write a few lines on the uncertainty of human fortunes, we should probably come much nearer to my imaginary sentence than to the one from *Ecclesiastes.*

As I have tried to show, modern writing at its worst does not consist in picking out words for the sake of their meaning and inventing images in order to make the meaning clearer. It consists in gumming together long strips of words which have already been set in order by someone else, and making the results presentable by sheer humbug. The attraction of this way of writing is that it is easy. It is easier—even quicker, once you have the habit—to say *In my opinion it is a not unjustifiable assumption that* than to say *I think.* If you use ready-made phrases, you not only don't have to hunt about for words; you also don't have to bother with the rhythms of your sentences, since these phrases are generally so arranged as to be more or less euphonious. When you are composing in a hurry—when you are dictating to a stenographer, for instance, or making a public speech—it is natural to fall into a pretentious, latinised style. Tags like *a consideration which we should do well to bear in mind* or *a conclusion to which all of us would readily assent* will save many a sentence from coming down with a bump. By using stale metaphors, similes and idioms, you save much mental effort, at the cost of leaving your meaning vague, not only for your reader but for yourself. This is the significance of mixed metaphors. The sole aim of a metaphor is to call up a visual image. When these images clash—as in *The Fascist octopus has sung its swan song, the jackboot is thrown into the melting-pot*—it can be taken as certain that the writer is not seeing a mental image of the objects he is naming; in other words he is not really thinking. Look again at the examples I gave at the beginning of this essay. Professor Laski (1) uses five negatives in 53 words. One of these is superfluous, making nonsense of the whole passage, and in addition there is the slip *alien* for akin, making further nonsense, and several avoidable pieces of clumsiness which increase the general vagueness. Professor Hogben (2) plays ducks and drakes with a battery which is able to write prescriptions, and, while disapproving of the everyday phrase *put up with,* is unwilling to look *egregious* up in the dictionary and see what it means. (3), if one takes an uncharitable attitude towards it, is simply meaningless: probably one could work out its intended meaning by reading the whole of the article in which it occurs. In (4) the writer knows more or less what he wants to say, but an accumulation of stale phrases chokes him like tea-leaves blocking a sink. In (5) words and meaning have almost parted company. People who write in this manner usually have a general emotional meaning—they dislike one thing and want to express solidarity with another—but they are not interested in the detail of what they are saying. A scrupulous writer, in every sentence that he writes, will ask himself at least four questions, thus: What am I trying to say? What words will express it? What image or idiom will make it clearer? Is this image fresh enough to have an effect? And he will probably ask himself two more: Could I put it more shortly? Have I said anything that is avoidably ugly? But you are not obliged to go to all this trouble. You can shirk it by simply throwing your mind open and letting the ready-made phrases come crowding in. They will construct your sentences for you—even think your thoughts for you, to a certain extent—and at need they will perform the important service of partially concealing your meaning even from yourself. It is at this point that the special connection between politics and the debasement of language becomes clear.

In our time it is broadly true that political writing is bad writing. Where it is not true, it will generally be found that the writer is some kind of rebel, expressing his private opinions, and not a "party line". Orthodoxy, of whatever colour, seems to demand a lifeless, imitative style. The political dialects to be found in pamphlets, leading articles, manifestos, White Papers and the speeches of Under-Secretaries do, of course, vary from party to party, but they are all alike in that one almost never finds in them a fresh, vivid, home-made turn of speech. When one watches some tired hack on the platform mechanically repeating the familiar phrases—*bestial atrocities, iron heel, blood-stained tyranny, free peoples of the world, stand shoulder to shoulder*—one often has a curious feeling that one is not watching a live human being but some kind of dummy: a feeling which suddenly becomes stronger at moments when the light catches the speaker's spectacles and turns them into blank discs which seem to have no eyes behind them. And this is not altogether fanciful. A speaker who uses that kind of phraseology has gone some distance towards turning himself into a machine. The appropriate noises are coming out of his larynx, but his brain is not involved as it would be if he were choosing his words for himself. If the speech he is making is one that he is accustomed to make over and over again, he may be almost unconscious of what he is saying, as one is when one utters the responses in church. And this reduced state of consciousness, if not indispensable, is at any rate favourable to political conformity.

In our time, political speech and writing are largely the defence of the indefensible. Things like the continuance of British rule in India, the Russian purges and deportations, the dropping of the atom bombs on Japan, can indeed be defended, but only by arguments which are too brutal for most people to face, and which do not square with the professed aims of political parties. Thus political language has to consist largely of euphemism, question-begging and sheer cloudy vagueness. Defenceless villages are bombarded from the air, the inhabitants driven out into the countryside, the cattle machine-gunned, the huts set on fire with incendiary bullets: this is called *pacification.* Millions of peasants are robbed of their farms and sent trudging along the roads with no more than they can carry: this is called *transfer of population* or *rectification of frontiers.* People are imprisoned for years without trial, or shot in the back of the neck or sent to die of scurvy in Arctic lumber camps: this is called *elimination of unreliable elements.* Such phraseology is needed if one wants to name things without calling up mental pictures of them. Consider for instance some comfortable English professor defending Russian totalitarianism. He cannot say outright, "I believe in killing off your opponents when you can get good results by doing so". Probably, therefore, he will say something like this:

> While freely conceding that the Soviet régime exhibits certain features which the humanitarian may be inclined to deplore, we must, I think, agree that a certain curtailment of the right to political opposition is an unavoidable concomitant of transitional periods, and that the rigours which the Russian people have been called upon to undergo have been amply justified in the sphere of concrete achievement.

The inflated style is itself a kind of euphemism. A mass of Latin words falls upon the facts like soft snow, blurring the outlines and covering up all the details. The great enemy of clear language is insincerity. When there is a gap between one's real and one's declared aims, one turns as it were instinctively to long words and exhausted idioms, like a cuttlefish squirting out ink. In our age there is no such thing as "keeping out of politics". All issues are political issues, and politics itself is a mass of lies, evasions, folly, hatred and schizophrenia. When the general atmosphere is bad, language must suffer. I should expect to find —this is a guess which I have not sufficient knowledge to verify—that the German, Russian and Italian languages have all deteriorated in the last ten or fifteen years, as a result of dictatorship.

But if thought corrupts language, language can also corrupt thought. A bad usage can spread by tradition and imitation, even among people who should and do know better. The debased language that I have been discussing is in some ways very convenient. Phrases like *a not unjustifiable assumption, leaves much to be desired, would serve no good purpose, a consideration which we should do well to bear in mind,* are a continuous temptation, a packet of aspirins always at one's elbow. Look back through this essay, and for certain you will find that I have again and again committed the very faults I am protesting against. By this morning's post I have received a pamphlet dealing with conditions in Germany. The author tells me that he "felt impelled" to write it. I open it at random, and here is almost the first sentence that I see: "(The Allies) have an opportunity not only of achieving a radical transformation of Germany's social and political structure in such a way as to avoid a nationalistic reaction in Germany itself, but at the same time of laying the foundations of a co-operative and unified Europe." You see, he "feels impelled" to write—feels, presumably, that he has something new to say—and yet his words, like cavalry horses answering the bugle, group themselves automatically into the familiar dreary pattern. This invasion of one's mind by ready-made phrases *(lay the foundations, achieve a radical transformation)* can only be prevented if one is constantly on guard against them, and every such phrase anaesthetises a portion of one's brain.

I said earlier that the decadence of our language is probably curable. Those who deny this would argue, if they produced an argument at all, that language merely reflects existing social conditions, and that we cannot influence its development by any direct tinkering with words and constructions. So far as the general tone or spirit of a language goes, this may be true, but it is not true in detail. Silly words and expressions have often disappeared, not through any evolutionary process but owing to the conscious action of a minority. Two recent examples were *explore every avenue* and *leave no stone unturned,* which were killed by the jeers of a few journalists. There is a long list of fly-blown metaphors which could similarly be got rid of if enough people would interest themselves in the job; and it should also be possible to laugh the *not un-* formation out of existence,[3] to reduce the amount of Latin and Greek in the average sentence, to drive out foreign phrases and strayed scientific words, and, in general, to make pretentiousness unfashionable. But all these are minor points. The defence of the English language implies more than this, and perhaps it is best to start by saying what it does *not* imply.

To begin with, it has nothing to do with archaism, with the salvaging

[3]One can cure oneself of the *not un-* formation by memorising this sentence: *A not unblack dog was chasing a not unsmall rabbit across a not ungreen field.* [Author's footnote.]

of obsolete words and turns of speech, or with the setting-up of a "standard English" which must never be departed from. On the contrary, it is especially concerned with the scrapping of every word or idiom which has outworn its usefulness. It has nothing to do with correct grammar and syntax, which are of no importance so long as one makes one's meaning clear, or with the avoidance of Americanisms, or with having what is called a "good prose style". On the other hand it is not concerned with fake simplicity and the attempt to make written English colloquial. Nor does it even imply in every case preferring the Saxon word to the Latin one, though it does imply using the fewest and shortest words that will cover one's meaning. What is above all needed is to let the meaning choose the word, and not the other way about. In prose, the worst thing one can do with words is to surrender to them. When you think of a concrete object, you think wordlessly, and then, if you want to describe the thing you have been visualising, you probably hunt about till you find the exact words that seem to fit it. When you think of something abstract you are more inclined to use words from the start, and unless you make a conscious effort to prevent it, the existing dialect will come rushing in and do the job for you, at the expense of blurring or even changing your meaning. Probably it is better to put off using words as long as possible and get one's meaning as clear as one can through pictures or sensations. Afterwards one can choose—not simply *accept*—the phrases that will best cover the meaning, and then switch round and decide what impression one's words are likely to make on another person. This last effort of the mind cuts out all stale or mixed images, all prefabricated phrases, needless repetitions, and humbug and vagueness generally. But one can often be in doubt about the effect of a word or a phrase, and one needs rules that one can rely on when instinct fails. I think the following rules will cover most cases:

i. Never use a metaphor, simile or other figure of speech which you are used to seeing in print.
ii. Never use a long word where a short one will do.
iii. If it is possible to cut a word out, always cut it out.
iv. Never use the passive where you can use the active.
v. Never use a foreign phrase, a scientific word or a jargon word if you can think of an everyday English equivalent.
vi. Break any of these rules sooner than say anything outright barbarous.

These rules sound elementary, and so they are, but they demand a deep change of attitude in anyone who has grown used to writing in the style now fashionable. One could keep all of them and still write bad English, but one could not write the kind of stuff that I quoted in those five specimens at the beginning of this article.

I have not here been considering the literary use of language, but merely language as an instrument for expressing and not for concealing or preventing thought. Stuart Chase and others have come near to claiming that all abstract words are meaningless, and have used this as a pretext for advocating a kind of political quietism. Since you don't know what Fascism is, how can you struggle against Fascism? One need not swallow such absurdities as this, but one ought to recognise that the present political chaos is connected with the decay of language, and that one can probably bring about some improvement by starting at the verbal end. If you simplify your English, you are freed from the worst follies of orthodoxy. You cannot speak any of the necessary dialects, and when you make a stupid remark its stupidity will be obvious, even to yourself. Political language—and with variations this is true of all political parties, from Conservatives to Anarchists—is designed to make lies sound truthful and murder respectable, and to give an appearance of solidity to pure wind. One cannot change this all in a moment, but one can at least change one's own habits, and from time to time one can even, if one jeers loudly enough, send some worn-out and useless phrase —some *jackboot, Achilles' heel, hotbed, melting pot, acid test, veritable inferno* or other lump of verbal refuse—into the dustbin where it belongs.

QUESTIONS FOR DISCUSSION

1. Orwell talks about the ways politics affects language and language affects politics. Selecting examples from current political speeches and writing, explain how the causality works in both directions.
2. In this article Orwell attacks the use of euphemisms, words that soften harsh realities and are employed by politicians in "defence of the indefensible." Discuss the use of euphemisms in other areas, such as in reference to the old, the poor, the uneducated, and the mentally weak or ill.
3. Orwell exhorts his readers to be careful of their language, to "put off using words as long as possible and get one's meaning as clear as one can through pictures and sensations." How might this be done?
4. Orwell ends his essay with a call for action. More specifically, what can students do to improve their English? How can teachers encourage better writing?
5. What would Orwell think of linguists who see language as the product of

culture? What would he think of the linguistic relativism that regards different dialects as equally legitimate? How would he regard the popular watchdogs of language who are always pointing out errors in grammar and usage?

6. Orwell sees political language as inevitably corrupting. Is politics the only institution whose use of language is corrupting? Can the languages of science and technology be corrupting too?

SUGGESTIONS FOR WRITING

1. Read over carefully the five passages of garbled English that Orwell quotes at the beginning of his essay. Rewrite them so that they make sense and meet Orwell's standards of clarity and directness.

2. Orwell claims that "political writing is bad writing." Find two political speeches, one by a public figure you admire and the other by one you do not; evaluate them according to Orwell's standards. Do you find that both are good writing, both are bad writing, or one is good and one bad? If you believe the one by the public figure you admired is the more effective speech, ask someone with different political sympathies to evaluate both speeches. What is that person's evaluation? How would you rewrite the poorly written speech?

3. To what extent does Orwell's own writing meet the criteria he suggests for good prose? Write an evaluation of his essay, using examples selected from his prose to illustrate whether he follows (or violates) the six rules he sets out at the end of it.

4. Find an example of what you consider good prose; draw on any area: politics, history, business, advertising, fiction, textbooks, research in your own field. Does your choice meet Orwell's standards? If it does, write an essay explaining what makes it good. If it does not, write an essay defending it on other grounds.

5. Find an example of what you consider poor prose, and rewrite it in a style you think Orwell would admire. Does it still say the same thing as the original? What differences in meaning do you detect? Show your rewrite and the original to an expert in the field and ask for a response.

6. Take a piece of writing you produced before you read Orwell's essay and revise it as you think Orwell would if he were doing it.

———————— ⇥»» ««⇤ ————————

Iridium Provides Clue to Dinosaurs' Extinction

REBECCA L. RAWLS

Certain scientific subjects have broad popular appeal, and perhaps none has more than the dinosaurs and anything having to do with them. The dinosaur halls of our museums are always thronged, and books about dinosaurs are among the most popular children's books. As a consequence any science writer would have an easy time popularizing the following causal argument: New evidence points to a most spectacular cause of the extinction of the dinosaurs and many other forms of life, an extinction that defines the shift between the Cretaceous and Tertiary eras in the earth's history.

    Rebecca L. Rawls, a science writer for Chemical and Engineering News, *did not have to glamorize her subject to the point of watering it down or falsifying it, as sometimes happens in popularizations. She could count on her readers having a special interest in the role played by a rare earth element in one of the greatest "whodunit" mysteries in science.*

Sixty-five million years ago, something happened on this planet to make it uninhabitable to a great many of its plants and animals. Estimates range as high as 75% of the species then living suddenly became extinct. Geologically speaking, this happened all at once, though whether it took a year or two or several thousand years is unclear.

    Chief among the animals that died out were probably the dinosaurs, which had dominated the planet for the previous 100 million years. But other important forms died out as well—the great marine reptiles, the flying reptiles, marine species like the ammonites and belemnites, and most of the marine phyto- and zooplankton. The event marks the boundary for geologists between the earlier Cretaceous period and the later Tertiary one.

    Some species survived. Among these were many of the land plants, organisms of the shallow coastal seas, and small land animals, including the early mammals—ratlike creatures whose progeny eventually came to replace the dinosaurs as the dominant animal species on the planet.

    This much is clear from the geological record. What the record doesn't say, at least very clearly, is what happened to cause this sudden mass extinction of so many different kinds of living things.

Theories, of course, abound. Over the years, the extinctions have been blamed on everything from destruction of the planet's ozone layer, which allowed too much ultraviolet light to reach the ground, to a spillover of relatively fresh water from the Arctic Ocean into the other oceans thereby changing their salinity so much that plants and animals could not survive, to a collision of the Earth with almost any heavenly body, including a supernova, a comet, or an asteroid.

The problem with almost all these theories is that they rest on very little physical data. In what seems like almost conscious perverseness, there is a gap in the rock strata that corresponds exactly with the Cretaceous-Tertiary boundary in most samples that have been examined. Whatever killed off so many life forms on the planet apparently washed away its own record in most places.

However, there is now a new burst of activity among earth scientists who study this event, and at least three different groups have published new and closely related theories within the past month. All are based on new physical evidence that has been pieced together by a team of geologists, physicists, and nuclear chemists at the University of California, Berkeley, and Lawrence Berkeley Laboratory.

The team is headed by geology professor Walter Alverez of the University of California, Berkeley, and includes his father, physics Nobelist and emeritus professor Luis W. Alverez of Lawrence Berkeley Laboratory, and two nuclear chemists, Frank Asaro and Helen V. Michel, also at LBL.

What the Berkeley group has found is an unusually high concentration of iridium in clay sediments at the Cretaceous-Tertiary boundary taken from three very different locations—one in Italy, one in Denmark, and one in New Zealand. In addition, an independent team of European geologists and geochemists has found a similar iridium anomaly at a fourth site in southeastern Spain.

This iridium, the researchers contend, is not of Earthly origin, but came from some other body within the solar system that struck the Earth at the same time as the Cretaceous extinction. They assume that these events are more than coincidental, and thus claim to have found some of the first solid evidence that an extraterrestrial catastrophe caused the end of the Cretaceous period.

How the Berkeley group discovered the anomaly is an interesting piece of scientific detective work. They were looking, not for evidence for the extraterrestrial origin of the end of the Cretaceous period, but for a better geologic clock with which to measure just how simultaneous the mass extinctions of that period were.

Iridium, along with the other platinum group elements—platinum, osmium, and rhodium—is much less abundant in the Earth's crust and upper mantle than it is in meteorites and other extraterrestrial solar system material. These elements are too heavy to be formed by any of the reactions that are taking place in the solar system now, and all these elements were once uniformly distributed throughout the solar system because of mixing of the protosolar gas cloud. On the larger masses of the solar system, such as Earth, gravitational attraction has long since pulled essentially all of these heavy elements into the core of the planet, leaving the outer layers extremely depleted in the elements. Small solar bodies—asteroids, comets, and the like—have weaker gravitational fields and have not become stratified in this way. Thus, these bodies have roughly 1000 times the iridium concentration found in the Earth's crust.

So complete is the stratification of the Earth's primordial iridium thought to be, that several earth scientists have suggested that all the iridium found in the Earth's crust had its source in dust that accumulates more or less constantly as meteors ablate in the Earth's atmosphere. Berkeley scientists proposed to use the concentration of iridium in the clay layer between the Cretaceous and Tertiary periods as an indication of how long this boundary period lasted. They selected iridium for their study because it can be analyzed fairly easily at low levels by neutron activation analysis. The other platinum group elements are more difficult to determine by this method.

What they found was much too much iridium in the boundary layer sediments. The first samples, taken near Gubbio in northern Italy, show 30 times the concentration of iridium in the boundary layer than in layers immediately above or below it. Analyses of 27 other elements across the boundary layer show less than a doubling of concentrations compared with the average behavior of rare-earth elements across this layer.

To test whether they had detected a unique concentration of iridium or a more universal feature of the Cretaceous-Tertiary boundary region, the scientists analyzed clay sediments from two other locations, one from Højerup Church, about 50 km south of Copenhagen, and the other near Woodside Creek in New Zealand.

The New Zealand samples show a 20-fold increase in iridium concentration in the boundary layer. The Danish samples show a 160-fold increase in iridium and substantial differences in the concentrations of 33 other elements at the boundary layer. Except for iridium and magnesium, which is depleted in the boundary layer, these differences can be satisfactorily explained by ordinary leaching and weathering processes that would be found in ocean bottom sediments, the Berkeley group argues. The iridium levels, however, like those in the Italian and New Zealand samples, are much too high to be explained by ordinary sedimentation.

Based on these findings, the scientists propose that the iridium found at the boundary layer did not come from ordinary accumulation of meteoric dust, but instead represents an extraordinary influx of extraterrestrial iridium. They propose that this came from the collision of the Earth with an asteroid about 10 km in diameter. The collision created an impact crater, and dust from the crater and the asteroid itself was thrown up into the stratosphere where it spread around the globe, much like the dust that was found in the atmosphere all around the planet when the Indonesian volcano Krakatoa erupted in 1883. The dust from the asteroid collision reduced the amount of sunlight reaching the Earth for several years, and many photosynthesizing plants and the food chains they support where thus wiped out.

The Berkeley group explains the selective destruction of plants and animals at the end of the Cretaceous by saying that the seeds of land plants would likely survive a few years of reduced solar influx, even if the parent plants died out.

Likewise, small animals that could feed on seeds and decaying vegetation could survive and organisms in the shallow coastal waters might even flourish, since they would be receiving a great increase of vegetable matter from the continental rivers as terrestrial plants died. Larger land animals, however, and those of the deep ocean would lose their food source and perish.

The object that struck the Earth and brought with it such an influx of iridium came from the solar system and not from more distant space, the scientists say. This conclusion is based on analysis of the isotope ratios of iridium in the boundary clays which match, within experimental error, those of iridium found elsewhere on the planet. This is evidence that the element was formed in the same nuclear reactions that formed the Earth's iridium. Matter from outside the solar system, such as that of a nearby supernova, for example, would almost certainly have a different isotope ratio, they argue.

A sense of the reaction of the rest of the earth science community to the Berkeley discovery is conveyed by Harvard geologist-biologist Stephen Jay Gould, writing in *Natural History:* "I care little whether the asteroidal scenario itself is correct," he says. "The remarkable aspect of the Alverezes' work—the part that has produced buzzing excitement among all my colleagues, rather than the ho-hum that generally accompanies yet another vain speculation—lies in their raw data on enhanced iridium at the very top of the Cretaceous . . . For the first time we now have the hope (indeed, the expectation) that evidence for extraterrestrial causes of mass extinction might exist in the geologic record. The old paradox that we must root against such plausible theories because we know no way to obtain evidence for them has disappeared."

Indeed, the Alverez findings have already led to at least two other laboratories' advancing theories to explain the Cretaceous extinctions based on the iridium anomaly. One group, that of Dutch geologist J. Smit of the Geological Institute in Amsterdam and J. Hertogen, a Belgian geochemist, proposes the same explanation as the Berkeley scientists—a meteorite of 5 to 15 km in diameter striking the Earth—but does so on the basis of independent evidence from sedimentation sample analysis from a site in southeastern Spain.

Smit and Hertogen have studied the Cretaceous-Tertiary boundary region in samples from Caracava, Spain, using radiochemical x-ray counting methods and neutron activation analysis. They find inexplicably high levels of iridium (450 times normal) and osmium (150 times normal) in the boundary layer samples. As the Berkeley group did with their Danish samples, they also find many other elements in very elevated concentration at the boundary layer, among them arsenic (110 times normal), cobalt, nickel, selenium, and antimony (all more than 10 times normal). However, with the exception of iridium and osmium, these elevated concentrations could have been derived from terrestrial rocks, they say. Osmium, like iridium, is a platinum group metal whose concentration would be expected to be increased greatly if a large meteorite struck the Earth.

Smit and Hertogen compared osmium isotopic ratios in their samples and found, as the Berkeley group did for iridium, that the ratio was the same as for terrestrial osmium within 0.1% experimental error.

The findings of the Berkeley group and Smit and Hertogen are entirely complementary, Walter Alverez says, each providing further evidence that the abnormally high concentration of platinum group metals at the Cretaceous-Tertiary boundary is a world-wide phenomenon. And the isotopic analysis of two different platinum elements also reinforces the idea that these higher levels of platinum group elements came from somewhere within the solar system.

A somewhat different explanation for the mass extinctions at the end of the Cretaceous period has been offered by Kenneth J. Hsü of the Geological Institute of the Swiss Federal Institute of Technology in Zurich. He postulates that it was not an asteroid but a comet that struck the Earth 65 million years ago.

Hsü suggests that a comet about the size of Halley's comet (about 10^{18} grams) would account for the increased iridium concentrations at the Cretaceous-Tertiary boundary in exactly the same way that the Alverezes' asteroid does. Its effect on planetary life, however, would be quite different.

Hsü first assumes that, since no crater has ever been discovered that corresponds to this collision, the comet must have fallen into the ocean. Much of the comet's energy would thus go into heating the ocean, rather than into forming a crater and throwing dust into the atmosphere. Further energy would likely be lost as heat as the comet passed through the Earth's atmosphere before reaching the ocean. Thus, the atmosphere may have been heated as much as 10° to 20° C and the ocean as much as 1° to 5° C. This latter heating is consistent with certain oxygen isotope data previously noticed in samples of ocean sediment at the Cretaceous-Tertiary boundary.

It is the likely chemical consequences of a comet's striking the Earth that Hsü finds particularly interesting. Although these must be somewhat speculative, since the chemical composition of comets is not well established, he bases his predictions on a well-known model in which comets are thought to be icy, solid bodies containing a large amount of carbon dioxide and carbon monoxide and about 10% cyanide. At this concentration, a 10^{18}-gram comet would contain enough cyanide to give the oceans a concentration of 0.1 ppm to 3 ppm, depending on the degree of mixing taking place.

The carbon monoxide and carbon dioxide from the comet temporarily would disturb the carbonate equilibrium in the oceans, Hsü suggests, and would alter the isotopic composition of the calcareous sediments in the oceans. This isotope change also has been observed in some ocean sediments, he says.

By Hsü's model, the plants and animals of the Cretaceous period could have been killed in three ways: large land animals by atmospheric heating, marine organisms by cyanide poisoning, and calcareous marine plankton by increased dissolved carbon dioxide disturbing the carbonate equilibrium in the seawater.

Strong evidence for any of the theories that involve collision of the Earth with a heavenly body would be to locate the crater the collision caused, if it still exists, Hsü says. Even more fundamental, says Alverez, is to locate more sites where the sedimentation record is intact across the Cretaceous-Tertiary boundary and discover whether the platinum group elements are always anomalously high at this boundary. Deepsea drilling projects are already looking for more sites where this boundary is intact, he says, so further data may soon be available.

Already the variation in iridium concentrations at various sites has raised some questions in the minds of some critics of an extraterrestrial explanation for the Cretaceous extinctions. A 10-km asteroid accounts nicely for the 20- to 30-fold increase in iridium found in New Zealand and Italian samples, but some sort of concentrating mechanism seems to be needed, or a larger asteroid, to explain the iridium concentrations found in Denmark and Spain.

For his part, Alverez says his group is still in a position of observing the pattern of iridium at the Cretaceous-Tertiary boundary. "It's premature to say it's wrong to have more iridium in one place than another," he says. "Right now, we are just looking to see what is there. We have no preconceived level that should be present."

QUESTIONS FOR DISCUSSION

1. What exactly does the iridium prove? What assumptions about the creation and distribution of matter in the solar system and on earth have to be accepted before the iridium becomes a "clue"? What role does coincidence play?
2. Reconstruct the chain of causes between the meteorite and the late Cretaceous extinction. What is the weakest link in this chain? How has the selective survival of some species been explained?
3. What is the importance of a lack of other explanations for the high concentration of iridium?
4. Why does Stephen Jay Gould say he cares little for whether the asteroidal scenario is in itself correct?
5. The interplay between theory and evidence is complex, but which must come first? Did the Alvarez group need a theory in order to find significance in their iridium data?
6. Why would this subject appeal to an audience of chemists and chemical engineers? What evidence do you see of accommodation to that particular audience? How could the subject have been popularized for a wider audience?

SUGGESTIONS FOR WRITING

1. The biggest piece of evidence (quite literally) missing from the case for a meteorite-caused extinction is the impact crater. However, an ingenious explanation has been put forward involving Iceland and plate tectonics. Investigate this subject and write a complete causal argument for lay readers about the meteorite-caused extinction, pulling together all the best evidence and theorizing.

2. Or read the dissenting opinions, particularly those from paleobotanists who claim that the meteorite-caused extinction (working through the agency of dust in the atmosphere and reduced sunlight) does not explain the survival of certain plant species across the Cretaceous-Tertiary boundary. Summarize their arguments in an essay refuting Rawls.

3. In the last decade or so the reptilian, cold-blooded nature of the dinosaurs has been questioned and theories have been advanced proposing that some species were in fact warm-blooded, like mammals. (For a popular account see Adrian J. Desmond's *The Hot-blooded Dinosaurs.*) For an audience predisposed to the meteorite theory, argue that a redefinition of the dinosaurs, the dominant species of the time, may either weaken or strengthen the case.

4. Compare Rawls' account of the iridium evidence with either the original scientific papers from Alvarez's group or with other popular accounts in science magazines or more general publications. What differences do you notice among the accounts? How is this topic made interesting to general readers?

5. Write a popularized account of a scientific model explaining the causes of a phenomenon or event such as acid rain, the 1983 drought caused by El Niño, the frequent mudslides in California, or any other at least primarily natural event. Try to use the chain of causes and make each link clear to your inexpert readers.

6. Write an evaluation argument (see the next section for a description and examples of this type) in which you defend the value of research aimed at purely specuative questions such as the causes of the late Cretaceous extinction. Aim your argument at an audience of newspaper readers.

————————— ⇝⤐ ⬿⇜ —————————

How Women's Diets Reflect Fear of Power

KIM CHERNIN

The following article is an excerpt from the author's book, The Obsession:
Reflections on the Tyranny of Slenderness. *The article appeared originally in
the* New York Times Magazine, *a publication directed at highly literate
readers. Kim Chernin probes for the social and psychological causes of a
phenomenon so widespread it almost escapes notice: women's obsessive
pursuit of slenderness.*

*There have been many articles on such eating disorders as anorexia
nervosa and bulimia, but few see these aberrations as extreme forms of that
more widespread eating disorder known as compulsive dieting. To look for
the causes of something so widespread requires a broad cultural and historical
perspective.*

*As you read Chernin's characterization of attitudes toward women, their
bodies, their status, their power, ask yourself how these general assumptions
can operate as motives for individual behavior.*

The locker room of the tennis club. A tall woman enters, removes her
towel; she throws it across a bench, faces herself squarely in the mirror,
climbs on the scale, looks down.

"I knew it," she mutters.

"Up or down?" I ask, hoping to suggest that there might be lands
and cultures where gaining weight would not be considered a disaster.

"Two pounds," she says, ignoring the suggestion. "Two pounds!"

Then she turns, grabs the towel and swings out at the mirror,
smashing it violently, the towel splattering water over the glass.

"Fat pig!" she shouts at her image in the mirror. "You fat, fat pig!"

The Harvard Medical School Health Letter estimates that some 20
million Americans are on a "serious" diet at any given moment. According to the sociologist Natalie Allon, these dieters are spending $10 billion
dollars a year in the process, much of it at hundreds of spas and health
farms that charge from $185 to $3,000 a week. Diet books enrich their
authors—"Never-Say-Diet Book," for example, out just a year, has spent
35 weeks of that time on the best-seller list and sold 560,000 copies.

Two facts make the current obsession with weight extraordinary. One is the scope of it. Throughout history, there have been dieters, including Roman matrons, who were willing to starve themselves. But there has never been a period when such large numbers of people have spent so much time, money and emotional energy on their weight. Weight Watchers, for example, holds more than 12,000 individual classes every week and has enrolled 13 million members since its founding in 1963.

The other extraordinary aspect of today's diet phenomenon is the degree to which it is focused on women. The nation has its share of fat men, of course, and many American men seek to lose excess weight. But interviews with physicians and psychologists make it clear that the truly obsessive dieter is almost inevitably female. Representatives of diet organizations acknowledge that 95 percent of their members are women. According to Dr. Hilde Bruch, professor emeritus of psychiatry at Houston's Baylor College of Medicine and an expert on eating disorders, more than 90 percent of those suffering from anorexia nervosa, a personality disorder that leads to self-starvation, are female. Bulimia, a condition in which periods of heavy eating are followed by self-induced vomiting, is almost entirely limited to women.

Why? Why have so many millions of American women, over the last decade, become so concerned about their weight? The subject has not received much attention, except on a superficial level. It deserves better.

There is, for example, the medical explanation: Women diet because of the long-proclaimed correlation between obesity and ill health. Yet that fails to cover the intense upset many women experience because of two or three pounds of overweight. And in any event, medical opinion has changed dramatically in recent years. Dr. Reubin Andres, clinical director of Baltimore's National Institute on Aging, has found, for example, based on his review of 40 world wide studies involving six million people, that "there's something about being moderately overweight that's good for you."

The psychological explanation tends to be shallow, to trivialize the problem, as though women go on periodic binges of eating and dieting simply to relieve the standard frustrations and unhappinesses of their lives. "Food is so fundamental," writes James Hillman, former director of studies at the C. G. Jung Institute of Zurich, "that it is astounding to realize the neglect of food and eating in depth psychology."

Even more astounding, perhaps, is the neglect of the modern woman's obsession with weight by today's feminist leaders—this despite the fact that the weight-watching movement and the women's liberation movement both developed during the 1960's. Indeed, in my view, this obsession involves some of the most fundamental questions feminists themselves have raised—core issues of women's identity, of the child's relationship to the mother, of the society's response to women's claims for power.

My experience of obsession began in 1957, when I was 17 years old. I was on vacation in Berlin, sitting at the table with my German landlords. I remember the day vividly: The wind was blowing; the curtain lifted on the window and a beam of sunlight crossed the room and stopped at the spout of the teapot. I felt that I was about to remember something and then, unaccountably, I was moved to tears. But I did not cry, I ate. Then, while no one was looking, I stuffed two rolls into my pocket, stood up from the table and left the room. Once out of the house, I began running, from street stall to street stall, buying cones of roasted chestnuts and pounds of chocolate.

Today, I can sit down at a meal without computing calories. My body, my hunger, my food, the things that once seemed like enemies, now have begun to look like friends. But for 20 years after that day in Berlin, compulsive eating was my routine, alternating with an equally compulsive addiction to dieting. My weight ranged from 90 to 130 pounds, and I became familiar with all those extravagant hopes and dismal failures experienced by every woman who tries to diet. Until I changed.

There were two moments of breakthrough. The first occurred when I was 26 years old. I had awakened around midnight, wondering how I could possibly be hungry, since I had eaten a great deal that day. Yet when I opened the refrigerator, I realized almost immediately that I wasn't interested; in fact, I wasn't really hungry. I was actually restless, frightened and confused. I didn't know if I wanted to continue at the university, if I wanted to marry the man who wanted to marry me, if I would be able to earn a living. I understood that food was not what I was hungering for.

Many of life's emotions—from loneliness to rage, from a love of life to a first falling in love—can be felt as appetite. And some would explain the obsession with weight in these easy, familiar terms. But there are deeper levels of understanding to plumb. That night, for example, standing in front of the refrigerator, I realized that my hunger was for larger things, for identity, for creativity, for power, for a meaningful place in society. The hunger most women feel, which drives them to eat more than they need, is fed by the evolution and expression of self.

My second moment of insight into the meaning of this obsession occurred almost 10 years later. I was again lying in bed. My attention was vaguely focused upon my round body. I fantasized my body's transformation to a consummate loveliness, the flesh trimmed away, stomach flat, thighs like those of the adolescent boy I had seen that day running in the park.

Such fantasies of transformation had occupied me often before, but this time I recognized that they were prompted by a bitter contempt for the female nature of my own body. The physical ideal for a woman in America today, I realized, was a man's body. The very curves and softness I had been trying to diet away were the natural qualities of a woman's body. Hips rounding, belly curved, thighs too large for an adolescent boy—what had driven me to deny this evidence of my woman's body?

Most Americans define their degree of "overweight" on the basis of those charts that hang on doctors' walls. In 1959, one of the most widely used of the charts was published by the Metropolitan Life Insurance Company. The tables of desirable weights for different heights, ages and builds were based upon data gathered by 26 insurance companies. The same data led experts to conclude that there was a correlation between excess weight and various chronic illnesses, particularly heart disease. Since then, it has become routine for physicians to tell us to take off those 10 or 15 pounds that exceeded the appropriate figure on the chart. "You'll look better," they said. "You'll feel better. And it's healthier."

Today, experts have their doubts. Says Dr. Andres, of the National Institute on Aging: "Those charts on doctors' walls are not desirable if you want to live longer." In fact, the insurance companies will be bringing out new charts within the next few months. The companies acknowledge that the weight guidelines will shift upward, but they are not telling by how much. Some researchers, including Dr. Andres, believe that the norms should rise by 10 percent.

The correlation between obesity—a condition generally defined as 35 percent or more above average body weight—and heart disease has been strongly challenged. Stacey C. FitzSimmons, of the Department of Epidemiology at the University of California at Berkeley, has reviewed more than 60 studies that support the correlation. She concludes that the findings, with few exceptions, are "fragmentary, inconsistent and contradictory" because of severe methodological problems. One example: The data assembled by the various insurance groups, did not take into account such variables as use of tobacco, exercise or socioeconomic status. Moreover, Miss FitzSimmons claims that no distinction was made between being overweight and being obese, a failure all too common in the medical literature.

In 1980, The Journal of the American Medical Association published the results of a 24-year study of 5,000 men and women in Framingham, Mass. The researchers found that the greatest risk to the health of those studied, as far as weight was concerned, was among the very lean. A person who was more than 10 percent below average body weight faced the greatest danger of suffering from heart disease. The next greatest risk was among people 35 percent above average body weight.

Dr. George Mann, investigator for the United States Department of Health and Human Services, has written in the New England Journal of Medicine: "There is little to support the widespread dogma of health education programs that regard obesity as a cause of high blood pressure." He also cautioned that weight reduction "has rarely been shown to be a useful treatment of any of the chronic diseases."

All of which does not mean, however, that obesity is a desirable state, nor should it suggest that we now understand all the medical effects of being overweight. Researchers continue to have trouble distinguishing association from causation. There is disagreement not only about what one's optimum weight should be but even about how best to measure body weight—some, for example, would ignore the scale and measure skin-fold thickness. According to Dr. Frederick H. Epstein, an epidemiologist at the University of Zurich, recent findings seem once again to establish a definite relationship between obesity and high blood-cholesterol levels—yet not between obesity and coronary illness.

This much seems clear. By and large, an extra 10 pounds beyond the figure on the old insurance-company chart is not harmful, and it may even be good for you. The weight obsession of the modern American woman cannot be dismissed as simply a medical issue.

The woman who lies in bed of a morning and counts over the number of calories she ate the night before, wondering whether her body has added substance to itself at the expense of her will, is actually pursuing a line of philosophical inquiry. The duality of mind and body has occupied scholars for ages. And for all their differences on other issues, the ancient Greeks, Hebrews and Buddhists agreed about this:

The mind is noble, close to God, and the body is lowly and ignoble, to be controlled by the mind.

Of course, we strive for a balance—the old Greek standard of a healthy mind in a healthy body. And many a woman who rises early, drinks a glass of protein liquid and jogs out to play tennis is living out that ideal, in tune with the modern emphasis on sports and diet. There are, however, many thousands of American women who perform those same activities for very different reasons. Sports and diet have taken over their lives. In their obsession with weight, they are alienated from bodies they perceive to be ugly. They are driven by the compulsion to impose their will upon these offending bodies.

Signs of the dualist quandary can be seen in virtually every weight-loss program. The publicity brochure for Lean Line Inc., for example, shows an arrow pointing to a woman's forehead and prominently displays the company's motto: "Mind Over Matter." Among women who have become obsessive about their weight, this idea is experienced as a contempt for the body.

"Little by little," one woman told me, "I began to be aware that the pounds I was trying to 'melt away' were my own flesh. These 'ugly pounds' which filled me with so much hatred were my body." The very language in which the authors of books on diet address their readers reveals how little we have overcome the repressive and fearful attitudes that guided our forebears. "You are sentenced to death row in a prison of your own adipose tissues," says a typical diet book in rhetoric reminiscent of Puritan preachers of the fire-and-brimstone school.

For the obsessive dieter, then, overweight is a philosophical, moral issue. The society may seek to trivialize the problem, we may snicker at cartoons of fat women, but it is far from a laughing matter—for the afflicted woman or for society, itself. The phenomenon raises two basic questions: Why has the age-old ambivalence about the human body focused upon the female body? And why has the obsession with weight assumed such prominence in our own time?

Psychological thought has always paid due attention to the mother's body. Erich Neumann, for example, the Jungian scholar, described the great-mother archetype and the enormous significance her body holds for the child's cultural and psychic life. Melanie Klein, the late pioneer child psychoanalyst, claimed that the early super-ego, the beginnings of conscience, develops when the child learns to control the rage he feels upon being weaned from the mother's breast.

Few of us have very clear memories of our earliest years, but it is not difficult to imagine the great power and magical force a woman's body must once have had for each of us as an infant. In a childhood typical of our culture, the mother is experienced as a great presence. And yet, as the Rutgers psychologist Dorothy Dinnerstein argues in "The Mermaid and the Minotaur," it is toward this same maternal body that our first serious exercise of will and struggle for control is directed.

Here we have another kind of ambivalence, not philosophical but physical and elemental. We feel the warmth and comfort of our mother's flesh; we feel awe at the very quantities of it, at our mother's size and power; we feel terror because of our own helplessness relative to her size and power.

Different societies react differently to the mother's body. The anthropologist Margaret Mackenzie has long studied the attitudes of various cultures. In Western Samoa, she found that the women tended to gain weight with each pregnancy. By middle age, they were by our standards distinctly fat. But being fat, Dr. Mackenzie says, is not regarded as a problem in Samoa.

Our culture has another kind of response to the awesome girth and power of woman that we experienced in our infancy. We have strong, ambivalent feelings about the relationship between a woman's power and her size, and they are reflected in our dislike for large, fleshy women.

Thus the male-dominated culture calls for slender women, unconsciously seeking to limit the symbolic physical expression of their power. And women themselves accept this tyranny of slenderness not only in submission to the male but because of their own ambivalence about their bodies.

As long as our culture maintains its traditional, male-centered balance, there may be some limited variation in the acceptable weight of women. At the turn of the century, for example, the prevailing mood favored some excess weight, and the fashions in clothing were—as usual —a clear reflection of the psychological state of the culture. Our grandmothers were permitted to wear flowing clothes, cut on the bias, to complement their ample hips.

In the 1920's, a shift in fashion signified the arrival of a major cultural change. The suffragette movement was approaching the culmination of its efforts to obtain the vote for women. Suddenly, women were supposed to look like boys. They bound their breasts and bobbed their hair.

When women are clearly subordinate, when they are not seeking to change their social status, men seem free to delight in them as physical beings. At such a time, voluptuous women may be welcome. But in an age when women assert their claim to power and autonomy, men have a different response. The culture calls for fashions that reflect a distinct male fear of a mature woman's power, particularly as it expresses itself through a woman's large body, with its capacity to remind men of a time when they depended upon a woman for their very survival.

Moreover, these new, boyish fashions are welcomed by women, for a variety of mostly unconscious, psychological reasons. By physically denying their womanness, by making themselves smaller, they seek to appease the male. They also express their own childhood hostilities toward their mother's abundant body. And finally, by taking on the angularity of a male, they are symbolically asking for the social rights, such as autonomy, that are traditionally reserved for men—much as George Sand wore male attire in order to move freely in masculine society.

On the afternoon of Sept. 7, 1968, picketers marched around the Atlantic City Boardwalk outside Convention Hall to protest the Miss America contest that was taking place inside. The demonstrators, who belonged, as one newspaper reported, "to what they called the Women's Liberation Movement," set down a huge "freedom trash can" and threw into it bras and girdles and curlers and false eyelashes and wigs. The posters they carried deplored "the degrading mindless-boob-girlie symbol" of Miss America and stated that the only "free" woman is one "no longer enslaved by ludicrous beauty standards." They were declaring war on the dictates of fashion.

Yet, in the years that followed, feminist theorists failed to make any serious effort to focus upon the esthetic of slenderness as a similar oppression of women. That failure is particularly ironic because the two decades that witnessed the growth and development of the feminist movement were also the period when fashion was proclaiming a new ideal of feminine beauty, an ideal that was boyish and childlike. It was also a period of revolution in the attitude of women toward food.

During the 1960's, we suddenly became aware of a startling increase in the incidence of anorexia nervosa. It primarily involved young girls who, as Dr. Hilde Bruch puts it, "willingly undergo the ordeal of starvation, even to the point of death." Moreover, within the last five years, she has seen a dramatic rise in the number of women afflicted in their late 20's. During the 1970's, we became aware of another medical

phenomenon: bulimia, sometimes known as bulimarexia. Marlene Boskind-White and William White, the husband-and-wife team of psychologists who began to study the condition in 1974, define it as "a
gorging, purging syndrome." Periods of extreme gluttony are followed
by laxative abuse and self-induced vomiting. Marlene Boskind-White
estimates that there are "tens of thousands of American women" who
suffer from this condition. She knows of few males who are so afflicted.

The last two decades have seen an amazing change in the society's
standards for the size of women. In 1959, when Marilyn Monroe made
the film "Some Like It Hot," she was voluptuous, as large as a woman
in a painting by Renoir. For those of us who fell in love with her then
and yearned, as adolescent girls, to look like her, that film today is a
revelation. She was, by modern standards, fat.

Now, the fashion model Kristine Oulman sets the standard for
women's beauty. Her image has been on the cover of *New York* magazine. She poses for photographs in the traditional seductive postures that
sell consumer goods in our culture.

We get to see a television program about Kristine that takes us
behind the scenes. We see her in a room filled with people who are
combing her, making her up, preparing her to wear the latest in sophisticated clothing. When their labors are done, we see the result: a preado-
lescent girl, with slender arms and shoulders, undeveloped breasts and
hips and thighs, whose body has been covered in sexy clothes, whose face
has been painted with a false allure and whose eyes imitate a sexuality
she has, by her own confession, never experienced. Kristine is 13 years
old.

And this is the message fashion conveys, the lesson that society
teaches, as to what a mature woman should attempt to look like. A
woman who wishes to conform to her culture's ideal, in this age of
feminist assertion, will not be large, mature, voluptuous, strong or powerful. She, who has the knowledge of life and birth, is to make herself
look like an adolescent girl if she wishes to appease her culture's anxiety
about female power.

During the last two decades, our society has witnessed the emergence of two significant movements among women. Because of the
women's liberation movement and the weight-watching movement, the
question of how large a woman is permitted to be has come to occupy
our lives in both a literal and a metaphorical form. We have heard much
about the metaphorical side; it is past time that we gave serious attention

to the implications of our very literal obsession with women's weight and size.

There are qualities about a woman's body that are natural. It is natural for her body to grow fuller before the menstrual cycle, taking on water and rounding itself out as if passing through a pregnancy, eating more food to sustain body and emotions. It is natural for women to grow larger with the body's knowledge of life and of birth, for the hips to be larger and the breasts heavier after bearing children. As years pass, it is natural for a softness to come to the flesh. Yet millions of women are compelled to conquer the nature in their bodies, and we should know why.

A woman obsessed with the size of her body, who wishes to make her breasts and belly smaller and less apparent, may be expressing the fact that she feels uncomfortable being female in this culture.

A woman obsessed with the size of her appetite, who wishes to control her hungers and urges, may be expressing the fact that she has been taught to regard her emotional life, her passions and "appetites," as dangerous, requiring control and careful monitoring.

A woman obsessed with the reduction of her flesh may be revealing the fact that she is alienated from a natural source of female power and has not been allowed to develop a reverential feeling for her body.

This social malaise, this tyranny of slenderness, is expressed in unhealthy dieting, in ever-more-widespread eating disorders, in the dictates of fashion. For millions of women, it is a cause of unremitting pain and shame. And it cannot be obliterated unless we address ourselves to resolving some of the most basic conflicts of our culture.

QUESTIONS FOR DISCUSSION

1. Like many of the essays in this section, this causal argument begins with a brief CP argument establishing the existence of the trend whose causes are being investigated. Why is this a common opening gambit in causal argument?

2. Kim Chernin is interested in the causes of a widespread and general phenomenon, yet personal experience and anecdote become an important and poignant kind of evidence. Why?

3. As a preliminary stage in your comprehending this argument, try to build a causal model from it. What are the main causes of women's obsessive dieting? How are they related to each other? If the causes are abstract and

impersonal cultural forces, how do they reach down to the individual? What, in other words, is agency?

4. What role do men have in women's dieting, according to this argument?

5. What is the role of the women's movement in the dieting obsession? Is it what you would expect?

6. What kind of expert opinion does Chernin use to bolster her argument? What does her use of these authorities reveal about her estimation of her audience?

SUGGESTIONS FOR WRITING

1. Write an essay for your classmates in which you compare the standards of feminine beauty in any two eras (or even decades). You might look at old movie or fashion magazines. Consider what might have caused some of the changes. Do standards of male attractiveness fluctuate in the same way?

2. What is the current standard of beauty for women? For men? What combination of factors has brought it about? Write an article whose purpose is to defend or criticize that standard.

3. If you do not find Chernin's account of the causes of neurotic dieting completely convincing, what causes do you think she has left out? Is her inital premise about the cultural ideal of thinness incorrect? Address your response to Chernin.

4. Do a survey among your dieting friends about their motives. If their reasons are different from those offered by Chernin, would she consider them refutation of her argument? Write up your results and consider your essay either a confirmation or a refutation of Chernin's.

5. Is there a parallel pursuit of thinness among men? How would Chernin explain it? How would you? Direct your essay at readers of a men's magazine, like *Esquire* or *Gentleman's Quarterly.*

6. Try your hand at predicting the cultural ideal of beauty ten years from now. The plausibility of your argument will depend on your identifying what has happened in the past and what similar trends exist in the present that could influence the future. Aim your article at readers of one of the women's fashion magazines.

—————————— ->>> <<<- ——————————

The Prognosis for this Patient Is Horrible

BERTON ROUECHÉ

In many ways the search for the origin of a disease or illness is a model of causal investigation in its purest form. Medical science believes firmly in discoverable causes; imagine the state of medicine if our physicians did not. The artful narrative below tells of a medical investigation that has all the excitement of a detective story. Clues, like the repetition of a middle name, build ominously, yet the author manages never to hint too much, leaving the surprising twist to its natural place as the discovery of the causal agency of death leads to the detection of a human agent.

The writer who tells us the true story with the skill of such mystery writers as Dorothy Sayers or Georges Simenon is Berton Roueché. Roueché has for years written elegantly on medical and scientific subjects for The New Yorker, *where "The Prognosis for this Patient Is Horrible" appeared.*

At around two o'clock on the afternoon of Tuesday, September 12, 1978, an eleven-month-old boy named Chad Shelton, the only child of Bruce Shelton, a television repairman, and his wife, Sallie Betten Shelton, was admitted to Immanuel Medical Center, in Omaha, Nebraska, for evaluation of persistent vomiting. Chad, his parents told the admitting physician, had been vomiting off and on for two days—since early Sunday evening. They added that they, too, had become sick Sunday evening, with severe abdominal cramps, diarrhea, and vomiting, but had now pretty well recovered.

The determination of the cause of an ailing infant's illness can be a serious diagnostic challenge. The diagnostician, being unable to elicit any account of how the patient feels or where he hurts, can make a judgment only on the observable and measurable signs of abnormality. The admitting physician at Immanuel Medical Center noted and recorded that Chad was "irritable," that his "right tympanic membrane was red," and that his tonsils were red and somewhat swollen. On the basis of these rudimentary findings, together with the information provided by the Sheltons, he recorded three tentative diagnoses: gastroenteritis, otitis media (inflammation of the middle ear), and tonsillitis. He also, as is usual in such ambiguous cases, sought the opinion of a consultant. The consulting physician's observations were entered on Chad Shelton's chart the following day. He observed that the patient was "somnolent through the evening, and this morning was noted to be poorly responsive." He noted what appeared to be multiple "bruises." Preliminary laboratory tests were generally normal, with two striking exceptions. One showed abnormal liver function. The other was the blood-platelet count. Platelets are protoplasms intricately involved in the salvational coagulation of blood that normally follows trauma. A normal platelet count ranges from a hundred and fifty thousand to three hundred thousand and upward. Chad's platelet count was nineteen thousand. That would seem to explain the "bruises." They were hemorrhages. The consultant noted his preliminary impression: "This may be a Reye's syndrome." Reye's syndrome, an entity of recent recognition, is a disease of still uncertain origin that largely afflicts young children and is characterized by vomiting, central-nervous-system damage, and liver damage. The production of platelets is a function of the bone marrow, and a low platelet count may reflect defective production or disordered distribution. The latter can be the result of a rush of platelets to a damaged organ—for example, the liver. The consultant recommended that more definitive tests be made and that the patient be transferred to the intensive-care unit of Children's Memorial Hospital.

Chad was admitted to Children's Hospital late that afternoon. He arrived there in a coma. It was noted on his chart that "within an hour after admission, the child's respiratory status began to deteriorate and it was necessary to place him on a ventilator. . . . A repeat platelet count at 4:30 P.M. revealed a platelet count of 18,000 [and] support was begun with platelets and whole blood. . . . During the evening and early morning hours, bleeding problems became increasingly difficult to control. The child's condition continued to deteriorate, and he was pronounced dead at 4:30 A.M. the morning of September 14th." An autopsy was performed. It revealed an "essentially complete necrosis of the child's hepatic [liver] cells, with very little fatty infiltration." The opinion of the pathologist was that "this pattern is more consistent with a toxic ingestion of an unknown agent rather than Reye's syndrome or other infectious etiologies." The final diagnosis reflected his opinion. It read, "1. Severe acute hepatic necrosis secondary to a toxic ingestion of an unknown agent. 2. Disseminated intravascular coagulation. 3. Cerebral hemorrhage secondary to #2. 4. Cerebral edema secondary to #1 and #2. 5. Terminal renal failure."

That was the beginning, but only the beginning. Shortly before noon that day—Thursday, September 14th, the day of Chad Shelton's death—a man named Duane N. Johnson, aged twenty-four and a trucker by trade, was admitted to Immanuel Medical Center by way of the emergency room. He was brought to the hospital by ambulance from the office of his family physician. He had collapsed in the waiting room there, and when he reached the hospital he was comatose. His wife, Sandra Betten Johnson, accompanied him. She told the admitting physician that her husband had become ill on Sunday evening. He had had an attack of chills, then diarrhea, then vomiting. He vomited several times on Monday and again on Tuesday. Yesterday, Wednesday, he had a severe nosebleed. This morning, he felt even worse—he was still vomiting, his head ached, light hurt his eyes, he was exhausted—and he arranged to see their doctor. Mrs. Johnson was frightened and confused. Her husband had never been sick a day in his life. Now he was lying there unconscious. And not only that, Sherrie, their three-year-old daughter, was also sick. Not as sick as Duane, but she had complained of stomach pains, and she had vomited several times. The last few days had been a nightmare. Mrs. Johnson didn't know what was happening. Her sister Sallie and her husband had also been sick this week—sick to their stomachs, like Sherrie. And only last night—early this morning—Chad, her sister's little baby, had died at Children's Hospital. They said he might have been poisoned. The admitting physician pricked up his ears. Chad? Was her nephew named Shelton? That's right—Chad Shelton. Did the doctor know about him? The doctor said he did. He said it was he who had admitted him to the hospital here on Tuesday. The doctor stopped and reflected. He reminded himself that Chad had suffered multiple hemorrhages. And Johnson had had a nosebleed. He asked himself if there might be some connection here. And Mrs. Johnson had said that their daughter was sick. He asked Mrs. Johnson to bring her daughter around to the hospital. He thought he ought to take a careful look at her.

Johnson remained comatose. The results of the admitting physician's preliminary examination were both unrevealing and alarming. The pupil of Johnson's right eye was "dilated and fixed," he wrote in his report. "Left pupil was pinpoint. Evidence of some conjunctival hemorrhage bilaterally. There was some blood in the pharynx." The physician again felt that a second opinion would be helpful. The consultant's findings, refined by a series of laboratory tests, fully justified the admitting physician's alarm. He noted on Johnson's chart, "There is no motor movement. There is no response to painful stimuli. . . . He is on a respirator. He has had an intracranial hemorrhage. . . . A CAT scan shows an intracerebral hematoma." Johnson's platelet count was a mere six thousand. An S.G.O.T. test was performed. This is a test that determines the concentration in the blood of an enzyme whose excessive presence is indicative of liver damage. A normal S.G.O.T. count is from five to eighteen units. Johnson's count was nine hundred and ten. The consultant concluded his report, "The patient, I think, has essentially gone into . . . a neurological situation from which he cannot be retrieved." Nevertheless, in the hope of retrieval, Johnson was transferred late that day to another hospital, Bishop Clarkson Memorial Hospital, where a technical procedure not available at Immanuel Medical Center could be performed. He was examined at Clarkson by a second consultant. It is usual for a physician confronted by a hopeless or near-hopeless case to note on the patient's chart some easy euphemism like "The prognosis is guarded." Johnson's condition jolted the consultant at Clarkson into the open. He concluded his report, "The prognosis for this patient is horrible."

Meanwhile, as requested by the physician who had admitted her husband that morning, Sandra Johnson returned to Immanuel Medical Center with her daughter, Sherrie. Sherrie was still in pain, still vomiting. She was admitted there at around two o'clock in the afternoon. The preliminary physical examination revealed a scattering of small intradermal hemorrhages on her eyelids and on her lower legs. Her liver was found to be tender and somewhat enlarged. Her platelet count was thirteen thousand. Her S.G.O.T. was seven hundred and two. An exchange blood transfusion was ordered. Following that, in the late afternoon, Sherrie was moved to Children's Hospital and placed in the intensive-care unit there.

Mrs. Johnson saw Sherrie settled at Children's Hospital. There was nothing more that she could do. She then visited her comatose husband at Clarkson Memorial Hospital. There was nothing that she could do there, either. She went home. But at least she did not go home to an empty house. Her second sister, Susan Betten Conley, was then staying with the Johnsons. The two distraught young women talked—about Duane, about Sherrie, about Chad. It was hard for them to believe that this was happening. Nothing in this terrible day seemed quite real. They later drove over to the Sheltons' house. The Sheltons were not as well recovered from their gastrointestinal troubles as they had tried to persuade themselves. Chad's pathetic illness and then his shattering death had distracted them from their own illness. Now they realized that they were far from well. Sallie Shelton, especially, felt poorly. She had abdominal pain, diarrhea, and nausea. Shelton and the three sisters talked. It was suggested that maybe Sallie should be hospitalized. Susan and Sandra left. They felt even more bewildered after talking with their sister and brother-in-law. They couldn't understand why they themselves were not sick—why they alone of the two families, the two households, were well. Sandra drove back to Children's Hospital. Sherrie was asleep, and her condition was described as stable. Sandra drove on to Clarkson Memorial. Her husband was still in a coma. There had been no improvement in his condition. He was almost certainly dying. She settled down to an all-night vigil.

Sallie Shelton spent a restless night. She awoke the next morning —Friday, September 15th—feeling very definitely ill. As she and her husband were dressing, the telephone rang. It was Sandra Johnson. Duane was dead. He had died about an hour ago, without recovering any degree of consciousness. That decided the Sheltons. They drove to Clarkson Memorial Hospital. Mrs. Shelton was examined in the emergency room. Her son's death and its cryptic nature were remembered. She was admitted for observation and testing. Then, as a precaution, it was decided to also admit her husband. The indicated tests revealed that Bruce Shelton's S.G.O.T. was mildly elevated (a hundred and twenty-five units) and his platelet count was a hundred and twenty-three thousand, or a little low. Sallie Shelton's condition was found to be more serious. She was still nauseated, still diarrheic, she had a headache, she was running a fever, and she was noticeably lethargic. Her S.G.O.T. level was eighty-five, and although her initial platelet count was a hundred and sixteen thousand, only a little lower than her husband's, subsequent evaluations showed an ominous downward trend.

Later that day, with Mrs. Johnson's permission, an autopsy was performed on Duane Johnson. The immediate cause of death was found to have been a cerebral hemorrhage. The pathologist's report also noted an almost total lack of platelets, and massive liver damage "of unknown etiology."

A memorandum dated September 18, 1978, from J. Lyle Conrad, director of the Field Services Division, Bureau of Epidemiology, Center for Disease Control, in Atlanta, reads:

On September 15, 1978, Alan Kendal, Ph.D., Respiratory Virology Branch, Virology Division, Bureau of Laboratories, C.D.C., received a call from Paul A. Stoesz, M.D., State Epidemiologist, Nebraska, concerning two recent deaths in a group of families in Omaha, Nebraska. . . . Dr. Stoesz related that 2 people, an 11-month-old child and a 30-year-old [*sic*] man, had died within the past 2 days of an illness characterized by vomiting and diarrhea. Clinical information on the child indicated a death from hepatic failure. No information was available on the cause of death in the man, although an autopsy was being performed. . . . Both toxic and infectious etiologies are being considered as possible causes for these deaths.

Dr. Stoesz, on behalf of Henry D. Smith, M.D., Director of Health, Nebraska State Department of Health, and Warren Jacobson, M.D., Director, Douglas County Health Department, invited C.D.C. to assist in an investigation of the situation. . . . After further discussions about potential etiologies for the outbreak, Dr. Conrad then contacted . . . John P. M. Lofgren, M.D., E.I.S. [Epidemic Intelligence Service] Officer in Jefferson City, Missouri. . . . Dr. Lofgren departed for Omaha the evening of September 15.

"Yes," Dr. Lofgren says. "I got Dr. Conrad's call at about three o'clock in the afternoon. Omaha and Jefferson City are not that close together, but apparently I was the nearest E.I.S. officer to the scene. Anyway, I got the call and went home and packed and took off. I drove the rest of the day and part of the night. I got to Omaha—to a motel room that the doctors there had reserved for me—at about 2 A.M. There was a message waiting for me. There was to be a big meeting the next morning in the conference room at Clarkson Memorial Hospital, and one of the local doctors would pick me up. Which he did. At the meeting, there were about thirty people—the attending physicians, house officers and medical students involved in the case, lab people and pathologists, hospital social workers, the staff of the county health department, and the state epidemiologist and his staff. We settled down to work in good order. We had the two autopsy reports and the charts on the three surviving patients. It was a strange case, and very wide open. But there were a few conclusions that we could be comfortable with. It seemed clear that we were dealing with a disease that was not epidemic, that was limited to just the Johnson and the Shelton families. Then we defined the disease. Our case definition required these symptoms: vomiting, an increased S.G.O.T., and a decrease in platelets.

"The state and county epidemiologists had made a good beginning.

A setting had begun to take shape. The Johnson home seemed to be the site of the trouble. The outbreak had its origin there on the afternoon of Sunday, September 10th, sometime between three and four o'clock. The two families had not been together in about a week until then. But that afternoon the three Sheltons—Bruce, Sallie, and the baby, Chad —dropped in on the Johnsons and Susan Conley. They visited about an hour. At about three-fifteen, Sandra Johnson went to the refrigerator and took out a white plastic pitcher of lemonade. She added ice and filled some glasses. Bruce Shelton took a couple of swallows from his glass and then poured about three-quarters of an inch in a glass for little Chad, and Sallie Shelton finished off the rest. Sandra didn't like lemonade, and she drank none. Neither did her sister Susan. Duane Johnson and the little girl, Sherrie, both drank some of the lemonade. It was suggested that Duane might have drunk two glasses. The Sheltons left to make another call and then started home. On the way home, Bruce and Sallie began to feel sick to the stomach. A few minutes after they got home —at about six o'clock—Sallie vomited. That made her feel a little better. Then, at about seven o'clock, Bruce vomited, and then little Chad. Then Sallie vomited again, and she and her husband vomited again and again during the next four hours. But Chad vomited only that once that night. The two Johnsons—Duane and his daughter, Sherrie—had much the same experience. The investigation had shown that Sandra Johnson had made the lemonade. She had made it a day or two before Sunday —maybe as early as the previous Thursday. But she had made it as she always did—a packaged mix with water and sugar. It was uncertain whether all the lemonade was drunk or whether some was left and thrown out. In any event, the pitcher was empty. The fatal lemonade was gone.

"I say 'fatal' because, as unlikely as lemonade sounds as a cause of poisoning, we were satisfied that the outbreak was an outbreak of poisoning, and that the lemonade was the vehicle. There had been some toxic material in it. The onset of illness was compatible with poisoning by some organic poison. The incubation period was all wrong for an infectious disease. Much too short. Later, after the meeting, I went out to the Johnson house and had a look around. It was a lower-middle-class house on low ground and in bad repair. The plumbing was poor. The house had already been carefully searched, and I was provided with samples of everything that could be even remotely connected with the trouble. One of these possibilities was some firecrackers. Firecrackers contain yellow phosphorus, and its taste could have been masked by the lemonade. There was no indication of how the phosphorus might have got into the lemonade. So that's where we stood. We had a clear clinical syndrome and a likely vehicle. But we didn't have any idea of what the toxic agent might have been. The answer, if we were going to get one, would seem to be up to the laboratory people. John Wiley, the Douglas County epidemiologist, was very helpful. We arranged for samples of everything found in the Johnson house that could be analyzed and sent them off to C.D.C. We also sent off blood and urine samples taken from all the patients, and frozen liver, brain, lung, kidney, and spleen specimens from Duane Johnson. That was about the end of my role in the investigation. I went back to Jefferson City and wrote up my report."

The samples gathered for Dr. Lofgren by Mr. Wiley and his staff were received at C.D.C.—at the Toxicology Branch of the Bureau of Laboratories—in three installments, on September 20th, 21st, and 25th. It was a comprehensive and a very considerable collection. It numbered thirty-four items, including a packet of twenty firecrackers. Animal experiments were at once begun. A group of laboratory rats were fed (by gavage) various materials found in the Johnson kitchen—tap water, sugar, lemonade mix. Other rats were injected with material taken from the several patients. The plastic pitcher in which the lemonade had been made was treated with a citric-acid solution in the hope of extracting some minuscule remains of the lemonade, and the solution was fed to another group of rats. The firecrackers were anatomized. They were found to contain only an insignificant quantity of yellow phosphorus. The laboratory animals were sacrificed at intervals during the next week or so, and their kidneys, livers, and other organs and tissues were examined for eloquent pathological changes. None were found. Liver tissue obtained from Johnson at autopsy was further analyzed for the presence of selenium, a substance that in large concentrations has a toxic affinity for the liver, and for arsenic. The results were essentially normal. Urine samples taken from Bruce and Sallie Shelton at the peak of their illness were analyzed for evidence of a dangerous herbicide called paraquat. The results again were negative.

The toxicological examination of the various samples and specimens relating to the Omaha outbreak was monitored and its results were evaluated by a research medical officer in the Toxicology Branch of C.D.C. named Renate D. Kimbrough. Dr. Kimbrough, a native of Germany and a graduate in medicine of the University of Göttingen, is the wife of a research chemist and the mother of three children. She is also a pathologist and a toxicologist of national distinction. She found the laboratory results, for all their negativity, both useful and interesting.

"One thing was particularly noteworthy," Dr. Kimbrough says. "The liver was the only affected organ. That eliminated a good many possible poisons. Most toxic chemicals that cause severe liver damage also cause damage to other parts of the body. As a matter of fact, it is unusual to find only liver damage—to find the liver destroyed and none of the other organs affected. There were also other limiting factors to consider. One was that the poison had to be something that was easily soluble in water—in lemonade. Another was that it had to be more or less tasteless and odorless. There was no indication that the Johnson lemonade had either a funny taste or a funny smell. Well, those factors eliminated a number of other compounds. In fact, they narrowed the field to a group of readily modifiable hydrocarbons called alkylating agents. This was not an area in which I felt very much at home, but I knew someone who did. I knew an expert. I put in a call to Ronald C. Shank. Dr. Shank is associate professor of toxicology in the Department of Community and Environmental Medicine at the University of California at Irvine. I told him my story and what I needed. Could he give me a list of water-soluble alkylating agents? No problem. He gave me a list of eight—methyl methane sulfonate; dimethyl sulfate; dimethylnitrosamine; N-methyl-N'-nitro-N-nitrosoguanidine; 1, 2 dimethylhydrazine; methyl chloride; methyl bromide; and methyl iodide. Then I went to work. It was another process of evaluation and elimination. I ruled out methyl chloride, methyl bromide, and methyl iodide almost at once. They are all weak alkylating agents, and they are lethal only in very large amounts—amounts too large to go undetected in a glass of lemonade. Moreover, the initial impact of those agents is on the brain, so the initial effect is mental confusion. That had not been noted in any of the Omaha cases. I could also rule out 1, 2 dimethylhydrazine. It causes severe damage to the red blood cells, and no such damage was noted in any of the Omaha reports. Then I eliminated methyl methane sulfonate. The kind of liver damage it produces is quite different from that observed in Duane Johnson and Chad Shelton. The same was true of dimethyl sulfate and N-methyl-N'-nitro-N-nitrosoguanidine. And the latter, again, is lethal only in very large amounts. That left dimethylnitrosamine.

"I think I knew almost at once that dimethylnitrosamine was the answer. It perfectly met all the required criteria. It is a liquid, and it is well miscible with water. It is largely odorless and tasteless. It is extremely toxic in very small amounts. The lethal dose for a medium-sized adult is less than two grams, and for a small child about one-third of a gram. A third of a gram is about seven drops, or less than half a teaspoonful. And dimethylnitrosamine is peculiarly liver-specific. It attacks the liver and only the liver, and the lesions it causes are quite distinctive. I studied the textbook lesions caused by dimethylnitrosamine. Then I examined under the microscope the liver specimens taken at autopsy from Duane Johnson and Chad Shelton. The Johnson and Shelton lesions were identical with the textbook examples. Now, let me move ahead for a moment. I was satisfied that the poison involved was dimethylnitrosamine, but I wanted to be more than that. I wanted to be absolutely sure. This was not an accidental poisoning. Everyone involved in the matter was certain that the poison had been deliberately added to the lemonade. It was a case of murder. Well, I called Dr. Shank again. Dimethylnitrosamine is very rapidly metabolized and excreted—within a couple of days of ingestion. So there was no possibility of turning up any trace of it in the liver samples. Its presence in the liver, however, causes certain chemical changes that can be measured by a high-pressure liquid-chromatography procedure that was recently developed by Dr. Shank. I asked him if he would perform his test on a group of liver tissues. This was to be, of course, a blind test. I supplied Dr. Shank with eight coded vials of material. They consisted of liver tissue taken from Duane Johnson, kidney tissue taken from him, and six liver and kidney specimens taken from cases in our storage file—three of them from alleged cases of methyl-bromide poisoning and three from cases of Reye's syndrome. Dr. Shank reported that one specimen of the eight was positive for dimethylnitrosamine. That was the coded sample of liver tissue taken from Duane Johnson. And that was definitive.

"But all this, as I say, came later. Much later—in August of 1979. So now let's go back to where we were—to October of 1978. I was reasonably satisfied that dimethylnitrosamine was the poison involved, and I acted on that assumption. The next question was: How did it get in the lemonade? And where did it come from? It certainly didn't come from the corner drugstore. Dimethylnitrosamine is not an everyday compound, and its uses are rather limited. It was originally developed in England, as a solvent for use in the automobile industry, and it may have some other highly specialized industrial uses, but it is also known to be a powerful carcinogen. That quality has given it a certain vogue in cancer research. It is widely used to induce cancer in laboratory animals. I thought about that, and I thought about Omaha. Omaha is not a great industrial center; it is a great insurance center. And it is something of a medical center. It has Creighton University School of Medicine and the University of Nebraska Medical School, and it has the Eppley Institute—the Eppley Institute for cancer research.

"I had talked with John Wiley, the Douglas County epidemiologist, a time or two in the course of the investigation. So now I called him again. I told him what I had in mind. I don't believe I actually singled out dimethylnitrosamine. I think I simply said that I was convinced that the poison involved was an alkylating agent, and that it might very well be one used in cancer research. I suggested that it might be a good idea to check and see if anybody connected with the Johnson or Shelton families had any connection with the Eppley Institute. He said he would. And he did. And there was a connection—a very direct, a very real connection."

The criminal investigation of the deaths of Chad Shelton and Duane Johnson was directed by Samuel W. Cooper, the Deputy Douglas County Attorney, together with Lieutenant Foster Burchard, of the Homicide Division of the Omaha Police Department. Much of the field work, and most of the most productive work, was done by a detective in Lieutenant Burchard's command named Kenneth G. Miller.

"It was a strange case," Cooper says. "Our investigation was the third phase of three quite distinct phases. There was first the medical investigation, then Renate Kimbrough's toxicological investigation, and then our homicide investigation. And even our phase was unusual. It was never, from our point of view, a simple case of whodunit. By the time we came into the picture, it had been established that the murder weapon was a toxic substance. So it was more a case of how-he-dunit. It took us a good long time to build up a provable case, but we had both the who and the how, and even the why, in only a matter of days. That was where Ken Miller came in. Miller had been working closely with John Wiley at the Health Department, and Wiley told him about his conversation with Dr. Kimbrough and her suggestion about a possible link between the families involved and the Eppley Institute. Miller was smart enough to take her suggestion seriously. He went back to his office and ran the Johnsons and the Sheltons through the computer file we have on victims of some sort of criminal act. And almost at once he found a lead. It involved the Johnsons—Duane and Sandra—and Sandra's mother and brother. One night in June of 1975, Duane and Sandra

—they weren't the Johnsons yet, they were only going together—and her mother and brother went to the movies. Afterward, they were standing together out in front of the Betten house, talking, when a car drove up and a man jumped out and opened fire with a shotgun. One of the pellets hit Sandra's mother, and Sandra's brother was nicked a couple of times, but neither was really hurt. The man drove off, but there was no big mystery about the attack. The man had been a high-school sweetheart of Sandra's. He was jealous and crazed, furious that she had dropped him for another man, and his intended victim may have been Duane Johnson. His name was Steven Roy Harper, and he was a rather familiar type. Good student, quiet, never drank, smoked, or used drugs. The records showed that Harper was arrested, pleaded no contest to a charge of shooting with intent to kill, and was sentenced to one to five years in prison. That was on December 6, 1976. He was paroled on November 16, 1977. Ken Miller absorbed all that and then moved on the Eppley Institute. It was almost too much. Harper had worked at the Eppley Institute. He had found a job there a few months after his release, and his job was one that put him in the vicinity of various chemical compounds, including alkylating agents, including dimethylnitrosamine. He had held the job for about five months, until August 18, 1978, when he resigned to take a better-paying job as a construction worker. That was the bare bones of our investigation. There was, of course, a great deal more—a lot of legwork, a lot of interviewing of Sandra Johnson and others, a lot of detail. Harper had been in Omaha at the time of the lemonade party, but now he was on a construction job in Beaumont, Texas. Miller and a couple of other detectives and I flew down to Beaumont with a warrant. We arranged for the F.B.I. to pick Harper up, and we took him into custody."

That was on Friday, October 13th, less than a month after the deaths of Chad Shelton and Duane Johnson. After his arrest, Harper made an informal declaration to a homicide detective in Cooper's entourage named Greg Thompson. Thompson's transcript of it reads, in its essentials:

> Harper states that he is still in love with Sandra Johnson, that his life has been miserable for the past four years, and everything built up in him until it came to this point. While working in the Gene Eppley Cancer Care Center [sic], he took a chemical which he called DMNA [dimethylnitrosamine], a carcinogen. . . .

Harper stated that he remembers driving up by the Johnson house, looking and seeing that no one was there, drove past it and parked down the street, around the corner. Harper then got out and walked back up the street, around the corner to the Johnson house, walked all the way around the Johnson house, looking for a way to get in. Harper states that he thought he went in the side door, but he may have went in the window, he can't really remember. Or maybe he just left by the side door. He remembers going into the house, opening up the refrigerator, taking the small vial, which he described to be between two (2) and three (3) inches long and maybe a half-inch (½) diameter, pouring it into the lemonade in the refrigerator. . . . Harper then left the residence.

Harper denied in his statement to Thompson that he had poisoned the lemonade with murderous intent. He told Thompson that "he didn't believe that it [the dimethylnitrosamine] was toxic, that it would only cause cancer." If such was his intention, he may have been not entirely unsuccessful. Of the three surviving victims of his poisoned lemonade, Bruce and Sallie Shelton were discharged from the hospital as fully recovered—he after four days of treatment, she after a stay of sixteen days. Sandra Johnson's daughter, Sherrie, was less fortunate. She was hospitalized for three weeks and then was followed for several months as an outpatient. The most recent record of her condition noted "continuous hepatosplenomegaly [enlargement of the liver and spleen] and elevated liver enzymes, and a liver biopsy obtained three months after exposure showed chronic active hepatitis." A liver so damaged is often eventually hospitable to the development of cancer.

Harper was returned to Omaha. His case was presented at a preliminary judicial hearing, after which the presiding judge charged him with two counts of murder in the first degree and three counts of poisoning. On October 5, 1979, after a three-week trial in which Cooper served as prosecuting attorney and Dr. Kimbrough appeared as a key witness for the state, Harper was found guilty on all five counts and sentenced to die in the electric chair.

QUESTIONS FOR DISCUSSION

1. Roueché's medical mystery follows chronological order (with the exception of one very clearly marked spot where the story gets ahead of itself). Could any other arrangement of the facts have been used? What effect does the arrangement he chose have on the material and thus on the audience?

2. How did the epidemiologists rule out an infectious disease?
3. What procedures were followed once a toxic agent was indicated and why?
4. Why were the unique physiological effects so important in the identification of the cause?
5. What role did the process of elimination play at various points in the investigation?
6. Why does Roueché include so many circumstantial details, even those that hardly seem important to the case, such as Dr. Lofgren's account of his travel arrangements?

SUGGESTIONS FOR WRITING

1. Write an argument for those who have read this story in which you argue for the main cause of the tragedy, and place that main cause in the context of contributing causes such as, perhaps, chance, human emotions, and ignorance.
2. Recount in detective story fashion for readers of the *New Yorker* the discovery of any causal agent of disease or death. Be sure to include the circumstantial details that give life to the story.
3. Carefully examine the details of this story and argue, again for an audience that has read the account, what absent blocking causes could have prevented it from happening. Do any agencies or people seem to have been irresponsible?
4. Give a detailed description, for the purpose of teaching someone the methods of causal argument, of a process of elimination that you have gone through in trying to find the cause of a surprising event—perhaps the cause of an allergic reaction or of car trouble or of something's turning up where it did not belong.
5. Investigate how the public health department in your town, county, or state works. How would it handle a case like that which faced officials first in Omaha and then in the state of Nebraska? What routine matters do public health officials investigate? What preventive powers do they have? Under what circumstances do they report to the Center for Disease Control in Atlanta? Write a report or an evaluation for a local newspaper audience.
6. Is the United States free from the possibility of an epidemic today? If not, where is our society vulnerable? Defend your opinion for an audience of newsmagazine readers.
7. Investigate the success epidemiologists have had in tracing the cause of AIDS or Legionnaire's Disease. Write an account of either for lay readers, stressing the methods of causal investigation that researchers used.

---------------- ⇒⟫ ⟪⇐ ----------------

Why We Live in the Musical Past

EDWARD ROTHSTEIN

Edward Rothstein was a frequent contributor of music criticism to the New
York Times. *Although the point of departure of this essay is classical music,
anyone interested in any kind of music will find Rothstein's argument
provocative.*

*Like other essays in this set, Rothstein sets up a causal model that
describes the operation of large cultural forces on very specific human
behavior. The childish desire for repetition and reassurance becomes a reason
for the frequent appearance of Mozart's name on concert programs. As you
read, keep in mind Rothstein's definition of music, and ask yourself whether
Rothstein's claims for the satisfaction classical music offers might also hold
for other kinds of music.*

We are living in a most peculiar musical age. Musical life is booming,
audiences are growing, seasons are expanding, conservatories are turning
out virtuosos. In New York, well over a *hundred* concerts are given every
week. There is an extraordinary bustle and whirl in the music world and
its accompanying business. But in the midst of all that activity, there
is a certain stillness, an immovable center. For our musical life is based
upon repetition.

In recent weeks, for example, the New York Philharmonic and the
Metropolitan Opera have announced their programs for the coming
season. At the Philharmonic, there are, of course, some unusual offerings. A concert performance of Janacek's "From the House of the
Dead" is planned as are programs devoted to Shostakovich and to the
Polish modern, Witold Lutoslawski—all reflecting growing interest in
Slavic and Eastern European composers. There is also a "retrospective"
of six compositions by Schoenberg planned, concentrating on his earliest
music.

But the repertory of the Philharmonic is actually dominated by
familiarly repeated works of the 19th-century musical tradition—including Mozart on one end and a few moderns like Rachmaninoff on the
other. Out of the more than 90 compositions the Philharmonic is per-

forming in 125 concerts with more than 35 different programs, only *six* works will be new to New York; *three* of those will be world premieres. The most heavily represented composers are Mozart, with seven works, including four popular piano concertos, and Beethoven with six works, including three familiar symphonies. Brahms is among the next most often scheduled composers, represented by the First Piano Concerto, First Symphony, Violin Concerto and Tragic Overture. Schumann is also heavily represented.

Many of the scheduled works—including Schubert's "Unfinished" Symphony, Mussorgsky's "Pictures at an Exhibition," Tchaikovsky's Fifth Symphony—are the musical equivalents of "best-sellers." Each season they are repeatedly played, if not by the Philharmonic then by another local or visiting orchestra. Apart from such other 19th-century masters as Berlioz, Bruckner, Liszt, Wagner, Strauss and Dvorak, there are a few familiar "modern" works—Barber's Adagio for Strings, Debussy's "La Mer"—a few selections by other repeated moderns like Elgar, Walton, Sibelius and Bernstein, and a handful of novelties by Carter, Druckman and others.

At the Metropolitan Opera, programming is similar. There are new productions of Strauss's "Arabella," Verdi's "Macbeth" and Mozart's "Idomeneo." The acclaimed production of Mussorgsky's "Boris Godunov" will return as will Debussy's "Pelléas et Mélisande" and the "Parade" trilogy, with its ballet and two 20th-century operas. But 12 out of the 21 operatic productions being offered next season—over *half* the repertory—were premiered in the 55 years between 1830 and 1885; five of those are by Verdi. Only *three* works premiered after 1905; one is the familiar "Der Rosenkavalier."

The seasons at both the Met and the Philharmonic, then, are intensely focussed on the 19th-century repertory. That policy is a resounding success: halls are filled to over 90 percent of capacity; at least 12,000 seats are filled at the four weekly Philharmonic concerts; more than 25,000 tickets are sold to the seven weekly Met performances. This programming speaks for the tastes of the musical mainstream.

Elsewhere, the same repertory is also repeated by popular demand. The Mostly Mozart Festival will soon return as well, with its repetitive festivities. The massive replays of Classical and Romantic music, occasionally interrupted by a new or recent work, have become an accepted part of the musical scene.

But as we know, in previous centuries new works were the rule and not the exception. Bach had a new cantata ready every Sunday, Mozart composed new concertos for his important appearances. 19th-century concert halls and opera houses thrived on premieres. Something changed in this century. The repertory congealed. Our institutions have become repetitive museums.

There is, of course, repetition in the other arts as well. But only in music is the new so sweepingly rejected and the old so worshipfully celebrated. New plays are at the heart of every theater season, new paintings appear on living room walls with insouciant ease, fiction is read hot off the presses. To get an idea of the peculiarity of our musical life, imagine most movie theaters as re-run houses; imagine if most publishers specialized in Dickens and Thackeray.

Still more peculiar is the restricted historical range of our musical life. The 19th-century supplies nearly all of our repertory. For most audiences, the Baroque era is worth only an occasional visit, the Renaissance is a novelty, the Middle Ages an eccentricity.

Of course, the 19th-century repertory is a great achievement of Western European culture; it is extraordinarily profound and exciting, worthy of living with, not just listening to. Given its immense riches many listeners hardly will risk an evening on a third-rate new composition. The repetitive musical culture has, in fact, been attributed to a failure of contemporary composition. Other explanations blame the lack of adventurous listeners, the stodgy institutions, the commercialization of classical music or the stagnation of the recording industry.

Each of these explanations has some validity. But they reduce an exceedingly complex cultural phenomenon to matters of taste and commerce. They do not explain why repetition has become so extensive in its own right, and why those repetitions should be so exclusively centered upon the 19th-century tradition.

We do not, for example, turn to this repertory simply because the "new" is unappreciated; in fact, for most audiences, the "new" is unnecessary. The 19th century satisfies our musical needs; it has a special meaning. This is not just because 19th-century music is "great" or has beautiful melodies—the melodies of the Renaissance are just as beautiful, largely unperformed early music just as "great." The point is that the 19th-century has actually come to *define* our ideas of what music should be. The Philharmonic and the Metropolitan Opera were founded in the 19th-century; the symphony orchestra, the concert hall and grand opera have their origins in the same period. We live in a 19th-century musical culture.

Why then, is this music so tirelessly repeated? There are the obvious reasons—because it is pleasurable, rewarding, beautiful. But our repetitions are also similar to the demands made in childhood, demands to hear a story told again and again; such demands are echoed in many of the repetitions of culture and religion.

As children we did not ask for retellings in order to learn more; we simply wanted to hear tales told again. Children ask to hear the stories they know the best, stories they know so well, they could easily tell them themselves.

Sigmund Freud referred to the "child's peculiar pleasure in constant repetition." In "Beyond the Pleasure Principle," he writes: "If a child has been told a nice story, he will insist on hearing it over and over again rather than a new one; and he will remorselessly stipulate that the repetition shall be an identical one and will correct any alterations of which the narrator may be guilty."

Of course, contemporary musical audiences are not merely children listening to papa composers tell stories. But the requests are similar; certain works are selected as "favorites"—Beethoven's Fifth Symphony, Chopin's Waltzes, Verdi's "La Traviata." These are known best, demanded most and varied least. Recordings also offer musical tales in precise, unaltered repetitions.

Freud linked compulsions to repeat to the nature of instinct—the effort "to restore an earlier state of things." Repetition of a story, in this view, involves an attempt to comprehend or restore a dramatic or psychological situation contained within the tale.

Both Bruno Bettelheim and Erich Fromm have continued this argument, demonstrating that stories contain conflicts and situations which the child is attempting to master or understand. In "Hansel and Gretel," for example, a struggle with parental figures is enacted in the children's exile from home and their overcoming of the witch. Particular moments are always psychologically significant to a child—when the prince rescues the sleeping beauty, when the wolf in grandma's clothing bares his teeth. "Tell it to me again," says the child, "the part where. . . ." Psychologists remind us: the child is never just listening to a story; he is dreaming of his own life.

The story involves not just fantasy, but the real world of parents, authority, conflict; that is why children prefer that stories be told by a parent instead of read in a book or recited by a friend. It may be that our repeated listening to music involves a similar state-of-mind. "Play it again," say our concert audiences, "the Beethoven 'Emperor'." We reflect on psychological or social situations embodied in the music, which take on additional power when told in their social setting, the concert hall.

What is special about our chosen repertory? First of all, 19th-century music really is written in the form of a story, with elaborate narrative programs. While programs in Baroque repertory centered on *images*, such as the warbling of a bird, Romantic and late Classical programs allude to narrative *journeys*, invoking Faust, Shakespeare, literary adventures.

These programs are supported by a narrative musical style. In a Baroque fugue, basic thematic material is an unchanged part of a complex musical architecture; but the dominant musical forms of our repertory treat a theme as if it were a character in a novel, subject to events which affect its character, until it is restored, transformed, all tensions resolved. Early sonatas by Haydn, for example, with their surprising wit and dramatic character can be compared to picaresque novels or opera buffa; later sonatas, by Lizst or Brahms, with their passionate mediations, can be compared to the Romantic confessional literature.

That is why we treat these works as stories and listen with rapt attention. If we also respond so strongly, it is because of their meanings. Music after early Classicism was not written for a patron, a court performance, church service or folk celebration; it was the first music written for "the public"—the new middle class—to be heard in concert halls. These musical narratives are similar to the novel which came to maturity in the same period. The novels of Austen, Dickens, or George Eliot were precisely observed tales about the social order and the willful individual, about the middle-class public and its ambitious, desirous and reflective citizens. Musical narratives by middle-class composers have the same spirit.

The symphonic repertory is suffused with psychological detail and epic tension, with encounters between public order (massive blocks of sound, regular harmonies, sturdy resolutions) and more unstable private passions (surprising dissonances, melancholy melodies, rhythmic disruption). These conflicts are the themes of grand opera as well. In "Don Carlo," an individual's desires threaten the social and familial order; in "Macbeth," ambition does the same. The heroic Siegfried is the savior and destroyer of the order of the gods. In grand opera, stable social hierarchies are threatened by the hero's yearning, or (as in "Carmen") by a woman outside the social order who inspires troubling desires and ambitions.

These were then, forms of bourgeois theater that spoke directly to the new public. The 19th-century concerto, with its heroic soloist pitted against a grand orchestral order, can be almost Dickensian in its melodramatic confrontations and coincidences. The charismatic conductor binding the orchestra into a single society, and the flamboyant virtuoso, victoriously braving instrumental dangers, embody the dreams of the middle-class.

Music has always been written for a specific audience. The music of the 19th-century was directed at the bourgeoisie. Even today, a century later, we treasure these tales; our audience is still the middle-class. As children do with resonant stories, we demand the repetition of this music, attempting to savor and master its situations and resolutions.

But this music is more than just social adventure. The anthropologist Claude Lévi-Strauss has suggested that this repertory has a *mythological* function in society.

In "Myth and Meaning," Mr. Lévi Strauss asserts that after the 16th-century, myth receded in importance; the novel and music took its place. "The music that took over the traditional function of mythology," he argues, "reached its full development with Mozart, Beethoven, and Wagner in the 18th and 19th centuries."

One function of myth, in Mr. Lévi-Strauss's view, is to show how a culture's customs of marriage, government or economy are related to more universal natural forces. Prometheus brings fire from the gods; Moses brings down laws from Mt. Sinai; medicine, in many myths, is taught to man by animals. In his musical analogy the anthropologist suggests that our repertory serves this mythological function: it dramatizes how bourgeois society is connected to the primal forces which lie outside it.

In opera, this was, in fact a major theme, not just in Wagner's overtly mythic "Ring." Again and again, opera shows the social order both animated and threatened by primal passions. The bourgeois family, for example, is one arena for mythic tensions. Carmen—a gypsy on the outskirts of the social order—seduces the soldier away from familial responsibilities; in "Il Trovatore," another gypsy steals a child from an aristocratic father; in "La Traviata," the "fallen woman" is a threat to Germont, the bourgeois father; in "Robert le Diable" the father is the devil himself.

Similar concerns with irrational forces lying behind a rational order can be heard throughout the symphonic music of the 19th-century. The figure of the devil in 19th-century music is just one example of the music's mythic concerns—in Berlioz's "Symphonie Fantastique," in Liszt's "Faust" and "Mephisto." Even the "virtuoso"—a favorite 19th-century persona—was a figure with frightening powers from outside the musical and social order; Paganini was considered demonic.

So when we listen to this repertory with as much avidity and passion as we do, it is not merely because it is "great." The foundations of contemporary society lie in the 19th-century; we share its mythology. Even today, musical myths speak with authority about our rational bourgeois society, its fragility and its strengths.

The mythological nature of the repertory also provides insight into our musical repetitions. Mircea Eliade, a historian of religion, has explained that in ancient cultures, myths are connected with ritualist repetitions. Even in contemporary religion, for example, the ritual of Mass regularly enacts the myth of the Eucharist, Sabbath rituals regularly recall the myth of God's rest after the Creation. Through these repetitions, societies act "to regenerate themselves periodically."

This is precisely what happens in our secular musical world. If 19th-century music has the function of myth in our society, the concert hall is a cross between a theater and a temple. The concert has the airs of a repeated ritual, communally celebrated in our modern religion of high art. The musical myths, telling of our social origins and our connections with primal forces, are told and retold.

The "great" 19th-century composer himself becomes a mythic figure in these rituals. The heroes of myth, Mr. Eliade points out, are not just individuals who lived at a particular time and place; they are representative of primal forces. Moses and Jesus and Mohammed, in the mythologies of three religions, speak for the divine realm. So too with Mozart, Beethoven, Wagner; no matter how program notes describe their lives or surroundings, we treat the music as if it derived from a transcendental source. In Peter Shaffer's Broadway play "Amadeus," this split between music and the historical individual is taken as self-evident: Mozart is crude and awful; his music is magical, a revelation.

Musically, then, we have turned these "great" composers into a pantheon of gods who lived at the beginning of our musical age. They stand outside of history, delivering regenerative messages from the musical beyond. And we honor their messages with unstinting devotion at every concert. When we repeat these myths we invoke our gods and celebrate our mythological past, regenerating ourselves with the concert ritual.

Of course, nuances and qualifications have to be added to these speculations about myth and story in the 19th-century; Mozart, for example, needs slightly different treatment. Clearly, the art works of a century cannot be treated only with sweeping abstractions. But in repeating this repertory with such regularity, we have already acknowledged its shared meanings. The expansion of middle-class audiences in recent decades has solidified the repertory's secure position.

Meanwhile the 19th-century forms of grand opera and symphony orchestra remain alien to the mainstream of contemporary expression. Music has moved on to other things, alienated and private statements, complex illuminations, attempts to recreate ritual in the repetitions of Minimalism. The middle-class is no longer its subject or its audience.

So our repetitions of 19th-century repertory have a darker, more disturbing side. On a vast scale, we mythologize the 19th-century. We anxiously savor music at its most heroic moment, before it went awry with the beginnings of modernism. We attempt, perhaps, to "restore an earlier state of things." We define what music should be by repeating the works of a single European century. Like myths, these works give our origins; like fairy tales, they offer us promises. But there is something in the present that they miss; they do not show us the future.

QUESTIONS FOR DISCUSSION

1. In his opening demonstration (CP) section, Rothstein claims that "our musical life is based on repetition" and that the program of the Metropolitan Opera and the New York Philharmonic "speaks for the musical mainstream." What do these statements tell you about his audience? Can you question this characterization of current musical taste?

2. One motive for investigating causes is the perception of an unusual state of affairs. How does Rothstein introduce the notion that there is something unusual in the popularity of nineteenth-century music?

3. How does Rothstein clear the decks for his own causal nominee? How convincing is his elimination of rival causes? Has he forgotten any potentially strong ones?

4. Find all the places where Rothstein concedes points to a potential opposition. What is the effect of granting arguments to the other side?

5. How does Rothstein manage to link up a Freudian view of childish demands

for repetition, the rituals of religion, and the perpetuation of a particular style of music?

6. Take a close look at Rothstein's style, particularly his manipulation of sentence length and parallelism. Look at the variety of sentence length in one of the longer paragraphs. How does he exploit shorter sentences?

SUGGESTIONS FOR WRITING

1. Take one of the causes that Rothstein dismisses and argue for Rothstein's *New York Times* readers its primary importance in perpetuating the nineteenth-century musical repertory.

2. Rothstein seems to limit twentieth-century music to the kind of avant-garde creation occasionally performed in concert halls. What would happen if he expanded his definition of twentieth-century music to include the works of composers such as Lennon and McCartney, Cole Porter, or Duke Ellington? Either confirm or refute Rothstein's argument using an expanded definition of twentieth-century music. Aim your argument at those who would be convinced by Rothstein's.

3. With his limited definition of twentieth-century music (as the last question suggests), Rothstein sees the music scene as quite different from that of other art forms. Is it really different? Argue that the same kind of repetition occurs in other arts if we narrowly restrict our definition of their twentieth-century forms.

4. Rothstein spends considerable time characterizing nineteenth-century music as programmatic, narrative, and mythic. Support or refute his definition by reference to particular works. Remember that the challenge will be in defining these attributes. Address your argument to fellow music students.

5. Is there a tendency to live in the musical past in other types of music such as rock, country, or jazz? Write a response to Rothstein, comparing some other type of music to the type he discusses and speculating on the reasons for similarities and differences.

6. If nineteenth-century creations (in whatever art form) reflect the taste of the middle class, and middle-class cultural taste still dominates, where else should we expect to see nineteenth-century art forms or taste perpetuated? Do we? Write an essay about some other art form explaining why nineteenth-century standards do or do not dominate.

———————— →» «← ————————

The Politics of Crime

RICHARD NEELY

*Richard Neely is especially well qualified to write on the intertwining of law
and politics that has produced the criminal justice system in our country.
Neely has a law degree from Yale, was a member of the West Virginia
legislature, was elected a justice of the West Virginia Supreme Court of
Appeals in 1972, and served as its chief justice in 1980. Yet despite his
eminent position, Neely also believes in the responsibility of our jurists to
speak on legal matters to average citizens, as his book,* How Courts Govern
America, *and the following article show.*

*Causal investigations often begin with the perception of an anomaly—of,
for instance, two apparently contradictory things holding true. How can it be
that people are outraged by crime and yet nothing is done about it? Neely
reasons backwards to discover the causes in a widespread interest in keeping
the judicial system as small as possible.*

Through at least the past decade, no public problem has worried Americans more persistently than crime. When people are asked in opinion
surveys to list the problems that concern them most, the threat of crime
typically comes at or near the top of the list. But when the same people
list the issues on which they'll decide which candidate to vote for, crime
usually comes behind half-a-dozen other subjects. The explanation they
offer most frequently is that a candidate's statements about crime are
unimportant—no one can do much about the problem.

What is misguided about this attitude is that it *is* possible to do
something about crime. Although the evidence lacks scientific precision,
certain facts of criminal-law enforcement are clear:

In many big cities, where the limit on crime is the presence of the
police (as opposed to family members, watchful neighbors, and the like,
who limit crime elsewhere), more officers on the streets or in the subways
means fewer criminals who dare to act. But in courtrooms, most accused
criminals go free because the system cannot afford to have it any other
way. Everyone involved in the criminal courts is overtaxed, from the
policemen, who must take time off the beat to testify, to the prosecutors,
who need to dispose of cases as quickly as possible, to the judges, who
know as they make their sentencing decisions that the prisons are already

overcrowded. The result of this pressure is the plea-bargain, in which a man who faces, for example, a ten-year sentence with a three-year minimum term if convicted of armed robbery will instead plead guilty to grand larceny and end up serving one year in jail.

Many people complain that plea-bargaining returns criminals to the streets, but few have considered the statistics that lie behind this practice. There are nearly 104,000 felony arrests in New York City every year. New York City has facilities for only about 5,000 full-blown jury trials per year, so it is forced to do what nearly all city courts must: find some way to dispose of the surplus, usually through plea-bargaining or dropped charges. Many of the people thereby freed undoubtedly belong in jail, and the crime rate would undoubtedly fall if they were imprisoned. All that is required is money—for police, prosecutors, judges, and jails.

Why, then, have we not taken steps we know would have some effect? The answers are complicated, but chief among them is that for every proposal that might be made to reduce crime, there is a powerful, organized interest that opposes it. These obstructive groups often include the most influential force of all, the middle-class interests that so frequently complain about the threat of crime.

This problem is intimately connected with the general difficulties of American courts, but not the courts as they are usually conceived. When lay people speak of the courts, they often mean judges and attendant judicial staffs of clerks and secretaries. However, the term "courts" must be expanded when we talk of criminal law to encompass all of the supporting agencies that either feed criminals to the judges or receive them after conviction. When courts are understood in this way, it becomes clear that improving their operations can be costly. Doubling the number of policemen and prosecutors would spare many people the costs they now bear as victims of crime, but it would increase the costs many others would pay in taxes.

As is often the case, the people who stand to gain the most from this protection are the ones with the least say about how public money is spent. The primary victims of crime pay the lowest taxes. Most victims of crime live in ghettos or declining working-class neighborhoods, and they work at low-wage jobs in places such as all-night diners or gas stations, which are easy to rob. But the taxpayers who would bear the cost of better protection for these victims are themselves seldom victims —they are instead large corporations with privately retained security forces, or middle-class taxpayers who live in well-protected neighborhoods and send their children to safe neighborhood schools or private schools.

Although it might not seem in the interest of the middle class to pay for increased enforcement, the cost of crime in the United States runs to hundreds of billions of dollars every year—much more than increased enforcement would cost. Shoplifting alone accounts for a loss of between 3 and 7 percent of all merchandise inventoried for sale by large chain stores, which means we all pay 3 to 7 percent more for our routine dry-goods purchases.

Moreover, criminal courts and their supporting agencies—unlike most government operations—actually generate revenue. At the simplest level, traffic courts and magistrate courts make more money from fees and fines than it costs to operate them. When state or local business regulations are enforced, the fines augment the treasury. Low crime rates also contribute to a desirable climate for industry, commerce, and residences, which in turn means higher property values and a stronger tax base. Lack of funding for the courts must be something more than just a reflection of overall budget constraints; while budget considerations do play a part, underfunding is often deliberate, purposeful, and unrelated to the budget.

One simple example should illustrate the point. Cheating on federal and state income taxes is pervasive in all classes of society; except among the compulsively honest, cheating usually occurs in direct proportion to opportunity. Why, then, do we not expand the Internal Revenue Service and its state counterparts? Every new revenue agent pays his salary and overhead at least eight times. The answer is that we do not really want Rhadamanthine enforcement of the tax laws. As long as the IRS is overworked and understaffed, everyone except the scrupulously honest will enact his own personal tax-reform program. The IRS's understaffing also guarantees that all but the most flagrant evaders will escape with a payment of back taxes and possibly a civil penalty.

Overworked United States attorneys cannot spend their time arguing every questionable deduction in tax court. The IRS will challenge a businessman's deductions, only to cede most of its points at settlement conferences. The mediocre enforcement of the tax codes stems not only from the IRS's lack of staff but also from a lack of U.S. attorneys, U.S. district court judges, and court-of-appeals judges. Without an increase in the personnel of supporting agencies, there is a limit to the effectiveness of new IRS agents, but there is no question that such an increase will bring in more money than it costs.

Since more rigorous enforcement will inspire a higher level of "voluntary" compliance, it must be obvious that some people out there do not want better enforcement. I am probably one. I actually do pay every cent I owe in taxes, and since I am a public official, I get audited about every four years. Notwithstanding my annoyance with those who cheat, I do not want to be audited more than once every four years, because it is a nuisance. Quite frankly, I prefer to let my neighbor cheat a little rather than be bothered with a yearly audit.

Most people probably feel as I do about forgiving their neighbors' tax trespasses in return for minimal personal harassment by Uncle Sam, but a similar philosophy of live and let live does not exist about violent crime. Why, then, do we not double the number of cops and courts?

The reason is both ideological and financial. Policemen, in my experience, are by nature bullies as well as heroes, and the smaller the police force, the more policemen tend to exhibit the characteristics of heroes rather than bullies. But the more policemen who are "cracking down on crime," the greater the likelihood that individual citizens will suffer abuse of their civil liberties. Work in any bureaucracy tends to expand to fill the time allocated to do it. If the police are not busy with serious crime, they may meddle in such citizen activities as private poker games, where no one wants their help. Consequently, a silent, even unconscious alliance exists between pro-civil-liberties liberals, who want small police forces for ideological reasons, and conservative taxpayers, who do not want to pay the costs of what from their point of view amounts to social services for others.

My favorite illustration of the diverse alliances that oppose improvements in the criminal-justice system is the repeated failure of a bill that is perennially introduced in the West Virginia Legislature. The bill, which is introduced at the request of the state attorney general, would give the attorney general statewide prosecutorial powers. Under the current system, each West Virginia county elects a prosecutor who has absolute discretion concerning what crimes will be prosecuted in his county. The attorney general handles criminal cases on appeal, defends the state's interest in federal habeas corpus proceedings, and represents the state's agencies in civil litigation; however, the attorney general has no power to initiate prosecutions at the trial-court level in the fifty-five counties. Why should there not be a statewide prosecutorial agency, particularly since many local prosecutors are reluctant to enforce the law against their political friends?

The answer is quite simple. The position of attorney general has historically been a stepping-stone to the governorship. Since 1936, four out of ten governors held the office of attorney general immediately before their election as governor. High elected office has tended to go to media stars since the demise of well-organized political machines. Only certain types of political antics, however, attract media attention; these include crusades against political corruption and white-collar crime. Everyone who is actively involved in either business or government is aware of the public-relations value of an anti-corruption crusade, yet even the consummately honest prefer not to be bothered by one. Zealous investigations demand the production of documents, testimony by employees on company time, and a costly disruption of normal business operations. None of these costs is borne by the government; all must be borne by the private sector.

The important facts are that there is less than universal support for the enforcement of most laws, from consumer fraud to drug use, and that lack of consensus about the value of some types of law enforcement is seen in the legislature's failure to establish a statewide enforcement agency.

In West Virginia's four northernmost counties, the population is composed largely of the children of Italians, Greeks, Poles, Hungarians, and other non-Anglo-Saxon peoples. The biggest illegal gambling institutions used to be the churches, which held regular, illegal bingo parties and raised significant revenues (bingo games for charitable organizations were recently legalized). Other social institutions similarly rely on slot machines and football pools; it is a way of life completely different from that of the predominantly fundamentalist southern part of the state. Local prosecutors in those counties are elected by citizens who expect a policy of conspicuous non-enforcement of the gambling laws, at least as they apply to churches and social clubs. The last thing on earth they want is a statewide strike force destroying their churches and clubs.

In 1977, when John D. Rockefeller IV became governor, his new chief of the state police attempted to enforce the gambling laws in the northern counties. Within a month, the state police were instructed to back off, because it became obvious that continued enforcement would anger every member of the legislature from those counties and that, in retaliation, those legislators would torpedo the governor's legislative program.

Every effort at improvement in the criminal justice system will seem either helpful or threatening, depending on the perspective of some political-interest group. Thus an increase in the number of policemen means more protection to some, more bullying to others. If, for example, the staffs of prosecuting attorneys are increased so that they can diligently prosecute armed robbers, murderers, and dope peddlers, they will also be available to ferret out consumer fraud, anti-trust violations, and political corruption. Since prosecuting attorneys are usually elected and, therefore, are lawyers with political ambitions, they will be tempted, as in West Virginia, to play to the press by prosecuting white-collar crime. These campaigns are middle-class morality plays that assuage the newspaper reader's sense of unrecognized merit. They are usually less attractive to the political establishment, however resolute it may be about cracking down on murder and armed robbery. Even firebrand political reformers use questionable tactics at election time, and the prospect of an elaborate enforcement bureaucracy falling into enemy hands is horrifying to politicians.

A classic example of frivolous white-collar-crime prosecution took place recently in Pittsburgh. A county commissioner, who was also the county Democratic Party chairman, was charged with theft of services during his tenure as county coroner. At that time, in addition to being coroner, he owned a private laboratory, which did pathology and toxicology testing. It was alleged that he brought tissue specimens from his lab to the morgue, where they were processed by morgue employees on the county payroll, thereby "stealing" $115,000 worth of county services.

The case had all the trappings of a political trial. The defendant, Cyril H. Wecht, was highly placed in county politics, so prosecuting him would bring much publicity—adverse for Wecht, angelic for the prosecutor. Wecht had political enemies even within his own party, and some of them were involved in initiating and developing the investigation. Others used the investigation and trial as a reason to force him to withdraw from the party chairmanship. And the district attorney responsible for the prosecution, perhaps trading on the publicity it generated, was running for the state supreme court bench at the same time.

Political or not, theft of government services is not a trivial charge. But this case certainly was not one of those occasions when an expensive jury trial was warranted by any cost-benefit analysis of the "public good." Fortunately for Wecht, he was able to hire the nationally known trial lawyer Stanley Preiser to defend him. After six weeks of exhaustive testimony and with thirty-two cartons of documentary evidence, the jury deliberated for ten hours and acquitted Wecht.

The investigation and trial took nearly two years and involved ten investigators and seven lawyers from the district attorney's office at one time or another. The trial lasted six weeks, and the whole affair was estimated to have cost the county about $1.5 million—more than ten times the value of the services said to have been stolen. The money spent on the trial could have bought almost forty prosecutors for a year at an annual salary of $40,000, and they each could have been prosecuting fifty violent crimes and property crimes such as murder, rape, arson, armed robbery, and larceny–the ones that affect the average citizen's life.

As long as we are talking only about the criminal courts, the questions are comparatively simple. But when we add the complications created by the civil courts, all bets are off. Devoting more money to the *criminal* courts would return economic dividends to the public, but increased funding for the entire court system has a much more mixed effect. Indeed, for certain groups, including local governments, businesses, unions, landlords, and even tenants, a better-functioning court system would be a calamity.

Consider the case of New York City, which is notorious for its long court delays. In the abstract, most New Yorkers would like to have an efficient court system so that criminals would be sent away. To the casual observer, New York's felon problem would appear easy to solve by increasing the number of policemen and prosecutors, and by expanding the court system.

The hitch, however, is that a New York trial-court judge is empowered to hear both criminal and civil cases; if the number of judges is increased, more civil cases can be heard. Of 25,589 civil cases concluded in New York City in the first forty weeks of the 1979–1980 fiscal year, 5,523 were against New York City itself. New York City has been on the verge of bankruptcy since 1975, and the policies of the Reagan Administration threaten even greater financial strains in the next two and a half years. The potential liability for New York City from the civil suits currently awaiting trial runs to billions of dollars. New York City cannot afford an efficient court system, because it would be bankrupt beyond bail-out if all these suits came to trial in one or two years.

New York is an extraordinary example, but legal-aid and other public-interest lawyers elsewhere are bringing suits challenging the standards of operation in mental hospitals, prisons, schools, and other state and local facilities. When courts take action in these areas, it can mean that local governments must spend millions or even billions of dollars they never planned to. In New Jersey, for example, the state supreme court ordered the legislature to enact an income tax to support the public schools. This required the allocation of state money to projects that judges wanted rather than to projects that the governor and the legislators wanted.

The moral of these stories is that the costs of creating more courts, along with all their supporting staff, are but a fraction of the total amount of money that an expansion of the courts will eventually involve. Typically, the entire judicial branch of government takes less than 2 percent of any state's budget. In New York City, the cost of doubling the number of judges, prosecutors, city attorneys, courtrooms, and supporting staff would be small compared with the cost of paying the judgments the new courts would render against the city.

In other parts of the United States, there are powerful private interests in the same position as New York City: they are not in the least interested in improving the efficiency of civil courts. If, for instance, litigation against insurance companies takes eight years to complete, the company has the use of its money for eight years, and can invest it during that period at between 10 and 18 percent. Furthermore, delay alone is a powerful force to inspire settlements for low sums. Since most federal and state courts are unified criminal and civil tribunals, in which any judge can hear either type of case, the positive economic effect for the general public of improved criminal courts is almost always offset by increased costs on the civil side for those who have the most political power. The public takes its accustomed beating.

If expanding the courts has varied effects, some of them welcomed and some of them abhorred by powerful political groups, the logical solution would be to separate the courts' various functions. We might create institutions that would work in areas where there is broad agreement— such as fighting violent crime—while avoiding other areas. Everyone wants violent criminals prosecuted and the streets made safe. During the 1960s and 1970s, there were numerous programs that attempted to get at the root causes of crime—slums, broken families, unemployment. While we have not abandoned these efforts, there is an increasing awareness that we do not have either the resources or the knowledge to reduce violent crime through preventive means, and this lack should not be used as an excuse for doing nothing.

New institutions will not be developed, however, until there is an organized citizen lobby that makes campaign contributions, sends out direct-mail newsletters about how elected officials perform in the area of court reform, and has representatives entering into the give-and-take of political bargaining in the committee rooms and the corridors of legislatures. Until there is such a lobby around which political support can coalesce, politically workable plans will not be generated. Since there is no active citizen lobby for court reform, and since, to the contrary, all of the day-to-day political rewards go to those who oppose court reform, the legislative branch is entirely indifferent to the courts. In fact, I cannot think of any other subject of major social concern that intrudes itself less upon the imagination of the average legislator than the courts. Yet court reform, albeit in simplistic terms, is the frequent subject of campaign rhetoric, which gives the illusion that politicians have some continuing interest in the subject. Sadly, the courts are usually regarded in the same light as is the Federal Reserve Board—as an institution that is to be reviled and attacked but ultimately to be left unchanged.

The history of the environmental movement suggests the direction that a citizens' movement could take. Environmental and conservation issues used to be as low a legislative priority as court reform is today. But in the early 1960s, the whole question of pollution control and conservation of unspoiled wilderness captured the imagination of the college-educated middle class. Suddenly, defense of the environment took on the aura of a religious crusade. Groups such as the Sierra Club organized on the national level, and in every state local groups developed and kept in communication with one another.

The reform of the criminal law may be ripe for the same type of crusade that the environmentalists led fifteen years ago. Most street crime is, to be sure, perpetrated upon the poor, because they must live where the criminals are. But crime has risen to a level that intrudes itself into the lives of many middle-class citizens on a daily basis. It is the middle class that has organizational and political skills, along with a spare hundred dollars to contribute to a political-action group. It was essentially the middle class that accomplished the environmental revolution.

The beginnings of a citizen lobby for better law enforcement can already be perceived. In West Virginia last year, the relatives of persons killed by drunk drivers organized themselves to make the drunk-driving penalties more severe. In general, the enforcement of the drunk-driving laws in the United States is a disgrace. But last year, the public outcry against drunk drivers was such that the West Virginia Legislature made drunk driving a serious offense, amending the law to include a no-nonsense procedure for enforcement.

West Virginia's decision to crack down on drunk driving was not unique; several other states amended their laws last year with spectacular results. In California, for example, after a new drunk-driving law went into effect, the highway death toll during the Christmas season was reduced by 50 percent over the previous year.

Drunk driving differs from other criminal questions in that it is a comparatively easily understood problem and there is no political pressure to protect drunk drivers. Although there is no pressure to protect any criminal who strikes at random, the more a criminal activity looks like a regular business—car theft, gambling, drug sales—the more criminals organize to influence the political process. Even more important in the passage of the drunk-driving laws, perhaps, was the lack of debate about what would reduce drunk driving. Everyone agreed that strict sanctions, quickly applied, would do the trick for the occasional drunk, and that permanent revocation of their licenses would keep most of the habitual drunks off the road. Like the environmental movement, the lobby against drunk driving knew just what it wanted.

By contrast, efforts within the political system to improve the criminal-justice system often stall because of the timeless debate about stricter enforcement versus elimination of the root causes of crime. The advantage of a citizen lobby seriously concerned with an improved criminal-justice system is that citizens want protection—they are content if the symptoms of the disease can be controlled, and that is probably the practical approach for the foreseeable future.

It is important to differentiate between traditional law-and-order rhetoric and real criminal-law reform. Traditional law-and-order rhetoric addresses itself primarily to the decisions of the United States Supreme Court since *Miranda* v. *Arizona* in 1966, when the Supreme Court began the wholesale reform of the criminal law in order to further civil rights and civil liberties. A return to police brutality, official harassment of the lower socio-economic class, and kangaroo-court summary convictions by forced guilty pleas is not my idea of criminal-law reform. It is possible to have a well-functioning system of criminal-law enforcement without the violations of personal integrity inherent in the police state. But it would be expensive.

In my estimation, a good criminal-justice system that reduces violent and petty crime to roughly one fifth of their current level could be established with substantially less political activism than was required for environmental reform. Furthermore, the costs to the nation of criminal-law reform would be dramatically less than those of the environmental movement, although they would *all* be borne directly by the taxpayers instead of being paid for through the inflation of consumer prices, as was the case with most environmental reforms. Cleaning up the environment exacted its costs through lost jobs, higher utility bills, and more expensive automobiles. Criminal-law reform will cost higher taxes.

It is not necessary that everyone suddenly become interested in criminal-law reform. After all, the number of voters who were actively dedicated to the ecology revolution was comparatively small. Extremely effective interest groups—the National Rifle Association, for example—are comparatively small in terms of active members. It must be remembered that politicians are not concerned with influencing everyone who is eligible to vote—just the 21 to 65 percent, depending on the election, who actually come to the polls. It is the militant and not the indifferent voter who must be satisfied first.

QUESTIONS FOR DISCUSSION

1. Where does Neely enter the argument as "I" and why? Why does he not introduce his professional qualifications into his argument?
2. Outline Neely's causal argument as he "backs up" to the significant causes. What blocking causes does Neely find missing? Why is there no money to put these into place?
3. Do you agree with Neely that blocking causes in the form of an enlarged police force and criminal justice system would significantly reduce crime?
4. Do the reasons Neely gives for why people do not want more police seem plausible? Would such a cause convince anyone or only those who have had some experience of the police as bullies? In other words, what is the *agency* that makes this cause operate?
5. What is the plea bargaining Neely talks about (and defines with an example)? Why does the criminal justice system resort to it? How does this point support his overall causal reasoning?
6. Note all the places where Neely introduces what he calls "illustrations." Are these illustrations really supporting examples? How does Neely get around the problem of the typicality of his evidence? Do we simply recognize these cases as typical of many more like them and therefore as constituting a large substratum of evidence for Neely's case?
7. Why does Neely introduce references to the Sierra Club, to lobbying for stiffer drunk-driving penalties, and even to the National Rifle Association toward the end of his argument? What purpose other than causal argument does he have and hint at?

SUGGESTIONS FOR WRITING

1. Investigate the docket of pending civil cases in the nearest county, state, or federal court. What interest groups stand to lose, as Neely suggests, if these cases are tried efficiently? Use the evidence you collect to support or refute Neely's argument that many public and private groups "are not in the least interested in improving the efficiency of civil courts" and therefore are a cause blocking that improvement. Send the results to your local newspaper.

2. Look at the statistics for violent crime in 1983, 1984, and 1985. Do they indicate a real (rather than merely apparent) decline in violent crime? What has been the cause of any change you find? Have we had some of the criminal law reform that Neely advocates? Write an essay in which you account for whatever changes have taken place.

3. What is mandatory sentencing? Has it been effective in reducing the rate of violent crime? Address an essay on the consequences of mandatory sentencing to Neely.

4. Neely suggests that "the more a criminal activity looks like a regular business —car theft, gambling, drug sales—the more criminals organize to influence the political process." Investigate the penalties (distinguishing laws on the books from sentences actually given) against drug dealing. If you find that drug pushers are handled inconsistently or not as severely as they might be, what might be the causes of such discrepancies? Write an essay in which you speculate about possible blocking causes.

5. Support or refute Neely's contention that "we do not have either the resources or the knowledge to reduce violent crime through preventive means."

6. Write a public argument for a local newspaper, a flyer to be stuffed in mail boxes, or a community newsletter in which you begin to create that "active citizen lobby" for court reform that Neely says is now missing.

—>>> <<<—

Dreams of the Death of Persons of Whom the Dreamer Is Fond

SIGMUND FREUD

Sigmund Freud's The Interpretation of Dreams *has been one of the most influential books of the twentieth century. In this selection from it, Freud argues for a causal connection between dreams of the deaths of loved ones and suppressed childhood wishes. Working backward from the recounted dreams of adult patients and from observations of children's hostility toward parents and siblings, Freud is actually arguing for a causal agency, for the connecting link of suppressed thoughts between childhood wishes and adult dreams.*

Since the time of Freud, this agency has become widely accepted, but in this piece we see Freud working on a resistant audience who would be horrified at the notion that children could have sexual impulses or wish for the deaths of baby brothers and sisters.

To support his causal argument, Freud uses a surprising source of evidence, the great tragedies of Oedipus Rex and Hamlet. He attributes the power of these plays to their expression of the unconscious motives of their heroes and their audiences.

Another group of dreams which may be described as typical are those containing the death of some loved relative—for instance, of a parent, of a brother or sister, or of a child. Two classes of such dreams must at once be distinguished: those in which the dreamer is unaffected by grief, so that on awakening he is astonished at his lack of feeling, and those in which the dreamer feels deeply pained by the death and may even weep bitterly in his sleep.

We need not consider the dreams of the first of these classes, for they have no claim to be regarded as 'typical.' If we analyse them, we find that they have some meaning other than their apparent one, and that they are intended to conceal some other wish. Such was the dream of the aunt who saw her sister's only son lying in his coffin. . . . It did not mean that she wished her little nephew dead; as we have seen, it merely concealed a wish to see a particular person of whom she was fond and whom she had not met for a long time—a person whom she had once before met after a similarly long interval beside the coffin of another nephew. This wish, which was the true content of the dream, gave no occasion for grief, and no grief, therefore, was felt in the dream. It will be noticed that the affect felt in the dream belongs to its latent and not to its manifest content, and that the dream's *affective* content has remained untouched by the distortion which has overtaken its *ideational* content.

Very different are the dreams of the other class—those in which the dreamer imagines the death of a loved relative and is at the same time painfully affected. The meaning of such dreams, as their content indicates, is a wish that the person in question may die. And since I must expect that the feelings of all of my readers and any others who have experienced similar dreams will rebel against my assertion, I must try to base my evidence for it on the broadest possible foundation.

I have already discussed a dream which taught us that the wishes which are represented in dreams as fulfilled are not always present-day wishes. They may also be wishes of the past which have been abandoned, overlaid and repressed, and to which we have to attribute some sort of continued existence only because of their re-emergence in a dream. They are not dead in our sense of the word but only like the shades in the Odyssey, which awoke to some sort of life as soon as they had tasted blood. In the dream of the dead child in the 'case' . . . what was involved was a wish which had been an immediate one fifteen years earlier and was frankly admitted as having existed at that time. I may add—and this may not be without its bearing upon the theory of dreams—that even behind this wish there lay a memory from the dreamer's earliest child-hood. When she was a small child—the exact date could not be fixed with certainty—she had heard that her mother had fallen into a deep depression during the pregnancy of which she had been the fruit and had passionately wished that the child she was bearing might die. When the dreamer herself was grown-up and pregnant, she merely followed her mother's example.

If anyone dreams, with every sign of pain, that his father or mother or brother or sister has died, I should never use the dream as evidence that he wishes for that person's death *at the present time*. The theory of dreams does not require as much as that; it is satisfied with the inference that this death has been wished for at some time or other during the dreamer's childhood. I fear, however, that this reservation will not appease the objectors; they will deny the possibility of their *ever* having had such a thought with just as much energy as they insist that they harbour no such wishes now. I must therefore reconstruct a portion of the vanished mental life of children on the basis of the evidence of the present.

Let us first consider the relation of children to their brothers and sisters. I do not know why we presuppose that that relation must be a loving one; for instances of hostility between adult brothers and sisters force themselves upon everyone's experience and we can often establish the fact that the disunity originated in childhood or has always existed. But it is further true that a great many adults, who are on affectionate terms with their brothers and sisters and are ready to stand by them today, passed their childhood on almost unbroken terms of enmity with them. The elder child ill-treats the younger, maligns him and robs him of his toys; while the younger is consumed with impotent rage against the elder, envies and fears him, or meets his oppressor with the first stirrings of a love of liberty and a sense of justice. Their parents complain that the children do not get on with one another, but cannot discover why. It is easy to see that the character of even a good child is not what we should wish to find it in an adult. Children are completely egoistic; they feel their needs intensely and strive ruthlessly to satisfy them—especially as against the rivals, other children, and first and foremost as against their brothers and sisters. But we do not on that account call a child 'bad,' we call him 'naughty'; he is no more answerable for his evil deeds in our judgement than in the eyes of the law. And it is right that this should be so; for we may expect that, before the end of the period which we count as childhood, altruistic impulses and morality will awaken in the little egoist and (to use Meynert's terms . . .) a secondary ego will overlay and inhibit the primary one. It is true, no doubt, that morality does not set in simultaneously all along the line and that the length of non-moral childhood varies in different individuals. If this morality fails to develop, we like to talk of 'degeneracy,' though what in fact faces us is an inhibition in development. After the primary character has already been overlaid by later development, it can still be laid bare again, at all events in part, in cases of hysterical illness. There is a really striking resemblance between what is known as the hysterical character and that of a naughty child. Obsessional neurosis, on the contrary, corresponds to a super-morality imposed as a reinforcing weight upon fresh stirrings of the primary character.

Many people, therefore, who love their brothers and sisters and would feel bereaved if they were to die, harbour evil wishes against them in their unconscious, dating from earlier times; and these are capable of being realized in dreams.

It is of quite particular interest, however, to observe the behaviour of small children up to the age of two or three or a little older towards their younger brothers and sisters. Here, for instance, was a child who had so far been the only one; and now he was told that the stork had brought a new baby. He looked the new arrival up and down and then declared decisively: 'The stork can take him away again!'[1] I am quite seriously of the opinion that a child can form a just estimate of the

[1] [*Footnote added* 1909:] The three-and-a-half-year-old Hans . . . exclaimed shortly after the birth of a sister, while he was suffering from a feverish sore throat: 'I don't *want* a baby sister!' [Freud, 1909*b*, Section I.] During his neurosis eighteen months later he frankly confessed to a wish that his mother might drop the baby into the bath so that she would die. . . . At the same time, Hans was a good-natured and affectionate child, who soon grew fond of this same sister and particularly enjoyed taking her under his wing.

set-back he has to expect at the hands of the little stranger. A lady of my acquaintance, who is on very good terms today with a sister four years her junior, tells me that she greeted the news of her first arrival with this qualification: 'But all the same I shan't give her my red cap!' Even if a child only comes to realize the situation later on, his hostility will date from that moment. I know of a case in which a little girl of less than three tried to strangle an infant in its cradle because she felt that its continued presence boded her no good. Children at that time of life are capable of jealousy of any degree of intensity and obviousness. Again, if it should happen that the baby sister does in fact disappear after a short while, the elder child will find the whole affection of the household once more concentrated upon himself. If after that the stork should bring yet another baby, it seems only logical that the little favourite should nourish a wish that his new competitor may meet with the same fate as the earlier one, so that he himself may be as happy as he was originally and during the interval.[2] Normally, of course, this attitude of a child towards a younger brother or sister is a simple function of the difference between their ages. Where the gap in time is sufficiently long, an elder girl will already begin to feel the stirring of her maternal instincts towards the helpless new-born baby.

Hostile feelings towards brothers and sisters must be far more frequent in childhood than the unseeing eye of the adult observer can perceive.[3]

In the case of my own children, who followed each other in rapid succession, I neglected the opportunity of carrying out observations of this kind; but I am now making up for this neglect by observing a small nephew, whose autocratic rule was upset, after lasting for fifteen months, by the appearance of a female rival. I am told, it is true, that the young man behaves in the most chivalrous manner to his little sister,

---

[2][*Footnote added* 1914:] Deaths that are experienced in this way in childhood may quickly be forgotten in the family; but psycho-analytic research shows that they have a very important influence on subsequent neuroses.

[3][*Footnote added* 1914:] Since this was written, a large number of observations have been made and recorded in the literature of psycho-analysis upon the originally hostile attitude of children towards their brothers and sisters and one of their parents. The [Swiss] author and poet Spitteler has given us a particularly genuine and naïve account of this childish attitude, derived from his own childhood [1914, 40]: 'Moreover there was a second Adolf there: a little creature who they alleged was my brother, though I could not see what use he was and still less why they made as much fuss of him as of me myself. I was sufficient so far as I was concerned; why should I want a brother? And he was not merely useless, he was positively in the way. When I pestered my grandmother, he wanted to pester her too. When I was taken out in the perambulator, he sat opposite to me and took up half the space, so that we were bound to kick each other with our feet.'

that he kisses her hand and strokes her; but I have been able to convince myself that even before the end of his second year he made use of his powers of speech for the purpose of criticizing someone whom he could not fail to regard as superfluous. Whenever the conversation touched upon her he used to intervene in it and exclaim petulantly: 'Too 'ickle! too 'ickle!' During the last few months the baby's growth has made enough progress to place her beyond this particular ground for contempt, and the little boy has found a different basis for his assertion that she does not deserve so much attention: at every suitable opportunity he draws attention to the fact that she has no teeth.[4] We all of us recollect how the eldest girl of another of my sisters, who was then a child of six, spent half-an-hour in insisting upon each of her aunts in succession agreeing with her: 'Lucie can't understand that yet, can she?' she kept asking. Lucie was her rival—two and a half years her junior.

In none of my women patients, to take an example, have I failed to come upon this dream of the death of a brother or sister, which tallies with an increase in hostility. I have only found a single exception; and it was easy to interpret this as a confirmation of the rule. On one occasion during an analytic session I was explaining this subject to a lady, since in view of her symptom its discussion seemed to me relevant. To my astonishment she replied that she had never had such a dream. Another dream, however, occurred to her, which ostensibly had no connection with the topic—a dream which she had first dreamt when she was four years old and at that time the youngest of the family, and which she had dreamt repeatedly since: *A whole crowd of children—all her brothers, sisters and cousins of both sexes—were romping in a field. Suddenly they all grew wings, flew away and disappeared.* She had no idea what this dream meant; but it is not hard to recognize that in its original form it had been a dream of the death of all her brothers and sisters, and had been only slightly influenced by the censorship. I may venture to suggest the following analysis. On the occasion of the death of one of this crowd of children (in this instance the children of two brothers had been brought up together as a single family) the dreamer, not yet four years old at the time, must have asked some wise grown-up person what became of children when they were dead. The reply must have been: 'They grow wings and turn into little angels.' In the dream which followed upon this piece of information all the dreamer's brothers and sisters had wings like

---

[4][*Footnote added* 1909:] Little Hans, when he was three and a half, gave vent to a crushing criticism of his sister in the same words. It was because of her lack of teeth, he supposed, that she was unable to talk. [Freud, 1909b, Section I.]

angels and—which is the main point—flew away. Our little baby-killer was left alone, strange to say: the only survivor of the whole crowd! We can hardly be wrong in supposing that the fact of the children romping in a *field* before flying away points to butterflies. It is as though the child was led by the same chain of thought as the peoples of antiquity to picture the soul as having a butterfly's wings.

At this point someone will perhaps interrupt: 'Granted that children have hostile impulses towards their brothers and sisters, how can a child's mind reach such a pitch of depravity as to wish for the *death* of his rivals or of playmates stronger than himself, as though the death penalty were the only punishment for every crime?' Anyone who talks like this has failed to bear in mind that a child's idea of being 'dead' has nothing much in common with ours apart from the word. Children know nothing of the horrors of corruption, of freezing in the ice-cold grave, of the terrors of eternal nothingness—ideas which grown-up people find it so hard to tolerate, as is proved by all the myths of a future life. The fear of death has no meaning to a child; hence it is that he will play with the dreadful word and use it as a threat against a playmate: 'If you do that again, you'll die, like Franz!' Meanwhile the poor mother gives a shudder and remembers, perhaps, that the greater half of the human race fail to survive their childhood years. It was actually possible for a child, who was over eight years old at the time, coming home from a visit to the Natural History Museum, to say to his mother: 'I'm so fond of you, Mummy: when you die I'll have you stuffed and I'll keep you in this room, so that I can see you *all* the time.' So little resemblance is there between a child's idea of being dead and our own![5]

To children, who, moreover, are spared the sight of the scenes of suffering which precede death, being 'dead' means approximately the same as being 'gone'—not troubling the survivors any longer. A child makes no distinction as to how this absence is brought about: whether it is due to a journey, to a dismissal, to an estrangement, or to death.[6] If, during a child's prehistoric epoch, his nurse has been dismissed, and

[5][*Footnote added* 1909:] I was astonished to hear a highly intelligent boy of ten remark after the sudden death of his father: 'I know father's dead, but what I can't understand is why he doesn't come home to supper.'

[6][*Footnote added* 1919:] An observation made by a parent who had a knowledge of psycho-analysis caught the actual moment at which his highly intelligent four-year-old daughter perceived the distinction between being 'gone' and being 'dead.' The little girl had been troublesome at meal-time and noticed that one of the maids at the pension where they were staying was looking at her askance. 'I wish Josefine was dead,' was the child's comment to her father. 'Why dead?' enquired her father soothingly; 'wouldn't it do if she

if soon afterwards his mother has died, the two events are superimposed on each other in a single series in his memory as revealed in analysis. When people are absent, children do not miss them with any great intensity; many mothers have learnt this to their sorrow when, after being away from home for some weeks on a summer holiday, they are met on their return by the news that the children have not once asked after their mummy. If their mother does actually make the journey to that 'undiscover'd country, from whose bourn no traveller returns,' children seem at first to have forgotten her, and it is only later on that they begin to call their dead mother to mind.

Thus if a child has reasons for wishing the absence of another, there is nothing to restrain him from giving his wish the form of the other child being dead. And the psychical reaction to dreams containing death-wishes proves that, in spite of the different content of these wishes in the case of children, they are nevertheless in some way or other the same as wishes expressed in the same terms by adults.

If, then, a child's death-wishes against his brothers and sisters are explained by the childish egoism which makes him regard them as his rivals, how are we to explain his death-wishes against his parents, who surround him with love and fulfil his needs and whose preservation that same egoism should lead him to desire?

A solution of this difficulty is afforded by the observation that dreams of the death of parents apply with preponderant frequency to the parent who is of the same sex as the dreamer: that men, that is, dream mostly of their father's death and women of their mother's. I cannot pretend that this is universally so, but the preponderance in the direction I have indicated is so evident that it requires to be explained by a factor of general importance.[7] It is as though—to put it bluntly—a sexual preference were making itself felt at an early age: as though boys regarded their fathers and girls their mothers as their rivals in love, whose elimination could not fail to be to their advantage.

---

went away?' 'No,' replied the child; 'then she'd come back again.' The unbounded self-love (the narcissism) of children regards any interference as an act of lèse majesté; and their feelings demand (like the Draconian code) that any such crime shall receive the one form of punishment which admits of no degrees.

[7][Footnote added 1925:] The situation is often obscured by the emergence of a self-punitive impulse, which threatens the dreamer, by way of a moral reaction, with the loss of the parent whom he loves.

Before this idea is rejected as a monstrous one, it is as well in this case, too, to consider the real relations obtaining—this time between parents and children. We must distinguish between what the cultural standards of filial piety demand of this relation and what everyday observation shows it in fact to be. More than one occasion for hostility lies concealed in the relation between parents and children—a relation which affords the most ample opportunities for wishes to arise which cannot pass the censorship.

Let us consider first the relation between father and son. The sanctity which we attribute to the rules laid down in the Decalogue has, I think, blunted our powers of perceiving the real facts. We seem scarcely to venture to observe that the majority of mankind disobey the Fifth Commandment. Alike in the lowest and in the highest strata of human society filial piety is wont to give way to other interests. The obscure information which is brought to us by mythology and legend from the primaeval ages of human society gives an unpleasing picture of the father's despotic power and of the ruthlessness with which he made use of it. Kronos devoured his children, just as the wild boar devours the sow's litter; while Zeus emasculated his father and made himself ruler in his place. The more unrestricted was the rule of the father in the ancient family, the more must the son, as his destined successor, have found himself in the position of an enemy, and the more impatient must he have been to become ruler himself through his father's death. Even in our middle-class families fathers are as a rule inclined to refuse their sons independence and the means necessary to secure it and thus to foster the growth of the germ of hostility which is inherent in their relation. A physician will often be in a position to notice how a son's grief at the loss of his father cannot suppress his satisfaction at having at length won his freedom. In our society today fathers are apt to cling desperately to what is left of a now sadly antiquated *potestas patris familias;* and an author who, like Ibsen, brings the immemorial struggle between fathers and sons into prominence in his writings may be certain of producing his effect.

Occasions for conflict between a daughter and her mother arise when the daughter begins to grow up and long for sexual liberty, but finds herself under her mother's tutelage; while the mother, on the other hand, is warned by her daughter's growth that the time has come when she herself must abandon her claims to sexual satisfaction.

All of this is patent to the eyes of everyone. But it does not help us in our endeavour to explain dreams of a parent's death in people whose piety towards their parents has long been unimpeachably established. Previous discussions, moreover, will have prepared us to learn that the death-wish against parents dates back to earliest childhood.

This supposition is confirmed with a certainty beyond all doubt in the case of psychoneurotics when they are subjected to analysis. We learn from them that a child's sexual wishes—if in their embryonic stage they deserve to be so described—awaken very early, and that a girl's first affection is for her father and a boy's first childish desires are for his mother. Accordingly, the father becomes a disturbing rival to the boy and the mother to the girl; and I have already shown in the case of brothers and sisters how easily such feelings can lead to a death-wish. The parents too give evidence as a rule of sexual partiality: a natural predilection usually sees to it that a man tends to spoil his little daughters, while his wife takes her sons' part; though both of them, where their judgement is not disturbed by the magic of sex, keep a strict eye upon their children's education. The child is very well aware of this partiality and turns against that one of his parents who is opposed to showing it. Being loved by an adult does not merely bring a child the satisfaction of a special need; it also means that he will get what he wants in every other respect as well. Thus he will be following his own sexual instinct and at the same time giving fresh strength to the inclination shown by his parents if his choice between them falls in with theirs.

The signs of these infantile preferences are for the most part overlooked; yet some of them are to be observed even after the first years of childhood. An eight-year-old girl of my acquaintance, if her mother is called away from the table, makes use of the occasion to proclaim herself her successor: '*I*'m going to be Mummy now. Do you want some more greens, Karl? Well, help yourself, then!' and so on. A particularly gifted and lively girl of four, in whom this piece of child psychology is especially transparent, declared quite openly: 'Mummy can go away now. Then Daddy must marry me and I'll be his wife.' Such a wish occurring in a child is not in the least inconsistent with her being tenderly attached to her mother. If a little boy is allowed to sleep beside his mother when his father is away from home, but has to go back to the nursery and to someone of whom he is far less fond as soon as his father returns, he may easily begin to form a wish that his father should *always* be away, so that he himself could keep his place beside his dear, lovely Mummy. One obvious way of attaining this wish would be if his father were dead; for the child has learnt one thing by experience—namely that 'dead' people, such as Granddaddy, are always away and never come back.

Though observations of this kind on small children fit in perfectly with the interpretation I have proposed, they do not carry such complete conviction as is forced upon the physician by psycho-analyses of adult neurotics. In the latter case dreams of the sort we are considering are introduced into the analysis in such a context that it is impossible to avoid interpreting them as *wishful* dreams.

One day one of my women patients was in a distressed and tearful mood. 'I don't want ever to see my relations again,' she said, 'they must think me horrible.' She then went on, with almost no transition, to say that she remembered a dream, though of course she had no idea what it meant. When she was four years old she had a dream that *a lynx or fox was walking on the roof; then something had fallen down or she had fallen down; and then her mother was carried out of the house dead*—and she wept bitterly. I told her that this dream must mean that when she was a child she had wished she could see her mother dead, and that it must be on account of the dream that she felt her relations must think her horrible. I had scarcely said this when she produced some material which threw light on the dream. 'Lynx-eye' was a term of abuse that had been thrown at her by a street-urchin when she was a very small child. When she was three years old, a tile off the roof had fallen on her mother's head and made it bleed violently.

I once had an opportunity of making a detailed study of a young woman who passed through a variety of psychical conditions. Her illness began with a state of confusional excitement during which she displayed a quite special aversion to her mother, hitting and abusing her whenever she came near her bed, while at the same period she was docile and affectionate towards a sister who was many years her senior. This was followed by a state in which she was lucid but somewhat apathetic and suffered from badly disturbed sleep. It was during this phase that I began treating her and analysing her dreams. An immense number of these dreams were concerned, with a greater or less degree of disguise, with the death of her mother: at one time she would be attending an old woman's funeral, at another she and her sister would be sitting at table dressed in mourning. There could be no question as to the meaning of these dreams. As her condition improved still further, hysterical phobias developed. The most tormenting of these was a fear that something might have happened to her mother. She was obliged to hurry home, wherever she might be, to convince herself that her mother was still alive. This case, taken in conjunction with what I had learnt from other sources, was highly instructive: it exhibited, translated as it were into different languages, the various ways in which the psychical apparatus reacted to one and the same exciting idea. In the confusional state, in which, as I believe, the second psychical agency was overwhelmed by the normally suppressed first one, her unconscious hostility to her mother found a powerful *motor* expression. When the calmer condition set in, when the rebellion was suppressed and the domination of the censorship re-established, the only region left open in which her hostility could realize the wish for her mother's death was that of dreaming. When a normal state was still more firmly established, it led to the production of her exaggerated worry about her mother as a hysterical counter-reaction and defensive phenomenon. In view of this it is no longer hard to understand why hysterical girls are so often attached to their mothers with such exaggerated affection.

On another occasion I had an opportunity of obtaining a deep insight into the unconscious mind of a young man whose life was made almost impossible by an obsessional neurosis. He was unable to go out into the street because he was tortured by the fear that he would kill everyone he met. He spent his days in preparing his alibi in case he might be charged with one of the murders committed in the town. It is unnecessary to add that he was a man of equally high morals and education. The analysis (which, incidentally, led to his recovery) showed that the basis of this distressing obsession was an impulse to murder his somewhat over-severe father. This impulse, to his astonishment, had been consciously expressed when he was seven years old, but it had, of course, originated much earlier in his childhood. After his father's painful illness and death, the patient's obsessional self-reproaches appeared —he was in his thirty-first year at the time—taking the shape of a phobia transferred on to strangers. A person, he felt, who was capable of wanting to push his own father over a precipice from the top of a mountain was not to be trusted to respect the lives of those less closely related to him; he was quite right to shut himself up in his room.

In my experience, which is already extensive, the chief part in the mental lives of all children who later become psychoneurotics is played by their parents. Being in love with the one parent and hating the other are among the essential constituents of the stock of psychical impulses which is formed at that time and which is of such importance in determining the symptoms of the later neurosis. It is not my belief, however, that psychoneurotics differ sharply in this respect from other human beings who remain normal—that they are able, that is, to create something absolutely new and peculiar to themselves. It is far more probable—and this is confirmed by occasional observations on normal children—that they are only distinguished by exhibiting on a magnified scale feelings of love and hatred to their parents which occur less obviously and less intensely in the minds of most children.

This discovery is confirmed by a legend that has come down to us from classical antiquity: a legend whose profound and universal power to move can only be understood if the hypothesis I have put forward in regard to the psychology of children has an equally universal validity. What I have in mind is the legend of King Oedipus and Sophocles' drama which bears his name.

Oedipus, son of Laïus, King of Thebes, and of Jocasta, was exposed as an infant because an oracle had warned Laïus that the still unborn child would be his father's murderer. The child was rescued, and grew up as a prince in an alien court, until, in doubts as to his origin, he too questioned the oracle and was warned to avoid his home since he was destined to murder his father and take his mother in marriage. On the road leading away from what he believed was his home, he met King Laïus and slew him in a sudden quarrel. He came next to Thebes and solved the riddle set him by the Sphinx who barred his way. Out of gratitude the Thebans made him their king and gave him Jocasta's hand in marriage. He reigned long in peace and honour, and she who, unknown to him, was his mother bore him two sons and two daughters. Then at last a plague broke out and the Thebans made enquiry once more of the oracle. It is at this point that Sophocles' tragedy opens. The messengers bring back the reply that the plague will cease when the murderer of Laïus has been driven from the land.

> But he, where is he? Where shall now be read
> The fading record of this ancient guilt?

The action of the play consists in nothing other than the process of revealing, with cunning delays and ever-mounting excitement—a process that can be likened to the work of a psycho-analysis—that Oedipus himself is the murderer of Laïus, but further that he is the son of the murdered man and of Jocasta. Appalled at the abomination which he has unwittingly perpetrated, Oedipus blinds himself and forsakes his home. The oracle has been fulfilled.

Oedipus Rex is what is known as a tragedy of destiny. Its tragic effect is said to lie in the contrast between the supreme will of the gods and the vain attempts of mankind to escape the evil that threatens them. The lesson which, it is said, the deeply moved spectator should learn from the tragedy is submission to the divine will and realization of his own impotence. Modern dramatists have accordingly tried to achieve a similar tragic effect by weaving the same contrast into a plot invented by themselves. But the spectators have looked on unmoved while a curse or an oracle was fulfilled in spite of all the efforts of some innocent man: later tragedies of destiny have failed in their effect.

If *Oedipus Rex* moves a modern audience no less than it did the contemporary Greek one, the explanation can only be that its effect does not lie in the contrast between destiny and human will, but is to be looked for in the particular nature of the material on which that contrast is exemplified. There must be something which makes a voice within us ready to recognize the compelling force of destiny in the *Oedipus*, while we can dismiss as merely arbitrary such dispositions as are laid down in [Grillparzer's] *Die Ahnfrau* or other modern tragedies of destiny. And a factor of this kind is in fact involved in the story of King Oedipus. His destiny moves us only because it might have been ours—because the oracle laid the same curse upon us before our birth as upon him. It is the fate of all of us, perhaps, to direct our first sexual impulse towards our mother and our first hatred and our first murderous wish against our father. Our dreams convince us that that is so. King Oedipus, who slew his father Laïus and married his mother Jocasta, merely shows us the fulfillment of our own childhood wishes. But, more fortunate than he, we have meanwhile succeeded, in so far as we have not become psychoneurotics, in detaching our sexual impulses from our mothers and in forgetting our jealousy of our fathers. Here is one in whom these primaeval wishes of our childhood have been fulfilled, and we shrink back from him with the whole force of the repression by which those wishes have since that time been held down within us. While the poet, as he unravels the past, brings to light the guilt of Oedipus, he is at the same time compelling us to recognize our own inner minds, in which those same impulses, though suppressed, are still to be found. The contrast with which the closing Chorus leaves us confronted—

> . . . Fix on Oedipus your eyes,
> Who resolved the dark enigma, noblest champion and most wise.
> Like a star his envied fortune mounted beaming far and wide:
> Now he sinks in seas of anguish, whelmed beneath a raging tide . . .

—strikes as a warning at ourselves and our pride, at us who since our childhood have grown so wise and so mighty in our own eyes. Like Oedipus, we live in ignorance of these wishes, repugnant to morality, which have been forced upon us by Nature, and after their revelation we may all of us well seek to close our eyes to the scenes of our childhood.

There is an unmistakable indication in the text of Sophocles' tragedy itself that the legend of Oedipus sprang from some primaeval dream-material which had as its content the distressing disturbance of a child's relation to his parents owing to the first stirrings of sexuality. At a point when Oedipus, though he is not yet enlightened, has begun to feel troubled by his recollection of the oracle, Jocasta consoles him by refer-ring to a dream which many people dream, though, as she thinks, it has no meaning:

> Many a man ere now in dreams hath lain
> With her who bare him. He hath least annoy
> Who with such omens troubleth not his mind.

Today, just as then, many men dream of having sexual relations with their mothers, and speak of the fact with indignation and astonishment. It is clearly the key to the tragedy and the complement to the dream of the dreamer's father being dead. The story of Oedipus is the reaction of the imagination to these two typical dreams. And just as these dreams, when dreamt by adults, are accompanied by feelings of repulsion, so too the legend must include horror and self-punishment. Its further modifi-cation originates once again in a misconceived secondary revision of the material, which has sought to exploit it for theological purposes. . . . The attempt to harmonize divine omnipotence with human responsibility must naturally fail in connection with this subject-matter just as with any other.

Another of the great creations of tragic poetry, Shakespeare's *Hamlet,* has its roots in the same soil as *Oedipus Rex.* But the changed treatment of the same material reveals the whole difference in the mental life of these two widely separated epochs of civilization: the secular advance of repression in the emotional life of mankind. In the *Oedipus* the child's wishful phantasy that underlies it is brought into the open and realized as it would be in a dream. In *Hamlet* it remains repressed; and—just as in the case of a neurosis—we only learn of its existence from its inhibiting consequences. Strangely enough, the overwhelming effect produced by the more modern tragedy has turned out to be compatible with the fact that people have remained completely in the dark as to the hero's character. The play is built up on Hamlet's hesitations over fulfilling the task of revenge that is assigned to him; but its text offers no reasons or motives for these hesitations and an immense variety of attempts at interpreting them have failed to produce a result. According to the view which was originated by Goethe and is still the prevailing one today, Hamlet represents the type of man whose power of direct action is paralysed by an excessive development of his intellect. (He is 'sicklied o'er with the pale cast of thought.') According to another view, the dramatist has tried to portray a pathologically irresolute character which might be classed as neurasthenic. The plot of the drama shows us, however, that Hamlet is far from being represented as a person incapable of taking any action. We see him doing so on two occasions: first in a sudden outburst of temper, when he runs his sword through the eavesdropper behind the arras, and secondly in a premeditated and even crafty fashion, when, with all the callousness of a Renaissance prince, he sends the two courtiers to the death that had been planned for himself. What is it, then, that inhibits him in fulfilling the task set him by his father's ghost? The answer, once again, is that it is the peculiar nature of the task. Hamlet is able to do anything—except take vengeance on the man who did away with his father and took that father's place with his mother, the man who shows him the repressed wishes of his own childhood realized. Thus the loathing which should drive him on to revenge is replaced in him by self-reproaches, by scruples of conscience, which remind him that he himself is literally no better than the sinner whom he is to punish. Here I have translated into conscious terms what was bound to remain unconscious in Hamlet's mind; and if anyone is inclined to call him a hysteric, I can only accept the fact as one that is implied by my interpretation. The distaste for sexuality expressed by Hamlet in his conversation with Ophelia fits in very well with this: the same distaste which was destined to take possession of the poet's mind more and more during the years that followed, and which reached its extreme expression in *Timon of Athens*. For it can of course only be the poet's own mind which confronts us in Hamlet. I observe in a book on Shakespeare by Georg Brandes (1896) a statement that *Hamlet* was written immediately after the death of Shakespeare's father (in 1601), that is, under the immediate impact of his bereavement and, as we may well assume, while his childhood feelings about his father had been freshly revived. It is known, too, that Shakespeare's own son who died at an early age bore the name of 'Hamnet,' which is identical with 'Hamlet.' Just as *Hamlet* deals with the relation of a son to his parents, so *Macbeth* (written at approximately the same period) is concerned with the subject of childlessness. But just as all neurotic symptoms, and, for that matter, dreams, are capable of being 'over-interpreted' and indeed need to be, if they are to be fully understood, so all genuinely creative writings are the product of more than a single motive and more than a single impulse in the poet's mind, and are open to more than a single interpretation. In what I have written I have only attempted to interpret the deepest layer of impulses in the mind of the creative writer.

QUESTIONS FOR DISCUSSION

1. Creating something of a dialogue with his readers, Freud anticipates and voices their reactions to his argument. Go through the essay and characterize the points at which he feels this tactic is necessary.
2. Although Freud's argument is of great philosophical significance, it is filled with stories and anecdotes used as evidence. Why do these work? What is their appeal even to an audience separated by time and culture from the writer?
3. How does Freud present himself in this excerpt as an authority with the right to make this argument?
4. In arrangement, this essay works backwards, from effect (dreams of the death of loved ones) to cause in childhood fantasies. Construct a causal model of Freud's reasoning and assess the strength of the links in the chain.
5. How convincing are Freud's analyses of *Oedipus* and *Hamlet*, not just as literary interpretations but as evidence for his thesis?
6. Compare Freud's investigative techniques with those of the researchers on identical twins (see "Identical Twins Reared Apart"). How do the methods of these two schools of psychology differ?

SUGGESTIONS FOR WRITING

1. Freud claims that relations between siblings are commonly fraught with dissension and hostility. From your own observation and experience, how accurate would you say his generalization is? Write a response to Freud, based on your own experience.

2. Students of literature may choose to attempt a pyschoanalytic interpretation of any work dealing with relations between siblings, parents, and children.
3. If you are a vivid dreamer, you might keep a journal of your dreams and at the end of several weeks try to characterize them for an imaginary Dr. Freud by identifying recurrent patterns or elements.
4. Even in this short selection, you can see many of the basic assumptions first articulated by Freud that are now widely held: that children experience sexual feelings, that childhood experiences are formative, remaining in the unconscious even if seemingly forgotten, and that dreams express this unconscious residue. Trace the influence of such Freudian conceptions in any current practices of raising, teaching, and disciplining children or young adults. Address your essay to people who would be surprised to hear this account of Freud's influence.
5. In his arguments, Freud does not distinguish between examples drawn from patients and examples from acquaintances and others not under treatment. Write an essay in which you explore what Freud's method implies about the distinction between normal and abnormal behavior.

Three

ARGUMENTS
THAT EVALUATE

Suppose your friend raves to you about a new restaurant, La Casa del Corazón del Fuega, that serves fantastic Mexican food; after eating there, you need a year's supply of Alka Seltzer. Or suppose you extol the merits of your favorite science fiction writer to another friend only to have your friend find the author's exposition of an ideal society in the year 2500 terminally dull and void. Were these initial laudations arguments? Did they fail because their audiences ultimately disagreed with them? Most people would dismiss such praise of a restaurant or writer, a movie or health spa, a quiche or vegetable soup recipe as mere statements of personal opinion, expressions of one person's taste, completely different from arguments about the existence and nature and causes of things such as we have looked at so far.

But claims about value can achieve the status of argument. The difference between an expression of personal taste and an argument about value depends on how they are carried on. If your enchilada-loving friend did no more than affirm enthusiastically "I liked the salsa, I liked the refried beans, and the tacos were great," then you would indeed have only a declaration of personal taste in the form of various ingenious restatements of the same point: "I like what I like." But if the restaurant critic gave reasons for a preference, grounded on points that you or any other listener *could* agree with, then you would have an argument, as much an argument as one based on definition or causality. If, to continue with our example, your friend set up the criteria for a good restaurant or for good Mexican food, and then demonstrated that the Casa and its menu lived up to those standards, then a convincing argument would be underway. Your head might agree then, even though your stomach never could.

It can, however, be difficult, sometimes even impossible, to differentiate expressions of personal taste from arguments for value because too often we do not separate the act of perceiving from the act of judging. Instantaneously, we recognize objects, events, people, or acts not simply as what they are but as surrounded by an aura of value. They are immediately beautiful or ugly, moral or immoral, good or bad, right or wrong. Our ability to make swift judgments is a useful one; we certainly could not survive without it. But when we want to convince a reader or listener to judge or evaluate as we do, we cannot always simply say, "Look how wrong this is," or "See how beautiful that is." Such bare claims work only if the audience sees with our eyes and judges with our principles. If they do not, then we must engage in an argument to convince them to make the same judgment. An argument supporting a value judgment is called an *evaluation*.

How do we actually evaluate? We do not seem to go through a lengthy set of mental steps before we turn away from an offensive sidewalk spectacle or decide to attend the exhibition of a particular artist. Yet even these quick evaluations require the application of *general criteria* to a *particular case*. When we evaluate, we have in mind something like an ideal of what a good thing—pianist, painting, or professor—should be and do, and we apply that ideal to the individual instance before us. If it lives up to our standards, the evaluation is positive; if it does not, the response is negative. Sometimes the review can come in mixed. Our seemingly automatic judgments grow from years of education and conditioning in the standards of our family, group, profession, and country and in the unique profile of our own experiences. In evaluation argument we often need to bring our standards of judgment out in the open and apply them.

Where do these criteria come from? The criteria that make evaluation possible come from two sources and demand two forms of argument: CP and causal, hinging once again on definition and agency. We can illustrate with a simple example of evaluating a sales manager. First for the CP. A want ad describing the position might define a good manager as one who has a degree in marketing, years of experience in the field, a history of promotions, a personable appearance, and good communication skills. But a candidate who fulfilled all these criteria and was hired might be re-evaluated as a failure after six months if sales declined, customers complained, and subordinates quit in record numbers. In other words, we have come to our second source of criteria: evaluation by effects. It is not enough for our subject to fit the ideal definition of "good sales manager"; the director of sales must also be the agent that produces good results.

Although all criteria belong to the general categories of definition and cause, specific criteria will uniquely fit the subject under consideration. If we are evaluating a material object—a toaster, for example—it gets evaluated in its own class, that of toasters; a personal computer is evaluated in its own category. We are all familiar with this sort of evaluation from *Consumer Reports*, where practical objects are evaluated according to functional criteria: a good widget ought to have qualities x, y, and z; brand A widget has x, y, and z; therefore, brand A is a good widget.

But we certainly do not expect every object and experience around us to serve a practical purpose. We do have painting, poetry, movies, music, and sculpture, and we consider design apart from function in clothing, buildings, and interiors. In other words, we make aesthetic judgments as well as practical ones on whether something is beautiful or ugly, pleasing or disturbing, on whether it has or lacks artistic value. For such evaluations we often have to invoke certain "formal" criteria, acknowledging or appealing to the general standards that great art fulfills, such as proportion, variation, harmony, contrast, craftsmanship, or historical association, and to special criteria unique to each art form. To use these usually calls for CP argument: color schemes, for example, can please if they are harmonious; the colors in this painting are subtle variations in the brown tones; therefore, the color scheme in this painting is pleasing. (The opposite criterion, contrast, can also be invoked.)

Sometimes, however, aesthetic evaluations rely on cause and

effect arguments, appealing to the consequences that a work of art might have. If, for example, a reviewer labels a movie "heart-warming," that is a way of evaluating it favorably because it produces positive sentiments and heartening thoughts in its viewers, effects that are self-evidently good. Similarly, if a TV series is called "decadent" or "indulgent," then chances are its reviewer condemns it for failing to display moral uplift; it depresses viewers with its sour outlook on human life and conduct. Among the readings in this section, John Russell's praise for Thomas Eakins as America's greatest painter clearly grows from such a consequence argument: ". . . we prize him [Eakins] above all for the new dimension of moral awareness that he brought to American painting." Russell's other criterion is largely formal: Eakins is a superb and accurate draftsman; his paintings can be "trusted" as faithful representations. But notice how the two criteria interconnect; faithful representation morally invigorates the beholder. Tom Wolfe's condemnation of modern architecture is largely formal; he damns it for its blandness, repetitiveness, cheapness of materials, and lack of appropriateness in conveying the grandeur of this age. But he too clinches his argument against the style he loathes when he describes its effects on the welfare residents of a modern housing project in St. Louis.

Unlike aesthetic objects, actions such as policy decisions are usually judged primarily by their consequences. What is a good diplomatic mission? Obviously it is one that has good effects, that brings about a cease-fire, a decline in tensions, a program of future meetings and accords. In our readings, Alston Chase evaluates the National Park Service negatively because its policy of bear management has apparently led to a drastic decline in the bear population at Yellowstone, the opposite of its intended effect.

Events and trends, too, are usually evaluated by effects, but they can also be measured against an ideal standard. Against ideals of harmony and stability, for example, the high rate of divorce in the United States might be considered a disaster; we may have a sense that a good society is one in which most couples live satisfactorily ever after. A particular divorce case, however, might be evaluated not according to an ideal standard for a whole society, but according to the effects it may have on an individual couple caught in an intolerable situation. In his appeal to officers of the A. H. Robins Company, Judge Miles W. Lord considered not only the potentially dangerous consequences to individuals from the company's products, but the standards of corporate behavior and responsibility to the public. Such standards that set the mark for right conduct, whether public or private, social or personal, we call ethics.

People too are subjects of constant evaluation. We judge each other and ourselves according to the roles we attempt. We even evaluate one another on whether or not we are good people living good lives, a much more challenging task than arguing about whether someone is a good teacher, travel agent, bank executive, or hamburger chef. In such a complete way Hugh Sidey evaluates the achievement of our first chief executive, George Washington. Large entities too—such as cities, governments, and universities —do not escape praise or condemnation. But these grandiose institutions are often broken down into their component people, actions, and things in order to be evaluated.

The criteria we have discussed so far are fairly abstract. Another kind of standard is worth mentioning. This is the exemplar, the ideal member of a class, the one we cannot imagine anyone or anything improving on. The exemplar becomes the standard against which all later instances are judged. Thus pianists are compared to Rubinstein, presidents to Lincoln, prestige luxury cars to the Rolls Royce. Rachel Flick uses an exemplar when she judges the Girl Scouts against the Boy Scouts, assuming somehow that they should be alike, that the Boy Scouts represent a standard the Girl Scouts should adopt.

Let's suppose that an arguer has in mind the best standards for evaluation. What techniques are then used to bring these criteria before an audience? First and most important is word choice. The skillful arguer chooses words that convey just the implicit values that will foster the desired judgment. We call such language "slanted" or "loaded" when we are contesting an evaluation, as though all such manipulation were deceptive. But it is not wrong in itself because virtually any word in our language can be tinged. Such words as *progressive, traditional, artificial,* and *conflicting* provoke immediate value associations, though the connotations might be modified or even inverted in different contexts. To call something "practical," for example, may praise it to some audiences and damn it to others. An evaluation can rely solely on word choice if its intended audience has in mind the same criteria the words suggest and applies them without hesitation.

The power of word choice has an important consequence. It becomes possible for a CP or causal argument, with its warrants of definition or agency, to nevertheless affect its audience as an evaluation if it is rendered in words that mesh with the audience's sense of values. Look back, for example, at Bob Teague's article, "To Get a Story, 'I Flimflammed a Dead Man's Mother,' " in the CP section. Most directly, this article aims to convince its readers that a certain practice exists among TV news reporters, but no one can read those examples touching on human grief and tragedy, and therefore on our basic values, without judging somewhat harshly the reporters who meddle in them. In fact, toward the end of the piece, Teague tries to defuse the reader's predictable evaluative response by justifying the reporters as simply meeting the expectations of their interviewees.

In another technique of evaluation argument the arguer openly states the criteria and openly appeals for audience agreement. You will see this clear appeal in Rachel Flick's evaluation of the Girl Scouts. No one has the slightest doubt what it is about the fifty-year-old movement that bothers the author, though readers may not agree with her conclusion. (Flick has not gone the extra step of justifying her criteria of judgment.) Similarly, Bertrand Russell is very clear about the criteria by which he judges the greatness of Albert Einstein.

But an audience may want more. They may want an explanation, and further, even a defense of the criteria themselves. Why should Einstein be judged by Russell's criteria and not by another set? An evaluation that defends its criteria can be very full indeed: It must establish criteria of judgment, defend them, and then apply them to the subject at hand. We see that full process self-consciously in action in Mary Jureller's "The Wisdom of Common Sense."

Actually supporting the criteria in an evaluation argument calls for another evaluation argument. Among the readings, Thomas Bender's "One for the Books" is primarily a defense of the criterion of diversity because it ensures liberty. If we agree with him that that principle, first defined by James Madison, ensures the success of our political institutions, we will more readily apply it in judging the case of censorship in a high school library. Sometimes an argument can be almost entirely a defense of criteria by which other evaluations can be made. Sissela Bok, in "Paternalistic Lies," raises her argument to the level of a defense of basic principles.

Evaluation, particularly negative evaluation, moves inexorably into the next category of argument, the proposal. We naturally feel that if a situation is wrong, or is not the best it could be, we should do something, anything, to correct it. Thus the arguments in this section could function as calls to action if they met with readers willing and able to act. Neal Devins and Roy Herron's piece on the death penalty, for example, if read by a juror or judge, might have practical consequences beyond effecting a change in attitude. The proposal arguments in Part Four are designed to move their readers through evaluation to feasible, effectual action.

—≫≫ ≪≪—

The Greatness of
Albert Einstein

BERTRAND RUSSELL

This essay presents us with one famous man's praise of another. A noted British mathematician and philosopher, Bertrand Russell received the Nobel Prize in Literature in 1950 for his writings "as a defender of humanity and freedom of thought." Russell is famous for diverse activities, for his contributions to symbolic logic, for his active pacifism, which often landed him in jail, and for his prose style, his ability to explain complex subjects to lay audiences. Thus in this evaluation, Russell speaks with unique authority about Einstein's contributions to science and humanity.

Einstein was indisputably one of the greatest men of our time. He had in a high degree the simplicity characteristic of the best men of science —a simplicity which comes of a single-minded desire to know and understand things that are completely impersonal. He had also the faculty of not taking familiar things for granted. Newton wondered why apples fall; Einstein expressed "surprised thankfulness" that four equal rods can make a square, since, in most of the universes that he could imagine, there would be no such things as squares.

He showed greatness also in his moral qualities. In private, he was kindly and unassuming; toward colleagues he was (so far as I could see) completely free from jealousy, which is more than can be said of Newton or Leibniz. In his later years, relativity was more or less eclipsed, in scientific interest, by quantum theory, but I never discovered any sign that this vexed him. He was profoundly interested in world affairs. At the end of the First World War, when I first came in contact with him, he was a pacifist, but Hitler led him (as he led me) to abandon this point of view. Having previously thought of himself as a citizen of the world, he found that the Nazis compelled him to think of himself as a Jew, and to take up the cause of the Jews throughout the world. After the end of the Second World War, he joined the group of American scientists who were attempting to find a way of avoiding the disasters to mankind that are threatened as a result of the atomic bomb.

After Congressional committees in America began their inquisitorial investigations into supposed subversive activities, Einstein wrote a well publicized letter urging that all men in academic posts should refuse to testify before these committees or before the almost equally tyrannical boards set up by some universities. His argument for this advice was that, under the Fifth Amendment, no man is obliged to answer a question if the answer will incriminate him, but that the purpose of this Amendment had been defeated by the inquisitors, since they held that refusal to answer may be taken as evidence of guilt. If Einstein's policy had been followed even in cases where it was absurd to presume guilt, academic freedom would have greatly profited. But, in the general *sauve qui peut*, none of the "innocent" listened to him. In these various public activities, he has been completely self-effacing and only anxious to find ways of saving the human race from the misfortunes brought about by its own follies. But while the world applauded him as a man of science, in practical affairs, his wisdom was so simple and so profound as to seem to the sophisticated like mere foolishness.

Although Einstein has done much important work outside the theory of relativity, it is by this theory that he is most famous—and rightly, for it is of fundamental significance both for science and for philosophy. Many people (including myself) have attempted popular accounts of this theory, and I will not add to their number on this occasion. But I will try to say a few words as to how the theory affects our view of the universe. The theory, as everyone knows, appeared in two stages: the special theory in 1905, and the general theory in 1915. The special theory was important both in science and philosophy—first, because it accounted for the result of the Michelson-Morley experiment, which had puzzled the world for thirty years; secondly, because it explained the increase of mass with velocity, which had been observed in electrons; thirdly, because it led to the interchangeability of mass and energy, which has become an essential principle in physics. These are only some of the ways in which it was scientifically important.

Philosophically, the special theory demanded a revolution in deeply rooted ways of thought, since it compelled a change in our conception of the spatio-temporal structure of the world. Structure is what is most significant in our knowledge of the physical world, and for ages structure had been conceived as depending upon two different manifolds, one of space, the other of time. Einstein showed that, for reasons partly experimental and partly logical, the two must be replaced by one which he called "space-time." If two events happen in different places, you cannot say, as was formerly supposed, that they are separated by so many miles and minutes, because different observers, all equally careful, will make different estimates of the miles and minutes, all equally legitimate. The only thing that is the same for all observers is what is called "interval," which is a sort of combination of space-distance and time-distance as previously estimated.

The general theory has a wider sweep than the special theory, and is scientifically more important. It is primarily a theory of gravitation. No advance whatever had been made in explaining gravitation during the 230 years since Newton, although the action at a distance that it seems to demand had always been repugnant. Einstein made gravitation part of geometry; he said that it was due to the character of space-time. There is a law called the "Principle of Least Action," according to which a body, in going from one place to another, chooses always the easiest route, which may not be a straight line: It may pay you to avoid mountain-tops and deep valleys. According to Einstein (to use crude language, misleading if taken literally), space-time is full of mountains and valleys, and that is why planets do not move in straight lines. The sun is at the top of a hill, and a lazy planet prefers going round the hill to climbing up to the summit. There were some very delicate experimental tests by which it could be decided whether Einstein or Newton fitted the facts more accurately. The observations came out on Einstein's side, and almost everybody except the Nazis accepted his theory.

Some odd things have emerged as a consequence of the general theory of relativity. It appears that the universe is of finite size, although unbounded. (Do not attempt to understand this unless you have studied non-Euclidean geometry.) It appears also that the universe is continually getting bigger. Theory shows that it must be always getting bigger, or always getting smaller; observation of distant nebulae shows that it is getting bigger. Our present universe seems to have begun about 2 billion years ago; what, if anything, there was before that, it is impossible to conjecture.

I suppose that, in the estimation of the general public, Einstein is still reckoned as a revolutionary innovator. Among physicists, however, he has become the leader of the Old Guard. This is due to his refusal to accept some of the innovations of quantum theory. Heisenberg's principle of indeterminacy, along with other principles of that theory, has had very curious results. It seems that individual occurrences in atoms do not obey strict laws, and that the observed regularities in the world are only statistical. What we know about the behavior of matter, according to this view, is like what insurance companies know about mortality. Insurance companies do not know and do not care which of the individuals who insured their lives will die in any given year. All that matters to them is the statistical average of mortality. The regularities to which classical physics accustomed us are, we are now told, of this merely statistical sort. Einstein never accepted this view. He continued to believe that there are laws, though as yet they have not been ascertained, which determine the behavior of individual atoms. It would be exceedingly rash for anyone who is not a professional physicist to allow himself an opinion on this matter until the physicists are all agreed, but I think it must be conceded that on this matter the bulk of competent opinion was opposed to Einstein. This is all the more remarkable in view of the fact that he had done epoch-making work in quantum theory, which would have put him in the first rank among physicists even if he had never thought of the theory of relativity.

Quantum theory is more revolutionary than the theory of relativity, and I do not think that its power of revolutionizing our conceptions of the physical world is yet completed. Its imaginative effects are very curious. Although it has given us new powers of manipulating matter, including the sinister powers displayed in the atom and hydrogen bombs, it has shown us that we are ignorant of many things which we thought we knew.

Nobody before quantum theory doubted that at any given moment a particle is at some definite place and moving with some definite velocity. This is no longer the case. The more accurately you determine the place of a particle, the less accurate will be its velocity; the more accurately you determine the velocity, the less accurate will be its position. And the particle itself has become something quite vague, not a nice little billiard ball as it used to be. When you think you have caught it, it produces a convincing alibi as a wave and not a particle. In fact, you know only certain equations of which the interpretation is obscure.

This point of view was distasteful to Einstein, who struggled to remain nearer to classical physics. In spite of this, he was the first to open the imaginative vistas which have revolutionized science during the present century. I will end as I began: He was a great man, perhaps the greatest of our time.

QUESTIONS FOR DISCUSSION

1. In what category or categories does Russell evaluate Einstein?
2. How is Einstein evaluated as a scientist? Could a scientist whose theories did not affect future work be considered great?
3. How much knowledge of science does Russell assume in his audience? He refers to what "everyone knows," but does he leave anything unexplained?
4. Would this evaluation be as convincing if it were not written by Bertrand Russell? What special authority does his voice bring to the praise of Einstein?
5. Normally, an evaluator makes whatever concessions are necessary toward the beginning of the argument, before the strongest favorable points are revealed. Russell does not do this. Why does he leave until the end (all but the last paragraph) Einstein's reluctance to accept quantum theory?
6. For what human qualities does Russell praise Einstein? And what qualities of his own character does Russell reveal in this essay?

SUGGESTIONS FOR WRITING

1. Write comparative evaluations of two individuals in the same profession, one who excels professionally and the other who excels for human traits. Direct your essay to someone within the profession.
2. Rehabilitate the reputation of a scientist, innovator, or inventor whose work has never been properly appreciated, perhaps because he or she worked in an unorthodox fashion or belonged to a minority.

3. Instead of evaluating a person in a career, evaluate the career itself for an audience of fellow students. What is the value—to the individual, the community, the human race—in the work of a plumber, computer systems analyst, horticulturist, dancer?

4. This section contains several evaluations of people (such as the essay on Washington and the one on Eakins). Compare and evaluate for fellow students of argument the criteria used to assess these outstanding individuals.

5. Using Russell's praise of Einstein as a starting point, establish a set of criteria for goodness in a person, regardless of that person's profession or role in life. Address yourself to general readers. What would you include that Russell omits? Defend your criteria.

6. Examine several issues of *Sports Illustrated* for articles that praise athletes. For what qualities are they admired? Is it only their skill at their particular sport that is admired? Think of your essay as a column to appear in that magazine, either criticizing or defending the standards by which individuals have been evaluated.

The Injustice of the Death Penalty

NEAL DEVINS AND ROY BRASFIELD HERRON

Some issues are of interest to all citizens of a society, and for us the death penalty is one of them. In 1984, 1,300 prisoners sat on death row in this country. Although we will probably never reach complete agreement about this issue, it should remain continually open to debate, subject to thoughtful arguments from all sides.

The following essay represents one line of argument against the death penalty. The authors are both lawyers, Devins a former research associate at the Institute for Public Policy Studies at Vanderbilt University, and Herron a teacher of law and divinity at Vanderbilt. Herron's law practice has included work on several death penalty cases.

Notice how this evaluation seems to imply a solution to the unfair administration of the death penalty without actually stating that solution. How can an argument mean more than it says this way?

Judicial safeguards for preventing the arbitrary administration of capital punishment are not working. The recent United States Supreme Court decision to delay the execution of Thomas Barefoot illustrates the courts' inability to administer death sentences fairly.

The Supreme Court has decided to review again the standards for delaying executions. Yet our nation's experiences with capital punishment suggest that no procedures will illuminate the arbitrary administration of death.

Charlie Brooks Jr. is the latest victim of this arbitrariness. On Dec. 7, 1982, Brooks was executed by injection in a Texas prison. Also in the prison was Brooks's partner, Woodie Loudres, likewise convicted of the same capital offense. Loudres, however, will be eligible for parole in six and a half years. Only he knows whether he or Charlie Brooks shot and killed a Fort Worth mechanic.

Prosecutor Jack Strickland, who persuaded jurors to give Brooks the death penalty, recently said that the state would never know if it executed the man who fired the fatal shot. "It may well be, as horrible as it is to contemplate, that the State of Texas executed the wrong man."

Strickland had been unable to persuade the Texas Board of Pardons and Paroles to grant Brooks a 60-day reprieve. He argued that the extremely different sentences were unfair since each defendant was convicted on the same evidence of the same acts.

Former prosecutor Strickland is right; it is not fair. Unfortunately, it is also not unusual that death sentences are administered with freakish unfairness.

Brooks was one of two Americans executed in the last 15 years who were still pursuing appeals. The other was John Spenkelink. Spenkelink, like Brooks, was one of two persons charged with first-degree murder. The prosecution offered to let Spenkelink plead guilty to second-degree murder. He refused the offer, maintaining that only in self-defense had he shot the professional felon who had assaulted and sodomized him.

Spenkelink testified. The other man accused of murder did not. The other man was released. John Spenkelink was electrocuted.

Late last year another telling occurrence unfolded, this time in Mississippi. Prosecutors were eager to convict and condemn a controversial black political leader named Eddie Carthan. They accused Carthan of contracting to have a political rival murdered.

The district attorney agreed not to prosecute a capital murder charge and five other charges against David Hester, one of the two men who admittedly planned and participated in the robbery and killing. Instead, in return for Hester's testimony against Carthan, the prosecution allowed Hester to plead guilty to a single charge of aggravated assault on a police officer. He will be eligible for parole in eight years.

Carthan ultimately was found not guilty. Yet, if he had been convicted, Carthan could have been executed while Hester, the killer who said he had been hired to shoot the victim, would have been released from prison.

The cases of Charlie Brooks, John Spenkelink, and Eddie Carthan are not isolated instances of disparate treatment in capital cases. Instead, they form a microcosm of the inconsistent application of the death penalty.

Such arbitrariness and capriciousness were what caused the Supreme Court to overturn the country's death penalty laws in 1972 in *Furman v. Georgia*. In 1976, however, the Court in *Gregg v. Georgia* approved certain statutes with specific safeguards designed to remove the arbitrariness and capriciousness.

Death penalty abolitionists argue that because of the strict precautions required by the Supreme Court, the death penalty is likely to be applied very rarely and thus always will appear arbitrary and freakish. This contention is supported by Justice Department and FBI statistics. In 1978 some 18,755 persons were arrested for murder and nonnegligent manslaughter and 197 persons were sentenced to die. In 1979 some 16,955 offenders were identified in connection with murders and 159 persons were sentenced to die. That averages about one death sentence for each hundred murder arrests.

Of course sentences will vary and one cannot throw out all punishments because of disparities. But the death penalty in fact differs from other punishments. According to Supreme Court Justice William Brennan: "Death is truly an awesome punishment. The calculated killing of a human being by the state involves, by its very nature, a denial of the executed person's humanity."

The late Justice Felix Frankfurter similarly noted, "The taking of life is irrevocable. It is in capital cases especially that the balance of conflicting interests must be weighted most heavily in favor of the procedural safeguards of the Bill of Rights."

But our attempts at fairness have been inadequate. Death has been combined with such disparities as in the cases of Brooks and Spenkelink. Death is meted arbitrarily and capriciously to less than one percent of those committing homicides.

Capital punishment still is administered with such rarity that no execution goes unnoticed. But as federal judge Doug Shaver noted:

"1983 will bring some more. So many (of the 1,200) on death row are ripe. They've . . . been through all the (legal) processes."

The Supreme Court may revise those processes in the Barefoot case now before it. Still, whether someone lives or dies will be determined by things largely beyond the control of the Supreme Court such as the adequacy or inadequacy of attorneys, plea bargains, and who sits on the jury.

The point is clear: the death penalty is not administered evenhandedly. Regardless of one's views on the morality or constitutionality of capital punishment, the death penalty cannot rightly be continued in this fashion. A country whose jurisprudence is based on notions of fairness ought to recognize this and act accordingly.

QUESTIONS FOR DISCUSSION

1. What are the authors' grounds for evaluating the death penalty? Do they appeal to principle or consequence or both?
2. Suppose you are convinced by the authors that the death penalty is unfairly administered. What course or courses of action could follow from this belief?
3. What do the authors mean when they appeal to a principle of fairness? Do they define it? Do they need to support the use of such a principle, and if so, how could they support it?
4. In the introduction to this section on evaluation argument, we talk about the use of various emotional appeals. What elements in this argument seem to appeal to the reader's emotions?
5. The authors use no personal voice in the text, nor do they establish their own professional authority. Should they have? Have they found another way to make appeals to authority? Why do you think Herron does not refer explicitly to his own experience on death penalty cases?
6. The authors cite three examples and give statistical evidence. What is the force of the examples? How do the authors try to strengthen them? What is the relation between the examples and the statistics?

SUGGESTIONS FOR WRITING

1. Writing in 1983, Devins and Herron predicted many more executions. Has their prediction come true? Has the rate of execution gone up in the last few years? Write an essay reporting on whatever trend you perceive and projecting the future of the death penalty.
2. Select a particular conviction that ended in an execution. Analyze the details

of the case to determine whether the sentence was fair or unfair. Write up your argument as an editorial appearing in a newspaper in the community where the case was tried.

3. What criteria, besides fairness, might be invoked for evaluating the death penalty? Can you construct arguments from consequence? From other principles? Evaluate the death penalty using arguments different from Devins' and Herron's but for the same audience.

4. Can you refute Devins' and Herron's appeal to unfairness? Is the death penalty necessarily unfair if only 1 percent of murderers are executed? Address your response directly to the authors.

5. Is there another law that you could argue is unfairly administered? What should be done about it? Is the unfair administration of a law a reason to rescind it? Write a newspaper editorial calling attention to an unfairly administered law and suggesting an appropriate course of action.

6. Explore the issue of what is the fair application of the law. Do we want laws to be uniformly applied, with no consideration of the particular circumstances of a case, as advocates of mandatory sentencing argue? What factors might justifiably affect the application of the law? Try answering these questions for readers who have never thought about these issues.

————————— ⟶⟩⟩ ⟨⟨⟵ —————————

A Draft Isn't Needed

DOUG BANDOW

Even in peacetime, the issue of the draft is alive for students. Young people are the ones most affected by the draft but they have little say in the making of policies. This article, which appeared in the New York Times, *is part of the ever-current debate. The author, a special assistant to President Ronald Reagan for policy development, is defending the status quo in 1982—no draft but mandatory registration of all eligible males. Bandow is, in effect, evaluating a hypothetical policy, one he does not want. If he can discredit the policy he does not favor, the argument for change in the present policy is weakened.*

The All-Volunteer Force was created in 1973, but the issue of how to man our military has not died. Despite the success of the All-Volunteer Force, there are still many people calling for a draft to strengthen our national defense.

A draft, however, would do nothing of the kind. Coercing people to serve would increase costs, decrease retention of military personnel, fail to improve both the quality of the armed forces and the degree to which they represent a cross-section of our society, create national disunity, and destroy fundamental values that make America worth defending.

Conscripting labor doesn't reduce costs; it increases and shifts them. Instead of paying a volunteer, say, $15,000—enough to convince him to forego or delay other career opportunities—the Pentagon would pay a draftee, say, $7,500. That means that the draftee in effect is taxed $7,500. Indeed, a defense cost supposedly too great to be borne by the entire society would instead be borne by 18- to 26-year-old males. Such economic expediency is unworthy of a free society.

A draft would not even significantly reduce budgetary costs. Though more than half of the military budget goes to personnel—$80 billion out of $156.1 billion in fiscal 1981—most of that is for career servicemen, civilians, and retirees. Only $6.6 billion was used to pay first-term active-duty servicemen—those who would be drafted.

Thus, if draftees' pay were slashed 50 percent, the savings would be only $3.3 billion. Cuts in recruiting costs might save a half billion dollars more. But there would be added costs of registration, classification, induction, and enforcement of the draft, as well as higher training costs caused by the inevitable decline in retention of first-termers.

A draft would also exacerbate the military's severest personnel problem: retaining skilled noncommissioned officers. The draft cannot directly increase the number of skilled career noncoms because it brings in only untrained 18-year-olds. Also, it hikes the cost of retaining a career force of a set size because of higher turnover among first-termers. This is so because draftees, resentful, re-enlist in smaller numbers than volunteers.

Reinstituting the draft would not increase the quality of armed forces personnel. The proportion of 1981 enlistees scoring highest in intelligence tests is as high today as it was during the draft in the 1960's and 1970's. In 1981, 81 percent of the people entering the armed forces were high school graduates.

Since the military already is nearly a cross-section of our society, conscription would be unlikely to increase that representativeness. For example, the overall educational attainment of military personnel is higher than that of their civilian counterparts: 69 percent as against 36 percent are high school graduates, and 14 percent as against 16 percent are college graduates.

Moreover, the parents of young servicemen are only slightly more blue-collar and less-educated than parents of the servicemen's civilian contemporaries, according to an Ohio State University poll. The educational aspirations of the young servicemen exceed those of their civilian counterparts, it shows.

Finally, though blacks are overrepresented in the military—while 12 percent of the population is black, 19 percent of the overall military and 30 percent of the army is black—the proportion of those serving edged downward in 1981. Indeed, because qualified blacks volunteer and re-enlist in greater numbers than whites, a draft would significantly affect the military's composition only if virtually no volunteers were accepted and if blacks were actively discouraged from re-enlisting.

As for coercion, with the history of violence and controversy it has engendered, it would seriously divide America again. To face the possible challenges in years ahead, we need to forge a consensus on foreign and defense policy. Reinstituting conscription would make acquiescence, let alone consensus, unattainable.

Most important, a draft is inimical to the fundamental principles that constitute the foundation of our country. We have manned our forces with volunteers for most of our history, and for good reason: Requiring involuntary service violates fundamental individual rights.

Indeed, even if free citizens in a free society owe service to the state, why should only the young be liable? National defense benefits everyone; therefore, everyone should be liable. A volunteer military financed by universal taxation, and not the draft, spreads the burden.

A draft will not enhance our national security. Indeed, if America has lost the moral authority to persuade its people to voluntarily defend their freedom, then it has lost something that no amount of coercion will restore.

QUESTIONS FOR DISCUSSION

1. Notice the order of Bandow's arguments as predicted in the second paragraph of this essay. Nothing compels that order. Why then did Bandow choose it for his audience?
2. How would you characterize the style of this piece? What impression does it give of its author?

3. Categorize the appeals Bandow makes in this negative evaluation of the draft. Which appeals are to consequence, which to ethics? Does he ever use one kind of appeal to back up another?
4. Notice that Bandow uses many different arguments against the draft while Devins and Herron use only one against the death penalty. What is the effect of multiplying arguments on your impression of the arguer and on your response to specific arguments?
5. Scan the essay for those word choices that carry an emotional charge. Does the author invoke positive or negative emotions?
6. Bandow is not arguing against an entrenched policy but is speaking out at a time when there is no draft. What does he have to do to make the issue come alive for his readers? How, in other words, does he create an occasion for this piece? Might he have a purpose other than arguing against a policy not in force anyway?

SUGGESTIONS FOR WRITING

1. Do some basic research to clarify your thinking on the issue of the draft. What countries currently have a draft? What is the nature of the service expected? Who is included in the draft and who is exempt? Report to your classmates on your findings, comparing the relative effectiveness of different policies.
2. When in this century has the draft been instituted in the United States? Why, in any particular instance, was it instituted and why was it discontinued? Your essay will be an evaluation of past policies, again for fellow students.
3. Examine the techniques of selection and exemption for the draft during the Vietnam War. How fair was the draft then and how fairly was it administered? Write an essay in which you explore the impact of past policy on the present.
4. Assuming that your fellow students would be skeptical, try to convince them that a peacetime draft is a socially useful policy.
5. Argue for or against registering or drafting women as well as men. Address your argument to a particular audience (e.g., women over thirty, young women of draftable age) since audience will inevitably affect your choice of appeals.
6. Bandow begins with an assumption of the success of the all-volunteer army. Either challenge or support that assumption.

———————— →>> <<<— ————————

Minor Art Offers
Special Pleasures

EVA HOFFMAN

It is unusual to read an argument as general as Eva Hoffman's. She is writing to an audience of New York Times readers who will undoubtedly be able to supply concrete examples of major and minor art to flesh out her argument. Her audience, and indeed most of us, have been educated in a tradition that labels certain works timeless and great and others ephemeral. A parallel distinction is drawn between intellectually and spiritually demanding works and those that are merely entertaining—between, in other words, High Art and Popular Art. Ask yourself whether such a chasm has to exist.

When we first read "War and Peace," we are bound to know that we are in the presence of greatness—and to be perplexed. Just what is the nature of Tolstoy's achievement? The novel seems hardly written. It is simply like life itself. When we hear our first Mozart sonata, we may recognize in it a kind of perfection. But the perfection seems utterly natural. It is there, like a landscape or a lovely face—just itself, as if it had always existed and could not be otherwise. And it is just such peak artistic experiences that point to the uses of the less than great.

We all have our favorite "minor" painters, or composers, or novelists —artists who don't reach for the "big statement," or make exalted claims for themselves, but whose particular flavor, or sensibility, or the imaginative world they delineate pleases or interests us. But just why do we call some art "minor" as opposed to "great"? Needless to say, such distinctions are bound to be somewhat artificial, susceptible to changing standards, and advisably flexible. Nevertheless, we feel that the distinctions exist, and that they describe real, if hard to define differences.

There are, for starters, entire genres that we think of as hovering somewhere between "art" and "entertainment"—the musical, the operetta, the detective novel or theatrical farce—genres defined by circumscribed conventions, and designed to give essentially lighthearted pleasure. Even in such "minor" modes, certain works can attain a level of excellence which raises them to the status of classics and makes us say that "they transcend their genre"—one need only think of a musical like "My

Fair Lady," or a mystery by Simenon. But there are also, of course, minor works in the major modes—a Saint-Saëns concerto, say, or a lesser Noel Coward play—works which don't aspire to the highest seriousness of purpose and which don't penetrate to the most intense levels of perception and form—but which create their own, well-circumscribed territory and take us there by means of good, honest craftsmanship.

Why some artists remain "minor" in spite of their best efforts, while the small, dashed-off bagatelles by Schumann, say, or Picasso, still bear the marks of something more inspired, is surely one of the more fundamental, if vexing esthetic questions. And it is particularly difficult to distinguish the "minor" from the "major" achievement in the present —particularly, maybe, in this particular present, when even the categories implied by such adjectives are coming under intense scrutiny, and when some of the most innovative art is designed to question the very idea that art is a privileged enterprise.

But when it comes to the art of the past, we can usually recognize works in the minor mode; and while such works may be presented to us as of secondary importance, we should not underestimate their pleasures—or their uses. There is, of course, the practical reason that the lesser works will always predominate, for accepting them and getting from them what we can. But compromises of pragmatism aside, the minor work can be an esthetic eye-opener, a possibly more useful key to the secrets of art than the more completely achieved one.

This is in part because a minor work shows its construction, its artifice, much more easily. All works of art are artifacts, all are made by people who make deliberate decisions. But in the most accomplished works, those choices are difficult to perceive. In terms of how it is put together, "War and Peace" challenges us to take apart its seamless fabric, but it never quite reveals itself. But take a novel by Graham Greene, or by Iris Murdoch, and all of a sudden much becomes clear. We see a character introduced, a description of the social setting, then a bit about the landscape, because those are such easy and satisfying bits for an author to do. Then a mysterious event occurs, some other characters come in and we know that our author has us launched on a most pleasantly rollicking journey. We can see the writer turn his characters and twists of plot this way and that; we can say, "Ah, so this is how it's done." And we can appreciate the skill and the intelligence—the craft in the art—with which everything keeps moving along, all the threads are tied up together and our interest is kept pricked at just the right— less than fever-pitch—temperature.

As for the acolyte to a new art—someone who is coming, say, to painting or to music as a curious innocent—to dwell only with the greatest works is to assure wonder, perhaps, but also bafflement. That light in Rembrandt, those ineffably perfect textures in Ingres—how are they done with an artist's brush? Well, perhaps it's perfectly easy. It looks just like our world repeated in finer tones. But then one looks at some perfectly nice landscape by Rosa Bonheur, say, or one of the minor Venetians, in which the painter is trying to achieve an effect of falling light; there are golden tones in the foreground, and darker ones in the background, but there's something not quite right about the refraction; the brush strokes have not refined themselves sufficiently to become light. And then we understand that we're in fact in the presence of a canvas, a two-dimensional piece of fabric on which warmth of skin and falling shadows are achieved only through considerable skill; and from there, we can go on to see that a canvas is an object on which other effects, like Cézanne's luminous serenity, or Van Gogh's tortured flux, are achieved only through a unifying vision.

Aside from the edifications of minor art, there is also the question of enjoyment. We've all had the experience of appreciating a canonized work only out of a sense of duty, and guiltily enjoying some piece of music or a movie which we officially feel obliged to dismiss as second-rate. Great art, in order to be experienced fully, takes concentration and an effort of receptivity. Yes, we can sit back and relax to the great, and by now familiar arias in "Don Giovanni," but to grasp the structure of the opera—to meet it halfway by following the interweavings of its motifs and intuiting the meanings of its somber moods—that requires a gesture of will, a reaching-out of consciousness and feeling. To really read "The Magic Mountain" means to enter into a dialogue with it; to pause every few moments in order to consider the justice or truthfulness of the arguments between its protagonists, in order to consider where they might lead, how they hold together, what impulses—what view of life they spring from.

Such stretching, such a sense of being taken out of oneself, is of course, the intense pleasure of great art. It is the pleasure—and, in the end, also the accomplishment—of entering a full vision which we may not have articulated, but which we recognize as profoundly true. Ultimately, great art not only takes us beyond ourselves—it also recalls us to ourselves, to those levels of the psyche where we don't usually dwell, or which we don't know consciously.

But, by the very nature of our energies and capacities, we do not live by spirit—or even spiritual effort—alone. Our repertory of needs and enjoyments encompasses many other levels, and sometimes a comfortable trip through those more easily accessible landscapes of experience is precisely what we want from our art. There are times when we say to ourselves, "All I want this evening is a plain meat-and-potatoes movie." There are authors who are just what's needed when we're recovering from an illness, because they can be taken in without those great strainings of the spirit—yet they provide enough vivacity, or drama, or wit, to keep us interested—to help us forget ourselves in the simplest way and give us the stimulus of more amusing, or lively, sensations than we're able, for the moment, to summon on our own. There are times when a Puccini opera seems like a most excellent diversion—easy to follow, pleasantly stirring of the emotions without requiring too much thought.

In our madly archivist age, much of even the minor art of the past is familiar. But sometimes, minor art can still give us that special pleasure of discovery. We come to the great monuments of art in the wake of countless pilgrimages, with clouds of preconceived ideas, and obligatory admiration swirling through our heads; it sometimes takes a reverse process of clearing our minds in order to perceive the most famous works with our own senses. But when we stumble on a painter or novelist who has led a more secluded existence, we can experience the great pleasure of surprise; we can come to such artists with fresh perceptions, notice their particular charm—in a word, make them ours.

And it may be that one of the more pleasurable attributes of minor art is in fact the quality of particularity, the emphasis on the immediate and immediately recognizable circumstances. A more profound work in any medium—a Beckett play, say, or a David Smith sculpture—may penetrate more deeply into the heart of its time and each epoch's version of the human condition. But the minor works, precisely because they remain closer to the surface, can often reflect more vividly, perhaps more mimetically, the glitter and noise of each time's vanity fair.

Surely that's one of the reasons we like to go to the movies—those works of "art" or "entertainment" whose very status as an art is still in flux and which are, for the most part, made only for the day, with no great aspirations to eternal glory. This does not mean, of course, that the movies haven't produced their gems, or their classics. But whether they're ambitious and provocative, or small and openly unpretentious, the movies show us how our particular place and moment in time looks; its furnishings, its clothes, its gestures and faces—those contingent and forever beguiling surfaces which give our world its familiar feel and flavor.

Perhaps that's why many of us are more tolerant of ordinary, not-so-great films than we are of mediocre plays; the movies are the medium of our time, capable of reflecting accurately certain common conditions —the sweep of our cities, the speed of our days, the mobility of our movements, the bigness of our landscapes as seen from an airborne point of view.

It is another pleasure of the movies that they are an art which is growing up with us. We've observed its expansions of technique, we've seen how montage, or cutting, or special effects have been added to film before our eyes; and we can therefore participate more fully—or identify with—the processes which go into the making of the work. Such identification is—in any medium—more easily afforded by the minor and self-disclosing work than by the sublime, and often opaque, accomplishments.

To achieve even these effects, a work of art has to have a considerable amount of intelligence and skill. Below a certain level, "art," or entertainment, has effects opposite of pleasurable. A silly sit-com may attract us like bad candy, but like bad candy, leaves us with an unpleasant aftertaste, as if we had taken in something that renders us a little more stupid and a little more dull than we really are. Perhaps that's why the quality of "having fun" at a really awful movie or a musical often sounds so hysterical; one can hear in it the strain of overcoming the ambivalence of those unpleasant, sometimes even degrading, sensations.

Good minor art probably thrives at times when artists in a particular medium have a modest idea of their occupation—when they think of it as an outgrowth of craft; thus, the large volume of good, unassuming Baroque music written by those journeymen composers who thought they were just doing their job. When artists develop a more exalted image of themselves, one is bound to get more attempts at greatness— and more attempts that fail. One need only think of the mystique of the "great American novel"—by now reduced to a sort of joke, but once a stimulus to a lot of bombast—as well as to ambitious and energetic writing.

There is nothing more satisfying than art in which a large vision is fulfilled in the substance and the execution. But works with unsupported pretensions to greatness can be irritating in a particular way; we feel manipulated by the demand they make on us to take them seriously, or cheated by empty suggestions of significance. Conversely, a work which makes modest claims and circumscribes a manageable, well-defined territory, predisposes us to sympathy, and offers unexpected satisfactions.

In any case, for the critic, and even more so for the constant reviewer, the capacity to identify with, or be intrigued by, the more ordinary creations is—given that the minor achievements are at any time likely to be far more prevalent than great ones—essential for psychic survival and the sustenance of energy. For the aspiring artist, the minor, the unfinished, or even the botched work, may be a more instructive model for how things should—and should not be done. For the amateur spectator, such works are the daily fare which provide good, honest nourishment—and which can lead to appreciation of more refined, or deeper pleasures.

QUESTIONS FOR DISCUSSION

1. Would this author ever drink a beer? To put it another way, what is your perception of Eva Hoffman's personality as revealed in her argument? Do her personal tastes seem to come close to the surface of her argument?
2. This evaluation depends heavily on a number of key terms. What does Hoffman seem to mean by *genre, convention,* or *classic?*
3. By what criteria can a work of art be judged "major" or "minor"? How can we tell whether these qualities reside in the works or in the perceivers?
4. This argument begins with a number of references to the books "we" read, the music "we" listen to, the art "we" are familiar with. Who are "we"? In other words, what are the characteristics of the ideal audience for Hoffman's evaluation?
5. Do you notice a difference in the language when Hoffman talks about major versus minor works? When is she more specific? What happens to her style when she confronts a major work?
6. Why does Hoffman claim that it is more difficult to distinguish the major from the minor in contemporary art? Is this observation incompatible with the distinction she tries to maintain between major and minor art?

SUGGESTIONS FOR WRITING

1. Hoffman implies that works in certain genres, such as detective fiction or Broadway musicals, could never be considered major art. Support or refute this contention for *New York Times* readers.
2. Extract Hoffman's criteria for a major work and apply them to a particular work. You might nominate a surprising candidate for elevation to the status of "major," or dethrone one that most people would value more highly.

3. Do you agree with Hoffman's characterization of the movies as "made only for the day" or showing us "how our particular place and moment in time looks," and thus without the potential to be major art? Using movies you are familiar with as examples, write a response to Hoffman.
4. Refute Hoffman's position that major works possess special qualities that always distinguish them from minor ones. Could an inferior appreciation reduce a major work to minor status, or a superior appreciation raise a minor work to major? Try doing one or the other for an audience with conservative artistic tastes.
5. Can you agree with Hoffman that there is a category of art or entertainment below minor, one that gives no pleasure at all? Offer an example (perhaps a TV show, a movie, a particular kind of music) and give a negative evaluation. Or turn this whole question around and argue that no such evaluation could be supported, that taste in such matters is wholly personal. Your audience might be people who never bother with the conscious evaluation of the art they consume.

—»» ««—

A Plea for
Corporate Conscience

JUDGE MILES W. LORD

The following selection is unique in this reader because it was originally a speech, delivered live to its audience on February 29, 1984. The speaker, Judge Miles W. Lord of the Federal District Court in Minneapolis, had just approved a $4.6 million product-liability suit against the A.H. Robins Company for injuries caused by one of its products, the Dalkon Shield intrauterine contraceptive device (IUD), a decision that satisfied 7 of the 9,000 claims that have been brought against the company. The judge then made the following remarks to three officials of the company: E. Claiborne Robins Jr., the firm's president; Carl D. Lunsford, senior vice president for research and development; and William A. Forrest Jr., vice president and general counsel.

Judge Lord's remarks also have the distinction of being cast in the strongest, most emotional language to be found in any argument in this reader. Here the notion of "responsibility as cause" (discussed in the introduction to our section on causal argument) comes alive as we hear the judge's voice condemning and yet pleading with the agents he finds guilty of cruelty, legal evasion, and hard-heartedness.

Mr. Robins, Mr. Forrest, and Dr. Lunsford: After months of reflection, study, and cogitation—and no small amount of prayer—I have concluded that it is perfectly appropriate to make this statement, which will constitute my plea to you to seek new horizons in corporate consciousness and a new sense of personal responsibility for the activities of those who work under you in the name of the A.H. Robins Company.

It is not enough to say, "I did not know," "It was not me," "Look elsewhere." Time and again, each of you has used this kind of argument in refusing to acknowledge your responsibility and in pretending to the world that the chief officers and directors of your gigantic multinational corporation have no responsibility for its acts and omissions.

Today as you sit here attempting once more to extricate yourselves from the legal consequences of your acts, none of you has faced up to the fact that more than 9,000 women claim they gave up part of their womanhood so that your company might prosper. It has been alleged that others gave their lives so you might prosper. And there stand behind them legions more who have been injured but who have not sought relief in the courts of this land.

I dread to think what would have been the consequences if your victims had been men rather than women—women, who seem, through some quirk of our society's mores, to be expected to suffer pain, shame, and humiliation.

If one poor young man were, without authority or consent, to inflict such damage upon one woman, he would be jailed for a good portion of the rest of his life. Yet your company, without warning to women, invaded their bodies by the millions and caused them injuries by the thousands. And when the time came for these women to make their claims against your company, you attacked their characters. You inquired into their sexual practices and into the identity of their sex partners. You ruined families and reputations and careers in order to intimidate those who would raise their voices against you. You introduced issues that had no relationship to the fact that you had planted in the bodies of these women instruments of death, of mutilation, of disease.

Gentlemen, you state that your company has suffered enough, that the infliction of further punishment in the form of punitive damages would cause harm to your business, would punish innocent shareholders, and could conceivably depress your profits to the point where you could not survive as a competitor in this industry. When the poor and down-trodden commit crimes, they too plead that these are crimes of survival and that they should be excused for illegal acts that helped them escape desperate economic straits. On a few occasions when these excuses are made and remorseful defendants promise to mend their ways, courts will give heed to such pleas. But no court will heed the plea when the individual denies the wrongful nature of his deeds and gives no indication that he will mend his ways. Your company, in the face of over-whelming evidence, denies its guilt and continues its monstrous mischief.

Mr. Forrest, you have told me that you are working with members of the Congress of the United States to find a way of forgiving you from punitive damages that might otherwise be imposed. Yet the profits of your company continue to mount. Your last financial report boasts of new records for sales and earnings, with a profit of more than $58 million in 1983. And, insofar as this court has been able to determine, you three men and your company are still engaged in a course of wrongdoing. Until your company indicates that it is willing to cease and desist this deception and to seek out and advise the victims, your remonstrances to Congress and to the courts are indeed hollow and cynical. The company has not suffered, nor have you men personally. You are collec-tively being enriched by millions of dollars each year. There is no evidence that your company has suffered any penalty from these litiga-tions. In fact, the evidence is to the contrary.

The case law suggests that the purpose of punitive damages is to make an award that will punish a defendant for his wrongdoing. Punish-ment has traditionally involved the principles of revenge, rehabilitation, and deterrence. There is no evidence I have been able to find in my review of these cases to indicate that any one of these objectives has been accomplished.

Mr. Robins, Mr. Forrest, Dr. Lunsford: You have not been rehabili-tated. Under your direction, your company has continued to allow women, tens of thousands of them, to wear this device—a deadly depth charge in their wombs, ready to explode at any time. Your attorney denies that tens of thousands of these devices are still in women's bodies. But I submit to you that he has no more basis for denying the accusation than the plaintiffs have for stating it as truth. We simply do not know how many women are still wearing these devices because your company is not willing to find out. The only conceivable reasons that you have not recalled this product are that it would hurt your balance sheet and alert women who have already been harmed that you may be liable for their injuries. You have taken the bottom line as your guiding beacon and the low road as your route. That is corporate irresponsibility at its meanest. Rehabilitation involves an admission of guilt, a certain contrition, an acknowledgment of wrongdoing, and a resolution to take a new course toward a better life. I find none of this in you or your corporation. Confession is good for the soul, gentlemen. Face up to your misdeed. Acknowledge the personal responsibility you have for the activities of those who work under you. Rectify this evil situation. Warn the potential victims and recompense those who have already been harmed.

Mr. Robins, Mr. Forrest, Dr. Lunsford: I see little in the history of this case that would deter others. The policy of delay and obfuscation practiced by your lawyers in courts throughout this country has made it possible for you and your insurance company to put off the payment of these claims for such a long period that the interest you earned in the interim covers the cost of these cases. You, in essence, pay nothing out of your own pockets to settle these cases. What corporate officials could learn a lesson from this? The only lesson they might learn is that it pays to delay compensating victims and to intimidate, harass, and shame the injured parties.

Your company seeks to segment and fragment the litigation of these cases nationwide. The courts of this country are burdened with more than 3,000 Dalkon Shield cases. The sheer number of claims and the dilatory tactics used by your company's attorneys clog court calendars and consume vast amounts of judicial and jury time. Your company settles those cases out of court in which it finds itself in an uncomfortable position, a handy device for avoiding any proceeding that would give continuity or cohesiveness to this nationwide problem. The decision as to which cases are brought to trial rests almost solely at the whim and discretion of the A.H. Robins Company. In order to guarantee that no plaintiff or group of plaintiffs mounts a sustained assault upon your system of evasion and avoidance, you have time after time demanded that, as the price of settling a case, able lawyers agree not to bring a Dalkon Shield case again and not to help less experienced lawyers with cases against your company.

Another of your callous legal tactics is to force women of little means to withstand the onslaughts of your well-financed team of attorneys. You target your worst tactics at the meek and the poor.

If this court had the authority, I would order your company to make an effort to locate each and every woman who still wears this device and recall your product. But this court does not. I must therefore resort to moral persuasion and a personal appeal to each of you. Mr. Robins, Mr. Forrest, and Dr. Lunsford: You are the people with the power to recall. You are the corporate conscience.

Please, in the name of humanity, lift your eyes above the bottom line. You, the men in charge, must surely have hearts and souls and consciences.

Please, gentlemen, give consideration to tracing down the victims and sparing them the agony that will surely be theirs.

QUESTIONS FOR DISCUSSION

1. Go through the judge's speech to find all the uses of emotional language. In particular, at what points do you seem to catch the intonation of a human voice, even on the printed page? Why does Judge Lord feel justified in using such strong, dramatic language?
2. What effect did Judge Lord expect to have on the three defendants in the courtroom? Did he perhaps have other audiences and effects in mind as well?
3. Judges and juries often consider the "quality" of an act, beyond simply determining who is responsible for it. A murder, for example, can be further judged as "aggravated" or "mitigated" depending on the precise circumstances surrounding it. Judge Lord clearly feels he has an aggravated case on his hands. Why?
4. How does Judge Lord elaborate the villainy of the defendants? What stereotypes of the weak against the powerful does he make the two sides in this case conform to?
5. Why does the judge make what he calls a "personal appeal" and try out "moral persuasion" in a court of law? Is he speaking beyond or within his prerogative?
6. What, according to Judge Lord, would be responsible action from the Robins officials? According to what corporate ethics does he want them to behave?

SUGGESTIONS FOR WRITING

1. Investigate the case of Robins versus IUD users for yourself. Do you agree with Judge Lord's determination that in this case responsibility lies solely with the manufacturer? What about the responsibility of the government agency that

permitted sale of the devices, the physicians who advised their use, and the women who chose to use them? Write a causal argument nominating a legally responsible agent who should be prosecuted under the law.

2. Do the same kind of causal investigation suggested above on a similar case where problems with a product have led or not led to the indictment of the manufacturer. Why, for example, are cigarette manufacturers not held legally responsible for deaths from lung cancer?

3. Read again or for the first time Richard Neely's argument on "The Politics of Crime" in Part Two. Write an essay for your classmates discussing whether the details of the Robins case support or refute Neely's characterization of how powerful entities can use the cumbersome procedures of the courts to their advantage.

4. Look carefully at Judge Lord's definitions of *punishment* and *rehabilitation*. Use these definitions to assess for newspaper readers the effectiveness of a particular court ruling in either a civil or criminal trial (one in which you were involved or one that achieved newspaper notoriety). Were the procedure and the verdict effective in achieving these two ends?

5. Write the speech that the three Robins officials might have made defending themselves in response to Judge Lord's remarks. Their options for responding could be many, ranging from intransigent refusal to acknowledge the judge's point to compliance with the judge's request while at the same time exonerating themselves, with many other possibilities.

6. What should be the code of ethics of a public corporation that produces consumer goods? To whom is the corporation's first responsibility? Should its code of ethics exceed or coincide with its legal liabilities? (You may either write a general response to this question or argue into place a code of ethics for a specific corporation.)

Above All, the Man had Character

HUGH SIDEY

Hugh Sidey is a regular columnist for Time, *one of our most familiar news weeklies. His essay on George Washington is an example of what the ancient Greeks would have called* epideictic, *or ceremonial, rhetoric—that is, a piece prepared for a special occasion, either praising or blaming a character or event. The occasion here is the lukewarm holiday of George Washington's birthday, usually unnoticed except for department store sales. It gives Sidey an excuse for writing and a subject to write about, but it also gives him a problem because there is little new to say about Washington on his 251st birthday. Notice how Sidey nevertheless uses his subject as a vehicle for contemporary commentary.*

Each year George Washington gains more luster in our reveries on how we got where we are. Our sophisticated scholarship and painstaking restoration, which so often dismantle heroes, have revealed the human dimensions of the father of the country but have failed to dim the aura of greatness that clings to Washington, whose 251st birthday we mark next week.

His contemporaries felt the same awe and wonder. In Washington's last years, Mount Vernon became a mecca for the great and the grateful, for the curious and the ambitious. So many people arrived at the doorstep that Washington, who would turn none away, finally engaged a social secretary to handle the flow. Sometimes he did not attend the dinners he gave because the company was so numerous and foreign to him. One night when he dined alone with Mrs. Washington, the event was so unusual he made a note of it in his diary.

The legend of the man is safely sheltered these days behind high fences of respect. Were the real Washington on hand today, that might not be the case, and therein may lie a lesson. We have in this nation erected standards for our public people that dim anyone's glow if he or she falls short of perfection. It is reasonable, then, to wonder if people can enter public life and make a difference as they did in the first years of the Republic. Even as our expectations have grown, our respect for and sympathy with Presidents have diminished.

By our modern measures, George Washington did not read the right books. He relished how-to-do-it texts, with their new ideas on the use of manure, turning soil and animal husbandry. But he did not delve very far into art, philosophy or science. When John Kennedy was coaxed into supplying a list of his ten favorite books, the collection was heavy with history, biography and geopolitics, the kind of reading that he knew critical journalists would admire. Twenty years ago, we took Presidents at their word. The suspicion now is that the list was a bit fraudulent.

Washington knew no foreign languages (Thomas Jefferson spoke or read five). Washington never traveled to Europe, while Benjamin Franklin, John Adams and Jefferson all spent years there. He was not an accomplished public speaker. His military achievements were judged for their perseverance rather than their brilliance. Yet the battle of Trenton might have been as important a battle as this nation ever won. The Trenton victory brought the Revolution back to life. The colonies dared hope again for independence. France began to look with more favor on the American struggle, and Britain began to lose heart. But the battle was technically a shambles.

Three columns were to have crossed the Delaware River. Only Washington made it across. The powder of his troops was soaked by a freezing rain, so they could not fire their arms. They had to depend on bayonets several times during the night. Washington's officers pleaded with him to call off the attack. The story goes that he stood on an old beehive in a muddy New Jersey field and turned aside every entreaty. The battle of Trenton was won by the determination of one man, but certainly not by his military expertise. Would he have done what he did on that miserable night if the failing campaign had been on the evening news with closeup shots of the ragged men?

Washington sometimes looked on his 22 years of public service as a kind of prison sentence that took him away from his land. Washington was not one of the boys. The thought of him in blue jeans around the graceful drives of Mount Vernon is, thank goodness, still shattering. Once, when Gouverneur Morris, a friend and supporter, put his hand on Washington's shoulder to show doubters how close he was to the chief, Washington coldly took Morris's hand and removed it. Nobody in Washington's inner circle tried that again. Sometimes, the stories go, when Washington was with his old Army friends and had a few glasses of wine, he became what they called "merry," and he would talk and reminisce into the night. But that was rather rare, according to the scholars. With this kind of record, one wonders how George Washington might have fared in the Style section of the Washington *Post* under the arch questioning of Sally Quinn: "Mr. President, do you and Mrs. Washington have separate bedrooms?"

George Washington accumulated nearly 100,000 acres of land in his last years and was judged one of the wealthiest men in the nation. He would have been suspected of conflict of interest at every turn. Investigative reporters would have been in clover—literally, perhaps, because Washington might have cornered the clover-seed market and been nabbed for restraint of trade.

Washington was meticulous about dress, selecting with care his shoes and their buckles, the cloth for his suits and shirts. In our time we are a little uneasy with Presidents who pay too much attention (or too little) to their dress. That may be changing. Grubbiness has proved less of a political asset than some thought a few years back. Still, any hint of vanity is deplored. John Kennedy became angry when the fashion magazine *Gentlemen's Quarterly* put him on its cover and announced that he had posed for the magazine in his new two-button suit. Kennedy told an astonished group around his desk that he would now be remembered as the President who posed in his new suit, just as Calvin Coolidge was most renowned for having been pictured in an Indian war bonnet.

Mount Vernon was almost totally George Washington's creation, another dimension of the man that would have been of dubious value in this age. Correspondents would have reported during the war that after a battle (with the fortunes of America ebbing, soldiers hungry and sick) the Commander in Chief sometimes penned many pages of instructions to his plantation manager, telling him what to build and plant and harvest. Neglect of duty? Washington designed his home, laid out the drives, selected the colors (green was his favorite), chose the trees, plants and flowers. The only decorating that Martha did was to choose some curtains. Surely today's social analysts would have been delighted at such domestic concern by Washington, but just as surely there would have been criticism of such dominance by the general of his wife.

Washington's favorite recreation was fox hunting. Consider that now: a President pounding over the hills on horseback, his hounds in full cry after a scraggly fox. Environmentalists would have jumped out at him from behind every hedge, waving placards. A "save the foxes" society would have been organized. Columnist Ellen Goodman would have rushed to detail the plight of the ill-fed, ill-housed, ill-treated foxes of Fairfax County. Newsmagazines might have noted that photographs of Washington mounting his horse revealed he had wide hips. The temptation would have been too much: "President Washington, displaying a broad beam and a narrow mind, last week chased a 10-lb. fox to an unseemly death in the lovely hills of Virginia."

Washington cannot be reconstituted and placed in our century, of course, nor would he want to be. His time and his land were not necessarily more simple, but they certainly were different. The nation had 4 million people and only six cities of more than 8,000 souls each. The Federal Government, when Washington ran it, had 350 civil employees. If numbers and complexity were not the adversaries, then distance, time, disease, weather, Indians and ignorance were. It took a week to get to New York City. Early death stalked almost everyone. Washington was remarkably durable for his time—and lucky. His horses and uniforms were riddled with bullets at Braddock's defeat in the French and Indian War. He was untouched. But even his luck ran out finally. He died at 67 of a throat inflammation. A young physician in attendance wanted to open the trachea but was overruled by his seniors, still fearful of the new technique. A sturdy figure like Washington might have been around many more years with only a little bit of today's medical knowledge.

Writers who journey through the accounts of his life almost always confess some bafflement about why he was such a great figure in his time and remains so in ours. British historian Marcus Cunliffe points out that Washington was a good man but not a saint, a competent soldier but not great, thoughtful but not brilliant like Alexander Hamilton. He was a respectable administrator but certainly not a genius. All this and more his biographers have put down. Washington was a prudent conserver but not a brilliant reformer. He was sober unto dullness. He lacked the common touch so much that not even his British enemies had a derogatory nickname for him during the war. He could strip off his coat and help the field hands, but he had no very close friends. The Marquis de Lafayette, his French ally, was as close as anyone. To humanize Washington, suggests Cunliffe, would be to falsify him, though of course many have tried to do that in the past two centuries.

We would do well in this age of total and instant analysis to ponder why it is we honor George Washington as we do, why the legend goes on in the face of the reservations and doubts that scholars keep raising. It is true that simply being an American and being around for the start of the United States would have assured Washington some place in history. There was more.

The sum of his rather normal parts added up to an exceptional figure. George Washington had character. That is easily said but not easily defined. Writers have been trying to do it since time began, but character defies scientific analysis. Duke University's James David Barber based an entire book about Presidents on the analysis of character. It was fascinating. But Barber raised as many questions as he answered. Nobody is quite certain what character is, but everybody captures a piece of the truth. Here are a few thoughts from Washington's contemporaries and his later biographers about the qualities that lifted him above others.

One writer noted Washington's "cool dignity." Washington's aloofness and reserve made him stand out from other men, several authors insisted. Washington understood power, wrote one. Another claimed simply: "Washington had quality." From there the scholars get more subjective. Washington merged his honor with that of America, recounted a writer, not to mention his fortune and everything he planned and built. During the Revolution, a British raiding party sailed up the Potomac and at Mount Vernon received some provisions from the farm manager. When Washington heard about it (he was off leading the Army), he was disturbed. He wrote that his people should have let the raiders burn down the place before they aided the enemy. Biographers have written that "Washington proved the soundness of America" and that he "had a true American vision." By that they meant that he, almost alone among those great men, understood in totality the wealth and strength of the land that lay before him and how it formed and held a society together. "The man is the monument; the monument is America," wrote Cunliffe with a poetic touch. Those nine words may say as much as anything about the source of our reverence.

George Washington was sensible and wise. He was not the most informed or imaginative of men. But he understood himself and this nation-to-be. That understanding came from the many elements that make up any person. His heart and mind were shaped by his family, his land, his community and the small events that touched him every day. Those were the normal experiences. They were added to his natural endowments. Only one power can fully fathom such a formula—God. Washington had the tolerance of a landsman, the faith that comes with witnessing the changing seasons year in and year out, the sensitivity that accumulates from watching buds burst and colts grow. Optimism, perseverance, patience and an eager view of the distant horizon have always been a gift of the earth to those who stayed close to it.

We pay too much attention these days to college degrees, to public displays of so-called brilliance. We are overawed by the listings in *Who's Who*, by prizes and travels and speeches. We pay too much heed to organizational charts, office tension, human friction and how paper flows or does not. We busy ourselves too much in searching for minor flaws in our Presidents, finding petty shortfalls and mistakes, relishing pratfalls and humiliations.

The presidency to this day still rests more on the character of the person who inhabits the office than on anything else, try as we may in our books and papers to develop formulas and charts that explain success and failure. The founding fathers designed it that way. It was their idea to find a man in America with a great character and let him invest a tradition and shape a national character. They found George Washington. He did his job splendidly. He might even have known what he was doing. When he took the presidency he wrote, "I walk on untrodden ground. There is scarcely any part of my conduct which may not hereafter be drawn into precedent." That is at once beautiful and profound. It is no wonder he succeeded, entering office with such a code of conduct.

Our task is to rekindle the tradition, to search in our system, for people of great character and then bring them to power and rally behind them; not blindly, to be sure, but with understanding and even sympathy and tolerance. Character like Washington's is not a blend of everything that is perfect. In fact, we have not done too badly through 39 men who became President. Even today, in the midst of great national worry, the quality in the presidency that helps keep a beleaguered nation together is the character of the man we glimpse in the White House. Over these past decades some of our Presidents have had more than others. We have not always been alert to those who have had outstanding characters, and sometimes we have been fooled by those who did not have the depths of character we thought they had. Character has come in different sizes and shapes, and some Presidents seemed to have enlarged it as time went on, while others have appeared to lose character under stress.

More than all the other Presidents, George Washington has marched through our centuries untouched by critics, growing larger under the baleful eye of history. An uncommon man made from common parts remains our grand legacy and our hope in this moment of bewilderment in our third century.

QUESTIONS FOR DISCUSSION

1. What is the purpose of this essay? Is it only praise for Washington or does the essay have more contemporary applications?
2. Why does Sidey spend so much time at the beginning of his essay listing Washington's defects? What difference would it have made if he had first argued for Washington's greatness?
3. Sidey praises Washington for his character. How does he define that term and connect it with specifics in Washington's career?
4. What attitudes can Sidey assume his audience already holds about Washington? Does the typical attitude toward Washington make Sidey's job as an evaluator more or less difficult?
5. Sidey has to conform to the style of *Time*, which is carefully controlled for its readability. How would you characterize his style for sentence length, word choice, and level of difficulty?
6. What part of the argument strikes you as the most emotional? Why is the emotion concentrated there, and how is it conveyed?

SUGGESTIONS FOR WRITING

1. Select a public figure and evaluate that person's character for *Time* magazine's readers, either in the specific office or role filled or as a coherent personality.
2. Take the qualities of Washington as Sidey has presented them and measure another president against them.
3. Is the kind of comparison you would undertake in suggestion 2 a valid one? Or do the criteria for evaluating a president's character change over time or even with every person in office? Write a response to Sidey, either upholding or questioning the value of comparing other presidents with Washington.
4. The reputations of historic figures rise and fall. Pick a historical figure whose reputation has fluctuated and try to explain to students of history the causes for such fluctuation. Why, for example, has the assessment of President Truman varied? What leads one age to reinterpret the past?
5. Reassess the reputation of a historical figure who has been either overrated or underrated. Address your re-evaluation to those holding the mistaken view.
6. Find two analogous incidents in the careers of two presidents. (You may have to argue that the incidents are indeed comparable.) Compare the press coverage (same newspapers or news weeklies) for the "understanding, sympathy, and tolerance" that Sidey recommends. Do you see significant differences in the way the presidents are treated? Address your analysis to readers unaware of differences in press coverage.

The Wisdom of Common Sense

MARY GIEGENGACK JURELLER

In the following evaluation, Mary Jureller defends the landmark legislation passed in 1975 that mandates the mainstreaming of handicapped children in public schools. Perhaps in your school career you have observed the effects of this law. Not only does Jureller praise a particular law here; she also exposes the criteria by which she evaluates it. Notice how she blends both appeals to consequence and appeals to moral principle in her argument while

demonstrating a very realistic sense of the difficulties this controversial
legislation will create.
  Mary Jureller teaches philosophy and medical ethics. Her original
audience for this piece were the alumnae of her college; the essay first
appeared in the College of New Rochelle Quarterly.

At the beginning of every ethics course I ask each of my students to give
an example of an immoral action and to explain what it is that makes
that action wrong. The examples are usually the easier ones for all of us
to categorize: wanton killings, blatant obstructions of justice, acts of
prejudice and discrimination which ruin the lives of others, and grossly
unfair distributions of this world's goods. To the question, why are these
actions wrong, the answers come back: the action violates some human
right (or fails to fulfill a duty) and/or the action has harmful consequences for people.

  Without yet realizing it, the students have outlined the two major
approaches to ethical theory: what is called the deontological approach
—from the Greek word "deon," meaning "duty"—and the teleological
approach—from the Greek word "telos," meaning "end, goal, purpose."
Many of us have studied Immanual Kant as a prime example of the
deontological approach and John Stuart Mill or John Dewey as examples
of the teleological approach. The natural law ethics of St. Thomas
Aquinas is an attempt to synthesize these two approaches within a
religious perspective.

  Whatever ethics course we have taken, we have become aware that
moral philosophers ask questions about the "right" and the "good" and
about the relationship between them. As we contemplate the implications of the Education of All Handicapped Children Act of 1975, we
can all assume the stance of moral philosophers. We can ask what rights
and duties this law recognizes and what consequences, both for individuals and for the society at large, it is likely to bring about.

  In order for our actions to be moral, Immanuel Kant requires that
we "treat humanity, in our own person, or in the person of another,
never only as a means to some end (extrinsic to the person), but always
also as an end in him or herself." Obviously, we use many persons as
means to extrinsic ends—bus drivers, salespersons, doctors, teachers are
all means we use to achieve our own ends. But we err if we treat these
persons *only* as means without respecting their autonomy as moral
agents and their right to direct their lives by their own values. This
fundamental requirement of treating all person as ends—Kant calls it a

"categorical imperative"—is binding regardless of the consequences that follow from it.

Public Law 94–142 takes a major step in the direction of respecting others as ends in themselves. It recognizes that every child has a right to a public education, consonant with his or her needs. The needs of the child rather than the needs of the institution or of the society are to determine the placement of the child and the program which the child follows. A handicapped child may not be denied equality before the law because her handicaps make it more difficult to teach her or because his progress takes place at a different pace from that of "normal" children. Such a child may not be used as a means to some extrinsic end. Displacement from the mainstream must henceforth be justified in terms of enhancing the child's opportunities and not in terms of the convenience of the mainstream institution, the personal preferences of teachers, or the cost (within reasonable limits) to the local school board.

Kant would applaud a stance which thus puts the intrinsic value of persons before the extrinsic value of a variety of consequences.

In the view of a utilitarian like John Stuart Mill, however, the morality of our actions is determined solely by the consequences. An overall balance of foreseeable good consequences over bad consequences for all the people involved is the only justification of our actions. So we must weigh the bad against the good. The mainstreaming of children with special needs may mean that they will receive *less* attention than they would in separate classes; it may overburden teachers who are already pressed by the demands of a diversified class; it may isolate the child in a corner of the regular classroom more than he or she is now isolated in a special classroom. And it may cost the taxpayers far more money than will be returned to them by the contributions of these individuals. We cannot be sure that these bad consequences will not follow.

What are the good consequences that are envisioned? It seems to me that the major goal of the legislation is to enable handicapped persons to assume as full a role in society at large as possible. The world they must take their place in when their schooling is over is a world of so-called "normal" people (though we are all aware of the moral problems involved in defining such norms and in applying them to persons). Sooner or later they will have to either "hack it" in the cold, competitive world of American capitalism and individualism or withdraw to institutions in which many opportunities will not be available to them. If fewer of them are institutionalized, an immediate financial benefit will ensue.

How much better prepared they will be, the proponents of Public Law 94-142 may say, if they have been able to adjust to life in the same schools which their neighbors attend. And how much better prepared their "normal" neighbors will be to receive them and interact with them comfortably in adult life. The mysterious child down the block who disappeared every September into a distant school for the mentally retarded, the emotionally disturbed, the blind, or the deaf and who came home in June to watch their summer antics from afar, is now in their music class, their school play, their little brother's first grade reading group. That child now has a real personality, strengths which they can admire, burdens which they begin to understand and to want to lighten. Fears and prejudices can be gradually eliminated on both sides. Perhaps eventually all of us can live more comfortably with our own limitations because we have lived with the limitations of others.

While good consequences such as these may be what we hope for, they will not be achieved unless we choose the right means. The law must be implemented with care. The "regular" teachers will need to deal with the special children who will join their classes permanently or for selected periods during the day. The "special ed" teachers will also need help. Many of them will be asked to assume new roles in the schools—moving from class to class and assisting the regular teachers with particular children; serving on teams to draw up the individualized educational programs which will have to be designed for each special child, dealing with PTAs and the larger public to explain what is being done and to help people to adjust to new situations. Some regular teachers will feel overburdened; some special ed teachers will feel supplanted. Conflicts may arise about assignments. Differences of opinion will arise about the best program for an individual child.

The special children will need help to adjust to new environments. And the "normal" children will need to be *taught* how to interact with some children. Children will feel frustrated and will make mistakes. There will be days on which nothing goes right and everyone goes home with a tension headache. Parents will be tempted to get on the phone and call someone to task for the day's mistakes.

All of these situations will require moral courage. As in all human endeavors, the goal may be lost sight of as we battle over the means. The goal, of course, is the growth and development of the children—all the children. Yet to create an atmosphere of growth, the adults involved must have the support they need. As parents, or friends, or neighbors, we may be able to provide that for them.

Our "will to believe" must create possibilities where they do not yet exist. All who participate will learn much that they did not expect. We may succeed in righting some of the wrongs we have done to disadvantaged children, and our own horizons may be expanded in the process.

We might even hope for other long-range social consequences. We live in a society which has increasingly separated the sick, the elderly, the dying, the mentally disturbed from the mainstream of American life. As a people, we have almost become accustomed to shutting our problems out of sight and hoping thereby to solve them. We have accepted the view that problems which were once considered rather normal are now the province of specialists. The wisdom of common sense is not allowed to compete against advanced degrees in psychology, medicine, or gerontology, to mention only a few. Genetic counseling has made it possible to determine in some cases whether or not our children will be retarded or afflicted with genetic diseases. There is strong pressure on many parents to practice selective abortion and thereby to rid themselves—and society—of unnecessary burdens. Questions are being raised about the responsibility of society to help support a retarded child whom the parents refused to abort or to give welfare to an unwed mother who refused sterilization.

Against such a background the passage of Public Law 94-142 is perhaps more of a triumph than it first appeared. It seems to go strongly counter to the trends we have just mentioned. Besides declaring that our special children must not be separated more than *their* needs require, it casts a vote in favor of the wisdom of common sense (vested in our experienced teachers of "normal" children), without denying the necessary contribution of specialists. It also recognizes that ideally the entire human family ought to help every human being to achieve that degree of self-fulfillment he or she is capable of.

The return of special children to our midst may cause us to question our need to isolate them and wish they would go away. Perhaps a new dawn is breaking in which our notions of "normalcy" may be reevaluated and we may claim as our own those whom the society has labeled as "other."

QUESTIONS FOR DISCUSSION

1. Jureller uses the unusual tactic of explaining to her readers just what the techniques of evaluation argument are. What does she gain by such a strategy?

2. How does Jureller's argument to support Public Law 94-142 use both what she calls deontological and teleological approaches? Which approach dominates?
3. Identify the emotional appeals in this argument. Could Jureller have used more? What audiences would find more emotional appeals on this issue persuasive? What audiences would be less responsive to them?
4. Jureller points out many potential bad consequences of the mainstreaming law and admits the problems in its implementation. Why does she include so much that seems to work against her argument?
5. Jureller talks about the possible long-range social consequences of Public Law 94-142. What is the relation between such consequences and a moral ideal? In other words, how do deontological and teleological arguments merge?
6. Jureller identifies herself as a teacher. What is there in her style and personal voice that reinforces that identification?

SUGGESTIONS FOR WRITING

1. Write up the assignment that Jureller gives her ethics class. Identify an action you regard as immoral and use her criteria to support your evaluation.
2. From your own experience or from research, consider the impact of mainstreaming one particular kind of handicapped child. You will need to distinguish among the mentally retarded, physically or emotionally handicapped, and learning disabled. You might want to persuade parents and school administrators that differences among these categories are so great that generalizations about programs for the "handicapped" can be misleading.
3. Write two short arguments evaluating the same subject (preferably an action). Make one depend entirely on consequence arguments and the other entirely on moral ones.
4. Try a case study approach. Interview a handicapped person (not necessarily a child) and do a causal analysis of how that person's educational opportunities helped or hindered him or her. Write up your findings as a feature article for a newspaper or magazine.
5. On some issues, principles and consequences conflict. An action can have desirable consequences but be immoral. Plagiarism or cheating on exams are examples. Write an argument on academic honesty (or a topic involving such conflict) in which you defend the moral principle to the person who would reap the good consequences of the immoral action.
6. Professions such as medicine have codified their ethical standards. Draw up a code of ethics, a set of principles that could be used to evaluate particular actions for a profession or field or role (some possibilities: a football team member, a telephone solicitor, fast food clerk, owner of a pet store).

—≫≫ ≪≪—

One for the Books

THOMAS BENDER

In April of 1976, the school board in the Long Island community of Island Trees banned eleven books from the high school and junior high school libraries in the district. Two books were restored a few months later (Laughing Boy by Oliver La Farge and Black Boy by Richard Wright), but nine books remained censored: Slaughterhouse Five, by Kurt Vonnegut Jr.; The Fixer, by Bernard Malamud; A Hero Ain't Nothing But a Sandwich, by Alice Childress; Go Ask Alice, author anonymous; The Best Short Stories by Negro Writers, edited by Langston Hughes; The Naked Ape, by Desmond Morris; Down these Mean Streets, by Piri Thomas; Soul on Ice, by Eldridge Cleaver; and A Reader for Writers—A Critical Anthology of Prose Readings, by Jerome W. Archer. Eventually, the American Civil Liberties Union, the New York State Supreme Court, and the United States Supreme Court intervened in what began as a nearly unanimous decision by a group of local citizens to purge their schools of books they considered "offensive to Christians, Jews, Blacks, and Americans in general."

Thomas Bender's argument begins on the issue of censorship, but it moves quickly away from the Island Trees case (which the author assumes his audience is familiar with) to ponder what "community" means in America. Most evaluations aim their criteria at some subject for judgment; this one spends its time defending a single criterion, one that could be applied in a censorship case but to many other issues as well.

"One for the Books," which relies on the authority of James Madison, is also made by an authority. Thomas Bender is a professor of humanities at New York University and author of Community and Social Change in America.

The controversy over removal of nine books from the Island Trees school district's high school library points directly to fundamental questions about the nature of community in modern American society and about our political tradition.

When the legal case that emerged from this conflict on Long Island is argued before the United States Supreme Court in March, it will mark the first time that the Court has considered a case concerning censorship in school libraries. Until now, the presumption that communities, through elected boards, should control their schools has gone unchallenged in the Court. Underlying this notion is the proposition that education is a local, not a Federal responsibility. But the opponents in this case insist that in a free society there must be limits on a board's power to indoctrinate the young.

Island Trees is thus a historic case, and one that encourages historical reflection. The issues are large ones of the sort James Madison considered in the "Federalist Papers." Among the Founding Fathers, Madison was the most acute in understanding that the diversity of values and interests in our society provided a basis for political freedom. Political theorists from Aristotle to Rousseau had assumed that free, republican government could survive only in small communities where there was a consensus of values. Otherwise, it was feared, conflict between groups would tear the society apart and open the way to order under tyranny. Madison, however, grasped a radically new, modern idea, one rooted in American society. Diversity itself could secure freedom and stability in a republic.

In the "Federalist Papers," Madison argued for an "extensive" republic, one containing diversity rather than the consensus assumed or preferred by opponents of the Constitution. He explained that with our society "broken into so many parts . . . the rights of individuals, or of the minority, will be in little danger from interested combinations of the majority." Recognizing that religious diversity nourished religious freedom in America, he argued: "In a free government the security for civil rights must be the same as that for religious rights. It consists in the one case in the multiplicity of interests, and in the other in the multiplicity of sects."

Freedom and diversity had been linked some 30 years earlier, as Madison knew, when William Livingston of New York, in a series of brilliant newspaper essays, argued against denominational control of the proposed King's College, now Columbia University. He argued that since there were at least three major religious groups in New York, the college should not be under the influence or custody of any. The curriculum, he said, should be "liberal" so that students (the age of today's high school students) could "have an unrestrained Access to all Books in the Library, and that free Conversations upon polemical and controverted Points in Divinity, be not discountenanced."

In view of this political tradition, the question raised by Island Trees is whether today's school district is a community with a consensus of values, such as Aristotle or Rousseau envisioned, or whether even localities have the elements of diversity Madison posited as a fact of nature in society. Is it not obvious that the degree of economic, ethnic, religious, and cultural diversity in even the smallest American political jurisdictions easily matches what Madison had in mind in 1787 for the nation as a whole?

Localities are no longer communal in the sense assumed by premodern theorists, and assumed in any school board claim to establish a community orthodoxy. Today, the kind of consensus implied by the traditional idea of local politics hardly extends beyond the circle of family and friends, and has not for at least a century.

The wisdom of Madison's understanding of the Constitution was to see in it a means of transforming diverse minority interests into the basis of freedom for an extensive republic. Today, local political jurisdictions and the courts, too, must seek ways of preserving such interests, and this implies jettisoning the notion that community is defined by geography alone. To allow or encourage any one group to assume or demand a consensus of local opinion, even as a triumphant majority, invites precisely the sort of civil conflict Madison sought to avoid.

A few basic facts about the Island Trees school district illustrate my point. First of all, the district comprises parts of four towns. Even if one tried to argue that a town represented a community of values, this district of four towns, not one, must accommodate itself to fundamental diversity. Second, the vote in school board elections there has reflected the essential diversity of our political culture. At Island Trees, winning totals in the two elections held since the controversy began in 1976 have not exceeded 53 percent of the vote. In a community where consensus is possible or in a totalitarian state, 90 percent majorities are common, but in a free society, where voting reflects a variety of concerns, winning margins are seldom wide. The result is that very large minority interests must be respected. An intelligent response to these interests, as Madison demonstrated, provides the foundation of our free institutions.

QUESTIONS FOR DISCUSSION

1. Bender does not apply his argument to the opening case, the censorship of books at Island Trees. Express his argument fully. How does a criterion of diversity justify a negative evaluation of censorship?
2. Bender claims that all communities in America today are diverse. Do you agree? Do you know of exceptions? (There are two hard-to-pin-down but critical terms in this argument, *community* and *diversity*.)
3. Is there a contradiction in Bender's argument? If consensus is impossible

because of diversity, and all communities are diverse, then how does any community agree on any course of action?

4. Suppose that a hypothetical community agreed unanimously to ban nine books from its high school library. Would their action then be right according to Bender's argument?

5. Why does Bender return to the Constitution for authority to back his premise about diversity and government? How does he make James Madison's authority supersede that of Aristotle and Rousseau?

SUGGESTIONS FOR WRITING

1. Read any one of the nine banned books and defend or refute the decision of the Island Trees school board to ban it as "offensive to Christians, Jews, Blacks, and Americans in general." Address your argument to the group supposedly offended.

2. Find out what the U.S. Supreme Court's ruling was in the Island Trees case and read the justices' opinions. Characterize their arguments and spell out your agreement or disagreement.

3. Choose nine books that you think should not be present in a high school library. (They need not be there already.) Now, can you convince anyone else of your evaluation on impersonal grounds? Would you remove the same nine books from a public library?

4. Although American schools are still controlled by local school boards, what forces work for unity or homogeneity and against local differences in education? Write an essay in which you discuss how these forces for homogeneity affect education for good or ill.

5. Characterize the diversity in your own community. (If you live in a large city, you could define a smaller section of it as a community.) What do people differ about? Are they more alike than different? Address your characterization to members of the community.

6. Bender makes one kind of constitutional argument against censorship. Can you make other arguments against it for your classmates on the basis of consequence or principle? Apply your arguments to the Island Trees case.

7. Bender was not addressing his argument to the Island Trees School Board; he was writing to a broader audience. Rewrite his argument to convince the local board to change its policy.

8. Suppose a minority wants to ban a book from a library. Consider, for example, *Huckleberry Finn*, which many black groups find objectionable. Does the majority have a right to keep the book in school or public libraries? Does the protection of minorities' rights necessarily work *against* censorship rather than for it as Bender suggests? Present several possible ways to deal with a case like this one and assess their relative merits for either the majority or minority interests.

---------------- →>> «<< ----------------

The Truth about Girl Scouts

RACHEL FLICK

*Rachel Flick's article, as its title suggests, belongs in the tradition of
muckraking journalism, which investigates the corrupt inner workings of
institutions and exposes them to the censure and ridicule of outsiders. This
kind of journalism has often aimed at such heavies as oil monopolies, the
meat-packing industry, and industrial polluters. Here it takes on the
all-American Girl Scouts.*

*As you read this entertaining essay, you might ask yourself some of the
following questions: Why does the author, a professional speech writer in
Washington, keep such a low profile in her article? What standards of
judgment does she assume her readers will share, and which does she invoke?
And finally, what would she have the Girl Scouts be?*

On March 11, 1982, fifty-two Girl Scouts assembled at the United
Nations to present a "Gift of Water" to the world. It was a lovely
ceremony. Water donated to the scouts from each of the states and from
Puerto Rico and the District of Columbia was ceremoniously poured
into a common vessel, the contents of which were to be spilled, a few
months later, at the ceremonial planting of a tree at a new scout conference center. Certificates explaining the waters' origins and importance
were on display at the U.N., which has declared the 1980s the International Drinking Water and Sanitation Decade. Mrs. Gouletas-Carey
appeared on behalf of her husband, the governor of New York, to
proclaim Girl Scout Week in the state.

The occasion was the seventieth anniversary of the Girl Scouts of
the United States of America, and the ceremony epitomized the organization it celebrated. Like Girl Scouting, it was pretty. It was feminine.
It was pregnant with symbolism. It expressed the virtues of charity and
service, with overtones of national and international harmony. And most
of all, it was uncontroversial—nobody, but nobody, could quarrel with
water. ("I think water is so important," explains Frances Hesselbein,
national executive director of GSUSA, "because without it, there's no
life.") The ceremony, in short, was the ideal Girl Scout Event.

It was an auspicious moment for a successful event. At that point,
the 1980s were looking good. Hopes were high, for the first time in about

twelve distressing years. The Seventies had been terrible, and scouting wasn't used to terrible. Never during its first fifty years had GSUSA seen a single year of falling enrollment. In 1950, in recognition of its solid and worthy position in the national life, Congress had even conferred upon it a congressional charter, that it might "continue to inspire the rising generation with the highest ideals of character, patriotism, conduct, and attainment." In 1969, the peak year of its enrollment, it had claimed a membership of 3,921,000, which made it the largest girls' organization in the world. The thing had looked impregnable. And then in 1971 the numbers had just started falling. . . . A few years later, GSUSA had lost fully a million girls.

Action was called for, and was undertaken. The Seventies were a time of change—big change—and apparently to good effect, for in 1979 the decline seemed finally to have been arrested.

So it was with well-earned pride and confidence that GSUSA undertook this grand new endeavor for the Eighties. It was announced that day at the U.N. that scouts all over the nation planned a variety of water projects to last for the next ten years. Some scouts would "conserve, clean, and care about" water; some would cook seafood dishes; others would "help people cope" with hurricanes. For scouts all over the land, the 1980s were declared to be the Decade of Water. Water could not have been a more appropriate symbol, for in its frantic attempts to anticipate and accommodate to the needs of a changing world, the organization threw out much of what had been best in it and offered girls who wanted to be scouts something very like water—colorless, tasteless, and liquid.

The Girl Scouts began in England as the female counterpart to the Boy Scouts, created at the turn of the century by Lord Robert Baden-Powell, a hero of the Boer War. "I had used scouting—that is, woodcraft, handiness, and cheery helpfulness—as a means for training young soldiers when they first joined the army," wrote Baden-Powell, "to help them become handy, capable men and able to hold their own with anyone instead of being mere drilled machines." After returning home from South Africa, he decided that this kind of training—militaristic in style, religious in outlook, and character-building in intent—would be useful for "troops" of civilian boys "throughout the free world," under the guidance of adult volunteers.

Central to Baden-Powell's program were three statements that expressed what he really wanted to teach boys. The first two he claimed to have taken from the code of the knights of old: the Boy Scout Motto, "Be Prepared" (when asked for what, he explained, "Why, for any old thing"), and the Boy Scout Law, "A Scout is Trustworthy, Loyal, Helpful, Friendly, Courteous, Kind, Obedient, Cheerful, Thrifty, Brave, Clean, and Reverent." The third, the Boy Scout Oath, he worked up from the oath taken by youths of ancient Athens upon becoming citizens (graciously described in the Boy Scout handbook as "the only oath out of the past that ranks with the Boy Scout Oath"):

> On my honor I will do my best
> To do my duty to God and my country
> And to obey the Scout Law;
> To help other people at all times;
> To keep myself physically strong,
> Mentally awake, and morally straight.

In 1908, when Baden-Powell published these statements and his program in *Scouting for Boys,* the book was an immediate best-seller, and Scouting the Movement was on its way. But it wasn't just English boys who yearned to join; 6,000 girls also applied. Baden-Powell turned them over to his sister, Agnes, to organize, stipulating only that a uniformed girl not so much as greet a uniformed boy in public, and that the girls' organization not use the Scout name.

Thus were born the Girl Guides, which attracted the attention of Mrs. Juliette ("Daisy") Gordon Low. A highly intelligent but deaf and wretchedly unhappy American woman who had recently been released from a miserable marriage by the death of her husband, a wealthy, philandering Englishman, Mrs. Low had plenty of time, money, and passion, and no sense of direction.

By chance she had met Baden-Powell while she was wandering through Europe; fired by what she took to be his selflessness, discipline, life of action (and perhaps, as one biographer suggests, a more personal, though repressed, passion), Mrs. Low adopted him as her spiritual model and teacher.

She met Agnes in England and then returned to her estate in Scotland, where she recruited seven local village girls. She taught them to spin, cook, and raise chickens for sale—skills she thought would be useful to them later in life. Then she set sail for America. On her first night home, in Savannah, Georgia, she telephoned a cousin and announced, in words often quoted by Girl Scouts ever since, "I've got something for the girls of Savannah and all America and all the world, and we're going to start it tonight."

She did not scruple to use the name of Scouting, though she did modify the Law and Promise for girls. To Mrs. Low, a Girl Scout was "Truthful, Loyal, Helpful, Friendly, Courteous, Kind, Obedient, Cheerful, Thrifty, and Pure in Thought, Word, and Deed," and Promised on her Honor to "Do my duty to God and my Country, to help other People at all Times, and to Obey the Girl Scout Law."

Wearing what was, in those frilly days, an ostentatiously sensible uniform designed by Mrs. Low herself, early Girl Scouts camped outdoors and studied tracking, the Morse code, knot-tying ("A knowledge of knots is useful in every trade or calling," claims the first handbook), shooting ("It is one of the best ways to 'Be Prepared' "), and archery ("excellent practice for the eye, and good exercise for the muscles. It makes no noise, does not disturb game or warn the enemy"). They also Cultivated the Faculty of Remembering Time, Observed Details of People ("It is very instructive to note the different people we meet and try to form estimates of their character and disposition by their look and clothes"), and dealt "with small natural bits of information likely to escape any but specially trained eyes and senses." All this was seasoned with the "true life" examples of Girl Scout heroines who triumphed over adversity and danger by following the Law—"Brave girls whose pluck we admire."

And she wasn't kidding about wanting Girl Scouting to be for all girls; within a few years of her phone call in Savannah, Mrs. Low had set up a three-tiered national structure to deliver her program. All Girl Scout troops were to be members of regional councils, and all councils were to be chartered by a single national office (GSUSA). GSUSA itself was to operate no troops. Rather, its full-time job was to provide the basic idea and program materials—it was to be, so to speak, the R&D of scouting.

Councils sprang up everywhere. Growth was explosive. There were eight American Girl Scouts in 1912; in 1915 their numbers had risen to 5,000, and by 1920, to something like 42,000. This growth continued unabated. For if there was one fact about scouting that was true from day one, it was this: *girls like it.* They took to it like ducks to water.

It was inevitable that Girl Scouting should eventually feel the effects of the upheavals of the 1960s. Major changes had, of course, already been made since the days of Mrs. Low; when I was a scout in the mid-Sixties, for example, we were no longer Cultivating the Faculty of

Remembering Time (weaving acrylic potholders, as I recall, was more our thing). Yet despite such changes, much of the Girl Scout program was simply not fashionable in the post-Sixties world ("Pure in Thought, Word, and Deed"?). So it was not really surprising that enrollment took a plunge. (The situation with the Boy Scouts, which in 1974 lost 10.6 percent of its youth membership, is comparable.) Nor, for that matter, was it unreasonable that GSUSA should decide some further changes were necessary if the organization was to stay current. But what *was* surprising, considering the program's incredibly successful history, was the extent and character of this change.

The organization adopted a "managerial idea," installing a "corporate planning system," which operated on the notion—as explained by Mrs. Hesselbein, who has published on the subject in *Philanthropy Monthly*—that management and planning are synonymous, and that planning has to be based on "hard data, demographic research, and local council experiences" about the "expressed preferences" of girls and leaders.

In line with its new principle, GSUSA began asking its constituency what it preferred. It began seeking statistics. It held discussion groups. It sent around surveys. It started offering "try-its"—"new ways of applying the basic principles." By 1977 the results—the "hard data"—were in. It remained only to take the "action steps," i.e., to revise.

The revisions were complete in 1980, and GSUSA enthusiastically presented its redesigned program, which consists of seven new books for girls and leaders, including new handbooks, to the councils at a series of national program conferences.

Throughout the process of revision GSUSA had made a point of saying that it wasn't going to touch the basics, but the new program begins with an emphatically new Promise and Law. And the character of the change in these principles is fundamental. "Trying to live by the Girl Scout Law" appears, nowadays, to mean thinking about it a lot. Scouts are now asked to consider: "What parts of the Girl Scout Law do I value most?" The Promise, too, is now read less than unequivocally. "Investigate," a scout book urges, "the way the Girl Scout Promise and Law help you show your feelings about serving God and your country and your pledge to be a good citizen."

Perhaps the one value that is not treated subjectively is a sort of deferential appreciation for other cultures. This comes in handy, for example, in treating religion, which is now something of a sticky wicket. As one leader quite reasonably points out, scouting's nondenominational policy makes religion difficult to take on in any serious way. "The only common ground is belief in God, and who's to say who God is? One person's god is not another person's god." Scouting, she feels sure, "would get a lot of flack from parents" if it got too specific about religion. So nowadays God tends chiefly to be the occasion for learning about colorful native celebrations and handicrafts, some of which enterprising scouts can reproduce in their troops with pipe cleaners and yarn.

When the girls' own culture requires that He make an appearance —on camping trips that extend through Sunday mornings, for example —God is simply introduced without the use of theological language. One leader describes the religious services she holds on camping trips as "a quiet time when you appreciate a particular subject, such as love, or friendship, or nature, and they [the girls] talk about it, and maybe read a poem about it." While such subtlety solves the denominational problem, it also widens God to the innocuous breadth of a Hallmark card; one wishes the scouts would punt or get off the course.

Just as religion is defused, so is the uncomfortable question of patriotism. The first handbook, published in 1913, was titled *How Girls Can Help Their Country,* and it included this ringing passage:

> You belong to the great United States of America, one of the great world powers for enlightenment and liberty. It did not just grow as circumstances chanced to form it. It is the work of your forefathers who spent brains and blood to complete it. Even when brothers fought they fought with the wrath of conviction, and when menaced by a foreign foe they swung into line shoulder to shoulder with no thought but for their country. In all that you do think of your country first.

Instead of sending her scouts to pour water, Mrs. Low sent one group of her girls to give "patriotic instruction" to New Bedford mill workers, when "foreign labor threatened to fall prey to the epidemic of Bolshevism and industrial unrest."

Obviously, this level of patriotic zeal needed substantial toning down. Still, GSUSA may now have modified it too far in the other direction. Today's scouting is freighted with critical activism—not the sort of attitude with which a child should begin her life as a citizen.

For the new Girl Scouting, patriotism seems to mean, as one leader put it, thinking about "what it really means to have allegiance to your country, and at what point you might not agree with your government." The handbooks—with updated titles such as *Worlds to Explore* and

You Make the Difference—encourage scouts to learn how their communities operate, to think about what they'd like to change, and to get busy. Girls so young they might not even have memorized Washington's birthday are merrily invited to start fixing up their national fundaments. "Keep a record of all the laws you must follow. . . . Consider changing at least one of these laws so that more people would benefit. Write up your new law and be able to explain why your law is better. . . ."

The natural corollary of this is a vigorous and guilty concern for other countries. This concern figures heavily in a section of *Worlds to Explore* designated "The World Around You." Here girls are invited to play a game in which each of them is assigned to represent a different nation, and each is dealt, by a seemingly arbitrary hand, a specified number of raisins that (as nearly as I can make it out) is about proportionate to her GNP. "Were the raisins divided fairly?" the handbook asks. "How did you feel about the number you received? Why shouldn't every girl be given the same number of raisins? This may not make you feel very good inside, but it may help you to understand what it is like to be a child in some parts of the world." Not that there aren't hungry people in the world, and not that children shouldn't learn at some point of their existence, but such abject liberal guilt seems a hell of a thing to hand to a nine-year-old.

One of the differences between peoples that scouting does not celebrate, however, is gender. In a way, scouting has been "feminist" from the start. Seventy years ago, Mrs. Low enjoined her girls, "Be womanly. None of us like women who ape men. An imitation diamond is not as good as a real diamond." And her program made clear that this statement was positive as well as negative. Being "womanly" was different from being a man, but it was no less studied and energetic a pursuit, and she intended her scouts to do it proudly and well.

Scouts of the Eighties, though, practice the feminism of the Eighties, which is a completely different—and much more defensive—kettle of fish. The handbook for girls aged six to eleven, for example, includes a game in which scouts clip from magazines pictures representing "men's work," "women's work," and "both"—or at least, the handbook corrects itself, "what some photographer or artist showed as these kinds of work. What do you think—are they right? Ask yourselves, 'Who says so?' "

In line with the new Girl Scout feminism, the badge book, too, has been changed. A badge is still the same sort of thing it was when I was a scout in the mid-Sixties—an award received upon completion of an exploratory project on a specified subject. The badges are listed in a special book, each with its eight to ten requirements underneath it. I had the cooking badge, for example, which required me, among other things, to learn the four food groups, prepare a breakfast, and bake a cake; when I had done all of this I received an embroidered cloth patch to sew on my uniform.

The cooking badge, in fact, is a good example—it was popular in my troop but girls today can't earn it, because it's been excised from the book. Nowadays a scout can still earn such old favorites as "Hobbies and Pets" and "Books," but if she's interested in her kitchen, she has to shoot for either a badge called "Exploring Foods" (which requires her to prepare a meatless meal and some foods from other cultures) or another called "Healthy Eating" (which includes both trying new foods and keeping "a record of the texture, taste, look, and smell of each one," and some lessons in consumer skepticism: "In what way do commercials teach good or poor eating habits? . . .")

But no more sexist cooking. And no more sexist sewing, either—today's girls can study, instead, for their badges in "Textiles and Fibers" or "Art to Wear."

Girl Scouts now read just about every activity in vocational terms. Motherhood is considered a "career" choice—listed in the new Girl Scout book *Careers to Explore*, right along with Gas Station Attendant and President of the United States. And with such options, of course, it makes sense that a scout should get started young; so in the same book, six- to eleven-year-olds are invited to diagram their career potential: listing a favorite toy, for example, as well as who uses it and what job it helps you prepare for.

Even leaders who are enthusiastic about the career program agree that it has to be sold with a song and a dance; girls tend not to warm to it as is. "It's better," one says, "when you don't say 'careers'—the more we work them into just plain troop fun, the more they respond." For example, she says her girls really like the role-playing suggested in the career book. "We did the one that asked, 'What would you do if your boss was a man who insisted you get his cup of coffee?' There were a couple of girls who were quite insistent about 'Gee, well, let him get his own coffee,' and a couple who said, 'What if he fires me?' It was a lot of fun."

Browsing further through the book, one wonders how much fun her scouts would have with the following outstandingly ungirlish problem:

Imagine you are in your mid-twenties. You are married and have a two-year-old child. After two years at home, you're ready to return to full-time work. You find a job with hours from 9:00 to 5:00, five days a week, paying $11,111 a year. Now you will need to combine your roles as homemaker and parent with your full-time paying job.

In small groups, determine the daily household chores and activities that must be done by you and your husband on a typical working day. . . . Decide who will do each chore. . . . Does one person have more time than the other? . . . Or is the work evenly divided? . . . How much time is there for the child? . . . Ask a group of males in your age range to do this exercise. How do your results compare?

It would hardly be surprising if such remote lessons failed, on a personal level, to register. Sure enough, when every now and again the program does ask girls to "define their own career interests," the plight of the working mother is forgotten, and the old familiar song emerges straight from their own hearts and lives. These girls almost invariably want to "explore" modeling or the stage. "Fashions, Fitness, and Makeup," for example, was the career-exploration choice of the girls who enacted the secretary's coffee dilemma.

No matter what they choose to explore, they explore in the preferred Girl Scout mode, which is heavily documental. Girl Scouting has embraced social science. The scouts are fanatic chart-makers, graph-drawers, listers, and calculators, and this business of reduce-and-quantify is not limited to careers.

For example, girls are asked to fill out a "Me and Others Profile." This is a chart that lists on its vertical axis a lot of interpersonal skills ("I am able to: trust; consider the feelings of; give assistance when problems physical, mental, or emotional seem difficult for . . ." etc.), and on its horizontal axis, a lot of people ("Older females," "people from racial, ethnic, religious groups not my own," etc.). This allows a girl to, say, give herself a "2" in "asking for the help of" a "close friend." "Girls like this 'Know yourself' stuff," one leader explains casually. "This is easy."

When not contemplating herself, today's Girl Scout is supposed to be expressing herself. "Letting your feelings show can help make you feel better," a handbook claims. "Here are some ways to let feelings out that won't hurt you or anyone else." The list includes "Cry if you want to" ("A Scout is Cheerful"?) and "Draw a really ugly picture."

In the past, Girl Scouts were supposed to learn about themselves by

losing themselves in activity. Where the self was concerned, they preferred industry to analysis. The original handbook, for example, enjoins:
"Too soft a bed tends to make people dream, which is unhealthy and
weakening. Don't lay abed in the morning thinking how awful it is to
have to get up. Rouse out at once and take a smart turn of some quick
exercise." And then it proceeds directly to the mundane. "Learn to
breathe through your nose. Breathing through the mouth makes you
thirsty. So does chewing gum."

There is one subject on which the Girl Scout program has gotten
less rigorous and analytical, and that is nature. Instead of the detailed
instruction in outdoor skills and the study of plant and animal life that
characterized Low's program, today's handbook emphasizes "contemplation"—sitting in a circle and reciting Edna St. Vincent Millay.
Nature is pictured as a playground for a girl's fancy. "The next time your
troop is anywhere where there are a lot of flowers, pretend that all of
you are bees and butterflies. Zigzag from one flower to another. Look
at blossoms from the insect point of view. . . . Make friends with an
earthworm," it enthuses. "Stop and say 'thank you' to a tree."

This change is important, because the case can be made that nature
—or more specifically, camping—*is* Girl Scouting. "Girls are scouts for
lots of reasons, most of which are camping" the leader of a New Jersey
troop told me. "Camping is the glue that holds scouting together."

It is certainly true that time and again girls say that camping is what
they love most about the program—but not, it seems, for its inspira-
tional aspects. What they really love is playing messy games with their
friends ("shaving cream fights!") and learning outdoor skills.

Things may have gotten a bit soft in the Girl Scout program, but at
GSUSA headquarters they most definitely have not. In particular,
GSUSA is not soft about public relations. It has cultivated a genius for
gesture. In 1979, for example, it lent its endorsement to the United
Nations Year of the Child—children; how nice. Ever mindful of its
image, GSUSA has also been aware during the past decade of the need to
recruit minorities—and, of course, to make sure everyone knew of it.
Conferences were staged on "Girl Scouting for Black Girls" and on "Girl
Scouting—Mexican-American Style." GSUSA printed special literature
to speak to minorities in their own idioms. For its grand project in 1981 it
ran a survey, conducted by the National Urban League, to assess the
impact of minority participation on Girl Scouting and also the extent of
"Girl Scout and public awareness of minority participation in Girl Scouting." Most people, it turned out, thought it was all a real good idea.

At the same time, GSUSA began to realize it was losing a still more valuable minority—volunteers. There are 572,000 adults in scouting, and about one percent are paid staff. By 1979 there were 141 troops nationwide without leaders, and even more girls who wanted to be scouts for whom there were no troops at all. Women had begun returning to the work force, and it was suddenly necessary for GSUSA to motivate them to volunteer.

GSUSA's strategy was canny. It added a new perk to volunteering; now leading a troop was handy not just to a woman's soul but to her career. (Today a Girl Scout troop leader, tomorrow . . .) Put simply, the Girl Scouts entered adult education.

Of course, GSUSA had always offered various sorts of training to its volunteer leaders: in the skills of the outdoors, for example, in the Girl Scout philosophy, and even in the simple management of a group. Today, however, GSUSA offers courses ranging from "the arts to computer technology," from "camping to financial management." In 1980, GSUSA secured accreditation by the Council for Noncollegiate Continuing Education, a United States agency, to grant units of credit toward academic degrees to participants in these courses.

These units of credit, explains Mrs. Hesselbein, "are a kind of recognition, whether you are working toward a degree or whether you are a homemaker, of the importance of your contribution." Such recognition is not, however, awarded for the simple contribution of leading a troop; it is only awarded for the taking of classes. And what a volunteer learns in those classes need not have any effect on what she does with her scouts, but it may well help her to complete a degree or secure a paid position later. Apparently, voluntarism has yielded to careerism.

Nowhere is this change better exemplified than in the development of the Edith Macy Conference Center. "Camp Edith Macy," a training center for Girl Scout leaders, was established in Westchester County, New York, in 1926. Its donor dreamed that it would become "a university in the woods." In its early days, students "really roughed it" there, sleeping in tents and cooking out.

In 1980, however, GSUSA began construction of an $8 million, 200-person conference center on the Macy property. The center, now unfortunately called a "miniversity in the woods," features technologically up-to-the-minute conference facilities (video-complete, touch-of-a-button automatic, color-coded), rooms that would do a decent hotel proud, and complete food service in a luxury dining room. Still, it continues to claim "woodsiness" because, as its glossy-printed descriptive literature explains, the building's "wood and stone construction materials are in harmony with those found in the region."

Camp Edith Macy is not a bad metaphor for today's characterless scouting, which, in its urge to modernize, has lost its clear identity—the raison d'être and sense of mission that was uniquely its own and served generations of contented girls very well.

Girl Scouting's structure has something to do with this turn of events. The structure of the organization may have been what did it in. Right from the start, scouting has offered its local councils tremendous autonomy. This means that the organization is flexible beyond the ordinary, a quality that is both its strength and, currently, its weakness.

Girl Scout councils are separately incorporated and set up their own structures for instituting and negotiating with their troops. And although they must adhere to certain standards in order to use the Scout name, it is possible for councils to be permanently chartered. This has the happy effect of allowing them to adjust to regional preferences—potentially a source of great strength. But regional preferences are subject to considerable fluctuation, because local Girl Scouting is almost completely run by volunteers, and, as with any all-volunteer organization, no one has much control over the staff. Councils, therefore, are rather vulnerable to the fads or fashions that prevail in their communities. This vulnerability may explain the "hard data" that arrived in the 1970s—the data that led GSUSA to conclude, wrongly, that the assumptions on which the old program was based were obsolete.

In forming this conclusion, the organization bent to pressure from its councils but managed to overlook a substantial and persuasive argument for keeping things as they were—namely, the nature of the girls. Girls are not interested in making friends with an earthworm or making a "Me and Others Profile." Confronted with the new program, they plump determinedly for its most reassuringly traditional aspects.

Ask the members of any troop, anywhere, what badges they have and the answers are always the same: Camping, Child Care, First Aid, Books. They'll tell you, with sincere faces, that they enjoy the serious aspects of scouting, too—but what they mean is the old, volunteer-service sort of thing. A gum-chewing blonde named Heidi clasps her hands together—glittery-blue nail polish gleaming—when she talks about Christmas caroling at an old-folks home. "They smile at you and stuff," she says. A thirteen-year-old scout from the Bronx summed it all up beautifully. "The best part," she said, "is working with all of our friends and helping people out."

The message is clear: one generation does not a transformation make. Girls wandered away from scouting in the Seventies because of unusual times, not because they were unusual creatures. And their return to scouting in 1979 probably had more to do with societal changes than it did with the trendy new program—which may be why, in 1980, after their exploratory blip upward, those numbers headed right back down again. In 1979, enrollment reached 2,961,000, but thereafter it declined and by 1982 had slid to 2,819,000. Tales of professional success have not, apparently, instilled staying power in today's Girl Scouts.

The example of the Boy Scouts seems to confirm this failure. Faced with a similarly declining enrollment, BSA, after some initial waffling, held fast to its traditional program, to the point at which the program looked positively quaint. But this quaintness, as it turns out, did not deter boys from becoming Scouts. Again, structure has a lot to do with it. There is relatively little regional variation in Boy Scouting: central control is strong, and as a result, the organization is stable and sturdy.

The cornerstone of Scouting's stability, however, is its doctrine. Of course BSA made some superficial changes to keep in step with the times. But its stated purpose remains, in the words of Ralph Derain, Scout Executive for the Greater New York Councils, "to help young people grow to responsible adulthood. We feel," he continues, "that whether it hurts or not, it is our responsibility to train kids to be better kids, and we have to stick to those principles."

This attitude is echoed in the 1979 edition of BSA's handbook, which still claims, with a straight face, to be second only to the Bible in offering "answers to the questions a boy wonders about." "Yes," it claims, "it's fun to be a Boy Scout!"

Despite its revisions, the handbook's language dates from the Forties: "Camp! There's a word that's filled with fun and adventure for every real boy!" And the graphics and typeface are out of the early Sixties—except that some of the scout faces are blackened in. On the frontispiece is a photo of the author: "William 'Green Bar Bill' Hillcourt, Author, Naturalist, and World Scouter," an old man pictured in a Boy Scout uniform, complete with short pants, knee socks, and neckerchief. The frontispiece also declares the Boy Scouts to be "four million strong for America." (The Girl Scout handbook's frontispiece is a misty pastel drawing of butterflies and flowers; it's a lot less alarming but it doesn't pack a fraction of the punch.)

It sounds like a joke, but they come in droves to read this book. In the three years since it has been out (data on 1982 are not yet available), BSA has not only reversed its decline, but has brought its numbers steadily back up each year, to a total of 3,246,000. Where careers have failed, the romance of old-style Baden-Powellism has succeeded. Tales of heroism and duty have sold a lot of kids on scouting in the past couple of years. As far as numbers are concerned, there can't be much question about which of the two scoutings took the right programmatic direction.

But the numbers aren't all—or even the most important part—of what's disappointing in the new Girl Scouting. A far more significant disappointment is the character of the changes. For although GSUSA clearly had to modernize (every organization needs to catch up, occasionally, with changing times), it modernized wrongly, and so suffered what might be called a loss of spirit. Some may say that today's Boy Scouting has its objectionable aspects, but everyone will agree that it is firmly, recognizably Boy Scouting. The new Girl Scouting, on the other hand, mirrors the conventional wisdom, and so looks just like everything else. To begin to look like everything else is to lose one's own spirit. At one point, the late Mrs. Low expressed the hope that "We will make scouting so much a part of the American life that people will recognize the spirit and say, 'Why of course. She is a Girl Scout.' " Sorry, Mrs. Low.

QUESTIONS FOR DISCUSSION

1. Go through this essay and identify all the explicit criteria Flick uses to evaluate the Girl Scouts (e.g. "—not the sort of attitude with which a child should begin her life as a citizen.")
2. Can you find an explicit criterion for judgment in each of Flick's areas of analysis: religion, patriotism, feminism, career choice, self-awareness, and nature study? Why, for example, does she dislike the new cooking badges?
3. Why does the essay open and close with a comparison between the Girl Scouts and Boy Scouts? To what extent are the Boy Scouts held up as an ideal?
4. Does Flick argue for or defend any of the criteria by which she evaluates the Girl Scouts? Does she assume that her intended audience shares her criteria? Do you share them?
5. Examine some of the language choices that serve Flick's evaluation. First look for loaded word choices in passages describing Girl Scout activities. Where does Flick use irony to invoke a reader's mockery of her target?
6. Flick announces her thesis at the end of the article's first section and emphatically restates it in the conclusion. What would the effect have been had she withheld the explicit statement of her judgment? Does the early statement of her thesis show confidence in her audience's agreement?

SUGGESTIONS FOR WRITING

1. Evaluate your personal scouting experience for a reader who has never been a scout (perhaps a class member) but who is curious about what scouts actually do. Remember that you are not simply expressing your personal taste but arguing on the basis of supportable criteria.
2. As an exercise in refutation, dismantle Flick's argument. You might go after the undefended criteria or write a defense of the Girl Scouts on other grounds. Or criticize some aspect of the Boy Scouts that Flick holds up for admiration. You might also write an essay praising the Boy Scouts of America.
3. Flick criticizes the Girl Scouts' handling of patriotism, religion, and feminism. How should an organization like the Girl Scouts, which aims to incorporate every element in our pluralistic society, respond to such issues? Direct your response either to Flick or the Girl Scouts.
4. Examine a current Girl Scout manual for its treatment of one of the critical issues Flick identifies. On what political and social assumptions does it seem to be built? Either defend the unit, or if you think it needs revising, propose an alternate approach to the Girl Scout organization.
5. Flick makes various uses of the facts about a decline in scouting over the last fifteen years. She blames "unusual times" rather than a change in girls' interests. Investigate the phenomenon more deeply and write a causal argument for Flick and her readers in which you identify significant contributing causes.
6. Flick addresses her argument to an audience likely to agree with her. Rewrite her essay for an audience of Girl Scout leaders, who would be likely to resist her argument.

Is Eakins Our Greatest Painter?

JOHN RUSSELL

English-born John Russell is an art critic for the New York Times, *and the occasion of his following encomium (a piece written to praise) is the opening of a major exhibit in Philadelphia featuring the nineteenth-century American painter, Thomas Eakins. Russell makes a "very large claim" for Eakins, perhaps not so much because Eakins is unappreciated by art critics as because he wants to alert a more general American audience to the merits of one of our own painters. To that end he devises a uniquely American set of criteria that places Eakins in a class by himself.*

In order to fully appreciate this essay, you might look at reproductions of the Eakins paintings mentioned by Russell.

There never was an American painter like Thomas Eakins, who was born in 1844, died in 1916, and is the subject of a great exhibition that has just opened at the Philadelphia Museum of Art. It is not simply that in his hands painting became an exact science, so that if he paints two men rowing on a river we can tell the month, the day and the hour that they passed under a certain bridge. We admire Eakins for that, but we prize him above all for the new dimension of moral awareness that he brought to American painting.

The question that he asks is not "What do we look like?" It is "What have we done to one another?" And it is because he gives that question so full and so convincing an answer that we ask ourselves whether Thomas Eakins was not the greatest American painter who ever lived. Even if the question strikes us as meaningless we find it difficult after an exhibition such as this to think of a convincing rival.

This is a very large claim. Let us see on what it is based. Eakins never had (nor ever craved) facility in paint. As a pupil of Jean-Léon Gérôme in Paris, he did not stand out. But as a 16-year-old draftsman he could draw a lathe, or any other piece of machinery, in such a way that we can see through it, and around it, and know exactly how it works. There is no arguing with work of that class. What we see, we trust.

That element of trust is not the whole of art, but it is difficult to conceive of a representational art in which it plays no part. And Eakins inspires it in the highest degree. We can say of him what Ralph Waldo Emerson said of Thoreau—that "his powers of observation seemed to indicate additional senses. He saw as with microscope, heard as with ear trumpet, and his memory was a photographic register of all that he saw and heard."

Eakins saw that particular capacity as a part of manhood, and one not to be talked of too much. "Every man should be able," he said, "to plot a field, to sketch a road or a river, to draw the outlines of a simple machine, a piece of household furniture, or a farming utensil, and to delineate the internal arrangement or construction of a house." To draw right is to live right, in other words.

Whence came the wonderful preliminary drawings with which Eakins foresaw every possible perspectival problem in his paintings of oarsmen. Once seen, those paintings stay with us forever as paradigms of American practicality, American physical vigor and American delight in the open air. We just *know*, without being told, that Eakins in those pictures left nothing to chance.

And, sure enough, when the late Theodor Siegl was cataloguing the Eakins collection at the Philadelphia Museum, he was able to prove that in the "Pair-Oared Shell" the size of the boat, the angle of its movement and its exact location in relation to the old Columbia Bridge on the Schuylkill River had been worked out to the nearest inch. More than that, we can be quite certain from the evidence of the painting that the boat passed under the bridge at precisely 7:20 P.M., Eastern time, on one of two summer evenings in either early June or mid-July in the year 1872.

Eakins could, of course, have made all those calculations and been no more than a first-rate engineering draftsman who couldn't bear to make a mistake. Throughout his life, as we see in the Philadelphia exhibition, he stood for an absolute exactitude. It was basic to his art that everything should be got exactly right, no matter whether it was the movement of a horse, the workings of a precision instrument, or the precise degree of squalor that comes over the bed linen in a rudimentary operating theater at the end of a long day.

It was the same with the human body. Eakins was not content with the traditional art-school approximations. Digging deep into human cadavers with his own two bare hands, he got to know their ins and outs as well as any surgeon. Though hampered hardly less than Cézanne by the pseudo-moral standards of the day, he also managed to work both from the living human body, male and female, and from photographs made by himself.

Among many of his contemporaries—above all perhaps among those who had not seen them—those photographs were thought to be outrageous in their matter-of-factness. That was not how Eakins saw them. Life for him was too important for prevarication. The artist was there to tell us how it was, and not to dress it up with bravura, like John Singer Sargent, or sprinkle it with confectioner's sugar, like Mary Cassatt.

Once again, this could have been a matter of objectivity fortified by conscientiousness. But Eakins was not just a man who simply kept the anatomical score. He was one of the great American moralists. Looking at his fellow human beings, whether singly or in groups, he remembered that there are truths that could cure, and truths that can kill. He also knew that it is our human duty to tell one from the other, difficult as that may very often be.

Walking from room to room in the Philadelphia exhibition—which was organized and catalogued by Darrel Sewell, the museum's curator of American art—we recognize a steadiness of moral purpose that shines out as much in the commissioned portrait of a well-to-do Philadelphian taking the air in his four-in-hand as it does in the two huge medical panoramas, "The Gross Clinic" and "The Agnew Clinic."

Those two panoramas were to Eakins what the "Night Watch" was to Rembrandt. They spell out the alphabet of attention with which grown men address themselves to weighty and often disagreeable tasks. To see them together is a prodigious experience, and one unlikely ever to be repeated. (The Philadelphia showing is through Aug. 1 only, and "The Gross Clinic" will not travel to the Boston Museum of Fine Arts, where the rest of the show can be seen from Sept. 22 through Nov. 28.)

In the two great medical panoramas, as in all the other symphonic subjects to which Thomas Eakins addressed himself, there is "more than meets the eye." In both "The Gross Clinic" and the big painting of the prize ring called "Between Rounds" there is, for instance, the figure of a man in sober black whose function it is to keep the record straight. Pen or bell in hand, he bends over his task. How can we doubt that he is more than a humdrum recorder? Is it not likely that he is to prose what the painter is to poetry, and that Eakins has included him as a point of reason and stability in a world given over to an ordered violence? Surgeon and bruiser are one, after all, in that their function is to spill blood as efficiently as possible.

But it is within four walls and on a one-to-one basis that Eakins the moralist is at his very best. It is relevant in that context that one of the few total failures in his career was the portrait of Walt Whitman that makes so unhappy an appearance in the Philadelphia show.

Everything was in favor of that painting. The No. 1 painter was faced with the No. 1 poet. What could go wrong? Even the photographs that Eakins took of the aged Whitman are unforgettable. But the painting just doesn't ring true. Whitman looks like a summer-stock Falstaff. That huge vacuous grin might reach to the rear mezzanine, but we don't for one moment believe that this is a great poet, let alone the man who took the whole of this country in his embrace in ways that are still valid.

We cannot doubt that Eakins was paralyzed by Whitman. He loved the work, he knew the man, but just for once he shuddered before the evidence of physical decline. As with the portraits of his father-in-law,

William H. Macdowell, he allowed a histrionic element to intervene. How much finer and more stringent are the other portraits in the show! Eakins was never better than when cataloguing the ways in which life in the end withdraws its benefits from those who have fought a good fight but have not come out on top. And when he was face to face with a young actress who had everything on her side—talent, money and looks—he made us feel exactly how anxious she was to get back to the full life that most of his sitters had never known.

So what Thomas Eakins sets before us is a touchstone of American truth. "Best" is a big word, but if there are better American paintings than these I for one cannot for the moment think which they are.

QUESTIONS FOR DISCUSSION

1. Part of the skill of evaluating is to find a limited set in which to place your subject. What is Russell arguing that Eakins is best of? What other sets, larger or smaller, might he have used?
2. What standards does Russell set for Eakins? Could a photographer meet them just as well as a painter?
3. Russell praises Eakins for his moral seriousness. In what sense can a painting or a painter's works be moral?
4. What qualities does Russell consider uniquely American about Eakins' art? Do these typically American characteristics appear in other art forms?
5. Does Russell defend his criteria of evaluation at all? Does he tell us, for example, why it is important for a painter to be as exact as a draftsman?
6. Do you get a sense from Russell's style (certain phrases and word choices) that he thinks he is making claims his readers will find outrageous?

SUGGESTIONS FOR WRITING

1. Compare the work of Eakins to some of America's other great and unique painters: Charles Willson Peale, John Singer Sargent, Winslow Homer, James McNeill Whistler, John Singleton Copley, Frederick Church, Asher Durand, Mary Cassatt, George Bellows, and Andrew Wyeth, for example. Would you argue for the same audience Russell addresses that any of them is as good as or greater than Eakins? Can you apply the same standards Russell uses?

2. Are there uniquely American standards of evaluation in any arts other than painting? Is there, for example, an American standard for excellence in music, film, architecture, or fiction? Argue for or against such a standard in an art form familiar to you for an American audience.

3. Find a good reproduction of one of Eakins' paintings and evaluate it by applying Russell's standards. Do you think some of its qualities could better be appreciated by applying other standards? Address your evaluation to students of art.

4. You might take exception to Russell's twin standards of representational fidelity and high moral seriousness. What characteristics of good art does he omit? How could we ever evaluate a nonrepresentational (i.e., abstract) painter by his standards? Either argue with Russell over the inapplicability of his standards, or apply at least one of his standards to an abstract painter.

5. Eakins is one of America's "establishment" painters. America also has a rich tradition of folk art that creates functional and beautiful objects such as quilts, primitive paintings, baskets, weather vanes, rugs, pottery, and country furniture. By what standards can any of these crafts be evaluated? Would any of Russell's standards apply? Evaluate a folk art for an audience not used to appreciating such objects as art.

6. Should museums in our country favor American art, no matter what the quality, over the art of other nations? Evaluate the collection of American art in a museum accessible to you. Perhaps you will want to use your evaluation to encourage the curators to expand their American holdings.

–≫≫ ≪≪–

Good Managers Don't Make Policy Decisions

H. EDWARD WRAPP

This essay on what makes a good manager was first published in the Harvard Business Review in 1967. Since then it has become one of that journal's most popular essays, as shown by the large number of reprints that have been requested. It was written by H. Edward Wrapp, who is now a retired professor of business policy at the Graduate School of Business, University of Chicago. Professor Wrapp writes from extensive experience in

*both academics and business. He has directed the University of Chicago's
executive program, served as associate dean for its management program, and
sat on the boards of many corporations. This ideal definition of the good
manager is based on Wrapp's observation of many managers at their work.
His subjects were neither preselected with research in mind nor told they were
being studied nor asked to formulate their own descriptions of what they did.
Professor Wrapp observed their actions in natural circumstances, when they
were not self-conscious about their jobs.*

The upper reaches of management are a land of mystery and intrigue.
Very few people have ever been there, and the present inhabitants
frequently send back messages that are incoherent both to other levels
of management and to the world in general.

This absence of firsthand reports may account for the myths, illusions, and caricatures that permeate the literature of management—for
example, such widely held notions as these:

Life gets less complicated as a manager reaches the top of the pyramid.

The manager at the top level knows everything that's going on in the
organization, can command whatever resources he may need, and therefore can be more decisive.

The general manager's day is taken up with making broad policy decisions and formulating precise objectives.

The top executive's primary activity is conceptualizing long-range plans.

In a large company, the top executive may be seen meditating about the
role of his organization in society.

I suggest that none of these versions alone, or in combination, is an
accurate portrayal of what a general manager does. Perhaps students of
the management process have been overly eager to develop a theory and
a discipline. As one executive I know puts it, "I guess I do some of the
things described in the books and articles, but the descriptions are
lifeless, and my job isn't."

What common characteristics, then, do successful executives exhibit
in reality? I shall identify five skills or talents which, in my experience,
seem especially significant.

KEEPING WELL INFORMED

First, each of my heroes has a special talent for keeping himself informed about a wide range of operating decisions being made at different levels in the company. As he moves up the ladder, he develops a network of information sources in many different departments. He cultivates these sources and keeps them open no matter how high he climbs in the organization. When the need arises, he bypasses the lines on the organization chart to seek more than one version of a situation.

In some instances, especially when they suspect he would not be in total agreement with their decisions, his subordinates will elect to inform him in advance, before they announce a decision. In these circumstances, he is in a position to defer the decision, or redirect it, or even block further action. However, he does not insist on this procedure. Ordinarily he leaves it up to the members of his organization to decide at what stage they inform him.

Top-level managers are frequently criticized by writers, consultants, and lower levels of management for continuing to enmesh themselves in operating problems, after promotion to the top, rather than withdrawing to the "big picture." Without any doubt, some managers do get lost in a welter of detail and insist on making too many decisions. Superficially, the good manager may seem to make the same mistake—but his purposes are different. He knows that only by keeping well informed about the decisions being made can he avoid the sterility so often found in those who isolate themselves from operations. If he follows the advice to free himself from operations, he may soon find himself subsisting on a diet of abstractions, leaving the choice of what he eats in the hands of his subordinates. As Kenneth Boulding puts it, "The very purpose of a hierarchy is to prevent information from reaching higher layers. It operates as an information filter, and there are little wastebaskets all along the way."[1]

What kinds of action does a successful executive take to keep his information live and accurate? One company president that I worked with, for example, sensed that his vice presidents were insulating him from some of the vital issues being discussed at lower levels. He accepted

Editors' note: The editors ask that whenever you read the word "he," "him," or "his," you take it to mean "she," "her," or "hers" as well.

[1]From a speech at a meeting sponsored by the Crowell Collier Institute of Continuing Education in New York, as reported in *Business Week*, February 18, 1967, p. 202.

a proposal for a formal management development program primarily because it afforded him an opportunity to discuss company problems with middle managers several layers removed from him in the organization. By meeting with small groups of these men in an academic setting, he learned much about their preoccupations, and also about those of his vice presidents. And he accomplished his purposes without undermining the authority of line managers.

FOCUSING TIME & ENERGY

The second skill of the good manager is that he knows how to save his energy and hours for those few particular issues, decisions, or problems to which he should give his personal attention. He knows the fine and subtle distinction between keeping fully informed about operating decisions and allowing the organization to force him into participating in these decisions or, even worse, making them. Recognizing that he can bring his special talents to bear on only a limited number of matters, he chooses those issues which he believes will have the greatest long-term impact on the company, and on which his special abilities can be most productive. Under ordinary circumstances, he will limit himself to three or four major objectives during any single period of sustained activity.

What about the situations he elects *not* to become involved in as a decision maker? He makes sure (using the skill first mentioned) that the organization keeps him informed about them at various stages; he does not want to be accused of indifference to such issues. He trains his subordinates not to bring the matters to him for a decision. The communication to him from below is essentially one of: "Here is our sizeup, and here's what we propose to do."

Reserving his hearty encouragement for those projects which hold superior promise of a contribution to total corporate strategy, he simply acknowledges receipt of information on other matters. When he sees a problem where the organization needs his help, he finds a way to transmit his know-how short of giving orders—usually by asking perceptive questions.

PLAYING THE POWER GAME

To what extent do successful top executives push their ideas and proposals through the organization? The rather common notion that the "prime mover" continually creates and forces through new programs, like a powerful majority leader in a liberal Congress, is in my opinion very misleading.

The successful manager is sensitive to the power structure in the organization. In considering any major current proposal, he can plot the position of the various individuals and units in the organization on a scale ranging from complete, outspoken support down to determined, sometimes bitter, and oftentimes well-cloaked opposition. In the middle of the scale is an area of comparative indifference. Usually, several aspects of a proposal will fall into this area, and here is where he knows he can operate. He assesses the depth and nature of the blocks in the organization. His perception permits him to move through what I call corridors of comparative indifference. He seldom challenges when a corridor is blocked, preferring to pause until it has opened up.

Related to this particular skill is his ability to recognize the need for a few trial balloon launchers in the organization. He knows that the organization will tolerate only a certain number of proposals which emanate from the apex of the pyramid. No matter how sorely he may be tempted to stimulate the organization with a flow of his own ideas, he knows he must work through idea men in different parts of the organization. As he studies the reactions of key individuals and groups to the trial balloons these men send up, he is able to make a better assessment of how to limit the emasculation of the various proposals. For seldom does he find a proposal which is supported by all quarters of the organization. The emergence of strong support in certain quarters is almost sure to evoke strong opposition in others.

SENSE OF TIMING

Circumstances like these mean that a good sense of timing is a priceless asset for a top executive. For example, a vice president had for some time been convinced that his company lacked a sense of direction and needed a formal long-range planning activity to fill the void. Up to the time in question, his soft overtures to other top executives had been rebuffed. And then he spotted an opening.

A management development committee proposed a series of week-end meetings for second-level officers in the company. After extensive debate, but for reasons not announced, the president rejected this proposal. The members of the committee openly resented what seemed to them an arbitrary rejection.

The vice president, sensing a tense situation, suggested to the president that the same officers who were to have attended the weekend management development seminars be organized into a long-range planning committee. The timing of his suggestion was perfect. The president, looking for a bone to toss to the committee, acquiesced immediately, and the management development committee in its next meeting enthusiastically endorsed the idea.

This vice president had been conducting a kind of continuing market research to discover how to sell his long-range planning proposal. His previous probes of the "market" had told him that the president's earlier rejections of his proposal were not so final as to preclude an eventual shift in the corridors of attitude I have mentioned.

The vice president caught the committee in a conciliatory mood, and his proposal rode through with flying colors.

CAUTIOUS PRESSURE

As a good manager stands at a point in time, he can identify a set of goals he is interested in, albeit the outline of them may be pretty hazy. His timetable, which is also pretty hazy, suggests that some must be accomplished sooner than others, and that some may be safely postponed for several months or years. He has a still hazier notion of how he can reach these goals. He assesses key individuals and groups. He knows that each has its own set of goals, some of which he understands rather thoroughly and others about which he can only speculate. He knows also that these individuals and groups represent blocks to certain programs or projects, and that these points of opposition must be taken into account. As the day-to-day operating decisions are made, and as proposals are responded to both by individuals and by groups, he perceives more clearly where the corridors of comparative indifference are. He takes action accordingly.

APPEARING IMPRECISE

The fourth skill of the successful manager is knowing how to satisfy the organization that it has a sense of direction without ever actually getting himself committed publicly to a specific set of objectives. This is not to say that he does not have objectives—personal and corporate, long-term and short-term. They are significant guides to his thinking, and he modifies them continually as he better understands the resources he is working with, the competition, and the changing market demands. But as the organization clamors for statements of objectives, these are samples of what it gets back from him:

"Our company aims to be number one in its industry."
"Our objective is growth with profit."
"We seek the maximum return on investment."
"Management's goal is to meet its responsibilities to stockholders, employees, and the public."

In my opinion, statements such as these provide almost no guidance to the various levels of management. Yet they are quite readily accepted as objectives by large numbers of intelligent people.

MAINTAIN VIABILITY

Why does the good manager shy away from precise statements of his objectives for the organization? The main reason is that he finds it impossible to set down specific objectives which will be relevant for any reasonable period into the future. Conditions in business change continually and rapidly, and corporate strategy must be revised to take the changes into account. The more explicit the statement of strategy, the more difficult it becomes to persuade the organization to turn to different goals when needs and conditions shift.

The public and the stockholders, to be sure, must perceive the organization as having a well-defined set of objectives and a clear sense of direction. But in reality the good top manager is seldom so certain of the direction which should be taken. Better than anyone else, he senses the many, many threats to his company—threats which lie in the economy, in the actions of competitors, and, not least, within his own organization.

He also knows that it is impossible to state objectives clearly enough so that everyone in the organization understands what they mean. Objectives get communicated only over time by a consistency or pattern in operating decisions. Such decisions are more meaningful than words. In instances where precise objectives are spelled out, the organization tends to interpret them so they fit its own needs.

Subordinates who keep pressing for more precise objectives are in truth working against their own best interests. Each time the objectives are stated more specifically, a subordinate's range of possibilities for operating [is] reduced. The narrower field means less room to roam and to accommodate the flow of ideas coming up from his part of the organization.

AVOID POLICY STRAITJACKETS

The successful manager's reluctance to be precise extends into the area of policy decisions. He seldom makes a forthright statement of policy. He may be aware that in some companies there are executives who spend more time in arbitrating disputes caused by stated policies than in moving the company forward. The management textbooks contend that well-defined policies are the sine qua non of a well-managed company. My research does not bear out this contention.

For example, the president of one company with which I am familiar deliberately leaves the assignments of his top officers vague and refuses to define policies for them. He passes out new assignments with seemingly no pattern in mind and consciously sets up competitive ventures among his subordinates. His methods, though they would never be sanctioned by a classical organization planner, are deliberate—and, incidentally, quite effective.

Since able managers do not make policy decisions, does this mean that well-managed companies operate without policies? Certainly not. But the policies are those which evolve over time from an indescribable mix of operating decisions. From any single operating decision might have come a very minor dimension of the policy as the organization understands it; from a series of decisions comes a pattern of guidelines for various levels of the organization.

The skillful manager resists the urge to write a company creed or to compile a policy manual. Preoccupation with detailed statements of corporate objectives and departmental goals and with comprehensive organization charts and job descriptions—this is often the first symptom of an organization which is in the early stages of atrophy.

The "management by objectives" school, so widely heralded in recent years, suggests that detailed objectives be spelled out at all levels in the corporation. This method is feasible at lower levels of management, but it becomes unworkable at the upper levels. The top manager must think out objectives in detail, but ordinarily some of the objectives must be withheld, or at least communicated to the organization in modest doses. A conditioning process which may stretch over months or years is necessary in order to prepare the organization for radical departures from what it is currently striving to attain.

Suppose, for example, that a president is convinced his company must phase out of the principal business it has been in for 35 years. Although making this change of course is one of his objectives, he may well feel that he cannot disclose the idea even to his vice presidents, whose total know-how is in the present business. A blunt announcement that the company is changing horses would be too great a shock for most of them to bear. And so he begins moving toward this goal but without a full disclosure to his management group.

A detailed spelling out of objectives may only complicate the task of reaching them. Specific, detailed statements give the opposition an opportunity to organize its defenses.

MUDDLING WITH A PURPOSE

The fifth, and most important, skill I shall describe bears little relation to the doctrine that management is (or should be) a comprehensive, systematic, logical, well-programmed science. Of all the heresies set forth here, this should strike doctrinaires as the rankest of all!

The successful manager, in my observation, recognizes the futility of trying to push total packages or programs through the organization. He is willing to take less than total acceptance in order to achieve modest progress toward his goals. Avoiding debates on principles, he tries to piece together particles that may appear to be incidentals into a program that moves at least part of the way toward his objectives. His attitude is based on optimism and persistence. Over and over he says to himself, "There must be some parts of this proposal on which we can capitalize."

Whenever he identifies relationships among the different proposals before him, he knows that they present opportunities for combination and restructuring. It follows that he is a man of wide-ranging interests and curiosity. The more things he knows about, the more opportunities he will have to discover parts which are related. This process does not require great intellectual brilliance or unusual creativity. The wider ranging his interests, the more likely that he will be able to tie together several unrelated proposals. He is skilled as an analyst but even more talented as a conceptualizer.

If the manager has built or inherited a solid organization, it will be difficult for him to come up with an idea which no one in the company has ever thought of before. His most significant contribution may be that he can see relationships which no one else has seen.

A division manager, for example, had set as one of his objectives, at the start of a year, an improvement in product quality. At the end of the year, in reviewing his progress toward this objective, he could identify three significant events which had brought about a perceptible improvement.

First, the head of the quality control group, a veteran manager who was doing only an adequate job, asked early in the year for assignment to a new research group. This opportunity permitted the division manager to install a promising young engineer in this key spot.

A few months later, opportunity number two came along. The personnel department proposed a continuous program of checking the effectiveness of training methods for new employees. The proposal was acceptable to the manufacturing group. The division manager's only contribution was to suggest that the program should include a heavy emphasis on employees' attitudes toward quality.

Then a third opportunity arose when one of the division's best customers discovered that the wrong material had been used for a large lot of parts. The heat generated by this complaint made it possible to institute a completely new system of procedures for inspecting and testing raw materials.

As the division manager reviewed the year's progress on product quality, these were the three most important developments. None of them could have been predicted at the start of the year, but he was quick to see the potential in each as it popped up in the day-to-day operating routines.

EXPLOITATION OF CHANGE

The good manager can function effectively only in an environment of continual change. A *Saturday Review* cartoonist caught the idea when he pictured an executive seated at a massive desk instructing his secretary to "send in a deal; I feel like wheelin'." Only with many changes in the works can the manager discover new combinations of opportunities and open up new corridors of comparative indifference. His stimulation to creativity comes from trying to make something useful of the proposal or idea in front of him. He will try to make strategic change a way of life in the organization and continually review the strategy even though current results are good.

Charles Lindblom has written an article with an engaging title, "The Science of Muddling Through."[2] In this he describes what he calls "the rational comprehensive method" of decision making. The essence of this method is that the decision maker, for each of his problems, proceeds deliberately, one step at a time, to collect complete data; to analyze the data thoroughly; to study a wide range of alternatives, each with its own risks and consequences; and, finally, to formulate a detailed course of action. Lindblom immediately dismisses "the rational comprehensive method" in favor of what he calls "successive limited comparisons." He sees the decision maker as comparing the alternatives which are open to him in order to learn which most closely meets the objectives he has in mind. Since this is not so much a rational process as an opportunistic one, he sees the manager as a muddler, but a muddler with a purpose.

H. Igor Ansoff, in his book, *Corporate Strategy*, espouses a similar notion as he describes what he calls the "cascade approach."[3] In his view, possible decision rules are formulated in gross terms and are successively refined through several stages as the emergence of a solution proceeds. This process gives the appearance of solving the problem several times over, but with successively more precise results.

Both Lindblom and Ansoff are moving us closer to an understanding of how managers really think. The process is not highly abstract; rather, the manager searches for a means of drawing into a pattern the thousands of incidents which make up the day-to-day life of a growing company.

CONTRASTING PICTURES

It is interesting to note, in the writings of several students of management, the emergence of the concept that, rather than making decisions, the leader's principal task is maintaining operating conditions which

[2]*Readings in Managerial Psychology*, ed. Harold I. Leavitt and Louis R. Pondy (Chicago: University of Chicago Press, 1964), p. 61.
[3]New York: McGraw-Hill, 1965.

permit the various decision-making systems to function effectively. The supporters of this theory, it seems to me, overlook the subtle turns of direction which the leader can provide. He cannot add purpose and structure to the balanced judgments of subordinates if he simply rubber-stamps their decisions. He must weigh the issues and reach his own decision.

Richard M. Cyert and James G. March contend that in real life managers do not consider all the possible courses of action, that their search ends once they have found a satisfactory alternative. In my sample, good managers are not guilty of such myopic thinking. Unless they mull over a wide range of possibilities, they cannot come up with the imaginative combinations of ideas which characterize their work.

Many of the articles about successful executives picture them as great thinkers who sit at their desks drafting master blueprints for their companies. The successful top executives I have seen at work do not operate this way. Rather than produce a full-grown decision tree, they start with a twig, help it grow, and ease themselves out on the limbs only after they have tested to see how much weight the limbs can stand.

In my picture, the general manager sits in the midst of a continuous stream of operating problems. His organization presents him with a flow of proposals to deal with the problems. Some of these proposals are contained in voluminous, well-documented, formal reports; some are as fleeting as the walk-in visit from a subordinate whose latest inspiration came during the morning's coffee break. Knowing how meaningless it is to say, "This is a finance problem," or, "That is a communications problem," the manager feels no compulsion to classify his problems. He is, in fact, undismayed by a problem that defies classification. As Gary Steiner, in one of his speeches, put it, "He has a high tolerance for ambiguity."

In considering each proposal, the general manager tests it against at least three criteria:

1 Will the total proposal—or, more often, will some part of the proposal—move the organization toward the objectives which he has in mind?

2 How will the whole or parts of the proposal be received by the various groups and subgroups in the organization? Where will the strongest opposition come from, which group will furnish the strongest support, and which group will be neutral or indifferent?

3 How does the proposal relate to programs already in process or

currently proposed? Can some parts of the proposal under consideration be added on to a program already under way, or can they be combined with all or parts of other proposals in a package which can be steered through the organization?

THE MAKING OF A DECISION

As another example of a general manager at work, let me describe the train of events which led to a parent company president's decision to attempt to consolidate two of his divisions.

Let us call the executive Mr. Brown. One day the manager of Division A came to him with a proposal that his division acquire a certain company. That company's founder and president—let us call him Mr. Johansson—had a phenomenal record of inventing new products, but earnings in his company had been less than phenomenal. Johansson's asking price for his company was high when evaluated against the earnings record.

Not until Brown began to speculate on how Johansson might supply fresh vigor for new products in Division A did it appear that perhaps a premium price could be justified. For several years, Brown had been unsuccessful in stimulating the manager of that division to see that he must bring in new products to replace those which were losing their place in the market.

The next idea which came to Brown was that Johansson might invent not only for Division A but also for Division B. As Brown analyzed how this might be worked out organizationally, he began to think about the markets being served by Divisions A and B. Over the years, several basic but gradual changes in marketing patterns had occurred, with the result that the marketing considerations which had dictated the establishment of separate divisions no longer prevailed. Why should the company continue to support the duplicated overhead expenses in the two divisions?

As Brown weighed the issues, he concluded that by consolidating the two divisions he could also shift responsibilities in the management groups in ways that would strengthen them overall. If we were asked to evaluate Brown's capabilities, how would we respond? Putting aside the objection that the information is too sketchy, our tendency might be to criticize Brown. Why did he not identify the changing market patterns in his continuing review of company position? Why did he not force the issue when the division manager failed to do something about new product development? Such criticism would reflect "the rational comprehensive method" of decision making.

But, as I analyze the gyrations in Brown's thinking, one characteristic stands out. He kept searching for the follow-on opportunities which he could fashion out of the original proposal, opportunities which would stand up against the three criteria earlier mentioned. In my book, Brown would rate as an extremely skillful general manager.

CONCLUSION

To recapitulate, the general manager possesses five important skills. He knows how to:

1 **Keep open many pipelines of information.** No one will quarrel with the desirability of an early warning system which provides varied viewpoints on an issue. However, very few managers know how to practice this skill, and the books on management add precious little to our understanding of the techniques which make it practicable.

2 **Concentrate on a limited number of significant issues.** No matter how skillful the manager is in focusing his energies and talents, he is inevitably caught up in a number of inconsequential duties. Active leadership of an organization demands a high level of personal involvement, and personal involvement brings with it many time-consuming activities which have an infinitesimal impact on corporate strategy. Hence this second skill, while perhaps the most logical of the five, is by no means the easiest to apply.

3 **Identify the corridors of comparative indifference.** Are there inferences here that the good manager has no ideas of his own, that he stands by until his organization proposes solutions, that he never uses his authority to force a proposal through the organization? Such inferences are not intended. The message is that a good organization will tolerate only so much direction from the top; the good manager therefore is adept at sensing how hard he can push.

4 **Give the organization a sense of direction with open-ended objectives.** In assessing this skill, keep in mind that I am talking about top levels of management. At lower levels, the manager should be encouraged to write down his objectives, if for no other reason than to ascertain if they are consistent with corporate strategy.

5 **Spot opportunities and relationships in the stream of operating problems and decisions.** Lest it be concluded from the description of this skill that the good manager is more an improviser than a planner, let me emphasize that he is a planner and encourages planning by his subordinates. Interestingly, though, professional planners may be irritated by a good general manager. Most of them complain about his lack of vision. They devise a master plan, but the president (or other operating executive) seems to ignore it, or to give it minimum acknowledgment by borrowing bits and pieces for implementation. They seem to feel that the power of a good master plan will be obvious to everyone, and its implementation automatic. But the general manager knows that even if the plan is sound and imaginative, the job has only begun. The long, painful task of implementation will depend on his skill, not that of the planner.

If this analysis of how skillful general managers think and operate has validity, then it should help us see several problems in a better light. For instance, the investment community is giving increasing attention to sizing up the management of a company being appraised. Thus far, the analysts rely mainly on results or performance rather than on a probe of management skills. But current performance can be affected by many variables, both favorably and unfavorably, and is a dangerous base for predicting what the management of a company will produce in the future. Testing the key managers of a company against the five skills described holds promise for evaluating the caliber of a management group. The manager who is building his own company and the man who is moving up through the hierarchy of a larger organization require essentially the same capabilities for success.

In today's frenzy of acquisitions and mergers, why does a management usually prefer to acquire a company rather than to develop a new product and build an organization to make and sell it? One of the reasons can be found in the way a general manager thinks and operates. He finds it difficult to sit and speculate theoretically about the future as he and his subordinates fashion a plan to exploit a new product. He is much more at home when taking over a going concern, even though he anticipates he will inherit many things he does not want. In the day-to-day operation of a going concern, he finds the milieu to maneuver and conceptualize.

Scarcely any manager in any business can escape the acutely painful responsibility to identify men with potential for growth in manage-

ment and to devise methods for developing them for broader responsibilities. Few line managers or staff professionals have genuine confidence in the yardsticks and devices they use now. The five skills offer
possibilities for raising an additional set of questions about management appraisal methods, job rotation practices, on-the-job development assignments, and the curricula of formal in-house management
development programs.

One group of distinguished executives ignores with alarming regularity the implications of the five skills. These are the presidents of
multidivision companies who "promote" successful division managers
to the parent company level as staff officers. Does this recurring phenomenon cast doubt on the validity of my theory? I think not. To the
contrary, strong supporting evidence for my thesis can be found in the
results of such action. What happens is that line managers thus "promoted" often end up on the sidelines, out of the game for the rest of
their careers. Removed from the tumult of operations, the environment which I contend is critical for their success, many of them just
wither away in their high-status posts as senior counselors and never
become effective.

QUESTIONS FOR DISCUSSION

1. Do the five criteria for good management that Wrapp sets forth seem to be
   of equal importance? If you had to weight them, which would you consider
   of greatest or of least significance?
2. Notice that Wrapp does not name particular managers he admires or identify
   the businesses with which they are associated. Why do you think he made
   that choice? What are the advantages of remaining general? Do they offset
   the disadvantages? Does Wrapp use any special techniques to avoid excessive
   generality?
3. Can the management techniques described by Wrapp be applied to fields
   other than business? What can other professionals learn from this essay?
4. Wrapp's first criterion is that managers be well-informed about the details
   of their companies. Is this consistent with his second criterion, that managers
   be able to focus attention on the few projects that require direct attention
   and delegate responsibility for the others?
5. How might the skills that Wrapp identifies in good managers be taught to
   business students?
6. What does Wrapp assume about his audience? Does he think they are
   disposed to accept or to reject his argument?

SUGGESTIONS FOR WRITING

1. Evaluate a manager you are familiar with according to Wrapp's stated criteria. You might select someone for whom you once worked or an acquaintance who is willing to be followed around for at least a day. Your evaluation could be aimed at the manager himself (perhaps a difficult audience), at employees, or at fellow students of management tactics.
2. Is Wrapp's good manager a manipulator? Write an essay for readers of Wrapp in which you either attack him for advocating a kind of Machiavelli of the board room or defend him from that accusation.
3. If you are familiar with various theories of management, you might want to take on Wrapp's argument and defend a technique such as "management by objectives." Write your essay as a response to be published in the *Harvard Business Review*.
4. Students interested in fields other than business can try creating their own ideal definitions of successful professionals in areas they are familiar with. Do you discover any unexpected qualities when you think about what makes a good musician, an effective salesperson, a great athlete, a superb teacher? Write an ideal definition for students or professionals in the field of your choice.
5. Drawing either on your own experience or on research, consider a specific instance of bad or good management in a particular situation. Write a report, addressed to a superior in that company, in which you explore the reasons why the strategy failed or succeeded.
6. Follow a continuing story about some company in a paper such as the *Wall Street Journal*, and do some supplementary research to familiarize yourself with the company involved. Compare the management strategies the company uses with those advocated by Wrapp. Address your evaluation to the company you have studied.

From Bauhaus to Our House

TOM WOLFE

Tom Wolfe is one of the most gifted stylists writing in America today. With a doctorate in American Studies from Yale and a brilliant career in journalism to his credit, Wolfe has produced a series of books that give Americans a look at themselves in cinematic words. His works include The

Kandy-Kolored Tangerine Flake Streamline Baby *(1965)*, The Electric
Kool-Aid Acid Test *(1968)*, *and* The Right Stuff *(1979)*, *the book that
spawned the movie of the same title.*

*Wolfe is also an artist, able to capture the American scene in pictures as
well as words, and in his 1981 book* From Bauhaus to Our House, *he uses
his background in art to take on the establishment in American architecture.
Wolfe vilifies those modern architects who have given us so many rectangular
glass skyscrapers as mindless followers of the Bauhaus, or Workers' Housing,
style that originated in Germany in the 1920s, a style that forbade all
decoration and insisted that every element be functional. Even if you
ultimately disagree with Wolfe's negative evaluation of modern architecture,
you will enjoy the panache with which he uses every resource available to an
arguer to carry it off. This selection is adapted from "Escape to Islip."*

This has been *the American century,* in the same way that the seventeenth might be regarded as the British century. This is the century in
which America, the young giant, became the mightiest nation on earth,
devising the means to obliterate the planet with a single device but also
the means to escape to the stars and explore the rest of the universe. This
is the century in which she became the richest nation in all of history,
with a wealth that reached down to every level of the population. The
energies and animal appetites and idle pleasures of even the working
classes—the very term now seemed antique—became enormous, lurid,
creamy, preposterous. The American family car was a 425-horsepower,
twenty-two-foot-long Buick Electra with tail fins in back and two black
rubber breasts on the bumper in front. The American liquor-store deliv-
eryman's or cargo humper's vacation was two weeks in Barbados with
his third wife or his new cookie. The American industrial convention
was a gin-blind rout at a municipal coliseum the size of all Rome
featuring vans in the parking lot stocked with hookers on flokati rugs for
the exclusive use of registered members of the association. The way
Americans lived made the rest of mankind stare with envy or disgust but
always with awe. In short, this has been America's Elizabethan era, her
Bourbon Louis romp, her season of the rising sap—and what architecture has she to show for it? An architecture whose tenets prohibit every
manifestation of exuberance, power, empire, grandeur, or even high
spirits and playfulness, as the height of bad taste.

We brace for a barbaric yawp over the roofs of the world—and hear
a cough at a concert.

In short, the reigning architectural style in this, the very Babylon of
capitalism, became worker housing. Worker housing, as developed by a

handful of architects, inside the compounds, amid the rubble of Europe in the early 1920s, was now pitched up high and wide, in the form of Ivy League art-gallery annexes, museums for art patrons, apartments for the rich, corporate headquarters, city halls, country estates. It was made to serve every purpose, in fact, except housing for workers.

It was not that worker housing was never built for workers. In the 1950s and early 1960s the federal government helped finance the American version of the Dutch and German *Siedlungen* of the 1920s. Here they were called public housing projects. But somehow the workers, intellectually undeveloped as they were, managed to avoid public housing. They called it, simply, "the projects," and they avoided it as if it had a smell. The workers—if by workers we mean people who have jobs —headed out instead to the suburbs. They ended up in places like Islip, Long Island, and the San Fernando Valley of Los Angeles, and they bought houses with pitched roofs and shingles and clapboard siding, with no structure expressed if there was any way around it, with gaslight-style front-porch lamps and mailboxes set up on lengths of stiffened chain that seemed to defy gravity—the more cute or antiquey touches the better—and they loaded these houses with "drapes" such as baffled all description and wall-to-wall carpet you could lose a shoe in, and they put barbecue pits and fishponds with concrete cherubs urinating into them on the lawn out back, and they parked the Buick Electras out front and had Evinrude cruisers up on tow trailers in the carport just beyond the breezeway.

As for the honest sculptural objects designed for worker-housing interiors, such as Mies' and Breuer's chairs, the proles either ignored them or held them in contempt because they were patently uncomfortable. This furniture is today a symbol of wealth and privilege, attuned chiefly to the tastes of the businessmen's wives who graze daily at the D & D Building, the major interior-decoration bazaar in New York. Mies' most famous piece of furniture design, the Barcelona chair, retails today for $3,465 and is available only through decorators. The high price is due in no small part to the chair's worker-housing honest nonbourgeois materials: stainless steel and leather. Today the leather can be ordered only in black or shades of brown. In the early 1970s, it seems, certain bourgeois elements were having them made in the most appalling variations . . . zebra skin, Holstein skin, ocelot skin, and *pretty fabrics*.

The only people left trapped in worker housing in America today are those who don't work at all and are on welfare—these are the sole inhabitants of "the projects"—and, of course, the urban rich who live in places such as the Olympic Tower on Fifth Avenue in New York. Since the 1950s the term "luxury highrise" has come to denote a certain type of apartment house that is in fact nothing else but the *Siedlungen* of Stuttgart, Berlin, and Zehlendorf, with units stacked up thirty, forty, fifty stories high, to be rented or sold to the bourgeoisie. Which is to say, pure nonbourgeois housing for the bourgeoisie only. Sometimes the towers are of steel, concrete, and glass; sometimes of glass, steel, and small glazed white or beige bricks. Always the ceilings are low, often under eight feet, the hallways are narrow, the rooms are narrow, even when they're long, the bedrooms are small (Le Corbusier was always in favor of that), the walls are thin, the doorways and windows have no casings, the joints have no moldings, the walls have no baseboards, and the windows don't open, although small vents or jalousies may be provided. The construction is invariably cheap in the pejorative as well as the literal sense. That builders could present these boxes in the 1950s, without a twitch of the nostril, as luxury, and that well-educated men and women could accept them, without a blink, as luxury—here is objective testimony, from those too dim for irony, to the aesthetic sway of the compound aesthetic, of the Silver Prince and his colonial legions [Gropius and the architects of the compound], in America following the Second World War.

Every respected instrument of architectural opinion and cultivated taste, from *Domus* to *House & Garden,* told the urban dwellers of America that this was *living.* This was the good taste of today; this was modern, and soon the International Style became known simply as modern architecture. Every Sunday, in its design section, *The New York Times Magazine* ran a picture of the same sort of apartment. I began to think of it as *that apartment.* The walls were always pure white and free of moldings, casings, baseboards, and all the rest. In the living room there were about 17,000 watts' worth of R-40 spotlights encased in white canisters suspended from the ceiling in what is known as track lighting. There was always a set of bentwood chairs, designed by Le Corbusier, which no one ever sat in because they caught you in the small of the back like a karate chop. The dining room table was a smooth slab of blond wood (no ogee edges, no beading on the legs), around which was a set of the S-shaped, tubular steel, cane-bottomed chairs that Mies van der Rohe had designed—the second most famous chair designed in the twentieth century, his own Barcelona chair being first, but also one of the five most disastrously designed, so that by the time the main course arrived, at least one guest had pitched face forward into the lobster bisque. Somewhere nearby was a palm or a dracena fragrans or some other huge tropical plant, because all the furniture was so lean and clean and bare and spare that without some prodigious piece of frondose Victoriana from the nursery the place looked absolutely empty. The photographer always managed to position the plant in the foreground, so that the stark scene beyond was something one peered at through an arabesque of equatorial greenery. (And *that apartment* is still with us, every Sunday.)

So what if you were living in a building that looked like a factory and felt like a factory, and paying top dollar for it? Every modern building of quality looked like a factory. That was *the look of today.* You only had to think of Mies' campus for the Illinois Institute of Technology, most of which had gone up in the 1940s. The main classroom building looked like a shoe factory. The chapel looked like a power plant. The power plant itself, also designed by Mies, looked rather more spiritual (as Charles Jencks would point out), thanks to its chimney, which reached heavenward at least. The School of Architecture building had black steel trusses rising up through the roof on either side of the main entrance, after the manner of a Los Angeles car wash. All four were glass and steel boxes. The truth was, this was inescapable. The compound style, with its *nonbourgeois* taboos, had so reduced the options of the true believer that every building, the beach house no less than the skyscraper, was bound to have the same general look.

And so what? The terms *glass box* and *repetitious,* first uttered as terms of opprobrium, became badges of honor. Mies had many American imitators, Philip Johnson, I. M. Pei, and Gordon Bunshaft being the most famous and the most unabashed. And the most unashamed. Snipers would say that every one of Philip Johnson's buildings was an imitation of Mies van der Rohe. And Johnson would open his eyes wide and put on his marvelous smile of mock innocence and reply, "I have always been delighted to be called Mies van der Johnson." Bunshaft had designed Lever House, corporate headquarters for the Lever Brothers soap and detergent company, on Park Avenue. The building was such a success that it became the prototype for the American glass box, and Bunshaft and his firm, Skidmore, Owings & Merrill, did many variations on this same design. To the charge that glass boxes were all he designed, Bunshaft liked to crack: "Yes, and I'm going to keep on doing boxes until I do one I like."

For a hierophant of the compound, confidence came easy! What did it matter if they said you were imitating Mies or Gropius or Corbu or any of the rest? It was like accusing a Christian of imitating Jesus Christ. . . .

. . . In 1958, the greatest single monument to the architecture of the Dutch and German compounds went up on Park Avenue, across the street from Lever House. This was the Seagram Building, designed by Mies himself, with Philip Johnson as his assistant. The Seagram Building was worker housing, utterly nonbourgeois, pitched up thirty-eight stories on Park Avenue for the firm that manufactured a rye whiskey called Four Roses. In keeping with the color of the American whiskey bottle, the glass for this greatest of all boxes of glass and steel was tinted brownish amber. When it came to the exposed steel—well, since brownish steel didn't exist, except in a state of rust, bronze was chosen. Wasn't this adding a *color*, like poor Bruno Taut? No, bronze was bronze; that was the way it came, right out of the foundry. As for the glass, all glass ended up with a tint of some sort, usually greenish. Tinting it brown was only a machine-made tint control. Right? (Besides, this was *Mies.*) Exposing the metal had presented a problem. Mies' vision of ultimate nonbourgeois purity was a building composed of nothing but steel beams and glass, with concrete slabs creating the ceilings and floors. But now that he was in the United States, he ran into American building and fire codes. Steel was terrific for tall buildings because it could withstand great lateral stresses as well as support great weights. Its weakness was that the heat of a fire could cause steel to buckle. American codes required that structural steel members be encased in concrete or some other fireproof material. That slowed Mies up for only a little while. He had already worked it out in Chicago, in his Lake Shore apartment buildings. What you did was enclose the steel members in concrete, as required, and then reveal them, *express* them, by sticking vertical WF-beams (wide-flange) on the outside of the concrete, as if to say: "Look! Here's what's inside." But sticking things on the outside of buildings . . . Wasn't that exactly what was known, in another era, as applied decoration? Was there any way you could call such a thing *functional?* No problem. At the heart of functional, as everyone knew, was not *function* but the spiritual quality known as *nonbourgeois.* And what could be more nonbourgeois than an unadorned WF-beam, straight out of the mitts of a construction worker?

The one remaining problem was window coverings: shades, blinds, curtains, whatever. Mies would have preferred that the great windows of plate glass have no coverings at all. Unless you could compel everyone in a building to have the same color ones (white or beige, naturally) and raise them and lower them or open and shut them at the same time and to the same degree, they always ruined the purity of the design of the exterior. In the Seagram Building, Mies came as close as man was likely to come to realizing that ideal. The tenant could only have white blinds or shades, and there were only three intervals where they would stay put: open, closed, and halfway. At any other point they just kept sliding.

No intellectually undeveloped impulses, please. By now this had become a standard attitude among compound architects in America. They policed the impulses of clients and tenants alike. Even after the building was up and the contract fulfilled, they would return. The imitators of Le Corbusier—and there were many—would build expensive country houses in wooded glades patterned on Corbu's Villa Savoie, with strict instructions that the bedrooms, being on the upper floor and visible only to the birds, have no curtains whatsoever. Tired of waking up at 5 A.M. every morning to the light of the summer sun, the owners would add white curtains. But the soul engineer would inevitably return and rip the offending rags down . . . and throw out those sweet little puff 'n' clutter Thai-silk throw pillows in the living room while he was at it.

In the great corporate towers, the office workers shoved filing cabinets, desks, wastepaper baskets, potted plants, up against the floor-to-ceiling sheets of glass, anything to build a barrier against the panicked feeling that they were about to pitch headlong into the streets below. Above these jerry-built walls they strung up makeshift curtains that looked like laundry lines from the slums of Naples, anything to keep out that brain-boiling, poached-eye sunlight that came blazing in every afternoon . . . And by night the custodial staff, the Miesling police, under strictest orders, invaded and pulled down these pathetic barricades thrown up against the pure vision of the white gods and the Silver Prince. Eventually everyone gave up and learned, like the haute bourgeoisie above him, to take it like a man.

. . . Not even the bottom dogs, those on welfare, trapped in the projects, have taken it so supinely. The lumpenproles have fought it out with the legions of the Silver Prince, and they have won a battle or two. In 1955 a vast worker-housing project called Pruitt-Igoe was opened in St. Louis. The design, by Minoru Yamasaki, architect of the World Trade Center, won an award from the American Institute of Architects. Yamasaki designed it classically Corbu, fulfilling the master's vision of highrise hives of steel, glass, and concrete separated by open spaces of green lawn. The workers of St. Louis, of course, were in no danger of getting caught in Pruitt-Igoe. They had already decamped for suburbs such as Spanish Lake and Crestwood. Pruitt-Igoe filled up mainly with recent migrants from the rural south. They moved from areas of America where the population density was fifteen to twenty folks per square mile, where one rarely got more than ten feet off the ground except by climbing a tree, into Pruitt-Igoe's fourteen-story blocks.

On each floor there were covered walkways, in keeping with Corbu's idea of "streets in the air." Since there was no other place in the project in which to *sin* in public, whatever might ordinarily have taken place in bars, brothels, social clubs, pool halls, amusement arcades, general stores, corncribs, rutabaga patches, hayricks, barn stalls, now took place in the streets in the air. Corbu's boulevards made Hogarth's Gin Lane look like the oceanside street of dreams in Southampton, New York. Respectable folk pulled out, even if it meant living in cracks in the sidewalks. Millions of dollars and scores of commission meetings and task-force projects were expended in a last-ditch attempt to make Pruitt-Igoe habitable. In 1971, the final task force called a general meeting of everyone still living in the project. They asked the residents for their suggestions. It was a historic moment for two reasons. One, for the first time in the fifty-year history of worker housing, someone had finally asked the client for his two cents' worth. Two, the chant. The chant began immediately: "Blow it . . . *up!* Blow it . . . *up!* Blow it . . . *up!* Blow it . . . *up!* Blow it . . . *up!*" The next day the task force thought it over. The poor buggers were right. It was the only solution. In July of 1972, the city blew up the three central blocks of Pruitt-Igoe with dynamite.

That part of the worker-housing saga has not ended. It has just begun. At almost the same time that Pruitt-Igoe went down, the Oriental Gardens project went up in New Haven, the model city of urban renewal in America. The architect was one of America's most prestigious compound architects, Paul Rudolph, dean of the Yale school of architecture. The federal government's Department of Housing and Urban Development, which was paying for the project, hailed Rudolph's daring design as the vision of the housing projects of the future. The Oriental Gardens were made of clusters of prefabricated modules. You would never end up with more disadvantaged people than you bargained for. You could keep adding modules and clustering the poor yobboes up until they reached Bridgeport. The problem was that the modules didn't fit together too well. In through the cracks came the cold and the rain. Out the doors, the ones that still opened, went whatever respectable folks had gone in in the first place. By September of 1980 there were only seventeen tenants left. Five months ago the HUD itself began returning the Oriental Gardens' nonbiodegradable plastic modules to the free-floating molecular state from whence they came. They set about demolishing it. . . .

QUESTIONS FOR DISCUSSION

1. Wolfe has basically two standards for judging architecture and interior design. What are they?
2. Tom Wolfe is justly celebrated for his elaborate prose style. Give yourself a tour of Wolfe's style by noting how many sentences in a row begin with or repeat a similar structure, how many adjectives are occasionally piled up before a noun, how many series have more than three elements, and how many word choices take you by surprise. What is the effect of these devices?
3. Now notice the connection between Wolfe's criteria of evaluation and his style. For starters, underline all the words and phrases that characterize his targets negatively. (Note: Some negative connotations accrue to words as they are used in this essay.)
4. Which of Wolfe's pieces of evidence are tied to some source of external verification and which are not? How are you convinced by the evidence that is not tied down by references to particular places, times, and people?
5. Could Wolfe have used this same essay as a convincing evaluation with a non-American audience? What appeals would he have had to leave out? What would he have to emphasize?
6. This excerpt from Wolfe's book is a self-contained section. What internal structure does it have? Has Wolfe manipulated his evidence to shape a climax that carries along the readers' conviction on the crest of a wave?

SUGGESTIONS FOR WRITING

1. What are your standards for a comfortable place in which to live? Comfortable furniture? A comfortable decor? Do you like your surroundings cluttered or spare, colorful or monochromatic? Describe your ideal living space in such a way that your readers, perhaps your peers, will share your enjoyment. (You may describe either an imaginary or an existing place.)
2. Particularly in his descriptions of "that apartment" and of country houses designed like Corbu's Villa, Wolfe suggests that people will endure discomfort in order to be fashionable. In what other areas of life can you see this happening? Where else has fashion dominated over convenience and com-

fort? Write an essay either defending or attacking the dominance of fashion in some area other than housing for an audience that tries to live up to the fashion.

3. Evaluate for a campus newspaper a building on your campus for its beauty, its utility, or its appropriateness as part of an academic institution.

4. Examine the housing in your community. How many different standards are being followed? How many types of dwellings are there? Your fellow citizens will be interested in the results of your survey/evaluation.

5. What styles would Wolfe approve of as embodying the "American century"? You may choose to describe what you believe would be quintessential, Wolfe-okayed, American style for readers convinced by Wolfe's essay.

6. Defend or refute the concept of "public housing" to an audience of city planners. Wolfe cites two disastrous examples of housing projects. Have any ever been successful? Is style dictated from above inherently doomed to failure?

7. Is Wolfe entirely correct in his depiction of the sources of the glass box skyscraper? Would you revise his labeling of notable buildings as entirely Bauhaus-inspired after looking at the work of Louis Sullivan and others in Chicago around the turn of the century? Address your version of the history of the skyscraper to students of architecture.

8. Evaluate your workplace (and if you are a full-time student you have several) as an interior that serves either efficiency or employee satisfaction or both. Your evaluation, addressed to the persons responsible, can include suggestions for improvement.

--->>> <<<---

The Last Bears of Yellowstone

ALSTON CHASE

This substantial and readable argument takes as its subject the bear management policies in force in Yellowstone Park for over a decade. The park's policy came from an environmentalist philosophy that wanted to recreate Yellowstone as a perfectly natural, self-contained environment, uncontaminated by humans, a goal that meant the bears had to be weaned from their diet of human garbage. But in the absence of undisputable facts about the size of the bear population, a controversy surfaced about the effects of the bear policy. Chase argues that the park service may achieve its goal of preserving wild, free, natural bears when the last bear of Yellowstone is destroyed.

This evaluation, which appeared in The Atlantic Monthly, *is part of Alston Chase's book-length study on Yellowstone National Park.*

"In the Yellowstone," wrote a visitor in 1909, "bears are as the autumn leaves," and indeed, since Yellowstone Park was founded, in 1872, bears and Yellowstone have seemed inseparable. For three generations of Americans, coming to the Park was nearly synonymous with coming to see bears. For these travellers, it was the black bear—*Ursus americanus,* the impish, appealing, but destructive and sometimes dangerous clown who prowled the campgrounds and begged along the roads, blocking traffic and causing "bearjams"—that provided many a vacation's thrills.

Few ever saw the grizzly—*Ursus arctos,* or silvertip, as westerners call him. But he remained in Yellowstone as a remnant of a species that once roamed throughout western North America. Much larger than the black, ranging up to 1,200 pounds, wilder and more unpredictable, this bear, easily identified by its humped shoulders, long hind feet, broad muzzle, and long gray guard hairs, usually stayed away from human beings. But his presence was felt. It instilled in the hearts of backcountry hikers the most authentic of wilderness emotions: awe. Knowing the silvertip was there, they knew they were in truly untamed country. The grizzly—with its reputation for ferocity, its intolerance of human beings, its need for great range—had rightly become a symbol of wild America.

As you enter the Park today, you will still be reminded of the bears. At the entrance, a familiar sign reads, "Bears and other large Animals are Dangerous . . . View from a Safe Distance." At the gate, the ranger will give you an information packet that includes a yellow sheet, "About Bears," warning you to "enjoy them at a distance." As you drive through or as you hike in the backcountry, you will most certainly see elk, deer, antelope, bison, mountain sheep, eagles, and ospreys. But you almost certainly will not see any bears. Last summer, I drove more than 5,000 miles in Yellowstone. During each of the past dozen years, I have spent weeks in the Park. During the past decade, I have hiked more than 1,000 miles of the Yellowstone backcountry. Yet I have not seen a bear by a road in Yellowstone since 1972. I have not seen a bear in the backcountry since 1974. Nor have I met anyone, except National Park Service employees, who claims to have seen a bear along a road in years. Larry Roop, a bear biologist for the state of Wyoming and a member of the Interagency Grizzly Bear Study Team, who flies over the Park several times a week looking for bears in areas best suited for them, has not, he tells me, seen a black bear in two years.

Where have all the bears gone?

If you ask a ranger at one of Yellowstone's visitor centers where the bears are, he will tell you the bears have gone wild: that they are there, but out of sight. The Park, he will say, has for twelve years pursued a policy of weaning bears from human food, to produce free-ranging populations of blacks and grizzlies. This program has been successful, you will be told: now all bears are truly wild, afraid of man, and living in the backcountry.

If you want to study the situation, the ranger will supply you with "fact sheets." From these you will learn that "all our information indicates that about as many black bears inhabit the park now, approximately 650, as when the park was established," and that "an estimated 350 [grizzlies] inhabit the Yellowstone ecosystem."

Unfortunately, I'm afraid, there is not a shred of truth in what you will have been told. The bears have not gone wild. They are simply gone. There never was a scientific field study that claimed there were 650 black bears in Yellowstone, and no scientific study of the black bear has been done since 1967. According to Richard Knight, director of the Interagency Grizzly Bear Study Team, a group that for nine years has been conducting all Park research on the bears, fewer than 200 grizzlies inhabit the entire Yellowstone area; of these, fewer than seventy are adults and fewer than thirty are adult females. Nineteen cubs are born a year, and grizzly-bear fertility and longevity are declining. About thirty grizzlies, he thinks, are killed each year.

These grizzlies belong to a small population that inhabits parts of Montana, Wyoming, Idaho, and Washington. Currently, not more than 600 to 1,000 live south of Canada, and numbers throughout this area are declining. Although substantial populations still exist in Canada and parts of Alaska, most experts agree that their continued survival is in doubt.

For the Yellowstone grizzly this decline has been dramatic. As late as 1967, according to the National Academy of Sciences and the U.S. Fish and Wildlife Service, grizzly-bear populations in Yellowstone were "viable and self-sustaining." Yet by 1975 the grizzly was declared a "threatened" species in the lower forty-eight states. Since 1975, its decline has, if anything, accelerated. No one today in a position to know is optimistic about its future.

The decline of the black bear, although it has drawn less attention, has been even more precipitous. In 1965, according to the only study done on black bears, there were 899 sightings of black bears in one season along the roads of Yellowstone. Yet Knight, Roop, and other researchers confirm that there are today even fewer blacks in the Park than there are grizzlies.

What has happened to the bears?

The answer, as we shall see, is freighted with paradox.

During the winter of 1961–1962, the Park Service began what was intended to be a quiet hunt. Rangers were assigned the task of systematically culling the northern Yellowstone elk herd. Unfortunately, their work was neither quiet nor systematic. Many thought that the killing was indiscriminate, and word leaked out. Many elk that were to be butchered and sent to orphanages, prisons, and reservations were left to rot. Altogether 4,283 animals were killed. The public outcry was enormous.

This official hunt was part of a longstanding Park policy to contain the numbers of the northern Yellowstone elk. To prevent overgrazing, Park officials reduced the herd by periodic hunts such as this one, and by transfers of elk to zoos and game ranges. By the winter of 1961–1962, the herd had grown to more than 10,000 on a range then believed to have a carrying capacity of 5,000. The reduction of 1962 brought their numbers down to 5,700, but word of the slaughter spread, and so did demands that it never occur again.

The secretary of the interior, Stewart Udall, established a committee to evaluate the Park Service game-management program. This committee, the Advisory Board on Wildlife Management, was chaired by A. Starker Leopold, professor of zoology at the University of California and son of the great naturalist Aldo Leopold.

Leopold saw his charge in broad terms. "We knew," he recently told me, "the world was looking at us. If we were to recommend public hunting of elk, parks in Africa would feel pressed to permit the public hunting of elephant. We decided that we would develop a philosophy of management that could be applied universally."

In March of 1963, the "Leopold Report," as it came to be known, was sent to Udall. This report's recommendations, its authors admitted, were "stupendous."

"As a primary goal," it said, "we would recommend that the biotic associations within each park be maintained, or where necessary re-created, as nearly as possible in the condition that prevailed when the area was first visited by the white man."

Managing parks as original ecosystems, it continued, required that "observable artificiality in any form must be minimized and obscured in every possible way. Wildlife should not be displayed in fenced enclosures; this is the function of a zoo, not a national park. In the same category is artificial feeding of wildlife."

By these means, the report noted, "a reasonable illusion of primitive America could be re-created, using the utmost in skill, judgment and ecological sensitivity." Unfortunately, accomplishing this goal called for "a set of ecologic skills unknown in this country today." To develop these skills, the committee urged that "a greatly expanded research program, oriented to management needs, must be developed within the National Park Service itself. Both research and the application of management methods should be in the hands of skilled park personnel."

The committee, in short, was advocating that natural ecosystems be re-created while admitting that knowledge of how to do this did not exist. And at the same time it was advocating closing the parks to scientific research and putting research under control of the Park Service.

Udall was reluctant to accept the committee's findings. The report, Leopold said, "was so potentially controversial it scared the Secretary to death. But later that spring I presented it as an address to an environmental conference in Detroit. The environmental community received it so enthusiastically that Udall changed his mind. Within three months, it was official Park Service policy."

It is not surprising that the Leopold Report was so appealing, for it presented a credo that coincided with a sentiment shared by a growing number of Americans—distrust of human intervention in the natural world. The parks, the report was saying, should no longer be managed as they were at the turn of the century—as game preserves, where hunting was permitted, good animals were protected, and bad animals were exterminated. Nor should parks be run as they were during many decades of this century—as farms, where trees were planted, forest fires fought, pastures plowed and harvested. Nor should they any longer be zoos, where animals were fed for the benefit of tourists. We must play a humbler role, it was telling us, not presuming to make judgments about what species are good and what species are bad; not presuming to decide what lives and what dies. Man must stop meddling with nature.

This was philosophy, not science. It was not science that demanded a return to natural conditions. After all, what is an ecosystem? Few biologists, when they are pinned down, will claim to know. There are different ecosystems for every species. Some, like that of the Devil's

Hole pupfish, are no bigger than an average-sized living room; others, like that of elk, encompass hundreds of miles. The range of the grizzly, for instance, is huge. The home range of the average Yellowstone male grizzly is 318 square miles, and some individuals have ranges of more than 600 square miles. Is there any park in the country big enough to be a natural ecosystem for all the species it contains? According to a report of the First World Conference on National Parks, held in Seattle in July of 1962, "few of the world's parks are large enough to be in fact self-regulatory ecological units."

What about Yellowstone? As America's first national park, protected almost from the moment the white man found it, surely it could be a model of natural, primitive America, if any place could. Yet even Yellowstone was not large enough to be "self-regulatory," and, more important, it was no longer in original condition. The white man had changed it in countless ways. He drove off the Indians. He introduced exotic species of trout, many in waters originally barren of all fish, and eliminated several subspecies of arctic grayling and cutthroat trout. He killed all the wolves. He sprayed the forests with DDT and eliminated numerous species of insectivorous birds.

He nearly eliminated the mountain bison (paring its numbers from a historic level of 1,000 to twenty-three by 1902) and then spent fifty years breeding bison like cattle—plowing under the native grasses of the Lamar Valley to plant crested wheatgrass, and feeding the buffalo hay in winter.

The white man also fed the bears. For nearly a hundred years, garbage dumps were maintained in the Park, and there the bears—both grizzlies and blacks—came to feed. The bears, natural scavengers, became the welcome, wild camp followers of the Park.

Restoring Yellowstone to its original condition would have been an impossible task. It would also have been an unpopular one. It would have entailed bringing back the wolf—and that would send shivers down the spines of local citizens. It would have entailed the elimination of many fishes and perhaps the end of fishing in the Park—and fishing groups would not stand for it. And, although this was overlooked, it would require reintroducing the Indian. Instead, the Leopold philosophy was applied selectively.

In fact, little happened until Jack Anderson, the superintendent of Grand Teton National Park, was made superintendent of Yellowstone, in 1967. Anderson was the first superintendent in Yellowstone history to have, following the suggestion of the Leopold Report, his own "supervisory research biologist" to help develop and support management policies.

With Anderson's arrival, new policies were quickly put into effect, the most controversial of which were the changes in management of elk and bear.

The Park now decided that the elk could manage itself as a wild population. Reductions would be ended for all time. Park biologists were assuming that even in the absence of the wolf—the greatest elk predator —this herd possessed some biologically determined "population-limiting factors." Over the past fifteen years, however, the elk have not exhibited such traits. The herd has grown from around 4,000 in 1968 to more than 16,000 today.

There was no threat that the bears would overpopulate the Park. But, having grown accustomed to human food, they were seen, following the report, to be unnatural. So the Park Service decided, in 1967, to wean the bears from garbage and transform them into a wild, free-ranging population. Unfortunately, weaning the bears would mean in effect killing many of them. Here, as with the elk, the biological compensatory mechanisms were supposed to help. It was hypothesized that weaning the bears from garbage would improve their diet and increase their fertility.

The major effect of the new eco-philosophy, so far as Yellowstone was concerned, was to end the killing of elk, of which there were too many, and begin the killing of bears, of which there were too few.

Lying behind the new bear policy, however, was something other than ecological concern. As our society became more environmentally enlightened, its tolerance of bears diminished. There was a "bear problem," as Yellowstone officials called it. Bears sometimes damaged property or injured people. Very infrequently, they killed, though the extent of this danger has been greatly exaggerated. In the ninety-five years of Park history preceding the new bear policy, three people had been killed by bears in the national parks (all of them, as it happened, in Yellowstone). The last death had occurred in 1942. Yet, on average, each year around a half-dozen people die in Yellowstone from every conceivable cause: drownings, falls, traffic accidents. People are also gored by buffalo and savaged by moose and occasionally die from these mishaps.

In the 1950s, approximately one out of every 24,000 visitors was injured by a bear, according to my calculations based on Park Service figures. During the first seven years of the 1960s, this rate went down 50 percent. Yet as the rate went down, concern over it went up.

The first person known to be killed by a bear in the Park was a young man, in 1907, out for a walk with his wife. He chased a grizzly cub up a tree and began poking it with an umbrella. The sow appeared and tore out the man's breastbone and one lung with a single swipe. Although considerable pressure was put on the chief ranger (or scout, as he was then called) to kill the bear, he refused to do so. The bear, he said, had the right to protect her young. That was forest justice.

By the 1960s, the Park was less willing and less able to invoke forest justice. By that time, we had become a litigious people. If, as has happened, Sequoia National Park could be sued by the family of someone who was killed by lightning there, think what a liability the bear must be. He was to Park Service lawyers what icy doorsteps are to homeowners. A bear injury often resulted in a tort claim against the Park. So when a bear hurt someone, the bear was removed, to prevent further liability. The new policy, as described by Starker Leopold and Durward Allen, both of the National Parks System Advisory Board, was to be one that "protects the people from the bears; protects the bears from the people; and protects the National Park Service from tort cases in the event of mishap." In 1968, the Park began to phase out the garbage dumps, to "bearproof" waste containers, to increase efforts to educate visitors on sanitation and the danger of bears, to remove all "nuisance" bears.

During this time, the noted naturalists John and Frank Craighead, twins, had been conducting the first scientific study of the grizzly ever undertaken in the Park. Their research—independently financed—had begun in 1959. By 1968, employing techniques of tagging and radio tracking individual bears, they had accumulated a data base that even today provides the most complete information available on grizzly population, fertility, and behavior.

But the Craigheads were to run afoul of the new policy. The Park Service, which by this time had its own biologists, felt no need to follow the advice of independent researchers. It was, in fact, anxious to close out independent research on the grizzly. Its decision to change bear policy was made against the Craigheads' advice.

The grizzly population, the Craigheads argued, was fragile, numbering not more than 175 animals. Over the past century they had become dependent on garbage as an important source of food. Maintenance of the dumps in remote locations was the most effective way to keep bears away from human beings. And, the Craigheads argued, it was not necessarily unnatural to do so. Bears naturally eat almost anything, and probably have always eaten human garbage. To the Craigheads the dumps were "ecocenters"—centralized sources of high protein where bears might go at critical times of the year to develop the fat reserves necessary to survive hibernation. The grizzly that visited the dump, they argued, was no different from the Kodiak bear in Alaska that, at certain times of the year, goes to his favorite stream to catch salmon.

So long as the dumps were in remote areas, the bears did not associate garbage with human beings and were not tempted to invade human settlements. But if the dumps were closed, the bears, deprived of a traditional food source, would be forced to wander looking for food. This would bring them into contact with human beings, endangering both people and bears.

The Craigheads suggested a controlled, gradual closing of some dumps with a simultaneous careful study to monitor the effect on the bears. During the transition period, and longer if necessary, supplemental carrion feeding in remote areas, or the continued operation of some dumps, might be used to help the bears.

"We recognize," they said, in a 1967 report to the Park Service,

the artificiality of this [maintenance of the dumps] as a management technique. However, any purposeful management of wildlife populations or their habitats can be considered "unnatural." Moreover, within Yellowstone some of the natural population regulating processes have been so altered since the establishment of the park that these are not now effective. Since there is no possibility of these being wholly restored and since management must do the job, artificiality becomes inevitable. Maintenance or reestablishment of the natural situation, although a commendable ideal to work towards in national parks, and we fully endorse this concept, does nevertheless have limitations that must be recognized.

The Park Service rejected the Craigheads' advice on the basis of objections voiced by Glen Cole, the supervisory research biologist. The Natural Sciences Advisory Committee of the National Park Service, chaired by Starker Leopold, reviewed the issue in September of 1969 and declined to recommend reversal of the new program.

The underlying issue was, how do you count bears? They are not easily found. If walking through the woods you see five bears, have you really seen five different bears? The only way to avoid duplicate counting is to do what the Craigheads (and only the Craigheads) did: capture a bear and collar it. But when do you know that you have collared them all? You never do. If you somehow managed to put collars on so many bears that after continued search you found none without collars, you might assume that you had found them all, but you could not be certain. And by the time you had reached that point you would have no way of knowing if the first bears you counted were still alive.

Where do you go to find a bear? To collar bears, the Craigheads went to the dumps. Then, by conducting backcountry censuses, on the basis of the observed ratio of dump (collared) bears to those without collars, they concluded that the bears that came to the dumps amounted to 75 percent of all Yellowstone grizzlies.

This is where the Interior Department parted company with the Craigheads. There was, it said, a much greater backcountry population. The Craigheads had, it said, fed only garbage-dump data into their computer. "If you put garbage-dump data into the computer," Cole said, "you'll get garbage-dump data out." By killing large numbers of these bears, therefore, the Park Service would not be endangering the population. It would only be making room for the backcountry population of unspoiled bears the Craigheads never found.

Unfortunately, there was no sound evidence that this backcountry population existed. The Park Service claim was based on a study of black bears conducted between 1965 and 1967 by Victor Barnes and Olin Bray, both graduate research assistants at Colorado State University. During this study, researchers observed, but did not tag, twenty-seven grizzlies in the backcountry, only one of which had a Craighead collar. On the strength of this evidence, the Park argued that dump bears were only a small percentage of the population.

The use to which the Barnes and Bray study has been put by the Park Service has produced much misinformation. This study, which was not even concerned with grizzlies, could not rule out duplicate counting. The sample was also too small to have statistical significance. Part of the black-bear study was conducted in some of the best habitat of the Park, where researchers counted an average of one bear every 5.2 square miles. Government biologists took that density figure—among the best density figures researchers could find—and applied it to the entire Park. In this way they extrapolated a black-bear population of 650—a completely unscientific conclusion that is still the basis for official estimates.

By 1971, all the dumps were closed. In the same year, the Craigheads' research permit came up for renewal. The Park agreed to renew it only if they would sign an agreement not to speak to the public or publish without first obtaining Park Service permission. The Craigheads, seeing this as an infringement of academic freedom, refused. Their twelve-year study came to an end.

As the dumps were closed, the bears began to wander. More came into campgrounds. More people were injured. In response, the Park began to kill more bears. The number of "control actions," according to a report of the National Academy of Sciences, rose from an average of thirteen a year in 1967 and earlier to 63.3 a year between 1968 and 1970. The number of grizzlies reported to have been killed by control actions rose from an average of three a year before 1967 to nine per year in 1968–1970. In all, 189 grizzlies were reported to have been killed between 1968 and 1973.

This was a period that even by official estimates was bloody, but there is good reason to believe that not all bear kills were reported. According to Harry Reynolds, a district ranger in Yellowstone during the late sixties, "Cole, with or without the approbation of Superintendent Anderson, endorsed or initiated a Park practice of not making records of all 'controlled' or otherwise deceased grizzlies." Consequently, according to Reynolds, many bear kills went unrecorded, especially those due to an accidental overdose of tranquilizer. "By this time," he said, in a letter to the National Academy of Sciences, "bears were not infrequently killed in this way by the use of drugs in inexpert hands."

Reynolds's story has been confirmed by many working with the Park at this time. Others tell of finding burial pits filled with bear carcasses in the backcountry. James June, a biologist for the state of Wyoming, has told me of finding piles of bear carcasses near Turbid Lake on two separate occasions during the late sixties, when he was doing field research on geese.

According to Ben Morris, one of the helicopter pilots who transported bears during this period, grizzlies would be hauled to the backcountry three times. "If they came back a fourth time, they were killed. But so far as I could tell, if a black bear caused trouble they just killed it. The Park VIPs felt they couldn't waste helicopter time and money hauling black bears."

Usually, Morris says, they would take a grizzly to a steep divide on the Park border that sloped out of the Park. After the bear was revived from the tranquilizer, they would chase it downhill, out of the Park. "Many of the bears," he adds, "were killed by accidental overdoses of tranquilizer." The problem, he thinks, was inexperienced Park personnel. "But the people working with the drug called it a bad batch of tranquilizer." Morris recalls a time in 1971 when three grizzlies died in two days from tranquilizers, and he suspected there were more. He remembers also another pilot accidentally dropping a grizzly, killing it.

The Park has, or makes available, little information about this period. Superintendent Anderson, according to Park archivist Tim Manns, discontinued in 1967 the long-established practice of requiring monthly reports from district rangers. To this day, the Yellowstone archives have no records on bears after 1967. Whatever materials exist, according to Manns, are said to be in the research biologists' office. When he requested them, he was told they were still in use.

The lack of data from this period reflects the Park's declining interest in science. Immediately after the Craigheads' research terminated, the Park Service began to remove the collars from bears the Craigheads had studied. This was done, it was said, in preparation for the Park's centennial. Collars were considered unsightly and every effort was being made to spruce up bears for the celebration.

With the collars gone, there was no way to settle the numbers dispute between the Park and the Craigheads; there was no way to gather fertility or longevity figures; no further information on the bears' movements and population dynamics was available.

Three years into the new era of official government biology, science was moving relentlessly in the wrong direction. Now all population statistics were kept by Cole. These consisted of reported sightings by "qualified observers." This was a system that invited double counting; thus, not surprisingly, the Park came up with numbers that, if believed, were reassuring to those concerned about the bears.

The Craigheads, meanwhile, continued to sound the alarm. The grizzly-bear dispute became a public controversy. To settle it, the Interior Department created in 1973 the Committee on the Yellowstone Grizzlies, a division of the National Academy of Sciences.

The committee's report was nearly a complete confirmation of the Craigheads' conclusions. It described Cole's population estimates as possessing "little if any meaning." It suggested that he exaggerated the number of backcountry bears, agreeing with the Craigheads that the dump bears were between 65 and 75 percent of the population. It criticized lax record-keeping by the Park Service of both control actions and injury rates. It suggested that both black-bear and grizzly kills may have been higher than reported. It suggested that "uncontrolled sources of bias" in the figures on bear-caused human injuries "make any comparison of injury rates valueless." It asserted that man-caused mortality rates of grizzlies were too high; that by 1974 they were averaging more than thirty a year, and that the population could not, over the long run, endure a man-caused mortality rate greater than ten.

Included in the committee's recommendations were these: First, "we urge the creation of a nongovernmental coordinating body . . . directed toward the well-being of Yellowstone grizzlies. It must be chaired by a respected neutral individual." Second, "the National Park Service and the U.S. Forest Service [should] pursue a policy of supporting and encouraging independent research on Yellowstone grizzlies. The freedom of scientists to conduct research throughout the Yellowstone ecosystem is imperative if the data essential to successful management of Yellowstone grizzlies are to be obtained."

These recommendations of course conflicted with the policy of government control of scientific work in the Park, as laid down in the Leopold Report, and the Park Service rejected them both. It continued to make inflated population estimates on the basis of unscientific sightings by "qualified observers." It continued to prohibit radio collaring or tagging of bears, even by its own scientists, until 1976.

Meanwhile, in place of an independent research effort, the Interior Department had created, in 1973, the Interagency Grizzly Bear Study Team, composed of personnel from the Park Service, the Forest Service, the Fish and Game departments of Montana, Idaho, and Wyoming, and the U.S. Fish and Wildlife Service, and directed by a Park Service employee, Richard Knight. This team in turn is supervised by a Grizzly Bear Steering Committee, coordinated through Interior Department offices in Washington.

In 1975, seven years into the new bear-management program, the grizzly was declared a threatened species by the Fish and Wildlife Service. The Park Service objected to the classification, seeing it rightly as official acknowledgment that its bear program had failed. But bear policy did not change.

The plight of the bears worsened. Their hunger made many of them mean, and less afraid of man. Often invading human settlements in the Park, they became the victims of control actions and removals. More wandered out of the Park, to be killed by shepherds, ranchers, hunters, and poachers. More maulings occurred outside the Park. Bears wandered into border communities such as West Yellowstone and Cooke City, attracted by garbage dumps, where they were sometimes shot.

"Grizzly bears," Roop told me recently, "are wandering farther each year. We are finding them in the northern part of the Beartooth Mountains, also near Bozeman—seventy-five air miles from the Park. These are places where grizzlies haven't been seen in a hundred years."

As more moved out, the number killed outside the Park rose dramatically. John Craighead, using Park Service estimates of man-caused mortalities (excluding deaths due to legal hunting, which ended when the grizzly was declared a threatened species in 1975), recently calculated that the number of grizzlies killed outside the Park in the decade since the closing of the dumps is two and a half times what it was during the decade prior to the closing of the dumps.

Shortly after the study team began its real research, in 1976, disturbing trends began to surface. The life expectancy of bears was dropping, possibly due to poor nutrition as well as to human predation. The average life expectancy of bears studied by the Craigheads was more than twenty-five years. But the team was finding no bears over sixteen. "Few bears," the 1980 report noted, "are reaching the older age classes."

Contrary to the sanguine assumptions of Park biologists that biological compensatory mechanisms would lead to an increase in bear fertility, the team found that fewer cubs were being born, apparently because the quality of the bears' diet had declined.

There was a growing imbalance in the sex ratio, a dangerously low number of sows relative to boars. "It is evident," the team noted, "that females are being produced and recruited into the population at a lower rate than males and that they are dying at a higher rate than males." This, Roop told me, was probably a result of control actions. Sows, protective of their cubs, were often seen as nuisance bears, and were therefore more likely to be removed from the population.

Even Leopold and Allen began to sense that things were not working out as they had hoped. In 1977, as members of the National Parks Advisory Board, they wrote, "It would appear that progress in bear management is far from satisfactory. We seem to have grossly underestimated the problem. In the past 10 years grizzlies have killed more people in the parks than in the previous century. . . . The task ahead is still enormous."

Meanwhile, as the study team and the advisory board were becoming more pessimistic, the Park Service—particularly the staff biologists (and naturalists trained by these biologists)—was displaying fresh optimism. A 1980 paper by Mary Meagher (a former pupil of Starker Leopold's who by then had succeeded Cole as supervisory research biologist at

Yellowstone) and Jerry Phillips, a Yellowstone resource-management specialist, concluded that "the bear management program within Yellowstone National Park during the 1970s had achieved the goal of restoring populations of grizzly and black bears to natural foraging conditions. Concurrently the management program reduced bear-caused injuries to humans in developed areas." Likewise, the bear fact sheet used to train naturalists in 1982 states, "The results [of Yellowstone's bear management] thus far have been encouraging—for the first time in almost a century these truly magnificent creatures are living relatively wild and undisturbed lives."

Clearly, to Park Service officials, the operation is a success even as the patient is dying. How have they managed to persist in this delusion? In part by the way they measure success. Bureaucratic boundaries serve to limit responsibility. Park policy is to protect the bear *in the Park*—and to reduce human injuries caused by bears *in the Park*. There are fewer bear mortalities and maulings in the Park because there are fewer bears in the Park. Their bear program will be a total success when they have eliminated all bears: zero bears, zero bear mortality; zero bears, zero maulings.

Over the past few months, Knight has been stating in increasingly forceful terms that the number of grizzlies has reached critically low levels. But Interior Department officials have been reluctant to accept his conclusions. From Knight's point of view, this is merely because he is "coming up with the wrong numbers."

"They want me to continue with research," he told me recently, "until I find more grizzlies. They want to do this because as long as they can say 'We don't know enough' they can postpone making any management decisions. But I can't find any more grizzlies, because there aren't any more. Between the Craigheads and me, twenty-one years of research have been done on the grizzly. We have both, independently, come up with the same figures. But people in management still won't believe them. So they want more research. But enough research has been done. Now is the time for management to make some policy decisions that will end the killing of bears."

The Grizzly Bear Steering Committee has been pressing Knight to conduct a "saturation trapping" or "grid trapping" program on the grizzly. The idea is to trap every bear so as to settle the numbers dispute once and for all. Knight refuses to do it.

"I don't want to do the trapping," he has told me. "There is no way to remove all doubt about grizzly numbers. To put traps every place in the Park they want me to I'd have to use snares—because culvert traps can't be lifted by helicopter. But snares injure bears. Besides, every time you tranquilize a bear you risk killing it with an overdose."

Other bear experts agree with Knight. "Our studies have not shown that tranquilizers hurt the bear," John Craighead told me a few months ago, "but you cannot rule it out. The fact that few bears seem to be living past fifteen years suggests that they have been severely stressed by research and transfers. I agree with Dick Knight—we knew enough about the bear to save it fifteen years ago. Now the question is: Are we going to count bears until we have counted the last one?"

Hank Fabich, a Montana game warden and a veteran of eight years of trapping bears, believes trapping is the single greatest source of man-caused bear mortality. "Every time you catch a bear," he told me recently, "in a snare or culvert trap, you risk killing it. Sometimes you overdose it. Other times the bear goes berserk and breaks a leg or tears out its claws or teeth in the cage. I have found a couple with useless limbs because they had been hobbled and released with the hobbles on. How do you think bears without teeth or claws or good legs can make it? They can't hunt well. So they go into human settlements looking for easy food. They are hungry and mean—they have a reason not to like us. Then they are killed by administrative removals because they are nuisance bears. Others are never listed as being killed by humans. They just die of starvation. I've seen bears—young bears that should have been perfectly healthy—dying in their sleep, in hibernation. Why did they die? Well, some were missing teeth, others claws. One we found with a broken foot. I love the bear and I hate to see this happening. But you can't convince me that we are not doing this to the bear."

Nevertheless, saturation trapping is still on the steering committee's agenda.

The plight of the black bear has been all but forgotten, except by those Yellowstone visitors who look for the bears in vain. But today there is renewed interest in the grizzly. Last summer, a memorandum from the steering committee, reflecting Knight's view that the number of grizzlies had fallen below critical levels, was leaked to the press. For the first time in seven years, there are renewed public demands to do something to save the bears. Government agencies and environmental groups have rediscovered the problem and are jumping on the bandwagon.

Unfortunately, the bandwagon is heading in the wrong direction. The grizzly's problems are now perceived to lie outside the Park.

Black-bear hunters in Wyoming bait bears to their blinds and sometimes kill grizzlies "by mistake." The Forest Service continues its practice of leasing land for sheep-grazing around the edges of the Park, where shepherds shoot grizzlies. People who live in border communities shoot hungry bears visiting town dumps in search of food. Poachers continue to kill bears that wander out of the Park, so long as a carcass can bring $15,000 when sold in parts. (The pancreas, for instance, is prized in the Orient as an aphrodisiac.) Grizzly habitat around the Park is being nibbled to death by geothermal development, oil and gas exploration, construction of new ski resorts and summer homes, grazing, and increased backcountry use by hikers and sportsmen.

Indeed, all this activity now threatens bears, and every effort must be made to stop it, not only to protect the grizzly but to protect other wildlife and the Park as well. But the obstacles to success in halting these killings and this loss of habitat are enormous. Betting the future of the grizzly on our ability to control human behavior in this region is not fair to the animal.

Since bears have no respect for administrative boundaries, pursuing a coherent policy means achieving agreement among the states of Idaho, Montana, and Wyoming, five national forests, two national parks, and the Fish and Wildlife Service. No one knows how decisions on the bears are to be reached, much less how a coherent change of policy might be achieved.

It is no wonder, therefore, that the architects of present policy sound despairing.

"I wish I knew what the solution was," Leopold says. "If I knew, I'd be out there, banging on doors."

"The grizzly's decline," Mary Meagher says, "is part of a long-term trend, and there is little reason to believe it will be reversed."

"It may be too late to save the grizzly," Nathaniel Reed says, though he urges a last-ditch effort to end illegal hunting. (Reed, an assistant secretary of the interior under Presidents Ford and Nixon, was instrumental in the decision to implement the new bear policy, and is now on the board of directors of the National Audubon Society.)

Although various agencies are considering piecemeal measures, no one is optimistic. The Fish and Wildlife Service continues to lobby without success for stiffer legal penalties for poachers and better sanitation in border communities. The Audubon Society is offering a $10,000 reward for information leading to the arrest and conviction of poachers. The Wilderness Society and other environmental groups are lobbying

for legislation that would protect the greater Yellowstone ecosystem—
an area about twice as large as the Park. Wyoming is considering the
prohibition of black-bear hunting in its Jackson district and of bearbait-
ing in the Cody district.

As important as efforts to reduce human predation and to protect
wildlife habitat along Park boundaries may be, these actions alone will
not save the bears. For the source of the bears' decline lies not outside
the Park but inside it. Park policy is killing the bears, because it is driving
them into human settlements. And no matter how strong the efforts to
protect the bears outside the Park, if policy remains unchanged and they
continue to wander, they will continue to be killed.

For these reasons, nearly all biologists working with Yellowstone
grizzlies believe that saving the bears will almost certainly require,
among other things, a program of supplemental feeding to re-establish
the Park as an ecocenter. This need not mean reopening the dumps. It
might entail, as first suggested by the Craigheads in the sixties, killing
a few surplus elk and leaving their remains in a central, remote area of
the Park, to encourage grizzlies to stay there and to give them the
essential protein necessary to raise their reproductive rate and to endure
hibernation.

The concern of these men is not only that past Park policy has been
mistaken; they also note that the present grizzly habitat in the Park is
deteriorating. There may simply not be enough food to keep a fragile
population from perishing. The Park is now constructing a new settlement (Grant Village) on the site of five prime grizzly fishing streams.
In a few years, Knight says, the pine bark beetle, which is already
widespread throughout the Park, will begin to infest the whitebark pine,
whose nut is the principal fall grizzly food. When that happens, he says,
the effect on the grizzly will be "devastating."

Yet supplemental feeding, although it is sometimes mentioned, is
not likely to be made policy unless there is a public outcry. To introduce
supplemental feeding is to admit that a system of official government
biology has produced fifteen years of deception; that hundreds of bears
died in vain; that a beautiful environmental ideal does not work, and
worse, is responsible for the near elimination of a species; that prominent individuals, still influential in the Park Service and the environmental movement, were dreadfully mistaken.

In 1981, the late John Townsley, then superintendent of Yellowstone, an outspoken and powerful voice in the Park Service, tried unsuc-
cessfully to introduce supplemental feeding of the grizzly. Although

both Interior Department and independent biologists with whom I have talked reacted favorably when they heard of Townsley's plan, I cannot find anyone in management or in the environmental movement in favor of it. Many, confusing the symptoms with the cause, put all the blame on what is happening outside of the Park. Many still do not accept, or do not want to accept, Knight's numbers. Some are simply timid, not wanting to be the first to favor a radical departure from existing policy. Others suggest that supplemental feeding would not keep bears in the Park a significant length of time, or they note, perhaps rightly, that it may be too late to reverse the migration. Still others argue that favoring one animal group over another—killing elk to save bears—could destabilize both populations.

Yet the most common objection to supplemental feeding raised by those to whom I have talked is a philosophical one. They do not want to interfere with nature. "If we are not going to have wild bear," Durward Allen (who serves on both the National Parks System Advisory Board and the board of directors of the National Audubon Society) told me, "we are going to have no bear at all!"

To Mary Meagher, feeding the bears is unthinkable: "We cannot play God," she told me.

To Roland Wauer, chairman of the Grizzly Bear Steering Committee, and Christopher Servheen, grizzly-bear-recovery-plan coordinator for the Fish and Wildlife Service, the prospect of supplemental feeding poses a problem of classification. "We don't want to make Yellowstone a zoo," they said.

These people, and others working within Yellowstone wildlife management, are well intentioned and dedicated to the preservation of our wilderness species. It is both paradoxical and sad, therefore, that they are, in the case of the bear, pursuing an illusion. "Not playing God," "keeping the bears wild," and not "turning Yellowstone into a zoo" are the catchphrases of a philosophy that, slowly but surely, is killing black bears and destroying the grizzly as a species. It is based on a distorted environmental logic that claims it is natural to kill a bear but not natural to feed it, that it is not hubris to re-create an ecosystem but that killing an elk is playing God.

This philosophy is tripping over its own semantic distinctions because it is based on myth, yet myth so attractive that few want to be disillusioned. The vision of the pristine wilderness and the self-regulating ecosystem still holds many environmentalists in thrall. That is why we hear so little from those who might help the bear.

The story of the bears ought to tell us that pristine wilderness is gone forever. There is no place on earth that man has not touched, not changed. The grizzly, whose intolerance of man so aptly symbolizes true wilderness, is dying because we have driven him from his home.

There are many reasons why the death of wilderness is difficult to accept. The environmental ethic rejects the Judeo-Christian view that nature was created for our use, to be subdued or consumed. But having removed man from the center of the universe, environmentalists all too often do not know where to place him. Presumably human beings, too, are part of the great web of life, but all too often the environmentalist perspective excludes them. The Leopold Report excluded them when it implied that man was not part of the primitive scene. The Park Service excludes them when it rules that human garbage is an unnatural food for bears. This philosophy generates dichotomies, in which man and nature are kept apart. The world is divided into the wild and the tame, the natural and the unnatural.

This kind of thinking has theoretically given the bears but two options: to live in a zoo or to live in a natural ecosystem. Our national parks, however, are neither zoos nor natural ecosystems. They are, as John Townsley once suggested to me, social institutions. They are laboratories where we learn how we might coexist with other creatures. Yellowstone demonstrates for the rest of the country how a community that is visited by more than 2 million people a year can remain beautiful, so nearly unchanging; how a settlement that can generate 5 million gallons of sewage a day can still have pure water; how streams that receive hundreds of thousands of fishermen a year can still be natural fisheries. It is in this way, as a model society side by side with nature, that Yellowstone serves as hope for the future. It shows that what people touch need not be made ugly by the touching, and that there is still a place where we might live in peace with other creatures. I think it would be nice, too, if, once again, the bears were included in this scene.

QUESTIONS FOR DISCUSSION

1. Examine Chase's evaluation for the CP arguments it incorporates. What claims about the nature of things, such as the state of bear populations, does it make? What evidence is offered in support and how are contradictory CPs challenged?
2. What exactly is being evaluated in this essay? A negative evaluation fre-

quently implies a course of action. What policy is therefore being suggested, though not explicitly stated?

3. This argument is particularly rich in the sources of support it draws on. Find the uses of personal experience, hearsay, scientific authority, statistical reports, and documentary evidence.

4. Chase's argument depends on a tacit (unexpressed) evaluation of bears as worth saving. How does he create a positive image of the bears at the beginning of the essay and reinforce it throughout?

5. Park officials evaluated their bear policy positively on the basis of principle (or "philosophy" as Chase calls it) while Chase evaluates it negatively on the basis of consequence. Which criterion seems to you more defensible? Can the two be reconciled?

6. The two sides in the grizzly controversy disagree fundamentally about facts, about the situation to which their policies respond. Evaluate the means of verifying the bear population. When facts, such as the number of bears, are in dispute, how do prior assumptions shape belief?

SUGGESTIONS FOR WRITING

1. Readers of Chase's essay would find it helpful to grasp clear distinctions among some key terms: natural ecosystem, game preserve, zoo or farm, laboratory for learning coexistence. All are possible models for a national park. Write an essay in which you distinguish these terms from each other for readers of Chase's argument and indicate which is the best model for Yellowstone.

2. Evaluate a park or zoo you are familiar with as a habitat for animals or a spectacle for visitors or a laboratory for the advancement of science. If your evaluation is negative, address it to the people who could correct the situation; if positive, address it to potential visitors.

3. Chase distinguishes two attitudes toward humanity's place in nature: Either the two are opposed and humans destroy nature every time they intervene, or humans are part of nature from the beginning and cannot remove their imprint. Support either view to an audience that would presume the opposite.

4. Investigate and evaluate the policy for managing some other kind of wildlife, such as wolves, fish, deer, snakes, or alligators. What seems to be the aim of the policy and how effectively is it achieved? Write your response so that readers of Chase's essay could make comparisons.

5. Write a letter to the editor of a large-circulation newspaper arguing for the evaluation of an endangered or threatened species. Your purpose will be to convince an unaware or uninterested audience to favor committing public resources to your proposal.

6. Using Chase's evidence, write a defense of the Park Service's bear policy in Yellowstone. You might argue that their policy serves the most laudable goal and that it is best for the people who use the park.

————— →»» «««← —————

Paternalistic Lies

SISSELA BOK

In her book Lying: Moral Choice in Public and Private Life *(New York: Vintage Books, 1978), the moral philosopher Sissela Bok takes on the complex question of whether lies are ever justifiable. This chapter from her book deals with one kind of deception, the paternalistic lie, told ostensibly to protect and serve the best interest of the deceived. Notice how Bok uses examples from everyday life to relate her subject to the general reader, not just the academic specialist. At the same time, she maintains an analytic approach. She does not so much preach against lying as inspect it from various points of view.*

The first inference is that even if something which has a false significance is said to an infant or insane person no blame for falsehood attaches thereto. For it seems to be permitted by the common opinion of mankind that "The unsuspecting age of childhood may be mocked." Quintilian, speaking of boys, said: "For their profit we employ many fictions." The reason is by no means far to seek; since infants and insane persons do not have liberty of judgment, it is impossible for wrong to be done to them in respect to such liberty.

—Grotius, *The Law of War and Peace*

The abuse of truth ought to be as much punishment as the introduction of falsehood.

As if there were two hells, one for sins against love, the other for those against justice!

—Blaise Pascal, *Pensées*

Tell all the Truth but tell it slant—
Success in Circuit lies
Too bright for our infirm Delight
The Truth's superb surprise

> As Lightning to the Children eased
> With explanation kind
> The Truth must dazzle gradually
> Or every man be blind—
>
> Emily Dickinson, *Poems*

PATERNALISM

Conquest, birth, and voluntary offer: by these three methods, said Hobbes, can one person become subjected to another. So long as questions are not asked—as when power is thought divinely granted or ordained by nature—the right to coerce and manipulate is taken for granted. Only when this right is challenged does the need for justification arise. It becomes necessary to ask: When *can* authority be justly exercised—over a child for instance? And the answer given by paternalism is that such authority is at the very least justified when it is exercised over persons for their own good.

To act paternalistically is to guide and even coerce people in order to protect them and serve their best interests, as a father might his children. He must keep them out of harm's way, by force if necessary. If a small child wants to play with matches or drink ammonia, parents must intervene. Similarly, those who want to ride motorcycles are forced in many states to wear helmets for their own protection. And Odysseus asked to be tied to the mast of his ship when approaching the Sirens, who were "weaving a haunting song across the sea," bidding his sailors to take more turns of the rope to muffle him should he cry or beg to be untied. Paternalistic restraints may be brief and self-imposed, as in the case of Odysseus, or of much longer duration, and much less voluntary.

Among the most thoroughgoing paternalistic proposals ever made were those of Johann Peter Frank, often called the Father of Public Health, in eighteenth-century Germany. In his six-volume *System for a Complete Medical Policing* he proposed ways to "prevent evils through wise ordinances." Laws should be passed, he argued, in every case where they might further the health of citizens. Sexual practices, marriage, and child rearing were to be regulated in the smallest detail; a law should be passed to prohibit the tight clothing women wore, if it interfered with their respiration; control of disease should be attempted in every village. Frank even suggested a law to require those who had been to a country dance to rest before leaving, lest the cool evening air give them a cold after their exertions.

The need for some paternalistic restraints is obvious. We survive only if protected from harm as children. Even as adults, we tolerate a number of regulations designed to reduce dangers such as those of infection or accidents. But it is equally obvious that the intention of guarding from harm has led, both through mistakes and through abuse, to great suffering. The "protection" can suffocate; it can also exploit.

Throughout history men, women, and children have been compelled to accept degrading work, alien religious practices, institutionalization, and even wars alleged to "free" them, all in the name of what someone has declared to be their own best interest. And deception may well have outranked force as a means of subjection: duping people to conform, to embrace ideologies and cults—never more zealously perpetrated than by those who believe that the welfare of those deceived is at issue.

PATERNALISTIC DECEPTION

Apart from guidance and persuasion, the paternalist can manipulate in two ways: through force and through deception. I have already described large-scale manipulation by governments and its appeal to paternalism; in this chapter I shall focus on deception among family members and friends. It is here that most of us encounter the hardest choices between truthfulness and lying. We may never have to worry about whether to lie in court or as experimenters or journalists; but in our families, with our friends, with those whose well-being matters most to us, lies can sometimes seem the only way not to injure or disappoint. Far from the larger professional schemes of deceit for the public good or for the advancement of science, we are here concerned with the closest bonds human beings can share.

Lies to protect these bonds carry a special sense of immediacy and appropriateness. To keep from children the knowledge that their parents' marriage may be dissolving; to keep up a false pretense of good health; to reassure those struck by misfortune that all will be well again—in such situations, falsehoods may be told so as to shore up, comfort, protect.

Children are often deceived with the fewest qualms. They, more than all others, need care, support, protection. To shield them, not only from brutal speech and frightening news, but from apprehension and pain—to soften and embellish and disguise—is as natural as to shelter them from harsh weather. Because they are more vulnerable and more impressionable than adults, they cannot always cope with what they hear. Their efforts, however rudimentary, need encouragement and concern, rather than "objective" evaluation. Unvarnished facts, thoughtlessly or maliciously conveyed, can hurt them, even warp them, render them callous in self-defense.

But even apart from shielding and encouragement, strict accuracy is simply not very high on the list of essentials in speaking with children. With the youngest ones especially, the sharing of stories and fairy tales, of invention and play can suggest, in Erik Erikson's words, at its best "some virgin chance conquered, some divine leeway shared"—leaving the conventionally "accurate" and "realistic" far behind.

A danger arises whenever those who deal with children fall into the familiar trap of confusing "truth" and "truthfulness." It may lead them to confuse fiction and jokes and all that departs from fact with lying.* And so they may lose track of what it means to respect children enough to be honest with them. To lie to children then comes to seem much like telling stories to them or like sharing their leaps between fact and fancy. Such confusion fails to recognize the fact that fiction does not *intend* to mislead, that it calls for what Coleridge called a "willing suspension of disbelief," which is precisely what is absent in ordinary deception.

Equally destructive are those dour adults who draw the opposite

---

*The confusion of fiction and deception has long antecedents. Plato stated in *The Republic* (597E) that artists and playwrights are at "three removes" from nature. Augustine and others argued, on the contrary, that what they convey, and what is conveyed in the use of symbol and ritual, is not deceptive, because it is not intended to mislead. Samuel Coleridge, in *Biographia Literaria*, chap. 14, used the "willing suspension of disbelief" to stand for the poetic faith which fiction requires of its audience. Such a suspension of disbelief is a form of *consent*.

But even though fiction and lying are in themselves quite separate, there are, of course, a number of borderline regions and areas where one invades the other. If an author really means to manipulate through his writing, as in propaganda; if the author mingles fiction and purportedly factual statements without signaling where the "suspension of disbelief" is appropriate; if the conveyor of what the audience takes to be fiction or invention is presenting what to him is straightforward history, as when a schizophrenic recently published his daily journal; if the author of a play has no intention to deceive anyone but finds that a gullible enthusiast in the audience leaps to the rescue of a victim in distress on the stage; in all these cases, the elements of fiction and deception are interwoven.

Finally, there are times where deception is clearly present, as in plagiarism and forgery.

conclusion from their confusion of fiction and deception and who try to eradicate both from the lives of their children. They fear what they take to be the unreality and falsity of fairy tales. They see lies and perversion in the stories children tell. They stifle every expression of imagination at crushing costs to their families and to themselves. Edmund Gosse, in *Father and Son*, has described such an upbringing, uncommon only in its excess. Explaining that his parents had dedicated him at birth to the ministry, and that they wanted to make him "truthful," he wrote:

> I found my greatest pleasure in the pages of books. The range of these was limited, for story-books of every description were sternly excluded. No fiction of any kind, religious or secular, was admitted into the house. [. . .]
>
> [. . .] Never, in all my early childhood, did any one address to me the affecting preamble, "Once upon a time!" I was told about missionaries, but never about pirates; I was familiar with humming-birds, but I had never heard of fairies. Jack the Giant-Killer, Rumpelstiltskin and Robin Hood were not of my acquaintance, and though I understood about wolves, Little Red Ridinghood was a stranger even by name.

Another reason for paternalistic deception stems from the very desire to *be* honest with children or those of limited understanding. In talking to them, one may hope to produce, for their own good, as adequate an idea of what is at stake as possible, so that they will be able to respond "appropriately"—neither too casually nor too intensely if it is a present danger, and without excessive worry if it is a future danger. The truth will then be bent precisely so as to convey what the speaker thinks is the right "picture"; it will compensate for the inexperience or the fears of the listener, much as raising one's voice helps in speaking to the hard of hearing and translation conveys one's meaning into another language.

Such "translation" into language the child can understand may seem very wide of the mark to bystanders, yet not be intended to deceive in the least, merely to evoke appropriate response. But it can, of course, be mixed with deception—to play down, for instance, dangers about which nothing can be done, or to create, conversely, some terror in the child to make sure he stays away from dangers he *can* do something to avoid. In this way, parents may tell a child that medicine won't taste bad, or that dressing a wound won't hurt. And they may exaggerate the troubles that befall those who don't eat the "right" foods. In each case, part of what the child learns is that grownups bend the truth when it suits them.

All these factors—the need for shielding and encouragement, the low priority on accuracy, and the desire to get meaningful information across in spite of difficulties of understanding or response—contribute to the ease with which children are deceived. Milton expressed the tolerance so commonly granted to misleading the young and the incapacitated:

> What man in his senses would deny that there are those whom we have the best grounds for considering that we ought to deceive—as boys, madmen, the sick, the intoxicated . . . ?

Following Grotius, many have taken the step of arguing that children can be deceived because they have no right to truthful information in the first place. Since children have no "liberty of judgment" with respect to what is said to them, one cannot wrong them or infringe on their liberty by lying to them.

Whatever we may conclude about the rightness of paternalistic lying at exceptional times, the argument that it is all right to lie to children and to the incompetent simply *because* they belong to these groups is clearly untenable. Someone who lied to harm a child would surely be more to blame, not less, because the victim could not fully understand the danger. Children can be wronged by lies as much as, or more than, others. And liars themselves can be as injured by lying to children as to all others. Finally, the lie to a child often turns out to affect his family as well, either because family members participate in the deceit or because they are themselves deceived. The following is an example of how the deception of a child "for his own good" corroded the existence of an entire family:

> An adolescent boy has only one kidney, as a result of having had cancer as a baby. The parents, wishing to avoid the worries that this knowledge might cause him and his siblings, told them instead the following story: that the boy, when very little, had been swinging, watched over by an eight-year-old sister. He had fallen out and hurt himself so much that the kidney had been gravely injured and had been removed. The boy now has but one desire: to play contact sports. He knows he cannot do so with only one kidney. He is angry and resentful toward his older sister, who in turn feels deeply guilty.

But not only children and those in need of care are deceived on paternalistic grounds. We may weigh the same questions with respect to adults who are close to us or for whom we have some special responsibility—as teachers sometimes deceive their students in order not to hurt them, or as colleagues flatter failing judges that their acuteness is undiminished. We may express—falsely—assurance, approval, or love, to those who seek it so as not to let them down. This is especially likely in existing relationships, where a close bond is taken for granted—at work, for example, or between friends. To keep up appearances, to respect long-standing commitments, to refrain from wounding, lies are told which disguise and protect.

Even if an open rejection does take place—as when an applicant is denied work, a request for money is turned down, an offer of marriage refused—paternalistic lies may be told to conceal the real reasons for the rejection, to retain the civility of the interaction, and to soften the blow to the self-respect of the rejected. It is easier to say that one cannot do something, or that the rules do not allow it, than that one does not want to do it; easier to say that there is no market for a writer's proposed book than that it is unreadable; or that there is no opening for the job seeker than that he lacks the necessary skills.

An interesting contemporary development illustrating lies to conceal rejection is found in the choice not to allow one family member to donate a life-saving organ to another. It is known that a kidney given by a close family member is much more likely to be successfully transplanted than a kidney from an unrelated donor. Yet sometimes there is no one in the family who has a kidney suitable for donation; at other times, a family member may express a wish to give the kidney, yet at the same time be frightened, resentful, and unwilling to do so. Renée Fox and Judith Swazey describe one case as follows:

> Susan's mother expressed her willingness to be a donor, but the medical team had reason to believe she did not really want to give Susan a kidney. The team noted, for example, that while Mrs. Thompson was being worked up she developed gastro-intestinal problems and heart palpitations. As soon as she was told that she would not be the donor for her daughter, "she changed for the better." Mrs. Thompson does not know, nor does the daughter, that she was turned down for psychological reasons . . . Mrs. Thompson was told that she could not be a donor because she was "not a good tissue match."

All such deceptive practices claim benevolence, concern for the deceived. Yet in looking at them, the discrepancy of perspectives stands out once again. We can share the desire to protect and to support that guides so many paternalistic lies; and recognize the importance of not using the truth as a weapon, even inadvertently. But from the perspective of the deceived, the power of paternalistic deception carries many dangers. Problems may go unexplored, as for the mother who was deceived about her suitability as a donor for the kidney her daughter so desperately needed. False hopes may be maintained, as for graduate students who have spent long years studying without ever being told that they could not hope to advance in their fields or even find employment. Unnecessary resentments may linger, as for the boy who was told that his sister was to blame for what an illness had caused. And eroded marriages and friendships may wear away further in the absence of an opportunity for the deceived to take stock of the situation.

One reason for the appeal of paternalistic lies is that they, unlike so much deception, are felt to be without bias and told in a disinterested wish to be helpful to fellow human beings in need. On closer examination, however, this objectivity and disinterest are often found to be spurious. The benevolent motives claimed by liars are then seen to be mixed with many others much less altruistic—the fear of confrontation which would accompany a more outspoken acknowledgment of the liar's feelings and intentions; the desire to avoid setting in motion great pressures to change, as where addiction or infidelity are no longer concealed; the urge to maintain the power that comes with duping others (never greater than when those lied to are defenseless or in need of care). These are motives of self-protection and of manipulation, of wanting to retain control over a situation and to remain a free agent. So long as the liar does not see them clearly, his judgment that his lies are altruistic and thus excused is itself biased and unreliable.

The perspective of the deceived, then, challenges the "helpfulness" of many paternalistic lies. It questions, moreover, even the benefits that are thought to accrue to the liar. The effects of deception on the liars themselves—the need to shore up lies, keep them in good repair, the anxieties relating to possible discovery, the entanglements and threats to integrity—are greatest in a close relationship where it is rare that one lie will suffice. It can be very hard to maintain the deceit when one is in close contact with those one lies to. The price of "living a lie" often turns out not even to have been worth the gains for the liars themselves.

JUSTIFICATION?

The two simplest approaches to paternalistic lying, then, have to be ruled out. It is not all right to lie to people just because they are children, or unable to judge what one says, or indeed because they belong to any category of persons at all. And the simple conviction voiced by Luther and so many others that the "helpful lie" is excused by its own altruism is much too uncritical. It allows far too many lies to go unquestioned. Both of these views fail to take into consideration the harm that comes from lying, not only to the deceived but to the liars and to the bonds they share.

Are there other ways to sort out the few justifiable paternalistic lies, if they exist, from the many abuses of paternalism? A first possibility is to take into account the frequent parallels between force and deception noted throughout this book, and to ask: Is lying for paternalistic reasons justified whenever force is?

In a crisis, to be sure, where an innocent life is threatened, and other alternatives have been exhausted, deception would certainly seem to be warranted to the extent that force is. Both might, for example, be justified in rescuing a child too frightened to leave a burning building. Carrying him out by force, or falsely saying there is no risk in running out, might both be justified. But the parallel is not complete. The very fact that paternalism so often thrives in families and in other relationships of closeness and dependence has a special effect on the choice between manipulation by force and by deception. These relationships require more trust than most others, and over a longer period of time. As a result, whereas in many crises such as that of the murderer seeking his victim, it may be as good or better to lie than to attempt force, the opposite may well be the case in family crises and wherever trust obtains.

Consider, for example, two parents trying to keep a small child from falling into a pond. They may try distraction or persuasion and resort to force if these do not succeed. But what if they choose instead to tell the child there are monsters in the pond? While such a tale might effectively avoid the danger of drowning and save the parents a certain amount of physical exertion, the strategy does not bode well for the family in the long run. (If, on the other hand, the parents were too far away, or unable to move to lift the child away, deception might be acceptable as a last resort.)

Not only does paternalistic concern for those to whom we are close not *add* a new excuse to those few we have accepted earlier, such as lies in crises, truly white lies, or lies where the deceived have given their consent. On the contrary, the very closeness of the bonds turns out to *limit* the justifiability even of lies in those narrow categories. Crises, as we have just seen, should call forth paternalistic deception only if persuasion and force are useless. And trivial lies mount up within families, among neighbors, close friends, and those who work together as they never can among more casual acquaintances. They can thus gather a momentum they would not otherwise have. For all such lies, there is the added harm to the relationship itself to be considered, and the fact that, as some of the lies come to be discovered, the liar will have to live with the resultant loss in trust at close hand.

Most problematic of all is the status of *consent* in paternalistic lying. It is rare that children, friends, or spouses will have consented in advance to being deceived for their own good. A variation of the requirement for consent is therefore sometimes brought forth: implied consent. Some day, this argument holds, those who are rightly deceived will be grateful for the restraints imposed upon them for their own good. And those who are wrongly deceived will not. This expectation of future gratitude is likened to the ordinary consent given in advance of an action in the following way: If those who are now being deceived for what is truly their own good were completely rational, sane, adult, or healthy, they would consent to what is being done for them. If they were in the liar's position, they, too, would choose to lie out of this altruistic concern.

Can "implied consent" be used as a test of all the paternalistic lies told—in crises, under more trivial circumstances, to shelter or encourage or heal? It would then close the gap between the perspectives of liar and deceived; their aims—to benefit the deceived—would coincide. The way to tell rightful paternalistic lies from all the others would then be to ask whether the deceived, if completely able to judge his own best interests, would himself want to be duped. If he becomes rational enough to judge at a later time, one could then ask whether he gives his retroactive consent to the deceit—whether he is grateful he was lied to.

Sometimes the answer to such questions is clear. If someone asks in advance to be lied to or restrained, consent can often be assumed. Odysseus asked to be tied with ropes; some patients ask their doctors not to reveal an unhappy prognosis. At other times, there has been no prior consent, but every reasonable person would want to be thwarted, even lied to, for his own good. A temporarily deranged person who asks for a knife, or the child paralyzed with fear who has to be cajoled and lured out of a burning house, will not question the integrity of those who lied to them, once their good judgment has returned.

The questions work equally well to rule out cases where no one would give genuine consent to certain forms of coercion merely labeled paternalistic. To be incarcerated in mental hospitals in order to "help" one overcome political disagreement with a regime, for instance, is a fate for which there is no implied consent; and retroactive consent to such treatment is no longer free—it is the sign of a broken spirit.

Or take the example often cited in antiquity: that it is right to bring false reports of victory to soldiers wavering in battle, so that they will be encouraged and go on to defeat their enemy. Those who tell such falsehoods may have persuaded themselves that they are doing the soldiers a favor. And once victory is achieved, the deceived soldiers who happen to survive may think so, too. But before going into combat, they would not view matters so optimistically. They have reason to ask how such a course of action is justified if one does not know the outcome of the battle—how the liar can take it upon himself to consider future consent only after the outcome of victory, and only for the survivors. While the defense of such lies is phrased in paternalistic language, stressing the pride and future consent of the deceived soldiers once they have won, and their gratitude at having gained courage to fight on through a lie, there is little genuine concern for the soldier behind such words, nor is the view of the deceived soldiers as insufficiently rational to choose for themselves a tenable one. The lie is purely strategic, told entirely to advance the aims of those guiding the hostilities.

But many times it is not so clear whether or not a rational person might at some future time give consent to having been deceived. Paternalistic lies are so often told in very private circumstances, where intricate webs of long-standing dissimulation make it hard to sort out what is a realistic alternative, whether the deceived is in fact not able to cope with the truth, what will benefit or harm, even what is a lie in the first place.

Should parents, for example, who have adopted a child, pretend to him that they are his biological parents?* Should a critically ill wife, afraid of her husband's inability to cope, lie to him about her condition? If one looks at the many lies which have been told—and lived—to conceal these matters, the consequences of telling the truth are not at

---

*The current practice is to encourage parents to be open about this fact to an adopted child.

all uniform. Most, if told the truth, might well agree that they prefer to know; but some would grieve, and wish that they had never been told. Except in very clear cases, where all would *agree* to consent or to refuse consent, relying on implied consent is very different from having actual consent. Actual consent makes false statements no longer deceptive, as in a game to which the players have consented; the same cannot be said of implied consent. Whether or not one believes that such consent will be given, one must therefore still ask whether the lie is otherwise justified. The bond between liar and deceived does not in itself justify paternalistic lies, nor does the liar's belief in his good intentions, in the inability of the deceived to act reasonably if told the truth, and in the implied consent of the deceived. In assuming such consent, all the biases afflicting the liar's perspective are present in force.

If we assume the point of view of potential dupes, it becomes important to try not to fall into any predicament where others might believe that we ought to be deceived. It is possible to discuss in advance the degree of veracity that one can tolerate in a marriage, or friendship, or working relationship and to work out the ground rules well before there is much to conceal. With paternalistic lies, just as with white lies (and these often overlap), it may be difficult to eliminate from one's life all instances of duplicity; but there is no reason not to make the effort to reduce them to the extent possible, to be on the lookout for alternatives, to let it be known that one prefers to be dealt with openly. (Needless to say, however, it is as important here as with white lies not to imagine that abandoning deception must also bring with it the giving up of discretion and sensitivity.)

Such a working out of standards can succeed among spouses, friends, co-workers. But greater difficulties arise with respect to children and the retarded, who will not soon, perhaps never, reach the point where they will be able to discuss with others how honestly they want to be treated. Present consent to deceiving them is therefore difficult to obtain; and retroactive consent in the future either impossible or so distant as to be more unreliable than ever.

The difficulty for these groups is made greater still by the fact that the recourse to public debate has often worked especially poorly in protecting their interests. Eminently "reasonable" thinkers have supported the most brutal practices of manipulation and deception of the immature, the incompetent, and the irrational. Even John Stuart Mill, who spoke so powerfully for liberty, agreed that exceptions had to be made for children, those taken care of, and those "backward states in which the race itself may be considered in its nonage." He held that:

Despotism is a legitimate mode of government in dealing with barbarians, provided the end be their improvement, and the means justified by actually affecting that end.

The appeal to "reasonable persons" never has protected the interests of those considered outsiders, inferiors, incompetent, or immature. And they themselves have no way to distinguish between benevolent and malevolent motives for lying to them; nor would history give them many grounds for confidence that the benevolent motives predominate. Rather than accepting the common view, therefore, that it is somehow more justifiable to lie to children and to those the liars regard as being *like* children, special precautions are needed in order not to exploit them.

In summary, paternalistic lies, while they are easy to understand and to sympathize with at times, also carry very special risks: risks to the liar himself from having to lie more and more in order to keep up the appearance among people he lives with or sees often, and thus from the greater likelihood of discovery and loss of credibility; risks to the relationship in which the deception takes place; and risks of exploitation of every kind for the deceived.

It is nevertheless also the case that some would in fact prefer to be deceived for paternalistic reasons. The difficulty here is in knowing who they might be. If there is some reason why one cannot ask them, much rides on what in fact is likely to befall the deceived. It may not be fair or kind to a person to tell him certain falsehoods; but then, it may not be fair or kind to tell him the corresponding truths either. The very privacy of the communication in paternalistic deception only aggravates this difficulty, as does the failure to share the predicament of those who are less than ordinarily competent.

QUESTIONS FOR DISCUSSION

1. By what criteria does Bok evaluate paternalistic lies? Does she demonstrate the consequences of lying? What is her final evaluation of paternalistic lying? Is it implied or expressed?
2. What authorities does Bok invoke to support her argument? Are there any other authorities you might have expected her to use?
3. Bok explores the effects of paternalistic lies on both the deceiver and the deceived. What rights does she assume that the deceived has? What assumptions does she make about the motives of the deceiver?

4. At whom is Bok's essay directed? Does she imply that most people condone paternalistic lies or that most people condemn them?
5. Why does Bok include the example of Johann Frank right after defining paternalism? How does it affect your attitude toward paternalism?
6. Notice the range of examples that Bok introduces throughout her essay. From what areas are they drawn? Can you think of other kinds of situations in which paternalistic lies might be told?

SUGGESTIONS FOR WRITING

1. Think of an incident in your own life when someone told you a paternalistic lie. Was it really for your own good? Looking back, are you glad you were deceived? Would you have done the same if you were in the deceiver's shoes? Address your analysis to the person who once deceived you.
2. Write an essay in which you present two scenarios, one in which a paternalistic lie seems justifiable and one in which it does not. How do the two cases differ? Imagine yourself writing for Bok or her readers.
3. Think of an instance of paternalism in some other area, one that involves persuasion or guidance rather than deception. Assess the legitimacy of paternalism in that situation, again for Bok or her readers.
4. Bok introduces many examples in her discussion of lying. Extract one from the essay and assess the justifiability of lying in that particular circumstance or one similar to it. You may either support or refute Bok's evaluation.
5. Bok points out that children are frequently the victims of paternalistic lies. Should children be treated differently from adults where truth is concerned? Write an essay, addressed to parents, arguing for or against paternalistic lies to children.

Four

ARGUMENTS THAT PROPOSE ACTION

Making the world a better place is a powerful motive for action in our society. We all have schemes for reforming ourselves, getting our work done faster, making our households run more smoothly, improving our neighborhoods, purifying city politics, advising the president what to do in the latest crisis. So strong is our presumption that conditions can be made better that we have built regular changes of leadership into many of our institutions, assuming that a new person will mean a new start and a chance for improvement. This drive for improvement is strongest whenever we sense that something is wrong, whether in ourselves or in our whole political or social system. We do not suffer abuses, either personal or institutional, with patience. Perhaps the Declaration of Independence set the tone for us: After our founding fathers catalogued abuses, they proposed a new nation.

But convincing anyone—whether a few colleagues or the public in general—to take action requires argument. Basically, we have to convince an audience of two points: First, that something is wrong and needs to be fixed, and second, that the remedy we are proposing is a practical solution to the problem. These two demands suggest the typical arrangement of a proposal argument.

Obviously, an audience must first be convinced that a problem exists before they can work up the energy and commitment to do something about it. It takes a strong impulse to overcome the stubborn inertia of human nature. But how much the arguer has to do *within the argument* to arouse this desire for action depends entirely on the situation of the audience, or rather on the arguer's best assessment of it. If on the one hand the arguer addresses an audience immersed in a problem, perhaps even defined by their awareness of that problem, then very little need be done to arouse awareness; the arguer can proceed directly to the proposal. Take the case of a speaker addressing demonstrators gathered on the steps of a state courthouse to protest the early parole of a murderer. That arguer will have to do little to remind the audience of the problem; the problem is what brought them together. Such situations are probably more common in spoken than written argument; concrete audiences always assemble for a reason, while writers have to find and unite their potential readers.

On the other hand, an audience can be totally ignorant of the nature of a problem, far from feeling any desire to change it. Here the arguer faces the hardest job of all. First, the arguer has to make the audience aware of the situation that calls for change. This requires a CP argument demonstrating the existence of a situation: The number of whales has decreased in the last ten years; the infant mortality rate is higher in the United States than in most Western European nations; the township is adding five hundred new homes within the year. With some audiences, just a demonstration that a situation exists will be enough to move them toward action; with others, more may be necessary. The ecological activists in the Greenpeace movement, for example, will be galvanized to action by statistics on the whale population, but a more general audience would want to be convinced of the *wrongness* of a situation before they could be moved to act. They would, in other words, need an *evaluation argument*, either ethical or practical, to bring them to desire action.

The preceding section contains evaluation arguments that work in just this way, by bringing their readers to the brink of wanting to take action even though that action remains unspecified. The tactics in proposals are the same as those in evaluation arguments: The arguer shows the ethical wrongness or the bad consequences of the situation to be corrected. Thus the evaluation arouses the audience into clamoring for some action, any action; in that state they are likely to be receptive to the arguer's specific proposal.

The arguments collected in this section show great variety in handling this first requirement, demonstrating that a problem exists. In "Trauma in Detroit," the opening CP section dominates entirely, using value-loaded words to push the reader toward the most natural judgment of all the statistics of economic decline and social woe. Martin Esslin's "Beyond the Wasteland," however, completely lacks an argument evaluating American commercial TV; apparently the author believed his readers came prepared with that evaluation in their minds. What they needed to initiate reform was exactly what he provided: a detailed knowledge of the history and functioning of the BBC as a positive model and a harangue to move them to action.

Similarly, both Paul Goodman and John Kemeny begin immediately with their proposal theses, seeming to dispense entirely with any preliminary arguments to warm up their readers. Each author's choice, however, may serve a different purpose: Goodman puts his thesis first for its shock value: Grades should be abolished in colleges. In the course of defending this proposal he backtracks to describe the situation it would remedy. John Kemeny also puts his thesis for universal training in computer literacy at the top of his argument, but for different reasons. This arrangement suggests his massive calm and certainty about the inevitability of the computer revolution. Perhaps he foresees no possible disagreement from his audience; at least his arrangement conveys that persuasive effect. Every argument you read in this section has a different solution to the structural problem of initiating a proposal: when to assume that the audience comes ready for action or when to assume they need stimulus to action.

Once the audience is convinced that they want something done, the proposal arguer may then urge a course of action. Here too great variety is possible, from the arguer who lets the context itself suggest a patently obvious remedy to the arguer who goes into painstaking detail on the nature and feasibility of the specific proposal.

Basically, proposals receive support from a kind of "inverse," or turnaround, of the arguments that aroused the audience's desire for some remedy in the first place. If the problem situation is ethically wrong, for example, then the proposal will be ethically in the right. Or if the problem situation led to bad consequences, then the proposal will produce good ones. A proposal must bring about this kind of reversal, this flip-flop between the good and the bad; otherwise, why recommend it? All the proposals in this section have some form of the flip-flop. Notice the strategy in Edward Morris's "One-Term Presidency": All the unfortunate consequences of the four-year repeatable presidency will be eliminated by the six-year nonrenewable term.

Even with the impetus of ethical and consequence arguments for a proposal, more may be required to move an audience to action. After all, most people resist calls upon their time, energy, and money, all the things that proposal makers are usually after. In order to overcome human inertia the proposal maker often tries to convince readers that the recommended action will be easy to accomplish. People also tend to suspect that proposals that sound too good to be true are impractical, especially if they are aimed at long-standing problems, familiar evils that people have learned to live with. For both these reasons, proposers sometimes launch into elaborate demonstrations of *feasibility,* showing how action can realistically be taken. Such demonstrations of feasibility usually involve showing how the money, time, or actors are available or attainable, or by suggesting the sequence of steps to be taken in order to obtain the desired result.

Yet sometimes a proposer cannot reassure an audience that a solution will be easy to accomplish, cost little, take next to no time, and be extremely popular with everyone affected. When this situation occurs, the arguer engages in trade-offs, showing the audience in effect that although they must make a sacrifice, they will be more than compensated by the resulting benefits or by the extremely worthwhile nature of the proposal's outcome. "Yes, it may cost something, take time, and require effort, but look at the moral gain and at all the practical, long-term profits!"

The readings in this section represent subtle accommodations to the demand for feasibility. Harley Shaiken, in "Trauma in Detroit," does not deliver any suggested courses of action until the very end of his argument, which is primarily devoted to making a technically sophisticated audience aware of the devastation wrought by recession and plant automation in the states that depended on the automobile industry. This argument appeared in a journal, *Technology Review*, reaching a widely dispersed audience in unpredictable positions of influence. If the author wants results from this audience, the best he can do is broadly suggest a few alternatives, which some of them may be in a position to implement.

But in the same journal, in a long, featured article, Robert K. Bastian and Jay Benforado write an argument that is *primarily* feasibility. They assume that the problem they are trying to solve, disposal of the ever-increasing waste generated by our urban centers, is familiar to their readers. Indeed, in just a few paragraphs they dispense with the preliminary arguments; the waste has to be treated, and it has to be treated in a way that will have minimum impact on the environment. There are a number of systems that accomplish this doubly desirable result, and the rest of their article describes them and uses one of the most powerful pleas for feasibility: "The proposal is already in effect elsewhere." Thus "Trauma in Detroit" and "Waste Treatment" represent opposite structural solutions to the demands of the proposal argument.

Proposal writers may also try to give their audiences a final push to action. In "Rest in Pieces," David Owen must overcome natural human squeamishness at the thought of death and decay. He confronts those responses head on and, incidentally, includes names and addresses to ease the reader into actually taking action on his suggestion. Martin Esslin's "Beyond the Wasteland" offers yet another unique solution to the problem of encouraging action. Esslin assumes his audience identifies the deficiencies of American television and recognizes the superiority of the British version, just as he has. His problem as a proposal maker, the impediment in the way of action, he feels, is the apathy of his audience, their willingness to live with a familiar evil. So in place of more typical feasibility arguments detailing exactly how to improve American television, he exhorts his readers on the cowardice of inaction, making general appeals for reforming zeal. With few changes, his feasibility section could be tacked onto other arguments; it is a general appeal.

As you can see from this discussion, the intended readers of a proposal and the situation in which it first appears determine much of its content and strategy. Still, we have to ask ourselves one more interesting question: Why are proposals sometimes addressed to audiences that could not take action on them? Paul Goodman's argument on grading probably did reach the academic audience that could effect changes; David Owen's is meant for the literate if unconventional reader, which *Harper's* approximately 110,000 subscribers no doubt are; and Marilyn Gardner's "Letter to a Store President" is again a public argument, sensibly appearing in a wide-circulation newspaper. But why doesn't Edward Banfield, in "Art vs. Collectibles," write only to museum directors or art dealers who have the power to change what is hanging in galleries? Why doesn't Lewis Thomas address only the academic readers who control the premedical curriculum, and why doesn't Edward Morris try to find the widest possible audience for his crusade to change the Constitution? Full-scale proposals are often directed to the apparently "wrong" audience because they have a more general purpose than the one they seem to be arguing for. Even the most optimistic writers do not make proposal arguments with the expectation that every convinced reader will go out and act immediately. Often the most that can be realistically hoped for is a nod of agreement, a slight shift in attitude, a measure of growth in awareness, an expansion of public consciousness. Such states of mind are essential preliminaries to action, but public attitudes change slowly, and often one must argue very hard to raise consciousness even a little.

————— →»» «« —————

A Proposal to Abolish Grading

PAUL GOODMAN

Culture-critic Paul Goodman (1911–1972) was a popular campus advocate during the 1960s, championing students' rights to question the power of institutions over them. The ferment of the sixties is past, yet the issue

*Goodman raises in this proposal is one that will be with us as long as there
are cumulative grade averages and entrance requirements.*
"*A Proposal to Abolish Grading*" *is extracted from Goodman's book,*
Compulsory Mis-Education and the Community of Scholars *(1966), a work
aimed primarily at people in college communities. Do the arguments
Goodman puts forward for this perennially appealing issue still have force?
Or does our decade demand a different rhetoric about education, one more
concerned with the practical consequences of a college degree?*

Let half a dozen of the prestigious Universities—Chicago, Stanford, the
Ivy League—abolish grading, and use testing only and entirely for peda-
gogic purposes as teachers see fit.

Anyone who knows the frantic temper of the present schools will
understand the transvaluation of values that would be effected by this
modest innovation. For most of the students, the competitive grade has
come to be the essence. The naïve teacher points to the beauty of the
subject and the ingenuity of the research; the shrewd student asks if he
is responsible for that on the final exam.

Let me at once dispose of an objection whose unanimity is quite
fascinating. I think that the great majority of professors agree that
grading hinders teaching and creates a bad spirit, going as far as cheating
and plagiarizing. I have before me the collection of essays, *Examining
in Harvard College,* and this is the consensus. It is uniformly asserted,
however, that the grading is inevitable; for how else will the graduate
schools, the foundations, the corporations *know* whom to accept, reward, hire? How will the talent scouts know whom to tap?

By testing the applicants, of course, according to the specific task-
requirements of the inducting institution, just as applicants for the Civil
Service or for licenses in medicine, law, and architecture are tested. Why
should Harvard professors do the testing *for* corporations and graduate-
schools?

The objection is ludicrous. Dean Whitla, of the Harvard Office of
Tests, points out that the scholastic-aptitude and achievement tests used
for *admission* to Harvard are a super-excellent index for all-around
Harvard performance, better than high-school grades or particular Harvard course-grades. Presumably, these college-entrance tests are tailored
for what Harvard and similar institutions want. By the same logic, would
not an employer do far better to apply his own job-aptitude test rather
than to rely on the vagaries of Harvard section-men. Indeed, I doubt that
many employers bother to look at such grades; they are more likely to
be interested merely in the fact of a Harvard diploma, whatever that

connotes to them. The grades have most of their weight with the graduate schools—here, as elsewhere, the system runs mainly for its own sake.

It is really necessary to remind our academics of the ancient history of Examination. In the medieval university, the whole point of the gruelling trial of the candidate was whether or not to accept him as a peer. His disputation and lecture for the Master's was just that, a master-piece to enter the guild. It was not to make comparative evaluations. It was not to weed out and select for an extra-mural licensor or employer. It was certainly not to pit one young fellow against another in an ugly competition. My philosophic impression is that the medievals thought they knew what a good job of work was and that we are competitive because we do not know. But the more status is achieved by largely irrelevant competitive evaluation, the less will we ever know.

(Of course, our American examinations never did have this purely guild orientation, just as our faculties have rarely had absolute autonomy; the examining was to satisfy Overseers, Elders, distant Regents—and they as paternal superiors have always doted on giving grades, rather than accepting peers. But I submit that this set-up itself makes it impossible for the student to *become* a master, to *have* grown up, and to commence on his own. He will always be making A or B for some overseer. And in the present atmosphere, he will always be climbing on his friend's neck.)

Perhaps the chief objectors to abolishing grading would be the students and their parents. The parents should be simply disregarded; their anxiety has done enough damage already. For the students, it seems to me that a primary duty of the university is to deprive them of their props, their dependence on extrinsic valuation and motivation, and to force them to confront the difficult enterprise itself and finally lose themselves in it.

A miserable effect of grading is to nullify the various uses of testing. Testing, for both student and teacher, is a means of structuring, and also of finding out what is blank or wrong and what has been assimilated and can be taken for granted. Review—including high-pressure review—is a means of bringing together the fragments, so that there are flashes of synoptic insight.

There are several good reasons for testing, and kinds of test. But if the aim is to discover weakness, what is the point of down-grading and punishing it, and thereby inviting the student to conceal his weakness, by faking and bulling, if not cheating? The natural conclusion of synthesis is the insight itself, not a grade for having had it. For the important purpose of placement, if one can establish in the student the belief that one is testing *not* to grade and make invidious comparisons but for his own advantage, the student should normally seek his own level, where he is challenged and yet capable, rather than trying to get by. If the student dares to accept himself as he is, a teacher's grade is a crude instrument compared with a student's self-awareness. But it is rare in our universities that students are encouraged to notice objectively their vast confusion. Unlike Socrates, our teachers rely on power-drives rather than shame and ingenuous idealism.

Many students are lazy, so teachers try to goad or threaten them by grading. In the long run this must do more harm than good. Laziness is a character-defense. It may be a way of avoiding learning, in order to protect the conceit that one is already perfect (deeper, the despair that one *never* can). It may be a way of avoiding just the risk of failing and being down-graded. Sometimes it is a way of politely saying, "I won't." But since it is the authoritarian grown-up demands that have created such attitudes in the first place, why repeat the trauma? There comes a time when we must treat people as adult, laziness and all. It is one thing courageously to fire a do-nothing out of your class; it is quite another thing to evaluate him with a lordly F.

Most important of all, it is often obvious that balking in doing the work, especially among bright young people who get to great universities, means exactly what it says: The work does not suit me, not this subject, or not at this time, or not in this school, or not in school altogether. The student might not be bookish; he might be school-tired; perhaps his development ought now to take another direction. Yet unfortunately, if such a student is intelligent and is not sure of himself, he *can* be bullied into passing, and this obscures everything. My hunch is that I am describing a common situation. What a grim waste of young life and teacherly effort! Such a student will retain nothing of what he has "passed" in. Sometimes he must get mononucleosis to tell his story and be believed.

And ironically, the converse is also probably commonly true. A student flunks and is mechanically weeded out, who is really ready and eager to learn in a scholastic setting, but he has not quite caught on. A good teacher can recognize the situation, but the computer wreaks its will.

QUESTIONS FOR DISCUSSION

1. Who is Goodman's audience? Could it be parents? students? teachers? Find the places in the text where he either identifies or excludes members of his audience.
2. Given Goodman's audience, why does he place his thesis statement at the beginning of his argument? What would be the effect of placing it elsewhere?
3. Go through Goodman's essay and indicate what parts of the full proposal argument each paragraph represents (i.e., statement of the problem, bad consequences of the problem, concessions, feasibility, etc.) How does this arrangement serve Goodman's purpose with his audience?
4. Underline all the words in the essay that you think are emotionally charged. How do these word choices shape the value judgments that serve the argument?
5. Arguments are also affected by what they leave out. Can you think of other reasons why students fail besides those mentioned by Goodman? And what about students who do very well within a grading system? If these omissions were brought to Goodman's attention, how do you think he would deal with them?

SUGGESTIONS FOR WRITING

1. Extract from Goodman's essay his assumptions about the nature and purpose of education. Support your interpretation of Goodman with references to and quotations from his essay. Explore the further implications of his position for readers of his essay.
2. Could Goodman's proposal be effected on your campus? Try writing a similar proposal argument directed at the college students, teachers, or administrators on your campus.
3. Imagine that your institution is convinced of the desirability of abolishing grades and has asked you to write an extended statement on the feasibility of bringing about such a change on your campus. Your job is to anticipate and answer objections while showing the series of practical steps to be taken to implement the "no grades" policy.
4. Rather than abolishing grading entirely, you might want to recommend replacing an existing system with a better one (e.g., number averages instead of letter grades). Write a letter to the campus newspaper introducing your proposal in order to generate grass roots support.
5. What might be the long-term consequences of abolishing grading as Goodman suggests, and letting business, government, and higher education devise their own means of testing candidates for jobs or graduate school? Write a prediction argument sketching out the possibilities. Or argue with the insti-

tutions that now choose candidates on the basis of G.P.A. that there are better ways.

6. As a participant in your own education, you have the right and responsibility to question the policies of your institution. Write a proposal argument to those in power recommending a policy change for a significant problem that affects students' lives at your school.

7. Refute Goodman's argument.

———————— 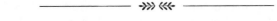 ————————

The One-Term Presidency

EDWARD A. MORRIS

Edward A. Morris, a lawyer practicing in San Francisco, has also served on the board of directors of the Robert Maynard Hutchins Center for the Study of Democratic Institutions, an organization devoted to promoting its founder's claim that "the real test of democracy is the extent to which everybody in the society is involved in effective political discussion." Morris's argument on the presidency, which follows, appeared in The Center Magazine, *published by the Hutchins Center as a nonpartisan forum for debate on legal and political issues.*

Morris's argument is not directed at constitutional lawyers or specialists on the presidency. Instead, Morris makes very broad, general appeals to include a wider audience, though he does not think it necessary to explain some things, such as how constitutional amendments actually get adopted or what the details of Mexican history are. Morris's argument has the quality of coming from a good citizen who is concerned over and has given some thought to public issues. Would his argument have a different effect if its author were a well-known politician?

Last year's Presidential election concluded two years of campaigning in which the President spent far too much time, energy, and attention trying to get re-elected. This concern for re-election has had top priority in the White House chiefly because of the Presidential primary elections, a phenomenon that in recent years has got completely out of hand. Back in 1952, only eight states had Presidential primaries. Then at the Democratic Convention in Chicago in 1968, supporters of the late Robert Kennedy were appalled to see Mayor Richard Daley and the political bosses wheeling and dealing for the delegates' votes. As a result, they adopted rule F-3-C which said that delegates henceforth must follow the will of the voters as expressed in primary elections. Then, more and more states changed their election laws. Today thirty-five states have primaries, and many that do not have primaries have caucuses and straw votes.

Another development which has caused Presidents to be especially concerned about their re-election was the state and federal election reform laws passed in the wake of Watergate. These require that campaign money be raised by small contributions from many, rather than, as in the past, by large contributions from a few. As a result, Presidential candidates must now have their campaigns in high gear months before the first primaries, in order to make impressive early showings so that financial support will come from thousands of small contributions. Candidates can thus qualify for additional funds from the federal government.

All these reforms may have resulted in a more open selection of the Presidential candidates, but apparently no one foresaw that with an increased emphasis on the primaries, the President must now devote almost all his attention for two years of his first four-year term to the winning of primaries if he hopes to be elected to a second term. Perhaps primaries and election reform laws should be retained, but they should not be allowed to cripple the American Presidency.

We should promptly amend the American Constitution, so that as soon as a President takes office, he is freed from the exhausting ordeal of the campaign trail, and is permitted to exercise greater courage and independence in the discharge of his duties. Running this nation requires a President's full time and attention. If America is to survive in the nineteen-eighties, it can no longer play "politics as usual." It can no longer require the President to spend two years crisscrossing the country, in a kind of circus-like atmosphere, surrounded by regiments of police and Secret Service men, risking assassination every time he reaches out into the crowd to touch the hands of those who came to see him.

What is it that we think a President will learn in this kind of spectacle? Will somebody in the crowd yell out, "Mr. President, did you know we have an unemployment problem in this country? Did you know we have an inflation problem in this country?" The President will not learn anything by this exercise that he could not learn by reading the newspapers in the Oval Office. This kind of situation would never be tolerated in business, or labor, or education, or in any of our major institutions. The university, union, or corporation president who spent half of his time away from his office, campaigning for his job, would be fired.

A simple amendment to the United States Constitution limiting the Presidency to a single six-year term of office would cure this problem. It has been proposed by many people in our history, starting in 1809 with Thomas Jefferson. A dozen Presidents since Jefferson have spoken in favor of it, including Jimmy Carter.

Bills calling for a single six-year term for the President have been introduced in Congress 147 times in our two-hundred-year history. These bills have been introduced by people who have seen politics firsthand. Senator J. William Fulbright drafted such a bill. Senator Everett Dirksen introduced a similar bill. The deans of both parties, Senator Mike Mansfield and Senator George Aiken, jointly sponsored one such bill. Testifying in 1971, Senator Aiken, who had served in Congress under six Presidents, said that "the six-year term will remove the President's worries over his own personal political standing, and allow him to make decisions free from the temptation of political expediency."

At one time, the single term for the President was a plank in the Democratic Party's platform. Among Republicans, President Ronald Reagan, former Presidents Richard Nixon and Gerald Ford, and Governor John Connally have all expressed support for the idea of a single six-year Presidential term.

Our nation's problems are monumental. They are not going to be solved by a President who spends half his time concentrating on winning delegates to a political convention. That may have been acceptable in a slower, gentler time, but in these turbulent days, where there is an international crisis almost every month, it is no longer tenable to have the most important leader in the Western world so engaged.

In his memoirs, President Lyndon Johnson wrote: "The old belief that a President can carry out the responsibilities of his office, and at the same time undergo the rigors of campaigning is, in my opinion, no longer valid." Johnson made that observation when Presidential campaigns were far fewer and less demanding than they are today.

A single six-year term is an idea whose time has come. Why, then, has it not become law? In recent years, when these bills were introduced, they never seemed to be able to get out of committee so that they could be fully debated on the floor of Congress. Perhaps congressmen fear that if the people start talking about the need to limit the tenure of a President, the same argument would apply to senators and representatives. In any case, these bills do not get out of committee.

What are some of the arguments against a single six-year term? One argument is that we could be stuck with a President like Jimmy Carter for six years instead of four. But Jimmy Carter's Administration might have been better if he had been free to choose his staff and to make all of his political appointments without concern as to whether or not those people would be able to help him in his bid for re-election. Also the news media would stop voicing suspicion of a President's motives every time he makes a speech or policy statement. Then, too, if there were no Presidential re-election, there would be more support for the President, and, as a result, we would see better leadership. Also, the Presidency is one of the most powerful unifying forces in the country, and a one-term Presidency would greatly augment that unifying power.

Unfortunately, the party that is out of office—the fraction less than fifty per cent of the nation—can never really get behind the President's ideas, no matter how good they are, because to do so almost guarantees his re-election. When half the nation is frequently against whatever the President is in favor of, foreign leaders wonder how firm American foreign policy can be.

Another argument against the single term is that the President would immediately become a lame duck. But when Senator Mansfield testified in favor of the single six-year term, he said that "lameness relates to the strength and quality of the person in office. If a President becomes a lame duck, it is not because of the single-term limitation; an unlimited number of terms would not sustain such a man." People who raise the lame-duck argument do not consider that putting a President into the second four-year term, in which there is no possibility for re-election, creates the same lame-duck situation. And the pathetic thing about it is that the President has to waste two years of his "good" term in order to get into the last four years, the "lame-duck" session.

Another argument concerns great Presidents. I was once asked, "Would we not lose years of the leadership of a man like Franklin D. Roosevelt if he could serve only a single six-year term?" The answer is that in January of 1939, near the end of six years in office, Franklin Roosevelt advised Congress that he had exhausted his ideas for social and economic reform. In other words, people who praise Roosevelt's New Deal are referring to just his first six years in office. Also, the

Twenty-second Amendment now limits all Presidents to eight years; but two years of the first term are now devoted, as I said, not to governing the nation but to seeking re-election. So even under our present system, we end up with only six effective Presidential years.

I am not suggesting a radical reform. Since Dwight Eisenhower, there has never been a President who has served longer than six years.

Furthermore, a great ex-President's talent need not be wasted. Since he could serve only one term, he would never be a "defeated" President. His successor might call him back to serve as a senior adviser.

Professional polls show that every year more of our citizens favor the single six-year term for the President. One poll taken a year ago showed that about thirty per cent of the American public was in favor of the six-year term for the President. If you ask someone on the street, without presenting any arguments in favor of this change, what they think about it, it is not surprising that only thirty per cent favor it. But I have found, when speaking on this subject, that when you ask for a show of hands after a speech and discussion, at least seventy per cent favor the idea.

Some countries have already adopted the single six-year term. Mexico has done so. Of course, Mexico still has the problem of having only one political party. Still, most people will agree that the single term has greatly improved the office of the Presidency in Mexico.

I am not a student of Mexican history, but if Mexico's first Constitution had limited its President to one term of six years, Mexico would be the third most prosperous country in the world today. It would still own California, New Mexico, Arizona, Texas, and all of Central America to the Panama Canal, almost all of which was sold off as its President struggled to keep himself in office for eleven Presidential terms.

Another example is Costa Rica which, in 1949, went to a single four-year term. Today that little republic has become the most prosperous country in Central America, while its neighbors are in economic chaos because of the revolutions and civil wars they have had to wage in order to get unpopular leaders out of the Presidential palace.

If the United States were to show the world that it can improve the quality of its leadership by going to a single six-year term for its Presidents, many other nations would do likewise. The world would thereby remove one of the main causes of coups and civil wars in more than eighty countries today.

QUESTIONS FOR DISCUSSION

1. How convincing is Morris's demonstration of the problem, that presidents spend two years out of their four-year terms in campaign activity? Test this generalization against a sampling of news coverage describing the activities of the last three presidents during the last two years of their terms.
2. Morris packs more than one argument into each paragraph. Examine the fourth paragraph, for example, for the complexity of its appeals. How are these carried on in the word choice? What unstated assumptions do they rely on? Identify places where you might substitute different words and get a different effect.
3. Notice the question that opens paragraph five. What objection does this question anticipate? Since this is probably not an objection that Morris would raise himself, why does he use "we" in the question?
4. How apt is the comparison between the president of the United States and the president of a university, union, or corporation? In what ways are the positions similar? In what ways are they different?
5. Find all the appeals to authority used by Morris. What is the principle of selection behind them?
6. How does Morris handle the following objection: If the one-term presidency has been suggested so often by such prestigious people, why has the proposal never succeeded?
7. Go through the essay and underline all the phrases that have a ring of familiarity to you (e.g., America can no longer play "politics as usual"). Why does Morris use language that borders on cliché? Does it help or hurt his argument?

SUGGESTIONS FOR WRITING

1. Morris uses very little evidence in demonstrating the existence of the problem he wants to reform. Can you make the case for him with evidence showing that recent presidents have been distracted by campaigning? Have they had other problems in foreign or domestic affairs because they were up for reelection? You may prefer to argue that they have not been hampered at all. Imagine yourself addressing Morris's readers.
2. Consider the differences between our system and a parliamentary system of government. Assess the advantages and disadvantages of both for an audience of average American citizens. Can you suggest a way to meld the advantages of both systems without incurring the liabilities of either?
3. Morris uses extended comparisons with the governments of Mexico and Central America. How strong are these arguments? Could you write a stronger supporting analogy? Could you refute his analogies? Try either option.

4. Morris suggests that Congress has never let his proposal out of committee because of self-interest. Can a similar case be made for limiting the terms of senators or even of representatives? Try making an argument for curtailing the re-election of members of Congress.

5. What is your explanation of why a bill that has been proposed 147 times in Congress has never passed? Write a response to Morris arguing that the bill will not pass on the 148th try or a letter to your representative in Congress seeking support for the bill.

6. Can you recommend a change in campaign rules or procedures that would alleviate the problem of a distracted, electioneering incumbent, without requiring the drastic measure Morris advocates? (For example, would it be feasible to limit campaigns to one month before an election?) Address your recommendation to those who could push for such changes.

--------------------------- →» «← ---------------------------

How to Fix the Premedical Curriculum

LEWIS THOMAS

From his stature as director of one of the foremost cancer treatment and research centers in the world, Memorial Sloan Kettering in New York, Lewis Thomas has achieved a second reputation as a science writer for the general public. He won the National Book Award for The Lives of a Cell *(1974), a collection of essays that originally appeared in the* New England Journal of Medicine.

The following argument is taken from his second collection, The Medusa and the Snail. *Using classical proposal form, Lewis asks for a sweeping fix of the premedical curriculum—by abolishing it—and proposes a radical revision of the core undergraduate curriculum in the process. Readers will have no trouble understanding what Thomas wants; their only problem will be deciding whether he really means it.*

The influence of the modern medical school on liberal-arts education in this country over the last decade has been baleful and malign, nothing less. The admission policies of the medical schools are at the root of the trouble. If something is not done quickly to change these, all the joy of going to college will have been destroyed, not just for that growing majority of undergraduate students who draw breath only to become doctors, but for everyone else, all the students, and all the faculty as well.

The medical schools used to say they wanted applicants as broadly educated as possible, and they used to mean it. The first two years of medical school were given over entirely to the basic biomedical sciences, and almost all entering students got their first close glimpse of science in those years. Three chemistry courses, physics, and some sort of biology were all that were required from the colleges. Students were encouraged by the rhetoric of medical-school catalogues to major in such nonscience disciplines as history, English, philosophy. Not many did so; almost all premedical students in recent generations have had their majors in chemistry or biology. But anyway, they were authorized to spread around in other fields if they wished.

There is still some talk in medical deans' offices about the need for general culture, but nobody really means it, and certainly the premedical students don't believe it. They concentrate on science.

They concentrate on science with a fury, and they live for grades. If there are courses in the humanities that can be taken without risk to class standing they will line up for these, but they will not get into anything tough except science. The so-called social sciences have become extremely popular as stand-ins for traditional learning.

The atmosphere of the liberal-arts college is being poisoned by premedical students. It is not the fault of the students, who do not start out as a necessarily bad lot. They behave as they do in the firm belief that if they behave any otherwise they won't get into medical school.

I have a suggestion, requiring for its implementation the following announcement from the deans of all the medical schools: henceforth, any applicant who is self-labeled as a "premed," distinguishable by his course selection from his classmates, will have his dossier placed in the third stack of three. Membership in a "premedical society" will, by itself, be grounds for rejection. Any college possessing something called a "premedical curriculum," or maintaining offices for people called "premedical advisers," will be excluded from recognition by the medical schools.

Now as to grades and class standing. There is obviously no way of ignoring these as criteria for acceptance, but it is the grades *in general* that should be weighed. And, since so much of the medical-school curriculum is, or ought to be, narrowly concerned with biomedical science, more attention should be paid to the success of students in other, nonscience disciplines before they are admitted, in order to assure the scope of intellect needed for a physician's work.

Hence, if there are to be MCAT tests, the science part ought to be made the briefest, and weigh the least. A knowledge of literature and languages ought to be the major test, and the scariest. History should be tested, with rigor.

The best thing would be to get rid of the MCATs, once and for all, and rely instead, wholly, on the judgment of the college faculties.

You could do this if there were some central, core discipline, universal within the curricula of all the colleges, which could be used for evaluating the free range of a student's mind, his tenacity and resolve, his innate capacity for the understanding of human beings, and his affection for the human condition. For this purpose, I propose that classical Greek be restored as the centerpiece of undergraduate education. The loss of Homeric and Attic Greek from American college life was one of this century's disasters. Putting it back where it once was would quickly make up for the dispiriting impact which generations of spotty Greek in translation have inflicted on modern thought. The capacity to read Homer's language closely enough to sense the terrifying poetry in some of the lines could serve as a shrewd test for the qualities of mind and character needed in a physician.

If everyone had to master Greek, the college students aspiring to medical school would be placed on the same footing as everyone else, and their identifiability as a separate group would be blurred, to everyone's advantage. Moreover, the currently depressing drift on some campuses toward special courses for prelaw students, and even prebusiness students, might be inhibited before more damage is done.

Latin should be put back as well, but not if it is handled, as it ought to be, by the secondary schools. If Horace has been absorbed prior to college, so much for Latin. But Greek is a proper discipline for the college mind.

English, history, the literature of at least two foreign languages, and philosophy should come near the top of the list, just below Classics, as basic requirements, and applicants for medical school should be told that their grades in these courses will count more than anything else.

Students should know that if they take summer work as volunteers in the local community hospital, as ward aides or laboratory assistants, this will not necessarily be held against them, but neither will it help.

Finally, the colleges should have much more of a say about who goes on to medical school. If they know, as they should, the students who are typically bright and also respected, this judgment should carry the heaviest weight for admission. If they elect to use criteria other than numerical class standing for recommending applicants, this evaluation should hold.

The first and most obvious beneficiaries of this new policy would be the college students themselves. There would no longer be, anywhere where they could be recognized as a coherent group, the "premeds," that most detestable of all cliques eating away at the heart of the college. Next to benefit would be the college faculties, once again in possession of the destiny of their own curriculum, for better or worse. And next in line, but perhaps benefiting the most of all, are the basic-science faculties of the medical schools, who would once again be facing classrooms of students who are ready to be startled and excited by a totally new and unfamiliar body of knowledge, eager to learn, unpreoccupied by the notions of relevance that are paralyzing the minds of today's first-year medical students already so surfeited by science that they want to start practicing psychiatry in the first trimester of the first year.

Society would be the ultimate beneficiary. We could look forward to a generation of doctors who have learned as much as anyone can learn, in our colleges and universities, about how human beings have always lived out their lives. Over the bedrock of knowledge about our civilization, the medical schools could then construct as solid a structure of medical science as can be built, but the bedrock would always be there, holding everything else upright.

QUESTIONS FOR DISCUSSION

1. Thomas's first proposal leads to a second, more radical one. How are these two proposals linked? Which is more challenging? Could the first be accomplished without the second?
2. Thomas's argument follows the standard proposal format, though in very condensed fashion. Find the parts of the proposal: the statement of the problem and its bad consequences (amounting to a negative evaluation), the causes of the problem, the proposal itself, the bad consequences that will be avoided if the proposal is followed, and the good consequences that will come from adopting the proposal.
3. Does Thomas's proposal have a feasibility section, a part that argues how his recommendation could actually be put into effect?
4. Why would Thomas make classical Greek the core of an undergraduate education? Could he have just as well chosen Sanskrit so long as everyone studies the same thing?
5. Thomas's books are read by people in all walks of life, but if this essay, as a serious proposal argument, has a set of ideal readers, people who could really take action on what he suggests, who would they be?

6. Is Thomas seriously proposing the changes put forward in this essay, or could he perhaps have other purposes in mind?

SUGGESTIONS FOR WRITING

1. Thomas feels that the premedical curriculum, fostered by the admissions policies of medical schools, is destroying "all the joy of going to college." Write a response to Thomas's accusation, indicating what that joy should be.
2. Why would it be an advantage, as Thomas maintains, for a would-be physician to have "general culture," a knowledge of literature, language, history, and in particular, the capacity to read classical Greek? Either support Thomas's contention or refute it by arguing that a doctor-to-be cannot know too much science.
3. Is it accurate to say, as Thomas maintains, that premed students "live for grades"? Can you find support for that CP from evidence gathered on your campus? Write a report for your campus newspaper.
4. Look at statistics on recent admissions to medical school. Is it still true, as Thomas maintains, that very few non–science majors are given the hotly contested places? Has the percentage changed at all recently? Report on your findings to the director of admissions of a medical school.
5. Read the two essays on the SAT in Part Five, Arguments and Refutations. Then find a sample of MCAT questions, perhaps in a preparation booklet in your library. What kind of knowledge is needed to score well on that test? Do you agree with Thomas that the MCAT could be abolished with no effect on the selection of the best candidates for medical school? If so, write up your argument for medical school admissions officers.
6. Support or refute Thomas's proposed alteration of the undergraduate curriculum for influential people in the university community. Could his ends so far as the medical profession is concerned be achieved by less sweeping means?

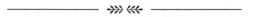

Trauma in Detroit

HARLEY SHAIKEN

When Harley Shaiken wrote this essay, he was a research associate in the Massachusetts Institute of Technology's "Program in Science, Technology, and Society," and a "specialist in the effects of technology on labor." Thus he writes with a great deal of institutional authority behind him. Furthermore, his essay appeared in Technology Review, *a journal originally addressed to MIT alumni, though now available to a wider audience. Readers of* Technology Review *tend to be technologically sophisticated people in positions of influence.*

Shaiken, writing in 1982, focuses on a problem once rampant in Detroit and offers only general suggestions for remedy. Notice that although his argument concentrates on the painful human consequences of economic dislocation, he avoids obvious emotional appeals and concentrates instead on statistical and factual evidence.

The collapse of the market for domestic automobiles has left a devastating trail of social dislocation: hundreds of thousands of autoworkers thrown out of work, dozens of plants permanently closed, communities torn apart, and economies disrupted. Detroit, once a symbol of the nation's special industrial triumph, now has come to symbolize economic depression.

Even if the automobile market improves, however, industry employment will likely stay depressed. For U.S. automakers, seeking to hold a significant market share in the face of devastating competition from overseas, are rushing to automate operations and "outsource" components—trade jargon for subcontracting from both domestic and overseas suppliers. For example, Donald E. Petersen, president of Ford Motor Co., feels that Ford may be able to meet market demand in the coming decade using 125,000 production-related workers in the United States and Canada, slightly above current employment but about 35 percent below the number employed by the company in 1978.

The industry's present economic trauma is greater than any since the Great Depression. This trauma, combined with the industry's effort to redesign its products, have resulted in a wave of plant closings and layoffs. Employment has plunged from 1,005,000 in the peak year of 1978 to only 734,000 in 1981—down 27 percent in three years.

Chrysler, which operated 57 factories in the United States and Canada in 1979, now has only 38 plants open and plans to shut down an additional 6 plants by the end of 1983. Its Huber Avenue Foundry in Detroit, a mammoth white concrete building trimmed in Chrysler blue that was completed in 1966, is now shuttered, a victim of the industry's lowered volume and reduced need for cast iron. A sign informs passersby that 1,114,000 square feet on 43.5 acres of land are for sale or lease. While the grass in front of the plant is still cut, three-foot-high weeds and abandoned homes across the street reflect the closing's impact on the city.

Ford has mothballed six plants and three distribution centers, and the fate of a number of others now hangs in the balance. Even General Motors has closed a number of plants and postponed some major investments, including a controversial new Cadillac plant in the Poletown section of Detroit.

But this is only the tip of the iceberg; suppliers have also been hard hit. Thousands of supplier industries, from mammoth steel mills to small tool-and-die shops, have been affected, and shock waves have reverberated throughout the U.S. economy. According to employment tables from the U.S. Department of Labor, for each auto worker laid off, 2.4 jobs are eliminated in the supplier networks and the community, including manufacturers of steel, tires and rubber products, and even fabrics and textiles. The Department of Transportation estimates that between 1979 and 1981, almost 100 supplier plants went down, idling over 80,000 workers. Some of these, now listed as excess capacity, may never be needed again.

ASSEMBLY LINES TO SOUP LINES

Unfortunately, the trauma has not been distributed evenly throughout the country. Some 80 percent of all motor-vehicle jobs are in five states, four of which—Illinois, Indiana, Ohio, and Michigan—now have 25 percent of the nation's unemployment. Michigan, dependent on automobiles for 55 percent of its manufacturing jobs in 1979, has experienced double-digit unemployment for over two years, with the rate still over 14 percent. And in 1980, over 250,000 people in that state exhausted all unemployment benefits. Indeed, conditions there have become so desperate that the state unemployment office has been compelled to furlough 22 percent of its 5,000-person staff since September 1981: workers assigned to find jobs for the unemployed are now themselves walking the streets.

Detroit is particularly hard hit because the troubled Chrysler Corp. is its largest employer. Chrysler's production-related employment in the area has plunged from over 50,000 in 1978 to 20,700 today, contributing to the 160,000 Detroit residents who are unemployed. One out of every three people in the city—some 400,000 individuals—now depends on some kind of public aid. The city once known for its assembly lines now has soup lines to feed the hungry. (Last year the Capuchin Fathers fed 18,000 families, compared with 6,000 in 1978.)

In Flint, Mich., its birthplace, General Motors' employment has slid to 60,000 from a 1978 peak of 78,000, propelling the unemployment rate to 23 percent, the highest for any major metropolitan area in the country. As recently as 1980, Flint's average annual pay of $18,704 was the second highest in the United States. Many of these highly paid industrial workers have found themselves without jobs virtually overnight—and with few alternatives.

FOUR CARS IMPORTED EQUAL ONE JOB LOST

The U.S. auto industry is now making major changes to reposition itself. *Business Week* reports that automakers have trimmed overhead costs by $9 billion and obtained $4 billion in wage concessions from the United Auto Workers, lowering their break-even point by 3 million cars. For example, Chrysler is now positioned to make a profit at a million fewer units than it could in 1979. Ford and General Motors are both aggressively pushing for changes in work rules that will lower labor requirements and increase flexibility.

The industry views this flexibility as critical for the efficient operation of the billions of dollars of highly automated equipment it is planning to install. Indeed, General Motors will purchase 20,000 robots in the next ten years. The company's experience is that each robot does the work of 1.7 workers in an assembly plant and 2.7 workers in a manufacturing plant, even after accounting for workers who install and maintain the robots. This means that robots alone could displace another 40,000 to 50,000 workers in the 1980s.

In another example, a Chevrolet engine assembly line scheduled to open in Flint at the end of the summer is targeted to produce 250 engines an hour with half as many workers as required in the 1970s. By 1990, computer-aided design is expected to be used in 90 percent of Ford's design and drafting work, significantly reducing the number of jobs there.

U.S. automakers are also seeking to pare costs by moving manufacturing operations overseas and buying components from suppliers instead of making them themselves. While 5 percent or so of a U.S.-built vehicle is now manufactured abroad, this could double or even triple in the next five years. Moreover, General Motors announced in June that its new mini-car will be built in Japan through its affiliate, Isuzu. The company will import upwards of 200,000 of these cars a year into the U.S. beginning in 1984. This is in addition to projected plans for Suzuki to build 100,000 G.M. mini-cars annually. Should these cars prove successful, far more could be imported.

According to Phillip Caldwell, Ford's board chairman, every four vehicles imported into the United States results in the loss of one U.S. manufacturing job. This means that G.M.'s plans in this area alone could imperil 75,000 jobs, a cost undoubtedly not included in the investment decision. Caldwell says that each foreign car sold costs the U.S. government about $2500 in unemployment benefits and lost taxes from autoworkers, manufacturers, and suppliers.

WHO PAYS?

Many analysts argue that unless the industry takes these drastic steps, even more jobs will be lost. But what happens to workers who are displaced during the industry's effort to become more competitive?

To the extent that such social costs are ignored, they will fall directly on those least able to pay—the unemployed workers and their devastated communities.

We need innovative strategies and different forms of industrial change to mitigate these social costs. This is particularly important since slow economic growth and increased automation may limit job opportunities in other sectors of the economy.

One approach might be to link the introduction of robots and other new technologies to reduced work time for employees, thus translating part of the potentially spectacular increases in productivity into more jobs rather than higher unemployment. In addition, public funds are needed to retrain and relocate workers into new jobs. Another unexplored option is governmental aid to stimulate alternative uses for idle auto industry capacity, perhaps involving new community- or worker-owned enterprises.

Legislation may be the only alternative to stem the rush of U.S. automakers to move production to lower-wage areas of the world. Such legislation would mandate that a major portion of every automobile— say 90 percent for manufacturers producing in volume—sold in the U.S. be built domestically. While this requirement could result in somewhat higher prices, it would clearly be less costly than the social disruption accompanying the erosion of the industrial base.

QUESTIONS FOR DISCUSSION

1. Shaiken aims his argument at a highly educated audience of policy planners, economists, and engineers. Imagine the same argument directed at an audience of TV viewers or at the readers of a Sunday newspaper magazine section. In what ways would the argument be livelier or more concrete?

2. Notice that Shaiken withholds his recommendations until the last few paragraphs. What is most of the argument devoted to? Why?

3. Shaiken makes a vague, general proposal and then follows it with four more specific suggestions. Why doesn't he argue for one proposal thoroughly? In what circumstances and for what audience would a specific proposal be most effective?

4. Go through the essay and underline all the statistics and specific details that support Shaiken's demonstration that a problem exists. What is the effect of using so many?

5. Notice the description of the Chrysler plant in paragraph four. What is the effect of making readers visualize the closed plant rather than merely reporting that it is closed? How does this picture symbolize Shaiken's point about the hidden human costs of the automotive recession?

6. In many ways Shaiken's argument does not have the arrangement of the typical proposal. Look especially at the opening and closing. What would be the effect of reversing them?

7. Sometimes a single word choice can have a tremendous impact on the force of an argument. Consider Shaiken's choice of the word *trauma*, both in the title and at significant points in the argument. What is the usual meaning of the word and to what is it usually applied?

SUGGESTIONS FOR WRITING

1. Write an essay for *Technology Review* readers assessing the extent to which Shaiken's characterization of the problem in Detroit is still valid now that the U.S. automotive industry is thriving again. Try to find the most recent values for the statistics he cites such as the rate of unemployment in Flint, Michigan, or the number of Japanese imports sold each year. If the situation has improved, what intervened?

2. Investigate whether any of Shaiken's proposals have been put into operation. If so, what has been their effect? If not, write a full proposal for one of his suggestions to an audience that could take action on it.

3. Shaiken predicts continued lower employment in the automobile industry because of the automation of plants with industrial robots. Explore some of the long-term social consequences of our increasing reliance on automation. See in which categories the number of jobs is increasing. Are we heading for a utopia where no one need do a dangerous or boring job, or for a society

divided into a technological elite and a substratum of service workers? Write a prediction argument for a general audience of American workers.

4. Select another industry that is facing stiff foreign competition and a declining work force (e.g., textiles, steel, electronics, small appliances). Write a proposal for alleviating its woes addressed to workers and management in that industry. Remember that extreme proposals, such as stopping all imports from another country, can have extreme repercussions.

5. Investigate the voluntary quota agreements between our government and nations that export a significant amount of goods to us. How do these agreements work and what are their consequences, good or bad? Write an essay either defending or attacking these agreements.

6. Assess the employment trends in your own community. What areas seem to have the best potential for the future? Write an essay in which you advise high school students who want to stay in the area of the most appropriate career choices.

Letter to a Store President

MARILYN GARDNER

This argument appeared as an open letter on the Living page of The Christian Science Monitor. *The Living page is devoted to consumer, home, and family issues, and the author was the editor of this section. The* Monitor *is neither sectarian nor local; it is a nationally circulated newspaper, famous for its analytical coverage of general and international news. It is read by people of every persuasion in all parts of the country. This broad audience means that the author, Marilyn Gardner, has to make very general appeals and yet, paradoxically, she chooses to write in a most personal voice and format. What she accomplishes is accessible to all of us. Her extraordinary ordinariness is a stance we could all often adopt—and maybe should.*

Many women across the country have had experiences that make them long to write a letter to the president of their favorite department store. If they did, it might go something like this:

Dear President ——————:

First the good news:
A little after noon yesterday I walked through the auto-

matic doors of your high-fashion department store. Apricot
carpeting cushioned my steps. Sleek display cases framed beautiful jewelry and leather. Expensive fragrance scented the air,
and music softened the hum of conversations and cash regis-
ters. You have created a monument to late-20th-century abundance, elegance, and sophistication—a fantasyland far removed
from the 9-to-5 routine of my working day.

Now the bad news. I arrived at the cosmetics counter and
waited. And waited. Ten minutes, according to the watch you
sold me last year. It seemed like 20, and the lone salesclerk,
casually chatting with another customer, still hadn't acknowledged my presence. What began as a simple errand—a lipstick
refill—consumed a lunch hour.

I filled the time rehearsing speeches I'd like to deliver to
you. "All I wanted was one $6 item," I would say in my calmest
voice. "Why should it be so hard to get a store to take my
money?"

I speak, Mr. President, for the ranks of working women—
time-short shoppers who must increasingly spend precious
lunch hours and evenings on routine errands. You have your
problems, too. I understand that. Faced with rising overhead
and lower profits, you and other store presidents must trim sales
staffs. But the result is one of the economic ironies of the '80s:
beautiful stores, dazzling displays, an abundance of merchandise, willing customers—and not enough clerks to serve them.
Cumulative evidence suggests that in some stores the old
motto, "Service with a smile," has been updated to read, "Service in a while."

Even the language signals a shift. Once you called us customers. Now you call us consumers—a cold, impersonal word
that seems to imply we will consume—buy—automatically,
without service.

But if the vocabulary has changed, my shopping needs have
not. There's a question of priorities here, Mr. President. Your
store designers have super-chic ideas, but do they have the
customer—I mean the consumer—in mind? They talk a good
game of "traffic pattern" and "logical adjacency," but sometimes you need a flashlight to see your "path of easy access."

Store designers refer to "darker tonalities" and "darker
light output." We consumers call it the twilight zone as we play

guessing games on how a new sport coat will look in broad daylight. If stores must be darker—for noble energy-saving reasons—good light (preferably incandescent rather than fluorescent) should still be plentiful in fitting rooms.

And speaking of fitting rooms, after trekking across all those apricot carpets and ballroom-like foyers, why must we end up

---

What Customers and Clerks Can Do . . .

AS A CUSTOMER:

I will be considerate of a clerk's time, especially during busy periods.
I will be as specific as possible about what I want.
I will keep young children in tow.
I will understand the reason for store policies. I won't expect clerks to make exceptions "just this once," or because I'm a regular customer.
I will realize that a request for identification or other information is store policy, not a personal affront.
I will discuss problems or complaints quietly with a clerk or the manager. Although the customer may not always be right, I know most stores try hard to resolve problems.
I will shop carefully, and return unwanted merchandise promptly in good condition. I realize that each return costs the store money; if merchandise is out of season or damaged, the store incurs a double loss.

AS A CLERK:

I will know enough about what I'm selling to be able to answer questions, and *care* enough to want to be of service. I know that honest enthusiasm (not to be confused with a hard-sell approach) is a powerful selling tool.
I will refrain from calling customers "dear" or "honey." Although a few customers may find the practice endearing, I realize most think it's condescending.
I will avoid telling a customer that something looks "stunning" or "gorgeous" when both of us know it doesn't. I know that quiet, honest comments win a customer's confidence and loyalty.
I will end personal telephone calls or conversations with other clerks when customers are waiting. I also understand that customers in the store take precedence over an inquirer (or a potential customer) on the phone.

—M. G.

in closets? "Room" has become a misnomer for many of these definitely unroomy spaces. One cubicle in the girls' department of an East Coast department store measures 2½ by 4 feet— manageable for a child, perhaps, but a nearly impossible squeeze when mothers need to help young daughters. Hooks (plural!), a seat, a mirror, and a shelf for handbag or briefcase should be standard equipment in every fitting room.

More on mirrors, Mr. President. When mirror-mirror-on-the-wall is hidden behind a mannequin, a giant schefflera plant, or a piece of contemporary sculpture, it's hard to tell which is the fairest garment of all. Even three-way mirrors, once common fixtures in every clothing department, are becoming an endangered species. Mirrors ought to be available where customers need them: near counters and clothing racks. (Those on ceilings and along escalators may be striking decorative elements, but they don't count.)

Then there's your little sport of keeping sizes and prices a state secret. Fumbling around for elusive size tags—checking necklines, waistlines, and seams—can discourage even the most enthusiastic shopper. Sizes should be clearly marked on every garment, preferably on a color-coded hangtag (purple for size 6, perhaps, yellow for size 8, etc.). Why should anyone have to decipher an obscure code known only to clerks and a few regular customers? Is 06214, for example, a size 4, a 14, or a 6?

Price tags discreetly tucked up in sleeves or down in necklines can be equally annoying. If the whole point of retailing is to sell, why be coy about making basic information easily available?

Also, whatever became of chairs? The bench here and there for a shopper to recoup on? Gone with the mirrors and the bright lights!

"Retailing is theater today," a Boston department store executive was quoted as saying on the eve of a lavish foreign promotion for his store. "We have to do special things to make it exciting to shop at our stores. I think you have to create the drama, the excitement, to get people to want to shop at your store versus somebody else's."

Some of us would argue that there's already enough excitement in shopping, with 86 different bed sheets to choose from when you add up all the selections of color, pattern, and fabric.

We would gladly settle for less theater and more clerks. Help, Mr. President, in every sense of the word.

I'm sure many shoppers enjoy all that marble sculpture and all those seminars every store sponsors nowadays. But I have to wonder: How many clerks' salaries do they cost?

Please consider all this in the nature of a suggestion box rather than a complaint department. There's much to like about your store, and this is merely one customer's attempt to help you and your staff make shopping the pleasure it can and should be.

Yours sincerely,

QUESTIONS FOR DISCUSSION

1. Marilyn Gardner's "letter" was never sent through the mail. It appeared in a newspaper. We call it an "open letter," and it is a tactic often resorted to. What are the advantages of this format?

2. Gardner is directly present in her argument as "I"; she uses personal experiences as evidence. And yet she claims to represent a larger constituency. What constituency is it and why that constituency?

3. Gardner seems to have a particular store in mind, and yet she does not name it. Why not? How typical is her example?

4. We can understand the advantages of Gardner's suggestions from the customer's point of view. What are the advantages for the store president who has to be moved to action? How does she present them?

5. Gardner makes many complaints and calls for several corresponding solutions. Would she have had a stronger argument if she had concentrated on one major problem, such as the lack of clerks? Or is she more likely to get one defect corrected by complaining about five?

6. To what extent does Gardner consider the feasibility of her suggestions? Would she have had to include more or less on feasibility if this letter had been addressed to someone other than a store president?

SUGGESTIONS FOR WRITING

1. Gardner quotes a Boston department store executive who claimed that "Retailing is theater today." What does the term *theater* mean in this CP? Addressing other customers, support or refute this CP from your own experience as a customer (or sales clerk).

2. If you have ever been a clerk in a store, write an open letter to your customers suggesting improvements in their behavior.
3. Write a specific version of Gardner's letter, addressed to a real store president and suggesting specific improvements in the environment of a store you patronize. Keep in mind that stores specializing in certain goods or serving a particular clientele may have special limitations.
4. Can you justify any of the practices Gardner criticizes? Is there, for instance, a reason for using size codes or for discreetly tucking price tags out of sight? Be a store president and write a letter to Gardner justifying these practices.
5. Use the open-letter format on a completely different issue. Address a well-known public figure calling for a specific reform, but plan to have your letter published in your local newspaper. Critical in this assignment will be your adoption of an appropriate persona, or "speaking" role, such as average citizen, ordinary consumer, interested spectator, avid fan.

—≫≫ ≪≪—

Rest in Pieces

DAVID OWEN

From the outrageous pun in the title to the "elbow-in-the-ribs" conclusion, David Owen gives us a most surprising proposal written in a most surprising style. The author (also represented in Part Five, Arguments and Refutations) was a regular contributor to Harper's as an investigative reporter. He is a generalist and a wry debunker who takes on topics ranging from the Educational Testing Service to management consultants to food freezing technology. He first became known for his book-length exposé, High School. *This essay will show you that serious subjects, attitudes, and resolutions can sometimes be effectively approached by unconventional means.*

My wife recently told me she intends to donate her body to science. I found the proposition ghoulish, even though it would relieve me (I intend to survive her) of the expense of disposal. I said that I was determined to have a more traditional send-off: a waterproof, silk-lined, air-conditioned casket priced in the sports car range, several acres of freshly cut flowers, a procession of aggrieved schoolchildren winding slowly through some public square, a tape-recorded compilation of my final reflections, and, local ordinances permitting, an eternal flame. But after a bit of research, I have come around to her point of view.

Two powerful human emotions—the fear of death and the love of bargains—inexorably conflict in any serious consideration of what to do with an expired loved one, all the more so if the loved one is oneself. Most people secretly believe that thinking about death is the single surest method of shortening life expectancy.

On the other hand, the appeal of the bargain intensifies when a third (though essentially unheard-of) emotion—the desire to do good for its own sake—is injected into the discussion. If, after one is entirely through with it, one's body can be put to some humane or scientific use, enabling life to be preserved or knowledge to be advanced, can one in good conscience refuse? And yet, the mortal coil recoils.

"No freezing in the winter. No scorching in the summer." Such are the advantages of booking space in an aboveground burial condominium, according to a flyer I received not long ago. Printed across the bottom of the page was this disclaimer: *"We sincerely regret if this letter should reach any home where there is illness or sorrow, as this certainly was not intended."* In other words, if this information has arrived at one of the rare moments in your life when it would actually be of immediate use, please ignore it.

That the funeral business is filled with smoothies, crooks, and con men has been well known since at least 1963, when Jessica Mitford published her classic exposé, *The American Way of Death.* Mitford's book is required reading for all mortals. Fit-A-Fut and Ko-Zee, she revealed, were the trade names of two styles of "burial footwear," the latter model described by its manufacturer as having "soft, cushioned soles and warm, luxurious slipper comfort, but true shoe smartness." The same company also sold special postmortem "pantees" and "vestees," enabling funeral directors to gouge a few extra dollars out of any family that could be dissuaded from burying a loved one in her own underwear.

Twenty years later, the death industry is unchanged in almost every particular except cost. Mitford found that the average funeral bill, according to industry figures, was $708. When I visited a local mortuary to price a simple burial for a fictitious ailing aunt, the director rattled off a list of probable charges that added up to more than $5,000, flowers and cemetery plot extra. His estimated included $110 for hauling her body two blocks to his establishment and $80 for carrying it back out to the curb. Pallbearing is a union job in New York City; family members can't lay a hand on a coffin without getting a waiver from the local. ("If they drop the casket, pal," a Teamsters spokesman told me, "you're gonna be in trouble.") Hairdresser, $35. Allowing "Auntie" (as he once referred to her) to repose in his "chapel" for one day—something he told me was mandatory, despite the fact that I said I didn't want a memorial service and that no relatives would be dropping by—would be $400. The largest single charge we discussed was for the casket. He used the word "minimum" as an adjective to describe virtually any model I expressed an interest in that cost less than $1,500. The single wooden coffin in his showroom was "very" minimum ($1,100). The whole genius of the funeral business is in making you believe you're buying a refrigerator or a sofa or even a car instead of a box that will be lowered into the ground and covered with dirt. Since there are no *real* criteria, other than price, for preferring one such box to another, you end up doing things like sticking your hands inside a few models and choosing the one with the firmest bedsprings. "Women seem to like the color coordination," my Charon said in reference to a 20-gauge steel model (I think it was called the Brittany) with a baby-blue interior. Since the women he was talking about are dead, that word "seem" is positively eerie.

Cremation is becoming a fairly popular choice among people who think of themselves as smart shoppers. The funeral industry has responded to this trend by subtly discouraging its customers from considering cremation and by making sure that cremation is very nearly as expensive as burial in a box. A pamphlet called "Considerations Concerning Cremation," published by the National Funeral Directors Association, Inc., and distributed by morticians, pretends to be evenhanded but is actually intended to horrify its readers. "Operating at an extremely high temperature [a cremation oven] reduces the body to a few pounds of bone fragments and ashes in less than two hours. . . . Most of the cremated remains are then placed in an urn or canister and carefully identified." This last sentence is the funeral director's equivalent of "Most newborn babies are then sent home with their proper mothers." Earth burial, in contrast, is "a gradual process of reduction to basic elements."

If the funeral business dislikes cremation, it positively abhors the donation of bodies to medical schools, because in such cases the opportunities for profiteering are dramatically reduced—though not, to be sure, eliminated. There is virtually nothing you can do, short of being disintegrated by Martians in the middle of the ocean, to keep a funeral director from claiming a piece of the action when you die. Once again, a pamphlet tells the story: ". . . essential to avoid the possibility of disappointment . . . more bodies available than the maximum required . . . rejection *is* permitted by state law . . . you can expect your funeral director to be of assistance. . . ."

One almost wishes one could die tomorrow, the sooner to savor the pleasure of taking one's business elsewhere.

Ernest W. April, associate professor of anatomy at Columbia University's College of Physicians & Surgeons, is the man in charge of superintending Columbia's supply of cadavers. Dr. April shares his office with Rufus, a huge red dog who wandered into his yard one day and doesn't like to be left alone. Also in Dr. April's office are some skulls, an old-fashioned radio, a human skeleton, a spine, a paperback book with a picture of a skull on it, some more skulls, a few microscopes, some big bones on a shelf, and a small plastic bone on the floor (for Rufus).

"Most medical students look forward to receiving their cadaver," Dr. April told me. "Once they have their cadaver they are, from their point of view, in medical school. It's something tangible. There's anticipation, trepidation. In the first laboratory exercise, the students basically come up and meet the cadaver, almost as if it were a patient."

As at all medical schools, Columbia's cadavers are donated. Prospective benefactors eighteen years of age and older fill out anatomical bequeathal forms and return them to the university. Hours, days, weeks, months, or years pass. "When the Time Comes," as one brochure puts it, the donor's survivors call the medical school's department of anatomy. "Within the greater metropolitan area," the brochure says, "arrangements for removal of the body can be made by the medical college. Alternatively, the family may engage a local funeral director to deliver the **unembalmed** body to the medical college at the address on the cover." Medical schools almost always require unembalmed bodies because ordinary cosmetic embalming, the kind sold at funeral homes, turns skin to the consistency of old shoes and doesn't hold off deterioration for more than a few days. Medical school embalming, on the other hand, is designed for the ages. "We've had some specimens that we've kept for over twenty years," one professor told me. "It's almost like the Egyptians."

Donated cadavers are stored in a refrigerated room until they're needed. Columbia has about 200 students in each class. The ideal student-cadaver ratio is four to one (which means "every two people get one of everything there's two of," a medical student explains). Contrary to what the funeral directors imply, Columbia, like many schools, has fewer bodies than it would like and so must assign five students to each. Ratios as high as eight to one are not unheard of. If the donor consents beforehand, a cadaver bequeathed to one institution may be transferred to another with greater need. New Jersey, for some reason, attracts almost as many cadavers as it does medical students and occasionally ships extras to New York. (That's extra cadavers, not extra medical students.) People who don't like the idea of being dissected by students at all can specify on their bequeathal forms that their bodies are to be used only for research.

"If a person donates his remains for biomedical education and research," Dr. April says, "there's a moral obligation on our part to utilize the body on this premises if at all possible, and only for that purpose. The only exception is that we occasionally do make material that has been dissected available to art students because, going back to the time of Leonardo da Vinci, Raphael, Titian, and Michelangelo, artists have had a real need to know and understand anatomy." Subscribers to public television, among others, should find this prospect irresistible: a chance to benefit science *and* the arts.

When Columbia's anatomy courses end, the cadavers are individually cremated and buried in a cemetery plot the university owns. All of this is done at the university's expense. (In comparison with funeral home rates, the cost of picking up, embalming, storing, cremating, and burying each cadaver is estimated by medical school officials at about $400.) If the family desires, the uncremated remains can be returned at the end of the course, as long as the family asks beforehand and agrees to cover any extra costs.

Nearly all medical schools operate donation programs much like Columbia's. All you have to do is call up the anatomy department at the nearest medical school and ask what the procedure is. A group called the Associated Medical Schools of New York, based at Manhattan's Bellevue Hospital, oversees donations to a dozen or so institutions around the state, including the New York College of Podiatric Medicine and the New York University School of Dentistry. You might think that a podiatry school and a dental school could happily share cadavers, but no school will take less than a whole body.

I sent away for donation information from dozens of medical schools and state anatomical boards. Studying the resulting avalanche of brochures has given me more than a week of intense reading pleasure, making me feel at times like a young girl poring over brides' magazines in hopes of discovering the perfect honeymoon. Comparison-shopping for a place to send one's corpse, like all consumer activities, quickly becomes a joy independent of its actual object. There are many factors to consider.

For example, I knew an elderly man who pledged his body to Harvard. When he died last year, his wife contacted a local funeral home to make the arrangements and was told that it would cost about $1,000 above and beyond the standard fee paid by Harvard. When the widow properly balked (all they had to do was drive the corpse fifty miles), the mortician supplied an eight-page letter justifying his charge. Among other problems, he wrote, was "the possibility that a body may be rejected by the Medical School." This conjures up unwanted images of admissions committees, and obliquely suggests that if my friend had aimed a little lower in the first place, the problem might never have arisen.

Medical schools do reserve the right not to honor pledges. All schools turn down bodies that have been severely burned, for obvious reasons. Other requirements vary. Pennsylvania rejects bodies that are "recently operated on, autopsied, decomposed, obese, emaciated, amputated, infectious, mutilated or otherwise unfit." Contagious diseases are particularly worrisome; anatomists keep a careful watch for Jakob-Creutzfeldt disease, a slow-acting virus that kills not only the occasional medical student but also cannibals who dine on the brains of their victims. All schools, as far as I can tell, accept bodies from which the eyes and thin strips of skin have been removed for transplantation. Removal of major organs, however, is almost always unacceptable, which means that organ donors (see below) generally can't also be cadaver donors. The state of Pennsylvania is more lenient in this regard. Most other schools want their cadavers intact, although the University of Kansas will accept bodies from which no more than "one extremity has been amputated."

Stanford's brochure is full of high sentence and King Jamesian resonances, the sort of prose selective colleges use to dishearten the hoi polloi. One section lists five grounds for rejection, each beginning with the phrase "The Division of Human Anatomy will not accept . . ." One thing the Division of Human Anatomy will not stand for is "the body of a person who died during major surgery," which sounds like the medical equivalent of refusing to cross a picket line. The section concludes, *"In summary, the Division of Human Anatomy reserves the right to refuse any body which is, in the opinion of the Division, unfit for its use."*

"Chances are, you have a long and healthy life to live. But a lot of other people don't. . . ." This strangely comforting thought comes from a pamphlet called "The Gift of Life," published by a Cleveland outfit called Organ Recovery, Inc. Since there's usually no way to tell whether your organs or your whole body will be more useful until When the Time Comes, the wisest course is to promise everything to everyone and leave it to the experts to sort things out later.

Organ donation has been given a lot of publicity in recent years. Drivers' licenses in most states now have tiny organ-pledge forms on the back. These forms don't have much legal meaning. At New York's Columbia Presbyterian Hospital, for instance, no one will remove an organ (or cart away a cadaver to a medical school) unless the next of kin give their consent. You could die with an organ-donor card in every pocket, and another one pasted on your forehead, and still no one would touch you if your current or separated but not divorced spouse, son or daughter twenty-one years of age or older, parent, brother or sister twenty-one years of age or older, or guardian, in that order, said no. Prince Charles carries a donor card; but if he dropped dead (God save the King) at Presbyterian, someone would have to get permission from Lady Di before removing anything. If you want to be an organ donor, carrying a card is much less important than making sure your relatives know your wishes.

No matter how thorough you are about clearing the way, however, the chances are slim that your heart, liver, kidneys, or lungs will ever be transplanted into somebody else. Only about one percent of all the people who die are potential kidney donors, for instance, and kidneys are actually removed from only one in five of these. The reason is that a suitable organ donor is that rarest of individuals, a person in marvelous health who is also, somehow, dead. Major organs for transplantation have to be removed while the donors' hearts are still beating, which means that all major-organ donors are brain-dead hospital patients on artificial respiration. The ideal donor is a young man who has played a game of basketball, run a few miles, and then had a safe dropped on his head.

John M. Kiernan, organ recovery coordinator at Columbia Presbyterian, explains that Karen Ann Quinlan is not a potential organ donor, because she is not dead. She is breathing by herself and there is activity in her brain. Every organ donor must be pronounced utterly and irretrievably deceased by two separate physicians who will not be involved in the ultimate transplantation. They are not goners; they are gone. This requirement is meant to reassure people who fear that signing organ-donor cards is the rough equivalent of putting out Mafia contracts on their own lives. I used to share these fears; now they strike me as silly.

The bookshelves in Kiernan's office hold volumes with titles like

Brain Death: A New Concept or New Criteria? Nearby are a few test tubes filled with darkish blood. Behind his door is a big blue-and-white picnic cooler that he uses to carry transplantable organs from donors to recipients. Big blue-and-white picnic coolers seem to be the industry standard for moving organs, whether across town or across the country. In a cover story on liver transplants last year, *Life* magazine published a picture of a man hoisting a cooler called a Playmate Plus into the back of a station wagon. The cooler contained a liver packed in ice.

If your major organs don't make it (because, say, you've lived a long time and faded away slowly in the comfort of your own bed), there's still hope for lesser service. Almost anyone can give skin, eyes, bone, often without hurting one's chances of getting into medical school. Small strips of skin (whose removal does not disfigure a cadaver) are used to make dressings for burn victims. These dressings help keep many people alive who might die without them. Several parts of the eye can be transplanted. There are perhaps 50,000 people now blind who would be able to see if enough of us followed the example of Henry Fonda and Arthur Godfrey and donated our corneas. Bone transplants eliminate the need for amputation in many cancer cases. The National Temporal Bone Banks Program of the Deafness Research Foundation collects tiny inner-ear bones and uses them in medical research.

None of these programs will save you burial costs the way donating your whole body will. Nor can you receive money for giving all or part of yourself away. Paying for bodies is widely held to be unseemly and is, in fact, against the law. On the other hand, physicians do not to my knowledge refuse payment for performing transplant operations. Maybe the law ought to be rewritten to include a little sweetener for the people who make the operations possible. On still another hand, the last thing Washington needs right now is a lobby for dead people, who only vote in Texas and Chicago as it is.

To find out more about these programs you can either ask your doctor or write to an organization called The Living Bank, P.O. Box 6725, Houston, Texas 77265. The Living Bank is a clearinghouse for organ and whole-body donation, coordinating anatomical gifts all over the country.

Making intelligent consumer choices usually entails trying out the merchandise. In this case, a test drive is out of the question. But since I had never so much as clapped eyes on an actual dead person before, I asked Columbia's Ernest April if he would give me a tour of his anatomy classroom. He agreed somewhat reluctantly, then led me down precisely the sort of stairway you would expect to be led down on your way to a room full of bodies. The classroom, by contrast, was cool and airy and had a high-priced view of the Hudson River. Blue walls, green floor, bright lights, a big blackboard, a lighted panel for displaying X rays, videotape monitors hanging from the ceiling, lots of enormous sinks for washing up.

Also, of course, the bodies. There seemed to be about thirty of them, each one lying on a metal table and covered with a bright yellow plastic sheet. The only noticeable odor in the room was the odor of new plastic, familiar to anyone who has smelled a beach ball. Since the course was drawing to an end, the shapes beneath the sheets were disconcertingly smaller than expected: as dissection progresses, students tag the parts they're finished with and store them elsewhere. To demonstrate, Dr. April pulled back the yellow sheet on the table nearest us, causing a momentary cessation of my heartbeat and revealing the top of a skull, a set of dentures, a long striated purplish thing, some other things, I'm not sure what else. But no arm, the object of his search. Far across the room, a few students were huddled over a dark form that suggested nothing so much as the week after Thanksgiving. My initial queasiness subsided and, with a sort of overcompensating enthusiasm, I asked if I could bound across the room for a closer look. Dr. April gently persuaded me to stay put. "This is late in the course," he said softly. "It's not particularly pleasant."

Unpleasant, yes; but is it disgusting or unbearable? Many people say they can't stand the thought of being dissected; much better, they say, to be fussed over by a funeral director and eased into a concrete vault, there to slumber intact until awakened by choirs of angels. But death is death, and every body, whether lying on a dissection table, baking in a crematorium, or "reposing" in a $10,000 casket, undergoes a transformation that doesn't lend itself to happy contemplation. In terms of sheer physical preservation, a medical school cadaver is vastly more enduring than the recipient of even the costliest ministrations of a funeral director. No casket ever prevented anyone from following the road that Robert Graves described in *Goodbye to All That:* "The colour of the faces changed from white to yellow-grey, to red, to purple, to green, to black, to slimy." The transformation takes hours, days.

Morticians sew corpses' lips together, bringing the needle out through a nostril. Lips are pinned to gums. Eyes are covered with plastic patches, then cemented shut. Orifices are plugged. To prevent loved ones from belching, howling, or worse as the accumulating gases of deterioration escape through any and all available exits, funeral home employees press hard on the abdomen immediately before and after family "viewings." Makeup is slathered on. Abdomens are drained. Leaks are patched. Unsightly lumps and bulges are trimmed away.

The trouble with death is that *all* the alternatives are bleak. It isn't really *dissection* that appalls; it's mortality. It may be gross to be dissected, but it's no less gross to be burned or buried. There just isn't anything you can do to make being dead seem pleasant and appealing. And barring some great medical breakthrough involving interferon, every single one of us is going to die. We should all swallow hard and face the facts and do what's best for the people who will follow us.

Which is why you would think that doctors, who spend their entire lives swallowing hard and facing facts, would be the eagerest anatomical donors of all. But they are not. Of all the people I interviewed for this article—including several heads of anatomical donation programs, a number of medical students, physicians, even the chief medical examiner of New York—only *one* of them, Ernest W. April, had pledged any part of his body to scientific study or transplantation. And April is a Ph.D., not an M.D. "I don't know of any medical student who is going to give his body," a medical student told me.

Do doctors know something? Does it, maybe, *hurt?* Of course not. Every profession lives in secret horror of its own methods. Most reporters I know can't stand the idea of being interviewed. But society would crumble if we weren't occasionally better than those who believe themselves to be our betters.

Morbid humor at their expense is one thing future cadavers worry about. Medical schools are aware of this and take great pains to keep jokes to a minimum. Still, a certain amount of horsing around is inevitable. Michael Meyers, the man who played Ali McGraw's brother in *Goodbye, Columbus* and went on to become a physician, described some dissection hijinks in a book called *Goodbye Columbus, Hello Medicine.* "By the second week of gross anatomy," Meyers wrote, "it was interesting to notice which members of the class really rolled up their sleeves and dug in (no pun intended—although one group of students did nickname their cadaver 'Ernest,' so they could always say that they were 'digging in Ernest') . . ." and so on and so on. This is a level of comedy that I do not, to be perfectly frank, find intimidating. And a cadaver donor who wanted to have the last laugh could arrange to have an obscene or hilarious message ("Socialized Medicine"?) tattooed across his chest. Beat them to the punchline. Humorous tattoos don't seem to be grounds for rejection, even at Stanford.

As for dissection itself, it's about what you would expect. "You work through the text," says a young woman just beginning her residency, "and by Halloween you've gotten to the hands. Well, we had a girl in our group who wanted to be a surgeon, and she did the most amazing thing. She dissected off the skin *in one piece*. It was like a glove. It was beautiful. And then there was mine. It looked like someone had been cracking walnuts. Little flecks, you know? And then this graduate student comes up and says, 'Have you found the recurrent branch of the medial nerve?' And I start looking through my pile . . ."

A first dissection, like a sexual initiation, is likely to be a botched job: long on theory and good intentions, short on practical knowhow. Results improve with practice, but early impressions linger. No wonder medical students don't like the idea of being dissected. For many of them, anatomy class is their first real experience of death. Maybe it's a good thing if physicians develop, right from the beginning, an overpowering abhorrence of cadavers. We are all better served if our physicians devote their energies to keeping us from turning into the things they hated to dissect in medical school. Anatomy classes, in a sense, trick grade-grubbing premeds into developing something like a reverence for human life.

Donating one's body is an act of courage, but it's not a martyrdom. Medical students may not immediately comprehend the magnitude of the gift, but so what? I confess I sort of like the idea of one day inhabiting the nightmares of some as yet (I hope) unborn medical student. And if my contribution means that my neighborhood mortician will go to bed hungry, shuffling off to his drafty garret in the Fit-A-Fut coffin shoes I decided not to buy, then so much the better. Dying well is the best revenge.

QUESTIONS FOR DISCUSSION

1. Did you find yourself laughing while reading about death and dismemberment? Why do you think Owen included so much humor?
2. Usually proposals tell other people what they should do. Owen begins this essay by telling readers what he is going to do. What is the reason for this

strategy? At what point do you realize that he is also encouraging his readers to do the same? (Does he ever use the pronoun *you?*)

3. Why does Owen spend so much time at the beginning of this essay debunking the funeral industry, even though he acknowledges that many readers are familiar with Jessica Mitford's book on the subject?

4. Most proposal arguments show the benefits of what they recommend to their audiences. It is also possible to argue that an audience should do something regardless of consequences simply because it is good or right. To what extent does Owen use both types of appeal on his readers?

5. What potential objections to his proposal does Owen raise and refute? Does he counter any objection that you would not have thought of on your own?

6. Why does Owen insist on describing the dissection room and the state of the cadavers "late in the course"? What is the intended effect of following this with a description of what funeral directors do to corpses?

7. Notice that Owen tells his readers how one goes about donating a body or organ. Why does he go into such precise detail (including addresses)?

8. What attitude toward death would Owen finally have his readers adopt?

SUGGESTIONS FOR WRITING

1. Owen mocks the notion of buying luxuries for the dead. Are funerals for the dead? What arguments can be made justifying the traditional rites of burial? Is there any society without burial ceremonies? Write an essay addressed to Owen and his readers defending the conventional funeral ritual.

2. Were you convinced by Owen's argument? If not, explain why. If yes, defend your personal decision to an audience of skeptics, perhaps an audience of family members.

3. Try making Owen's argument without humor. Or try making it with a direct appeal to "you the reader" throughout. Would you have to drop some of Owen's arguments or add new ones?

4. Owen makes a high-minded appeal to "do what's best for the people who will follow us." Choosing a different subject, can you make a similar ethical argument for an action against self-interest (e.g., for adopting the "unadoptable," for keeping aged parents in the home, for giving up career advancement in favor of family security)?

5. Try writing an argument whose sole purpose is to get people to change their attitudes about something—from horror to objectivity, from distaste to acceptance, or the reverse.

-->>> <<<--

Art Versus Collectibles:
Let Them See Fakes

EDWARD C. BANFIELD

Edward C. Banfield is not part of the "art world." He is George D. Markham Professor of Government at Harvard and the author of several books, among them The Democratic Muse: Visual Arts and the Public Interest *(1984), from which the following selection is taken, although it first appeared as an independent essay in* Harper's. *Banfield writes as an outsider, standing above the economic, political, and institutional interests of the art community. From that vantage point, he can make a revolutionary proposal on behalf of the public. Whether you are convinced by Banfield's proposal or you remain resistant to it, his argument will make you rethink aspects of the arts usually taken for granted.*

Throughout his long public career Nelson Rockefeller was a leading—some might say *the* leading—art advocate. As much as anyone, perhaps, he promoted measures to bring art to the people at the taxpayers' expense. At the end of his life he launched another venture to bring art to the people. This one, however, was to be supported not by the taxpayer but by people who would pay for what they got. Rockefeller invested $3.5 million in an enterprise to sell reproductions of art works from his private collection. To begin with there were ninety-six reproductions for sale at prices from $65 to $7,500. For $850, for example, one could buy by mail a top-quality photographic copy of Picasso's painting "Girl With Mandolin," a work for which Rockefeller had been offered $2 million.

One might think that the art world, or at least the art advocates with whom Rockefeller had labored so long, would have cheered him on and sung his praises even louder than before. Important works of art are accessible only to people who live in or near about a dozen of the largest cities, and then usually only if they join the throngs in the galleries of the major museums. To be sure, there are several hundred small museums, but few possess masterpieces and some have nothing that can compare to any one item in Rockefeller's private collection. Of more than a hundred college art museums, only a dozen have notable works in any number; even in the best university art departments, teaching is done mainly from slides. Except here and there in the big cities, public buildings contain no art of importance. In schools and libraries across the country there is bad art or none. Except for the wealthy, ownership of important originals is out of the question. Rockefeller could have donated "Girl With Mandolin" to, at most, one museum in one city. Instead, he made it potentially accessible to almost any public institution, and even to many private citizens.

This, however, is very far from the view that the art world took of Rockefeller's last enterprise. The man who all his life had endeavored to bring art to the public was showered with abuse because of it. "We have entered a new era of hype and shamelessness . . . ," declared Hilton Kramer, the chief art critic of *The New York Times*. Other notables of the art world added their words of vilification.

What so outraged the art world was that Rockefeller had challenged the widespread opinion—one on which much of the art world depends for its bread and butter—that a reproduction cannot possibly have the aesthetic value of an original. Reproductions are sold by the millions every year, of course. Art museums, in particular, sell as many as they can. But the size and quality of most copies assures that no one can possibly find in them anything approaching the aesthetic rewards of seeing the original. Three things made Rockefeller's copying business objectionable to the art world. First was the taint of commerce. This project was self-sustaining and even profitable, rather than an act of charity or government. Second, Rockefeller offered reproductions of much higher quality than usual. Third were Rockefeller's name and standing as a collector. If anyone could cause the public to doubt that only an original could be art, it was he. Rockefeller, Kramer wrote, certainly knew the "unbridgeable difference" between a work of art and a reproduction, but "apparently the temptation to cash in on the market for *haut schlock* has proved irresistible." Kramer could hardly have supposed that Rockefeller, generous and high-minded all his life, had suddenly turned unprincipled. More likely, what so upset Kramer was that Rockefeller had turned traitor to the art world.

The position of the art world is that only bad reproductions are good. "The truth is," Kramer explained, "that these [Rockefeller's] reproductions have nothing to do with the experience afforded by a genuine work of art. As an educational tool, reproductions serve as aids to memory. At best they are mementos of experience rather than the thing itself." *Time* magazine's critic, Robert Hughes, took the same line. After making the point about memory aids (he specified *cheap* reproductions as "indispensable" for this), he went on to say that "even the most perfect replication" is "intrinsically dead, like a stuffed trout." Ruth Berenson, writing in the *National Review*, incautiously remarked that often "there is no way even an expert can distinguish *ersatz* from *echt,*" but nevertheless dismissed Rockefeller's reproductions as "high-class fakes."

In a press release about the Rockefeller Collection, the Art Dealers Association of America asserted: "Although a reproduction is and can only be no more than an imitation of the original, replicas have an undisputed educational value as inexpensive reminders of important works of art. Photographs or other copies of paintings, sculpture or antiquities also have some decorative value, as with a poster which reproduces an important painting." A few months later the association presented its annual award for outstanding achievement in art history to the director of the Fogg Museum at Harvard. The award consisted of $5,000 and a bronze replica of a stabile by Alexander Calder.

Cultural commentators apply a curious double standard to the visual arts and music. People who sneer at a very good reproduction of a painting will praise a far inferior reproduction of a symphony. There is, one would think, a wider gulf between seeing and hearing an opera in an opera house and seeing and hearing it on a television screen than there is between seeing an original work of art and seeing one of Rockefeller's reproductions. Yet the National Endowment for the Arts has won great praise for sponsoring TV broadcasts of the Metropolitan Opera. Indeed, the bringing of "live" opera to millions who would never otherwise be able to see it was widely acclaimed as a cultural achievement. Samuel Lipman wrote in *Commentary*, "The medium's present limitations— principally the near-universality of small sets producing wretched sound, but also the more basic lack of three-dimensional visual representation —seem less significant than the possibility television presents of bringing operas in high-level productions to those who have little or no other opportunity to experience them."

Yet imagine the howls from the art world if someone were to propose that state and federal governments, rather than subsidizing the purchase of original works of art for museums and public buildings, sponsor an enterprise like Rockefeller's to make top-quality copies far more available than the originals could ever be. I go further. Why should public museums not substitute reproductions for originals, thus drastically reducing the presently high costs of security and conservation?

The fundamental economic fact about art is that works of high quality are scarce in relation to the demand for them. This would be true even if all of the demand came from art lovers whose interest was purely aesthetic. But in fact demand based on aesthetic considerations is only a trivial part of the total demand for art. Individuals and institutions pay large sums for works of art for reasons that have nothing to do with art as such—two reasons in particular. First, art (or "art") in any form is a "collectible," like wind-up toys, Mickey Mouse souvenirs, stoneware inkwells, beer cans, and almost everything else. For the rich, valuable art (or "art") is considered more suitable than, say, old toys. An important class of collectors are antiquarians: they attach value to whatever has some association with a famous person or event: they collect relics. It was as relics, not as art, that the Gilbert Stuart paintings of George and Martha Washington were deemed worth $6 million when purchased a few years ago by the National Portrait Gallery. The other nonaesthetic interest in the demand for art, and the most important one in setting the price, is the investment interest. The investor, as investor, views all engravings exactly as he does those on his stock certificates; he buys what he believes will increase in money value faster than other things that he might buy. (When this happens, it is thanks mainly to collectors and other investors.)

No criticism is intended of those who collect art or anything else, whether for pleasure or for profit. The point is that these nonaesthetic interests in the art market compete with the public interest in making the aesthetic experience of art more widely available and more frequent. The government, acting as proxy for the public as a whole, does not buy art on speculation or as a hedge against inflation. It does occasionally buy relics (the Stuart portraits, for example), but it does so on different public-interest grounds than those on which it usually buys art to stock its museums and decorate its public places.

From the standpoint of the public, it would be advantageous if the demand for art came only from those whose interest in it was purely aesthetic. In such a world, the price of art would be much lower, and the public could afford to enjoy it more. In reality, the public must compete for art in a market dominated by those whose interests are largely or entirely nonaesthetic. It would be greatly to the advantage of the public (and also of those individuals or institutions whose interest is, like the public one, purely aesthetic) if there were two markets for art: one for art as art, and the other for art as a collectible and for investment.

In effect, Rockefeller's enterprise achieved precisely this publicly advantageous separation of aesthetic from other values. By mass-producing high-quality copies of valuable originals, the Rockefeller Collection and similar enterprises make separate commodities of what would otherwise be joint ones: art as an aesthetic experience, and art as a collectible or investment. As an investment or collectible with aesthetic value, "Girl With Mandolin" may be worth $2 million. As a source of aesthetic satisfaction alone, it is worth something closer to $850 (with a suitable premium for whatever nuances of the original are lost in even the highest-quality reproduction). This suggests two things. First, $1,999,-150 of the ostensible value of Picasso's original has little to do with "art." Second, a public institution or individual interested only in the aesthetic value of Picasso's masterpiece can have most of that value for only $850, and can have $1,999,150 left over to purchase other sources of aesthetic satisfaction.

When there is only one example of a work of art, there is obviously no way to make it widely accessible. By bidding against each other, buyers do not increase the supply of art. They simply raise the price. Public institutions, using taxpayers' money, participate in this process, often bidding against one another for the existing supply. From the public standpoint, doesn't it make more sense to use tax dollars to *increase* the supply and *decrease* the price of art?

The art world will object at this point that a copy, however good, cannot have the artistic value of the original. But is this true? From a purely aesthetic standpoint, it can make no difference when, where, or by whom a work was produced: all that matters is its quality as art. A priori there is no reason to believe that a copy cannot be an even *better* work of art than a very good original. And in fact this is doubtless sometimes the case. Michelangelo, Vasari tells us, "made copies of various old masters, making them look old with smoke and other things so that they could not be distinguished from the originals." If these copies were not better than the originals, it is only because Michelangelo was attempting to make them "perfect."

In some cultures—admittedly ones utterly unlike our own, the ancient Egyptian and the Chinese, for example—no distinction was made between originals and copies. Indeed, instructions were generally provided for making copies. The Romans attached very little importance to the difference between an original and a copy. Most Roman sculpture (what is today "original" Roman sculpture) was copied by Greek slaves from Greek originals. The Emperor Hadrian had innumerable copies made of famous statues, which now enrich the museums of the world. During the Renaissance, an acknowledged imitation often brought as much as half the price of the original. There was no stigma attached to making or owning copies. The Holy Roman Emperor, Rudolf II, in about the year 1600, sent his court painters to copy what was best in Venice and Rome. They did their work so well that experts are still trying to decide which is which. "Until we reach modern times," the art historian Walter Pach writes, "copies, imitations, and even forgeries were made by men of such talent that the works possess qualities connoisseurs value in themselves."

Even today, many "original" works of art *are* copies in every sense except that of illicitness. It has been many years since most sculpture has been made that is in the strict sense "original"—that is, carved by the hand of the artist. The normal practice is for the sculptor to make a model in clay, wax, or some other plastic material. The model is then either sent to a foundry to be cast or recreated by workmen on the site where it is to be displayed. Often the dimensions of the finished work are very different from those of the model. Mechanical processes are used to enlarge or reduce the work, and the resulting artifact is at least slightly different from what the artist conceived. Some sculptors are very particular about the quality of the finished product but others—among them Henry Moore—sell objects that they have never seen.

One must stretch the concept "original" very far to include certain famous and very valuable works, including the seventy-odd Degas bronzes, all of which were cast after the artist's death, only three of them from plaster models that he made; the huge Arp tapestry commissioned by the National Gallery and made after his death from a small sketch; and the towering Picasso sculpture in Chicago, constructed from a small maquette of his design but never seen by him. Indeed a court refused to stretch the word far enough to include this last item: "The maquette," it ruled in 1970, "was an original work of art; the monumental sculpture was a mere copy."

Prints also usually involve a collaboration between the artist and one or more craftsmen. Holbein merely drew on a wood block, leaving the carving to others. There have always been artists who are very particular about the quality of every print that is "pulled," but there are also some who are willing to leave the judgment to the printer and to sell work that they have never seen. Despite the efforts of organized artists to establish standards, the word "original" now has no definite meaning with reference to a print.

To the assertion that a perfect copy has just as much artistic value as an original, the art world replies that a perfect copy is an impossibility. True enough, the history of art is filled with examples of "forgeries" that have been detected. And as a matter of simple logic, there is no record of a forgery that has deceived everyone. But there have been many cases where experts have mistaken copies for originals for long periods of time. Painters and sculptors now and then have been unable to distinguish their own works from copies. Rodin, for example, made the mistake of suing a dealer who had offered for sale a perfectly authentic work of his. The Metropolitan Museum displayed its three famous terra cotta Etruscan warriors under the label FIFTH CENTURY B.C. for forty years before discovering that they were modern works. The National Gallery displayed two "Vermeers" for years before discovering that they were fakes.

It is notorious that all forms of art have been successfully forged time and again. Robert Reisner's bibliography *Fakes and Forgeries in the Fine Arts* lists 859 references, not including newspaper articles, to forgeries in twenty-one art forms. Every important collection has been taken in on at least a few occasions. Recently the Morgan Library exhibited seventy-five works by the so-called "Spanish Forger," which it had gathered from the collections of (among others) J. P. Morgan, the Metropolitan, the Fogg Museum of Art, the Beinecke Library at Yale, and the Cincinnati Art Museum.

The Metropolitan Museum once found itself inadvertently *producing* forgeries, when it discovered that reproductions of early American glassware in its museum shop were turning up in antique stores for sale as originals. To prevent such embarrassments, the Met now stamps MMA on all but the very cheapest reproductions it sells. This device may help prevent copies from being passed off as originals, but the fact that it is necessary illustrates that the distinction is more commercial than aesthetic.

The identification of fakes depends very largely on the development of laboratory techniques. Chemistry and physics, not the discerning eye of the art lover, make the difference. Had it not been for the spectrograph that revealed manganese dioxide in black glaze, the Metropolitan's Etruscan warriors might still be on display. And had he not seen fit to confess, thereby bringing great numbers of works into the laboratories, the paintings of the supremely gifted forger van Meegeren (1889–

1947)—who sold six fake Vermeers for about $3 million—would be giving pleasure to countless museumgoers all over the world.

Van Meegeren confessed in 1945, in order to avoid prosecution for selling art treasures to the Nazis. But he had a hard time convincing the authorities that his beautiful "Vermeers" were not valuable art treasures, but rather worthless "fakes." According to W. K. Wimsatt, in his book *The Verbal Icon*, "The confession was officially accepted, more than two years later, only after the demonstrative painting by van Meegeren of a seventh Vermeer under court supervision and, what was of far more weight, the most rigorous radiographic, spectrographic, and microchemical testing of the forgeries by a large corps of Dutch, Belgian, British, and American technicians."

If the taboo against copies and reproductions were to be broken and mass duplication of masterpieces were to become widely accepted, all prints and most paintings and sculptures could be duplicated at per-unit prices within the reach not only of schools and libraries, but of average-income individuals. The fact that it is possible to copy most works of art "perfectly" (meaning so well that differences cannot be discovered without the use of sophisticated laboratory methods) does not suggest that perfection is always necessary. Except with prints and drawings, perfect copies cannot be cheap. If the copy is only "excellent" (meaning that no one but an expert can detect a difference with the naked eye) the cost will be much less. And if it is just "very good" (meaning that an experienced—but less than expert—viewer can tell the difference) the cost will be lower still. A reasonable person must ask in what circumstances the difference between "very good" and "excellent," or between "excellent" and "perfect," is worth what it costs.

Some in the art world will say that knowingly to accept anything short of perfection is philistinism. This, of course, is nonsense. We live in a world the nature of which requires at almost every moment that some amount of one good be traded off for some amount of another. Aesthetic, and for that matter moral, values are not exempt from this necessity. Once again, the double standard for music and the visual arts is enlightening. How many people would not dream of having a "fake" Rembrandt on their walls, however high its quality, yet own and enjoy record sets of the Beethoven symphonies?

Far from encouraging the widest possible dispersal of art reproductions of as high a quality as is practicable, our present government policy is exactly the opposite—that is, it aims to prohibit the making of copies that are not so poor as to be travesties of the originals. Intentional forgery of art works, of course, has always been illegal. The art community, however, wants legal and other restrictions against copies good enough to be *mistaken* for originals. "The more exact the reproduction," write two Stanford professors, "the greater the potential confusion and the consequent devaluing effect." They would require by law that reproductions of paintings, drawings, and fine prints be at least 20 percent larger or smaller than the originals and that they be clearly and indelibly labeled "reproduction." In the case of three-dimensional works, they would require a reduction in size of at least one quarter. The Art Dealers Association is the most vigorous supporter of laws and "professional standards" to limit the quality of reproductions; the College Art Association of America and the Association of Art Museum Directors are generally its allies. Since most "great" art is now in museums, obviously the museums are in a position to obstruct any large-scale effort to make high-quality copies.

It is sometimes argued that for perfect reproductions of masterpieces to become dirt cheap would be a cultural disaster. Familiarity would breed contempt. The painting before which one stood awestruck would become invisible. The Mona Lisa has been reproduced billions of times in the most preposterous contexts, but the crudeness of the imitations has helped to preserve the charm of the original. Would even the Mona Lisa survive widespread near-perfect reproduction? (In fact, there is a near-perfect version of the Mona Lisa sitting in a bank vault in New Jersey. The owners believe it is a later version by Leonardo himself, a claim that cannot be disproved by the experts. Naturally, the painting's value hinges completely on this presently unanswerable question.)

It has been suggested that something like this has happened to the great musical classics—that the Beethoven symphonies *are* degraded, the aesthetic joys of hearing them reduced, by too frequent hearing, however excellent the reproduction. But the purpose of encouraging reproduction of visual-art masterpieces is not to enable people to see them often enough to get sick of them, but to enable more people to see them at all. No one is going to travel around looking at "Girl With Mandolin" at dozens of different museums. Also, to the extent that having a copy of a classic in your house is like having Beethoven's Fifth Symphony playing all the time, it's true of those lucky enough to own originals now. Widespread reproduction would merely make both the pleasures and the possible perils of owning top-flight art more widely available.

Walter Benjamin argued in his essay "The Work of Art in the Age of Mechanical Reproduction" that works of art ought not be reproduced, because they were created to be confronted by the viewer in particular circumstances of time and place: to view them out of this intended context is to see them distorted. But, of course, almost all *original* works (except modern ones) *are* seen out of context. And, indeed, the culture having changed, it is impossible to experience a work from another time and place as it was intended to be experienced.

The real reasons for the cult of the original are cultural, not intellectual. Several powerful forces are at work to prevent the separation of artistic from pecuniary values. One consists of the individuals who own objects whose financial value would be reduced if reproductions lost their stigma and became legitimate alternatives to original works. If museums, which directly and, even more, indirectly (by virtue of the tax exemptions for wealthy donors) are among the mainstays of pecuniary values, were to substitute reproductions for originals, the multibillion-dollar art business would fall into an acute and permanent recession.

Artists themselves, it should be noted, get little benefit from present arrangements. Under American law, once a work leaves their hands, they have no right to share in the profit from future increases in the work's value, and no right to control or profit from reproductions. Artists would have nothing to lose if widespread reproduction slowed the appreciation of their past creations, and everything to gain, if—as part of an effort to encourage high-quality reproductions—the law were to assure the creator control over quality and part of the profit.

A second powerful force against acceptance of high-quality reproductions consists of that large part of the art world whose interest in art is historical rather than aesthetic. In the United States, the profession of art historian came into being early in the present century, when J. P. Morgan and others of the fabulously rich took to stocking their mansions and museums with the art treasures of Europe. In order for their kind of collecting to be a workable game, there had to be umpires whose authority all players in the game would accept. Bernard Berenson, working with Lord Duveen, was the first and most important of these. Soon every major collection had to have its own expert capable of proving that a work long thought to be minor was really major. Art historians, especially those trained at Harvard, became the curators, and sometimes the directors, of the big museums. Not surprisingly, in view of what they were trained and paid to do, art historians more often than not are more sensitive to historical than to artistic values. In their eyes the authenticity of a work is of supreme importance.

To a large extent, the art-interested public consists of college graduates who learned from books and courses by art historians. Much of the public has been taught to see art as part of this history of culture, rather than as something to be responded to aesthetically. The professional's respect for the authentic, however inartistic, and his contempt for the inauthentic, however artistic, has all too often been communicated to his students and readers.

Finally, it must be said as a fact of psychology that the aesthetic interest is probably not entirely separable from the pecuniary. "We find things beautiful," Veblen observed in *The Theory of the Leisure Class*, "somewhat in proportion as they are costly." That something is costly associates it in our minds with famous persons and places, with power and glory, with what stirs emotions of respect, reverence, and awe. These emotions may have no proper place in the aesthetic attitudes but they are likely to be there nonetheless. It would not be unduly cynical to say that many of the thousands who stood in line for a ten-second look at "Aristotle Contemplating the Bust of Homer," after the Metropolitan Museum paid $6 million to acquire it, would as willingly have stood to see the $6 million in cash. To the extent that these nonaesthetic feelings are linked with aesthetic ones, the public will not accept a perfect copy (labeled as such) as a perfect substitute for the original. Asked how people would respond to perfect reproductions identified as such, the associate director of a large museum said he thought they would accept some as a supplement to a display of originals but without any originals the display would fail for lack of glamour. "What would your wife say," he asked, "if you went home and told her you saw a woman who looks *just like* Elizabeth Taylor? Not what she'd say if you said you'd seen Elizabeth Taylor in person!"

QUESTIONS FOR DISCUSSION

1. Banfield often refers to an entity known as "the art world." Who belongs to this world and what do they do? How is identifying such a group a convenience for Banfield in his argument?

2. The essay begins with the story of Nelson Rockefeller's venture into selling art reproductions. Since Rockefeller's project was so widely criticized, why does Banfield feature it so prominently?

3. Banfield claims that Picasso's "Girl With Mandolin" is worth about $850 as "a source of aesthetic satisfaction alone." How does he arrive at this figure? Why not $250 or $2,000?
4. At several points Banfield makes an analogy between art and music. Explore this analogy further. Is the issue of reproduction really the same for both of these arts?
5. Locate the first appearance of the proposal thesis itself. Then look at the nature and proportion of arguments that come before and after. What is the effect of this scheme of arrangement?
6. Banfield distinguishes levels of reproduction, from the perfect to the excellent to the very good. Would describing how these different qualities of reproduction are achieved help his argument?
7. What distinction does Banfield make between the aesthetic, economic, and historical value of works of art? How clearly can the distinction between these values be maintained? Are there works of art that have one kind of value but not the others?

SUGGESTIONS FOR WRITING

1. Using Banfield's distinctions, select a familiar work of art (whether literary, visual, or musical) and write an argument for your classmates separating and assessing its economic, historical, and aesthetic value.
2. Suppose you agree with Banfield's thesis that museums should be filled with high-quality reproductions of works of great aesthetic value. Imagine yourself in charge of acquisitions for one of these new museums and write a letter to the Board of Directors justifying several of your purchases.
3. Building on the same scenario outlined in Suggestion 2, write a brochure for the public that will visit your museum, explaining why you have replaced its originals with reproductions of aesthetically finer works.
4. Explore the role of uniqueness as a criterion of value. Does the appeal of "the only one of its kind" exist only in the visual arts or among people with the funds to invest in uniqueness? Write an evaluation based on this appeal for those who might not appreciate rarity.
5. Try applying the issues raised in Banfield's argument to the world of fashion and clothing. Is originality of design prized and rewarded in the same way? What are the status and value of fashion reproductions at different levels of quality and fidelity? Address your argument to readers in the fashion industry.
6. Banfield assumes that it is a good idea to bring art to the widest possible audience. Take on that assumption and either confirm or refute it for a wider audience than Banfield addresses.

———————— →>> <<← ————————

Beyond the Wasteland: What American TV Can Learn from the BBC

MARTIN ESSLIN

The Boston Review, *where the following essay first appeared, is a publication sponsored by the National Endowment for the Humanities, a government agency that distributes funding to support the arts and scholarship. The author, Martin Esslin, is a professor of drama at Stanford University who has turned his attention to television. Another version of this article appears in Esslin's book,* The Age of Television *(1982).*

As you read Esslin's proposal, try to profile the audience for whom it was intended; notice especially what value judgments Esslin does not feel the need to defend because he assumes his audience shares them.

The invention of the printing press greatly increased man's capacity to communicate: information, facts, ideas, and opinions could be made available to far larger numbers of people at far lower costs than in previous epochs, when books had to be produced by scribes laboriously copying old manuscripts. It took a long time for the principle of freedom of the press to become established, however. Once this right was won in the more advanced countries of the Western world, this freedom became virtually limitless: almost anyone could get his ideas printed and distributed at relatively little expense. When the electronic mass media came into existence, they further enhanced mankind's capacity to communicate to even greater numbers at even greater speed. But they also presented a new and complex problem: there were only a limited number of channels available on the airwaves. If their number were increased above a certain limit, or their range increased by additional power, they would inevitably interfere with one another, there would be chaos, and the media's capacity to spread information and entertainment would break down altogether.

From the outset, the necessity of government control of the distribution of wavelengths and strength of broadcasting stations and the limitation of the number of stations created a problem for free speech and expression over the open airwaves. There could be as many printed forms of communication as anyone wanted, but only a limited number of outlets for broadcast communication. To whom should that privilege be given? And once those fortunate enough to be allocated such a channel of communication began to broadcast, how were they to finance their programs? Broadcasts could be received at no charge by anyone with a set; they could not be sold individually to each recipient as could a newspaper, pamphlet, or book.

In the infancy of radio the manufacturers of radio sets provided the programs at their own expense. They could not hope to sell their product unless they supplied something to be heard on the wonderful new contraptions. But after a while, when the thrill of hearing someone play a piano a hundred miles away had worn off, the public demanded more elaborate programming. And fulfilling that demand became ever more expensive.

Ways had to be found to finance the running and programming of radio stations. It is here that different solutions were found in Europe and in America.

In the United States every radio and television station has to be licensed by the Federal Communications Commission (FCC). Established by Congress in 1934, and headed by seven commissioners appointed by the president with the consent of the Senate, the FCC is empowered to regulate all interstate and foreign communication by wire and radio, including telegraph, telephone, and broadcast. In this respect radio and television are as much under government control in the United States as they are elsewhere.

In Britain the manufacturers of radio sets joined together to form the British Broadcasting Company, which began daily transmissions in November 1922. From the very beginning all listeners operating a radio set had to obtain a "broadcasting receiving license" (analogous to the license to operate a car in the United States and in most other countries). The license fee initially amounted to ten shillings (at that time two dollars) per annum. The general manager of the company was a young Scotsman, John Reith, the son of a clergyman, a brilliant administrator, and a person of the sternest moral fiber. Reith believed that this powerful new instrument for informing, educating, and entertaining the masses should be managed in the public interest, independent of interference from the state or business. To meet this requirement John (later Sir John, and later still Lord) Reith invented a new kind of public body:

an organization established by the state but independent of it in its daily operation, and financed directly by its users through the license fee. On January 1, 1927, the new British Broadcasting *Corporation* was set up under a royal charter, originally designed to run for ten years and to be renewable by Parliament at regular intervals thereafter.

How was the BBC's independence from government interference to be achieved? The corporation is controlled by a board of governors who are appointed by the queen for five-year terms of office. Their number has varied over the years—it is twelve at present. The BBC's charter stipulates that there must be at least one governor for each of the three non-English nations of the United Kingdom: Scotland, Wales, and Northern Ireland; and it has also become a practice that among the rest of the board there are always governors representative of the trade unions, business, women, the academic world, and the arts. Once appointed, the board of governors, under its chairman, is sovereign in its responsibility over the corporation. It is empowered to use the license fee according to its own judgment and to appoint the chief executive of the corporation, the director general. The executive function of the board of governors stops here: it is not meant to interfere in the daily operation of the administration and of the programs on radio and television. The royal charter also forbids the BBC to raise any revenue by advertising.

The board of governors has to ensure that the BBC remains wholly impartial in political matters. A balance must be maintained in the presentation of all responsible political views. During periods of general election campaigns the BBC has to allocate an agreed number of time slots for election broadcasts, which are provided by the political parties themselves and remain strictly outside the editorial control of the corporation (which, however, can be asked to furnish technical assistance in the form of studios, microphones, cameras, etc.). Between elections, similarly, there is an agreed number of "party political broadcasts" determined in a meeting of representatives of all the political parties in Parliament and on the basis of their strength in that body.

The royal charter of the BBC expressly specifies that the objective of the corporation is to disseminate "information, education and entertainment"—in that very significant order. The BBC thus regards itself as a public service with an important cultural and social role to play in the society.

The fixed license fee, which provided an ever-increasing and secure income while the number of radio sets continued to grow at leaps and bounds in the 1920s and 1930s, allowed the BBC to experiment not only in programming but also in technical innovation. It was the BBC that started the first regular daily television service in the world in 1936. To finance this fledgling TV service a television license fee was introduced. And as the number of television sets grew to saturation point, the radio license fee was abolished. Today some nineteen million British households pay a license fee amounting to some $90 for a color set, about $45 for a black-and-white set each year. That is to say, television costs the British household less than $2 per week for a color set, less than $1 for a black-and-white set. Compare this with the cost of television in the United States: in 1978 total revenues of all commercial stations in the United States amounted to some $7 billion; if one divides this sum by the roughly sixty million households in the country, the annual cost of television per household, which must come out of prices paid in the marketplace, also amounts to about $115—roughly $2.20 per week. The difference is that the BBC provides a service free from advertising and offering a much wider spectrum of programs.

The BBC as created by Reith became the model for most broadcasting organizations in Europe. Although commercial stations have also been licensed in most European countries (in Britain, for example, commercial television was introduced in 1954) and although some of the public broadcasting corporations in countries like France or Germany take a limited amount of advertising, the bulk of broadcasting expenses in Europe is still borne by the public broadcasting services. (In the Soviet-controlled parts of Europe, of course, all broadcasting is strictly government-run and controlled and merely an instrument of state propaganda.)

In the United States the development of broadcasting followed a completely different pattern. It may well have been a mere accident of history that there happened to be no equivalent to John Reith in America and that the problem of who should pay for the programming on radio stations was solved—on the analogy of the daily press—by the sale of advertising time on the air.

The situation in the United States was also basically different from that in Europe in that the vast size of the United States made it much more difficult to develop a centralized broadcasting service for the whole country. The great distances between the major centers of population favored a much more localized approach. In the smaller countries of Europe there was less scope for local stations that would not interfere with one another (at least with the state of technology as it existed in the 1920s and 1930s, before the advent of FM). In the United States it was possible to allocate a large number of relatively low powered stations to each major center of population. Nevertheless in radio—and later in television—a system of networking of the more ambitious program material had to develop simply because of the immense costs involved with producing high-standard programming, particularly in television. The U.S. system that evolved thus incorporated a considerable amount of local autonomy within a basic structure of three commercial networks financed entirely by advertising revenues.

So it came about that television in America became, in effect, a branch of the advertising industry. Whatever other qualities TV programs possess, they contribute to one basic purpose: to fill the gaps between advertisements, to induce people to turn on their sets so that they will see the advertisements. In his *New Yorker* profile of Johnny Carson, written in 1979, Kenneth Tynan quoted Carson as saying: "If you are selling hard goods—like soap or dog food—you simply can't afford to put on culture." One cannot put it more clearly or succinctly than that.

American commercial television, in generating enormous sums of money through advertising, has been immensely successful in producing programs of high technical quality and the widest popular appeal—not only within the United States but worldwide. However, it has effectively abdicated any positive cultural function. The FCC, under its charter, is charged with the responsibility of interpreting "the public interest" in broadcasting. It also is empowered to remove broadcasting licenses from stations that have "demonstrably failed to serve the public interest, convenience or necessity." But in practice these powers are hardly ever exercised. The concept of the public interest remains exceedingly vague and is rarely interpreted as meaning more than the provision of news, public announcements, or the granting of air time to spokesmen of various political bodies or pressure groups.

The deficiencies of this state of affairs, which in 1961 the then-chairman of the FCC, Newton Minow, described as "the vast wasteland" of commercial television, were recognized officially by the establishment of the Public Broadcasting Service (PBS) through the Public Broadcasting Act, which became law in 1967. The PBS evolved out of the educational broadcasting stations that had tried to fill the arid stretches of the cultural wasteland in the 1950s. The PBS is, in effect, an alliance of local community and educational stations financed by grants from the Corporation for Public Broadcasting, also established by the 1967 Act, and supplemented by grants from the National Endowments for the Humanities and the Arts, funds from university sources, public subscriptions, and donations from big corporations that regard sponsorship of culturally respectable programs as a form of discreet prestige advertising. Thus, while in theory there is no advertising on PBS, there is frequent mention of sponsoring corporations' names; and, in addition, the stations have to devote considerable time to soliciting voluntary subscriptions and gifts from their public. This necessitates frequent intrusions analogous to the commercials on the big networks, and emphasizes the dire financial straits public broadcasting has been in since its inception.

The congressional appropriation for public television through the Corporation for Public Broadcasting was set at $162 million for 1981. The appropriation proposed for the CPB in President Reagan's budget for 1982 was only about 75 percent of that sum. The total annual revenue of public broadcasting (television *and radio*) amounted to about $600 million in 1979. This compares with a total advertising revenue of commercial television and radio of more than *$12 billion* in the same year—that is to say, commercial broadcasting was more than twenty times richer than public sector broadcasting.

Paucity of financial resources—basically crippling as it is—is by no means the only organizational weakness of the PBS. Its decentralized structure makes genuine networking of programs very difficult and thus deprives public TV of the great advantages of national publicity. Under this decentralized method of programming, initiating a new series entails a lengthy and cumbersome process by which a sufficient number of stations must be convinced to support such projects in advance. In the big public television organizations of Europe decisions of this nature can be swiftly and efficiently taken at the center. There are considerable advantages in size and concentration in television—as, indeed, is the case in the closely related film industry.

What are the advantages and disadvantages of a public TV service as compared to a completely commercial system? One of the dangers inherent in a public service system is paternalism: some authority decides what the viewers should see and hear simply on the basis of what it arbitrarily feels would be good for them. Yet in countries where a highly developed public system exists alongside a commercial one, that danger is minimized because of the market pressure on the commercial system to give its audience what it wants. Indeed, in a dual system the danger is often that the public service may be tempted to ignore its stated purpose to serve the public interest and instead pander to mass preferences because of a sense of competition with the commercial networks.

Another problem that plagues public TV service is that it may run short of money, which in turn can increase its dependence on the government. The extent of government dependence is intimately connected to how the public broadcasting service is financed. In West Germany and Italy, for example, the public broadcasting service takes advertising, but it is usually confined to a clearly delimited area of the network's programming. In Britain the BBC, as noted, relies entirely on its annual license fee, which guarantees it a steady income and allows long-term planning. In periods of severe inflation, the license-fee system leaves the BBC in a dangerous position vis-a-vis the government, and the network's income may decline in real terms. In countries where the public broadcasting service is financed by an annual allocation in the national budget, long-term planning becomes more difficult and the dependence on the government is far greater. Nevertheless public TV services financed on that pattern, such as the ABC in Australia and the CBC in Canada, provide programs of high quality that are genuine alternatives to the fare on the numerous popular and prosperous commercial networks. In Canada, this includes programs from the three commercial American networks.

One of the most important positive features of services under public control is their ability to provide planned, high-quality viewing alternatives. The BBC, for example, has two television channels, BBC 1 and BBC 2. The program planning on these two networks is closely coordinated so that highly popular material on one channel is regularly paired with more specialized or demanding fare on the other. And though the percentage of the audience that tunes in to the challenging programming may be small, the scale of magnitude operative in the mass media is such that even a small percentage of the viewing audience represents a very large number of people indeed. A popular dramatic series on BBC 1, for instance, may reach an audience of 20 percent of the adult population of Britain—about ten million people. A play by Shakespeare on BBC 2 that may attract an audience of only 5 percent nonetheless reaches about two-and-a-half million people—a substantial audience for a work of art. It would take a theater with a seating capacity of 1,000 about seven years, or 2,500 performances, to reach an equivalent number of people! Nor should it be overlooked that this audience will include people whose influence may be greater in the long run than that of the ten million who watched the entertainment program. In this system, no segment of the viewing public is forced to compromise with any other. In our example, not only did BBC 1 provide a popular entertainment program as an alternative to the Shakespeare, but, in addition, the commercial network offered still another popular program. By careful—perhaps paternalistic—planning the general audience satisfaction was substantially increased.

One of the difficulties of the American situation is that the size of the United States favors decentralization and the fragmentation of initiatives for the more ambitious programming of the public service network. A revitalized PBS would need a strong central governing body that could allocate to local producing stations the substantial sums of money they require for ambitious projects—projects that could compete with the best offerings of the rich commercial competitors.

Using existing satellite technology, such a truly national network of public service television could be made available to the entire country. If a public service television organization was able to provide simultaneous, alternative programming along the lines of BBC 1 and BBC 2, the cultural role of television in the United States could be radically improved, and the most powerful communication medium in history could realize its positive potential to inform, educate, and provide exposure to diverse cultural ideas.

Is such a solution within the realm of practical possibility, or is it pure fantasy? To me, one of the most astonishing aspects of the American scene is its parochialism about its broadcasting system. Commercial television, with all its faults, is regarded by otherwise enlightened and responsible citizens almost as part of the natural order of things, so that the very idea of an alternative does not even surface. Yet just a glance across the borders of the United States into Canada reveals the possibility of a system that, though far from perfect, is in many ways preferable. British visitors to the United States are regularly surprised to be asked, and with great frequency, "Why is British TV so good?" This question almost seems to spring from a conviction that some undefinable sensibility is found on that little island that is beyond the grasp of the United States. Taking into account the great resources and talents of Americans, the reality is that a more rational method of financing programs that aim for artistic respectability would probably produce superior results equivalent to the best of British television. The American cinema, after all, has produced first-rate and highly artistic entertainment for decades.

There remains always this vexing question of financing such a public service: assuming that one advocates an annual TV license fee or an excise tax, why should people who don't want to watch certain types of programs be required to pay for them? Yet people who do not have children pay taxes that finance public schools and universities; people who do not visit museums pay for them through their taxes. The question, then, becomes: is a rationally structured mass communications service—radio as well as TV—as vital to the well-being of the nation as are libraries, museums, schools, and universities?

The answer to me seems beyond doubt. The absence of an adequately funded public television service in the United States in an age when other nations are in a position to make much fuller use of the positive potential of so powerful a medium amounts to no less than a national tragedy. To say that nothing can be done about the status quo and act as if it is a fact of life that television should continue to be geared to the intellectual level of a twelve-year-old child is a mixture of abject defeatism and dispirited complacency. In a democracy there are vast possibilities when enough people of intelligence and determination become convinced that changes are necessary—and take the initiative to make those changes.

And this is the crux of the matter: if it is realized that the present condition of the mass communication media in the United States constitutes a calamitous deficiency and might well entail very real dangers for the future economic well-being as well as cultural creativity and general standing of the nation, then surely there is a case for doing something about it. I find it deeply depressing that Lawrence Lichty, the author of a thoughtful and concerned article on the state of television in America, "Success Story," in the Winter 1981 issue of the prestigious *Wilson Quarterly*, can say about this matter:

> One still reads, from time to time, laments in the press or in academic journals about what television "could have been," as if it could have been any different than what it actually became. Its future, as a mass marketing tool, was determined well before its birth, in a very Darwinian sense. A fish cannot fly; it swims.

This strikes me not only as false because highly parochial—radio and television did become different elsewhere—but also as horrifyingly defeatist. Had the same attitude been taken about slavery, civil rights, the status of women, we would still have slaves, still have segregation in hotels, restaurants, and buses, still have women as chattels of their husbands or fathers. Surely the essence of a democracy lies in its ability to change conditions that have been recognized as immoral, harmful, or degrading. What is essential is the will to effect such a change and the determination to make the masses of the people—who are in the last analysis capable of intelligent and wise insights—realize the need for such change. The wasteland of television is not an unalterable feature of the American landscape. It is man-made and therefore not beyond the range of determined social and political action.

QUESTIONS FOR DISCUSSION

1. Compare Esslin's language at the opening and closing of this essay. You might choose several paragraphs and count the number of emotional and value-laden terms. How would you characterize the difference in tone between the beginning and the end? What effect would be lost if the beginning were more like the end?

2. At what point do you first become aware that this essay is a proposal argument? Is the actual thesis stated directly as a proposal? Before you became aware of the proposal, what did you expect to be the point of the essay?

3. What is the effect of opening this essay with an extended historical comparison between the development of British and American TV?

4. Could Esslin's essay have appeared in *TV Guide* as it is written? If it had, how do you think the *TV Guide* audience would have responded to it? If you think it could not have appeared as written, what changes would have been needed, what arguments included or omitted?

5. What is Esslin's assumption about the nature and value of American commercial TV? Why does he not argue explicitly and at length for his evaluation of it?

6. Find the paragraph beginning "What are the advantages and disadvantages of a public TV service as compared to a completely commercial system?" Try to unpack and paraphrase the arguments in that single paragraph.

7. Examine carefully the last three paragraphs of this essay. What does Esslin assume is the hardest thing to get from his audience?

SUGGESTIONS FOR WRITING

1. Writing in 1982, Esslin makes no mention of the impact of cable TV and video cassette recorders on the availability and quality of programming in the United States. Does the increasing popularity of cable TV and the widespread availability of video cassettes make the revitalization of PBS irrelevant? Update Esslin's argument for his readers.
2. Esslin describes how the BBC's charter ensures that it maintains a balanced presentation "of all responsible political views." Does such balance characterize American TV broadcasting? Direct your argument either way for an audience of American TV viewers.
3. Compare this essay to Edward Banfield's to discover shared assumptions about the public dissemination of culture. What do both authors seem to mean by *culture?*
4. Esslin claims that American commercial television has "effectively abandoned any positive cultural function." Can you defend American TV to Esslin as having the positive cultural effect he denies it? (Your definition of *cultural function* will be crucial here.)
5. Choose a single TV program and evaluate it either positively or negatively for its producers or potential viewers. Try beginning your evaluation as Esslin does with an apparently neutral explanation of the program's origins or evolution.
6. Watch a representative sampling of programming on PBS. Decide what audience it is appealing to. Write a proposal, perhaps in the form of a letter, recommending what PBS has to offer to someone who does not watch it.

→≫ ≪←

Waste Treatment: Doing What Comes Naturally

ROBERT K. BASTIAN AND JAY BENFORADO

Every proposal argument in this section of the reader represents a variation on the full proposal form described in the introduction, a variation made to fit the exact rhetorical situation the authors found themselves in. "Waste Treatment: Doing What Comes Naturally" is no exception. It is included because of its well-developed feasibility section, typical of the technical report that recommends practical action in the real world. Indeed, in the first few paragraphs the authors very quickly remind their readers of the problem to be remedied and the expensive and dangerous consequences of ignoring it; most of "Waste Treatment" attempts to convince readers that natural treatment systems are workable by showing how many are already in operation.

Both authors have advanced degrees in environmental science. Robert K. Bastian works in the Environmental Protection Agency's Office of Water in Washington, and Jay Benforado, an ecologist with The Conservation Foundation, has worked in the EPA's Office of Research and Development. Thus both men are highly qualified to suggest to city planners, engineers, and interested citizens in language anyone can understand the kinds of natural systems their communities might adopt.

Some 15,000 municipal sewage-treatment plants in the United States handle more than 26 billion gallons of wastewater each day, serving about 150 million people and at least 87,000 industries. Much of the treated wastewater—called effluent—flows after treatment into streams, lakes, and coastal waters—often to their detriment. The treatment plants also generate more than 17,000 tons (dry weight) of sludge, the solid material removed from the wastewater, every day. Sludge has traditionally been disposed of by incineration, burial in landfills, land application, and ocean dumping. But each option poses environmental concerns and economic barriers that in turn pose serious problems for many communities.

What's more, both wastewater and sludge are steadily increasing in quantity. This is because population is growing, municipal treatment plants are serving more industries, and federal and state regulations require more thorough treatment of sewage. Treatment plants in 1985 will handle about 15 percent more wastewater and sludge than they did in 1980, and treatment and disposal will also cost more as the prices of labor and energy continue to rise. At the same time, water pollution remains a serious national concern, and supplies of fresh water for irrigation, recharge of groundwater, and industrial and municipal uses are becoming scarce in some regions of the country.

Ironically, we can alleviate such problems by looking at municipal wastewater and sludge as valuable resources. By adopting "natural" treatment systems, many communities can handle their sewage more economically while recycling and reusing the materials productively. These materials are rich in important nutrients: a year's worth of treated wastewater and sludge contains an estimated 1.4 million tons of nitrogen, 300,000 tons of phosphorus, and 600,000 tons of potassium. This represents roughly 10 percent of the amounts of these nutrients now supplied by commercial fertilizers—worth about $950 million at current prices.

Wastewater and sludge also contain many micronutrients that are essential for plant growth, organic matter that is valuable as a soil conditioner, and enough water for one-sixth of the nation's irrigated land. In many cases, the "products" of natural waste-treatment systems can be used to improve farmlands, reclaim strip mines and other disturbed lands, create new recreational areas, recharge groundwater supplies, and produce marketable crops—all of which can help offset treatment costs.

The challenge is to learn how to manage natural ecosystems so that they can safely and effectively assimilate and recycle sewage wastes. With better understanding of how ecosystems function, we can also develop "artificial" natural systems that capitalize on the capabilities of these same processes. Some natural treatment systems are already widely accepted, and many others are being investigated in the United States and abroad. They make use of a diversity of ecosystems, including farmlands, forests, ponds, and wetlands, and they range from variations on traditional land-treatment concepts to intensive aquaculture systems.

BACK TO THE LAND

Applying wastewater and sludge to the land has evolved from the time-honored practice of recycling animal manures and agricultural residues. There are three major types of land-treatment systems for municipal wastewater.

SLOW-RATE LAND TREATMENT

Similar to conventional crop irrigation, this relatively popular alternative recycles nutrients and produces a potentially marketable crop while reclaiming wastewater. Partially treated wastewater is applied to vegetated lands, and the soil, plants, and microorganisms clean the water as it soaks in and gradually percolates to the groundwater. Systems used to irrigate farmlands, old fields, and forests are currently operating successfully in many parts of the country.

For example, Clayton County, Ga., located just south of Atlanta, recently started up a slow-rate system that will treat 20 million gallons of wastewater per day by applying it to a 2,400-acre forest of loblolly pines. Costing $43 million to construct, it is one of the largest systems operating year-round. The forest is divided into seven sections, and the water is sprayed through a network of sprinklers. Once a week, each section receives 2.5 inches of wastewater over a period of 12 hours. The trees, to be sold as pulpwood to help offset operating costs, will be harvested on a 20-year rotation cycle. Since the forest is located in the community's watershed, the wastewater eventually becomes part of the drinking-water supply. Other relatively large slow-rate systems—each treating more than 20 million gallons per day—have been installed in Michigan and Texas, while smaller systems operate in at least 40 states.

RAPID INFILTRATION

This system is usually used independent of agriculture and forestry operations. Wastewater is cyclically applied to basins containing coarse, highly permeable soil. Physical, chemical, and biological cleaning occurs as the wastewater drains through the soil to the groundwater. (All land-treatment systems use alternating wet and dry periods; this schedule optimizes microbial activity, prevents waterlogging and keeps the soil from becoming clogged with suspended solids.)

Rapid-infiltration systems are gaining in popularity but are still less widespread than slow-rate systems. They are somewhat more limited than slow-rate systems by the need for highly permeable soils and certain underground drainage patterns. Phoenix now uses a large system of this type, while smaller systems are operating in at least 24 states, including New York, Massachusetts, and New Jersey.

OVERLAND-FLOW LAND TREATMENT

Wastewater is applied at the top of grassy slopes, which are underlain by a relatively impervious soil layer. The water flows in a thin film down the slope and is cleaned by the soil, vegetation, and microorganisms at the soil surface. The water is collected in open ditches at the bottom for reuse or discharge to surface waters. The slopes must be steep enough to prevent "ponding" of the runoff, yet gentle enough to prevent erosion and allow the water enough time to be purified. The slopes must also be carefully graded and kept free from gullies to prevent channeling and allow uniform distribution of the water over the surface. Naturally rolling terrain is easily adapted to the network of slopes and terraces needed for an overland-flow system, minimizing land-preparation costs. Cities can install such systems to preserve green belts and open spaces. In other locations, the systems may be used to produce forage grass for feeding cattle. Perennial grasses with long growing seasons, high moisture tolerance, and extensive roots are best for this purpose.

The city of Davis, Calif., has installed one of the largest municipal overland-flow systems, which treats about 5 million gallons per day. Smaller or experimental systems are operating or are under construction in at least 15 states, including New Hampshire, South Carolina, Mississippi, Texas, and Illinois. The first systems were built in relatively warm climates, but recent advances in construction and design and greater operating experience have made them useful in cooler regions as well. Although overland flow has only recently been used to treat municipal wastewater, such systems have proved their worth in treating food-processing wastes for over 25 years.

Land-treatment systems can clean wastewater to a purity that equals or exceeds some of the most sophisticated conventional treatment processes. The systems also cost less to build and operate than more highly engineered systems—if enough land is conveniently available at reasonable cost. For small treatment plants handling less than 1 million gallons per day, a 25 percent savings in construction costs and 50 percent savings in operation and maintenance costs (partly because they use much less energy) have been fairly common. In larger metropolitan areas with very large volumes of wastewater, these systems may be less practical because of land availability problems. However, large slow-rate systems may be attractive in regions where water is needed to irrigate crops. A slow-rate system usually requires 50 to 500 acres per million gallons of wastewater handled daily. Rapid-infiltration and overland-flow systems require 2 to 50 acres and 15 to 100 acres per million gallons a day, respectively. Both the land requirements and performance of similar projects can vary considerably due to local factors such as soil properties, wastewater characteristics, application rates, crops grown, climate, and the desired level of treatment.

TURNING SLUDGE INTO GOLD

Processing and disposing of sludge frequently accounts for 50 percent or more of the costs of operating a typical sewage-treatment plant. And with the usual disposal methods limited by lack of acceptable sites, rising costs, environmental problems, and legal restrictions, some communities have turned from a philosophy of disposal to one of reuse. Indeed, about 20 percent of the nation's sewage-treatment facilities currently rely to some degree upon land application as a sludge-management practice. Sludge reuse projects are underway in many large metropolitan areas, including Milwaukee, Chicago, Denver, San Diego, Seattle, Philadelphia, and Washington, D.C., as well as in thousands of smaller cities and towns across the country, especially in the Midwest. The sludge is being recycled as a soil conditioner and organic fertilizer on cropland, pastures, sod farms, golf courses, parks, forests, and disturbed areas.

Raw sludge is 96 to 98 percent water; only 2 to 4 percent consists of solid material. It contains many microorganisms that can cause disease and material that can produce objectionable odors. Therefore, the sludge usually must be processed to "stabilize" it before it is applied to land. Sludge can be stabilized in a variety of ways, including composting, heat treatment, and digestion. "Anaerobic" digestion, in which sludge is decomposed by bacteria in the absence of oxygen, is the most widely used.

Stabilized liquid sludge can be sprayed directly onto the soil surface, incorporated into the upper soil layer by plowing, or injected beneath the soil surface with specially designed injection systems. However, sludge is frequently "dewatered" in drying beds exposed to the sun or with the aid of vacuum filters, centrifuges, filter presses, belt presses, and even thermal dryers. This concentrates the sludge solids and lowers transportation costs. Once the dewatered sludge is spread on the soil surface or mixed in, natural biological systems take over, breaking down the sludge and incorporating its nutrients and organic matter into the soil.

Sludge is most commonly applied to agricultural land. Many farmers long ago discovered the benefits of participating in sludge-reuse programs—their fertilizer costs decrease, crop yields increase, and soil quality improves. For example, municipal sludge from several Ohio cities is currently being supplied to farms in neighboring counties, under the direction of the Ohio Farm Bureau and other agricultural groups. Under a grant from the U.S. Environmental Protection Agency (EPA), researchers are measuring the resulting effects on crop yields as well as monitoring human and animal health. Improvements in yields and the lack of health effects noted so far have stimulated greater interest among both farmers and county agricultural extension agents. With success stories becoming more common, farmers may someday routinely approach municipal treatment plants to *buy* sludge for use as organic fertilizer.

There is also growing interest in the potential for using sludge to increase productivity in forests and reclaim damaged lands. For example, researchers in the Pacific Northwest applied about 40 tons of sludge solids per acre to a 50-year-old stand of Douglas fir located on relatively poor soil. Two years later, they recorded a 60 percent increase in growth over untreated sites, resulting in an extra $270 worth of timber per acre. The researchers also predict that the improvement in productive capacity of these forests will last at least five years and possibly longer. Sludge can benefit intensively managed tree "plantations" as well, often dramatically. At the Savannah River Laboratory near Aiken, S.C., researchers have found that applying sludge to loblolly pines may mean that three cuttings of pulpwood—rather than the normal two cuttings—can be harvested in a 20-year period.

However, not all species of trees appear to respond equally well to sludge. Red cedar and hemlock seedlings show high mortality rates when planted on recently treated sites, while Ponderosa pine seedlings survive but their growth doesn't increase significantly. Grasses and weeds in newly clear-cut areas, as well as low-growing "understory" plants in established forests, also grow more rapidly when sludge is applied. Thus, unwanted plants may have to be controlled to reduce competition with tree growth.

Compelled by the federal ocean dumping act to curtail disposing of sludge in the Atlantic, Philadelphia developed a master plan for managing sludge in 1975. The plan included using sludge to revegetate strip-mined lands, and the city is now reclaiming numerous spoil sites in western Pennsylvania. Because of initial opposition in mining areas, the city began with a pilot project, combined with a public-information program, to show local communities that the method was environmentally sound.

In June 1978, the state approved the application of sludge to a 10-acre barren site in Somerset County. Following grading and liming, 50 to 60 tons per acre of sludge solids were spread and mixed into the soil. The area was then seeded with a mixture of grass and legumes, and a lush green plant cover grew rapidly. Researchers monitored sludge, soil, and groundwater before, during, and after application, turning up no adverse effects on the environment. The city has since expanded the operation each year. About 1,100 acres were reclaimed in both 1981 and 1982, using nearly 140,000 tons of sludge annually.

The need for reclaiming abandoned strip mines is great—there are more than 250,000 acres of despoiled lands in Pennsylvania alone and several million acres nationwide. The costs of transporting sludge for such projects—a potential drawback—can be minimized by "backhauling" the sludge in the same trucks or railcars that bring coal from the mining areas to the city. Chicago, Birmingham, and Seattle are already using sludge to reclaim despoiled lands, while Knoxville, Pittsburgh, Tulsa, Baltimore, and several other cities are seriously considering similar sludge-management programs.

Sludge can also be put to good use at home, and one of the oldest sludge-reuse operations is run by the Los Angeles County Sanitation Districts. More than 100 tons of solids per day are composted after stabilization by digestion. The compost is then sold to a local company that screens, blends, and bags the material. The company, which has been in business for over 50 years, markets the sludge-derived product for home garden and horticultural use and to commercial nurseries. Demand is so great that the company must ration the material among selected customers.

While the benefits of recycling municipal sludge are well documented, there are also a number of concerns, especially for agricultural use. Most important is the possibility that pathogens or toxic chemicals that may be present in the sludge may contaminate the soil. If such contaminants accumulate beyond the soil's ability to assimilate them, the land could deteriorate rather than improve, groundwater quality could be degraded, surface water could be jeopardized, and crops could become unfit for consumption.

Researchers across the country have been developing management practices to help prevent such problems. Federal and state agencies, along with a number of universities, have issued detailed guidelines on the proper use of municipal sludge as a soil conditioner and fertilizer. For example, many sludges—especially those from treatment plants in heavily industrialized areas—contain elevated levels of heavy metals such as cadmium and lead and toxic organic chemicals such as PCBs. This has prompted the EPA and many state regulatory agencies to limit the levels of such contaminants in sludges and the amount that can be applied to the land. By following these guidelines—such as applying the sludge at predetermined rates and using "clean" sludges —communities should be able to recycle municipal sludge on land safely and effectively.

WASTES UPON THE WATERS

Managed aquatic systems are extremely attractive alternatives to conventional methods of treating wastewater because they can clean the effluent to about the same level but often can be considerably cheaper. Managers of relatively small treatment systems, especially those handling less than 1 million gallons per day, commonly report savings of 35 to 75 percent in construction, operation and maintenance, and energy costs. Although aquatic systems can require less space than some land-treatment methods, their use by large cities may still be limited by the cost or availability of land.

Full-scale aquatic treatment systems, as well as numerous research and development projects, are operating or under construction in at least 15 states as well as in several foreign countries. These include natural and constructed wetlands; treatment ponds; systems using floating aquatic plants grown in ponds, or ditches; and aquaculture operations involving a variety of freshwater or marine organisms, often in combination with other treatment processes. Aquatic systems may employ a number of physical, chemical, and biological mechanisms to clean the wastewater, ranging from sedimentation and filtration to uptake by plants and breakdown by bacteria.

Some of the wetlands being used or investigated include cypress swamps, bogs and other peatlands, "washes" in the West that fill with water after heavy rains, and both freshwater and salt marshes. Wetlands slow the movement of surface water passing through them, which promotes deposition of suspended particles. The wetland soil, plants, and associated microorganisms assist in the cleaning. Researchers at the University of Florida and the University of Michigan, sponsored by the National Science Foundation, have provided a good scientific basis for wetland treatment in a few types of wetlands, but additional large-scale systems representing other major wetland types need to be installed in different geographical regions. Monitoring them under various conditions will provide "real world" operating information and data needed for developing reliable design criteria. Not all wetlands are good candidates for wastewater treatment—some are too valuable in their undisturbed condition, some are too sensitive to change, and some do not provide much treatment. The EPA is currently evaluating several kinds of wetlands in the Midwest and the Southeast to determine their suitability.

"Artificial" wetlands are less restricted by user conflicts and potential environmental concerns than natural wetlands. They can be constructed almost anywhere—including on lands with limited alternative uses—and they offer greater flexibility in design and operation that can lead to superior treatment and reliability. They can be built in natural settings or they may entail extensive earthmoving, constructing impermeable barriers, or building containers such as tanks or trenches. Wetland vegetation is often established on an artificial substrate such as gravel or peat. Cattails and reeds appear to be ideal plants—they are hardy and widespread, and they propagate easily and grow quickly. In Ontario, for example, an experimental cattail marsh built on heavy clay soils provides efficient year-round treatment. There is only a slight decrease in performance during the winter, when ice forms on the marsh surface but wastewater continues to flow underneath.

Shallow ponds, usually less than two meters deep, can economically treat raw wastewater or remove additional contaminants from partially treated sewage. Such "stabilization ponds" are already widely used at many treatment plants. Bacteria play the major role by decomposing the organic matter in the wastes, and algae provide oxygen for bacterial respiration. Some pond systems are aerated mechanically to allow greater loadings of wastewater than could otherwise be handled.

The water hyacinth, a fast-growing, free-floating freshwater plant that is very efficient in removing nutrients and other materials, is the centerpiece in another aquatic system. About 15 acres of hyacinths, grown in ponds under controlled conditions, can treat 1 million gallons of wastewater to high levels per day. The plants take up nutrients and other chemicals as they grow, and their roots foster the growth of bacteria and higher organisms that assist in treatment. And by creating a blanket of vegetation that reduces wind and wave action on the water, they reduce unwanted growth of algae and help suspended solids settle to the bottom more quickly. Harvesting the hyacinths may be required to keep the system performing properly; 20 to 40 tons of plant material (dry weight) can be harvested per acre after about three months growth. The hyacinths can be digested to produce methane fuel or processed to produce organic soil conditioner or animal feed, but such recycling systems are not yet economical.

The use of water hyacinths was pioneered by scientists at NASA's laboratory in Bay St. Louis, Miss., where the plants have been cleaning domestic and chemical wastewaters since 1975. Systems are also being used or tested in other Southern areas, especially Florida, Texas, and California. For example, Walt Disney World near Orlando, Fla., has installed hyacinth ponds, and production of energy and soil conditioner from harvested plants is being evaluated. And San Diego is building a prototype system that will treat 1 million gallons per day, which will be used to study the potential of hyacinths for large-scale renovation of wastewater. Although hyacinths have proven effective in many locations, their use in colder climates and for treating very strong wastes is limited. The NASA researchers and other groups are now developing more versatile hybrid systems using other aquatic plants such as rushes, cattails, and reeds.

Aquaculture systems that both treat wastes and produce valuable aquatic plants and animals have potential but are farthest from widespread use. In one particularly ambitious project, scientists at Woods Hole Oceanographic Institute tested a marine "polyculture" system that used municipal wastewater. They grew marine algae in a mixture of seawater and sewage effluent, and then fed the algae to shellfish, including oysters, clams, scallops, and mussels. The algae removed nutrients from the wastewater and the shellfish removed the algae. Lobsters and fish such as flounder were then fed the wastes produced by the shellfish, and commercially valuable seaweed provided the final "polishing" of the effluent. The cost-effectiveness of the total system is questionable, but it does appear that the seaweed unit by itself may prove attractive economically.

In other projects, a variety of fish species have been grown in wastewater stabilization ponds. In Arkansas, for example, buffalofish, channel catfish, and several species of Chinese carp were raised in the last four stabilization ponds of a six-pond series in which municipal wastewater flowed from one to another. The fish got no other food. More than 3,000 pounds of fish per acre were harvested after eight months, and the quality of the water discharged from the system was improved. Another possibility is to use the cooling water discharged from power plants and industrial boilers, combined with various agricultural and industrial wastes, to support a commercial aquaculture system. Public utilities in at least ten states are exploring this prospect. However, it appears that aquaculture systems cannot be optimized for both food production and waste treatment in the same unit; systems involving higher forms of animals seem less efficient at treating wastewater and are more difficult to manage. But in some cases it should be possible to combine waste treatment with aquaculture systems to help decrease net costs.

WHAT'S NEEDED FOR SUCCESS?

Several problems stand in the way of widespread acceptance of natural treatment systems. Many natural areas have traditionally served as convenient sites for disposing of wastes, leading to serious environmental problems. Thus, many people automatically oppose integrating natural systems and waste-treatment projects. Also, adjoining landowners, government officials, and special-interest groups often express concern about potential odors, aesthetic problems, noise, and property values. And people often differ widely in their views about land use—such as whether to allow multiple use of public lands or how to balance environmental protection and development. Education in the form of public meetings and information campaigns is the way that many successful programs have approached community relations. Letting people know and see what to expect—the disadvantages as well as the advantages—helps gain public acceptance.

Even more important, researchers are still uncertain about the eventual fate and long-term impact of some contaminants in wastewater and sludge. The possibility that heavy metals, toxic organic chemicals, or disease-causing organisms may become concentrated in food chains, flow into local streams, or leach into groundwater supplies cannot be ignored. Nor can the potential for disease outbreaks and worker contamination caused by poor management or simple miscalculation—issues often raised when natural treatment systems are proposed. Research continues in these areas but needs more emphasis. However, natural treatment systems should not be singled out as having ecological problems; conventional treatment facilities release the same materials, merely to different ecosystems. In assessing natural treatment, environmental effects should be compared to those of available alternatives and not to "zero risk."

Good project design and management is the key. And appropriate siting and thorough monitoring will go far toward assuring both scientific and public confidence in these systems. Most, if not all, environmental problems can be avoided or mitigated by using proper management controls. For example, sludges can be treated to stabilize odor-causing organic materials and to reduce pathogens and toxic chemicals to acceptable levels. Wastewater and sludge can also be applied according to crop needs, weather conditions, and waste-production rates. And pretreating industrial wastes before they are put into the sewer system should greatly reduce contaminant concentrations in the effluent and sludge produced at many municipal treatment plants. Appropriate regulations and guidelines are also essential. These should allow a measure of flexibility that reflects how a system is used. Designers and managers of systems devoted primarily to sewage treatment—where the public has few opportunities to come into direct contact with waste—should have greater leeway in choosing application rates, pretreatment, and other procedures to hold down costs. For example, California's Department of Health has long allowed different uses of wastewater that has received different levels of treatment and disinfection. The degree of treatment required is tailored to the specific use: for example, whether it's for use on cropland, golf courses, or highway medians. Many states have also adopted regulations or guidelines for the controlled use of sludge in agriculture, and some have guidelines for forestry and land reclamation.

The purpose of a natural treatment system must be clarified early in the planning stage. Projects can be designed and operated solely for waste treatment and disposal or to achieve multiple benefits, including crop production, water conservation, and the like. The choice will determine how to balance technology and operations, costs and benefits. For example, if obtaining multiple benefits is the goal, project costs may be higher because more land and equipment is needed, application rates may be lower, and pretreatment may be more thorough. But under the right conditions, the value of marketed products or other benefits can offset such additional costs. On the other hand, if waste treatment is the only goal, simplified natural systems that cost less but don't provide other benefits may be more appropriate.

There are also a variety of more practical problems. Building all the components of a system—transmission lines, dikes, weirs, impoundments, storage facilities, access routes, and monitoring stations—without seriously disrupting natural areas can be difficult and expensive. This is especially true in wetlands and forests. And many sanitary engineers and public officials simply prefer dealing with established technologies for treating wastes. Despite recent government efforts to encourage use of innovative technologies, such as the EPA's construction grants program, few consulting engineers and equipment manufacturers have expressed interest. This is not entirely surprising. Natural systems require less equipment and feature simple engineering designs, so profit opportunities, at least in the short term, are not enormous. Natural treatment systems will be accepted slowly unless government agencies aggressively promote their development and use.

Sewage disposal is a complex task: done improperly, it can adversely affect the air, land, water, and ultimately, people. We must be careful not to simply shift the problem from one environmental medium to another. But properly managed natural ecosystems, although no panacea, do offer an ecologically acceptable way to deal with pressing water-pollution problems at reasonable cost.

QUESTIONS FOR DISCUSSION

1. The authors of this article never make direct claims about their expertise. Nevertheless, what sense do you have of their knowledge of the subject? How does that sense affect your faith in their argument?
2. Why do the authors use so many examples? Do they have the problem of supporting the typicality of their examples? Could this proposal have been made without any examples?
3. The proposal thesis of this argument is introduced very early. Where exactly is it? Why is so little space devoted to convincing readers that a problem exists?
4. What audience do Bastian and Benforado have in mind for this article, which appeared in *Technology Review?* Do they think of their readers as being automatically opposed to natural waste treatment systems? Are they writing for sanitation engineers?
5. Consider your answers to Questions 3 and 4 about the arrangement of this argument and the audience it seems to address. Now describe the overall purpose of Bastian and Benforado's proposal.
6. How are drawbacks to natural systems handled? Where are they mentioned in each section? Are the potential problems ever left unanswered?

SUGGESTIONS FOR WRITING

1. Investigate the waste treatment system being used in your community. Is it artificial, natural, or a combination of both? Characterize it in a CP argument for your uninformed fellow citizens.
2. If you live near or have access to one of the new types of waste treatment centers mentioned by Benforado and Bastian, investigate it in detail and write an evaluation of it for local officials. You may choose to evaluate it only

for its impact on the neighboring population. (Doing research in this case means getting out and talking to people, not simply looking things up in a library.)

3. If your community does not have a natural waste treatment facility or one that produces valuable by-products in addition to removing wastes, write a proposal addressed to average citizens advocating a change.

4. What is the extent of public knowledge about waste treatment in your community? Do a survey, sampling and questioning residents to see what they know. Write a characterization of the general level of ignorance or understanding you discover. If you find people generally uninformed, write an informative piece for your local newspaper, using the results of your survey as the lead.

5. At the end of their proposal, Bastian and Benforado make a short appeal for the aggressive promotion of natural systems by government agencies. Write a fully developed proposal for the role of government incentives in this area. First determine what problem the government intervention is supposed to cure. You may instead write a refutation of any role for government above the local level.

6. Compare and evaluate waste treatment practices in this country with those in one or more other highly developed countries. Is the United States behind or ahead and why?

->>> «<-

A Modest Proposal

JONATHAN SWIFT

"A Modest Proposal" is perhaps the most famous of all proposal arguments, and undoubtedly the most shocking. It was written by the Anglo-Irish satirist Jonathan Swift in 1729 and published anonymously. Of course, the very anonymity of such an essay would attract attention and set people talking about it, wondering who the author was. As you read it now, at a distance of 250 years, notice how Swift presents enough information to enable even a modern reader to reconstruct the political and economic plight of Ireland in the eighteenth century. We have included this essay for its persuasive power, which is only partially accounted for by its use of the standard format of the proposal. Swift's essay also demonstrates the persuasive force of irony and indirection.

FOR PREVENTING THE CHILDREN OF POOR PEOPLE IN IRELAND FROM BEING A BURDEN TO THEIR PARENTS OR COUNTRY, AND FOR MAKING THEM BENEFICIAL TO THE PUBLIC

It is a melancholy object to those who walk through this great town or travel in the country, when they see the streets, the roads, and cabin doors, crowded with beggars of the female-sex, followed by three, four, or six children, all in rags and importuning every passenger for an alms. These mothers, instead of being able to work for their honest livelihood, are forced to employ all their time in strolling to beg sustenance for their helpless infants, who, as they grow up, either turn thieves for want of work, or leave their dear native country to fight for the Pretender in Spain, or sell themselves to the Barbadoes.

I think it is agreed by all parties that this prodigious number of children in the arms, or on the backs, or at the heels of their mothers, and frequently of their fathers, is in the present deplorable state of the kingdom a very great additional grievance; and therefore whoever could find out a fair, cheap, and easy method of making these children sound, useful members of the commonwealth would deserve so well of the public as to have his statue set up for a preserver of the nation.

But my intention is very far from being confined to provide only for the children of professed beggars; it is of a much greater extent, and shall take in the whole number of infants at a certain age who are born of parents in effect as little able to support them as those who demand our charity in the streets.

As to my own part, having turned my thoughts for many years upon this important subject, and maturely weighed the several schemes of other projectors, I have always found them grossly mistaken in their computation. It is true, a child just dropped from its dam may be supported by her milk for a solar year, with little other nourishment; at most not above the value of two shillings, which the mother may certainly get, or the value in scraps, by her lawful occupation of begging; and it is exactly at one year old that I propose to provide for them in such a manner as instead of being a charge upon their parents or the parish, or wanting food and raiment for the rest of their lives, they shall on the contrary contribute to the feeding, and partly to the clothing, of many thousands.

There is likewise another great advantage in my scheme, that it will prevent those voluntary abortions, and that horrid practice of women murdering their bastard children, alas, too frequent among us, sacrificing the poor innocent babes, I doubt, more to avoid the expense than the shame, which would move tears and pity in the most savage and inhuman breast.

The number of souls in this kingdom being usually reckoned one million and a half, of these I calculate there may be about two hundred thousand couple whose wives are breeders; from which number I subtract thirty thousand couples who are able to maintain their own children, although I apprehend there cannot be so many under the present distresses of the kingdom; but this being granted, there will remain an hundred and seventy thousand breeders. I again subtract fifty thousand for those women who miscarry, or whose children die by accident or disease within the year. There only remain an hundred and twenty thousand children of poor parents annually born. The question therefore is, how this number shall be reared and provided for, which, as I have already said, under the present situation of affairs, is utterly impossible by all the methods hitherto proposed. For we can neither employ them in handicraft or agriculture; we neither build houses (I mean in the country) nor cultivate land. They can very seldom pick up a livelihood by stealing till they arrive at six years old, except where they are of towardly parts; although I confess they learn the rudiments much earlier, during which time they can however be looked upon only as probationers, as I have been informed by a principal gentleman in the county of Cavan, who protested to me that he never knew above one or two instances under the age of six, even in a part of the kingdom so renowned for the quickest proficiency in that art.

I am assured by our merchants that a boy or a girl before twelve years old is no salable commodity; and even when they come to this age they will not yield above three pounds, or three pounds and half a crown at most on the Exchange; which cannot turn to account either to the parents or the kingdom, the charge of nutriment and rags having been at least four times that value.

I shall now therefore humbly propose my own thoughts, which I hope will not be liable to the least objection.

I have been assured by a very knowing American of my acquaintance in London, that a young healthy child well nursed is at a year old a most delicious, nourishing, and wholesome food, whether stewed, roasted, baked, or boiled; and I make no doubt that it will equally serve in a fricassee or a ragout.

I do therefore humbly offer it to public consideration that of the hundred and twenty thousand children, already computed, twenty thousand may be reserved for breed, whereof only one fourth part to be males, which is more than we allow to sheep, black cattle, or swine; and my reason is that these children are seldom the fruits of marriage, a circumstance not much regarded by our savages, therefore one male will be sufficient to serve four females. That the remaining hundred thousand may at a year old be offered in sale to the persons of quality and fortune through the kingdom, always advising the mother to let them suck plentifully in the last month, so as to render them plump and fat for a good table. A child will make two dishes at an entertainment for friends; and when the family dines alone, the fore or hind quarter will make a reasonable dish, and seasoned with a little pepper or salt will be very good boiled on the fourth day, especially in winter.

I have reckoned upon a medium that a child just born will weigh twelve pounds, and in a solar year if tolerably nursed increaseth to twenty-eight pounds.

I grant this food will be somewhat dear, and therefore very proper for landlords, who, as they have already devoured most of the parents, seem to have the best title to the children.

Infant's flesh will be in season throughout the year, but more plentiful in March, and a little before and after. For we are told by a grave author, an eminent French physician, that fish being a prolific diet, there are more children born in Roman Catholic countries about nine months after Lent than at any other season; therefore, reckoning a year after Lent, the markets will be more glutted than usual, because the number of popish infants is at least three to one in this kingdom; and therefore it will have one other collateral advantage, by lessening the number of Papists among us.

I have already computed the charge of nursing a beggar's child (in which list I reckon all cottagers, laborers, and four fifths of the farmers) to be about two shillings per annum, rags included; and I believe no gentleman would repine to give ten shillings for the carcass of a good fat child, which, as I have said, will make four dishes of excellent nutritive meat, when he hath only some particular friend or his own family to dine with him. Thus the squire will learn to be a good landlord, and grow popular among the tenants; the mother will have eight shillings net profit, and be fit for work till she produces another child.

Those who are more thrifty (as I must confess the times require) may flay the carcass; the skin of which artificially dressed will make admirable gloves for ladies, and summer boots for fine gentlemen.

As to our city of Dublin, shambles may be appointed for this purpose in the most convenient parts of it, and butchers we may be assured will not be wanting; although I rather recommend buying the children alive, and dressing them hot from the knife as we do roasting pigs.

A very worthy person, a true lover of his country, and whose virtues I highly esteem, was lately pleased in discoursing on this matter to offer a refinement upon my scheme. He said that many gentlemen of this kingdom, having of late destroyed their deer, he conceived that the want of venison might be well supplied by the bodies of young lads and maidens, not exceeding fourteen years of age nor under twelve, so great a number of both sexes in every county being now ready to starve for want of work and service; and these to be disposed of by their parents, if alive, or otherwise by their nearest relations. But with due deference to so excellent a friend and so deserving a patriot, I cannot be altogether in his sentiments; for as to the males, my American acquaintance assured me from frequent experience that their flesh was generally tough and lean, like that of our schoolboys, by continual exercise, and their taste disagreeable; and to fatten them would not answer the charge. Then as to the females, it would, I think with humble submission, be a loss to the public, because they soon would become breeders themselves: and besides, it is not improbable that some scrupulous people might be apt to censure such a practice (although indeed very unjustly) as a little bordering upon cruelty; which, I confess, hath always been with me the strongest objection against any project, how well soever intended.

But in order to justify my friend, he confessed that this expedient was put into his head by the famous Psalmanazar, a native of the island Formosa, who came from thence to London above twenty years ago, and in conversation told my friend that in his country when any young person happened to be put to death, the executioner sold the carcass to persons of quality as a prime dainty; and that in his time the body of a plump girl of fifteen, who was crucified for an attempt to poison the emperor, was sold to his Imperial Majesty's prime minister of state, and other great mandarins of the court, in joints from the gibbet, at four hundred crowns. Neither indeed can I deny that if the same use were made of several plump young girls in this town, who without one single groat to their fortunes cannot stir abroad without a chair, and appear at the playhouse and assemblies in foreign fineries which they never will pay for, the kingdom would not be the worse.

Some persons of a desponding spirit are in great concern about that vast number of poor people who are aged, diseased, or maimed, and I have been desired to employ my thoughts what course may be taken to ease the nation of so grievous an encumbrance. But I am not in the least pain upon that matter, because it is very well known that they are every day dying and rotting by cold and famine, and filth and vermin, as fast as can be reasonably expected. And as to the younger laborers, they are now in almost as hopeful a condition. They cannot get work, and consequently pine away for want of nourishment to a degree that if at any time they are accidentally hired to common labor, they have not strength to perform it; and thus the country and themselves are happily delivered from the evils to come.

I have too long digressed, and therefore shall return to my subject. I think the advantages by the proposal which I have made are obvious and many, as well as of the highest importance.

For first, as I have already observed, it would greatly lessen the number of Papists, with whom we are yearly overrun, being the principal breeders of the nation as well as our most dangerous enemies; and who stay at home on purpose to deliver the kingdom to the Pretender, hoping to take their advantage by the absence of so many good Protestants, who have chosen rather to leave their country than to stay at home and pay tithes against their conscience to an Episcopal curate.

Secondly, the poorer tenants will have something valuable of their own, which by law may be made liable to distress, and help to pay their landlord's rent, their corn and cattle being already seized and money a thing unknown.

Thirdly, whereas the maintenance of an hundred thousand children, from two years old and upwards, cannot be computed at less than ten shillings a piece per annum, the nation's stock will be thereby increased fifty thousand pounds per annum, besides the profit of a new dish introduced to the tables of all gentlemen of fortune in the kingdom who have any refinement in taste. And the money will circulate among ourselves, the goods being entirely of our own growth and manufacture.

Fourthly, the constant breeders, besides the gain of eight shillings sterling per annum by the sale of their children, will be rid of the charge of maintaining them after the first year.

Fifthly, this food would likewise bring great custom to taverns, where the vintners will certainly be so prudent as to procure the best receipts for dressing it to perfection, and consequently have their houses frequented by all the fine gentlemen, who justly value themselves upon their knowledge in good eating; and a skillful cook, who understands how to oblige his guests, will contrive to make it as expensive as they please.

Sixthly, this would be a great inducement to marriage, which all wise nations have either encouraged by rewards or enforced by laws and penalties. It would increase the care and tenderness of mothers toward their children, when they were sure of a settlement for life to the poor babes, provided in some sort by the public, to their annual profit instead of expense. We should see an honest emulation among the married women, which of them could bring the fattest child to the market. Men would become as fond of their wives during the time of their pregnancy as they are now of their mares in foal, their cows in calf, or sows when they are ready to farrow; nor offer to beat or kick them (as is too frequent a practice) for fear of a miscarriage.

Many other advantages might be enumerated. For instance, the addition of some thousand carcasses in our exportation of barreled beef, the propagation of swine's flesh, and improvement in the art of making good bacon, so much wanted among us by the great destruction of pigs, too frequent at our tables, which are no way comparable in taste or magnificence to a well-grown, fat, yearling child, which roasted whole will make a considerable figure at a lord mayor's feast or any other public entertainment. But this and many others I omit, being studious of brevity.

Supposing that one thousand families in this city would be constant customers for infants' flesh, besides others who might have it at merry meetings, particularly weddings and christenings, I compute that Dublin would take off annually about twenty thousand carcasses, and the rest of the kingdom (where probably they will be sold somewhat cheaper) the remaining eighty thousand.

I can think of no one objection that will possibly be raised against this proposal, unless it should be urged that the number of people will be thereby much lessened in the kingdom. This I freely own, and it was indeed one principal design in offering it to the world. I desire the reader will observe, that I calculate my remedy for this one individual kingdom of Ireland and for no other that ever was, is, or I think ever can be upon earth. Therefore let no man talk to me of other expedients: of taxing our absentees at five shillings a pound: of using neither clothes nor household furniture except what is of our own growth and manufacture: of utterly rejecting the materials and instruments that promote foreign luxury: of curing the expensiveness of pride, vanity, idleness, and gaming in our women: of introducing a vein of parsimony, prudence, and temperance: of learning to love our country, in the want of which we differ even from Laplanders and the inhabitants of Topinamboo: of quitting our animosities and factions, nor acting any longer like the Jews, who were murdering one another at the very moment their city was taken: of being a little cautious not to sell our country and conscience for nothing: of teaching landlords to have at least one degree of mercy toward their tenants: lastly, of putting a spirit of honesty, industry, and skill into our shopkeepers; who, if a resolution could now be taken to buy only our native goods, would immediately unite to cheat and exact upon us in the price, the measure, and the goodness, nor could ever yet be brought to make one fair proposal of just dealing, though often and earnestly invited to it.

Therefore I repeat, let no man talk to me of these and the like expedients, till he hath at least some glimpse of hope that there will ever be some hearty and sincere attempt to put them in practice.

But as to myself, having been wearied out for many years with offering vain, idle, visionary thoughts, and at length utterly despairing of success, I fortunately fell upon this proposal, which, as it is wholly new, so it hath something solid and real, of no expense and little trouble, full in our own power, and whereby we can incur no danger in disobliging England. For this kind of commodity will not bear exportation, the flesh being of too tender a consistence to admit a long continuance in salt, although perhaps I could name a country which would be glad to eat up our whole nation without it.

After all, I am not so violently bent upon my own opinion as to reject any offer proposed by wise men, which shall be found equally innocent, cheap, easy, and effectual. But before something of that kind shall be advanced in contradiction to my scheme, and offering a better, I desire the author or authors will be pleased maturely to consider two points. First, as things now stand, how they will be able to find food and raiment for an hundred thousand useless mouths and backs. And secondly, there being a round million of creatures in human figure throughout this kingdom, whose sole subsistence put into a common stock would leave them in debt two millions of pounds sterling, adding those who are beggars by profession to the bulk of farmers, cottagers, and laborers, with their wives and children who are beggars in effect; I desire those politicians who dislike my overture, and may perhaps be so bold to attempt an answer, that they will first ask the parents of these mortals whether they would not at this day think it a great happiness to have been sold for food at a year old in the manner I prescribe, and thereby have avoided such a perpetual scene of misfortunes as they have since gone through by the oppression of landlords, the impossibility of paying rent without money or trade, the want of common sustenance, with neither house nor clothes to cover them from the inclemencies of the weather, and the most inevitable prospect of entailing the like or greater miseries upon their breed forever.

I profess, in the sincerity of my heart, that I have not the least personal interest in endeavoring to promote this necessary work, having no other motive than the public good of my country, by advancing our trade, providing for infants, relieving the poor, and giving some pleasure to the rich. I have no children by which I can propose to get a single penny; the youngest being nine years old, and my wife past childbearing.

QUESTIONS FOR DISCUSSION

1. What is Swift's real purpose in this essay? Is it actually to make a proposal, as he claims at the beginning? If so, how would he seriously propose to alleviate hunger in Ireland? If not, how might the essay's purpose be more accurately described?
2. Swift's essay has often been described as a classic of irony. It uses language to express something quite different from its literal meaning. As you were reading, at what point did you first become aware that this essay was not straightforward? Does Swift always mean the opposite of what he says?
3. What set of values does the speaker of this proposal count on his readers to share with him? How do they differ from the values of the author, Swift? How do the values of the speaker compare with your own? Where are they similar, and where are they different?
4. Characterize the speaker of the modest proposal. How does he see himself? What does the reader see in his character that he is unaware of?
5. Identify the elements of the proposal argument that are present in this essay. How does Swift arrange the standard components of the proposal to enhance his purpose?
6. Whom is Swift really attacking in this essay? What would he have the government of England do to solve the problem of hunger in Ireland? Why does he not argue directly?

SUGGESTIONS FOR WRITING

1. Pretending to address the same audience, write a straightforward version of Swift's real argument, without using irony. Using information he presents in his essay, construct an argument suggesting what should be done to alleviate the poverty of Ireland.

2. Choose a contemporary situation resembling the one Swift identifies, such as the abject state of some group of people, the suffering they endure, and the economic burden they cause. Construct an ironic proposal that will supposedly solve the problem but will actually reveal its magnitude. Address it to newspaper readers.
3. Take an economic perspective toward some problem your readers do not usually like to regard as economic (e.g., drunk driving or child abuse) and seriously defend that point of view.
4. Or take the opposite point of view: Consider a problem usually viewed as economic (e.g., the rate of unemployment or the cost of higher education) and argue that other values should be considered more important in defining and solving it.
5. Imagine that you are a public official who has just received Swift's modest proposal and you are unsure whether you are dealing with a madman or an ironist. Write a response to the author discussing the feasibility of his argument.
6. Take on the difficult task of constructing an argument for a position most people will find inhumane. What characterization of yourself do you have to project? What can you do to make such a position acceptable to an audience?

---------- →≫ ≪← ----------

The Case for Computer Literacy

JOHN KEMENY

Hungarian-born mathematician John Kemeny has had a distinguished career. In the 1940s he worked at Los Alamos and was a research assistant to Albert Einstein. He was a professor of mathematics and then president of Dartmouth. And among other public services, he headed the presidential commission investigating the nuclear-reactor accident at Three Mile Island. But he is perhaps most famous as the creator of BASIC, one of the simplest and most widely used of programming languages. Thus Kemeny brings considerable authority to the subject of computer literacy.

"The Case for Computer Literacy" appeared in Daedalus, *the organ of the American Academy of Arts and Sciences, which addresses an elite audience of educators and policy makers. As you read his argument, notice*

whether Kemeny anticipates any objections or resistance to computer literacy.
There is a tone of optimism and enthusiasm in this essay that is missing
from other proposals in this section. What is the source of Kemeny's
confidence?

The warning of English physicist and author C.P. Snow that the well
educated are splitting up into two cultures, that many in fact lack an
understanding of science, is certainly applicable to the United States
today. But while Snow deplored the indifference of the best educated
to the Second Law of Thermodynamics, here we complain that most
citizens do not understand even the most elementary physical science.
Other articles in this volume will deal with the sad state of scientific
literacy and with possible remedies. My task is to make the case for
widespread computer literacy.

One is tempted to be extremely pessimistic: if, in spite of decades
of trying to improve scientific education, most educated people are still
scientific illiterates, what hope is there to achieve literacy in a field as
new and strange as computer science? Will not the coming of computers
make the split between the two cultures worse and limit computer
literacy to a very small fraction of the population? After extensive
thought, I have rejected that proposition and instead have reached an
optimistic conclusion. On the one hand, I believe that computer literacy
is even more important than scientific literacy; on the other, I am
convinced that the former is much easier to achieve and that a substantial fraction of the population has a chance of doing so. I believe further
that widespread computer literacy will help to solve the problem of
scientific illiteracy.

THE NEED

Much has been written about the impact of the computer revolution
and the fact that the number of jobs requiring computer literacy is
increasing rapidly. Yet it would be a mistake to base the case entirely
on past and present experience, because a much stronger case can be
made for computer literacy in the future. In the next three decades,
intelligence will be built into most manufactured objects, and those who
lack even minimal computer literacy will have difficulty functioning in
everyday life.

All machines, from automobiles to ovens, will contain microprocessors capable of a substantial degree of intelligence. But I foresee intelligence also being incorporated into all kinds of manufactured objects that would not normally be classified as "machines." An important example may be the intelligent house.

Since buying a home is for most of us our single greatest investment, providing our home with a fairly high IQ is merely giving it no more than its due. Although the savings in energy alone should justify the cost of a microprocessor, there is much more that an intelligent house can do to protect and shelter us, and to keep us informed and entertained.

A computer system can control the source of heat in a much more sophisticated way than can the old-fashioned thermostat. It can also monitor smoke detectors and burglar alarms, and make a thoughtful decision on whether to call for help. It can control all those gadgets and appliances that now have some primitive intelligence built into them, such as videorecorders, microwave ovens, and radio alarms. One should be able to program, in a vastly more flexible way than is possible today, all of the instruments at a single central station. Our home control computer, for example, can memorize all our favorite recipes, and then, provided with a menu and the number of people for dinner, as well as the time when dinner should be ready, it could tell us how much we need of each ingredient and take over the entire processing of the dinner, with each dish ready at just the right time. Or it can provide a flexible alarm system that wakes us at different times on different days, sometimes to FM music and sometimes to an early morning program on television. And the system must be intelligent enough to know that whenever we cannot catch "Hill Street Blues," the program should be videorecorded for later viewing. (The first videorecorder that has sufficient intelligence to skip commercials will make a fortune. Unfortunately, the recognition of commercials is a very difficult problem in artificial intelligence, since some commercials are more interesting than the shows they interrupt.)

The gadgets and appliances now being marketed represent "halfway technology." Since each is limited to the intelligence built into it, and to its own means of communication, manufacturers are achieving much less than is possible. Yet it would be prohibitively expensive for each household article to have the capabilities of a personal computer as far as logic and memory and the way it communicates with human beings are concerned.

The key breakthrough will be to have a central computer in the home, with the various household gadgets, the "peripherals," hooked into it. The occupants of the home will have the luxury of a sophisticated and yet friendly personal computer to communicate with, and will be able to use similar methods for regulating all the appliances. It will also make the appliances affordable, since the capabilities of the personal computer need not be duplicated.

The drawback to recent "high technology" appliances is that they are quite hard to use, and a variety of them in the home means that the user will have to become familiar with their different conventions and programming methods. Each one, of course, comes with its own instruction manual, and it seems to be a law of nature that the one you need is the one that has been misplaced. This is surely an absurd way of storing and retrieving information in the age of computers.

If manufacturers could be persuaded that computer literacy is spreading rapidly and that computers capable of running appliances will soon become common in the home, they will start designing appliances that are peripherals for these computers. Someday in the not too distant future, instead of each appliance coming with an instruction manual, it will be delivered with a computer program to be added to the repertoire of the home computer. Then it will be the computer, not the human being, that learns how the new gadget operates. Once the program is inserted, the occupants of the house would be able to give instructions to the new appliance in a language and style that have become second nature. Furthermore, the home computer, by taking adequate safeguards, could prevent us from making dangerous mistakes. Only the absence of a sufficiently large buying public, with enough computer literacy to operate a personal computer intelligently, prevents the realization of this domestic paradise.

While the control of gadgets may justify the expense of an intelligent home, its potential for enriching our lives is much greater. The processor can serve as a computer and a word processor. And a powerful computer in the home can be the source of first-rate entertainment. While today's video games give an indication of the potential popularity of computer games, all the intelligence is used for spectacular visual images and very little for the games themselves. But the most important use of our home computer will be as an information center.

Access to key information can often mean the difference between success and failure in many endeavors. In our complex world, it is difficult to have that kind of access without the aid of computers. Sooner or later this nation must—and will—come up with a design for a national information network that any intelligent home will be able to access.

What kind of information is likely to be available? First of all, news distributed through home computers will replace printed newspapers. It will be quite cheap to store an enormous amount of information, ranging from international news that one normally gets in the *New York Times,* to the kind of personal details found only in a small-town newspaper. Once we can get the news this way, we will also have available a sophisticated means for finding items of interest and for doing selective reading. For example, the computer could alert us to news on topics of special interest to us and, depending on what we wish to see, let us choose a summary, a brief account, or complete details.

Further, a home terminal should be able to access a network of information on merchandise available in neighborhood stores and the programs of various theaters. It will provide information on medical and legal issues that do not require the services of a doctor or a lawyer, and give you the voting record of your Congressman.

Education will be one of the most important uses of a home information center, for children and adults alike. The problem with adult education on television is that the "student" is purely passive. With a computer terminal, one can engage actively in a program of continuing education. This is particularly true for what is perhaps the most important use of such a system, access to the research and reference materials of the great libraries of the country. It will be entirely possible to search the catalogue of the Library of Congress from your home terminal and to read articles and books right on the screen of your terminal.[1] (I shall discuss education in more detail later.)

I have avoided using the word "robot" because artificial intelligence must make much greater progress before we have "R2D2" available to us. And I do worry about the day when household robots first come on the market; someone is sure to tell the robot to dump out the bath water and forget to tell it to remove the baby first.

The problem of the baby in the bath water is very much to the point. Isaac Asimov has written most reassuringly about robots that have laws built into them to prevent their ever doing harm to human beings. I believe it is possible to do so—but we must first solve two problems: How does the machine recognize a human being, and how does the machine know what is harmful to human beings? A robot capable of recognizing a small mass of fat, uttering unrecognizable squeals, as a baby in the bathtub would be a very intelligent robot indeed.

The problems may not exist in the early stages when we will be provided with a small number of options within specified ranges for each

---

[1] I first proposed such a system in a talk at M.I.T. in 1961. For a later discussion, see chapter 8 of my book, *Man and the Computer* (New York: Scribner's, 1972).

gadget we own. But the whole point of programming a computer is to provide ourselves with vastly more freedom than we had previously. I am quite certain that we are going to *insist* that manufacturers provide us with that capability. The greatest satisfaction that can be had from a computer is to use it for something that the manufacturer has not even conceived of. And once we can do that, our home computer must either be intelligent enough to prevent us from making dangerous mistakes, or our home insurance policy is likely to have an escape clause not only for acts of God, but also for computer bugs.

If I am right that intelligent machines will invade the lives of all of us, then the need for computer literacy will be even more vital than it is today, and at a level of sophistication higher than that required for using a computer that merely calculates and retrieves information.

WHAT WILL HUMANS DO?

The Industrial Revolution fundamentally changed how most people in what became the modern world earn their living. From a society in which human labor was mainly physical, we have become one in which the majority of workers provide a service. Very few jobs now require exceptional physical powers, since machines can easily lift heavy weights, move much faster, and work longer hours than human beings. The coming of intelligent machines will further narrow the areas in which human beings excel.

A good example of this is how photoduplication, dictating machines, and, more recently, word processors have changed the secretary's job. And yet those changes are small compared to what the impact of an intelligent computer terminal will be. Most mail will be received electronically and filed in the memory of the computer. Hard copy may never be required, since any office having access to the information can always display the item on a computer screen. I would not dare to predict what sophisticated machinery will be available routinely to secretaries a generation from now. Many of their present skills will be irrelevant, and the secretary's most important asset will be the ability to communicate with intelligent machines and to make full use of their capabilities.

Today, universal literacy is demanded because the illiterate is unemployable, and indeed, has difficulty surviving. Someday computer literacy will be a condition for employment, possibly for survival, because the computer illiterate will be cut off from most sources of information. The human brain unaided by computers will appear feebleminded.

I have never been an advocate of "full automation" but rather of human beings and computers working as a team. We know the tasks at which computers outperform human beings; what we need to define are the tasks that are best left to humans. In the past, we have identified the traits unique to human beings by comparing ourselves to the higher animals. But that method of comparison is no longer satisfactory, because computers are even better at some of these "uniquely human" tasks. Just where the line is drawn between computer and human skills will determine not only how most people will be employed in the future, but what "human" skills will be most highly prized.

It is risky to speculate what these skills will be, but I will hazard a guess at some that are likely to be reserved to humans. First, although pattern recognition by machines will improve, I believe that, for some time to come, the best results will be obtained by human beings—assisted by computers. Second, computers will be invaluable in decision-making, but the final value judgments will be left to humans. And third, creativity will, for the indefinite future, be a uniquely human attribute.

Robert Jastrow ends *The Enchanted Loom* [2] with a gloomy picture of a future (not so far away) when computers will outperform human beings at all tasks. With all due respect to Professor Jastrow and his excellent book, I think that prediction is overly pessimistic. Computers will not catch up with us in all areas in the foreseeable future, and it is not obvious to me that they ever will. Biological evolution of the human race is entirely possible, but it is not our only defense. Thanks to the invention of the printing press, human beings advanced more in a few centuries than did most species in a million years. What capabilities will mankind develop once it fully masters the use of computers and intelligent machines?

COMPLEX SYSTEMS

The structure of our society has become so complex that human beings no longer seem able to manage its systems. The national economy, social security, higher education—we seem to make a mess of all long-range planning. Computers alone cannot of course solve the problems of planning for our complex systems, but neither can these problems be solved *without* the use of computers. Indeed, they require extremely sophisticated use. We need computer models, not only to answer our

[2]Robert Jastrow, *The Enchanted Loom* (New York: Simon & Schuster, 1981).

questions, but because in many cases, it is the model itself that helps to formulate the *right* ones.

The usefulness of computer models is still controversial; many of the existing models of complex human systems have flaws that are easy to identify—and therefore easy to ridicule. But the alternative is a set of hazily formulated assumptions, usually not even articulated, that may exist only in the mind of one human being. Since others do not have access to this "mental model," or only hear an extremely vague description of it, its flaws are much more difficult to discern. The only way to criticize it is by pointing out that the model leads to disastrous results.

To choose an example at random, I believe that such mental models characterize the way the Executive Branch and Congress think about the national economy, and about federal planning for energy, transportation, and health care—and not only are these models inadequate, but we seem to be making absolutely no progress with them. When something goes wrong, as it usually does, it is hard to pinpoint where the fault lies, and politicians can therefore blame the failure on something other than their own decision-making processes.

Computer models may appear risky to their users because their flaws *can* be pinpointed. Yet if one tests them carefully against experience, and tries to make an improvement every time the predictions turn out to be inaccurate, there will be significant progress in the long run. Anyone who doubts this should consider how far physics would have progressed if physicists had been limited to working in ordinary English.

But there are still more benefits from attempting to model a complex system by a computer program. Even the executive who thinks that he or she knows an enterprise very well may gain an entirely new perspective from the process of trying to model it. For this purpose, whether the eventual model is good, bad, or mediocre is almost irrelevant, for it is the discipline of describing precisely the organization's structure, and stating clearly the interrelationships between the various segments, that helps one to understand the enterprise better.

The modeling process itself will suggest a number of questions that have never been thought of before. During my years as president of Dartmouth, I gained a great deal from doing my own computer modeling. Sometimes the benefit was a highly useful model, but often it was a new line of thought or a new way of looking at the College that had not occurred to me (or to anyone else) before.

One tends to live with a number of "rules of thumb" that represent experience under "normal" conditions. As long as conditions are reasonably normal—whatever that may mean at the moment—one does not ask what combinations of factors have brought about the present situation and what new factors could change the situation dramatically. But if one attempts to build a computer model of the system, these questions are necessarily asked. Answering them turns out to be a valuable learning process, and sometimes the answers are vitally important.

Unfortunately, most decision-makers in government and industry today are computer-illiterates. Although computer systems are in place in most large organizations, they perform mostly routine bookkeeping functions and are used little, if at all, in decision-making. High-level executives, too embarrassed to expose their ignorance of computers by asking questions of the computing center, often leave important corporate decisions by default to computer programmers, who must fill in the gaps in the vague, general instructions they receive from top management.

A great deal of research needs to be done on computer modeling of complex systems, but research alone cannot solve the problem. Major organizations need among their senior decision-makers men and women who are computer literate and in tune with the computer age.

Nor is the problem limited to planning. Many of today's more complex pieces of technology are far behind the state of the art. From the control room of a nuclear power plant to systems of urban mass transportation, we find primitive levels of intelligence built into machines when the problem cries for highly intelligent equipment. Again, significant progress will not be made until we have a plentiful supply of human beings who are capable of designing, implementing, and operating large systems of artificial intelligence.

The United States is going through an extremely dangerous transition stage. Since most decisions in both the public and private sectors are made by individuals who were educated in the precomputer age, individuals who have not been able to readjust their thought processes, their fumblings are similar to what we would expect if a camel driver found himself at the controls of a modern ocean liner.

THE CHALLENGE

If we compare learning a computer language with learning a foreign language, we find similarities but also major differences. All languages are designed to express the same thoughts as in our own, using a different vocabulary, of course, and most often a different syntax. Learning a computer language, however, is more like learning to communicate with an alien, the essential difficulty of which is to adjust our thinking to the alien's.

The difference becomes even clearer if we compare learning a second foreign language with learning a second computer language. While there is no doubt that the second foreign language comes easier than the first, it still takes a couple of years to read and write the language at all well. In contrast, all the major difficulties are mastered with the learning of one's first computer language, and one can become reasonably expert in a second language within a month. Learning a computer language is not primarily a linguistic achievement; rather, it requires an adjustment in the way we think.

Achieving computer literacy, however, has its obstacles. Many grown-ups, for example, when forced to sit down at a computer terminal, exhibit the kind of fear that reflects the adult wariness of experiences that are new and hence "strange." But such fear is not innate, since children, who greet new experiences with anticipation and delight, take great joy in being allowed to use a computer, and seem to master its mysteries with remarkable speed.

But fear is by no means the only obstacle. Human language abounds in vagueness and ambiguity, features that are essential for human endeavors ranging from poetry to puns. Computers, however, require a precision of expression rare in ordinary language. In normal discourse we assume some shared experiences, and hence need not dot every "i" and cross every "t." (For this reason, individuals from drastically different cultures *do* have difficulty in communicating.) And we assume that the listener has common sense. Unfortunately, computers have not shared our experiences and have absolutely no common sense!

There are many simple examples. Using "legal" words and the correct syntax, we ask a computer to work out a long problem, but what we forget to tell it is that we want to know the answer, which the computer meticulously finds—and keeps a secret from us. (When I tell this story, I can always spot the experienced computer users in the audience—they are the ones who are *not* laughing. It has happened to us too often.) Or we assume, in speaking, that our listener will mentally correct small slips of the tongue, will guess the intent of dangling references and accept a wave of the hand or a facial expression for an omitted phrase. None of these works with computers.

A final obstacle is that we have to learn to think in terms of algorithms, which are precise recipes for solving problems or for accomplishing a task. A computer program describes an algorithm; it tells us "how to get there." Although algorithms were used and studied in mathematics in the past, there is today a strong prejudice in favor of formulas—that is, achieved results. But computers are forcing us all, even mathematicians, to readjust our thinking.

This is easier said than done, for we perform many tasks that we would find difficult to explain. Humans excel at pattern recognition, yet it is very difficult to teach this to computers. This is true whether one speaks of a numerical pattern, a geometric shape, or a piece of furniture. Children learn how to walk, but we would have great difficulty explaining to an alien species exactly what we do with each muscle.

That is why "easy" and "difficult" take on new meaning when dealing with a computer. The difficulty of writing a given computer program has less to do with the inherent complexity of the problem being solved (complexity as perceived by humans) than it has to do with how hard we find it to explain the method of solution to an alien intelligence.

LET THE PUNISHMENT FIT THE CRIME

For generations, mathematics teachers have preached to their students the necessity for clarity, precision, and logical thinking—and for generations, most students have failed to respond. One of the most common experiences in teaching mathematics is to have a student come up after a test and say, "I really understand the material, but I made some careless mistakes." Sometimes the mistakes are indeed carelessness, such as being wrong by a factor of ten, but at other times, the student thinks he or she understands the material but actually has missed an important point. What will these students do if they get into decision-making positions? Will a doctor get the dose of medicine wrong by a factor of ten? Will a business leader only *think* that he understands the needs of his corporation, and through a slight misunderstanding, bankrupt it? Will a decision-maker in government commit a small logical error and cause untold suffering to millions of people?

Whatever else computers may be good for, they are a marvelous means of counteracting the human tendency to be sloppy. A bit of carelessness in writing a complete program will result in a gentle message pointing out the error, in language simple enough for a human being to understand. A program that is based on "almost understanding the problem," or that commits a small logical mistake, will very likely result in a computer producing tons of results—all of them wrong. Computers, in short, are designed to let the punishment fit the human crime.

We humans suffer only slight embarrassment when others detect errors in our work, yet it is quite humiliating to be chided by an electronic box for carelessness, or after many hours of hard work, to have complicated garbage pouring out of the computer. For anyone who desires to learn computer programming, a few sessions with the computer will do much more to teach him or her about the necessity for precise logical thinking than any amount of human preaching could. One need not present a hypothetical case to show how a quite small mistake can ruin a very large project. Every computer programmer knows this from unhappy personal experience.

What are the skills necessary to become a good computer programmer? The first is the ability to express one's thoughts in a very simple language. A computer language like BASIC, with its small vocabulary and limited number of clearly defined concepts, is extremely simple compared to any human language. When beginners say they have trouble learning a computer language, what they really mean is that, although they can learn the language easily enough, expressing their needs in so slight a number of concepts is much more difficult. Most people write in a complex style primarily because they have trouble expressing their thoughts simply. One hears frequent complaints about this from the world of business, and the writing style prevalent in government is the subject of an endless number of jokes.

Once a programmer crosses this linguistic barrier, the next obstacle is to explain to the computer how to solve a problem—and to do so without appealing to shared experiences or to intuition. If, in instructing a computer, you use the phrase "you know," you will be in trouble, because the computer does *not* know—unless whatever the phrase refers to is clearly explained. In the process, the programmer will discover that he has either not truly understood the method of solution or is unable to articulate it clearly.

In teaching computer programming, we place great stress on the ability to divide complex tasks into small, clearly understood components. But breaking down a procedure into simple steps, and then being able to understand the precise, logical relation among them, is a skill that human beings seldom acquire. Yet once the skill is mastered, it influences the way a person thinks in all kinds of situations that have nothing whatever to do with computers. Here are two quite different examples.

First, let us consider medical diagnosis. A doctor giving an annual checkup needs to carry out a large number of small steps. These range from executing advanced procedures, such as electrocardiography, to looking carefully through the pupils of the eye, or simply talking to the patient. And if any procedure leads to results other than what the doctor would normally expect, further tests will be necessary. In effect, the doctor is working his or her way through a complex algorithm, where future steps depend on the outcomes of earlier tests. Since most tests are not in themselves conclusive, to reach a reasonable diagnosis the doctor must understand the interrelations between a large number of small steps. Although some physicians are able to diagnose a wide variety of illnesses accurately, "bugs" in medical procedures, leading either to an erroneous diagnosis or the failure to spot a disease, must be quite common. How far computers can go to help doctors in their diagnosis is a fascinating topic. However, this is not my current concern. Instead, I am suggesting that the doctor who has had serious exposure to computer programming is likely to be a much more successful diagnostician.

Next, consider an executive managing a complex enterprise. It is axiomatic that the executive must learn how to delegate—to divide each job into a number of separate tasks, assigning many of them to other individuals, and explaining clearly what is expected. In a large organization, delegation may proceed to the next lower level, then the next, and so on. This is similar to writing a large computer program in hierarchical form, where, through several levels, larger tasks are divided into smaller ones, always making sure that the communication, both "from the top down" and "from the bottom up," is good.

The most annoying problems seem to crop up about three levels below the chief executive, where there may be someone who does not understand the task assigned and how it fits into the overall goals of the institution, or where two people are working at cross purposes, or where the chain of communication has broken down. A period of serious exposure to computer programming would, I think, improve the quality of managers.

Finally, a skill that all computer programmers must acquire is "debugging." For a large computer program, consisting of several levels of smaller and smaller tasks, one must be able to infer, from the overall program malfunction, where to look for the source of trouble, and if the answer is not clear, to work down the hierarchy until the "bug" is found. The acquisition of such skills would be invaluable for those charged with the management of complex systems, particularly organizations of human beings.

In sum, learning computer programming has a beneficial effect on human thinking, because it teaches skills that are fundamental to most professions.

A NEW CONCEPTUAL FRAMEWORK

In the major challenge to computer scientists, that of enabling millions of people to program intelligent machines, discussions tend to focus on the significant improvements that have been made from early—and primitive—computer languages, or the relative merits of currently popular languages. I would like to focus the discussion instead on the emergence of *new types of concepts* within languages.

The early languages were designed to deal exclusively with arithmetic and primitive logic. As computers acquired large memories, they had to be able to read and write files. With the coming of time-sharing, users were able to interact with computers while their program was running; thus computer languages had to include commands that allowed two-way communication. Still later, when graphics terminals became easily available, concepts had to be added to languages for the drawing of pictures. I cite these developments, because I believe that to enable computers to manipulate all kinds of machines, an entirely new set of concepts must be invented.

Another trend has been to improve the structure of languages. A good language both makes it easy for a beginner to start writing programs and accommodates the needs of the advanced programmer. The development of "structured languages" in recent years has been a giant step forward. A good structured language helps an inexperienced person avoid many of the usual kinds of mistakes and helps the expert to write a large, complex program that is readable and reasonably easy to debug.

Yet not all the developments have been favorable. Complexity usually brings chaos in its train. In computer graphics, the lack of standardized terminals is a great nuisance. Furthermore, it is not reasonable to expect everyone to become expert on the peculiarities of particular devices, for all freshmen, for example, to learn the idiosyncrasies of the various kinds of graphics terminals available on campus. The complexity we will face when computers have to manage a variety of machines will be far worse than any problem we have solved so far. One possible solution lies in the ingenious way graphics are handled at Dartmouth.

BASIC at Dartmouth is a highly structured language of great power, with simple commands for drawing pictures built into it. These commands cover the commonest features available on graphics terminals and can be used easily by beginners. The user may, by a single command in the program, specify the kind of plotting device he or she is using. If the same program is to be run on a different device, only one line need be changed. This simple solution works because systems programmers have written a set of routines for each kind of graphics terminal the college has acquired. These routines translate the graphics instructions into the special codes that activate the drawing of pictures on that particular terminal. By specifying within the program the name of the terminal, the system knows which particular set of routines to provide for the user. If an entirely new terminal comes along—which happens frequently—the sole requirement is for one programmer to write a new set of routines. The new terminal can then be used by someone simply inserting its name in the appropriate place in the program.

Could such a solution work for communication with intelligent machines? I can conceive—at least vaguely—of a conceptual framework rich enough to allow communication with arbitrary machines. One could build appropriate commands to cover these concepts into a language and then leave it to systems programmers (or to the manufacturers of particular devices) to implement routines that apply these concepts to a particular machine. Thus the same home computer, using the same computer language, could be used to instruct an oven, a TV recorder, a burglar alarm, and an information retrieval system. The major breakthrough that is necessary is to invent a new conceptual framework, a challenge that I predict will be far greater than any we have faced so far.

EDUCATION IN THE COMPUTER AGE

Once computers are available in the classroom, we will be forced to rethink what to teach and how to teach it. First, the right way to solve a problem may be different in the computer age. Second, certain traditional topics have become useless. Third, the computer is a powerful tool for solving problems, available both to the instructor and the student. Fourth, programming a computer is an important learning experience for the programmer. Points one and two affect *what* we should teach to students, while three and four should drastically change *how* we teach.

Although some topics are taught for their intrinsic value, many of the things we teach, at all levels of education, are means to an end. And since these means were designed in the precomputer age, a good many have become obsolete. Why teach the "skill" of interpolation in a trigonometric table, when the value of a trigonometric function can be found in ten seconds on a pocket calculator? Once the student is freed from this arithmetic bondage, it is much more likely that he or she will understand the principles of trigonometry and learn to enjoy them.

Again, the most hated portions of a calculus course deal with messy techniques that were necessary in an age of hand calculation, as, for example, the many steps required to arrive at a numerical value for a complicated definite integral. But there is no justification in teaching these transformations when a computer can find the same numerical value in a fraction of a second. A modern calculus course should concentrate on the fundamental concepts of the calculus—which are among the greatest creations of the human mind—teach only the most basic techniques, and lead the student to the appropriate computer programs for obtaining answers.

We can revolutionize the teaching of sciences by substituting the power of the computer for the memorization and application of complex mathematical formulas. Although knowledge of the basic concepts of the calculus is necessary to understand Newton's laws, students poor at arithmetic or algebra should not be discouraged from pursuing the physical sciences. While differential equations frighten many students, a computer program that incorporates the laws of motion and gravitation is much simpler to understand. And spending an hour in front of a computer screen trying to put a satellite into orbit around the earth, or landing a space ship on the moon, will do vastly more for a student's physical intuition than trying to solve complicated equations—a particularly good example, since the complete solution of the path of a rocket is not possible without a computer. Nothing is gained by taking the student through very complicated calculus-type arguments before turning to the computer. For such reasons, computer literacy cannot help but bring about a much wider understanding of the principles of physical science.

So, too, with the teaching of the biological and social sciences. Much of the latter deals with the retrieval and analysis of vast data bases, techniques that the modern computer enables elementary students to master. A freshman sociology student who already knows how to use computers can in one term learn an enormous amount about the formulation of hypotheses and their testing against actual data. In a sense, the computer provides a laboratory for the social sciences and allows the instructor to concentrate on basic principles and major techniques, rather than drilling the student in messy statistical procedures involving arduous, time-consuming calculations. And for the first time, it allows students to check the conclusions of "experts" and to demand that sweeping assertions be backed up by facts.

How will the methods of teaching change? It will no longer be possible—or desirable—to teach a mathematics course without giving computer demonstrations in the classroom. In the courses I teach, I use the classroom terminal for working out significant examples, rather than the usual trivial ones, to enable me to teach important applications and to walk the students through the steps of a complex algorithm. And a computer-drawn graph is worth a thousand words.

I can ask my students to use the same programs to solve problems, to modify the programs to handle different applications, or to write programs of their own. Programming is an invaluable learning experience, a point that cannot be stressed too strongly. Even after more than three decades of teaching, I acquire a deeper understanding of well-known techniques by writing a computer program for them. For students unacquainted with the technique, it is an even more important learning experience. Something as familiar as the quadratic formula takes on new meaning if one is forced to write a program. The so-called formula is shorthand for three entirely different cases that must be treated completely differently. This fact has confused generations of students. Since one is forced in a computer program to identify the cases clearly, and to treat each by an appropriate method, the student arrives at a clearer understanding of the quadratic formula than did most students in the past.

As I said before, we must break away from an emphasis on formulas, or achieved results, for in most cases, teaching the algorithm—the method of *achieving* a result—is what is important. Instead of stressing that equations of higher degree do not have formulas similar to the quadratic, we should teach a simple method that will find the roots of any equation, to any desired degree of accuracy.

A colleague of mine developed a probability theory course for sophomores that enables them to learn topics usually reserved for more advanced courses. The secret is the use of the computer to build up a student's intuition about probability and to enable him or her to apply advanced mathematical techniques.

The greatest hindrance to moving rapidly to the stage where computers are regularly available for the teaching of all science courses and many social science courses is not the cost of the equipment, but the need to train and retrain teachers to use computers competently and to be comfortable in their use in the classroom. With a computer, human beings can share in the vast accumulation of knowledge, not just in the sense of information retrieval, but in being able to use problem-solving techniques developed by others.

The computer's single most important impact on education will be in allowing the student to participate much more actively in the educational process. In much of education, the student is a passive absorber of knowledge, and there is only an occasional opportunity to work out a "canned" exercise. When spending hours at the computer terminal becomes a routine part of education, the student will be an active participant, able to initiate changes and influence the direction of his or her education. At no level is this more significant, perhaps, than in adult education. If the home computer can be used in conjunction with lectures on television or videotapes, many of the current weaknesses of continuing education will disappear. And we can look forward to still greater technological breakthroughs that will further revolutionize the educational process. At some point, a marriage will occur between personal computers and videodisc technology, allowing a richness of sight, sound, information retrieval, and computing power whose full effects none of us can foresee.

There are of course some bottlenecks to be overcome. Inexpensive computers are now widely available at the precollege level, but the software is often very poor. It is therefore essential that manufacturers of good, inexpensive computers provide standardized versions of one or more of the popular teaching computer languages. Once this happens, first-rate teachers will find it worthwhile to develop high-quality educational software, not only for the improved teaching it will afford, but also for the substantial financial benefits. The writing of good software may in the future become as lucrative as the writing of textbooks has been during the last few decades.

We must also accelerate the training and retraining of teachers. But just as good textbooks help improve the teaching of a weak teacher, good software can play the same role until a sufficiently large corps of trained teachers is developed. On the college level, much more rapid progress should be expected.

Many colleges now offer an elementary introduction to computers. A question frequently asked is whether such an elementary introduction suffices, and if not, how room for further computer courses in an already overcrowded curriculum can be made. We can answer this question by comparing the achievement of computer literacy to that of writing skills. Although freshman English is very important, it cannot carry the total responsibility for the teaching of writing. Unless there are courses throughout the curriculum that assign a substantial amount of writing —and in which professors are willing to hold students responsible for doing it well—the majority of graduates will write poorly. Similarly, if computer assignments are routinely given in a wide variety of courses —and faculty members expect students to write good programs—then computer literacy will be achieved without having a disproportionate number of computer science courses in the curriculum.

Where a good time-sharing system is easily available to faculty and students, the rest happens almost automatically. But there is still enormous diversity in the computer capabilities available for instruction on various campuses. Many years ago I proposed that the lack of adequate computer capability should be cause for a college to lose its accreditation, just as an inadequate library is today. But my suggestion has not been implemented. Accrediting committees are very conservative, particularly when a new rule might mean disaccrediting some very famous institution.

Initially, we all guess that only students with an interest in mathematics and a demonstrated talent for it will be good at computers. But the evidence is overwhelming that computers may appeal to students who have never shown any talent for mathematics and, indeed, may have hated the subject. I knew a religion major at Dartmouth, with a strong antiscience bias, who became a computer scientist.

We are going through a difficult bootstrap operation. A generation untrained in computers is trying to introduce this powerful new technology into the classroom and to educate a new generation that will feel completely comfortable in the computer age. It is essential that we rethink what is worth teaching today and how we can improve the process of instruction by means of computers. I hope that the federal government and private foundations will be prepared to underwrite the very substantial transition costs, and that computer manufacturers will be enlightened enough to see the enormous long-term benefits they can achieve by helping to accelerate the spread of computer literacy. The transition to full use of computers and intelligent machines is inevitable. Our only choice is whether, through intelligent reform of our educational system, we make the transition a relatively painless one.

AN OPPORTUNITY FOR MANKIND

One proposal for achieving computer literacy is to enable users to communicate with computers in "ordinary language." I consider this a mistake and am worried that mankind will miss a major opportunity. No, I have not changed my mind about making systems easy and pleasant to use, but the substitution of ordinary language for simple computer languages is *not* a step in the right direction.

Ordinary languages have developed, without any particular rhyme or reason, through a long series of historical accidents. Vaguenesses and ambiguities are tolerated, and grammarians are more interested in history than in logic. The extensive drilling in their native language that students receive at an early age may be wonderful preparation for the appreciation of literature, but it teaches them very poor habits for scientific thinking. The early introduction of a computer language might be a healthy antidote.

To some extent, this counterbalancing role has been played historically by mathematics. It is called "the language of science," and students are warned not to attempt the more rigorous sciences without first acquiring a strong mathematical background—which, unfortunately, takes a discouragingly long time. Yet children are learning computer programming at a remarkably early age, and loving it. Therefore, while ordinary languages will continue to be used for daily discourse and literature, and mathematics will certainly remain an important subject, much more of the teaching of mathematics and science should be in the language of algorithms, and hence taught as computer programs.

We have a unique opportunity to improve human thinking. If we recognize the areas of human knowledge where ordinary languages are inappropriate, and if computer literacy is routinely achieved in our schools, we can aspire to human thought of a clarity and precision rare today. This development would be of immense value for science, for the organization and retrieval of information, and for all forms of decision-making. Forcing humans to develop such thought processes may be the major fringe benefit of the coming of computers.

One of the oldest dreams of mankind is a universal language. It is notable that computer languages seem to cross national boundaries without difficulty. Thus the first universal language may turn out to be neither English nor Esperanto, but a language like BASIC.

QUESTIONS FOR DISCUSSION

1. Kemeny's title, "The Case for Computer Literacy," states directly the nature of his proposal. Exactly what does computer literacy entail, as Kemeny defines it?
2. Kemeny assumes that learning computer skills improves one's thinking in other areas, the way learning geometry purportedly improves one's logical reasoning. Does your own experience support this assumption? That is, have you noticed carryover from any subject area to another, especially from computer courses?
3. Notice that Kemeny states his thesis and forecasts his supporting arguments in the first two paragraphs. Might such a strategy alienate skeptical readers? Is Kemeny worried about convincing the skeptical?
4. Kemeny's proposal differs from others in this section because of its reliance on predictions rather than on the demonstration of a present problem as a motive for action. How does he make his scenarios of the future seem inevitable?
5. Find the occasions where Kemeny forecasts or summarizes the course of his argument. What is the effect of emphasizing the outline of the argument in this way? Is the length of his argument a factor?
6. Kemeny sees human language as limited in its ability to solve certain kinds of problems, in part because of its inherent vagueness and ambiguity. Is Kemeny ever vague or ambiguous? Does he come close to achieving in this argument the clarity and precision characteristic only of computer programs? Is his language here distinctly different from that of any other proposal argument in this section?

SUGGESTIONS FOR WRITING

1. Look up some of the early predictions, from the late forties and early fifties, of the promise of that amazing new technology, television. Report on whether time has confirmed or refuted those predictions.
2. Writing in 1983, Kemeny makes many predictions about how computers will transform our lives at home, school, and work. Have any of his predictions been fulfilled, or are they close to fulfillment? Write an essay indicating the extent of the impact computers have had on your life. (Think of indirect as well as direct effects.)
3. Write a short proposal showing how computer application will solve a specific problem for an audience that will benefit from the remedy.
4. Kemeny makes a careful distinction between human and computer skills, conceding that computers do not excel in pattern recognition, value judgments, and creativity. Can you write a set of instructions that would enable

a computer operator to recognize when a problem calls for these human skills and cannot be handled by a computer?

5. Kemeny sees great scope for computers as an aid to education. Can you argue that computers could assist in the writing process? Look at some of the available programs that claim to aid invention, editing, spelling, or other verbal skills, and evaluate one of them for your fellow writing students.

6. Take just one of Kemeny's predictions, such as his claim that computers will replace newspapers; explore and evaluate the consequences of such a change.

—————————— →≫ ≪← ——————————

Habit

WILLIAM JAMES

William James was a member of the brilliant and idiosyncratic James family of nineteenth-century America, brother of the novelist Henry James. After obtaining a polyglot education in Europe and America and a medical degree, James became an instructor in physiology at Harvard. His career and writings show the wonderful ferment of disciplines at the time, so that James extended his studies from physiology to psychology to philosophy, establishing the first laboratory in America for experimenting on the relation between physiology and psychology. He also helped to found the American Society for Psychical Research. While believing that all mental phenomena would some day have detailed physical explanations, James also struggled to preserve his faith in the spirit and the will: "My first act of free will shall be to believe in free will." His rational study of religion appears in his book, The Varieties of Religious Experience *(1902).*

The following selection on "Habit" comes from Chapter 4 of James's textbook Principles of Psychology *(1891), but the tone and voice are not at all like modern textbooks. Obviously James imagined himself in a much richer relationship with his readers than most modern textbook writers do.*

In a section of the chapter omitted here, James tried to describe how paths in the brain could be forged, following "our usual scientific custom of interpreting hidden molecular events after the analogy of visible massive ones," and he supported two generalizations about habit: "habit simplifies the movements required to achieve a given result," and "habit diminishes the conscious attention with which our acts are performed."

When we look at living creatures from an outward point of view, one of the first things that strikes us is that they are bundles of habits. In wild animals, the usual round of daily behavior seems a necessity implanted at birth; in animals domesticated, and especially in man, it seems, to a great extent, to be the result of education. The habits to which there is an innate tendency are called instincts; some of those due to education would by most persons be called acts of reason. It thus appears that habit covers a very large part of life, and that one engaged in studying the objective manifestations of mind is bound at the very outset to define clearly just what its limits are.

The moment one tries to define what habit is, one is led to the fundamental properties of matter. The laws of Nature are nothing but the immutable habits which the different elementary sorts of matter follow in their actions and reactions upon each other. In the organic world, however, the habits are more variable than this. Even instincts vary from one individual to another of a kind; and are modified in the same individual, as we shall later see, to suit the exigencies of the case. The habits of an elementary particle of matter cannot change (on the principles of the atomistic philosophy), because the particle is itself an unchangeable thing; but those of a compound mass of matter can change, because they are in the last instance due to the structure of the compound, and either outward forces or inward tensions can, from one hour to another, turn that structure into something different from what it was. That is, they can do so if the body be plastic enough to maintain its integrity, and be not disrupted when its structure yields. The change of structure here spoken of need not involve the outward shape; it may be invisible and molecular, as when a bar of iron becomes magnetic or crystalline through the action of certain outward causes, or India-rubber becomes friable, or plaster "sets." All these changes are rather slow; the material in question opposes a certain resistance to the modifying cause, which it takes time to overcome, but the gradual yielding whereof often saves the material from being disintegrated altogether. When the structure has yielded, the same inertia becomes a condition of its comparative permanence in the new form, and of the new habits the body then manifests. *Plasticity*, then, in the wide sense of the word, means the possession of a structure weak enough to yield to an influence, but strong enough not to yield all at once. Each relatively stable phase of equilibrium in such a structure is marked by what we may call a new set of habits. Organic matter, especially nervous tissue, seems endowed with a very extraordinary degree of plasticity of this sort; so that we may without hesitation lay down as our first proposition the following, that *the phenomena of habit in living beings are due to the plasticity of the organic materials of which their bodies are composed.*

. . .

"Habit a second nature! Habit is ten times nature," the Duke of Wellington is said to have exclaimed; and the degree to which this is true no one can probably appreciate as well as one who is a veteran soldier himself. The daily drill and the years of discipline end by fashioning a man completely over again, as to most of the possibilities of his conduct.

There is a story, which is credible enough, though it may not be true, of a practical joker, who, seeing a discharged veteran carrying home his dinner, suddenly called out, "Attention!" whereupon the man instantly brought his hands down, and lost his mutton and potatoes in the gutter. The drill had been thorough, and its effects had become embodied in the man's nervous structure.[1]

Riderless cavalry-horses, at many a battle, have been seen to come together and go through their customary evolutions at the sound of the bugle-call. Most trained domestic animals, dogs and oxen, and omnibus- and car-horses, seem to be machines almost pure and simple, undoubtingly, unhesitatingly doing from minute to minute the duties they have been taught, and giving no sign that the possibility of an alternative ever suggests itself to their mind. Men grown old in prison have asked to be readmitted after being once set free. In a railroad accident to a travelling menagerie in the United States some time in 1884, a tiger, whose cage had broken open, is said to have emerged, but presently crept back again, as if too much bewildered by his new responsibilities, so that he was without difficulty secured.

Habit is thus the enormous fly-wheel of society, its most precious conservative agent. It alone is what keeps us all within the bounds of ordinance, and saves the children of fortune from the envious uprisings of the poor. It alone prevents the hardest and most repulsive walks of life from being deserted by those brought up to tread therein. It keeps the fisherman and the deck-hand at sea through the winter; it holds the miner in his darkness, and nails the countryman to his log-cabin and his lonely farm through all the months of snow; it protects us from invasion by the natives of the desert and the frozen zone. It dooms us all to fight out the battle of life upon the lines of our nurture or our early choice, and to make the best of a pursuit that disagrees, because there is no other

[1] Huxley's *Elementary Lessons in Physiology,* lesson xii.

for which we are fitted, and it is too late to begin again. It keeps different social strata from mixing. Already at the age of twenty-five you see the professional mannerism settling down on the young commercial traveller, on the young doctor, on the young minister, on the young counsellor-at-law. You see the little lines of cleavage running through the character, the tricks of thought, the prejudices, the ways of the "shop," in a word, from which the man can by-and-by no more escape than his coat-sleeve can suddenly fall into a new set of folds. On the whole, it is best he should not escape. It is well for the world that in most of us, by the age of thirty, the character has set like plaster, and will never soften again.

If the period between twenty and thirty is the critical one in the formation of intellectual and professional habits, the period below twenty is more important still for the fixing of *personal* habits, properly so called, such as vocalization and pronunciation, gesture, motion, and address. Hardly ever is a language learned after twenty spoken without a foreign accent; hardly ever can a youth transferred to the society of his betters unlearn the nasality and other vices of speech bred in him by the associations of his growing years. Hardly ever, indeed, no matter how much money there be in his pocket, can he even learn to *dress* like a gentleman-born. The merchants offer their wares as eagerly to him as to the veriest "swell," but he simply *cannot* buy the right things. An invisible law, as strong as gravitation, keeps him within his orbit, arrayed this year as he was the last; and how his better-bred acquaintances contrive to get the things they wear will be for him a mystery till his dying day.

The great thing, then, in all education, is to *make our nervous system our ally instead of our enemy.* It is to fund and capitalize our acquisitions, and live at ease upon the interest of the fund. *For this we must make automatic and habitual, as early as possible, as many useful actions as we can,* and guard against the growing into ways that are likely to be disadvantageous to us, as we should guard against the plague. The more of the details of our daily life we can hand over to the effortless custody of automatism, the more our higher powers of mind will be set free for their own proper work. There is no more miserable human being than one in whom nothing is habitual but indecision, and for whom the lighting of every cigar, the drinking of every cup, the time of rising and going to bed every day, and the beginning of every bit of work, are subjects of express volitional deliberation. Full half the time of such a man goes to the deciding, or regretting, of matters which ought to be so ingrained in him as practically not to exist for his consciousness at all. If there be such daily duties not yet ingrained in any one of my readers, let him begin this very hour to set the matter right.

In Professor Bain's chapter on "The Moral Habits" there are some admirable practical remarks laid down. Two great maxims emerge from his treatment. The first is that in the acquisition of a new habit, or the leaving off of an old one, we must take care to launch ourselves with as strong and decided an initiative as possible. Accumulate all the possible circumstances which shall re-enforce the right motives; put yourself assiduously in conditions that encourage the new way; make engagements incompatible with the old; take a public pledge, if the case allows; in short, envelop your resolution with every aid you know. This will give your new beginning such a momentum that the temptation to break down will not occur as soon as it otherwise might; and every day during which a breakdown is postponed adds to the chances of its not occurring at all.

The second maxim is: *Never suffer an exception to occur till the new habit is securely rooted in your life.* Each lapse is like the letting fall of a ball of string which one is carefully winding up; a single slip undoes more than a great many turns will wind again. *Continuity* of training is the great means of making the nervous system act infallibly right. As Professor Bain says:

> The peculiarity of the moral habits, contradistinguishing them from the intellectual acquisitions, is the presence of two hostile powers, one to be gradually raised into the ascendant over the other. It is necessary, above all things, in such a situation, never to lose a battle. Every gain on the wrong side undoes the effect of many conquests on the right. The essential precaution, therefore, is so to regulate the two opposing powers that the one may have a series of uninterrupted successes, until repetition has fortified it to such a degree as to enable it to cope with the opposition, under any circumstances. This is the theoretically best career of mental progress.

The need of securing success at the *outset* is imperative. Failure at first is apt to dampen the energy of all future attempts, whereas past experience of success nerves one to future vigor. Goethe says to a man who consulted him about an enterprise but mistrusted his own powers: *"Ach!* you need only blow on your hands!" And the remark illustrates the effect on Goethe's spirits of his own habitually successful career.

Prof. Baumann, from whom I borrow the anecdote, says that the collapse of barbarian nations when Europeans come among them is due to their despair of ever succeeding as the new-comers do in the larger tasks of life. Old ways are broken and new ones not formed.

The question of "tapering-off," in abandoning such habits as drink and opium-indulgence, comes in here, and is a question about which experts differ within certain limits, and in regard to what may be best for an individual case. In the main, however, all expert opinion would agree that abrupt acquisition of the new habit is the best way, *if there be a real possibility of carrying it out.* We must be careful not to give the will so stiff a task as to insure its defeat at the very outset; but, *provided one can stand it,* a sharp period of suffering, and then a free time, is the best thing to aim at, whether in giving up a habit like that of opium, or in simply changing one's hours of rising or of work. It is surprising how soon a desire will die of inanition if it be *never* fed.

One must first learn, unmoved, looking neither to the right nor left, to walk firmly on the strait and narrow path, before one can begin "to make one's self over again." He who every day makes a fresh resolve is like one who, arriving at the edge of the ditch he is to leap, forever stops and returns for a fresh run. Without *unbroken* advance there is no such thing as *accumulation* of the ethical forces possible, and to make this possible, and to exercise us and habituate us in it, is the sovereign blessing of regular *work.* [2]

A third maxim may be added to the preceding pair: *Seize the very first possible opportunity to act on every resolution you make, and on every emotional prompting you may experience in the direction of the habits you aspire to gain.* It is not in the moment of their forming, but in the moment of their producing *motor effects,* that resolves and aspirations communicate the new "set" to the brain. As the author last quoted remarks:

The actual presence of the practical opportunity alone furnishes the fulcrum upon which the lever can rest, by means of which the moral will may multiply its strength, and raise itself aloft. He who has no solid ground to press against will never get beyond the stage of empty gesture-making.

[2] J. Bahnsen: *Beiträge zu Charakterologie* (1867), vol. I, p. 209.

No matter how full a reservoir of *maxims* one may possess, and no matter how good one's *sentiments* may be, if one has not taken advantage of every concrete opportunity to *act*, one's character may remain entirely unaffected for the better. With mere good intentions, hell is proverbially paved. And this is an obvious consequence of the principles we have laid down. A "character," as J. S. Mill says, "is a completely fashioned will"; and a will, in the sense in which he means it, is an aggregate of tendencies to act in a firm and prompt and definite way upon all the principal emergencies of life. A tendency to act only becomes effectively ingrained in us in proportion to the uninterrupted frequency with which the actions actually occur, and the brain "grows" to their use. Every time a resolve or a fine glow of feeling evaporates without bearing practical fruit is worse than a chance lost; it works so as positively to hinder future resolutions and emotions from taking the normal path of discharge. There is no more contemptible type of human character than that of the nerveless sentimentalist and dreamer, who spends his life in a weltering sea of sensibility and emotion, but who never does a manly concrete deed. Rousseau, inflaming all the mothers of France, by his eloquence, to follow Nature and nurse their babies themselves, while he sends his own children to the foundling hospital, is the classical example of what I mean. But every one of us in his measure, whenever, after glowing for an abstractly formulated Good, he practically ignores some actual case, among the squalid "other particulars" of which that same Good lurks disguised, treads straight on Rousseau's path. All Goods are disguised by the vulgarity of their concomitants, in this work-a-day world; but woe to him who can only recognize them when he thinks them in their pure and abstract form! The habit of excessive novel-reading and theatre-going will produce true monsters in this line. The weeping of a Russian lady over the fictitious personages in the play, while her coachman is freezing to death on his seat outside, is the sort of thing that everywhere happens on a less glaring scale. Even the habit of excessive indulgence in music, for those who are neither performers themselves nor musically gifted enough to take it in a purely intellectual way, has probably a relaxing effect on the character. One becomes filled with emotions which habitually pass without prompting to any deed, and so the inertly sentimental condition is kept up. The remedy would be, never to suffer one's self to have an emotion at a concert, without expressing it afterward in *some* active way. Let the expression be the least thing in the world—speaking genially to one's aunt, or giving up one's seat in a horse-car, if nothing more heroic offers—but let it not fail to take place.

These latter cases make us aware that it is not simply *particular lines* of discharge, but also *general forms* of discharge, that seem to be grooved out by habit in the brain. Just as, if we let our emotions evaporate, they get into a way of evaporating; so there is reason to suppose that if we often flinch from making an effort, before we know it the effort-making capacity will be gone; and that, if we suffer the wandering of our attention, presently it will wander all the time. Attention and effort are, as we shall see later, but two names for the same psychic fact. To what brain-processes they correspond we do not know. The strongest reason for believing that they do depend on brain-processes at all, and are not pure acts of the spirit, is just this fact, that they seem in some degree subject to the law of habit, which is a material law. As a final practical maxim, relative to these habits of the will, we may, then, offer something like this: *Keep the faculty of effort alive in you by a little gratuitous exercise every day.* That is, be systematically ascetic or heroic in little unnecessary points, do every day or two something for no other reason than that you would rather not do it, so that when the hour of dire need draws nigh, it may find you not unnerved and untrained to stand the test. Asceticism of this sort is like the insurance which a man pays on his house and goods. The tax does him no good at the time, and possibly may never bring him a return. But if the fire *does* come, his having paid it will be his salvation from ruin. So with the man who has daily inured himself to habits of concentrated attention, energetic volition, and self-denial in unnecessary things. He will stand like a tower when everything rocks around him, and when his softer fellow-mortals are winnowed like chaff in the blast.

The physiological study of mental conditions is thus the most powerful ally of hortatory ethics. The hell to be endured hereafter, of which theology tells, is no worse than the hell we make for ourselves in this world by habitually fashioning our characters in the wrong way. Could the young but realize how soon they will become mere walking bundles of habits, they would give more heed to their conduct while in the plastic state. We are spinning our own fates, good or evil, and never to be undone. Every smallest stroke of virtue or of vice leaves its never so little scar. The drunken Rip Van Winkle, in Jefferson's play, excuses himself for every fresh dereliction by saying, "I won't count this time!" Well! he may not count it, and a kind Heaven may not count it; but it is being counted none the less. Down among his nerve-cells and fibres the molecules are counting it, registering and storing it up to be used against him when the next temptation comes. Nothing we ever do is, in strict scientific literalness, wiped out. Of course, this has its good side as well as its bad one. As we become permanent drunkards by so many separate drinks, so we become saints in the moral, and authorities and experts in the practical and scientific spheres, by so many separate acts and hours of work. Let no youth have any anxiety about the upshot of his education, whatever the line of it may be. If he keep faithfully busy each hour of the working-day, he may safely leave the final result to itself. He can with perfect certainty count on waking up some fine morning, to find himself one of the competent ones of his generation, in whatever pursuit he may have singled out. Silently, between all the details of his business, the *power of judging* in all that class of matter will have built itself up within him as a possession that will never pass away. Young people should know this truth in advance. The ignorance of it has probably engendered more discouragement and faint-heartedness in youths embarking on arduous careers than all other causes put together.

QUESTIONS FOR DISCUSSION

1. Why does William James begin with so broad a definition of *habit*, extending it to "the habits of an elementary particle of matter"? Why should an attempt to define *habit* lead immediately to a consideration of the "fundamental properties of matter," and why is the notion of "plasticity" important to his definition of *habit?*
2. Are habits changeable or aren't they? Does James seem to contradict himself?
3. What does James mean when he defines *habit* metaphorically as the "enormous fly-wheel of society"? (First make sure you know what the term "fly-wheel" would have meant to James.) Do you agree that habit is responsible for all the effects he lists following his metaphoric definition?
4. Do you agree with James that, on the whole, personal habits are set by the age of twenty and professional and intellectual habits by thirty? Have you known cases where either kind of habit has been radically and permanently altered in older persons? If so, what was the impetus?
5. What changes come over James's language as the essay reaches its climax? What does this chapter from a learned psychology text begin to sound like?
6. Why is James so adamant that no emotion be allowed to evaporate without expressing itself in some action? If good impulses must find expression to strengthen a person's resolve, what makes it difficult to follow this advice? What does it mean that "Good lurks disguised"?

SUGGESTIONS FOR WRITING

1. Write an essay comparing this selection from James to a self-help or advice book or article familiar to you. Is there any similarity in the advice? In the language? Go on to explain the source of the consistent appeal of such books to readers addicted to them.

2. Do you know someone who would profit from James's advice on habit? Try to personalize his advice and make it palatable to this person in a letter.

3. Would you want to have a "completely fashioned will," to borrow the phrase that James borrows from John Stuart Mill? Can the formation of habits go too far? Write a refutation addressed to James.

4. Such terms as *habit* and *instinct* have undergone considerable redefinition, thanks to the work of ethologists (students of animal behavior) and sociobiologists. Write a modern definition of either of these terms, one that would be acceptable to psychologists today. Address your definition to students in an introductory psychology class, but make it more interesting and entertaining than the kind of definition they would find in a textbook.

5. Compare the view of human nature and habit that James advocates with the view implied by the research conducted on identical twins (see "Identical Twins Reared Apart" in Part Two). Which view is more reassuring?

6. James seems to feel that the ultimate habit is that of making an effort, a habit that should be kept alive by doing something you dislike every day or two. Could you argue that everyone, and especially university students, must practice this habit daily? Your argument may take the form of a parody of advice giving.

Five

ARGUMENTS
AND
REFUTATIONS

In its everyday meaning, *argument* suggests conflict. Two people arguing maintain contradictory theses, back and forth, hurling unverified facts, declarations of personal taste, and perhaps even insults at one another. All too often neither one's mind changes, no issue is clarified, and feelings get hurt. No wonder many of us grow up under the injunction that arguing, especially about politics and religion, is somehow impolite and always to be avoided.

Yet nothing is more characteristic of a healthy intellectual and civic life than argument properly engaged in. All societies have found ways to institutionalize or regulate "argument" in the sense of disagreement between several parties. The courtroom, for example, requires ritualized procedures between conflicting parties and, most important, introduces a third party disengaged from the contending points of view, the judge or jury, to decide which party has the better argument. In legislative bodies, from city councils to the United States Congress, the assembled members present arguments to each other and, supposing they can be moved by motives other than personal loyalty or interest, they also become judges of the pro and con arguments offered to them. Organized debate, practiced in high schools and colleges, simulates the courtroom and legislative setting with its third-party judge and rules about proper procedure. And argument occurs in other situations where it is less structured: in scholarly journals in all fields, where experts offer their views and expose them to the judgment of their peers; in institutions, where past programs must be assessed and future ones planned; and of course in the media, where varying interpretations and predictions of events are offered.

All these kinds of argument are concerned with probable claims, not with provable ones. If we could know for certain the truth about a statement—or convince ourselves that we did—we would not waste time arguing. We would look up the answer, write the proof, and print Q.E.D. at the end, just as we do after demonstrations in geometry. But for most situations in life we cannot come up with one right answer that disallows all others; human conduct and the entire future are two such enormous areas. So we argue, not necessarily against any one person but simply to test how convincing, how plausible we can make a statement by adducing reasons to support it. The proposal, "We should send an astronaut to Mars for this reason, and that reason, and the other reason," will sound much more probable with support behind it than the naked statement will.

We do this kind of arguing all the time, identifying and testing our grounds of belief, seeing how good a case can be made for a position. But every proposition that we care to formulate (such as "Jupiter is a planet") can bring into being a host of other propositions, including the contrary ("Jupiter is not a planet") and the contradictory ("Jupiter is a brown star"). In other words, every arguable proposition evokes its own potential rivals, and a case might be made for one of them. A case for an opposite (whether a contrary or a contradictory proposition) either amounts to a refutation of the first, or it calls for reconciliation with it. We cannot maintain, for example, both that "Senator X should be elected president" and that "Governor Y should be elected president." If we can find a vantage point from which to judge one of these hostile arguments as better, then the other is refuted.

But refutation is more than just a contest between opposed propositions to see which one wins. It is essential in establishing the soundness of any argument. Remember we said earlier that arguments concern matters that cannot be proven beyond a shadow of a doubt. They can only be maintained with the best possible case. How can we know what the best possible case is? Logicians and philosophers maintain that the best test of the validity of an argument is its ability to withstand the assaults of refutations, both those aimed directly at the argument itself and those upholding rival theses. Since no additional support will ever make an argumentative thesis a certainty, the most that can be done to confirm or dislodge it is to aim the best possible counterarguments at it. If it is still standing after the crossfire, it will continue to attract our agreement. We will "believe" it in that special way we believe propositions that can never be matters of fact. As winners by default, many of the liveliest concepts in all fields thus stand firm because they are unrefuted—so far.

Refutation comes in two forms. In the first, an arguer bent on refutation takes hammer and chisel to the edifice of an established argument and starts chipping away. Even if the whole structure of the argument is not demolished, it may nevertheless be weakened by the attack, at least enough so that many would-be adherents will be lost. For a familiar example of this process we can take the famous case of the Warren Commission's Report on the assassination of President John F. Kennedy. The report's conclusion, that Lee Harvey Oswald acted alone and without obvious motivation, has been seriously challenged by the ballistic facts inferable from Kennedy's wounds and by investigations of Oswald's past. Critics of the Warren Commission Report have offered alternative explanations, but none of them has been complete, coherent, or convincing enough to replace the findings of the Warren Commission. Nevertheless, the opponents of the report have attacked so many of its assumptions and interpretations that the doubt cast on its arguments has been sufficient to shake many adherents. If we can cast doubt on the verification of facts in an argument or on the assumptions underpinning it or on the authority of the arguer, we have often successfully refuted it, at least for readers who have no personal stake, emotional or financial, in the argument.

Many people mistakenly believe that refutation solely depends on detecting *fallacies*, special faults in reasoning or violations of the rules of evidence, and to aid such sleuthing countless manuals cataloging fallacies have been written. There is something attractive about the neat categories of fallacies (over one hundred in some books), often with impressive-sounding Latin names and concise, one-sentence examples illustrating their use. Just pop in an instance from an argument, snap down the lid of the fallacy detector, and out pops refutation. But pure logic does not apply to matters of value or probability, and many fallacious arguments remain powerfully convincing to some audiences. The most fruitful hunting ground for the fallacies is logical demonstration; they are less successfully applied to arguments that convince specific audiences of the probability of a contingent thesis. The actual process of refutation, as the essays in this section demonstrate, is a much messier, less certain undertaking than the citation of fallacies.

What then is this process of refutation that aims to weaken an argument? First, we must point out that the tactics of supporting a counterargument against a proposition are exactly the same as those used in support of the original proposition. We can see this process in action in the first selection of this unit, Osamu Nakashima's "Why the West Should Let Japanese Eat Whale," which appeared as an editorial in a "Speaking Out: A Citizen's View" section of a newspaper. Several weeks later the paper printed a sampling of the many letters written to refute Nakashima's argument. Like a dartboard in a pub, his defense of the Japanese customs of whale hunting and eating drew pointed attacks all over its surface. These refutations aim separately at Nakashima's definitions, categorizations, analogies, assumptions of value, and more—all of which they counter with their own definitions, categories, analogies, and assumptions. In fact, it is astounding how many spots in his brief argument attracted the darts of rebuttal. When Nakashima speaks of the Western anti-whaling movement, he is reminded that non-Western nations participate in it; when he speaks of inevitable differences in cultural values, he is reminded that we all share a rather small planet. His implicit analogy between Japanese whale-eating and Christian pork-eating seemed to rankle especially, and the letters point out in many ingenious ways that whales are not domesticated animals raised for humane slaughter, that whales do not breed with the fecundity of domestic animals, and that cattle and hogs are not endangered species. Nor do Nakashima's readers allow to stand unchallenged his thesis that eating whale meat is simply a matter of cultural taste and that the Japanese should be left alone to continue it. Notice, though, that not one of the refuters invokes some automatic formal fallacy, even though many of their points could be fit into certain broadly defined fallacies. Rather they challenge the argument point for point—substantively, ethically, and even personally.

Effective refutation must go after the very substance of an argument. Thus Samuel Florman defines and takes on the antitechnology mentality; the critics of Camilla Benbow and Julian Stanley patiently try to disentangle the issues involved in the apparent mathematical inferiority of girls; and John Ciardi rises to the defense of his critical principles. At its best, refutation can inspire the most eloquent formulation of an author's point of view, as in Martin Luther King, Jr.'s impassioned defense of his tactics, undertaken in response to the criticisms of eight Alabama clergymen.

Each kind of argument has its own special susceptibilities to refutation. Since CP arguments, the first kind, depend on a tie between definition and evidence, they may be undone by attacks on critical terms and on the representative power of the evidence. Notice that challenges to definition rarely take the form of outright disagreement over a word's designation. What is often refuted instead is its area of signification. Thus, to go back to the Nakashima example, neither the first writer nor his host of attackers basically disagree over the denotation of *whale* as a large cetaceous mammal. But the Japanese writer describes this whale as a native culinary delicacy, while to his Western respondents it is a splendid endangered animal.

Refuters also ask whether the evidence gathered really supports the categorization, as in the claim that girls are weaker in mathematical ability than boys. They question whether scores on the SAT exam given to seventh-graders really indicate the nascent mathematical ability of girls. They ask, does the test really "test" for mathematical reasoning, or could other factors operate to inhibit the expression of the girls' ability? Is it strained to base so large a claim on such small evidence? Everything depends on how representative that evidence seems. David Owen performs similar surgery on the claims of the Educational Testing Service to produce a meaningful indicator of college applicants' aptitude for further study.

Causal arguments, our second category, stand or fall on the plausibility of agency, the assumption about what can cause what, and on the evidence they muster to support a claim. Perhaps their weakest flank is the plausible rival cause that a refuter can suggest. Thus when Camilla Benbow and Julian Stanley suggest that the poor showing of girls on the mathematical talent search test is due to innate intellectual differences between boys and girls, perhaps related to spatial reasoning, a chorus of voices chimes in to point to an overlooked factor: the socialization of girls away from the more abstract sciences, a process that may take place before seventh grade.

Similarly, evaluations stand or fall on the acceptability of their criteria to the audience addressed. John Ciardi, for instance, based his first review of Anne Morrow Lindbergh's poetry on criteria he assumed his audience would share: grammaticalness, sensitivity to meaning, aptness of metaphor. His review raised howls of protest, not because his readers denied the legitimacy of his criteria but because they held other standards that they weighted more heavily. In evaluation arguments that appeal to the good or bad consequences of that which is being evaluated, disagreement can arise over which consequences seem more plausible. For example, in the R. L. Mead and Margaret Logan essays about video games presented in this section, the arguers come to different conclusions about the effects, good or bad, of the games on their players. Which argument you find more persuasive will depend on which set of consequences you believe is most convincingly linked with the games.

Since proposal arguments draw on their readers' sense of shared definitions, plausible consequences, and commonly held values, they must defend all those elements against possible refutation. In addition, proposal arguments are especially vulnerable on the flank of feasibility: Can this proposal really be implemented? Is the person making the argument ready, willing, and able to take action? What kinds of obstacles must be overcome in order to bring about the desired state of affairs? Does the proposed action convincingly follow from the analysis that precedes it? Both the Declaration of Independence and the Seneca Falls Declaration present their resolutions after outlining the set of grievances that drove their framers to the manifesto. Their success as arguments depends partly on the extent to which they have made their proposed solutions seem inevitable, even though the ideals they suggest are difficult to achieve. It also depends on what kind of position these arguments would force their refuters to take in order to attack them. The two declarations show how arguments that articulate their most basic assumptions help their readers to take them seriously.

Refutation is thus both a component of arguments, as writers anticipate objections and incorporate potentially hostile points of view into their texts, and a method of responding to arguments others have framed. Far from being a wholly negative activity, it is a way of discovering the basic components of any argument and part of the process by which effective arguments are constructed.

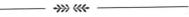

Why the West Should Let Japanese Eat Whale

OSAMU NAKASHIMA

On Eating Whale,

RESPONSES TO OSAMU NAKASHIMA

The following set of arguments illustrates the workings of one of the best institutions any society could have, the free exchange of pro and con opinions in the editorial columns of a newspaper. In this case, a Japanese journalist,

Osamu Nakashima, wrote a defense of his country's practice of eating whale, which was published as the Speaking Out column in the Opinion and Commentary section of the Christian Science Monitor. *Several weeks later the newspaper printed in the Readers Write column a selection of the barrage of letters received in response to Nakashima's opinion.*

The clash of arguments that follows shows how culturally bound most of our values are. Things are right to us because they are right to the group we belong to. To argue across cultures requires finding higher values, values that any human, regardless of cultural affiliations, would acknowledge.

"Why the West Should Let Japanese Eat Whale"

Whale songs enchanted a Boston audience recently as an orchestra performed a piece entitled "And God Created Great Whales."

A listener might almost have heard the scream of the whale in the songs, imploring, "Don't kill us, please." As a Japanese, I also enjoyed it, but I was reminded of a different matter: the Western anti-whaling movement aimed at the Japanese whaling industry.

Last year the International Whaling Commission (IWC) ordered an experimental whaling moratorium starting in 1985, running for as long as five years. The purpose of this proposal is clear: a total and permanent ban.

"Why can't we eat whales?" most Japanese ask. For us, eating whale is a deep cultural tradition.

The tragedy is that antiwhaling activists don't know this. Generally they are very innocent and good-hearted people. They believe in their righteous goals based on Western values, not knowing—even hardly imagining, I am afraid—that they are cultural imperialists.

It reminds me of an old joke.

An American lady once heard about the Japanese dish *sashimi* and remarked: "Eat fish raw? Oh, poor Japanese, we must teach them how to cook."

Just before leaving my country, I went to *Kujira-ya* (a famous whale restaurant in Tokyo) because I knew I would not be able to eat whale in the United States. Moreover, I was not quite sure if I would be able to eat whale when I returned to Japan after a couple of years.

I like whale meat. Many Japanese do. How did we come to appreciate it? The history is simple: we have been eating whale, as well as fish and shellfish, for thousands of years. It was almost a necessary dish since Japan's rulers did not allow the people to eat four-legged animals from the 7th to the 19th century.

Part of the history is wrapped up in the word *sukiyaki*, a popular Japanese meat dish. "Suki" means plow and "yaki" means cook, in this case. The name came from the fact that some Japanese violated the prohibition against eating four-legged animals by cooking on a plow blade in a field so as not to contaminate their homes with the smell.

Hindus don't eat beef because Hinduism says cows are holy. Jews and Muslims don't eat pork since both Judaism and Islam consider pigs unclean. How would Christians feel if these religious sects tried to forbid the eating of beef or pork?

In the same way, the Japanese feel imposed upon. What makes it difficult is that we do not debate the issue in international society, unlike Americans, since that would go against our nature.

Western values are not the only ones that should be accepted on this planet. People with different histories and cultures have different values. No one can judge another's value based on his own, even when he doesn't like it.

Americans may have forgotten an ironic historical fact. In 1852, Commodore Matthew Perry visited Japan in his famous black ships. His gun-ship diplomacy scared the Shogun's government into opening several ports, giving up a two-century isolation. Why did America demand that Japan open its door? One main reason was to get water, food, and fuel for American whalers!

"On Eating Whale: Responses to Osamu Nakashima"

... While Mr. Nakashima makes no mention of the scientific and ecological concerns presented by the continued operation of the whaling industry, he also ignores the international makeup of the growing community dedicated to ending whaling (such "Western" nations as India and the People's Republic of China have recently joined the International Whaling

Commission. . .). His argument that whaling is a cultural right for Japan is unfortunately similar to the defense of a vast number of social and environmental problems, extending back to the days when John C. Calhoun warned the US Senate that the abolition of slavery would change forever the culture of the South.

Finally, the human consumption of whale meat in Japan is a trifle, consisting of less than 1 percent of that nation's protein intake. If this were quite so important, why did Japan's whalers concentrate their efforts on the inedible sperm whale in the 1970s?

Washington   *Greenpeace USA*

Mr. Nakashima asks that Japan be allowed to continue to eat whale because it is part of the Japanese culture. Certainly eating traditions change; the Aztecs and other societies ate human flesh. Whether it was a cultural or nutritional need is not relative; the value placed on human life caused most peoples, by force, acculturation, or diffusion, to relinquish this practice.

The Japanese culture has changed dramatically during its history. Gone are the shoguns, divine emperors, seppuku (ritualistic suicide), and the extreme reverence for their elders. I, therefore, fail to understand the great need to perpetuate this cultural bias of eating whale.

Current data supports the belief that whales are intelligent and even caring animals, a belief supported by scientists as well as environmentalists.

Boise, Idaho

Osamu Nakashima defends the Japanese appetite for whale meat and asks: "How would Christians feel if these religious sects [Judaism and Islam] tried to forbid eating of beef and pork?"

This comparison might even be valid if the whales multiplied as abundantly and as availably as cows and pigs. That they do not, needless to say.

Sanibel, Fla.

Mr. Nakashima missed the whole point of the anti-whaling movement. Our objections to the killing of whales by the USSR and Japan are not ethnocentric, but logical and humane. We are not trying to change the diet of the Japanese, or anyone else; we are trying to keep the whales from extinction.

Pittsburgh

No one is trying to tamper with your eating habits, Mr. Nakashima. . . . it is none of the West's business what you choose to eat. As long as there are vast supplies of whatever it is.

But not whales, Mr. Nakashima. Not whales because whales are endangered as a species, and if something is not done, will soon be totally extinct. Not whales, because whales do not belong to the Americans or to the Japanese. Whales belong to the entire earth. As stewards of the earth it is our responsibility to hand to the future generations of our children a world that is as intact as we can keep it.

Pittsburgh

A majority on the International Whaling Commission voted for a moratorium on whaling starting in 1985. Democratic values are not necessarily just Western values. The United States recognizes the damage its whalers did to the Cetacea family over the last centuries. That is why the US does not "whale" today.

Milwaukee

Surely Mr. Nakashima can see the difference between eating the meat of a wild creature that is becoming endangered, —whose very existence as a species is in question—and the eating of pork, beef, chicken, and other such animals raised in great numbers for the sole purpose of supplying those who eat meat. And surely he can see the difference between the mostly humane slaughter of animals in slaughterhouses around the world and the barbaric, unconscionable methods (the exploding harpoons, et al.) used to kill whales.

If cattle were wild animals that had to be caught and killed in the wild, and if they were becoming extinct, we would be banning their slaughter as well.

La Grange, Ill.

Does [Mr. Nakashima] really believe any culinary tradition worth the destruction of a species? We in the West once enjoyed our own similarly inviolable traditions—including the hunting of buffalo and passenger pigeon—with obvious results.

Washington

What do the Japanese plan to eat when the magnificent whales are extinct? They will have to turn to other food eventually, so why not do it now and preserve the whales for those who take pleasure in watching them . . . and enjoy just knowing that they are still in existence?

Pembroke, N.H.

What is so alarming about Mr. Nakashima's view is his blindness to the fact that man is just an infinitesimal part in the whole grand scheme of life on this planet. This lack of awareness is a form of arrogance that dooms not only whales, but presages ominously our fate as a species.

Marblehead, Mass.

[*Osamu Nakashima replies:* No one wants whales to be extinct. The Japanese would agree to any preservation as long as it was required scientifically. Also, the catching method should be improved.

[These are *not* the real points, however, because everyone can agree on them.

[The real issue is that the hardliners of the major anti-whaling movements are those who argue that whales not be eaten based on their own values. That is why I call them cultural imperialists.

[If they would approve other people's values—and right to eat whales unless the whales are in danger of becoming extinct —we could then drain emotion from the issue, leave it to scientists, and cooperate with each other.]

QUESTIONS FOR DISCUSSION

1. What are the points of definition at contention between Nakashima and his refuters?
2. Nakashima argues for eating whale as a cultural right. What values do his refuters hold as higher? How are these higher values hierarchically ordered?
3. Why does Nakashima invoke Commodore Perry? How does his view of America's whaling past conflict with his refuters' view?
4. Which one of the respondents do you think is the most emotional in tone? What are the signs in the language by which we sense the emotion of the writer?
5. Which of the respondents do you consider to have the strongest argument? (There are two perspectives from which to judge "strongest argument": that of Nakashima or that of the *Monitor's* readers.)
6. What does Nakashima concede in his final statement? What does he retain as his strongest argument? Why does he invoke the authority of science to solve a problem of value?
7. What attitude toward change and tradition is implied in Nakashima's argument? How does the attitude of his refuters differ from his?

SUGGESTIONS FOR WRITING

1. The arguments in the letters responding to Nakashima are brief and fragmentary (no doubt in part because the newspaper exercised its right to condense respondents' letters). Drawing on their various suggestions, write a unified, sustained refutation of Nakashima's argument.
2. Or come to Nakashima's aid and write a stirring defense of his position from a Western point of view.

3. Argue for the protection of a species from commercial exploitation, such as elephants, rhinoceroses, seals, egrets, or sea turtles. Aim your argument at the readers of the *Monitor*.

4. Argue for the preservation of an endangered species, refuting the claim that if it died out, nothing would happen. Or take the opposite position and argue that extraordinary efforts should not be made to protect an endangered species; rather, it should be allowed to die out. In each case, direct your argument at a resistant audience.

5. Write an argument evaluating the values expressed or implied on either side of the whale argument. How would you defend to your fellow students the right to cultural practices or the right to oppose them in the name of higher values?

6. Justify one of our cultural practices that might be considered odd by an outsider predisposed against it, such as our preference for eating rare meat, or painting eyelids various unnatural colors, or even the outrageous practice of allowing young people to choose their own marriage partners.

⇉⟫ ⟪⇇

In Defense of Pac-Man

R.L. MEAD

⇉⟫ ⟪⇇

Et in Arcadia Video

MARGARET LOGAN

As hard as it is to believe now, just a few years ago the rising phenomena of computer game parlors and home video game systems aroused a flurry of discomfort in many parents and educators. Some communities went so far as to ban computer game centers. Just why the suspicion of video games, as well as much of the fad, has passed away is itself an interesting subject for speculation.

The two articles below were not aimed at one another, but they represent opposing evaluations of the computer game craze. Though they were published at roughly the same time (August and October 1982 respectively), they are aimed at completely different audiences. "In Defense of Pac-Man" (Does anyone remember Pac-Man?) appeared over the signature of editor R.

L. Mead in Technology Illustrated, *a mass circulation publication; "Et in Arcadia Video," by novelist Margaret Logan, came out in the* Boston Review, *a publication sponsored by the National Endowment for the Humanities, which reaches a very select audience. Both arguments conduct readers on a virtual tour of the techniques of evaluation. The relaxed and autobiographical "Defense" defuses any fear of video games by associating them with things familiar and harmless. The erudite and serious "Et in Arcadia Video" explores the definition of play and the consequences of the games on the human spirit. Both arguments were designed to fit their respective audiences.*

"In Defense of Pac-Man"

"We got trouble, right here in River City . . ."

I remember the first and only time I was hustled at the pool table. It was a Saturday night in early summer about 25 years ago. I arrived with two friends at Ames pool hall on Manhattan's West Side about 9:30, and we went up and got a table and a rack of balls. Then, with all the nonchalance I could muster, I pulled the pieces of my grandfather's inlaid, ebony pool cue from its black leather carrying case, screwed the stick together, and started lagging the cue ball at our corner table. You really need only two other details to get the scene. Ames pool hall was as unregenerate a commercial establishment as 99 percent of the population would ever want to experience. The fact that *The Hustler* with Paul Newman and Jackie Gleason as Minnesota Fats was shot at Ames may have lent the place some celebrity, but it did nothing to improve its ambience. The second fact is that I had graduated from prep school two days before. Although I had played pool off and on since I was 13, I walked into Ames that night with my custom cue, dressed in my chino pants, polo shirt, and penny loafers—all 17 years of me—ripe for the plucking.

I got plucked, all right, by Dino Defasio from Astoria, Queens. Dino wasn't any older than me, but he'd been around the block a few times, as they say, and had been playing pool, he told me later, every day since he was seven. But to me, warmed up and ready to shoot straight pool, Dino looked easy. We started playing at a buck a ball, and I broke and ran maybe eight balls. Dino jumped down from the windowsill where he had been sitting cleaning his nails and ran a little more than three racks. So it went. I lost nearly $50 ($20 of my own and every cent my friends had with them). We left Ames at 1:30 A.M. and walked home. We couldn't even stop for Cokes.

Through most of high school and college, pool was my game. For my brother-in-law, 12 years my junior, pinball was the rage. Now it's Pac-Man. Pool, pinball, Pac-Man—manual, mechanical, electronic—the point doesn't seem to have changed: Kids will get together and try to outscore each other pushing little globes around a rectangular frame. Such games of skill aren't dangerous or particularly expensive to play (if you're any good at Pac-Man, you can play all afternoon for a couple of quarters). They create spaces that are exciting to go to, places to see others and to be seen. Granted, there is an intensity in the Pac-Man phenomenon that is unparalleled. But I suspect that says more about the era we live in—its rapidly obsolescing technology—than about our kids. In the same way that Space Invaders (an electronic incarnation of another old standby, the shooting gallery) was zapped out of video-arcade preeminence after a lifetime counted in months, the kids know that as Pac-Man crests, the next wave is forming. And they're ready to jump.

Still, it's nothing short of mania, equally visible in parents. They're reacting true to form: "We got trouble . . . with a capital T and that rhymes with P and that stands for . . ." Pac-Man. Across the country town councils, boards of aldermen, and other official guardians against civic turpitude are closing arcades and impounding the machines, thus restoring to pizza parlors, bus stations, bowling alleys, and other after-(school)-hours spots their former uplifting atmospheres. Where the kids congregate to play wicked games, evil will transpire.

To the right-minded it must be a relief to see Pac-Man come into the home, where its use can be supervised. . . . Coleco's stock raced to the front of the Wall Street pack in the first quarter of 1982 with the announcement that it was introducing a home version of Pac-Man.

I'm not surprised by the Pac-Man hysteria, on the part of the kids or their parents. And the home version of Pac-Man will undoubtedly continue to enjoy record sales until the next wave overtakes it. But those right thinkers shouldn't let down their guard. I doubt if Coleco or Atari, which is marketing a home-computer version of Pac-Man, will be any more successful domesticating youthful energies than Sears was in my day selling pool tables for the family rec room.

The last time I saw Defasio he was studying to be a CPA. Wherever he is today, if he's a parent, I'll bet his kids are Pac-Man champs. And I'll bet he hasn't increased their allowance one dime, either.

"Et in Arcadia Video"

The Charlie Chaplin classic *Modern Times* has our hero, wrench in either hand, tightening bolts on a factory assembly line. The line speeds up, wrenches fly, and Chaplin manages—barely—to hang in. The pace increases yet again. Overwhelmed, Chaplin goes berserk.

Berzerk happens to be the name of a video machine. Like all these games, *Berzerk* begins briskly enough, then speeds up. To "stay alive," as they say in the arcades, you must keep pace with each escalation of the computer-driven machine. Lasting seven minutes is no mean feat.

How has Chaplin's nightmare vision become a pleasing fantasy? Why are the nation's citizens (mostly male) of all ages (mostly adolescent) voluntarily, not to say addictively, paying in number (twenty billion quarters last year) for the pleasure of contending with machines relentless beyond Chaplin's wildest fears?

To understand the arcade, it is important first to see how computer control interferes with traditional concepts about play. The machine's demands—its pace, its fixed program—virtually eliminate daydreaming, invention, and fantasy, all cited by Freud, Erikson, and others as significant benefits of true play. Equally impossible is the exploratory play that Einstein believed was fundamental to productive scientific thought. In no real sense does a kid in an arcade freely choose or create his own objectives and methods, refining or discarding these as he goes along, limited only by his own imagination.

Computer control has also altered our notion of "game." Chance, that intractable complicator of every other contest, is totally absent. Although the frenetic activity on the screen usually bewilders neophytes, each program eventually proves to be predictable, manageable, unwaveringly "fair." In the arcade, you do not test your skill against an opponent's. Your opponent, after all, is a computer; infallible, it can't lose. Ironically, the appeal of video games may lie in this bleak truth. With standard games and sports, the worst kind of opponent is one who "plays like a machine" and makes you feel like a fool for even hoping to win. The video machine removes both the burden of that hope and its possible disappointment. Instead of trying to win, you set your own scoring standards and try to surpass them. "The machine doesn't judge you," Arcadeans will say approvingly.

With invention, fantasy, chance, and the hope of winning subtracted, the one element of traditional play left is order. As historian Johan Huizinga points out in *Homo Ludens: A Study of the Play-element in Culture,* all play creates order and thus "gratifies the human aesthetic impulse—the impulse to create orderly form." The video machine obviously delivers order, in spades. The kid who achieves a degree of mastery, the reward of many hours and countless quarters, dwells for an interval in a flawlessly consistent universe. He knows precisely when a belt of asteroids will swarm onto the screen and threaten his space ship. He knows precisely how to maneuver Pac-Man through a tricky maze. No wonder if confused teenagers and harassed adults, unable to deal with the world's unpredictability, find the arcade so therapeutic.

Indeed, the arcade's social atmosphere is orderly and remarkably harmonious. Differences of race or sex, which might trigger powerful reactions elsewhere, are eclipsed by the all-absorbing games. Computer control and precise scoring preclude fights about cheating, poor sportsmanship, and doctored scores. The arcade is, in fact, a milieu for our troubled times. It's a place to congregate with one's fellows in a state of pleasurable, intense excitement without incurring the hazards of intimacy likely to spring from such situations.

"I like the total anonymity," confesses an educational planner, changing another dollar. "When people watch it breaks my concentration," a teenager complains. Though players learn programs by watching others play them, post-game wrap-ups and strategy sharing are severely limited. There is a strong ethos that one "plays his own game." Real Arcadeans scorn trots like *How to Win* (sic) *at Pac-Man:* "That's like starting with the last chapter of a mystery," they complain.

Defenders of video games invariably answer worries about creeping solipsism by introducing the option of doubles. But doubles are only sequential: I play my own game until I lose a man, then you play your own game until you do. Doubles aren't taken seriously by true Arcadeans. "You're just hacking around with friends," says one boy. "You get better scores alone," says another. "More for your quarter. I'm there to blank everything else out. I never play doubles."

Much has been said about the violence of video games, but here, too, the reductive, orderly principle dominates. The scenarios of the games, unlike street, domestic, or political violence, are canned. However incessantly reenacted, the bombardment, ambush, mutation, and annihilation cannot exceed what was fixed on the memory chip. Nothing is random, all is satisfactorily controlled by a player's mastery. Nevertheless, even teenaged Arcadeans will question a culture in which so many are playing out agons of this nature. And the language of the arcade is dire. The screen reads GAME OVER, but kids call it dying. Mastery was defined for me by one twelve-year-old as "not worrying about dying."

In *Modern Times*, Chaplin and his "gamine" never settle for the narrow view of life's possibilities. Although the satisfactions of work have been undermined by machines repressive of every natural impulse, the world of imaginative play remains intact. Like artless children absorbed in the game of "house," the pair invent their domestic arrangements. Later, set loose in a department store closed for the night, they explore its riotous potential. Play in this movie is more than a consolation or an escape from the alienating workplace. It is the way we touch and know our moral and human center. Ultimately it releases the artist, the free spirit.

Against this, the activity of the arcade seems not only reductive but pernicious. The most complete mastery belongs to individuals most capable of submission to a machine's fixed program. And once a kid is persuaded that the workings of his own imagination cannot match the adrenalin-rich thrills supplied by Atari's R&D department, he has lost more than his quarters, grievously more. The immense popularity of video machines is a warning. We should be alerted to the fragility of children's confidence in their own imaginative powers—powers we must soon draw on to continue struggling with problems the arcade simply distracts us from.

Only a dedicated conspiracy theorist would believe that video machines are deliberately "designed" to promote habits of submission and to spawn docile workers, voters, and consumers. Nevertheless, this may prove to be their long-term effect. Their limited, canned programs will nurture few apostates, heretics, innovators, prophets or conscientious objectors, to use Huizinga's list of imaginative spoil-sports who refuse to obey the rules. But then, if we really valued such people, would we embrace the video machine? Aren't we saying, with every quarter we put in the slot, that everything would run more smoothly without them?

QUESTIONS FOR DISCUSSION

1. Characterize the projected personalities of the authors of these articles. That will seem easier to do for R. L. Mead, who talks a great deal about himself, but even Margaret Logan, who does not use the first person, nevertheless writes in an identifiable voice.

2. Both authors base part of their arguments on comparisons to movies, Mead implicitly by quoting lyrics and Logan explicitly and extensively. What do they gain by these comparisons?
3. What different definitions of *play* underlie each of these arguments? What do these appeals show about their respective audiences?
4. These two essays characterize the social atmosphere of arcades quite differently. Which do you think is more correct? Could both be correct?
5. What are the authors' views on the competition provided by video games? Do they agree or disagree about the value of competition?
6. Extract the appeals to authority underpinning Logan's argument. Where does authority lie in Mead's essay?

SUGGESTIONS FOR WRITING

1. Adopt the personal voice of Mead and make a direct response to Logan's argument.
2. Both essays characterize video games and the atmosphere of the video arcade very differently. Write your own characterizations of either or both for an uninitiated audience.
3. Select one game, not necessarily a video game, that you are familiar with and evaluate it positively or negatively according to the criteria of Logan or Mead. Does the game foster friendly or destructive competition, encourage or stifle creativity, socialize participants or isolate them? Address your evaluation to players of the game.
4. Both essays depend heavily on definitions of *play*. Think back to your own experiences as a child and examine the play you engaged in. Were there different kinds of play with different purposes, or did all forms of play seem to have the same elements? Write a comparison of the kind of play you engaged in as a child with the kind of play you do now. Your essay might emphasize either similarities or differences.
5. According to Mead, "kids will get together and try to outscore each other pushing little globes around a rectangular frame." Now that the Pac-Man craze has died out, is there a current or perennial version of this "globe and rectangle" impulse? Identify a game that is currently popular and make a case for the sources of its appeal.
6. Logan says that chance is an element in all games. Do you agree? To write an extended answer to this question you will need to create a working definition of *chance*.

--- →» «← ---

The SAT

JAY AMBERG

--- →» «← ---

1983: The Last Days of the ETS

DAVID OWEN

Every college student knows what the SAT is and how much time, money, and anxiety it costs. But you may not know what all the effort is for. Did your SAT score actually help or hinder your chances of getting into the college of your choice? The SAT has become so much an institution, such a fixture in high school life since even sophomores now take the PSAT to sharpen their skills, that basic questions about the test tend to be ignored. Is it worth all the effort and anxiety? Does it serve any valuable individual or social purposes?

The pair of essays reprinted here come up with opposite answers to the question of the SAT's value. To Jay Amberg, writing largely to the academic community in Phi Beta Kappa's The American Scholar, *the test remains "a fair, uniform, and judiciously administered exam." His conclusion follows a detailed look at the test and a reexamination of what it actually measures. To David Owen, writing for the iconoclastic readers of* Harper's, *the SAT is anything but fair, uniform, and judiciously administered. In fact, Owen doubts that the test scores make any difference in the vast majority of admissions decisions. The final verdict on the SAT is up to the readers of these essays.*

"The SAT"

At any rate they keep out the half-witted.
          —Lord Bloomfield on competitive examinations.

Parents at a suburban high school open house ask an English teacher what he is doing to prepare their son for the Scholastic Aptitude Test —not for college, but for the SAT. A senior in high school writes in an essay, "Although being an upperclassman is often a lot of fun, taking the SAT causes tension and aggravation." Parents of high school seniors, talking at a party, compare their children's SAT scores—as though high scores certify intelligence and low scores suggest stupidity. A senior in high school who has just received average SAT scores announces to a friend that she will never amount to anything in life. A young man sues the Educational Testing Service, the creators of the SAT, because he feels he has been discriminated against by ETS. During a job interview, an employer asks a twenty-four-year-old graduate student what her SAT scores were.

Applying to American colleges is often a confusing and frustrating rite of passage—perhaps *the* American rite of passage. Many students, their parents, and much of the American public believe that the SAT is the crucial factor, the gatekeeper, in this rite. Many students consider the day they receive their SAT scores the second most important day in their educational lives. (The first is the day they are actually accepted or rejected at the college of their choice.) Anyone who doubts this needs only to talk to high school seniors—or to browse through the scores of articles that appear yearly in popular magazines and in newspapers.

In European countries, standardized tests have historically been the gatekeepers to higher education. In France all students graduating from public schools must take standardized state examinations. Those students, for example, who attend the lycées, the academic secondary schools, must take the *baccalauréat* examination. Those who pass the *baccalauréat* (sometimes as few as 60 percent of those taking it) are admitted to most French universities. In Great Britain, the "eleven-plus" examination was until recently administered to all students at the age of eleven. Those who failed the "eleven-plus," about four-fifths of the students, went on to secondary modern schools, which offered a general education, or to technical schools, which provided vocational training. Those who passed the "eleven-plus" attended academic grammar schools in preparation for the universities. Even though the "eleven-plus" is no longer required in most locales and comprehensive high schools offering all three programs have begun to replace the segregated schools, secondary school students planning to attend college still must take the Advanced Level General Certificate of Education (GCE) examinations administered by the universities. Although SAT scores are by no means the sole—or even the most important—admissions criterion used by American colleges, many Americans have come to believe that the SAT is as crucial to their children's educational future as the *baccalauréat* is to the French or the Advanced Level GCE is to the British.

The current public confusion about the SAT suggests a number of questions about the test itself, the Educational Testing Service, and the College Entrance Examination Board, the original creators of the SAT: How is the SAT used—and how *should* it be used—by American college admissions officers? Is the SAT a *fair* measure of scholastic aptitude? For that matter, what is the SAT—and what exactly does it attempt to measure? What, if anything, can or should young people do to prepare for the test? Why has the public concern about and criticism of the SAT intensified in the last decade? Do ETS and the College Board have the sort of gatekeeping power attributed to them? And finally, to put all of these questions into historical perspective, why was the SAT created in the first place?

The need for a standardized college admissions examination became obvious at the turn of the century. Admissions requirements to American colleges in the seventeenth and eighteenth centuries had been classical: applicants had only to demonstrate that they could read and write Latin and Greek. During the nineteenth century admissions requirements expanded considerably (Harvard, for example, added arithmetic in 1807; the University of Michigan added United States history in 1869), but there was little standardization. Before 1870 a student wanting to go to college had to take a separate admissions test for each school. There was no substantial agreement among leading colleges about how much preparation was needed—or even what subjects were required. In 1870 Michigan set up the first accrediting system requiring applicants to present a diploma or secondary school certificate. Nonetheless, admission to American colleges was still chaotic in the 1890s.

In 1900 a group of educators formed the College Board to standardize college admission procedures and to act as a liaison between secondary schools and colleges. A major responsibility of the College Board was the creation of examinations, "these to be thorough, fair, uniform, and judiciously administered by a board of national recognition." The College Board today includes as members more than twenty-five-hundred colleges and universities, secondary schools, and education associations and agencies, but its original purpose still guides the organization. A 1977 report of the Committee on College Board Mission and Accountability concluded, "The purposes of the College Board as stated in the Charter remain consonant with the needs and purposes of the contemporary American educational system." Chief among the purposes listed in the charter is "the continuance and development of a program of tests and examinations."

In the late 1940s, the College Board contracted with the Educational Testing Service (ETS), a private nonprofit corporation, to produce the SAT and other standardized tests. ETS today provides a variety of services, including a substantial amount of educational research, but it remains best known for its standardized tests. Each year more than a million and a half high school students take the SAT; another million and a quarter high school juniors take the PSAT, a preliminary scholastic aptitude test used to determine qualifications for National Merit Scholarships. More than a million additional students take other ETS tests, including the Graduate Record Examination (GRE), the Law School Admission Test (LSAT), and the National Teacher Examination (NTE). As the number of persons taking the ETS exams increases, so does ETS revenue. In 1980 ETS reported revenue of almost $107 million and assets of $47 million. Even though ETS is not the only producer of standardized tests and the SAT is not the only standardized test used by college admissions officers, ETS and the SAT have received most of the public attention and criticism of standardized admissions tests over the last few years.

Much of the public concern about the SAT has focused less on the test itself (most people remain confident that the test measures something akin to academic aptitude) than on the uses of the test by college admissions officers. Although many Americans believe that the SAT is a national gatekeeper similar to the *baccalauréat* or the Advanced Level GCE exam, neither ETS nor the College Board tells admissions officers how to use the test. Michael Kean, Midwest director of ETS, says: "ETS is not a gatekeeper. The SAT plays a role in admissions selection, in the gatekeeping process, but the term 'gatekeeper' suggests that ETS ultimately decides who is accepted in college. This is simply not true." What is true is that 86 percent of four-year public colleges and 90 percent of four-year private colleges consider standardized test scores an important factor in admissions. Yet only 1 percent of four-year private colleges and 2 percent of four-year public colleges claim they consider the scores "the single most important factor." In contrast, an applicant's academic performance in high school is considered the single most important factor in 39 percent of four-year private colleges and 43 percent of four-year public colleges. James Alexander, past president of the National Association of College Admissions Counselors, puts these statistics into perspective when he notes: "Admissions officers at selective colleges tend to use a variety of factors to determine who will be admitted. High school performance is the best predictor; the addition of standardized test scores, as well as other factors, will improve prediction. Very few schools will accept or reject a student on the basis of test scores alone."

How this variety of factors to determine admissions works in practice is best shown through examples of particular colleges' admissions procedures. At Princeton University, for instance, 50 percent of the admissions decision is based on academic credentials and 50 percent on nonacademic factors. The academic portion is based on a variety of criteria: grades and rank in high school, SAT scores, achievement-test scores, and recommendations. Nonacademic factors include "leadership activities," school activities, sports, and personal interviews. Special attention is given to students in certain categories: prospective engineers, athletes, minorities, and alumni and faculty children. (James Wickenden, Princeton's director of admissions, admits, "We took forty-five percent of those alumni children who applied, but only twenty percent of all others.") Within this context, the SAT is used as an admission requirement that cuts across all applicants—it is the single unifying measure. A high SAT score does not, however, guarantee admission to Princeton. Less than 52 percent of the applicants for the class of 1984 with SAT verbal scores between 750–800 (the test scores are reported on a 200–800 scale) and less than 39 percent of those with similar SAT math scores were offered admission. Conversely, approximately 18 percent of those with SAT verbal scores between 550–599 and over 19 percent of those with similar SAT math scores were admitted. In fact, a few applicants with verbal and math scores below 350 were accepted. Wickenden concludes, "The SAT scores, while important, are far from being determining factors in the admission process."

At the University of Michigan, the academic part of an applicant's record is most carefully evaluated. Donald Swain, assistant director of admissions, says, "We begin by looking at the academic record of an applicant as reflected by grades on a transcript. We give a little extra weight in our process to those students who have taken honors or advanced placement courses. Consistency of grades and improvement of grades are important factors." Extracurricular activities and recommendations are not strongly considered at Michigan. Alumni children and minorities receive some extra consideration, as do students who come from geographical areas not overly represented at the university. The combined SAT verbal and math scores or the composite ACT score (American College Testing Assessment published in Iowa City, Iowa) are considered important. Swain says:

> We use whatever set of scores is to the applicant's advantage. There is a tremendous range of test scores. In the liberal arts college, where we get many more applicants than we can accommodate, we hold tighter to a grade average or a test range—but there is no cutoff score. Our priority is with students who have done well day by day in class. An application that shows an outstanding record will likely, although not necessarily, counterbalance low SAT scores.

Despite what college admissions officers say about the SAT, many Americans remain convinced that the Scholastic Aptitude Test measures something innate, something akin to inborn academic ability. Although "aptitude" means "a natural or acquired capacity or ability," ETS and the College Board use the term to mean only *acquired* ability. The 1981/82 SAT guide sent to students states: "The SAT measures developed verbal and mathematical reasoning abilities that are involved in successful academic work in college; it is not a test of some inborn and unchanging capacity." Why then the use of the ambiguous term "aptitude"? Rex Jackson of ETS writes: "The SAT is described as an aptitude test because, unlike a traditional achievement test, it is not tied to a particular course of study, and because it is designed to assist in predicting future academic performance." The SAT, then, is a test that, despite its dubious title, measures acquired academic ability unrelated to a specific course—and nothing more. It does not purport to measure motivation, creativity, or other traits generally associated with success in college and life.

The SAT is a multiple-choice test composed of four separately timed, half-hour verbal and mathematics sections (each SAT also includes a half-hour Test of Standard Written English and an experimental verbal or mathematics section that is not scored with the others). The two verbal sections of the SAT include antonym, analogy, sentence-completion, and reading questions. The examples that follow are from the 1981 ETS publication *Taking the SAT*, which is available to students.

The antonym questions, designed to test a student's vocabulary, ask the students to choose from among five words the word that is most nearly opposite in meaning to a word in capital letters:

DENOUNCE: (A) overstate (B) acclaim (C) destroy (D) refuse (E) hasten.

The vocabulary that is tested ranges from ordinary words like "ordinary" to difficult—and the critics would suggest esoteric—words like "exculpate," "ebullient," and "vestigial."

The analogy questions are designed to test a student's "ability to see a relationship in a pair of words, to understand the ideas expressed in the relationship, and to recognize a similar or parallel relationship":

YAWN : BOREDOM :: (A) dream : sleep (B) anger : madness (C) smile : amusement (D) face : expression (E) impatience : rebellion

A student's ability to answer many of the analogy questions is less dependent on a knack for recognizing word relationships than on a rich vocabulary, a fact tacitly admitted by ETS in that the analogy scores are reported as part of a "vocabulary subscore." For example, "particle: aggregate," "enigma: mysterious," and "whelp: dog" (three of ten analogies in one SAT section) all present relatively simple, indeed almost simpleminded, word relationships, a point that is obvious only to those who happen to know the meanings of *aggregate, enigma,* and *whelp.*

The sentence-completion questions are designed to test a student's ability to recognize the relationships among parts of a sentence. As with the analogies, it helps to have a rich vocabulary:

Although Spalding --- the importance of the physical necessities of life, her most successful endeavor was the --- of the condition of the impoverished.
(A) deprecated . . alleviation
(B) emphasized . . investigation
(C) accentuated . . amelioration
(D) epitomized . . delineation
(E) disregarded . . desecration

A typical SAT verbal section includes two or three 300–500-word reading selections from the humanities, sciences, or social studies. The three to five questions following each selection require students to understand, analyze, and interpret what they have read. No prior knowledge of the content is necessary, however; all of the questions may be answered solely on the basis of what is stated or implied in the selection.

The SAT mathematical sections include two types of problems—

standard multiple-choice word problems ("If x is a positive integer and $x^2 + x = n$, which of the following could be the value of n? (A) 14 (B) 15 (C) 18 (D) 23 (E) 30") and quantitative comparison questions. The quantitative comparison questions emphasize the concepts of equalities, inequalities, and estimations. Although they generally require less computation than the standard multiple-choice questions, the quantitative comparison questions sometimes confuse students:

$$x + y = 8$$

$$x - y = 12$$

Column A   Column B
  y 0

Answer: A if the quantity in Column A is greater;
        B if the quantity in Column B is greater;
        C if the two quantities are equal;
        D if the relationship cannot be determined from the
          information given.

According to ETS pamphlets, the only mathematical preparation needed for the SAT is a year of high school algebra and some geometry. Although this is technically true, the form of the problems, particularly the quantitative comparisons, is quite different from the form of the problems students have experienced in high school classes. Many students become confused by the questions on the SAT; indeed, less than half of the students taking the test are able to answer even half of the mathematics questions correctly.

Between 1963 and 1980, the average SAT mathematics score declined thirty-six points (on the 800–200 scale), from 502 to 466. The average SAT verbal score declined even more dramatically–fifty-four points, from 478 in 1963 to 424 in 1980. (The average scores for 1981, 425 verbal and 468 math, marked the first reversal in this downward trend.) During the 1960s, much of the decline was attributable to changes in the composition of the student group taking the SAT. Students from minority groups who had not traditionally gone to college began taking the test as part of the admissions process. During the 1970s, however, the decline continued, even though the composition of the student group did not change significantly. The statistics showing this second phase of the decline in no way intimated causes for the decline, a fact that has allowed a variety of people to draw their own conclusions about the decline. Indeed, many of the reasons put forth for the decline reflect personal bias rather than informed opinion: decline in modern foreign language study, stress on independent study, "parental coddling," increased encroachment of the courts (including, of course, busing), growing rejection of traditional Western religions and interest in Eastern religions, use of drugs by students, subversive political activities, women's liberation, more married female teachers, and the influx of male teachers into the "female domain" of school. The College Board, in a 1977 examination of the decline, suggested that six general factors, including the changing role of the family, the influence of television, and "the disruption in the life of the country," were at work —a rather grand and long-winded admission that they, too, did not have the foggiest notion about the specific causes of the decline.

Whatever the real causes, the decline itself has directed unprecedented attention toward the SAT. With this attention has come criticism of a surprisingly virulent nature. (Ralph Nader, for example, begins the preface of his study group's report on ETS, *The Reign of ETS,* with, "The conception of this report on the Educational Testing Service began with the *victims* of standardized testing." [Emphasis added.]) Although criticism of the SAT has been offered since the test's inception, the recent criticism has been more widely reported in the popular media. ETS and the SAT have become something of a magnet for criticism of standardized tests and of college admissions.

The College Board and ETS recommend that SAT scores be used as a supplement to students' high school records in the admissions process. This use of the SAT is based on the assumption that it validly predicts first-year college grades. No one at the College Board or at ETS suggests that the test predicts success in college or in life beyond college years. Yet, some critics, notably Warner V. Slack and Douglas Porter of Harvard Medical School, believe that the SAT does not serve even this limited function well. In the *Harvard Education Review* (May 1980) Slack and Porter conclude: "The validity coefficient of the [SAT] tests, together with high school records, is, on the average, only 0.06 higher than that of the high school record alone." Similarly, the Nader report states that the SAT increases predictive ability over high school records alone by only 3 to 5 percent. The College Board and ETS, using different methods, reject both the Slack and Porter and the Nader conclusions. Rex Jackson of ETS states that the improvement in predictability of the tests in conjunction with the high school record over the high school record alone is 27 percent. George H. Hanford of the College Board puts the matter more dramatically: "Thousands of validity studies prove that the SAT increases predictive efficiency by 40 to 50 percent when it is used in *helping* to estimate first-year college grades —not the paltry 3 to 5 percent that Ralph Nader suggests." Because the researchers use different methods—and sometimes different figures—conclusions about the SAT's predictive ability are likely to remain contradictory. The underlying issue, however, is not what the exact percentage of improvement the SAT offers is, but how the scores are used by admissions officers. As we have seen, admissions officers at selective colleges tend to use SAT scores as a supplementary factor that cuts across all students regardless of their backgrounds. Used as a counterbalance to the differences in high school curricula and the subjectivity of grades, the SAT scores, admissions officers believe, have a usefulness that transcends the argument about the percentage of increase in predictive ability.

The fact that SAT scores are used to compare students from different backgrounds, however, prompts other criticism. An ostensibly simple fact about the SAT is that the scores of minority students are lower than those of other students. Robert L. Williams, among other critics, makes the point that the scores are not fair standards of comparison because the test discriminates against blacks and other minority students, who are not altogether familiar with mainstream American culture and with standard written English. In an attempt to demonstrate his point, Williams wrote a test called the "Black Intelligence Scale of Cultural Homogeneity" (BITCH). All of the items for the BITCH were drawn exclusively from black experience. When Williams administered the test to blacks and whites, the scoring pattern, not surprisingly, was the reverse of the SAT—blacks had higher scores. Whatever Williams' results might suggest about American culture, it is erroneous to conclude, as Williams did, that because he was capable of creating a biased test, the content of the SAT is therefore biased. Every item on the SAT is checked for bias by minority reviewers—and then checked again. Indeed, anyone familiar with the content of the SAT is aware that there are no items biased against blacks or other minorities. Any items *about* minorities are uniformly positive in nature.

Williams's point about the language of the SAT is more interesting. He is perfectly correct in assuming that the test contains no black slang— or any other slang, for that matter. The language of the SAT is standard written English—the English used in most college classes, required in most college papers, and used in most American businesses. Including nonstandard English on the SAT might help minority students score better, but it would not help college admissions officers determine who would likely do well in college classes, which is, of course, what the test is designed to do. The fact that black students score well on the BITCH suggests that they know black English better than they know standard written English. Blacks and other minorities certainly have a right to their language, but such usage will not likely help them to succeed in selective American colleges or in most businesses.

Statistical evidence concerning SAT scores suggests that the argument about minority discrimination is really an argument about social class in the United States. The correlation between SAT scores and family income, the critics point out, is embarrassingly high. The following table of average SAT scores for 1973/74 seniors does, in fact, show that the mean scores are higher among high income groups.

Student's Score	Student's Mean Family Income
750–800	$24,124
700–749	21,980
650–699	21,292
600–649	20,330
550–599	19,481
500–549	18,824
450–499	18,122
400–449	17,387
350–399	16,182
300–349	14,355
250–299	11,428
200–249	8,639

This information leads some critics to conclude that the SAT is a substantial barrier to equal educational opportunity. Spokesmen for ETS, however, categorically deny this. An ETS pamphlet states as fact that the "use of admissions tests has also contributed to increased access of disadvantaged students to higher education," but fails to muster any evidence to support that assertion.

That students from wealthier families tend to score higher than students from poor families cannot be denied, but it is still somewhat misleading. The use of average SAT scores and median incomes ignores the full range of SAT scores. Many students from the highest income level have low scores, and nearly one-third of the students from the lowest income group (below $6,000) score in the upper half of the total group. Further, most other measures of educational achievement—from reading scores to college grades—show a similar relationship between achievement and family income. One should not conclude, however, that wealthy people are more intelligent than poor people. (A dim-witted *Fortune* editorial about the SAT, for example, asked rhetorically, "Are rich people smarter than poor people?" and answered, "Yes, obvi-ously.") Rather, one has to ask what effects poverty has on learning (the SAT, after all, measures acquired ability). Implicit in this question is the assumption that wealthy people also tend to be better off educationally —an assertion that is less than shocking to anyone who has visited a variety of schools. In *College Admissions and the Public Interest,* B. Arden Thresher wrote: "Social class, which we in the United States like to ignore, or take note of only shamefacedly, plays a powerful part in access to education." James Loewen, who would agree with this ap-praisal, created the "Loewen Low Aptitude Test" that measures "expo-sure" to working-class life. The test, he says, is "designed to show my urbane white students some of the forms of test bias." And, like the BITCH, it works. Also like the BITCH, however, it, too, misses the point. The SAT test may be "biased" in favor of those "urbane" stu-dents who have had "exposure" to high culture and standard written English, but it is exactly this "bias"—in favor of culture and correct English—that colleges should be trying to preserve in our nation. Ralph W. Tyler puts the matter most succinctly: "Putting snobbism aside, the 'elite culture' is an important resource for a democratic society. . . . The scholarly heritage is a great and vital resource which schools and colleges should help students discover and learn to use."

In some ways, the most radical criticism of the SAT is that it is "coachable," that students can raise their scores by taking SAT prepara-tion courses. Until recently ETS and the College Board have denied that coaching could improve scores at all. A 1968 College Board pamphlet, for example, stated, "Changes in scores occur in about the same degree and with the same frequency *whether or not a student is coached.*" A 1977 ETS booklet asserted, "The abilities measured by the SAT develop over a student's entire academic life, so coaching—vocabulary drill, memorizing facts, or the like—can do little or nothing to raise the student's scores." Slack and Porter's survey of published research, a National Education Association study, and a Federal Trade Commission report all flatly contradict these statements. Indeed, an internal FTC memorandum suggested, "The representations of ETS and its clients regarding the susceptibility of their standardized admission examinations to coaching are false, misleading, deceptive." While there is little evidence to suggest malfeasance on the part of ETS or the College Board, there is evidence, some of it from ETS itself, that their earlier statements were incorrect. Recently ETS has begun to hedge on those earlier, unequivocal statements. In a response to Slack and Porter's conclusion that "coaching for the SAT can result in gains in scores," Rex Jackson stated: "In making their case the authors fail to draw clearly the critical distinction between programs of short-term drill and practice designed to yield quick increases in scores, and longer term educational programs designed to have lasting effects." This distinction between education and cramming is echoed throughout recent ETS publications and also by Neal Samors of ETS, who says, "With more schooling, you're likely to increase your aptitude—and your performance in college."

This distinction between long-term and short-term work is, of course, educationally valid, but it still implies that short-term work is futile—an assertion that recent studies and my own experience in tutoring students would suggest is erroneous. Students I have worked with over periods of months have invariably improved their scores, but even some of those whom I have worked with for only short periods of time have improved remarkably. One girl, for example, raised her SAT math score one hundred points after only three hours of tutoring. She had understood algebra and geometry well enough, but had not known how to answer the word problems, particularly the quantitative comparisons, on the SAT. This sort of short-term work on test-taking skills, what some critics call "test-wiseness," is often beneficial to students—a point ETS concedes. In fact, each year ETS publishes a bulletin for students that includes a full practice test and advice on how to answer the various types of SAT questions. The problem is, as ETS spokesmen acknowledge, that most students do not read the bulletin, much less take the practice test. Some of the same students, however, do take short-term preparation courses, during which they learn test-taking methods—and subsequently improve their scores.

ETS spokesmen also insist that the mean scores of students taking preparation courses are not significantly higher than the scores of those who do not take such courses. The truth of this assertion is debatable (the NEA study and the FTC report conclude that coaching does help), but even if it were true, it is still deceptive. Just as there is a wide range of scores despite a mean that correlates scores with family income, there is certainly a wide range of scores despite a mean that correlates scores with preparation courses. ETS spokesmen insist that the former range is extremely important, but conveniently ignore the latter range. Many students, among them those who are unfamiliar with test-taking strategies, those who suffer from "test anxiety" (and therefore need to know exactly the kinds of questions they will be asked), and those who are not self-motivated enough to work through ETS bulletins and SAT preparation texts, benefit from short-term coaching—even if general conclusions drawn by ETS suggest otherwise.

The fact that the SAT is susceptible to coaching does not imply that it is a poor test. Students are likely to do better on any standardized test, or for that matter on any test, if they understand the form of the test —if they have developed test-wiseness. Further, the abilities measured by the SAT—critical reading, vocabulary, and mathematical reasoning skills—are, as ETS so insistently points out, *acquired.* One way to develop test-wiseness and to acquire these abilities is to receive coaching. That coaching helps does suggest, however, that those economically advantaged students who can afford preparation courses are likely to improve on the cultural and educational advantages that they already have, an instance of the rich getting, if not richer, then at least brighter. This poses an ethical issue concerning the use of the SAT in the college admission process. Quite simply, the SAT is not quite the unifying factor it seems to be; it cuts differently across various ethnic and economic groups. Again, this does not suggest that the SAT itself discriminates, but rather that certain uses of the SAT by admissions officers at American colleges may be discriminatory. The use of cutoff scores, for example, quite likely discriminates against the poor and minorities, as does the use of the scores to compare students from different economic and cultural backgrounds. But the use of SAT scores as a supplementary item within the context of other admissions factors and the use of scores to compare students from similar backgrounds remain valid, indeed valuable, for admissions officers at selective American colleges. The SAT itself remains, in the words of the College Board charter, a fair, uniform, and judiciously administered exam.

"1983: The Last Days of ETS"

Tennis courts, a swimming pool, a baseball diamond, a private hotel, 400 acres of woods and rolling hills, cavorting deer, a resident flock of Canadian geese—I'm loving every minute here at the Educational Testing Service, the great untaxed, unregulated, unblinking eye of the American meritocracy.

ETS is best known as the Princeton, New Jersey, manufacturer of the Scholastic Aptitude Test, the two-and-a-half-hour multiple-choice examination that helps determine where (or whether) more than a million young Americans will go to college every year. ETS is also responsible for, among other things, the Graduate Record Examinations (for graduate school candidates), the Graduate Management Admission Test (for business school candidates), and part of the Law School Admission Test (for future attorneys, many of whom will later take ETS-written bar exams).

. . .

The business of deciding who goes where in American society is so vast and various that during peak grading season ETS's "scanners," the machines that score answer sheets at the rate of 200 a minute, are never turned off. Day after day, night after night, ETS's computers process and consume an unceasing stream of information, giving the company one of the largest compilations of private data about individuals in the world. "Maybe only the CIA," an ETS memorandum once asserted with pride, "has greater and better capacities."

The Central Intelligence Agency may have greater capacities, but even that resourceful institution knows when it needs outside help. The CIA buys ETS tests. So do the Defense Department, the National Security Council, the government of Trinidad and Tobago, the Institute for Nuclear Power Operations, the National Contact Lens Examiners, the International Council for Shopping Centers, the American Society of Heating, Refrigerating and Air-Conditioning Engineers, the Commission on Graduates of Foreign Nursing Schools, the Malaysian Ministry of Education, the National Board of Podiatry Examiners, and the Institute for the Advancement of Philosophy for Children.

You can't become a golf pro without passing an ETS exam (sample item: "The distance from the center line of a shaft hole to the farthest front portion of the face is the (A) hosel offset (B) loft (C) lie (D) face progression (E) length"*). In at least some parts of the country you also can't become a real-estate salesman, a certified moving consultant, a certified auto mechanic, a merchant marine officer (the same holds true in Liberia), a fireman, a travel agent ("with the ultimate expectation of improving public confidence in the travel industry," according to ETS), a certified business-form consultant, or, in Pennsylvania, a beautician or a barber.

Old-fashioned thinkers may wonder whether a multiple-choice test

*Answer: (D).

is really a better measure of barbering skills than a haircut is, or what great social cost would be exacted if a few untutored individuals were suffered to trim the sideburns of Pennsylvanians. But no such befuddlement hampers executives at ETS. A COPA promotional pamphlet makes prominent mention of the barber exam, and also of tests for, among others, office managers, architects, social workers, and gynecologists.

ETS had revenues of $115 million in 1981. As a "nonprofit" institution, ETS does not make profits as such. But these revenues support a very comfortable life and generous salaries for ETS's 2,200 employees. They also support research studies to further the cause of testing.

Just about half of ETS's annual revenues come from the SAT and related college admissions tests conducted for the College Board. Every penny of that sum, $55 million in 1981, as well as much of the College Board's revenues, came from students who paid to take the tests. Most of the rest of ETS's budget also came from people required to pay for the privilege of submitting to ETS exams in order to pass various checkpoints in America's social hierarchy.

ETS is a monopoly, probably the most powerful unregulated monopoly in America. People who wish to advance in almost all walks of life have no choice but to pay its fees and take its exams. Corporations and institutions with far less power have had to submit, in the public interest, to government regulation over the last half century, but ETS has managed to resist, flourish, and spread into markets where none but the brave would have imagined a need.

What started as a small organization performing a narrow service has taken on a life of its own. Although ETS does not hire its own executives on the basis of test scores, its guiding philosophy is that people's selection of comestibles on the buffet of life should be governed by a series of multiple-choice exams. In evangelizing its tests, ETS may merely be following the institutional imperative of survival and growth. But at the same time, it is promoting the notion that human superiority and inferiority can and should be measured scientifically and rewarded accordingly.

ETS has big plans for the future. Its researchers are working on a computerized version of the SAT that will take only a few minutes to administer. "We have the technology virtually ready to go," an ETS executive told College Board members at a conference last fall. "We expect we're going to be getting rapidly out of the paper transfer business." ETS president George Anrig is looking forward to a day when Americans will be able to take ETS tests on their television sets. Other people at ETS are working on computerized teaching programs that will make the testing company a powerful presence in schools, enabling it both to teach what it tests and to test what it teaches. Still others are tinkering with scoring systems that will replace numbers with "narrative," providing test-takers with computer-written paragraphs detailing all there is to know about their "aptitude." The day is coming, the company hopes, when you'll scarcely be able to get out of bed without some ETS statistician offering his considered opinion as to whether you've really got what it takes.

On the other hand, perhaps not. In fact, we may be seeing the beginning of the end of the Educational Testing Service. After several decades of steady growth in tax-free revenues, ETS suffered its first small deficit in fiscal 1980. The company more than made up for the shortfall in 1981, but that brief encounter with red ink put the fear of the almighty dollar in ETS executives. The company substantially reduced its research staff in a series of large-scale firings. As recently as two or three years ago, ETS executives were known to grow pale if unthinking workers described their employer as a "company" instead of an "institution." But in 1982, President Anrig inaugurated his term of office by commissioning a $500,000 "strategic plan" from Booz, Allen & Hamilton, Inc., a New York-based management consulting firm. In connection with the study, Anrig divided key ETS personnel into a dozen "revenue growth teams" charged with identifying new opportunities for short-term profits. Anrig also issued a confidential "corporate plan" calling for, among other things, "corporate intelligence gathering, external relations and government relations focused to provide a positive climate and receptive clients for ETS marketing initiatives."

The hard times at ETS aren't just economic. In recent years the company has endured its first sustained public criticism in areas it had come to believe were sacrosanct: the quality, meaning, and use of its tests. Vocal critics of standardized testing have been around for years, arguing that tests like the SAT measure little more than absorption of white upper-middle-class culture and penalize both the economically disadvantaged and the unusually bright. But the new onslaught caught ETS by surprise. In the late 1960s, researchers at the University of Michigan discovered a blood test that appeared to be better than the SAT at predicting which students would ultimately graduate from school. The

Federal Trade Commission released a report taking issue with ETS's long-standing claim that the SAT could not be coached. A group funded by Ralph Nader published a 500-plus–page report accusing ETS of misrepresenting its tests.

Several ETS employees I spoke with told me they resented the tendency of people like Nader to compare ETS to the CIA. But readers with above-average verbal aptitude will remember that the CIA comparison I quoted several paragraphs ago originated not with a detractor but with ETS itself. In fact, ETS has always cultivated its image as an organization whose ways passeth all understanding and whose methodology is not only above reproach but also exempt from public scrutiny. In 1979 it published a pamphlet called "The War on Testing," in which criticism of standardized tests was referred to as "an attack on truth itself."

Because this aura of mystery is so important to ETS, the greatest blow came in 1979, when New York State passed a "truth-in-testing" law. This law required, among other things, that ETS make test questions and graded answer-sheets available to the students who take its tests. Until 1980, when the law went into effect, no one besides ETS could check whether the scores that could determine people's places in life had even been added up correctly, let alone whether the questions were faulty. ETS has since admitted under challenge that several of its "right" answers have, in fact, been wrong.

When ETS cites "scientific studies" supporting its side of various controversies, it is almost always referring to research performed by people in its own employ. Until 1980, nobody besides ETS could assess the value of the tests for their ostensible purposes, since nobody but ETS could see them except while actually taking them. To make outside assessment possible, the New York truth-in-testing law also required ETS to publish information about the "validity" of its exams, and about the correlation between test scores and family background, income, race, and other factors.

While the bill was being considered, ETS and the College Board pelted college presidents, high school principals, headmasters, and legislators with letters, mailgrams, and phone calls warning of dire results that would ensue if the New York legislature had its way. Their most serious charge was that disclosing SAT tests would lead to huge increases in test fees and sharp reductions in the number of times tests could be given, since ETS would no longer be able to reuse test questions. ETS itself, though, had compiled the figures that refute this claim: a 1972 study had shown that less than 5 percent of student fees go into the writing of tests and that few questions were ever reused. In a memorandum labeled URGENT and dated May 11, 1979, the College Board also alleged that "the bill encroaches on institutional autonomy by requiring testing agencies to disclose confidential information, such as validity information, which is *the property of the colleges and universities.*" (My emphasis.) This is a curious claim, since ETS's "validity" studies are paid for entirely out of students' fees and provided free of charge, along with reams of other information, to colleges and universities that want them. If ETS's "validity" information is the property of anyone, it is the property of the students who pay for it.

Having predicted the collapse of civilization if the truth-in-testing law passed, ETS did not, in the event, collapse itself. In fact, it adapted easily. Test fees in New York are only fifty cents higher than in other states and test schedules were not dramatically changed.

Smiling ETS executives today claim that the furious response to the truth-in-testing law was the work of a few excitable individuals and not representative of the company as a whole. This argument is not persuasive to anyone who has sifted through the reams of official documents ETS and the College Board churned out while the bill was being considered. In fact, ETS *still* hands out a pamphlet, published in 1981 (a year after the bill went into effect), that purports to tell "The Truth about Truth-in-Testing." The pamphlet, which is printed in the form of a multiple-choice test, points out, among other things, that less than 2 percent "of students identifying themselves as black, Mexican-American or Puerto Rican have requested copies of their SAT questions and answers," a statistic perhaps not entirely unrelated to the fact that ETS charges $6.50 for every such report. For the final question in the brochure—"Should other states considering legislation similar to the New York State testing law approve it?"—ETS offers only one possible response: "(A) The only reasonable answer is 'no.'"

ETS has responded to every challenge to its mission and methods the same way it responded to truth-in-testing. This response takes the form of a series of contradictory assertions, known to lawyers as "arguing in the alternative." A man is accused of borrowing and breaking his neighbor's kettle. His lawyer argues in his defense: 1) he didn't take the kettle; 2) it was already broken when he took it; 3) he returned it in perfect condition. Whatever the issue, ETS argues: 1) it has done nothing wrong; 2) it has fixed the problem; 3) nothing has changed. Truth-in-testing makes this elusive stance increasingly hard to maintain.

It would be impolitic for ETS, as a semipublic institution, to refuse all outside scrutiny, but it is extremely cautious about outsiders. I was accompanied on all my interviews in Lawrenceville by at least one emissary from the company's bustling Information Division, who generally took copious notes. Employees of the Information Division do not hesitate to inject themselves into conversations if they perceive that the actual interviewee is being insufficiently ingenious in his defense of his employer. After a while I almost expected passing secretaries to come sailing through open doorways, thrusting sheaves of paper at me and saying, "What he *really* means is . . ." When I interviewed President Anrig, I was preceded by a bundle of my previous articles, which someone in Information had dutifully dug up. Anrig had also requested a list of the questions I intended to ask him. I replied that ETS doesn't hand out its questions ahead of time, and neither do I.

The oldest controversy involving ETS concerns the validity of multiple-choice tests. Without such tests, which can be graded and scored by machines, assessing the abilities of millions of people every year would be impossible, and ETS would go out of business. More important, widespread acceptance of testing depends on the perception that it is scientifically neutral and objective, which only a test with "right" and "wrong" answers can be.

In the early 1950s, ETS was criticized in educational circles for presuming to assess writing skills with a multiple-choice "achievement" exam called (then as now) the English Composition Test. Still at its peak of institutional self-confidence, ETS set out to silence the critics by demonstrating that a multiple-choice test is actually a better measure of essay-writing ability than writing an essay is. Together with the College Board, ETS designed a three-year experiment to compare the ECT with both an all-essay achievement exam (called the General Composition Test) and the verbal portion of the SAT. These three tests were judged against general essay-writing ability as measured over a year or more by actual teachers of the students taking the tests.

Now, ETS has long held that teachers' opinions are deceiving, since they are highly subjective and reflect all sorts of unconscious prejudices and expectations. This, indeed, is the justification for giving Scholastic Aptitude Tests. But faced with the need to measure the validity of its tests against *something*, ETS had nowhere else to turn.

In 1957, when ETS tallied the results of its experiment, the all-essay GCT, as ETS had predicted, came in last. The two multiple-choice tests, the verbal SAT and the ECT, came in first and second, respectively. ETS and the College Board announced the findings triumphantly, and proceeded as before.

But there was something very odd about these results, as Banesh Hoffmann, a distinguished mathematician, pointed out a few years later in a wonderful book called *The Tyranny of Testing.* If the experiment proved to ETS's satisfaction that its multiple-choice English Composition Test was better than an essay test, it also proved that the verbal part of the SAT was a better test of English composition ability than the ECT. Yet ETS continued to administer the ECT (to customers who'd already paid to take the SAT), perhaps realizing that if necessary an experiment could be devised to demonstrate the superiority of the ECT. ETS is singularly adept at proving the excellence of whatever test it happens to be peddling at the moment, even if these proofs perforce contradict one another.

In later years, ETS retreated to the position that multiple-choice tests are only *just as good* as essay tests, and it offered new experimental results to prove this thesis. In a 1980 article about standardized testing in the *Atlantic Monthly,* James Fallows wrote: "Hunter Breland, an ETS research psychologist, explained that to get statistically reliable results from an essay exam, students had to write five separate essays, with five readers each. 'We found we could do as well with fifty multiple choice questions in a thirty-minute test,' Breland said. *'We got the same people in the same order.'* " (My emphasis.)

The same people in the same order? This must be a typical ETS exaggeration. After all, ETS calculates that one SAT-taker in three will score more than thirty-three points higher or lower than his hypothetical "true score." Not even two administrations of the SAT would produce "the same people in the same order." Hunter Breland, it seems, was trying to make his argument sound stronger than it was.

But let's ignore this point and address Breland's major assertion, which is that a statistically reliable essay exam requires five separate essays, each of them evaluated by five graders.

Strange to report, ETS has been giving essay exams for years. Back in the 1960s, the company bowed to continued criticism from educators and began offering students the option of writing an essay as part of the English Composition Test. The essay was not graded, because ETS had proved that a grade on a single writing sample was not reliable. Student compositions were merely passed along to college admissions officers, who apparently could be trusted to submit them to five separate readers before passing judgment.

But the critics were not appeased, and ETS was eventually forced to take the next step down this fatal road. In 1977, it began to offer, once a year, an optional version of the ECT with one graded twenty-minute essay question in place of some of the usual multiple-choice items. Both versions of the test last an hour overall, and scores on both are reported as single numerical grades on ETS's familiar 600-point scale. On tests with an essay, the essay counts for one third of the score.

The single ECT essay is graded not by the five readers Breland calls for, but by two. "Readers are instructed to read essays quickly," a College Board publication explains, "and to score immediately while the impression the total essay creates remains fresh." Time is money in the testing business. ETS refers to this grading system as "holistic." It instructs graders to read each essay only once and not to be overly concerned with spelling, punctuation, or grammar. "The first thing we tell our readers," an ETS executive told me, "is that this is not creative writing. We don't expect a brilliant political essay." Each reader assigns a grade of 1, 2, 3, or 4. The two readers' scores are then added together to produce a final range of 2–8, which, when multiplied by 100, provides a no-frills approximation of the standard ETS scale.

Contrary to what you may believe, ETS essay tests are not graded by Irving Howe, Northrop Frye, and whatever other distinguished scholars happen to be passing through New Jersey at scoring time. In fact, ECTs are graded by the sort of high school English teachers and low-level college instructors who can be tempted away from Shakespeare and Milton by the prospect of spending five days in a gymnasium reading 1,500 or so one-page adolescent responses to a single question in return for $310. Periodic calibrating sessions are held in which all the graders read sample answers and indicate their grades with a show of hands. This continues until everyone's back on the same wavelength.

Let's take a holistic look at a College Board booklet called "The English Composition Test with Essay," which contains the essay assignment from the 1978 exam, along with some responses. The 1978 assignment was to discuss the quotation "We have met the enemy and he is us." ("What does this quotation imply about human beings? Do you agree or disagree with its implications?") The first sample essay, which the booklet describes as "a well-written response taking a psychological approach," begins: "The quotation I am to discuss implies a dual nature for human beings, both at the individual and at the collective level." A

Take This Simple Test

To help convince you that what ETS tests test is the ability to take ETS tests, I've composed a short Scholastic Aptitude Test Aptitude Test (SATAT). The five items below are taken from a reading-comprehension portion of an actual SAT. In answering them, reach back in your mind to the days when you took your own SATs and then look for the kinds of answers that you think would appeal to a test-writer at ETS.

Oh, yes: I've left out the reading passage that the items refer to. I've also mixed up the order of the items and eliminated all references to the actual novelist and books the reading passage discusses. You need to know only that the novelist, though dead, has a name you would recognize, and that "the author" referred to in several of the items is the author of the reading passage, not the author of the novels.

So that you will approach this test in a properly anxious frame of mind, I will tell you that when I administered it to myself, after many hours spent reading SATs, I had no trouble getting all of the answers right. And I *still* haven't read the passage.

1. The main idea of the passage is that
   (A) a constricted view of [this novel] is natural and acceptable
   (B) a novel should not depict a vanished society
   (C) a good novel is an intellectual rather than an emotional experience
   (D) many readers have seen only the comedy in [this novel]
   (E) [this novel] should be read with sensitivity and an open mind
2. The author's attitude toward someone who "enjoys [this novel] and then remarks 'but of course it has no relevance today' " (lines 21–22) can best be described as one of
   (A) amusement
   (B) astonishment
   (C) disapproval
   (D) resignation
   (E) ambivalence
3. The author [of the passage] implies that a work of art is properly judged on the basis of its
   (A) universality of human experience truthfully recorded
   (B) popularity and critical acclaim in its own age
   (C) openness to varied interpretations, including seemingly contradictory ones
   (D) avoidance of political and social issues of minor importance
   (E) continued popularity through different eras and with different societies

4. It can be inferred that the author [of the passage] considers the question stated and restated in lines 8–13 to be unsatisfactory because it
   (A) fails to assume that society and its standards are the proper concern of a novel
   (B) neglects to assume that the novel is a definable art form
   (C) suggests that our society and [this novelist's] are quite different
   (D) fails to emphasize [this novelist's] influence on modern writers
   (E) wrongly states the criteria for judging a novel's worth
5. The author [of the passage] would probably disagree with those critics or readers who find that the society in [this novelist's] novels is
   (A) unsympathetic
   (B) uninteresting
   (C) crude
   (D) authoritarian
   (E) provincial

When I administered this test to four people at a *Harper's* editorial meeting, the youngest member of the staff, who has just emerged from the world of ETS exams, also got all the answers. Two older editors got three correct. The worst score—one out of five—was that of an editor from England, who has never taken (or even seen) an SAT test. Thus there was a perfect (1.0) correlation between test scores and familiarity with the ETS mentality.

CORRECT ANSWERS:

1. E 2. C 3. A 4. E 5. B

bit thick, that, when you consider that the quotation under discussion was originally uttered by a talking possum in a cartoon strip about the animal inhabitants of a swamp. On the other hand, the student has clearly demonstrated a thorough knowledge of how to sucker a high school English teacher.

Is the ECT with essay a better measure of writing skills than the ECT without? This is a thorny question, since giving a definite answer would require throwing out one or the other version. If one test is better, why give the other? If the tests are the same, why give both? In an exercise that is supposed to rank people scientifically on a scale from 200 to 800, how can you offer a choice of tests? But throwing out the all-multiple-choice version would imply what ETS has always denied: that an essay test, especially a teeny one, is *better* than a multiple-choice test. On the other hand, getting rid of the essay would amount to a confession that all this "holistic grading" business is just a bunch of hooey; it would also defeat the *true* purpose of the essay, which is to pacify all those skeptics out there who don't believe you can learn very much about students' ability to write without asking them to write something.

So does the essay make the ECT better, worse, or what? "Essentially, we're looking at writing style, not creativity, conceptualization, and what have you," says Richard Noeth, director of ETS's Admissions and Guidance Programs. "That's different, I think—though I'm not saying better or worse—different than an item-by-item analysis of ability to recognize something in a particular sentence, or the ability to restate something in a different way, or what have you. We're looking at essentially a very holistic analysis of a student's ability in this area. So I think that's different, and I think that adds a different component to what we can assess."

The test was fine all along; but the essay adds something; but it makes no difference to your score.

Lock up the kettle, folks.

In contrast to messy essay tests, ETS would have you think, its multiple-choice questions and answers are designed by scientific methods so complex and so exacting that outsiders can't hope to comprehend them. In fact, ETS tests are written by ordinary people who quite possibly didn't do as well on their SATs as you did on yours. Until 1980, it was impossible for any outsider to evaluate ETS's tests, since only a few sample questions were made available. But New York's truth-in-testing law changed that.

The first challenge came almost immediately, when a high school student named Daniel Lowen protested ETS's scoring of the now famous "pyramid problem." The problem showed a picture of two pyramids, one with a square base and four triangular sides, the other with a triangular base and three triangular sides. All the triangles were equilateral, and all were the same size. The question asked: "If the two pyramids were placed together face-to-face with the vertices of the equal-sized equilateral triangles coinciding, how many exposed faces would the resulting solid have?" The answer ETS wanted was seven, since the two touching faces would disappear when the pyramids were joined, leaving seven of the original nine. But Lowen realized that there would actually be only five faces left, since four of the original triangles would merge into two parallelograms. (Try it yourself if you don't believe him.) ETS admitted its mistake and raised 240,000 scores, even though few of these 240,000 could have gotten the answer "wrong" for the "right" reason. On the other hand, ETS did not *lower* any scores, apparently reasoning that students shouldn't be punished for failing to see something ETS didn't see either. Nor did ETS go back and rescore any of the earlier tests that included the same question.

ETS eventually took steps to tighten its question-checking procedures (without, of course, admitting that it had been negligent before, or that truth-in-testing laws might be a good thing), but bad questions continue to surface. Not many, of course, since few students will bother to make the enormous effort required to challenge a question. But even a few errors tarnish ETS's claims to scientific perfection, and the impossibility of ETS's making a logically consistent response when a faulty question is found puts those claims in a nice comic light.

No one has ever successfully challenged an SAT verbal question. The reason is obvious: outside mathematics, ETS's "right" answer cannot be proved definitively "wrong," because the questions are inherently ambiguous, precisely what ETS must deny in defending the scientific accuracy of its tests. But a study of SAT verbal questions confirms the obvious.

One of the first tasks the creator of a multiple-choice test faces is how to make people miss questions whose subject matter they actually understand. This sounds silly, but it's important. One way it's done is by limiting the time allowed. (Veteran test-takers know, for instance, that the key to doing well on SAT math items lies in finding *quick* solutions; if you have to perform a complex or lengthy calculation, you've probably missed the trick.) Another way is to write questions that are misleading. Test-makers don't always do this intentionally, but they always do it, in part because it's very hard not to. Many of the verbal items ETS calls most difficult are in fact merely ambiguous, since writing a genuinely difficult multiple-choice item is much harder than writing a confusing one. This was one of Banesh Hoffmann's main points in *The Tyranny of Testing.*

In order to get people to miss the right answer, as of course some must if the test is to be useful, it's necessary to make another answer look equally or more attractive. One way to do this is to make the question so hard that students have no idea what the desired response is. The drawback to this method is that if only a very few students understand the question, more will get it right for the wrong reason or through luck than for the right reason, and it won't be testing what it's supposed to test. The alternative is to make the question ambiguous. It's revealing to note, as Hoffmann points out, that in the jargon of standardized testing, "incorrect" answers are known as "distractors."

One of the few scientific studies of test ambiguity was performed in 1980 by Walt Haney and Laurie Scott of the Huron Institute in Cambridge, Massachusetts. Haney and Scott did something that ETS never does in checking its tests, which was to ask a group of children *why* they had chosen their answers. In one of the experimental items, for example, taken from a published Stanford Achievement Test, young children were shown a picture of a potted flower, a cabbage, and a potted cactus and asked, "Which plant needs the least amount of water?" The desired answer was the cactus, which nine of eleven children chose. But one child chose the head of cabbage, explaining that it would need water "only when you clean it." Since there was nothing in the drawing to indicate that the cabbage was growing in a garden and not sitting in a refrigerator, the child's answer was at least as rational as the desired answer, and it was arguably a good bit more intelligent, since it indicated that the child had delved further into the question than the other children had. But on an actual administration of the test, of course, his score would have been lower. That clever child will have to learn, in his test-taking career, that delving further is a fatal mistake.

If ETS allowed challenges to nonmathematical questions, there'd be no end to it. Only in math can the occasional Daniel Lowen be allowed to dig deeper and mess up the test results. But the principle that ambiguous questions undermine ETS's claims to be measuring something with scientific precision is the same, no matter what the topic.

How many cabbage questions are there on, say, a Scholastic Aptitude Test, ETS's biggest seller? ETS would say virtually none, and can haul out statistical studies to "prove" it. But the statistics only show that people who did well on the rest of the exam tended to get this question "right"—that is, to see the question the way the testmakers saw it. Indeed, this is the way ETS assures itself of the quality of all its tests. But statistics cannot spot errors of the sort Daniel Lowen found.

The only reliable way to evaluate the testmakers is to look at an actual test. The purpose is not to suggest that ETS discriminates against the brilliant Daniel Lowens of the world (they generally figure out how to give ETS what it wants), but to assess ETS's claims to scientific accuracy, and to ask whether what ETS tests is anything other than the ability to take ETS tests.

In the days before ETS was required by law to disclose its tests, actually examining the questions was impossible. But nowadays people who can spare $6 can order a College Board publication called *6 SATs*. This booklet, which was published in 1982, contains six SAT tests that were administered a year or two before. Since ETS has never thrown out a verbal item, we'll confine our investigation to verbal items. So ETS won't be able to claim we're nitpicking, let's look only at the first section of the first test in the booklet. This section contains forty-five items and has a time limit of thirty minutes.

Here's the first item that caught my eye, a sentence completion:

> Unfortunately, certain aspects of democratic government sometimes put pressure on politicians to take the easy way out, allowing ——— to crowd out ———.
> (A) exigencies . . necessities
> (B) immediacies . . ultimates
> (C) responsibilities . . privileges
> (D) principles . . practicalities
> (E) issues . . problems

This is a particularly interesting item, because it is an example not only of ambiguity but also of cultural bias.

How you respond to this item will depend on what you think politicians do when they "take the easy way out." Unlike most ETS sentence completions, this one doesn't contain a contextual clue. We are told only that "certain aspects" are at fault, that they only "sometimes" have an effect, and that when they are in force all they do is allow one thing to "crowd out" another.

The answer ETS is looking for here is (B). This produces a plausible sentence, and one that is only slightly vaguer and more badly written than the uncompleted version. (Back in my test-taking days, I used to think that badly written items and reading passages in ETS tests served some diabolical but scientifically precise assessment purpose; it was thus something of a shock to learn, as I did on visiting Lawrenceville, that ETS actually tries hard to write sturdy, well-crafted prose.) "Immediacies" and "ultimates" are two words that, in this context at least, don't willingly divulge much solid meaning. I suppose, however, that the finished sentence could be translated into English as something like this: "In a democratic society, considerations of the moment unfortunately sometimes distract politicians from contemplating fundamental principles." Certainly we've all heard a sentiment like this before, perhaps from our high school civics teacher, who was also, quite possibly, the football coach. To get this question "right" requires a dead ear for the language combined with a belief in conventional wisdom (or, of course, a wily understanding of the ETS mentality).

Is the ETS answer correct? Consider an example from contemporary political life. The United States government is currently running a large deficit. Politicians from both parties agree this is bad. What should be done? One possibility would be to do something "immediate": raise taxes, slash spending. But these steps affect voters' lives and are unpopular. So instead we have a president who wants neither to raise taxes nor to slash spending but rather to add a balance-the-budget amendment to the Constitution. This doesn't affect anybody right now. It is a fundamental statement of principle. President Reagan is unfortunately taking the easy way out, letting an "ultimate" crowd out "immediacies."

By this reasoning, a better answer is (D). President Reagan is letting the principle of a balanced budget crowd out the practicalities of actually balancing the budget.

For that matter, why not (E)? Nuclear disarmament is an extremely popular issue at the moment. Overcrowded prisons are a tenacious and unpopular problem. If you invite Teddy Kennedy to speak to your breakfast club next week, which topic do you think he'll be more likely to address? The fact that unglamorous problems like prison reform almost always take a backseat to (important but) nebulous and generally intractable issues like nuclear disarmament is, I would argue, an unfortunate aspect of democratic government. When a politician wants to avoid a problem, there's always an issue to hide behind.

A case could even be made for (A). The point, though, is that getting this question "correct" depends less on understanding its verbal content than on subscribing to ETS's locker-room idealism about the way things ought to work. If—for cultural, ideological, or practical reasons—you think it's just fine that elected representatives don't spend more time lounging on the steps of the Capitol asking, "And what is Truth, Socrates?" then you're just plain out of luck. Yet ETS contends that, through questions like this one, it can rank people precisely on a 600-point scale of "aptitude."

Let's try another. Here's an analogy. In SAT analogy items, students are given a pair of words and asked to select, from among five choices, another pair "that *best* expresses a relationship similar to that expressed in the original pair." (Original emphasis.) This one reads as follows:

THREAT : HOSTILITY ::
(A) plea : clemency
(B) promise : benevolence
(C) lampoon : praise
(D) capitulation : malice
(E) compliment : admiration

ETS suggests that students approach analogy questions by forming a sentence using the words in capital letters (known to testmakers as the "stem") and then plugging in the lettered choices to see which fits best. If we form our sentence as "A threat is an expression of hostility," we probably won't have much difficulty in settling on (E), which is the desired answer, or "key." A compliment, after all, is an expression of admiration.

But suppose we form our sentence in a slightly different way and say, "A threat produces hostility." Isn't this every bit as true as the other sentence is? Working from this statement, (A) now seems like the best choice (with [D] a nearly elegant and possibly profound runner-up).

When I discussed this and other questions with Pamela Cruise, an ETS official in charge of putting together verbal SAT tests, she told me that an analogy is no good "if you have to use 'sometimes' " (even though ETS itself hides behind a "sometimes" in the sentence-completion question discussed above). A threat only *sometimes* produces hostility. But ETS's answer doesn't work without "sometimes" either. After all, a compliment is only *sometimes* an expression of admiration. Compliments are uttered for all sorts of reasons, and sincere admiration may not even be the most common one. Can ETS honestly argue that a student who understood all of the words in this item, and could formulate the possible relationships between them, might not be justified in selecting (A) as his answer?

Let's try another. Here is part of a reading-comprehension passage, along with one of the questions that follow it:

> Suppose that a rod is moving at very high speed. At first it is oriented perpendicular to its line of motion. Then it is turned through a right angle so that it is along the line of motion. The rod contracts. This contraction [*is*] known as the FitzGerald contraction. . . .
>
> [*This*] may seem surprising. . . . If the rod is thought of as continuous substance, extending in space because it is the nature of substance to occupy space, then there seems to be no valid cause for a change of dimensions. But the rod is really a swarm of electrical particles moving

about and widely separated from one another. The marvel is that such a swarm should tend to preserve any definite extension. . . .

30. When the author refers to the idea that a solid rod is "continuous substance" (lines 13–14), he implies that this idea is which of the following?
I. A common conception of the nature of solid matter
II. A concept that is not particularly useful for explaining the Fitz-Gerald contraction
III. An accurate description of some kinds of matter
(A) I only   (B) III only   (C) I and II only   (D) II and III only
(E) I, II, and III

We have no trouble agreeing with I and eliminating III. But what about II? We could agree with it immediately if it were worded differently: "A concept that does not explain the FitzGerald contraction." But ETS says "not particularly useful." Is ETS getting at something? Why, after all, does the author bring up the "continuous substance" idea? Surely because he finds it useful, if only in a negative way, for explaining the FitzGerald contraction. Writers, orators, and advertisers do this all the time. It's a run-of-the-mill rhetorical device.

When I administered this test to myself, I pondered Item 30 for a very long time and then finally settled on (A) as my answer. I knew that the author of the passage didn't think the "continuous substance" idea *explained* the FitzGerald contraction, but that wasn't what the item asked. The item asked whether *referring* to the "continuous substance" idea helped *the author* to explain the FitzGerald contraction.

As you must have guessed already, this line of thinking didn't win me any points with ETS. The "correct" response is (C). I am left to conclude that ETS didn't realize how sloppily the item was written. Perhaps ETS ought to be required to print, on the cover of every SAT test, the names and SAT scores of all the people who contributed to it.

Here's one last item:

MAGNET : IRON ::
(A) tank : fluid
(B) hook : net
(C) sunlight : plant
(D) spray : tree
(E) flame : bird

You probably didn't have any trouble in selecting (C), the answer ETS wants. But if you thought harder (a mistake, of course), you might notice that the analogy is stated incorrectly: magnet*ism* is to iron as sunlight is to plant—or magnet is to iron as *sun* is to plant.

In an ETS pamphlet called "Preparing for Tests," students who are about to take the SAT are told, "Be careful to eliminate those relationships that are not exactly parallel to the relationship of the original pair."

Is there a better answer? How about (B)? You can pick up a net with a hook, just as you can pick up a piece of iron with a magnet. You can also pick up a hook with a net, as you can a magnet with a piece of iron. Plants, by contrast, do *not* attract sunlight. Unlike a plant and sunlight, but like a magnet and iron, the relationship between hook and net remains true no matter how long you keep them apart. Hook and net are both inanimate and both made of matter. And so on and so on.

Why is (B) a worse answer than (C)? Pamela Cruise of ETS: "It doesn't really strike me as an analogy. I mean, there's a reason for pairing magnet and iron. I mean, that's the kind of thing that seems to go together. You've done it yourself, you've picked up pieces of iron or pins or something with a magnet. God, I've done it millions of times. But you don't really think of hook and net in that same kind of sense. I mean, if you had suggested that as a stem and key for an analogy, I would say that doesn't really strike me as an analogy."

In other words, it's so *obvious* what the answer is.

To see the inherent flaw in questions like this, all you have to do is put them in a different context. Suppose I typed out the magnet item on a piece of paper, handed it to you, and said, "Here's an analogy problem that's got all the fellas up at MIT bamboozled. See what you can make of it." Wouldn't you hesitate before selecting (C) as your answer? Might you not discover that you could make a case for one of the other choices? Might you not begin to lean toward this new answer if you thought the tester was looking for something more than an ability to think conventionally? And what is an item like this doing in a test of *verbal* skills in the first place? All you need to answer it is a little first-grade physics, so that you know how magnets work, and a little fourth-grade biology, so that you know how plants grow.

A student of even moderate ability who chooses an "incorrect" response for this item (and ETS considers it fairly difficult) probably does so not because he doesn't understand the words or the relationships among them, but because his ability to read the mind of Pamela Cruise has momentarily faltered and he has read more into the item than was intended.

Let's suppose, for the sake of argument, that I really have found four bad items in a single section of a single SAT verbal test (and I think there are more than four). The test may not be perfect, but it's still useful if the majority of ETS's other questions are valid, isn't it? Not really. The great drawback of a multiple-choice test is that you can't use a single item to measure a *range* of performance. Every question you add to your test increases the *test's* range of measurement (assuming that each new question measures something different from what the previous one did), but each *question* adds only a single piece of information to the total picture. Suppose, for instance, you want to find out how high a group of test-takers can count, up to an upper limit of, say, eighty-five. In a free-response test you could simply say, "Write out all the whole numbers between 0 and 86 in order." But in a multiple-choice test (that is, a test that can be given to millions and graded by a machine) you'll need eighty-five items ("The first whole number larger than 0 is (A) 5 (B) 44 (C) 1 (D) 20 (E) 13; The second whole number is . . ." and so on). Assuming you remember not to number your questions, you'll end up with a similar picture of your group's counting ability. But the quality of your results will depend on how well you wrote all your questions. If "85" is not one of the choices on the eighty-fifth item, you won't be able to distinguish a person who can count up to eighty-five from one who can only count up to eighty-four. (A flaw like this will cause other measurement errors, too.)

A verbal SAT test, as it happens, consists of eighty-five items. Each of these has its own difficulty rating, known as its "delta," which is just a fancy-sounding way of expressing the percentage of test-takers who get it "correct." Since each item has its own delta, you can take all eighty-five items and line them up, from 1 to 85, in order of their difficulty ratings, the same way we arranged the items in our counting test. In fact, ETS does essentially this in building its exams. Every SAT test is constructed according to a standard set of specifications that dictate how many items of a certain difficulty rating will be included, what their subject matter will be, and where they will be placed. Every test, section, and subsection is arranged so that it tends to increase in difficulty from beginning to end. Test-takers who understand this know that it is foolish to spend a lot of time puzzling over the last few items in a given subsection, since the first few items in the next subsection will almost certainly be easier.

It may seem crudely simplistic to compare an SAT test to the multiple-choice counting test I described earlier, but the two tests are intended to perform in exactly the same way. If the SAT test is functioning just as it is supposed to, each student will climb the delta ladder, answering questions correctly precisely up to the limit of his "aptitude," and then he will be able to answer no more.

Even ETS does not expect a real test to behave in this ideal manner. But by ETS's own criteria, a test must be viewed as flawed precisely to the extent that it fails to do so. Suppose, for instance, that you and I take an SAT verbal exam and that we each miss five items. We'll both receive the same score, in this case 750. But suppose that the five items you missed were the five "easiest" items on the test, while the ones I missed were the five most "difficult." In my case, the test behaved exactly as it was supposed to. I missed the items that a person who scores 750 is supposed to miss. But in your case, something went wrong. Our performances on the test don't mean the same thing. In the test's own terms, my score is more reliable than yours is, because the "errors" I made—once again in the test's own terms—were more meaningful than yours. But of course there's no way to tell us apart by looking at our scores.

On any single SAT test that is functioning exactly as it should, there are only two important items: the last one on the delta ladder that the student gets correct, and the first one that he misses. For a student who scores 750 on an ideal SAT, the first seventy-nine items on the delta scale are superfluous, because all the information his score conveys about him is conveyed exclusively by his performance on the eightieth and eighty-first items. We can now think of a verbal SAT test not as a single eighty-five-item exam but as a large number of very much smaller exams, all of which have been lumped together in a single booklet in order to make it more convenient for ETS to measure, at one sitting, more than a million people of widely disparate backgrounds, abilities, and levels of education. All those easy "tests" at the bottom of the scale don't add any reliability to the score of someone who performs at the very top; all they can do is subtract from it, by failing to convey the information that the logic of the test says they should. And for someone who scores near the bottom of the scale, the questions at the top can only reduce the reliability of his score, by giving him the opportunity to beat chance in guessing at the answers.

For any given SAT-taker, the true "test" that determines ETS's assessment of his "scholastic aptitude" is actually very much smaller than the entire eighty-five-item example. If the real business of determining your score is actually being done by five or ten difficult questions, the quality and content of individual items begin to take on an immense significance.

No college would ever consider creating, say, a ten-minute, ten-item multiple-choice test (with two sentence completions, two analogies, two antonyms, and two reading-comprehension passages with two questions each) and then using it to determine anything at all about its applicants, much less their "scholastic aptitude." The idea is ridiculous. And yet all selective schools do essentially this very thing every time they allow an admissions decision to be affected by an SAT score.

To get an idea of what ETS *really* thinks about the "accuracy" of SAT tests, all you have to do is look at its method of detecting cheating. ETS's scoring computers are programmed to set aside the answer sheets of students who, in taking the SAT for the second time, score suspiciously higher or lower than they did the first. In order to set off the computers in this way, there has to be a 250-point difference between the first verbal or math score and the second.

If you take the SAT verbal and score 500 on it, and then you take it again and score either 260 or 740—scores that encompass all but 120 points of the total scale—ETS's computers won't bat an eye. (If the difference is more than 250 points, ETS will look for irregularities in your signature or similarities to the answer sheets of students who sat near you. In most cases, ETS says, no damaging evidence is found and the scores are allowed to stand.) If a 250-point difference in scores on two versions of the same test isn't cheating, what is it? Does ETS think that "scholastic aptitude" is so volatile that it can grow or shrink by 50 percent in less than a year?

ETS's recent history as a public institution has consisted almost entirely of a not always orderly retreat from prior enthusiasms. On no subject has the retreat been more dramatic than on the issue of what exactly it is that the SAT tests. Carl Campbell Brigham's two great contributions to Western civilization were the Scholastic Aptitude Test, of which he was the primary author, and the Immigration Restriction Act of 1924, for which his book *A Study of American Intelligence* provided the major theoretical justification. Both these monuments to his insight grew out of the infamous Army Alpha and Army Beta examinations of "innate intelligence," which Brigham helped administer to new recruits at the time of America's entry into World War I. Brigham's work with the soldiers convinced him that Catholics, Greeks, Hungarians, Italians, Jews, Negroes, Poles, Russians, Turks, and a great many others were innately less intelligent than people whose ancestors were born in countries that abounded in natural blonds. After the war he addressed himself to the problem of how to keep these people out of the American mainstream, if not out of America entirely, and the SAT and the Immigration Act were two of the results. Today Brigham is little remembered, except by historians of mental measurement and by users of the Carl Campbell Brigham Library, the principal repository of enlightenment and learning at the Educational Testing Service.

The army mental tests were ludicrously flawed, relying on questions like the following: "Crisco is a: —patent medicine, —disinfectant, — toothpaste, —food product." But Brigham rubbed his hands and drew dark conclusions from his results. "We must face a possibility of racial admixture here that is infinitely worse than that faced by any European country today," he wrote, "for we are incorporating the negro into our racial stock, while all of Europe is comparatively free from this taint."

The idea of mental measurement struck a chord deep in the American psyche and had a profound effect on the life of the nation. The innate superiority of individuals, countries, races, and even entire hemispheres could now be proven scientifically. "Within two or three years after the war," writes Brigham's biographer in a celebratory volume published by ETS in 1961, "intelligence testing had developed a new and wide popularity in secondary schools, colleges, and universities across the country."

Brigham field-tested the Army Alpha exam on students at Princeton University, then created a more challenging version of his own. In 1925 Princeton made Brigham's test a requirement for admission.

Brigham's experiments sent a shiver of foreboding through the College Entrance Examination Board. The College Board had been established in 1900 to prepare and administer standardized admissions exams for a handful of prestigious Eastern colleges. High school students across the country could take a single essay test and have the results accepted at any school that participated in the program (973 young people took the College Board's first exam, in 1901). But now that intelligence testing had taken hold in the popular imagination, the board's very existence was in danger. It took the only logical step and put Brigham on its payroll. His first "Scholastic Aptitude Test," the direct descendant of the Army Alpha exam, was administered, alongside the board's usual essay exam, in 1926. The two tests were given together until 1942, when the essay exam was discontinued for the duration of World War II, and never resumed.

Brigham, who died in 1943 at the age of fifty-two, created the culture of standardized testing. He is responsible for the 200–800 scale, the "delta" difficulty rating system, the practice of testing new questions by burying them in actual tests, the statistical "equating" of tests from one year to another, and so on.

Carl Brigham publicly recanted the racism of his youth in 1930, seven years after the publication of *A Study of American Intelligence*, four years after the first SAT. His interpretation of the army data, Brigham conceded, had been wrong. His recantation was properly applauded as the act of courage that it was. But it had virtually no effect on the new social attitudes, now widely held, that Brigham had been instrumental in creating. The Immigration Restriction Act was not repealed. The Scholastic Aptitude Test was not abandoned. The methodology of testing did not change.

Henry Chauncey, ETS's president from its founding in 1947 until 1970, was a bony-jawed New England aristocrat and former Harvard dean who was fascinated with the idea of assessing mental powers. In the Army Alpha exam and other intelligence tests, he whiffed the inebriating spoor of *science*. Writing in 1963 about the early intelligence experiments of Alfred Binet, Chauncey commented:

> [*Binet's*] method was truly scientific and remarkably like the method used by physicists forty years later to detect and measure the forces released by the atom. The cloud chamber does not permit the physicist to see the atom or its electrically charged components, but it does reveal the tracks of ionizing particles and thus permits the scientist to deduce the nature of the atom from which the particles emanate.

Intelligence, for Chauncey, was a hard, smooth nut, buried somewhere deep in the brain, that cast off particles of merit. One might never hope to squirrel out the thing itself, but if one were scientific enough, the nature of the nut might be deduced from its "emanations." Chauncey did not doubt the significance of his mission. In ETS's *Annual Report* for 1949–50, he described "an urgent need for a national census of human abilities," which, he said, would be "of critical importance for the National Military Establishment" and would also provide information about "the ability difference between men and women, and the trends of employment as between the sexes. . . ." ETS's tests, furthermore, would serve society by dampening the unreasonable aspirations of the unfit. "Life may have less mystery," Chauncey wrote, "but it will also have less disillusionment and disappointment. Hope will not be a lost source of strength, but it will be kept within reasonable bounds."

Chauncey thought of the SAT as essentially an IQ test. No one at ETS would publicly claim that today. Indeed, the company is reluctant even to refer to the Scholastic Aptitude Test as an *aptitude* test. You can read "Taking the SAT" from cover to cover and not find the word "aptitude" in it anywhere except in the name of the test the booklet purports to describe. The new euphemism is "developed ability," and ETS is now careful to say, for instance, that the SAT "is not a test of some inborn and unchanging capacity."

ETS hasn't always been so careful. In 1959 it published a booklet called "YOU: Today and Tomorrow" to help *grade school* students plan out the rest of their lives on the basis of their performance on ETS aptitude tests. "Your scholastic ability is like the engine," the booklet said: "it is the source of your power and speed in school. It tells you how fast and how far you *can* go." (Original emphasis.) Everything was so simple in those days. "Can you measure scholastic ability?" the booklet asked. "This is where you can use your 'magic mirror!' Take a good look at the facts about your scholastic ability *now.*" These days ETS often says that it abhors the "common misconception" that the company's aptitude tests measure something innate and unchanging. But if this is a misconception, no one has worked harder to make it a common one than ETS.

ETS's slow abandonment of the notion of innate aptitude has required any number of dike-plugging operations as the foundations sink and the floodwalls start to crack. One involves the issue of coaching. In recent years, a lively and profitable industry has grown up offering coaching books, live training, and practice sessions for the SAT, LSAT, and other ETS exams. Many high schools have also started coaching programs. These developments threaten ETS in at least two ways. First, they add weight to the frequent charge that ETS tests simply reinforce social and economic advantages. The students who get coaching are the ones whose parents are disposed toward it and can afford to pay. Second, and more important, coaching lends credence to the suspicion that all ETS really tests is the trick of taking ETS tests. Should major decisions about people's lives really turn on scores that can be affected by a few weeks' (some would say a few hours') practice?

ETS's traditional position, therefore, has been that SAT scores cannot be improved by coaching. More recently, as numerous independent researchers have published findings to the contrary, ETS has retreated a bit. ETS officers are now careful to say that coaching "as we define it" is ineffective, and coaching as ETS now defines it is "the short drill." How short is short? Answers to this question tend to be vague. Last year in *The New York Times,* George Hanford, the president of the College Board, said, "Coaching is at one end of a continuum, with teaching and a good education at the other. The distinctions are hard to make."

The short drill may not help, but in 1978 ETS itself began publishing a practice booklet called "Taking the SAT," which was intended, according to an ETS document, "to improve candidates' familiarity with the Scholastic Aptitude Test." Then, with that imperviousness to irony so necessary to an authentic kettle defense, ETS set about proving that this new coaching tool doesn't do students any good. An experiment was hastily designed. About 1,000 high school juniors were mailed prepublication copies of the booklet; their SAT scores were later compared with those of a group of students who had not received it. Although relatively few of the students who had received the booklet bothered to take and score the sample test that it contained, the comparison was based on the entire group. ETS proudly announced that the students who had not received the booklet scored slightly higher on their SATs than the students who had. The gentlemanly response to this discovery, certainly, would have been to recall all extant copies of the booklet and burn them. But ETS continues to publish "Taking the SAT." And ETS officials continue to cite their "study" as proof that coaching doesn't work.

Of course it's perfectly obvious to anyone who's ever taken an ETS test that coaching and practice help. In 1981, for example, ETS did something it had never done before: it analyzed, item by item, an entire school's performance on a PSAT (Preliminary SAT, given to high school juniors) and compared the results with the national average. One unexpected discovery was that the students at this particular school apparently weren't guessing the answers to items they didn't know. It turned out that the administrator of their exam had told them not to. In fact, you *are* supposed to guess, if you can eliminate one obviously wrong answer. A student who doesn't do this will earn a lower score than a student who does. The students at this school were penalized because they hadn't known the proper way to take the test. That's one thing they drill into you in coaching school.

The SAT wouldn't enjoy the stature it does today if college admissions officers didn't think of it as something not unlike an absolute measure of intellectual worth. (Admissions officers refer to people who do well in school but poorly on SAT tests as "overachievers," not as "undertesters.") But ETS has never officially claimed more for the SAT than that it is a slightly less reliable predictor of freshman grades than an applicant's high school performance is. "Your high school record," says "Taking the SAT," "is probably the best evidence of your preparation for college." How well does the SAT actually predict freshman grades?

George Hanford, president of the College Board, was quoted in *The New York Times* last year as saying, "Most studies show validities for the SAT and for the high school record of .52 (each, separately)." The number Hanford mentioned is known as a correlation coefficient. I don't know where he got his figure, unless he did a study of his own. In a booklet ETS published in 1980 in response to the Nader report, the correlation between SAT scores and freshman grades was given as .41. An ETS statistician told me it has since risen to about .43. A perfect positive correlation—which would exist if you could line up everybody at any given college according to their SATs and the order turned out be exactly the same as if you'd lined them up by grades—is 1.0. A correlation of under .5 is pretty modest.

If the SAT is not even as good a predictor as high school grades of the one thing it claims to predict—college freshman grades—what's the purpose of it? The correct function of the SAT, many people would say, is to enable college admissions officers to find promising students who might otherwise be lost in the shuffle. The SAT, this argument goes, puts minority students on an equal footing with white students, giving a uniform, color-blind test on which to demonstrate "aptitude."

This is a cheerful thought, but I challenge anyone to prove it. As ETS finally acknowledged with published statistics in 1982, there is a considerable gap between the average SAT performance of whites and that of blacks, Mexican-Americans, and Puerto Ricans, and between that of people whose families have a lot of money and people whose families don't. In 1981, 8,239 whites scored 700 or above on the verbal SAT; so did 70 blacks. In the same year, 57,686 whites scored 600 or above on the verbal SAT; so did 887 blacks. (The test population included 719,383 whites and 75,434 blacks.) The mean score for whites on the verbal SAT was 442; the mean score for blacks was 332.

If colleges actually used the SAT as a "color-blind" indicator of academic ability, you wouldn't find many minority students enrolled in selective schools. Most minority applicants who are admitted to selective colleges are admitted *in spite of* their SAT scores, not because of them. Admission to college in these circumstances carries with it a built-in slap in the face: you can come to our school, but you're not really entitled to.

Whether the SAT is culturally biased against minorities is another hardy perennial controversy in which ETS takes the kettle position: the tests were never biased; they've now been fixed; but the changes have had no effect. ETS naturally says that it has proved statistically that its tests aren't biased. Just to make sure, for the last few years it has used "an actual member of a minority" (as one ETSer told me) to read every test before it's published. This minority reader presumably scours each test booklet, scrupulously scratching out the word "nigger" wherever he finds it, and then affixes his actual-minority-member seal of approval. All this has less to do with test integrity than with public relations. The same is true of ETS's decision in 1970 to add "minority-oriented" reading passages to SAT verbal tests.

While making both of these gestures, ETS continues to insist that its tests can be "equated": this month's SAT is supposed to perform just like last month's SAT, which allegedly performs just like last year's SAT, which allegedly performs just like the SAT in 1965. This is why ETS claims it can actually compare average SAT scores from 1982 with average SAT scores from, say, 1969. But if this is true, you can't add a "minority-oriented" reading passage to an SAT unless it performs just like a non-minority-oriented reading passage, since non-minority-oriented passages are what the SAT always *used* to have. In the same sense, you can't remove the word "nigger" from one item unless you find some way to sneak it into another. Otherwise, you couldn't "equate" the tests over time, and editorial writers wouldn't be able to moan about one-point SAT-score declines.

In 1974, a writer for *New York* magazine interviewed ETS executive Marion Epstein about the new "minority-oriented" reading passages.

Q. If the texts weren't culturally biased in the first place, why did you make the change?
A. Because minorities feel at ease reading this kind of passage.
Q. If they feel at ease reading this one, does that mean they *don't* feel at ease reading the six or seven other passages in the text?
A. No. It just means they feel more comfortable with this one.

Q. Well, if they feel more comfortable, does that mean their scores will be higher?
A. No, I don't think there will be any difference in "scores."

Is the SAT biased against blacks? A senior research scientist at ETS, who asked not to be identified, told me that black students tend to do better in college than their SAT scores predict they will. If you have a black student and a white student with identical scores, he said, you can expect the black student to earn a higher grade-point average than the white student. No doubt the motive for this assertion is high-minded: to rebut accusations that unqualified blacks are getting into selective schools because of favored treatment. But if the assertion is true, the SAT test is literally racist: it systematically gives black students lower SAT scores than they deserve in terms of the sole criterion by which the test's validity is judged.

But maybe the research scientist was wrong. When I asked Arthur M. Kroll, an ETS vice president in charge of College Board programs, if the SAT penalized blacks, he said, "If you mean, Does the SAT predict as well how minority students are going to do in college as majority students, then the SAT has done as effective a job for blacks as for whites." If I understand Kroll correctly (why do so many people at ETS seem to have so much trouble with syntax?), this means that the SAT is not biased either for or against blacks. A different story. So I asked the same question of Ernest Kimmel, who's in charge of test development for ETS's College Board programs. "I guess I'll disagree slightly with my boss," he said. "The scores do not work exactly the same with whites and blacks. If an admissions officer uses a single admissions equation based on a mix of white and black students with the same scores and the same high school rank, he's going to predict the same grade averages. But in actuality the black students in about 80 percent of the studies seem to do a bit worse." In other words, blacks get worse grades than their SATs would predict; the test is biased against whites.

I now had three apparently contradictory explanations. I took them to Richard Noeth, the ETS official who had told me that essay exams are different from multiple-choice exams, but are neither better nor worse.

"The thing is," Noeth said, "to my knowledge, there's supporting evidence for each of the three positions that you mentioned. I tend to —I believe them all. I'm sure they're all true."

Well, we've certainly cleared up this bias business. But we're left with the disparity in scores. Now that ETS has abandoned "aptitude" in favor of "developed ability" as its rallying cry, no one seriously disputes the explanation. Obviously a student's SAT scores are very heavily affected by the quality of the education he has received up until the time he takes the test. Private school students do better on SATs than public school students, and so on. Since most black children attend worse schools than most white children, it would indeed be surprising if black children did as well as white children on SATs.

It's equally obvious (though ETS cannot concede this) that white middle- and upper-class children have a big advantage because they are familiar with the ins and outs of ETS-test-taking. Students in good schools pick up test-taking skills almost by osmosis, because standardized tests are a constant presence in their lives. They know when to guess and when not to, they know where to find easy items, they know the kind of predictable answers ETS usually looks for, they know not to give up if they run into a string of questions they can't answer, they know the instructions and the different types of questions.

ETS regards the disadvantages some children bring to the SAT as part of the hard facts of life. It says that it bears no more responsibility for the low scores that result than a thermometer does for a fever. But what is left of the rationale for the SAT if it cannot filter out the hard facts of life? Remember, ETS concedes that the SAT does not predict college freshman grades (the only thing ETS claims the test *does* predict) as well as high school grades do. The rationale for the SAT has been that it could see past the prejudices and disadvantages and lift up promising students who haven't had the opportunities they deserve. But if black students do poorly on the SAT because they've gotten a lousy education, or because they haven't mastered the code the test is written in, their scores won't tell you a thing about their "scholastic aptitude." All the scores will do is to make it a bit less likely that they'll ever be given the chance to find out what the big secret was all about.

In March 1980, the *Bulletin of the American Association for Higher Education* published a paper that, in cautious academic prose, threatens the very existence of the Educational Testing Service. The paper, written by Rodney T. Hartnett and Robert A. Feldmesser, two senior research scientists at ETS, was entitled "College Admissions Testing and the Myth of Selectivity." It pointed out the curious fact that although virtually all American colleges require their applicants to take a standardized admissions test, hardly any actually use the scores in making admissions decisions.

"Many of the institutions that accept large proportions of their applicants nevertheless require the applicants to submit an admissions-test score," the paper said. "Ninety-two percent of all institutions in the random sample from the [College Board's] *College Handbook* had such a requirement; even among those accepting at least 90 percent of their applicants, 88 percent had such a requirement. . . . These figures put admissions tests in a new light and raise interesting questions about the role they are playing in the admissions policies and practices of particular colleges and universities, and in higher education generally."

The overwhelming majority of colleges and universities in this country require standardized admissions tests, but aren't using the results. "There's no way they could be," Hartnett says. "If you look at the distribution of American institutions of higher education with regard to selectivity, you'd probably be amazed to learn how many of them are either open-door institutions or ones that accept virtually everybody who applies. They may turn away kids who have some record of drug abuse or something."

Hartnett and Feldmesser's paper was really a call for further research, a call that ETS was understandably reluctant to heed. ETS and the College Board, Hartnett says, pressured them to reconsider their findings. They refused. Later, both were given the choice of either leaving the company or accepting new jobs outside of research. Hartnett, who had been at ETS fifteen years, quit. Feldmesser decided to stay and was put to work writing test questions, something ETS also hires college students to do. Both actions were officially described as cost-cutting moves, but because ETS has a university-style tenure system, Hartnett had to be given a generous severance settlement and Feldmesser continued to be paid his old salary. More recently, he also quit.

ETS essentially confirms Hartnett and Feldmesser's thesis. Ernest Kimmel, the director of test development for ETS's College Board programs, told me that there are only "fifty or sixty colleges and universities that are still selective." But ETS, characteristically, shies away from the implications.

What are the implications? Well, as we've seen, the entire meaning (whatever it may be) of an SAT score, if the test is functioning the way ETS says it is supposed to, derives not from the entire test but from just a few questions. Now it turns out that SAT scores are used not by the hundreds of colleges that require them but by just a few dozen schools. All of those schools use other factors besides the SAT in deciding whom to admit, factors (like grades) that correlate roughly with the SAT anyway; so the SAT makes the crucial difference in only a fraction of admissions decisions even at selective schools.

In other words, the entire portentous and expensive apparatus of the Scholastic Aptitude Test is irrelevant for its stated purpose of determining who should go to which college, except for a very few questions asked of a very few students applying to a very few schools. If colleges required only the scores they really used, the cost would be prohibitive. The SAT —cornerstone of the testing establishment and of ETS's finances— would go bust.

Why do colleges demand SAT scores that they don't really use? "We came to the conclusion," Hartnett says, "that most institutions require the test scores to maintain this aura of selectivity. One other reason they do it is that it doesn't cost them anything. It costs the kids. If, in fact, the institutions had to pay, you'd better believe they'd stop it in a hurry."

Contrary to what many people think, it doesn't cost an institution anything to require and receive your SAT scores, or your Achievement Test scores, or any other ETS score. In New York State in 1982–83, ETS charged you $11 for every SAT you took and $18.25 for every Achievement Test. (When I applied to college, I was told to take the SAT twice, and three different Achievements.) There is a slew of extra charges for things like late registration and extra score results. (If you apply to more than three colleges, you pay so the extra schools can find out your score.) Advanced Placement tests cost $42 each. And so on.

That's what you paid. What did you pay for? You paid for things like the subsidized lunches in ETS's employee cafeteria, and for mowing the grass on the baseball diamond, and for tidying up the little island in the middle of the goose pond. You also paid for dozens of ancillary studies and services that ETS provides to high schools and colleges— the real "customers"—free of charge, along with scores. You also paid for all those "validity" studies that ETS performs every year for the 200 or so colleges that request them. All of this information is less useful to the colleges than it is to ETS. ETS floods institutions with statistics in order to make itself seem indispensable and to uphold the "scientific" façade it has erected around its tests. If the colleges had to pay, few of them would bother.

An ETS employee I spoke to disagreed. "The colleges would just pay for it," he said, "and then pass the cost along to the students. It's no big deal. It's like: General Motors has to have airbags? Sure. So we'll add $300 to the cost of the car."

If memory serves, there are no airbags in General Motors cars. GM didn't think it could pass the cost along to consumers, so it resisted regulations requiring passive restraints in cars. The ETS employee's analogy does not best express the relationship between standardized tests and airbags.

Bowdoin College, a top liberal arts school in Maine, stopped requiring SAT scores in 1970, having found that it could build a better student body without them. If a college like Bowdoin can get by without SATs, how many schools in the country can convincingly argue that they can't? And if those schools really *do* believe they can't do without the SATs, shouldn't they have to pay for the luxury of requiring students to take them? Where is Milton Friedman when you need him?

One of the reasons Bowdoin got rid of SATs was that in the two years before its decision, only 31 percent of all its honors graduates had scored above the class average on both SATs, while 24 percent had scored below. SAT scores weren't telling Bowdoin much of anything it couldn't have figured out by simply, say, asking applicants how much their parents earned and whether their mothers had gone to college and where they spent their summer vacations.

Hartnett and Feldmesser's hypothesis that colleges require test scores they don't really need for reasons of "prestige" is on the right track, but perhaps too narrow. Life without the SATs and other such tests is simply hard to imagine. Ever since the Army Alpha exams of World War I, American society has been hypnotized by mental measurement. And no matter how much ETS protests that this isn't what it intends, test scores are taken by society and by the recipients themselves as proxies for "merit" and therefore for their proper place in the social hierarchy.

The more important test scores become, the more they tend to become self-fulfilling prophecies. A high score can give a great boost to self-confidence, giving a young person the courage to trust his judgment. But a low score has the opposite effect. A study at Duke University last year showed that the grades of struggling freshmen could be improved simply by telling them that their sophomore grades would probably be better. We'll never truly be able to discover how strong this effect is with ETS tests because ETS, like a bad doctor, buries its mistakes.

Leaving aside the technical debate over bias, the simple fact is that from the beginning—the Army Alpha exams—standardized testing has been associated with racial and cultural prejudice and has served to reinforce the established hierarchy rather than to shake it up. And even apart from who in particular is helped or hurt, the question remains as to why, in a democracy, it should be considered desirable to rank people from 200 to 800 every time they turn around.

Sprawled in the sauna at the Henry Chauncey Conference Center, mopping my humid brow, I reflect that there's no reason to accuse the people at ETS of some nefarious plot to enforce the social status quo. Institutional self-preservation is a more likely explanation for their eagerness to expand testing into new and ever less likely aspects of life, for their refusal to inquire what good all this testing does, for their casual indifference to the harm, and for the jerry-built reinforcements they construct every time another chunk of their ideological foundation collapses.

It can't last.

QUESTIONS FOR DISCUSSION

1. Both Amberg and Owen describe the history of the ETS and scholastic testing in the United States. If both accounts are accurate, how can they serve different evaluations?

2. Owen uses humor in his essay; Amberg does not. Does Owen compromise his authority by his penchant for irony? Does Amberg increase his by his seriousness? Which essay do you think has the more believable voice and why?

3. At what point while you are reading do you realize that Amberg is evaluating rather than simply explaining the SAT? Why does he leave his thesis statement to the very end?

4. Owen accuses the ETS of conducting what he calls a "kettle defense" of its practices (see page 543) in which it denies that an abuse exists and then claims to have corrected it. How many examples of such contradictions does he cite?

5. Both Amberg and Owen deal with questions of bias, predictability, validity, and the efficacy of coaching. How do they manage to reach such different conclusions about each of these?

6. Both arguments make the point that SAT scores are not the single most significant criterion for college admission. Yet 92 percent of colleges still require SAT scores. If the SATs cannot help you, can they hurt you? Could you afford not to take them?

SUGGESTIONS FOR WRITING

1. Obtain some sample SAT questions, perhaps from a coaching booklet, and analyze one or more of the verbal questions for the kinds of ambiguity Owen finds. Can you argue with the educational establishment that oversubtlety could defeat a test-taker?
2. The cultural bias of the SAT test (i.e., the correlation of scores with family income) is either acceptable or unacceptable depending on other cultural values about merit, access to opportunity, and the responsibility of families for their children's development. Can these values be in conflict? Argue pro or con to an audience of parents of college-bound students.
3. Think back on your own experience with the SAT. Do you think your scores accurately predicted your college performance or measured your aptitude to do college work? Did any of the skills you had to learn to take the test prove useful in college? Write a letter to high school seniors, imparting to them the benefits of your experience with the SAT.
4. Write a letter to your college admissions director arguing, on the basis of Owen's critique, that your school should drop its SAT requirement. Or write a letter to high school students arguing that they should take some special courses to prepare for their SATs.
5. Compare the way testing is used to qualify people for higher or professional education in the United States with the way it is used in another country, such as Great Britain or France. Argue to an audience of Americans which way seems preferable.
6. Evaluate a test you have taken in a college course and present to the instructor your assessment of its fairness.

─────────── ⋙ ⋘ ───────────

Math and Sex: Are Girls Born with Less Ability?

GINA BARI KOLATA

─────────── ⋙ ⋘ ───────────

Sex Differences in Mathematical Ability: Fact or Artifact?

CAMILLA PERSSON BENBOW AND JULIAN C. STANLEY

─────────── ⋙ ⋘ ───────────

Mathematical Ability: Is Sex a Factor?/Letters

RESPONSES TO BENBOW AND STANLEY

The following unit contains the original article by two Johns Hopkins University researchers, Camilla Benbow and Julian Stanley, suggesting the existence of sex differences in mathematical ability. It is preceded by an introductory article from the same issue by science writer Gina Bari Kolata, defining the controversy and presenting pro and con statements from various authorities. And it is followed by a series of letters arguing with Benbow and Stanley's conclusions, with a final word from the researchers themselves.

This is an important controversy with vocal adherents on both sides. The debate was conducted in a prestigious scientific journal, Science, where experts talk to experts. In such a format, evidence is presented in more detail and conclusions are more carefully qualified than they would be in the popular press.

"Math and Sex: Are Girls Born with Less Ability?"

Throughout history there have been very few women mathematicians, and this trend continues today. For example, when Edith Luchins, a mathematician at Rensselaer Polytechnic Institute, and Abraham Luchins, a psychologist at the State University of New York at Albany, asked mathematicians to list five famous contemporary women mathematicians, many could not. When Ravenna Helson, a psychologist at the University of California at Berkeley, set out in the 1960's to study creative women mathematicians, she reported that there were so few that she did not have to sample them—she could study all of them.

Since creativity in mathematics seems to be a talent, like musical or artistic ability, the question has been, why are there so few outstanding women mathematicians? Some researchers have said the answer lies in nurture rather than nature. Mathematics is viewed as a "masculine" field of study, and girls are discouraged from developing their mathematical abilities. But Camilla Benbow and Julian Stanley of Johns Hopkins University question this theory. They have evidence that extraordinary mathematical talent may be less prevalent in girls than in boys. The differences between the abilities of girls and boys are so striking, they say, that it is hard to imagine that they are entirely due to socialization. By sticking their necks out in this way, Benbow and Stanley seem to be asking for an attack. But, says Stanley, "We want our data out in the public domain so they can't be ignored."

The data are from Stanley's mathematics talent searches, the Study of Mathematically Precocious Youth. From 1972 to 1979, Stanley and his associates conducted six talent searches, looking for 7th and 8th graders who scored in at least the upper 2 to 5 percent in standardized mathematics achievement tests, such as the Iowa Tests of Basic Skills. They found 10,000 children, 43 percent of whom were girls, and invited them to take the mathematics and verbal portions of the Scholastic Aptitude Tests (SAT). Those who did extremely well on the math portion were encouraged to take accelerated mathematics courses at Johns Hopkins.

Stanley contends that the math SAT serves as an aptitude test when given to 7th and 8th graders because they have not been formally taught the principles that underlie the math problems. If they can do the problems, they must have unusual abilities.

In 1980, the Johns Hopkins group expanded its talent search and changed its eligibility criteria. Any 7th grader who scored in the 97th percentile or above in any standardized achievement test—whether the high score was in a math section or a verbal section or was a combined score—was invited to take the verbal and math SAT's. The researchers found 10,000 such students, making the total tested thus far 20,000.

Every year, the Johns Hopkins group has found that the girls and boys do equally well on the verbal SAT's but the boys do significantly better on the math SAT's. For example, more than twice as many boys as girls had math scores greater than 500. The greatest differences were between the top-scoring girls and boys. And in every talent search, the student with the highest math score was a boy.

"We began our talent searches to find gifted children. We had no expectations of sex differences," says Benbow. "We were surprised to see the differences in 1972 [the year of the first search] and we were really shocked when we saw them again in 1973." One possible explanation is that the talent search is somehow failing to reach the best girls. But, Benbow finds, "We have a better sample of girls than boys." Benbow also reports that girls who were invited to take the SAT's said they like math. "These are not girls with math anxiety," she says.

Jane Armstrong, of the Education Commission of the States, Denver, has results that, she thinks, confirm those of Benbow and Stanley. When the commission tested nearly 1800 high school seniors, the boys did significantly better than the girls in math, and this difference did not disappear when the number of math courses the students had taken was accounted for. The kinds of problems in which the boys excelled were those that tested reasoning, not computational or spatial visualization abilities. Armstrong says that the boys' higher scores seem to be due to a group of very bright boys who do so well that they pull up the boys' averages. "I definitely agree with Stanley that these are hard-core sex differences," she says. "A lot can be accounted for by socialization but it won't take care of all the differences."

Many take issue with this interpretation, of course. Mary Gray, a mathematician at American University in Washington, D.C., who is active in the Association for Women in Mathematics, says she cannot see on what basis Armstrong, Stanley, and Benbow draw their conclusions. Too little is known about the development of mathematical reasoning ability and how to test for it to jump to the conclusion that these sex differences are genetically based rather than solely a result of social factors.

Elizabeth Fennema, a member of the education department at the

University of Wisconsin in Madison, says, "I think they [the Johns Hopkins group] are on darned shaky ground when they draw conclusions about genetic differences." She and Julia Sherman, a psychologist at the University of Wisconsin, find no differences in boys' and girls' spatial visualization abilities. Spatial visualization, which includes picturing how objects will look after they are rotated or folded, is widely assumed to be correlated with mathematical reasoning ability—although some mathematicians, including Gray, disagree.

At Johns Hopkins, the researchers believe that social factors probably play some role in causing the talented girls to do less well on the math SAT's than the talented boys. Therefore, Lynn Fox, Diane Tobin, and Linda Brody of Johns Hopkins are looking into the backgrounds and upbringing of these students, asking such things as what toys the children played with, whether the mother or father helped them with their math homework, and what aspirations the parents have for their children. In addition, they want to know whether the talented boys and girls differ in test-taking strategies. Maybe the girls are less willing to guess at answers, for example. Yet, says Tobin, it is not clear whether they are asking the right questions or, even if they do see sex-related differences in the children's upbringing and behavior, what these differences mean.

Although fewer girls than boys qualify for the accelerated math courses at Johns Hopkins, even fewer girls enroll in them—and those who do tend to drop out. When Fox questioned the talented girls, she found that many declined to participate in the accelerated classes because they were afraid of being labeled "different" by their friends. They also said that the accelerated classes were dull and that the talented boys were "little creeps."

Fox, concerned that social factors may at the very least be preventing the talented girls from reaching their potential, tried to make the accelerated classes more appealing to girls. She organized an all-girl accelerated class taught by a woman and featuring talks by scientists on research involving mathematics and bearing on both social and theoretical problems.

At first, the results seemed encouraging. More girls who were invited participated and fewer dropped out than in the mixed-sex classes. But in the long run the all-girl class has been disappointing. The girls, now sophomores in college, are doing no better in math and are taking no more math courses than the control group of girls who were not invited to participate in the special class. "The girls may need constant intervention," Tobin speculates.

Although Stanley, Benbow, Tobin, and others at Johns Hopkins tend to think that the differences in ability they see in the very talented students also extend, in a less dramatic form, to average students, others are not so sure. "What their study means for women at large is very problematical," says Fennema. "There is no way that their data can explain why women do not take math in college and do not go into math and science professions."

Certainly, says Patricia Casserly of the Educational Testing Service in Princeton, New Jersey, the Johns Hopkins results do not mean that high school girls cannot score as well in math achievement tests as the boys. Although high school girls generally score lower than boys, there are some schools where the two sexes consistently score equally well. Casserly has studied 20 such schools in the past 8 years. These are a diverse group of public schools drawing students of widely differing backgrounds. Nonetheless, they share common features. For example, the teachers have science, math, or engineering backgrounds rather than backgrounds in education and they communicate a love of and enthusiasm for mathematics. Bright students are grouped together in math classes, the teachers place more than usual emphasis on reasoning, and the teachers counsel students.

But if there are genetically based differences in mathematical abilities between males and females, it may be more difficult for women to study math and it may be one reason why so few women receive Ph.D.'s in math. Benbow believes that socialization is a factor in women's math achievement but that it is not the only factor. Women, she says, would be better off accepting their differences and working to encourage girls to achieve as much as they can than to constantly blame their lesser achievements in mathematics solely on social factors. Tobin agrees with Benbow but admits that she finds such a view somewhat disconcerting. "As a woman, I don't want to think there is something about us that does not allow us to do math like the men do," she says.

"Sex Differences in Mathematical Ability: Fact or Artifact?"

Abstract. *A substantial sex difference in mathematical reasoning ability (score on the mathematics test of the Scholastic Aptitude Test) in favor of boys was found in a study of 9927 intellectually gifted junior high school students. Our data contradict the hypothesis that differential course-taking accounts for observed sex differences in mathematical ability, but support the hypothesis that these differences are somewhat increased by environmental influences.*

Huge sex differences have been reported in mathematical aptitude and achievement (*1*). In junior high school, this sex difference is quite obvious: girls excel in computation, while boys excel on tasks requiring mathematical reasoning ability (*1*). Some investigators believe that differential course-taking gives rise to the apparently inferior mathematical reasoning ability of girls (*2*). One alternative, however, could be that less well-developed mathematical reasoning ability contributes to girls' taking fewer mathematics courses and achieving less than boys.

We now present extensive data collected by the Study of Mathematically Precocious Youth (SMPY) for the past 8 years to examine mathematical aptitude in approximately 10,000 males and females prior to the onset of differential course-taking. These data show that large sex differences in mathematical aptitude are observed in boys and girls with essentially identical formal educational experiences.

Six separate SMPY talent searches were conducted (*3*). In the first three searches, 7th and 8th graders, as well as accelerated 9th and 10th graders, were eligible; for the last three, only 7th graders and accelerated students of 7th grade age were eligible. In addition, in the 1976, 1978, and 1979 searches, the students had also to be in the upper 3 percent in mathematical ability as judged by a standardized achievement test, in 1972 in the upper 5 percent, and in 1973 and 1974 in the upper 2 percent. Thus, both male and female talent-search participants were selected by equal criteria for high mathematical ability before entering. Girls constituted 43 percent of the participants in these searches.

As part of each talent search the students took both parts of the College Board's Scholastic Aptitude Test (SAT)—the mathematics (SAT-M) and the verbal (SAT-V) tests (*4*). The SAT is designed for able juniors and seniors in high school, who are an average of 4 to 5 years older than the students in the talent searches. The mathematical section is particularly designed to measure mathematical reasoning ability (*5*). For this reason, scores on the SAT-M achieved by 7th and 8th graders provided an excellent opportunity to test the Fennema and Sherman differential course-taking hypothesis (*2*), since until then all students had received essentially identical formal instruction in mathematics (*6*). If their hypothesis is correct, little difference in mathematical aptitude should be seen between able boys and girls in our talent searches.

Results from the six talent searches are shown in Table 1. Most students scored high on both the SAT-M and SAT-V. On the SAT-V, the boys and girls performed about equally well (7). The overall performance of 7th grade students on SAT-V was at or above the average of a random sample of high school students, whose mean score is 368 (8), or at about the 30th percentile of college-bound 12th graders. The 8th graders, regular and accelerated, scored at about the 50th percentile of college-bound seniors. This was a high level of performance.

A large sex difference in mathematical ability in favor of boys was observed in every talent search. The smallest mean difference in the six talent searches was 32 points in 1979 in favor of boys. The statistically significant t-tests of mean differences ranged from 2.5 to 11.6 (9). Thus, on the average, the boys scored about one-half of the females' standard deviation (S.D.) better than did the girls in each talent search, even though all students had been certified initially to be in the top 2nd, 3rd, or 5th percentiles in mathematical reasoning ability (depending on which search was entered).

One might suspect that the SMPY talent search selected for abler boys than girls. In all comparisons except for two (8th graders in 1972 and 1976), however, the girls performed better on SAT-M relative to female college-bound seniors than the boys did on SAT-M relative to male college-bound seniors. Furthermore, in all searches, the girls were equal verbally to the boys. Thus, even though the talent-search girls were at least as able compared to girls in general as the talent-search boys were compared to boys in general, the boys still averaged considerably higher on SAT-M than the girls did.

Moreover, the greatest disparity between the girls and boys is in the upper ranges of mathematical reasoning ability. Differences between the top-scoring boys and girls have been as large as 190 points (1972 8th graders) and as low as 30 points (1978 and 1979). When one looks further at students who scored above 600 on SAT-M, Table 1 shows a great difference in the percentage of boys and girls. To take the extreme (not including the 1976 8th graders), among the 1972 8th graders, 27.1 percent of the boys scored higher than 600, whereas not one of the girls did. Over all talent searches, boys outnumbered girls more than 2 to 1 (1817 boys versus 675 girls) in SAT-M scores over 500. In not one of the six talent searches was the top SAT-M score earned by a girl. It is clear that much of the sex difference on SAT-M can be accounted for by a lack of high-scoring girls.

A few highly mathematically able girls have been found, particularly

Table 1. Performance of Students in the Study of Mathematically Precocious Youth in each talent search (N = 9927).

TEST DATE	GRADE	NUMBER		SAT-V SCORE* ($\bar{x}$ ± S.D.)		SAT-M SCORES† $\bar{x}$ ± S.D.		HIGHEST SCORE		PERCENTAGE SCORING ABOVE 600 ON SAT-M	
		BOYS	GIRLS	BOYS	GIRLS	BOYS	GIRLS	BOYS	GIRLS	BOYS	GIRLS
March 1972	7	90	77			460 ± 104	423 ± 75	740	590	7.8	0
	8+	133	96			528 ± 105	458 ± 88	790	600	27.1	0
January 1973	7	135	88	385 ± 71	374 ± 74	495 ± 85	440 ± 66	800	620	8.1	1.1
	8+	286	158	431 ± 89	442 ± 83	551 ± 85	511 ± 63	800	650	22.7	8.2
January 1974	7	372	222			473 ± 85	440 ± 68	760	630	6.5	1.8
	8+	556	369			540 ± 82	503 ± 72	750	700	21.6	7.9
December 1976	7	495	356	370 ± 73	368 ± 70	455 ± 84	421 ± 64	780	610	5.5	0.6
	8‡	12	10	487 ± 129	390 ± 61	598 ± 126	482 ± 83	750	600	58.3	0
January 1978	7 and 8‡	1549	1249	375 ± 80	372 ± 78	448 ± 87	413 ± 71	790	760	5.3	0.8
January 1979	7 and 8‡	2046	1628	370 ± 76	370 ± 77	436 ± 87	404 ± 77	790	760	3.2	0.9

*Mean score for a random sample of high school juniors and seniors was 368 for males and females (8).
†Mean for juniors and seniors: males, 416; females, 390 (8).
‡These rare 8th graders were accelerated at least 1 year in school grade placement.

in the latest two talent searches. The latter talent searches, however, were by far the largest, making it more likely that we could identify females of high mathematical ability. Alternatively, even if highly able girls have felt more confident to enter the mathematics talent search in recent years, our general conclusions would not be altered unless all of the girls with the highest ability had stayed away for more than 5 years. We consider that unlikely. In this context, three-fourths as many girls have participated as boys each year; the relative percentages have not varied over the years.

It is notable that we observed sizable sex differences in mathematical reasoning ability in 7th grade students. Until that grade, boys and girls have presumably had essentially the same amount of formal training in mathematics. This assumption is supported by the fact that in the 1976 talent search no substantial sex differences were found in either participation in special mathematics programs or in mathematical learning processes (6). Thus, the sex difference in mathematical reasoning ability we found was observed before girls and boys started to differ significantly in the number and types of mathematics courses taken. It is therefore obvious that differential course-taking in mathematics cannot alone explain the sex difference we observed in mathematical reasoning ability, although other environmental explanations have not been ruled out.

The sex difference in favor of boys found at the time of the talent search was sustained and even increased through the high school years. In a follow-up survey of talent-search participants who had graduated from high school in 1977 (10), the 40-point mean difference on SAT-M in favor of boys at the time of that group's talent search had increased to a 50-point mean difference at the time of high school graduation. This subsequent increase is consistent with the hypothesis that differential course-taking can affect mathematical ability (2). The increase was rather small, however. Our data also show a sex difference in the number of mathematics courses taken in favor of boys but not a large one. The difference stemmed mainly from the fact that approximately 35 percent fewer girls than boys took calculus in high school (10). An equal proportion of girls and boys took mathematics in the 11th grade (83 percent), however, which is actually the last grade completed before taking the SAT in high school. It, therefore, cannot be argued that these boys received substantially more formal practice in mathematics and therefore scored better. Instead, it is more likely that mathematical reasoning ability influences subsequent differential course-taking in mathematics.

There were also no significant sex differences in the grades earned in the various mathematics courses (10).

A possible criticism of our results is that only selected mathematically able, highly motivated students were tested. Are the SMPY results indicative of the general population? Lowering qualifications for the talent search did not result in more high-scoring individuals (except in 1972, which was a small and not widely known search), suggesting that the same results in the high range would be observed even if a broader population were tested. In addition, most of the concern about the lack of participation of females in mathematics expressed by Ernest (11) and others has been about intellectually able girls, rather than those of average or below average intellectual ability.

To what extent do girls with high mathematical reasoning ability opt out of the SMPY talent searches? More boys than girls (57 percent versus 43 percent) enter the talent search each year. For this to change our conclusions, however, it would be necessary to postulate that the most highly talented girls were the least likely to enter each search. On both empirical and logical grounds this seems improbable.

It is hard to dissect out the influences of societal expectations and attitudes on mathematical reasoning ability. For example, rated liking of mathematics and rated importance of mathematics in future careers had no substantial relationship with SAT-M scores (6). Our results suggest that these environmental influences are more significant for achievement in mathematics than for mathematical aptitude.

We favor the hypothesis that sex differences in achievement in and attitude toward mathematics result from superior male mathematical ability, which may in turn be related to greater male ability in spatial tasks (12). This male superiority is probably an expression of a combination of both endogenous and exogenous variables. We recognize, however, that our data are consistent with numerous alternative hypotheses. Nonetheless, the hypothesis of differential course-taking was not supported. It also seems likely that putting one's faith in boy-versus-girl socialization processes as the only permissible explanation of the sex difference in mathematics is premature.

REFERENCES AND NOTES

1. E. Fennema, *J. Res. Math. Educ.* 5, 126 (1974); "National assessment for educational progress," *NAEP Newsl.* 8 (No. 5), insert (1975); L. Fox, in *Intellectual Talent: Research and Development*, D. Keating, Ed. (Johns Hopkins Univ. Press, Baltimore, 1976), p. 183.

2. For example, E. Fennema and J. Sherman, *Am. Educ. Res. J.* 14, 51 (1977).
3. W. George and C. Solano, in *Intellectual Talent: Research and Development,* D. Keating, Ed. (Johns Hopkins Univ. Press, Baltimore, 1976), p. 55.
4. The SAT-V was not administered in 1972 and 1974, and the Test of Standard Written English was required in 1978 and 1979.
5. W. Angoff, Ed., *The College Board Admissions Testing Program* (College Entrance Examination Board, Princeton, N.J., 1971), p. 15.
6. C. Benbow and J. Stanley, manuscript in preparation.
7. This was not true for the accelerated 8th graders in 1976. The N for the latter comparison is only 22.
8. College Entrance Examination Board, *Guide to the Admissions Testing Service* (Educational Testing Service, Princeton, N.J., 1978), p. 15.
9. The t-tests and P values for 7th and 8th graders, respectively, in the six talent searches were 2.6, $P < .01$; 5.3, $P < .001$; 5.1, $P < .001$; 5.2, $P < .001$; 4.9, $P < .001$; 7.1, $P < .001$; 6.6, $P < .001$; 2.5, $P < .05$; 11.6, $P < .001$; and 11.5, $P < .001$.
10. C. Benbow and J. Stanley, in preparation.
11. J. Ernest, *Am. Math. Mon.* 83, 595 (1976).
12. I. MacFarlane-Smith, *Spatial Ability* (Univ. of London Press, London, 1964); J. Sherman, *Psychol. Rev.* 74, 290 (1967).
13. We thank R. Benbow, C. Breaux, and L. Fox for their comments and help in preparing this manuscript. Supported in part by grants from the Spencer Foundation and the Educational Foundation of America.

"Letters in Response and the Authors' Defense"

MATHEMATICAL ABILITY: IS SEX A FACTOR?

Benbow and Stanley report that, over an 8-year period of studying selected samples of intellectually gifted students, their best male students outperformed their best female students. This is an observation that must be taken seriously because of the large number of volunteers involved and the consistency of the findings. What cannot be concluded from their data, although they speculate to this effect, is that there might be a genetic origin to these sex differences. . . . How then can their consistent findings of male "superiority" be accounted for?

In all the test populations studied by Benbow and Stanley, males outnumbered females. Benbow and Stanley argue, rightly, that we cannot assume the missing females (37 in one year, 418 in another, for example) would have been the highest scoring girls. But we can begin to wonder why fewer girls than boys always volunteered for the gifted programs. If we isolate as a variable "willingness to enter the talent search," we might argue that, although it isn't *likely* that the most talented girls refused to enter the talent search, it is *possible* that, having other options, they did not. Indeed, in research on the same populations, published some years ago, Fox writes (*1*) that it is difficult to get talented girls (and their parents) to agree to participate in a math class for gifted children because of fear of social ostracism. . . .

A second factor might be different out-of-class experiences. In taking mechanical items apart, participating in strategy-memory game-playing, competing in math contests, and playing geometrical or trigonometrical sports (sailing, billiards, and so forth) boys, more than girls, may develop and exercise math-like reasoning powers.

A third consideration is that 7th and 8th graders, however interested they are in mathematics (and the attitude questionnaire administered by the researchers did indicate about equal appreciation for, and interest in, the subject), are experiencing sudden and intense awareness of their adult sex roles and expected behaviors. In addition to the appearance of secondary sexual characteristics at this age (and because of them), 7th and 8th graders are very much aware of the values attached to "masculinity" and "femininity" and, according to many researchers (Fennema, Sherman, Bush), teenagers in general associate mathematics with masculinity (*2*). A question like "Is mathematics a more appropriate activity for boys and men than for girls and women?" might have revealed that there are comparable stereotypes even among the gifted and talented.

Finally, we know precious little about the components of mathematical reasoning and even less about how to test for it.

There is probably no way to conduct a true study of male and female mathematical aptitude so controlled for self-image, out-of-class experiences, and parental reinforcement (or nonreinforcement) that aptitude can be truly sorted out from performance. Moreover, there is no need to do this. If spatial visualization contributes to mathematical reasoning, teach it. Improve math teaching overall, and eliminate all the factors in the culture that discourage children of both sexes and all races from pursuing mathematical study with pleasure and reasonable expectations of success.

Department of Physics
University of Arizona   CARL TOMIZUKA

Overcoming Math Anxiety
Suite 203, 302 18th Street, NW
Washington, D.C. 20036   SHEILA TOBIAS

REFERENCES

1. L. H. Fox, *J. Ed. Gift,* 1 (No. 2), 24 (1978).
2. E. Fennema and J. Sherman, *Women and Mathematics: Research Perspectives for Change* (NIE Papers in Education and Work, No. 8, National Institute of Education, Washington, D.C., 1977); L. Bush, *Girls and Mathematics: The Problem and the Solution* (Apt Associates, Cambridge, Mass., 1980).

Benbow and Stanley "favor the hypothesis" that the sex differences they observed in performance on the Scholastic Aptitude Test in mathematics (SAT-M) "result from superior male mathematical ability, which may in turn be related to greater male ability in spatial tasks." They base this hypothesis, in part, on the contention that "boys and girls have presumably had essentially the same amount of formal training in mathematics," by the 7th grade. There are serious problems with this assumption, as represented by the following findings for elementary school students: girls receive less praise for correct answers than do boys (*1*); boys are praised for participation in academic activities more often than girls (*2*); and teachers sex-stereotype academic fields, making more academic contacts with girls in reading and with boys in math (*3*). From these observations, one would expect males to participate more effectively in academic activities, particularly in mathematics. Equivalence of formal training is therefore not a warranted assumption. . . .

We also note that Benbow and Stanley did not measure spatial ability themselves but cite two published sources for their argument. One of these (*4*) relies on studies now 20 or more years old; the other (*5*) has been superseded by a work (*6*) that clearly voices objection to the male superiority hypothesis.

Certainly this new massive study by Benbow and Stanley reemphasizes the sex differences in mathematical achievement that have been recognized as a serious social problem. Unfortunately, the hypothesis of superior male ability, favored but not substantiated by the authors, received widespread distribution in the popular media (*7*), which did not call attention to the complexity of the problem.

Lawrence Hall of Science   ELIZABETH K. STAGE
University of California   ROBERT KARPLUS

REFERENCES

1. J. Brophy and T. Good, *J. Ed. Psychol.* **61**, 365 (1970).
2. P. Delefes and B. Jackson, *Psychol. Schools* **9**, 119 (1972).

3. G. Leinhardt, A. Seewald, M. Engel, *J. Ed. Psychol.* **71**, 432 (1979).
4. I. MacFarlane-Smith, *Spatial Ability* (Univ. of London Press, London, 1964).
5. J. Sherman, *Psychol. Rev.* **74**, 290 (1967).
6. ———, *Sex-Related Cognitive Differences* (Thomas, Springfield, Ill., 1978).
7. *Time* **116**, 57 (1980); D. Williams and P. King, *Newsweek* **46**, 73 (1980).

. . . The most serious problem with the report by Benbow and Stanley is the underlying presumption that the concept of mathematical ability, as defined by the SAT-M, is theoretically defensible. Such tests sample performance in a domain of learned knowledge and skill: for this reason experts in testing generally recognize the difficulty of separating any measure of ability from achievement, the effects of schooling, and other experience (*1*). In a fundamental sense, we do not yet know what mathematical ability is. . . .

Another suggestion raised by Benbow and Stanley is that girls are particularly deficient in mathematical reasoning ability. The term "mathematical reasoning" also seems to say a great deal more than is justified by the reality of the testing behind it. It refers to performance on word problems. Often, girls—on the average—are reported to do less well on word problems. Before this difference is accepted as real, the possibility of sex bias in the content of word problems should be considered. Analyses of the content of SAT-M (*2*) and other test (*3*) problems have found the content to favor males in a way that can affect problem-solving performance (*4*). Good problem-solvers work with the content of the problem as much as with the mathematical form (*5*), using intuitive understanding of the content to guide choices of mathematical operations. Therefore, familiarity of problem content can make a difference. Girls perform well on tests of computation and algebra where such content bias is not a possibility. . . .

Should we ever discover a genetic and organic basis for mathematical ability, we can be certain at a minimum that some girls will have more ability than almost all boys—a subtlety that keeps getting lost in our "Boys are more or less *X* than girls" language. Why not let performance, with all its pragmatic importance, speak for itself?

National Institute of Education,
Department of Education   SUSAN CHIPMAN

REFERENCES

1. A. Anastasi, in *New Directions for Testing and Measurement*, W. B. Schrader, Ed. (Jossey-Bass, San Francisco, 1980).

2. T. F. Donlon, *Content Factors in Sex Differences in Test Questions* (Research Monograph No. 73-m, Educational Testing Service, Princeton, N.J., 1973).
3. ———, R. B. Ekstrom, M. Lockheed, *Comparing the Sexes on Achievement Items of Varying Content* (ETS Program Report 77–11, Educational Testing Service, Princeton, N.J., 1977).
4. R. G. Graf and J. Riddell, *J. Educ. Res.* **65**, 7 (1972).
5. J. R. Paige and H. Simon, in *Problem Solving: Research, Method and Theory*, B. Kleinmuntz, Ed. (Wiley, New York, 1966).

. . . An underlying fallacy that has been largely responsible for the unwarranted publicity in the popular media which the study by Benbow and Stanley has received is the notion that, if a trait is under genetic control, the expression of that trait is immutable. The genotype of an organism does not determine, in any trivial sense, a single complex phenotype that will be displayed in all environments. One has only to consider something as simple as the height of wheat to realize that a particular genetic strain of wheat will yield different ranges of height in different environments. A determination of the height in one environment will tell one nothing about the height in a substantially different environment. Unfortunately, the history of the past 100 years is replete with examples of deplorable social conditions being attributed to unchangeable innate human differences as an argument for accepting these conditions (*1*). . . . Similarly, medical research into the heritability of diseases would be quite ridiculous if the conclusion were that we should accept as incurable all those diseases which are heritable.

Benbow and Stanley have not shown heritability or innate sex-linked differences in mathematical ability. Even if they had, it would tell us nothing about how to boost the observed performance of girls in mathematics. The real issue is whether or not one wants to see such a change. Attempts to attribute this social difference to a biological difference that would then legitimize the social difference are fallacious at best. . . .

Rosenstiel Basic Medical Sciences
Research Center, Brandeis University   EDWARD EGELMAN

Department of Chemistry,
University of Massachusetts   JOSEPH ALPER

Department of Sociology-
Anthropology, Northeastern University   LILA LEIBOWITZ

Department of Microbiology and
Molecular Genetics,
Harvard Medical School   JONATHAN BECKWITH

Department of Zoology, University of
New Hampshire   REGINA LEVINE

Department of Anthropology,
Boston University   ANTHONY LEEDS

REFERENCES

1. A. Chase, *The Legacy of Malthus: The Social Costs of the New Scientific Racism* (Knopf, New York, 1977).

Kolata notes that many mathematicians whom we questioned did not know the names of five famous contemporary women mathematicians. Our research (*1–3*) does not support the thesis that girls are born with less math ability than boys. It does suggest that, both in and out of the classroom, environmental influences may be different for females than for males. For example, of the mathematicians whom we questioned, significantly more women than men said that they were discouraged by others in their efforts to become mathematicians, and that they were treated differently, as mathematics students and professionals, because of their sex (*1–2*). To cite another example: on an arithmetical problem-solving test, girls tended to interpret the instructions differently than boys and were more prone to give answers that they thought their teachers wanted (*3*). Such results hint at how difficult it is to control environmental or cultural factors and to ascribe observed differences sheerly or mainly to genetic differences. . . .

For more than a century, sex differences have been reported in mathematical ability, in spatial ability, and in verbal ability, some favoring males and others females (*2, 4*). There is often a large overlap in the distribution of the males' and females' scores on the tests, so that there are females with better scores on tests of mathematical ability or spatial ability or with lower scores on tests of verbal ability than males. It is not possible to make predictions from these studies for a particular male or female, nor has a genetic basis been established for any of the differences. Indeed, a genetic hypothesis that has been investigated for two decades—that an X-linked gene determines spatial ability—has been dismissed as unfounded in recent critical reviews (5).

The whole issue is reminiscent of the fruitless nature-nurture–IQ controversy, and conclusions about the meaning of differences in scores (between sexes or races) have the same ideological ramifications. Instead of arguing about whether sex differences in mathematical ability are due to heredity or environment, or whether they are "facts" or "artifacts" —particularly, if one means that they are immutable or changeable respectively—it seems more fruitful to study what happens to them under transformation of conditions. In particular, conditions of teaching and learning can be changed. Our studies (3) showed that girls responded better to verbal hints in geometric problems than did boys. Using Gestalt psychological principles, we found that spatial configurations could be presented in a structurally clear manner so as to improve their visualization and to eliminate sex differences. Attempts to enhance mathematical learning for both sexes may be challenging ways to channel some of the energy now being used in controversies over the nature and source of sex differences in mathematics.

Department of Mathematical Sciences,
Rensselaer Polytechnic Institute   EDITH LUCHINS

Department of Psychology,
State University of New York   ABRAHAM S. LUCHINS

REFERENCES

1. E. H. Luchins and A. S. Luchins, in *Women and the Mathematical Mystique*, L. H. Fox, L. Brody, D. Tobin, Eds. (Johns Hopkins Univ. Press, Baltimore, 1980).
2. E. H. Luchins, *Women in Mathematics: Problems of Orientation and Reorientation* (Final Report NSF GY. 11316, National Science Foundation, Washington, D.C., 1976); *Am. Math. Mon.* 86, 161 (1979); *ibid.*, in press.
3. A. S. Luchins, *Psychol. Monogr.* 54 (1942); _____ and E. H. Luchins, *Rigidity of Behavior* (Univ. of Oregon Press, Eugene, 1959); *J. Genet. Psychol.* 134, 255 (1979).
4. E. E. Maccoby, and C. N. Jacklin, *The Psychology of Sex Differences* (Stanford Univ. Press, Stanford, Calif., 1974).
5. M. G. McGee, *Psychol. Bull.* 80, 889 (1979); D. B. Boles, *Child Dev.* 51, 625 (1980).

The results of Benbow and Stanley on sex differences in mathematical achievement are similar to some results of mine on scientific achievement (1). In an international study of the achievement of 14-year-olds in physics, chemistry, and biology, I found that in all 14 countries studied boys scored higher than girls on average. It was also true that within each country the boys' advantage was most marked at the highest levels of achievement. However, the international aspect of the study revealed another dimension, not present in Stanley and Benbow's work. Girls in some countries did better than boys in other countries. When a standard corresponding to the international top 5 percent was defined, this was reached by 11 percent of Japanese girls and 9 percent of Hungarian girls, compared to less than 4 percent of boys in Belgium, the Netherlands, and Italy. It would, I suppose, be possible to argue that there is a genetic difference between children in different countries as well as between girls and boys. But it is equally plausible to suggest that the science education which children receive is responsible for the differences. Some countries teach science more efficiently than others; but in all the countries studied science has a masculine image and is taught in a way which is oriented toward boys rather than girls (2).

Department of Sociology,
University of Manchester   ALISON KELLY

REFERENCES AND NOTES

1. A. Kelly, *Girls and Science: International Study of Sex Differences in School Science Achievement* (Almqvist & Wiksell, Stockholm, 1978).
2. These ideas are explored in *The Missing Half: Girls and Science Education*, A. Kelly, Ed. (Manchester Univ. Press, Manchester, 1981).

RESPONSE

So little of our report is quoted directly that it seems desirable to reproduce its concluding paragraph: "We favor the hypothesis that sex differences in achievement and in attitude toward mathematics result from superior male mathematical ability, which may in turn be related to greater male ability in spatial tasks. This male superiority is probably an expression of a combination of both endogenous and exogenous variables. We recognize, however, that our data are consistent with numerous alternative hypotheses. Nonetheless, the hypothesis of differential course-taking was not supported. It also seems likely that putting one's faith in boy-versus-girl socialization processes as the only permissible explanation of the sex difference in mathematics is premature."

In this context, "superior male mathematical ability" and "greater male ability in spatial tasks" mean only that boys tend to score higher on the SAT-M and spatial tests (*1*) than girls do. Unfortunately, many readers (such as Stage and Karplus) interpret "superior ability" as meaning inherently, intrinsically, or genetically abler. As national norms show, girls tend to score lower on spatial tests, such as the Differential Aptitude Test (*1*), whether or not for environmental reasons.

We postulated that "endogenous" variables (*2*) *may* be involved. Endogenous sex differences have been documented in a wide variety of organisms, including humans (*3*). We have carried out more research and helped more able young girls mathematically (*4*) than most other investigators in the country. We believe that the last sentence of our brief report is consistent with the present state of knowledge.

Because the girls in our studies were bright, eager, volunteer participants in a mathematics talent search and were matched with boys on in-school mathematics tests, most of the proffered explanations that the sex differences are defects of the SAT-M as a measure of mathematical reasoning ability are irrelevant. The SAT is designed mainly for above-average 11th and 12th graders, 4 or 5 years older and more advanced in grade placement than participants in the Study of Mathematically Precocious Youth's (SMPY's) annual search for youths who reason extremely well mathematically. Thus, the SAT-M almost certainly functions far more at the analytical reasoning level for the SMPY testees, who have not had many formal opportunities to develop their abilities, than it does for high school juniors and seniors who have already studied rather abstract mathematics for several years.

Stage and Karplus challenge our assumption that our males and females received similar *formal* training in mathematics. We doubt that the studies they cite are relevant to the mathematical reasoning ability of our subjects, who are highly able and well motivated (*5*). In addition, Stage and Karplus object to our references relating sex differences in mathematical reasoning ability to spatial ability, saying that one was "20 or more years old" and the other had been "superseded." To their first objection we reply that research findings do not automatically become invalid with age. Their second objection has been in turn "superseded" by our own study of the spatial ability of a subset of SMPY examinees, as well as by other studies (*6*).

The male-female ratio of participants tended to be remarkably stable from year to year at about 57 to 43. We postulate that fewer girls could meet the qualifying score for the search, in addition to the fact that more boys than girls found entering a mathematics competition appealing. In eight talent searches thus far, involving about 34,000 participants, we have found no evidence that the ablest girls tend not to enter. Moreover, the January 1980 and 1981 searches involving 24,000 participants were based on verbal as well as mathematical qualifications, and the sex ratio of participants was 1 to 1. Nonetheless, the mean difference between sexes on the SAT-M was exactly the same (32 points) as in the January 1979 search, when one could qualify only on a mathematics test. Also, even if we accept a 1.3 boys to 1 girl bias in participation, that could not account for the great difference between boys and girls in *high scores* earned.

Egelman *et al.* erect a straw man we do not recognize from our report. For our groups, Chipman also seems to be grasping at straws, however relevant the ETS research she cites may be to 11th and 12th graders who take the SAT. . . . Kelly's observations about physics, chemistry, and biology may be more relevant to learning mathematical concepts and computation than to mathematical reasoning ability. Kelly has not established causal links between male images and the sex difference in ability.

The statement in the 16 January 1981 *Science* editorial by Schafer and Gray that "Not a single student identified by [SMPY] as mathematically precocious—boy or girl—has gone on to do graduate work in mathematics. . . ." is simply incorrect. For example, an 18-year-old is a 4th-year graduate student in "pure" mathematics at Princeton University. Two more are at the Massachusetts Institute of Technology. Three are, or were, at Berkeley, Stanford, and Johns Hopkins. As graduate students, SMPY's protégés have not yet been studied systematically. We know of only 19, a majority of whom major in mathematics, computer science, electrical engineering, physics, and other fields in which high mathematical ability is important.

We deeply regret that press coverage of our brief report confused the issues, rather than alerting people to the *magnitude* of the sex difference. The situation is far worse than most persons realize. For example, of the 7500 boys and 7500 girls in our current talent search (selected for overall intellectual ability), 23 boys and no girls scored 700 or more on the SAT-M. Our search nationwide found another 19 boys but no girls scoring 700 or more. Let's face these dismaying findings squarely and search hard for causes, whatever they may be. Our data clearly show a large, important sex difference *before* the well-documented and intensive socialization processes operating during puberty. Moreover, our data show that extensive boy-versus-girl socialization processes during this period seem to have little, if any, effect on mathematical reasoning ability. At the very least, one must discount differential course-taking. It would also seem prudent not to rule out endogenous explanations for these sex differences entirely.

It is not the method of science (or *Science*) to ignore published facts or provide a forum for subjective judgments and anecdotal evidence.

Department of Psychology,   CAMILLA PERSSON BENBOW
Johns Hopkins University   JULIAN C. STANLEY

REFERENCES AND NOTES

1. G. Bennett, H. Seashore, A. Wesman, *Manual for the Differential Aptitude Test* (Psychological Corporation, New York, ed. 5, 1974), forms S and T.
2. The word "endogenous" has a much broader meaning than "genetic"; the latter word does not appear in the report.
3. R. Goy and B. McEwen, *Sexual Differentiation of the Brain* (MIT Press, Cambridge, Mass., 1980); J. Levy, *The Sciences* 21 (No. 3), 20 (1981).
4. Thus far, the Johns Hopkins groups have reported their rationale and findings in seven books and more than 100 articles, including the following volumes published by the Johns Hopkins University Press: *Mathematical Talent* (1974), *Intellectual Talent* (1976), *The Gifted and the Creative* (1977), *Educating the Gifted* (1979), and *Women and the Mathematical Mystique* (1980).
5. C. Benbow and J. Stanley, in preparation.
6. C. Benbow, M. Kirk, L. Daggett, J. Stanley, in preparation; S. Burnett, D. Lane, L. Dratt, *Intelligence* 3, 345 (1979); S. Cohn, in preparation.

QUESTIONS FOR DISCUSSION

1. Carefully match the various points raised in refutation of Benbow and Stanley with contentions in the original article. Are they being challenged on hidden assumptions of value, definition, and causality, or on something else? Which points raised in refutation do you think are the strongest? Which do you think are the weakest?
2. Analyze the diction in the Benbow and Stanley article, circling all words that

seem to convey emotional or value-laden associations. Then examine the authors' final response, in which they try to clarify and justify their wording.

3. Benbow and Stanley assume that the education of boys and girls is not significantly different up to seventh grade. Recalling your own experience, what do you think?

4. Consider the arguments over the SAT in relation to the evidence cited by Benbow and Stanley. Do the analyses of Amberg and Owen (pp. 525–572) lead you to question the instrument used in the search for mathematically talented youngsters?

5. What are the social and educational consequences of assuming that Benbow and Stanley are correct (that nature accounts for the differences between boys and girls)? What are the consequences of assuming that their critics are correct (that nurture is a better explanation)?

6. Consider the argumentative appeals that spring from the status and the gender of all the participants in this controversy. Would it make a difference if the names and institutional affiliations of the writers were suppressed?

SUGGESTIONS FOR WRITING

1. Benbow and Stanley's original study appeared in December 1980 and the responses in April 1981. Track down published reports about the original study between those two dates in newspapers and widely circulated magazines. How accurately do the reports represent Benbow and Stanley's conclusions? Write up your findings in an argument characterizing science reporting for a mass audience.

2. Whether you are male or female, recall your own education in mathematics. Was it uniform for the sexes before the seventh grade? After? Was it reinforced in other subjects? Were you given special tests for mathematical ability? To what extent does your own experience reinforce any of the positions expressed in any of the articles or letters? Address your assessment to elementary and high school administrators.

3. Examine your curriculum, asking yourself whether different kinds of reasoning are called for in different courses. For example, does a computer course demand different mental skills than a writing course? Does a literature course call for a different reasoning approach than a business course? Your essay, addressed to your college faculty, will make a case for either the similarities or the differences in reasoning skills across the curriculum.

4. Benbow and Stanley offer yet another version of the familiar nature versus nurture controversy. In what other areas are sex or race used to explain differences in skill, aptitude, or status? What are the practical and ethical consequences of these explanations? Your findings here should be addressed to a large, general audience.

5. If you assume that there is a sex-linked difference between mathematical ability in boys and girls, why would that be a problem? Try arguing that such a difference does not matter, that arguments about such differences reflect an overvaluation of one mode of thought, or that average mathematical ability is sufficient for most purposes. Or maintain the reverse, that the suggestion of a sex-linked difference in mathematical ability is extremely damaging.

Public Statement by Eight Alabama Clergymen

Letter from Birmingham Jail

MARTIN LUTHER KING, JR.

Martin Luther King's famous "Letter from Birmingham Jail" was written in 1963 in direct response to the published statement of eight Alabama clergymen. He actually did write the letter in his jail cell, but he polished it slightly afterwards to make it ready for publication. On the one hand, King's letter is certainly a direct refutation of the position outlined by the clergymen, but at the same time King reaches out to them as fellow clergymen and brothers. He wants not just to win an argument by revealing the weakness in his opponents' position, but to move his audience to share his conviction. For King refutation is not negative or adversarial; he uses the occasion to plead for the creation of a larger community of shared values. The use of the letter format reinforces his purpose: The letter is actually addressed to the eight clergymen, but it also speaks to a wider audience.

"Public Statement by Eight Alabama Clergymen"

(April 12, 1963)

We the undersigned clergymen are among those who, in January, issued "An Appeal for Law and Order and Common Sense," in dealing with racial problems in Alabama. We expressed understanding that honest convictions in racial matters could properly be pursued in the courts, but urged that decisions of those courts should in the meantime be peacefully obeyed.

Since that time there had been some evidence of increased forbearance and a willingness to face facts. Responsible citizens have undertaken to work on various problems which cause racial friction and unrest. In Birmingham, recent public events have given indication that we all have opportunity for a new constructive and realistic approach to racial problems.

However, we are now confronted by a series of demonstrations by some of our Negro citizens, directed and led in part by outsiders. We recognize the natural impatience of people who feel that their hopes are slow in being realized. But we are convinced that these demonstrations are unwise and untimely.

We agree rather with certain local Negro leadership which has called for honest and open negotiation of racial issues in our area. And we believe this kind of facing of issues can best be accomplished by citizens of our own metropolitan area, white and Negro, meeting with their knowledge and experience of the local situation. All of us need to face that responsibility and find proper channels for its accomplishment.

Just as we formerly pointed out that "hatred and violence have no sanction in our religious and political traditions," we also point out that such actions as incite to hatred and violence, however technically peaceful those actions may be, have not contributed to the resolution of our local problems. We do not believe that these days of new hope are days when extreme measures are justified in Birmingham.

We commend the community as a whole, and the local news media and law enforcement officials in particular, on the calm manner in which these demonstrations have been handled. We urge the public to continue to show restraint should the demonstrations continue, and the law enforcement officials to remain calm and continue to protect our city from violence.

We further strongly urge our own Negro community to withdraw support from these demonstrations, and to unite locally in working peacefully for a better Birmingham. When rights are consistently denied, a cause should be pressed in the courts and in negotiations among local leaders, and not in the streets. We appeal to both our white and Negro citizenry to observe the principles of law and order and common sense.

Signed by:

C. C. J. Carpenter, D.D., LL.D., *Bishop of Alabama*

Joseph A. Durick, D.D., *Auxiliary Bishop, Diocese of Mobile, Birmingham*

Rabbi Milton L. Grafman, *Temple Emanu-El, Birmingham, Alabama*

Bishop Paul Hardin, *Bishop of the Alabama-West Florida Conference of the Methodist Church*

Bishop Nolan B. Harmon, *Bishop of the North Alabama Conference of the Methodist Church*

George M. Murray, D.D., LL.D., *Bishop Coadjutor, Episcopal Diocese of Alabama*

Edward V. Ramage, *Moderator, Synod of the Alabama Presbyterian Church in the United States*

Earl Stallings, *Pastor, First Baptist Church, Birmingham, Alabama*

*"Letter from Birmingham Jail"**

April 16, 1963

MY DEAR FELLOW CLERGYMEN:

While confined here in the Birmingham city jail, I came across your recent statement calling my present activities "unwise and untimely." Seldom do I pause to answer criticism of my work and ideas. If I sought to answer all the criticisms that cross my desk, my secretaries would have little time for anything other than such correspondence in the course of the day, and I would have no time for constructive work. But since I feel that you are men of genuine good will and that your criticisms are sincerely set forth, I want to try to answer your statement in what I hope will be patient and reasonable terms.

I think I should indicate why I am here in Birmingham, since you have been influenced by the view which argues against "outsiders coming in." I have the honor of serving as president of the Southern Chris-

---

*AUTHOR'S NOTE: This response to a published statement by eight fellow clergymen from Alabama (Bishop C. C. J. Carpenter, Bishop Joseph A. Durick, Rabbi Milton L. Grafman, Bishop Paul Hardin, Bishop Nolan B. Harmon, the Reverend George M. Murray, the Reverend Edward V. Ramage and the Reverend Earl Stallings) was composed under somewhat constricting circumstances. Begun on the margins of the newspaper in which the statement appeared while I was in jail, the letter was continued on scraps of writing paper supplied by a friendly Negro trusty, and concluded on a pad my attorneys were eventually permitted to leave me. Although the text remains in substance unaltered, I have indulged in the author's prerogative of polishing it for publication.

tian Leadership Conference, an organization operating in every southern state, with headquarters in Atlanta, Georgia. We have some eighty-five affiliated organizations across the South, and one of them is the Alabama Christian Movement for Human Rights. Frequently we share staff, educational and financial resources with our affiliates. Several months ago the affiliate here in Birmingham asked us to be on call to engage in a nonviolent direct-action program if such were deemed necessary. We readily consented, and when the hour came we lived up to our promise. So I, along with several members of my staff, am here because I was invited here. I am here because I have organizational ties here.

But more basically, I am in Birmingham because injustice is here. Just as the prophets of the eighth century B.C. left their villages and carried their "thus saith the Lord" far beyond the boundaries of their home towns, and just as the Apostle Paul left his village of Tarsus and carried the gospel of Jesus Christ to the far corners of the Greco-Roman world, so am I compelled to carry the gospel of freedom beyond my own home town. Like Paul, I must constantly respond to the Macedonian call for aid.

Moreover, I am cognizant of the interrelatedness of all communities and states. I cannot sit idly by in Atlanta and not be concerned about what happens in Birmingham. Injustice anywhere is a threat to justice everywhere. We are caught in an inescapable network of mutuality, tied in a single garment of destiny. Whatever affects one directly, affects all indirectly. Never again can we afford to live with the narrow, provincial "outside agitator" idea. Anyone who lives inside the United States can never be considered an outsider anywhere within its bounds.

You deplore the demonstrations taking place in Birmingham. But your statement, I am sorry to say, fails to express a similar concern for the conditions that brought about the demonstrations. I am sure that none of you would want to rest content with the superficial kind of social analysis that deals merely with effects and does not grapple with underlying causes. It is unfortunate that demonstrations are taking place in Birmingham, but it is even more unfortunate that the city's white power structure left the Negro community with no alternative.

In any nonviolent campaign there are four basic steps: collection of the facts to determine whether injustices exist; negotiation; self-purification; and direct action. We have gone through all these steps in Birmingham. There can be no gainsaying the fact that racial injustice engulfs this community. Birmingham is probably the most thoroughly segregated city in the United States. Its ugly record of brutality is widely known. Negroes have experienced grossly unjust treatment in the courts. There have been more unsolved bombings of Negro homes and churches in Birmingham than in any other city in the nation. These are the hard, brutal facts of the case. On the basis of these conditions, Negro leaders sought to negotiate with the city fathers. But the latter consistently refused to engage in good-faith negotiation.

Then, last September, came the opportunity to talk with leaders of Birmingham's economic community. In the course of the negotiations, certain promises were made by the merchants—for example, to remove the stores' humiliating racial signs. On the basis of these promises, the Reverend Fred Shuttlesworth and the leaders of the Alabama Christian Movement for Human Rights agreed to a moratorium on all demonstrations. As the weeks and months went by, we realized that we were the victims of a broken promise. A few signs, briefly removed, returned; the others remained.

As in so many past experiences, our hopes had been blasted, and the shadow of deep disappointment settled upon us. We had no alternative except to prepare for direct action, whereby we would present our very bodies as a means of laying our case before the conscience of the local and the national community. Mindful of the difficulties involved, we decided to undertake a process of self-purification. We began a series of workshops on nonviolence, and we repeatedly asked ourselves: "Are you able to accept blows without retaliating?" "Are you able to endure the ordeal of jail?" We decided to schedule our direct-action program for the Easter season, realizing that except for Christmas, this is the main shopping period of the year. Knowing that a strong economic-withdrawal program would be the by-product of direct action, we felt that this would be the best time to bring pressure to bear on the merchants for the needed change.

Then it occurred to us that Birmingham's mayoral election was coming up in March, and we speedily decided to postpone action until after election day. When we discovered that the Commissioner of Public Safety, Eugene "Bull" Connor, had piled up enough votes to be in the run-off, we decided again to postpone action until the day after the run-off so that the demonstrations could not be used to cloud the issues. Like many others, we waited to see Mr. Connor defeated, and to this end we endured postponement after postponement. Having aided in this community need, we felt that our direct-action program could be delayed no longer.

You may well ask: "Why direct action? Why sit-ins, marches and so forth? Isn't negotiation a better path?" You are quite right in calling for negotiation. Indeed, this is the very purpose of direct action. Nonviolent direct action seeks to create such a crisis and foster such a tension that a community which has constantly refused to negotiate is forced to confront the issue. It seeks so to dramatize the issue that it can no longer be ignored. My citing the creation of tension as part of the work of the nonviolent-register may sound rather shocking. But I must confess that I am not afraid of the word "tension." I have earnestly opposed violent tension, but there is a type of constructive, nonviolent tension which is necessary for growth. Just as Socrates felt that it was necessary to create a tension in the mind so that individuals could rise from the bondage of myths and half-truths to the unfettered realm of creative analysis and objective appraisal, so must we see the need for nonviolent gadflies to create the kind of tension in society that will help men rise from the dark depths of prejudice and racism to the majestic heights of understanding and brotherhood.

The purpose of our direct-action program is to create a situation so crisis-packed that it will inevitably open the door to negotiation. I therefore concur with you in your call for negotiation. Too long has our beloved Southland been bogged down in a tragic effort to live in monologue rather than dialogue.

One of the basic points in your statement is that the action that I and my associates have taken in Birmingham is untimely. Some have asked: "Why didn't you give the new city administration time to act?" The only answer that I can give to this query is that the new Birmingham administration must be prodded about as much as the outgoing one, before it will act. We are sadly mistaken if we feel that the election of Albert Boutwell as mayor will bring the millennium to Birmingham. While Mr. Boutwell is a much more gentle person than Mr. Connor, they are both segregationists, dedicated to maintenance of the status quo. I have hope that Mr. Boutwell will be reasonable enough to see the futility of massive resistance to desegregation. But he will not see this without pressure from devotees of civil rights. My friends, I must say to you that we have not made a single gain in civil rights without determined legal and nonviolent pressure. Lamentably, it is an historical fact that privileged groups seldom give up their privileges voluntarily. Individuals may see the moral light and voluntarily give up their unjust posture; but, as Reinhold Niebuhr has reminded us, groups tend to be more immoral than individuals.

We know through painful experience that freedom is never voluntarily given by the oppressor; it must be demanded by the oppressed. Frankly, I have yet to engage in a direct-action campaign that was "well timed" in the view of those who have not suffered unduly from the disease of segregation. For years now I have heard the word "Wait!" It rings in the ear of every Negro with piercing familiarity. This "Wait" has almost always meant "Never." We must come to see, with one of our distinguished jurists, that "justice too long delayed is justice denied."

We have waited for more than 340 years for our constitutional and God-given rights. The nations of Asia and Africa are moving with jetlike speed toward gaining political independence, but we still creep at horse-and-buggy pace toward gaining a cup of coffee at a lunch counter. Perhaps it is easy for those who have never felt the stinging darts of segregation to say, "Wait." But when you have seen vicious mobs lynch your mothers and fathers at will and drown your sisters and brothers at whim; when you have seen hate-filled policemen curse, kick and even kill your black brothers and sisters; when you see the vast majority of your twenty million Negro brothers smothering in an airtight cage of poverty in the midst of an affluent society; when you suddenly find your tongue twisted and your speech stammering as you seek to explain to your six-year-old daughter why she can't go to the public amusement park that has just been advertised on television, and see tears welling up in her eyes when she is told that Funtown is closed to colored children, and see ominous clouds of inferiority beginning to form in her little mental sky, and see her beginning to distort her personality by developing an unconscious bitterness toward white people; when you have to concoct an answer for a five-year-old son who is asking: "Daddy, why do white people treat colored people so mean?"; when you take a cross-country drive and find it necessary to sleep night after night in the uncomfortable corners of your automobile because no motel will accept you; when you are humiliated day in and day out by nagging signs reading "white" and "colored"; when your first name becomes "nigger," your middle name becomes "boy" (however old you are) and your last name becomes "John," and your wife and mother are never given the respected title "Mrs."; when you are harried by day and haunted by night by the fact that you are a Negro, living constantly at tiptoe stance, never quite knowing what to expect next, and are plagued with inner fears and outer resentments; when you are forever fighting a degenerating sense of "nobodiness"—then you will understand why we find it difficult to wait. There comes a time when the cup of endurance runs over, and men are no longer willing to be plunged into the abyss of despair. I hope, sirs, you can understand our legitimate and unavoidable impatience.

You express a great deal of anxiety over our willingness to break laws. This is certainly a legitimate concern. Since we so diligently urge people to obey the Supreme Court's decision of 1954 outlawing segregation in the public schools, at first glance it may seem rather paradoxical for us consciously to break laws. One may well ask: "How can you advocate breaking some laws and obeying others?" The answer lies in the fact that there are two types of laws: just and unjust. I would be the first to advocate obeying just laws. One has not only a legal but a moral responsibility to obey just laws. Conversely, one has a moral responsibility to disobey unjust laws. I would agree with St. Augustine that "an unjust law is no law at all."

Now, what is the difference between the two? How does one determine whether a law is just or unjust? A just law is a man-made code that squares with the moral law or the law of God. An unjust law is a code that is out of harmony with the moral law. To put it in the terms of St. Thomas Aquinas: An unjust law is a human law that is not rooted in eternal law and natural law. Any law that uplifts human personality is just. Any law that degrades human personality is unjust. All segregation statutes are unjust because segregation distorts the soul and damages the personality. It gives the segregator a false sense of superiority and the segregated a false sense of inferiority. Segregation, to use the terminology of the Jewish philosopher Martin Buber, substitutes an "I–it" relationship for an "I–thou" relationship and ends up relegating persons to the status of things. Hence segregation is not only politically, economically and sociologically unsound, it is morally wrong and sinful. Paul Tillich has said that sin is separation. Is not segregation an existential expression of man's tragic separation, his awful estrangement, his terrible sinfulness? Thus it is that I can urge men to obey the 1954 decision of the Supreme Court, for it is morally right; and I can urge them to disobey segregation ordinances, for they are morally wrong.

Let us consider a more concrete example of just and unjust laws. An unjust law is a code that a numerical or power majority group compels a minority group to obey but does not make binding on itself. This is *difference* made legal. By the same token, a just law is a code that a majority compels a minority to follow and that it is willing to follow itself. This is *sameness* made legal.

Let me give another explanation. A law is unjust if it is inflicted on a minority that, as a result of being denied the right to vote, had no part in enacting or devising the law. Who can say that the legislature of Alabama which set up that state's segregation laws was democratically elected? Throughout Alabama all sorts of devious methods are used to prevent Negroes from becoming registered voters, and there are some counties in which, even though Negroes constitute a majority of the population, not a single Negro is registered. Can any law enacted under such circumstances be considered democratically structured?

Sometimes a law is just on its face and unjust in its application. For instance, I have been arrested on a charge of parading without a permit. Now, there is nothing wrong in having an ordinance which requires a permit for a parade. But such an ordinance becomes unjust when it is used to maintain segregation and to deny citizens the First-Amendment privilege of peaceful assembly and protest.

I hope you are able to see the distinction I am trying to point out. In no sense do I advocate evading or defying the law, as would the rabid segregationist. That would lead to anarchy. One who breaks an unjust law must do so openly, lovingly, and with a willingness to accept the penalty. I submit that an individual who breaks a law that conscience tells him is unjust, and who willingly accepts the penalty of imprisonment in order to arouse the conscience of the community over its injustice, is in reality expressing the highest respect for law.

Of course, there is nothing new about this kind of civil disobedience. It was evidenced sublimely in the refusal of Shadrach, Meshach and Abednego to obey the laws of Nebuchadnezzar, on the ground that a higher moral law was at stake. It was practiced superbly by the early Christians, who were willing to face hungry lions and the excruciating pain of chopping blocks rather than submit to certain unjust laws of the Roman Empire. To a degree, academic freedom is a reality today because Socrates practiced civil disobedience. In our own nation, the Boston Tea Party represented a massive act of civil disobedience.

We should never forget that everything Adolf Hitler did in Germany was "legal" and everything the Hungarian freedom fighters did in Hungary was "illegal." It was "illegal" to aid and comfort a Jew in Hitler's Germany. Even so, I am sure that, had I lived in Germany at the time, I would have aided and comforted my Jewish brothers. If today I lived in a Communist country where certain principles dear to the Christian faith are suppressed, I would openly advocate disobeying that country's antireligious laws.

I must make two honest confessions to you, my Christian and Jewish brothers. First, I must confess that over the past few years I have been gravely disappointed with the white moderate. I have almost reached the regrettable conclusion that the Negro's great stumbling block in his stride toward freedom is not the White Citizen's Counciler or the Ku Klux Klanner, but the white moderate, who is more devoted to "order" than to justice; who prefers a negative peace which is the absence of tension to a positive peace which is the presence of justice; who constantly says: "I agree with you in the goal you seek, but I cannot agree with your methods of direct action"; who paternalistically believes he can set the timetable for another man's freedom; who lives by a mythical concept of time and who constantly advises the Negro to wait for a "more convenient season." Shallow understanding from people of good will is more frustrating than absolute misunderstanding from people of ill will. Lukewarm acceptance is much more bewildering than outright rejection.

I had hoped that the white moderate would understand that law and order exist for the purpose of establishing justice and that when they fail in this purpose they become the dangerously structured dams that block the flow of social progress. I had hoped that the white moderate would understand that the present tension in the South is a necessary phase of the transition from an obnoxious negative peace, in which the Negro passively accepted his unjust plight, to a substantive and positive peace, in which all men will respect the dignity and worth of human personality. Actually, we who engage in nonviolent direct action are not the creators of tension. We merely bring to the surface the hidden tension that is already alive. We bring it out in the open, where it can be seen and dealt with. Like a boil that can never be cured so long as it is covered up but must be opened with all its ugliness to the natural medicines of air and light, injustice must be exposed, with all the tension its exposure creates, to the light of human conscience and the air of national opinion before it can be cured.

In your statement you assert that our actions, even though peaceful, must be condemned because they precipitate violence. But is this a logical assertion? Isn't this like condemning a robbed man because his possession of money precipitated the evil act of robbery? Isn't this like condemning Socrates because his unswerving commitment to truth and his philosophical inquiries precipitated the act by the misguided populace in which they made him drink hemlock? Isn't this like condemning Jesus because his unique God-consciousness and never-ceasing devotion to God's will precipitated the evil act of crucifixion? We must come to see that, as the federal courts have consistently affirmed, it is wrong to urge an individual to cease his efforts to gain his basic constitutional rights because the quest may precipitate violence. Society must protect the robbed and punish the robber.

I had also hoped that the white moderate would reject the myth concerning time in relation to the struggle for freedom. I have just received a letter from a white brother in Texas. He writes: "All Christians know that the colored people will receive equal rights eventually, but it is possible that you are in too great a religious hurry. It has taken Christianity almost two thousand years to accomplish what it has. The teachings of Christ take time to come to earth." Such an attitude stems from a tragic misconception of time, from the strangely irrational notion that there is something in the very flow of time that will inevitably cure all ills. Actually, time itself is neutral; it can be used either destructively or constructively. More and more I feel that the people of ill will have used time much more effectively than have the people of good will. We will have to repent in this generation not merely for the hateful words and actions of the bad people but for the appalling silence of the good people. Human progress never rolls in on wheels of inevitability; it comes through the tireless efforts of men willing to be co-workers with God, and without this hard work, time itself becomes an ally of the forces of social stagnation. We must use time creatively, in the knowledge that the time is always ripe to do right. Now is the time to make real the promise of democracy and transform our pending national elegy into a creative psalm of brotherhood. Now is the time to lift our national policy from the quicksand of racial injustice to the solid rock of human dignity.

You speak of our activity in Birmingham as extreme. At first I was rather disappointed that fellow clergymen would see my nonviolent efforts as those of an extremist. I began thinking about the fact that I stand in the middle of two opposing forces in the Negro community. One is a force of complacency, made up in part of Negroes who, as a result of long years of oppression, are so drained of self-respect and a sense of "somebodiness" that they have adjusted to segregation; and in part of a few middle-class Negroes who, because of a degree of academic and economic security and because in some ways they profit by segregation, have become insensitive to the problems of the masses. The other force is one of bitterness and hatred, and it comes perilously close to advocating violence. It is expressed in the various black nationalist groups that are springing up across the nation, the largest and best-known being Elijah Muhammad's Muslim movement. Nourished by the

Negro's frustration over the continued existence of racial discrimination, this movement is made up of people who have lost faith in America, who have absolutely repudiated Christianity, and who have concluded that the white man is an incorrigible "devil."

I have tried to stand between these two forces, saying that we need emulate neither the "do-nothingism" of the complacent nor the hatred and despair of the black nationalist. For there is the more excellent way of love and nonviolent protest. I am grateful to God that, through the influence of the Negro church, the way of nonviolence became an integral part of our struggle.

If this philosophy had not emerged, by now many streets of the South would, I am convinced, be flowing with blood. And I am further convinced that if our white brothers dismiss as "rabble-rousers" and "outside agitators" those of us who employ nonviolent direct action, and if they refuse to support our nonviolent efforts, millions of Negroes will, out of frustration and despair, seek solace and security in black-national-ist ideologies—a development that would inevitably lead to a frightening racial nightmare.

Oppressed people cannot remain oppressed forever. The yearning for freedom eventually manifests itself, and that is what has happened to the American Negro. Something within has reminded him of his birthright of freedom, and something without has reminded him that it can be gained. Consciously or unconsciously, he has been caught up by the *Zeitgeist*, and with his black brothers of Africa and his brown and yellow brothers of Asia, South America and the Caribbean, the United States Negro is moving with a sense of great urgency toward the prom-ised land of racial justice. If one recognizes this vital urge that has engulfed the Negro community, one should readily understand why public demonstrations are taking place. The Negro has many pent-up resentments and latent frustrations, and he must release them. So let him march; let him make prayer pilgrimages to the city hall; let him go on freedom rides—and try to understand why he must do so. If his repressed emotions are not released in nonviolent ways, they will seek expression through violence; this is not a threat but a fact of history. So I have not said to my people: "Get rid of your discontent." Rather, I have tried to say that this normal and healthy discontent can be chan-neled into the creative outlet of nonviolent direct action. And now this approach is being termed extremist.

But though I was initially disappointed at being categorized as an extremist, as I continued to think about the matter I gradually gained a measure of satisfaction from the label. Was not Jesus an extremist for love: "Love your enemies, bless them that curse you, do good to them that hate you, and pray for them which despitefully use you, and persecute you." Was not Amos an extremist for justice: "Let justice roll down like waters and righteousness like an ever-flowing stream." Was not Paul an extremist for the Christian gospel: "I bear in my body the marks of the Lord Jesus." Was not Martin Luther an extremist: "Here I stand; I cannot do otherwise, so help me God." And John Bunyan: "I will stay in jail to the end of my days before I make a butchery of my conscience." And Abraham Lincoln: "This nation cannot survive half slave and half free." And Thomas Jefferson: "We hold these truths to be self-evident, that all men are created equal . . ." So the question is not whether we will be extremists, but what kind of extremists we will be. Will we be extremists for hate or for love? Will we be extremists for the preservation of injustice or for the extension of justice? In that dramatic scene on Calvary's hill three men were crucified. We must never forget that all three were crucified for the same crime—the crime of extremism. Two were extremists for immorality, and thus fell below their environment. The other, Jesus Christ, was an extremist for love, truth and goodness, and thereby rose above his environment. Perhaps the South, the nation and the world are in dire need of creative extremists.

I had hoped that the white moderate would see this need. Perhaps I was too optimistic; perhaps I expected too much. I suppose I should have realized that few members of the oppressor race can understand the deep groans and passionate yearnings of the oppressed race, and still fewer have the vision to see that injustice must be rooted out by strong, persistent and determined action. I am thankful, however, that some of our white brothers in the South have grasped the meaning of this social revolution and committed themselves to it. They are still all too few in quantity, but they are big in quality. Some—such as Ralph McGill, Lillian Smith, Harry Golden, James McBride Dabbs, Ann Braden and Sarah Patton Boyle—have written about our struggle in eloquent and prophetic terms. Others have marched with us down nameless streets of the South. They have languished in filthy, roach-infested jails, suffering the abuse and brutality of policemen who view them as "dirty nigger-lovers." Unlike so many of their moderate brothers and sisters, they have recognized the urgency of the moment and sensed the need for powerful "action" antidotes to combat the disease of segregation.

Let me take note of my other major disappointment. I have been so greatly disappointed with the white church and its leadership. Of course, there are some notable exceptions. I am not unmindful of the fact that each of you has taken some significant stands on this issue. I commend you, Reverend Stallings, for your Christian stand on this past Sunday, in welcoming Negroes to your worship service on a nonsegregated basis. I commend the Catholic leaders of this state for integrating Spring Hill College several years ago.

But despite these notable exceptions, I must honestly reiterate that I have been disappointed with the church. I do not say this as one of those negative critics who can always find something wrong with the church. I say this as a minister of the gospel, who loves the church; who was nurtured in its bosom; who has been sustained by its spiritual blessings and who will remain true to it as long as the cord of life shall lengthen.

When I was suddenly catapulted into the leadership of the bus protest in Montgomery, Alabama, a few years ago, I felt we would be supported by the white church. I felt that the white ministers, priests and rabbis of the South would be among our strongest allies. Instead, some have been outright opponents, refusing to understand the freedom movement and misrepresenting its leaders; all too many others have been more cautious than courageous and have remained silent behind the anesthetizing security of stained-glass windows.

In spite of my shattered dreams, I came to Birmingham with the hope that the white religious leadership of this community would see the justice of our cause and, with deep moral concern, would serve as the channel through which our just grievances could reach the power structure. I had hoped that each of you would understand. But again I have been disappointed.

I have heard numerous southern religious leaders admonish their worshipers to comply with a desegregation decision because it is the law, but I have longed to hear white ministers declare: "Follow this decree because integration is morally right and because the Negro is your brother." In the midst of blatant injustices inflicted upon the Negro, I have watched white churchmen stand on the sideline and mouth pious irrelevancies and sanctimonious trivialities. In the midst of a mighty struggle to rid our nation of racial and economic injustice, I have heard many ministers say: "Those are social issues, with which the gospel has no real concern." And I have watched many churches commit themselves to a completely otherworldly religion which makes a strange, un-Biblical distinction between body and soul, between the sacred and the secular.

I have traveled the length and breadth of Alabama, Mississippi and all the other southern states. On sweltering summer days and crisp autumn mornings I have looked at the South's beautiful churches with their lofty spires pointing heavenward. I have beheld the impressive outlines of her massive religious-education buildings. Over and over I have found myself asking: "What kind of people worship here? Who is their God? Where were their voices when the lips of Governor Barnett dripped with words of interposition and nullification? Where were they when Governor Wallace gave a clarion call for defiance and hatred? Where were their voices of support when bruised and weary Negro men and women decided to rise from the dark dungeons of complacency to the bright hills of creative protest?"

Yes, these questions are still in my mind. In deep disappointment I have wept over the laxity of the church. But be assured that my tears have been tears of love. There can be no deep disappointment where there is not deep love. Yes, I love the church. How could I do otherwise? I am in the rather unique position of being the son, the grandson and the great-grandson of preachers. Yes, I see the church as the body of Christ. But, oh! How we have blemished and scarred that body through social neglect and through fear of being nonconformists.

There was a time when the church was very powerful—in the time when the early Christians rejoiced at being deemed worthy to suffer for what they believed. In those days the church was not merely a thermometer that recorded the ideas and principles of popular opinion; it was a thermostat that transformed the mores of society. Whenever the early Christians entered a town, the people in power became disturbed and immediately sought to convict the Christians for being "disturbers of the peace" and "outside agitators." But the Christians pressed on, in the conviction that they were "a colony of heaven," called to obey God rather than man. Small in number, they were big in commitment. They were too God-intoxicated to be "astronomically intimidated." By their effort and example they brought an end to such ancient evils as infanticide and gladiatorial contests.

Things are different now. So often the contemporary church is a weak, ineffectual voice with an uncertain sound. So often it is an arch-defender of the status quo. Far from being disturbed by the presence of the church, the power structure of the average community is consoled by the church's silent—and often even vocal—sanction of things as they are.

But the judgment of God is upon the church as never before. If today's church does not recapture the sacrificial spirit of the early church, it will lose its authenticity, forfeit the loyalty of millions, and be dismissed as an irrelevant social club with no meaning for the twentieth century. Every day I meet young people whose disappointment with the church has turned into outright disgust.

Perhaps I have once again been too optimistic. Is organized religion too inextricably bound to the status quo to save our nation and the world? Perhaps I must turn my faith to the inner spiritual church, the church within the church, as the true *ekklesia* and the hope of the world. But again I am thankful to God that some noble souls from the ranks of organized religion have broken loose from the paralyzing chains of conformity and joined us as active partners in the struggle for freedom. They have left their secure congregations and walked the streets of Albany, Georgia, with us. They have gone down the highways of the South on tortuous rides for freedom. Yes, they have gone to jail with us. Some have been dismissed from their churches, have lost the support of their bishops and fellow ministers. But they have acted in the faith that right defeated is stronger than evil triumphant. Their witness has been the spiritual salt that has preserved the true meaning of the gospel in these troubled times. They have carved a tunnel of hope through the dark mountain of disappointment.

I hope the church as a whole will meet the challenge of this decisive hour. But even if the church does not come to the aid of justice, I have no despair about the future. I have no fear about the outcome of our struggle in Birmingham, even if our motives are at present misunderstood. We will reach the goal of freedom in Birmingham and all over the nation, because the goal of America is freedom. Abused and scorned though we may be, our destiny is tied up with America's destiny. Before the pilgrims landed at Plymouth, we were here. Before the pen of Jefferson etched the majestic words of the Declaration of Independence across the pages of history, we were here. For more than two centuries our forebears labored in this country without wages; they made cotton king; they built the homes of their masters while suffering gross injustice and shameful humiliation—and yet out of a bottomless vitality they continued to thrive and develop. If the inexpressible cruelties of slavery could not stop us, the opposition we now face will surely fail. We will win our freedom because the sacred heritage of our nation and the eternal will of God are embodied in our echoing demands.

Before closing I feel impelled to mention one other point in your statement that has troubled me profoundly. You warmly commended the Birmingham police force for keeping "order" and "preventing violence." I doubt that you would have so warmly commended the police force if you had seen its dogs sinking their teeth into unarmed, nonviolent Negroes. I doubt that you would so quickly commend the policemen if you were to observe their ugly and inhumane treatment of Negroes here in the city jail; if you were to watch them push and curse old Negro women and young Negro girls; if you were to see them slap and kick old Negro men and young boys; if you were to observe them, as they did on two occasions, refuse to give us food because we wanted to sing our grace together. I cannot join you in your praise of the Birmingham police department.

It is true that the police have exercised a degree of discipline in handling the demonstrators. In this sense they have conducted themselves rather "nonviolently" in public. But for what purpose? To preserve the evil system of segregation. Over the past few years I have consistently preached that nonviolence demands that the means we use must be as pure as the ends we seek. I have tried to make clear that it is wrong to use immoral means to attain moral ends. But now I must affirm that it is just as wrong, or perhaps even more so, to use moral means to preserve immoral ends. Perhaps Mr. Connor and his policemen have been rather nonviolent in public, as was Chief Pritchett in Albany, Georgia, but they have used the moral means of nonviolence to maintain the immoral end of racial injustice. As T. S. Eliot has said: "The last temptation is the greatest treason: To do the right deed for the wrong reason."

I wish you had commended the Negro sit-inners and demonstrators of Birmingham for their sublime courage, their willingness to suffer and their amazing discipline in the midst of great provocation. One day the South will recognize its real heroes. They will be the James Merediths, with the noble sense of purpose that enables them to face jeering and hostile mobs, and with the agonizing loneliness that characterizes the life of the pioneer. They will be old, oppressed, battered Negro women, symbolized in a seventy-two-year-old woman in Montgomery, Alabama, who rose up with a sense of dignity and with her people decided not to ride segregated buses, and who responded with ungrammatical profundity to one who inquired about her weariness: "My feets is tired, but my soul is at rest." They will be the young high school and college students, the young ministers of the gospel and a host of their elders, courageously and nonviolently sitting in at lunch counters and willingly going to jail for conscience' sake. One day the South will know that when these disinherited children of God sat down at lunch counters, they were in reality standing up for what is best in the American dream and for the most sacred values in our Judaeo-Christian heritage, thereby bringing our nation back to those great wells of democracy which were dug deep by the founding fathers in their formulation of the Constitution and the Declaration of Independence.

Never before have I written so long a letter. I'm afraid it is much too long to take your precious time. I can assure you that it would have been much shorter if I had been writing from a comfortable desk, but what else can one do when he is alone in a narrow jail cell, other than write long letters, think long thoughts and pray long prayers?

If I have said anything in this letter that overstates the truth and indicates an unreasonable impatience, I beg you to forgive me. If I have said anything that understates the truth and indicates my having a patience that allows me to settle for anything less than brotherhood, I beg God to forgive me.

I hope this letter finds you strong in the faith. I also hope that circumstances will soon make it possible for me to meet each of you, not as an integrationist or a civil-rights leader but as a fellow clergyman and a Christian brother. Let us all hope that the dark clouds of racial prejudice will soon pass away and the deep fog of misunderstanding will be lifted from our fear-drenched communities, and in some not too distant tomorrow the radiant stars of love and brotherhood will shine over our great nation with all their scintillating beauty.

Yours for the cause of Peace and Brotherhood,
MARTIN LUTHER KING, JR.

QUESTIONS FOR DISCUSSION

1. King addresses his letter to his eight fellow clergymen. What do you think their reaction was when they read it?
2. The statement of the eight clergymen is brief, and King's response is quite long. Could King have achieved his purpose in a short statement modeled more directly on the clergymen's document? How does King justify the length and elaborateness of his letter?
3. Letters, whether public or personal, reveal the character of their writers and that of their recipients. What kind of character sketch does King draw of his audience? What does he reveal of his own character? What does the Alabama clergymen's statement reveal about them?

4. Notice how often King anticipates the arguments of his opponents. In fact, he sometimes presents their positions very eloquently. Would he have been more or less effective if he were less generous to those who disagreed with him?

5. Look through King's letter and distinguish appeals to reason and appeals to emotion. How effective are the emotional appeals? How are they related to the more logical appeals? Do the two work together or separately? Do the eight clergymen use any emotional appeals?

6. Characterize the style of King's letter. Where would you place it on a scale running from the formal to the informal? From the plain to the elaborate? From the unself-conscious to the self-conscious? How would you characterize the style of the eight clergymen's statement?

SUGGESTIONS FOR WRITING

1. Put yourself in the position of the eight Alabama clergymen who just received King's letter. Write a response to him, of whatever kind you think appropriate.

2. Take a close look at King's metaphors, his Biblical and historical allusions, his use of repetitions and rhetorical questions. Write an essay for your classmates in which you assess the impact of such rhetorical and stylistic devices on King's argument.

3. Consider the distinction that King makes between just and unjust laws, and explain it carefully to someone who might never have thought about the subject. Then find an example of an unjust law and suggest what people should do to get it changed.

4. Try your hand at writing a letter on a subject of public interest or controversy. Address your letter to someone who is known to be associated with a particular position, but make yours an open letter, one that speaks to a larger audience of concerned citizens.

5. Write a follow-up to King's letter, assessing the position of blacks several decades after King wrote. Address your response to King, informing him of changes that have occurred, indicating what would please him and what he would still be concerned about.

6. King's approach in his letter is that of a clergyman talking to other clergymen, appealing to their common knowledge and interests. Place yourself in one of your roles (student, employee, member of a particular political, ethnic, or religious group) and write a letter of protest to someone within your group who you think has acted badly. Then try rewriting the letter, this time to an objective outsider.

———————— →>> <<‹- ————————

I Refute It Thus

SAMUEL C. FLORMAN

*In 1968, as he tells the story, Samuel C. Florman, a successful, practicing
civil engineer, was asked to speak at the monthly meeting of the engineering
division of the New York Academy of Sciences on engineering from a broad
philosophical perspective. The result was a paper entitled "The Existential
Pleasures of Engineering," which, in response to the praise of engineers
everywhere, became a book of the same title published in 1976. By
"existential pleasures" Florman meant "those irrational feelings that arise out
of the depths of our innermost being"; he maintains that engineering, as one
of the most satisfying of human activities, gives such emotional as well as
intellectual fulfillment.*

*The following excerpt is Chapter 5 of Florman's book, a chapter in
which he takes on the "antitechnologists," those who believe, among other
things, that technology is a demon beyond human control. Unlike all the
other refutations in this section of the reader, Florman's essay is not paired
with another taking a contrary position. He is not aiming at one specific
argument and dismantling it, point by point. Rather, he has the writings of
several antitechnologists in mind, as well as a general presumption against
technology that he believes has been "working its way into our popular
consciousness." Engineers, who have less time to write than their critics, have
found an able defender in Florman. His argument here will make you mull
over some of the large historical and social generalizations that underlie your
cultural values.*

If we are to build a new philosophy of engineering, we must start with
a rebuttal of antitechnology. Conceivably we could let the argument go
unanswered, except to respond that technology is a necessary evil. But
that would not be very satisfying. Besides, it would not give expression
to what we know in our hearts; that technology is not evil except when
falsely described by dyspeptic philosophers.

In the often-repeated story, Samuel Johnson and James Boswell
stood talking about Berkeley's theory of the nonexistence of matter.
Boswell observed that although he was satisfied that the theory was false,
it was impossible to refute it. "I never shall forget," Boswell tells us, "the
alacrity with which Johnson answered, striking his foot with mighty
force against a large stone, till he rebounded from it—'I refute it
thus.' "

The ideas of the antitechnologists arouse in me a mood of exasperation similar to Dr. Johnson's. Their ideas are so obviously false, and yet so persuasive and widely accepted, that I fear for the common sense of us all.

For a long time, many foolish things were said in praise of technology that should never have been said. Even now the salvation-through-technology doctrine has some adherents whose absurdities have helped to inspire the antitechnological movement. Also the growth as a serious discipline of the long-neglected history of technology has deposited layer upon layer of subtle thought upon what was once considered a fairly uncomplicated subject. Add to these absurdities and subtleties the malaise that is popularly assumed to prevail in our society, and you have the main ingredients of antitechnology.

The impulse to refute this doctrine with a Johnsonian kick is diminished by the fear of appearing simplistic. So much has been written about technology by so many profound thinkers that the nonprofessional cannot help but be intimidated. Unfortunately for those who would dispute them, the antitechnologists are masters of prose and intellectual finesse. To make things worse, they display an aesthetic and moral concern that makes the defender of technology appear to be something of a philistine. To make things worse yet, many defenders of technology are indeed philistines of the first order.

Yet the effort must be made. If the antitechnological argument is allowed to stand, the engineer is hard pressed to justify his existence. More important, the implications for society, should antitechnology prevail, are most disquieting. For, at the very core of antitechnology, hidden under a veneer of aesthetic sensibility and ethical concern, lies a yearning for a totalitarian society. But I am getting ahead of myself.

The first antitechnological dogma to be confronted is the treatment of technology as something that has escaped from human control. It is understandable that sometimes anxiety and frustration can make us feel this way. But sober thought reveals that technology is not an independent force, much less a thing, but merely one of the types of activities in which people engage. Furthermore, it is an activity in which people engage because they choose to do so. The choice may sometimes be foolish or unconsidered. The choice may be forced upon some members of society by others. But this is very different from the concept of technology *itself* misleading or enslaving the populace.

Philosopher Daniel Callahan has stated the case with calm clarity:

At the very outset we have to do away with a false and misleading dualism, one which abstracts man on the one hand and technology on the other, as if the two were quite separate kinds of realities. I believe that there is no dualism inherent here. Man is by nature a technological animal; to be human is to be technological. If I am correct in that judgment, then there is no room for a duality at all. Instead, we should recognize that when we speak of technology, this is another way of speaking about man himself in one of his manifestations.[1]

Although to me Callahan's statement makes irrefutable good sense, and Ellul's concept of technology as being a thing-in-itself makes absolutely no sense, I recognize that this does not put an end to the matter, any more than Samuel Johnson settled the question of the nature of reality by kicking a stone. There are many serious thinkers who, in attempting to define the relationship of technology to the general culture, persist in some form of the dualism that Callahan rejects.

It cannot be denied that, in the face of the excruciatingly complex problems with which we live, it seems ingenuous to say that men invent and manufacture things because they want to, or because others want them to and reward them accordingly. When men have engaged in technological activities, these activities appear to have had *consequences*, not only physical but also intellectual, psychological, and cultural. Thus, it can be argued, technology is *deterministic*. It causes other things to happen. Someone invents the automobile, for example, and it changes the way people think as well as the way they act. It changes their living patterns, their values, and their expectations in ways that were not anticipated when the automobile was first introduced. Some of the changes appear to be not only unanticipated but undesired. Nobody wanted traffic jams, accidents, and pollution. Therefore, technological advance seems to be independent of human direction. Observers of the social scene become so chagrined and frustrated by this turn of events —and its thousand equivalents—that they turn away from the old common-sense explanations, and become entranced by the demonology of the antitechnologists.

Once mysterious "technology" is invoked as a deterministic force, it becomes no longer intellectually respectable to say that our automobile culture has grown because people have always wanted to do the

---

[1]Daniel Callahan, *Proceedings of the Centennial Convocation of the Thayer School of Engineering at Dartmouth College,* held September 23–25, 1971, published by The Thayer School, Hanover, N.H., April 1972, p. 74.

things that automobiles now enable them to do. Even an engineering educator hastens to assure us that such a belief is a sign of immaturity: "Until he becomes a manager, the young engineer interprets his work largely as a means to ends chosen by other people. A neat separability of ends and means is basic to this view of the relation of technology and values." A more mature view, according to this professor, will not assume that technology is merely the servant of men's purposes, but will face the question: "What if technology is a generator as well as an instrument of those purposes?"[2]

The "young engineer" might argue that technology did not create in people the desire to move quickly and independently from one place to another. Such a desire has existed within the human heart for a long time. Technologists, knowing of this desire, were, in a sense, "commissioned" to invent the automobile. Today it is clear that people enjoy the freedom of movement of which they had previously dreamed. True, they are unhappy about traffic jams, accidents, and pollution, but they recognize that these unhappy developments result from human decisions, not from technological imperatives. With remarkable stubbornness, and contrary to technological good sense, people persist in drinking and driving recklessly, refuse to take commuter trains, even where good and speedy ones exist, and resist joining together in car pools, which would reduce traffic by more than half.

Another unfortunate development that was not foreseen is the transformation of the automobile from a plaything to a necessity through the growth of suburbia. But how can this be blamed on technology, when a technological search for efficiency would dictate that people live in the cities where they work? Something other than technology is responsible for people wanting to live in a house on a grassy plot beyond walking distance to job, market, neighbor, and school. Not that wanting to live in the suburbs is necessarily a bad idea. The trouble with it is that when myriads of people set about doing the same thing the result is a "sprawl" of shopping centers and gasoline stations.

However much we deplore the growth of our automobile culture, clearly it has been created by people making choices, not by a runaway technology. Some people have come to despise the automobile, but at the present time they are very much in the minority. As more and more citizens become disgruntled with the problems arising out of mass own-

[2]Donald W. Shriver, Jr., *Technology and Culture*, Volume 13, No. 4, October 1972, p. 534.

ership of the automobile, they are beginning to pass new laws controlling its use, and also to "commission" the technologists to devise different types of vehicles for individual and mass transport. Indeed, the technologists are already at work on their new assignment.

Of course, this is a superficial view of what has happened, but less superficial, I submit, than the antitechnological view, which sees a malignant technology "creating" choked and bloodied highways while the populace suffers in bewilderment.

There has been some attempt to find a middle ground in this dispute by resorting to the concept of a "soft" determinism. According to this view, technology provides new alternatives to society, and society then chooses which new path to follow. But even this misses the point, which is that a basic human impulse precedes and underlies each technological development. Very often this impulse, or desire, is directly responsible for the new invention. But even when this is not the case, even when the invention is not a response to any particular consumer demand, the impulse is alive and at the ready, sniffing about like a mouse in a maze, seeking its fulfillment. We may regret having some of these impulses. We certainly regret giving expression to some of them. But this hardly gives us the right to blame our misfortunes on a devil external to ourselves. We might, with equal lack of sense, blame wars on warfare.

Four decades ago, long before he became depressed by the atom bomb and other unfortunate technological developments, Lewis Mumford saw things more rationally than he and his fellow antitechnologists do today:

> Choice manifests itself in society in small increments and moment-to-moment decisions as well as in loud dramatic struggles; and he who does not see choice in the development of the machine merely betrays his incapacity to observe cumulative effects until they are bunched together so closely that they seem completely external and impersonal . . . Technics . . . does not form an independent system, like the universe: it exists as an element in human culture and it promises well or ill as the social groups that exploit it promise well or ill. The machine itself makes no demands and holds out no promises: it is the human spirit that makes demands and keeps promises.[3]

In recent times, Mumford has seen fit to absolve the human spirit of any consequential sins. He and his fellow antitechnologists would have

---

[3]Lewis Mumford, *Technics and Civilization,* Harcourt, Brace & World, Inc., 1934, Harbinger Books Edition, 1963, p. 6.

us believe that most of the unpleasant aspects of our life are caused, not by the human spirit, but by "technology"—a demon, a force, a thing-in-itself. This logical absurdity, which has been working its way into our popular consciousness, is the first antitechnological myth to be resisted.

In addition to confounding rational discourse, the demonology outlook of the antitechnologists discounts completely the integrity and intelligence of the ordinary person. Indeed, pity and disdain for the individual citizen is an essential feature of antitechnology. It is central to the next two dogmas, which hold that technology forces man to do work that is tedious and degrading, and then forces him to consume things that he does not really desire.

Is it ingenuous, again, to say that people work, not to feed some monstrous technological machine, but, as since time immemorial, to feed themselves? We all have ambivalent feelings toward work, engineers as well as antitechnologists. We try to avoid it, and yet we seem to require it for our emotional well-being. This dichotomy is as old as civilization. A few wealthy people are bored because they are not required to work, and a lot of ordinary people grumble because they have to work hard. Sociologists report that "job discontent is not currently high on the list of American social problems."[4] Or further: "It is clear that classically alienating jobs (such as on the assembly-line) that allow the worker no control over the conditions of work and that seriously affect his mental and physical functioning off the job probably comprise less than 2 percent of the jobs in America."[5] When the Gallup Poll asks the question, "Is your work satisfying?" the response is 80 percent to 90 percent affirmative. More sophisticated measures of job satisfaction, to be sure, uncover a great variety of complaints.[6]

The antitechnologists romanticize the work of earlier times in an attempt to make it seem more appealing than work in a technological age. But their idyllic descriptions of peasant life do not ring true. Agricultural work, for all its appeal to the intellectual in his armchair, is brutalizing in its demands. Factory and office work is not a bed of roses either. But given their choice, most people seem to prefer to escape from the drudgery of the farm. This fact fails to impress the antitechnologists,

[4]Harold L. Wilensky, "Work, Careers and Leisure Styles," *Harvard University Program on Technology and Society, 1964–1972, A Final Review,* p. 142.

[5]Based on an analysis of Bureau of Labor Statistics for job categories likely to have "assemblyline features." Noted in *Work in America,* Report of a Special Task Force to the Secretary of H.E.W., The M.I.T. Press, Cambridge, Mass. p. 13.

[6]*Ibid.* pp. 14–15.

who prefer their sensibilities to the choices of real people. As engineers, we cannot expect to resolve an enigma that is inherent in the human condition. We merely do what we can to solve real problems. We are interested in, and are participating in, industrial experiments which seek to make the work experience more fulfilling. We will leave to others lamentations for arcadian days that never were.

As for the technological society forcing people to consume things that they do not want, how can we respond to this canard? Like the boy who said, "Look, the emperor has no clothes," one might observe that the consumers who buy cars and electric can openers could, if they chose, buy oboes and oil paints, sailboats and hiking boots, chess sets and Mozart records. Or, if they have no personal "increasing wants," in Mumford's phrase, could they not help purchase a kidney machine which would save their neighbor's life? If people are vulgar, foolish, and selfish in their choice of purchases, is it not the worst sort of copout to blame this on "the economy," "society," or "the suave technocracy"? Indeed, would not a man prefer being called vulgar to being told he has no will with which to make choices of his own?

Engineers devote more time and energy to creating hi-fi equipment and concert halls than we do to creating motorcycles. But if people want motorcycles, we are happy to provide them. And we do not like being called technocrats for our pains.

Which brings us to the next tenet of antitechnology, the belief that a technocratic elite is taking over control of society. Such a view at least avoids the logical absurdity of demon technology compelling people to act against their own interests. It does not violate our common sense to be told that certain people are taking advantage of other people. But is it logical to claim that exploitation increases as a result of the growth of technology?

Upon reflection, this claim appears to be absolutely without foundation. When camel caravans traveled across the deserts, there were a few merchant entrepreneurs and many disenfranchised camel drivers. From earliest historical times, peasants have been abused and exploited by the nobility. Bankers, merchants, landowners, kings, and assorted plunderers have had it good at the expense of the masses in practically every large social group that has ever been (not just in certain groups like pyramid-building Egypt, as Mumford contends). Perhaps in small tribes there was less exploitation than that which developed in large and complex cultures, and surely technology played a role in that transition. But since the dim, distant time of that initial transition, it simply is not true that advances in technology have been helpful to the Establishment in increasing its power over the masses.

In fact, the evidence is all the other way. In technologically advanced societies there is more freedom for the average citizen than there was in earlier ages. There has been continuing apprehension that new technological achievements *might* make it possible for governments to tyrannize the citizenry with Big Brother techniques. But, in spite of all the newest electronic gadgetry, governments are scarcely able to prevent the antisocial actions of criminals, much less control every act of every citizen. Hijacking, technically ingenious robberies, computer-aided embezzlements, and the like, are evidence that the outlaw is able to turn technology to his own advantage, often more adroitly than the government. The FBI has admitted that young revolutionaries are almost impossible to find once they go "underground." The rebellious individual is more than holding his own.

The Establishment has potent propaganda techniques at its disposal, but this is more than offset by the increasingly free flow of information that the Establishment cannot control. And, as in the case of criminals, anti-Establishment movements have been quick to turn new techniques to their advantage. A generation ago it was the labor unions. More recent examples are the civil rights movement, the students' antiwar movement, and women's liberation. If members of the Establishment are indeed trying to persuade the masses to consume an oversupply of shoddy merchandise, then the consumer movement is a response that can be expected to grow, using advertising to combat advertisers, lobbyists to combat lobbies.

Exploitation continues to exist. That is a fact of life. But the antitechnologists are in error when they say that it has increased in extent or intensity because of technology. In spite of their extravagant statements, they cannot help but recognize that they are mistaken, statistically speaking, at least. The world was not "divided into two classes" starting in the nineteenth century, as Ellul contends. Reich is wrong when he says that "decisions are made by experts, specialists, and professionals safely insulated from the feelings of the people." (Witness changes in opinion, and then in legislation, concerning abortion, divorce, and pornography.) Those who were slaves are now free. Those who were disenfranchised can now vote. Rigid class structures are giving way to frenetic mobility. The barons and abbots and merchant princes who treated their fellow humans like animals, and convinced them that they would get their reward in heaven, would be incredulous to hear the antitechnologists theorize about how technology has brought about an increase in exploitation. We need only look at the underdeveloped nations of our present era to see that exploitation is not proportionate to technological advance. If anything, the proportion is inverse.

As for the role of technologists in the Establishment, it is ironic to hear ourselves called "high priests" and "technocratic elite" at the very time that we are complaining of a lack of prestige and power. Talk to any engineer or scientist, look into any professional journal, and you will learn quickly enough that the centers of power lie elsewhere. Technologists are needed, to be sure, just as scribes were needed at one time, or blacksmiths, or millers, or builders of fortresses. Some engineers have moved into positions of responsibility in industry and government, but their numbers are small compared to leaders trained in the law, accounting, and business. In any event, real power rests, not with the technologists, or with any special professional group for that matter, but with the wealthy, the clever, and the daring—and with their friends—just as it always has. How blind must one be not to see this obvious truth?

Nor do the technologists lord it over their fellows from a "citadel of expertise." That this myth persists is difficult to comprehend, but it appears to have a special place in the hearts of antitechnologists. John McDermott, in 1969, wrote a piece for *The New York Review of Books* entitled "Technology: The Opiate of the Intellectuals." It received quite a bit of attention at the time, and has since become a standard point of reference in the antitechnology literature. In agreement with the authors we have considered, McDermott asserted that "we now observe evidence of a growing separation between ruling and lower-class culture in America, a separation which is particularly enhanced by the rapid growth of technology." This is happening, according to McDermott, because "almost all of the public's business is carried on in specialized jargon," and "the new new language of social and technical organization is divorced from the general population."

This is persuasive rhetoric, but not in accordance with the facts. My teen-age sons read articles in *Scientific American* on computers, quasars, and laser beams with much readier comprehension than most of the pieces they are apt to find in *The New York Review of Books.* A typical plumber or gas station attendant, or even a bank teller who owns a secondhand car, knows more about society's technical systems and "the august mystery of science" (McDermott's phrase) than any dozen Establishment people such as bank presidents, political bosses, and Mafia godfathers. I pick up a book entitled *How Things Work*, intended for children of primary school age. It contains straightforward discussions of electricity and magnetism, internal combustion engines and rockets. With the help of simple diagrams, it explains the workings of carburetors, thermostats, transistors, and dozens of other devices. Where is all the mystery?

There are obscure specialties, to be sure, more than there have ever been. There was, for a time, much concern about a schism between the "two cultures," a phrase made famous by C. P. Snow in 1959. But Snow observed in 1963 that the divide seemed already to be closing, and with the growth of public concern about ecology and conservation, the general public is becoming more conversant with technological subjects rather than less so. (This can hardly be said, however, about the mysteries of economics, political science, and contemporary developments in the arts.) The average citizen, seated in front of his television set watching Walter Cronkite demonstrate the details of a flight to the moon, is not aware that he is being exploited by the mandarins of the technological elite. Nor are the technologists aware that they are the new mandarins. Both conditions exist mainly in the bizarre nightmares of the antitechnologists.

Next we must confront the charge that technology is cutting man off from his natural habitat, with catastrophic consequences. It is important to point out that if we are less in touch with nature than we were —and this can hardly be disputed—then the reason does not lie exclusively with technology. Technology could be used to put people in very close touch with nature, if that is what they want. Wealthy people could have comfortable abodes in the wilderness, could live among birds in the highest jungle treetops, or even commune with fish in the ocean depths. But they seem to prefer penthouse apartments in New York and villas on the crowded hills above Cannes. Poorer people could stay on their farms on the plains of Iowa, or in their small towns in the hills of New Hampshire, if they were willing to live the spare and simple life. But many of them seem to tire of the loneliness and the hard physical labor that goes with rusticity, and succumb to the allure of the cities.

It is Roszak's lament that "the malaise of a Chekhov play" has settled upon daily life. He ignores the fact that the famous Chekhov malaise stems in no small measure from living in the country. "Yes, old man," shouts Dr. Astrov at Uncle Vanya, "in the whole district there were only two decent, well-educated men: you and I. And in some ten years the common round of the trivial life here has swamped us, and has poisoned our life with its putrid vapours, and made us just as despicable as all the rest." There is tedium in the countryside, and sometimes squalor. No poet has sung the praises of Tobacco Road.

Nevertheless, I personally enjoy being in the countryside or in the woods, and so feel a certain sympathy for the antitechnologists' views on this subject. But I can see no evidence that frequent contact with nature is *essential* to human well-being, as the antitechnologists assert. Even if the human species owes much of its complexity to the diversity of the natural environment, why must man continue to commune with the landscapes in which he evolved? Millions of people, in ages past as well as present, have lived out their lives in city environs, with very little if any contact with "nature." Have they lived lives inherently inferior because of this? Who would be presumptuous enough to make such a statement?

The common domestic cat evolved in the wild, but a thousand generations of domesticity do not seem to have "denatured" it in the least. This is not the place to write the ode to my cat that should someday be written. Suffice it to say that although she never goes out of doors, she plays, hunts, loves, and eats with gusto, and relaxes with that sensuous peace that is uniquely feline. I submit that she is not more "alienated" than her wild sister who fights for survival in some distant wood.

The antitechnologists talk a lot about nature without clearly defining what they mean by the word. Does nature consist of farms, seashores, lakes, and meadows, to use Reich's list? Does not nature consist also of scorched deserts, fetid tropical forests, barren ice fields, ocean depths, and outer space—environments relentlessly hostile to human life? If farms and meadows are considered "natural" even though they have been made by men out of the stuff of the universe, what is "unnatural"? A stone wall and a farm cottage are still "good," I suppose, but a bridge and a dam become "bad," and a glass building façade becomes unnatural and dehumanizing, even though the glass has been made by man out of the sands of the earth.

Must one be in the wilds to be in touch with nature? Will not a garden in the back yard suffice? How about a collection of plants in the living room? Oriental artists have shown us how the beauty of all creation is implicit in a single blossom, or in the arrangement of a few stones. The assertion that men are emotionally crippled by being isolated from the wilds is, as I have said, unwarranted because of lack of evidence. But more than that, it does not take into account the multitude of ways in which "nature" can be experienced.

If pressed, the antitechnologists might grudgingly admit that the harm of being separated from nature can be mitigated if the separating medium is graceful and in harmony with natural principles, say like the Left Bank in Paris, or the Piazza Navone in Rome. But they point to the modern city as the epitome of everything that is mechanical and antihuman.

I will not here embark on a discussion of functionalism and modern architecture. But I will note in passing that there are millions of families who have lived happy years in nondescript high-rise apartments, and millions of people who have spent pleasant working lifetimes in the most modern office buildings. To claim that such passive environments are emotionally crippling is not to state a general truth, but rather to exhibit a personal phobia.

I have seen early-morning crowds pouring into a Park Avenue office building, into a spacious lobby, via a smooth-riding elevator to comfortable offices with thick carpets and dazzling window views. I have heard them chattering of personal concerns, a boyfriend who called, a child who scratched his knee, a movie seen, an aunt visiting from out of town. These people are no more dehumanized by their environment than are a group of native women doing their laundry on the bank of a river. I have seen them at their work, remarkably free to move about, exchange gossip, and gather at the water cooler. I have seen them promenading at lunch hour, looking into gaily decorated store windows, boys and girls eyeing each other, in time-honored fashion. I have shared in coffee breaks, drinking lukewarm coffee out of traditional cardboard and plastic cups with as much gusto as a peasant drinking his *vin ordinaire.*

I have also seen these office workers on a Monday morning comparing sunburns and trading tales about picnics, hikes, fishing trips, and various other sorties into the out-of-doors. The average person is not as isolated from nature as the antitechnologists would have us suppose. Ah, but this "pathetic weekend," as Dubos has told us, is not a true or meaningful relationship with nature.

There is a fussiness about the antitechnologists' abhorrence of the city, as if the drama of life could not unfold in anything but an idyllic setting. Saul Bellow, one of our leading novelists, has taken a more robust position. In his view, mankind is not about to be intimidated by anything as insignificant as a technological landscape:

> A million years passed before my soul was let out into the technological world. That world was filled with ultraintelligent machines, but the soul

after all was a soul, and it had waited a million years for its turn and did not intend to be cheated of its birthright by a lot of mere gimmicks. It had come from the far reaches of the universe, and it was interested but not overawed by these inventions.[7]

The next target of the antitechnologists is Everyman at play. It is particularly important to antitechnology that popular hobbies and pastimes be discredited, for leisure is one of the benefits generally assumed to follow in the wake of technological advances. The theme of modern man at leisure spurs the antitechnologists to such heights of derision that we cannot help but question their seriousness of purpose. Perhaps they are merely expressing a satirical impulse, from the barbs of which no human activity is exempt. I have a fondness for grand opera, yet I have seen this sublime art burlesqued by a dozen comedians—and I have been amused. In *Gulliver's Travels* Swift has shown us how human beings appear ludicrous when viewed from an aloof perspective, and grotesque when viewed from close up. If the antitechnologists wrote in this timeless tradition, it would be querulous to object. But satire is clearly not their mode. In dead earnest, and with a purpose in mind, they are determined to show that the ordinary man at leisure is a contemptible sight, and that he has been reduced to his lowly state by the trickery of the technocratic society.

There are many popular pastimes contemptuously referred to as mass-cult activities—bowling, for example—that are not to my taste. But how can one draw sweeping conclusions from such a fact? A joyous, obviously exhilarating hour in a bowling alley is certainly not inferior in the scheme of things to a torpid, nonattentive hour listening to string quartets. Also, is bowling, or any of the other pastimes that the antitechnologists disdain, inferior to entertainments of earlier days, such as bear baiting, cock fighting, and public executions?

In their consideration of recreation activities, the antitechnologists refuse to take into account anything that an actual participant might feel. For even when the ordinary man considers himself happy—at a ball game or a vacation camp, watching television or listening to a jukebox, playing with a pinball machine or eating hot dogs—we are told that he is only being fooled into *thinking* that he is happy.

It is strategically convenient for the antitechnologists to discount the

[7]Saul Bellow, "Machines and Storybooks," *Harpers Magazine*, August, 1974, p. 59 (a paraphrase by Bellow of a quote from Russian writer V.V. Rozanov.)

expressed feelings of the average citizen. It then follows that (1) those satisfactions which are attributed to technology are illusory, and (2) those dissatisfactions which are the fault of the individual can be blamed on technology, since the individual's choices are made under some form of hypnosis. It is a can't-lose proposition.

Under these ground rules, how can we argue the question of what constitutes the good life? If most people are fooled into desiring things they do not really desire, tricked into thinking they are free when they are really enslaved, mesmerized into feeling happy when true happiness forever eludes them, then clearly we are in a sorry state. But if the people themselves do not agree that their contentment is misery, what are we to conclude?

A character in a Gide novel remarks about the moment he first realized that "men feel what they imagine they feel. From that to thinking that they imagine they feel what they feel was a very short step!" Between feeling and imagining one feels, "what God could tell the difference?"

The antitechnologists fancy themselves to be the gods who can tell the difference. They charge technologists with having formed an elite class. But what is a little extra knowledge about machines compared to the godlike knowledge that they claim for themselves? Is it not clear that they consider themselves to be the elite of all elites?

They have complained that in the scientific worldview the scientist, seeking objectivity, cuts himself out of the picture, ignoring his own passions. The antitechnologists, however, in painting *their* picture of the true world, see nothing wrong with deleting the average man's passions. "As for the mass of urban workers," says Mumford, "they must have viewed their dismal lot, *if they were conscious at all,* with a feeling of galling disappointment." I have added the emphasis to the phrase which expresses so perfectly the antitechnologists' total scorn for anything that the average man might think, if indeed they credit him with thinking at all.

The idea that a man of the masses has no thoughts of his own, but is something on the order of a programmed machine, owes part of its popularity with the antitechnologists to the influential writings of Herbert Marcuse. In his *One-Dimensional Man,* Marcuse voices the disgust and frustration that are central to the antitechnological movement:

> If the individuals are satisfied to the point of happiness with the goods and services handed down to them by the administration, why should

they insist on different institutions for a different production of different goods and services? And if the individuals are pre-conditioned so that the satisfying goods also include thoughts, feelings, aspirations, why should they wish to think, feel, and imagine for themselves?

It is legitimate, of course, to speculate on the extent to which people's lives are dominated by debasing illusions. Ibsen's *The Wild Duck* and Eugene O'Neill's *The Iceman Cometh* are two dramatic works that deal with the theme of how our lives are made tolerable by self-deceit, and with the problem of what happens when simple people are abruptly confronted with "truth." But the antitechnologists are not creative artists speculating about the eternal problems of being human. They are polemicists determined to prove that life today is worse than it used to be. At the very least, one would expect them to give weight to such evidence as is available. However, they avoid the discussion of facts, preferring to rely on such subjective impressions as the "blank, hollow, bitter faces," that Reich fancies he sees on the white-collar and blue-collar workers of America.

When real people are actually asked about their lives, "they believe that technology is both good and bad, and for most of them . . . the good outweighs the bad."[8] In medical studies assessing the adverse impact on health of changes in a person's life, it has been found that timeless events such as marriage, divorce, and death in the family are far more significant than anything having to do with the rule of technology in the world.[9] This is not to say that there is no dissatisfaction with life or disenchantment with technology; we will come to that in a moment. But the essentials of life do not seem to have undergone changes as sweeping as the antitechnologists maintain.

I leaf through *The Family of Man*, a book reproducing the photographic exhibition assembled in 1955 by Edward Steichen. I see 503 pictures from 68 countries, representing man in every cultural state from primitive to industrial. I see lovers embracing, mothers with infants, children at play, people eating, dancing, working, grieving, consoling. Everything really important seems eternally the same—in cities and in jungles, in slums and on farms. Carl Sandburg's prologue attempts to put

[8]Irene Loviss, "A Survey of Popular Attitudes Toward Technology," *Harvard University Program on Technology and Society, 1964–1972, A Final Review,* p. 174.

[9]"Doctors Study Treating of Ills Brought on by Stress," *The New York Times,* June 10, 1973.

it into words: "Alike and ever alike, we are on all continents in the need of love, food, clothing, work, speech, worship, sleep, games, dancing, fun. From tropics to arctics humanity lives with these needs so alike, so inexorably alike." A few moments spent studying these photos make the attitudes of the antitechnologists seem peevish and carping. These are real people with real faces that give the lie to the antitechnologists' snobbish generalizations.

Steichen and Sandburg are yea-sayers, a refreshing and necessary breed to have around. That does not mean that there is no place for Cassandras. The antitechnologists have every right to be gloomy, and have a bounden duty to express their doubts about the direction our lives are taking. But their persistent disregard of the average person's sentiments is a crucial weakness in their argument—particularly when they then ask us to consider the "real" satisfactions that they claim ordinary people experienced in other cultures of other times.

It is difficult not to be seduced by the antitechnologists' idyllic elegies for past cultures. We all are moved to reverie by talk of an arcadian golden age. But when we awaken from this reverie, we realize that the antitechnologists have diverted us with half-truths and distortions. We can see no reason why the gratifications experienced in earlier cultures (if, indeed, they *were* experienced) should be considered real or valid, while the expressed gratifications of people in our culture are to be discounted. We cannot agree that an earlier culture "in a long-range sense reflects the beliefs and values of the people in it" (Reich), while our culture does not. If we have been "sold" on automobiles and television sets, were not these earlier men "sold" on rain dances and promises of heaven? Or, if they created their cultures to fill their needs, have we not done the same? Man creates and is created in a never-ending, complex process. But the way the antitechnologists have twisted this to their purposes is simply intellectual deception.

Setting aside this technique of applying double standards, it is fair to go on to ask whether or not life was "better" in these earlier cultures than it is in our own. How is one to judge? The harmony which the antitechnologists see in primitive life, anthropologists find in only certain tribes. Others display the very anxiety and hostility that antitechnologists blame on technology—as why should they not, being almost totally vulnerable to every passing hazard of nature, beast, disease, and human enemy? As for the peasant, was he "foot-free," "sustained by physical work," with a "capacity for a non-material existence"? Did he crack jokes with every passerby? Or was he brutal and brutalized, materialistic and suspicious, stoning errant women and hiding gold in his mattress? And the Middle Ages, that dimly remembered time of "moral judgment," "equilibrium," and "common aspirations." Was it not also a time of pestilence, brigandage, and public tortures? "The chroniclers themselves," admits a noted admirer of the period, tell us "of covetousness, of cruelty, of cool calculation, of well-understood self-interest. . . ."[10] The callous brutality, the unrelievable pain, the ever-present threat of untimely death for oneself (and worse, for one's children) are the realities with which our ancestors lived, and of which the antitechnologists seem totally oblivious.

There are aspects of earlier cultures that seem appealing, and to which we can usefully look in structuring our own lives. But the antitechnologists have distorted the picture shamelessly, glorifying the earlier cultures and at the same time defaming ours. Then, with the air of protecting the higher values and the nobler pursuits, they blame the fancied deterioration in society on the role supposedly played by technology.

QUESTIONS FOR DISCUSSION

1. In the refutation of a presumption—a prevailing view that may exist diffusely in many places—one of the refuter's first tasks is to characterize the opposition. This characterization can obviously be devised to serve the refuter, but if it is too far off the mark, we call it the strawman fallacy. List the assumptions that Florman claims the antitechnologists hold. (There are several main points, some with subsidiary points.) List also the arguments he uses in refutation, characterizing them according to type, such as CP or causal.
2. What tone does Florman take against his opposition? Is he dispassionate, enraged, or somewhere in between? Find evidence in the style (for instance, in his use of "I") for your characterization of his voice.
3. Who are included in the "we" that Florman uses? What audience is he writing for?
4. Florman uses many specifically "rhetorical" tactics of argumentation (though these are not easy to separate from the "logical"). Find the places where he creates a middle ground for himself, stigmatizes his opposition, creates a positive persona for himself, and builds a sense of solidarity with his audience.
5. Check off the sources of evidence that Florman appeals to and catalog the

[10]J. Huizinga, *The Waning of the Middle Ages,* St. Martin's Press, Inc., New York, 1949, Anchor Books, 1954, p. 67.

types (e.g., personal experience, authority). Does he rely primarily on one kind of evidence? To what extent does he assume that his points will be self-evidently valid to his readers?

6. What are the "ground rules" that make it so difficult for Florman to argue with his opponents about the "good life"? Are argument and counterargument impossible when parties have different standards of evidence?

SUGGESTIONS FOR WRITING

1. Florman expresses his thesis with one qualification: "technology is not evil except when falsely described by dyspeptic philosophers." Would you add other qualifications, perhaps garnered from elsewhere in Florman's argument? Address your additions to Florman's audience of antitechnologists.

2. Florman's chapter is filled with CPs that could themselves be theses for support or refutation (e.g., "Man is by nature a technological animal," and "A basic human impulse precedes and underlies each technological development"). Select one of these claims and support or refute it, perhaps incorporating strategies that Florman uses for an audience uninformed about technology.

3. Florman disagrees heartily with the antitechnologists' view that technology has served only to enslave the "masses." What does a comparison between developed and underdeveloped nations suggest? (Crucial to your inquiry will be a working definition of what it means to have less freedom.) You may direct your argument to Florman's audience.

4. Look yourself at one of the works that Florman rebuts, perhaps at McDermott's essay or at Marcuse's *One-Dimensional Man.* Try a refutation of part of one of these antitechnology pieces. Or defend it against Florman's attack.

5. Florman suggests that *Scientific American* is inherently clearer than the *New York Review of Books.* Compare these two periodicals (or two similar ones) yourself and report the results to readers of either journal.

6. Florman maintains that the general public is becoming increasingly conversant with technological subjects. How could this assertion be tested? How could we judge the general public's understanding of technical matters? Devise a means to test this assertion and present your results, supporting or refuting Florman's claim, to an audience interested in scientific and technological education. (Would a comparison of the technical vocabulary in news magazines twenty years ago and today be an adequate test?)

7. Following Florman's technique if not his subject matter, construct a refutation against a nebulous presumption, a floating misconception that you believe many people have about something. Your refutation will require you to first characterize an opposition before you can take it on.

—————————— ≫≫ ≪≪ ——————————

A Close Look at the Unicorn

—————————— ≫≫ ≪≪ ——————————

The Reviewer's Duty to Damn: Letter to an Avalanche

JOHN CIARDI

The pair of essays reprinted here are not arguments on contradictory sides of an issue; instead they are both on the same side. The second was written in defense of the first, refuting a barrage of criticism that the first received when it appeared in the Saturday Review. *The critic John Ciardi, an eminent poet himself and respected translator of Dante, gave a harsh reception to Anne Morrow Lindbergh's seventh volume of poetry,* The Unicorn and Other Poems. *As a result Ciardi received an "avalanche" of letters, taking him to task for his ungentlemanly conduct toward the lady's work. But Ciardi responded point by point to the charges made against him. He attempted to capture the higher ground and defended his original review in the name of Poetry—with a capital P. What he tried to do, in essence, was to show that he had made a valid evaluation argument (thus evaluating his evaluation) and not merely indulged in an expression of personal taste.*

"A Close Look at the Unicorn"

Anne Morrow Lindbergh's great personal distinction, together with the popularity of her six earlier volumes, some of poetry and some of prose, made it clear from the start that her latest volume of verse, *The Unicorn and Other Poems,* would sell widely. Poetry nevertheless is no reliable consort of either personal distinction or of book-store success. Everyone is in trouble when he looks at the stars, and under the stars I am as humanly eager to grant Mrs. Lindbergh the dignity of her troubles as I am to enjoin my own.

One of my present troubles is that as a reviewer not of Mrs. Lindbergh but of her poems I have, in duty, nothing but contempt to offer. I am compelled to believe that Mrs. Lindbergh has written an offensively bad book—inept, jingling, slovenly, illiterate even, and puffed up with the foolish afflatus of a stereotyped high-seriousness, that species of aesthetic and human failure that will accept any shriek as a true high-C. If there is judgment it must go by standards. I cannot apologize for this judgment. I believe that I can and must specify the particular badness of this sort of stuff.

I open to the first poem, a simple two-part piece titled "The Man and the Child." Stanza one develops the theme "It is the man in us who works"; stanza two, the theme "It is the child in us who plays"; and the two themes are resolved in the single final line, "It is the child in us who loves."

A simple pattern of idea but certainly not a bad one as such. One need only imagine what Blake might have done with such a structure to realize that poetry can remake any theme or series of themes if it can manage to deepen and to reinvigorate them. The measure of the poem is not in its assertion but in the performance of its own insight. As a definition of "performance" let me offer "the emotional enlargement of the starting insight by its re-creation within the artifice of the poem."

What of Mrs. Lindbergh's performance? Here are her starting lines:

> It is the man in us who works;
>
> Who earns his daily bread and anxious scans
> The evening skies to know tomorrow's plans;
> It is the man who hurries as he walks;
> Finds courage in a crowd; shouts as he talks;
> Who shuts his eyes and burrows through his task;
> Who doubts his neighbor and who wears a mask;
> Who moves in armor and who hides his tears.
> It is the man in us who fears.

I certainly must record as a first general impression that the details of the man's behavior seem exquisitely foolish. I wince over the opening clash of cliché in "who earns his daily bread," stumble over the tortured and rhyme-forced inversion of "and anxious scans" (Mrs. Lindbergh might at least have put commas around "anxious"), and proceed from there to a dull nothingness, only to be brought up with a real grating of the nerve by the absurdity of line eight, in which I am told that the man moves in armor and, so encased, goes to the trouble of hiding his already hidden tears. Or perhaps Mrs. Lindbergh thought of the man as wearing armor but with the vizor raised. But what can be the figurative force of "to move in armor" if it does not mean "to go carefully and completely on guard"? Knights in armor raised their vizors only in moments of relaxation or as a gesture of courtesy. Clearly neither possibility can apply here. And clearly, too, Mrs. Lindbergh asks no such questions of her language and metaphors. The more evident principle of the writing seems to be that "tears-fears" is an easy rhyme and that any other consideration may be thrown overboard so long as the jingle is saved.

At this point I have had enough of the first poem. I turn to the second and read the first two lines:

> Like birds in winter
> You fed me;

I wonder why there is no comma after "winter" and I am left to guess what I later confirmed, that Mrs. Lindbergh does not understand English usage of the comma. But, more urgently, who is "like birds in winter"? Grammatically rendered, the lines can only mean "You, like birds in winter, fed me," *i.e.*, a kind of coming of the ravens. Four lines later, however, the context makes it clear that these lines must be taken to mean "You fed me as one feeds birds in winter."

Once again I have had enough. I turn to the third piece, "The Little Mermaid," and I read:

> Only the little mermaid knows the price
> One pays for mortal love, what sacrifice
> Exacted by the Sea-Witch, should one choose
> A mermaid's careless liberty to lose.

Only the little mermaid—and Mrs. Lindbergh. But by now I am becoming accustomed to mindlessness, as I am to Mrs. Lindbergh's way of lunging for rhymes, for any rhyme. So I am prepared to pass over, as familiar ground, the rhyme-forced redundancy of "sacrifice," the similarly dictated inversion of line four, and the faulty parallel construction of the second clause.

There still remains a small harvest of clichés. From the next twelve lines of the poem I cull: "smoky cauldron," "restless waves," "dim pellucid depths," "unheard music," "light as foam," and "moon bright nights." The poem continues on to the overleaf but I do not. I begin to skip.

I try page eighteen and find this metaphoric flight in the first four lines:

> Burning tree upon the hill
> And burning tree within my heart,
> What kinship stands between the two,
> What cord I cannot tear apart.

I am not at all sure I know how that second burning tree got into Mrs. Lindbergh's heart, but to save time let me grant rather than dispute both the trees and the assertion that a kinship "stands" between them. I am next asked to believe that this kinship, by apposition, is a "cord" and that the cord, by carry-over of the parallel construction, "stands" between the two trees. I can only assume that Mrs. Lindbergh intends the construction "a cord stands between the two trees" to mean "a cord is tied from tree to tree." But if this is her intention—and no other seems remotely possible—I must certainly remind her that freshman English students are required to take remedial courses when they persist in such illiteracies. Mrs. Lindbergh continues with "What cord I cannot tear apart." Once again the grammar is faulty (as it is in poem after poem of those I sampled). Whether "cord" be taken as some sort of rope or as some sort of umbilicus, "to tear it apart" can only mean "to shred or to rip it," whereas the only possible sense in this context is not "to shred" but "to break." Am I to assume that Mrs. Lindbergh is actually illiterate? The contrary evidence is not overwhelming. But what is more evident—once again—is the fact that she is constantly in trouble with the simplest of rhymes (here "heart—apart") and that, lacking first a sound grammatical sense and second anything like a poet's sense of words and their shades of meaning, she is defenseless against her rhyme-schemes and will commit any absurdity while entangled in her own harness.

Nor is "absurdity" too strong a word. I can certainly sense the human emotion that sends Mrs. Lindbergh to the writing, but I can only report that what emerges in the writing is low-grade poetry and low-grade humanity. As a person Mrs. Lindbergh must certainly have richer resources than these, but whatever those personal resources the fact remains that they simply do not make their way through bad writing. I must believe that the art of poetry is more important than Mrs. Lindbergh or than you or than me, and that bad observance of that art is an assault on one of the most enduring sanctions of the total human experience. Believing that, I believe it to be absurd, and a violence against language, to write, as Mrs. Lindbergh does, for example, of a submerged stone "clogging" a stream. "Clog" is a distinct, meaningful,

and useful word, and as such it is as delightful to the senses as is the feel
of a well-made pair of pliers in the palm. For the first three reasons the
word is part of the total possibility of human understanding and communication. For the consequent sense of delight, it is a part of the relish
and art of language. For a person of poetic pretensions to misuse language itself in so slovenly a way is certainly akin to Original Sin, and in
the absence of the proper angel I must believe that it is the duty of
anyone who cares for the garden to slam the gate in the face of the sinful
and abusive.

Certainly it is the same sinful insensibility that permits Mrs. Lindbergh to offer for sale the following lines—as pedestrian, tone-deaf, and
silly a proposition in intellect as ever befuddled a high school valediction:

> For beauty, for significance, it's space
> We need, and since we have no space today
> In which to frame the act, the word, the face
> Of beauty, it's no longer beautiful.

(Characteristically, note the construction "space [dimensional] in which
to frame the word [oral].")

Or again in the following, in which the reader is asked to believe,
among other things, that earth lies between its own surface and some
neighboring planet:

> The planet in the sky,
> The sea-shell on the ground:
> And though all heaven and earth between them lie.

Or, finally, and as a sort of ultimate absurdity, what must certainly
be the neatest trick of the literary season:

> Down at my feet
>   A weed has pressed
> Its scarlet knife
>   Against my breast.

Compare the now classical examination answer that read: "Dante was
a great transitional figure: with one foot he stood in the Middle Ages,
while with the other he saluted the rising sun of the Renaissance." The
student could perhaps be forgiven—he was racing the clock. But what
will forgive Mrs. Lindbergh this sort of miserable stuff?

"The Reviewer's Duty to Damn"

A few weeks ago I reviewed in these pages Anne Morrow Lindbergh's *The Unicorn and Other Poems.*

Then came the avalanche. As it happens I am sitting the year out on a Fellowship to the American Academy in Rome and the avalanche descended on the New York office. The cable connects, however; the airmail has been flowing; and I have been receiving generous samples from the avalanche. SR tells me that hundreds of such letters have been received. The sampling that has been forwarded to me shows a remarkable consistency in language. The following phrases will serve to illustrate the whole range: "shocking . . . cruel . . . horrid person hitting below the belt . . . a mean low person . . . unfairness shouts aloud . . . totally unjust . . . gross discourtesy . . . lack of plain human decency . . . petty harshness . . . it leaves me with a sense of degradation for having read it."

The issues here—the first issues at least—are clear enough, but before addressing them, let me assure the avalanche of its own numerical strength and consistency. Of the hundreds of letters my review evoked, I have seen only two that might be called favorable. If there is reason in numbers, those who have been moved to object are certainly right. I am not yet persuaded, however, that the avalanches of indignation are an intellectual measure I can respect. If the excellence of poetry were determinable by a national election, I have no doubt that Edgar Guest would be elected the greatest poet in the English language—by a landslide. I doubt that he is, and I doubt the pertinence of the present avalanche.

The first issue is clearly enough the ever-present *ad hominem.* I have attempted to show by principle and evidence that Mrs. Lindbergh writes not simply bad poetry, but contemptibly bad poetry. The answer to that proposition, according to the avalanche, is: "You are a mean low horrid person." The avalanche may be right about me. But my character has nothing to do with the proposition I have put forth, and with the principles I have attempted to introduce as measures of Mrs. Lindbergh's poetry. These principles are not my invention. They would have existed in human reckoning had I never been born. Clearly, therefore, they do not depend on me for their validity. It may even be that I am unworthy of the principles I have offered for discussion. It is still the principles themselves that are at issue. If I have misstated these principles, let the statement be corrected; if I have misapplied them, let my procedure be challenged; if I have misused evidence, let my error be shown.

A second charge, already implicit in some of the phrases I have cited, is made explicit in the following passage from one letter:

> Mrs. Lindbergh is (as everyone except Mr. Ciardi knows) a sensitive and intelligent person; she would have understood a more subtly worded criticism; and so would the readers of *The Saturday Review,* who are now more prejudiced against Mr. Ciardi than against Mrs. Lindbergh. . . . It is not necessary to use a sledgehammer to demolish a fragile shell.

I think this would be a valid criticism were it a fact that the premise of my review was to make Mrs. Lindbergh understand, or that she is indeed a fragile shell. I shall have more to say below about the fragile shell, but one of the main reasons for selecting *this* book for damnation in so many words was the very fact that it was obviously destined for considerable sale and general acclaim; that far from being a fragile shell, it was almost certain of solid sales and praise, as poetry goes. For better or worse I thought it necessary to make my disagreement strong enough to counterbalance the general vague approval the book was bound to receive elsewhere.

The fact that I have expressed myself as contemptuous of Mrs. Lindbergh's poetry is, as far as I am concerned, a necessary accuracy. I regret—I have already regretted it in my review—that my final considered judgment leaves me no other choice. I think these are slovenly poems. The title under which I sent in the review was "The Slovenly Unicorn." I do not understand why the title was changed by other SR editors. Slovenliness I have always held to be the most contemptible of aesthetic sins. I think I have established the existence of slovenliness in these poems. If I have failed to establish the existence of such slovenliness, my charge must, of course, fall through. If I have established it, and if slovenliness is indeed (as I believe it to be) contemptible, what choice have I but to consider these poems contemptible? I am sorry if that conclusion hurts Mrs. Lindbergh, but I am even sorrier that she writes such stuff. I should, of course, be delighted to have her grasp my objections and profit by them. More urgently, however, I am trying to establish as a policy of this magazine that poetry is a serious, dignified, and disciplined human activity which is not to be debased in the name of a counterfeit sentimentality that will not bother to learn the fundamentals of its own art.

It is that line I mean to defend. That, and the proposition that the discussion must go by principle. I am not aware of any compulsion within myself to assault the character of persons not known to me, and I do not believe that I have done so. I chose to affirm principles. It is certainly significant to me that I was able to find only two letters in the total avalanche that showed even so much as an awareness that a principle was involved.

An avalanche, moreover, is not only a descending mass; it is a release of stored-up forces. "Insulting," says one letter and then cites the "idiotic verse" I have chosen for *SR* since I became Poetry Editor. One letter speaks of "the animus which darkens" my criticism, then goes on to say that I "should have attacked cummings and Eliot if what you crave is clarity of thought and meaningful use of words." One reader was moved to look up my own poems, and concludes that my recent poem to Dylan Thomas in this magazine is no good. Another says practically nothing about the present review but gleefully reports having found an unfavorable review of my own last book of poems in the most recent issue of *The Hudson Review*. (You missed another in the *Yale Review* a few issues back.) One argues that it is all wrong to "dissect" poetry in this way because it is "too living a thing for close criticism." (I thought that particular bit of nonsense had been disqualified even as a topic for sophomore bull sessions.) Another calls my review a "rude piece of writing" and goes on to schoolmarm me in the following way: "I shall watch *SR* for a poem by Mr. Ciardi and believe me if he doesn't make his ideas walk like good tin soldiers (with their *vizors down*) he'll come a cropper." (Dear Faithful Reader—I have had three poems in *SR* during the last year. I certainly hope none of them walk like good tin soldiers. Please send cropper.)

I have said that an avalanche is a release of stored-up forces. The alignment of those forces is not peculiar to *SR;* it is in fact descriptive of the fundamental split in all general discussion of poetry today. One vocal group believes basically that poetry must avoid all "difficulty," that it is offensive to discuss aesthetic principles, that to anatomize an art form is to destroy it, and that the real purpose of art is "to breathe forth BEAUTY." In practical application this attitude tends to become a kind of surviving Genteel Tradition.

The poetry of the surviving Genteel leans heavily to the big abstractions loudly proclaimed, to bluebirds, to "yet I know's" and "do but command's," and to the wonder the wonder the wonder of being fifty in a vague suburban way. For present purposes, let me summarize the opposite attitude with a line and a half from Browning: "Thoughts may be/ Overpoetical for poetry." Poets and readers of this persuasion (I have already described it in some detail in some of my earlier articles and need not repeat all the specifications here) tend to find the output of the Genteel Tradition to be mushy and mindless. And there is the division: one group wants poetry pretty, vague, and easily effusive. (Because easy effusion is subject to telling ridicule, the Genteel are naturally inimical to close criticism. The trouble is they can seldom if ever survive it.) The other group wants poetry to be real, physical, and disciplined. The stored-up forces of the present avalanche are simply the forces of the offended Genteel: when I took over as Poetry Editor of *SR* a year ago I began systematically to uproot Genteel poetry and to substitute whatever you want to call the other kind. I never imagined everyone would like it, but that remains my policy and it will be my policy for as long as I am its Poetry Editor.

One last charge delivered by the avalanche is that a reviewer commits a social impropriety, a somehow cowardly action, in expressing contempt for poems written by a socially gracious lady, *even if the poems justify such contempt.* It would be much better, runs this argument, to ignore the poems in silence. Clearly, however, to grant this argument is in effect to deny the reviewer the right to offer any but favorable reviews—a situation already dangerously prevalent in all our mass media.

I must insist in rebuttal that a reviewer's duty is to describe the book as accurately as he can. Twice in quite a number of years as a reviewer I have reviewed a book not simply harshly but contemptuously. It occurs to me that twice in something like fifteen or twenty years is not exactly a general compulsion to character assassination. If I come on another book as bad as Mrs. Lindbergh's, by an author whose name passes as that of a serious writer, I shall certainly review it in the same terms of contempt. I have only two reservations to make: the first is that the author's reputation be such that there is reasonable danger that the poems will be taken seriously; the second is that the more unfavorable a review happens to be, the more meticulously it must be documented.

What is the reviewer's contract with the author, the publisher, and his own readers? I think the author and the publisher are one in this: they, as part of their promotional process, offer the book for sale, and as part of their promotional process they send me a copy with the request that I state my considered opinion of the work in print. I do not ask for the book: it is sent to me. Moreover, if I say anything especially favorable about the poetry, there is an excellent chance that my remark will be excerpted and used in promotion for this book or on the dust jacket of the next. My contract with my readers is simple enough: to be honest.

Had I liked this book, I should certainly have said so, and all hands would have been happy. I did not like it, and I tried to say exactly how much I did not like it, and for what reasons.

I may be wrong in thinking Mrs. Lindbergh writes dismal stuff. But I have asked no one to take my word for it. Rather, I have tried to document point by point what I submit to be the slovenly incompetence of the writing.

Let me confess, moreover, that I had long been waiting for the proper chance to do an out-and-out unfavorable review. I was in no sense lying in wait for Mrs. Lindbergh. I had simply decided as basic policy that it was necessary for *SR* from time to time to publish a review in which a bad book was called bad in so many words and for carefully detailed reasons. In the course of the last six months or so, I have passed over many possible subjects on the grounds that they were too insignificant to be worth a real assault. Mrs. Lindbergh's book happened to fill the bill perfectly. To the extent that she cares anything at all about this review my pre-set decision was a misfortune. The real misfortune, however, is that these poems were ever written. I was especially ready to sail into them, first, because they provided an excellent opportunity to define further that sort of pernicious poetry I mean to have none of in *SR*, and, second, because they provided an opportunity to offer an essential challenge to the whole pussyfooting process of book reviewing in our national mass media. It is even possible that in my zeal to press these two charges I overstated my objections to Mrs. Lindbergh's poetry. I cannot feel that I did, however, and I must still rest my case on the critical methods of the review itself.

The fact is that reviewing in the United States seems to have succumbed to a mindless sort of approval of everything. The very fact that the author is a human being seems to plead that to dislike his writing would be to offend him. I have long been appalled by the national review standards (and lack of standards) and I have long been determined to do something about them as Poetry Editor of *SR*. I was especially delighted, therefore, to find in the current issue of *The American Scholar* an article by Geoffrey Wagner entitled "The Decline of Book Reviewing." Mr. Wagner argues tellingly a number of points I have often argued less well: (a) that different reviewing standards are often applied on the same page of a given periodical, (b) that it is almost impossible to find an unfavorable review in our mass media, and (c) that the reviewers themselves are forced to cheat their real opinions or to quit. Here is part of what Mr. Wagner says on that last point:

Who has not heard complaints from some friend who read a eulogistic review of what turned out to be a rotten novel? While there can be no question of the reviewer today not being allowed the free play of review, one cannot help observing that the big review media seem to employ extremely unexacting and optimistic men and women. There is even the suspicion abroad that a reviewer is dropped like a hot potato should he consistently "pan" the books he is sent. (The sourpuss! Some poor devil has to sell these things.)

Mr. Wagner goes on to point out how this process cannot help but corrupt the reading tastes of the masses. He then cites two instances of double-standard reviewing that fascinate me in their implications:

> Readers have seen *Marjorie Morningstar* reviewed on the front pages of *The New York Times Book Review* in a friendly notice by Maxwell Geismar, only to be followed by his sharp "criticism" of the same book in the pages of the *Nation*. Readers are also able to compare, if they wish, Edgar Johnson's kid-gloves review of Gordon Ray's recent book on Thackeray in *The New York Times Book Review* with his distinctly less cordial approach to Ray in *Publications of the Modern Language Association of America* for last March.*

I think I need hardly argue that the state of things Mr. Wagner describes is real, and dangerous to the standing of good literature in our society. I would add one further charge against the American book

---

*The March 23, 1957, issue of *SR* carried on the Letters to the Editor page the following remonstrance from Mr. Geismar: "It is too bad that John Ciardi, who is so right in principle, should be so wrong in language and feeling—an odd thing for a poet. To make matters worse, he has now repeated a silly tale about my two articles on Herman Wouk, and he brings to his fevered defense a rather frivolous article on book reviewing by Geoffrey Wagner in *The American Scholar.*

"From what bit of inaccurate gossip Mr. Wagner himself picked up this Wouk affair, I don't know. But if anybody had read my two articles with care, the following points would be clear: 1) The first review of *Marjorie Morningstar* in *The New York Times* could hardly have been called a 'friendly notice.' It was in fact a particularly severe review which the *Times* featured without changing a word, and I received—certainly not so many letters as Mr. Ciardi has—but enough to record its honesty and integrity; 2) My second article on 'The Age of Wouk' in the *Nation* was a sequel to this review—not a contradiction of it. That was why the *Nation* suggested it to me; and it dealt not with Mr. Wouk or his novel in themselves, but with the *Time-Life* version of this artist as the apostle of a new American literature. It was a satire.

"Come, come, Mr. Ciardi! It may also 'fascinate' you to know that I am including both articles in a forthcoming collection of critical essays because I happen to be proud of them, and see no fundamental difference in their values, or in those principles of criticism which I, too, share with the exacerbated Poetry Editor of *The Saturday Review.*"

reviewer: he has destroyed his own vocabulary. Our review media use the same terms for discussing the junk produced along the Spillane–Wouk axis as they do for the efforts—good or bad but at least seriously undertaken as living art—produced along the Hemingway–Thomas Mann axis. The publishers and their jacket-blurbing tradition are certainly partners in this guilt. (One of these days I mean to do a survey of book-jacket prose and let the chips and advertising contracts fall where they may.) Between them and the natural laziness of all sentimentality, book reviewing has confused even its own inner standards. Lacking any true sense of good and bad writing, lacking any standard by which they may feel justified in damning bad writing, the reviewers have tended to settle for gentle, meaningless, polite noises. They have become readers without conviction.

I damned *The Unicorn,* first, for the reasons stated in the review itself—because the poetry struck me as miserable stuff and because I am not willing to concede that personal distinction can compensate for slovenly performance. (Had Mrs. Lindbergh's performance been on Broadway instead of in the bookshops, imagine what the drama critics would have done to her.) I did so, more importantly however, because her book was bound to have a wide circulation and to receive many vague accolades. I cite a single example: *SR* in its issue of December 22 (my review, already written, was awaiting publication) undertook its annual "critics'" poll of the best books of the year. *The Unicorn and Other Poems* was tied for second place with three votes. You may be sure that the votes Mrs. Lindbergh received were all from "newspaper critics" and included none from the panel of experts who had been polled. (That distinction between "newspaper critics" and "experts" is not accidental.)

I submit that when a book I believe to be as certainly meritless as *The Unicorn* comes that close to winning even an informal national poll as the best book of verse of the year, then I conceive myself to have a duty to state my objection to this sort of stuff with no apology to the author or to the traditions of the Genteel. Should I wait till it wins the Pulitzer? I think it is time, rather, to cry Hellfire. Or there is no pulpit.

The principles on which I reviewed *The Unicorn* are the principles on which I hope to see all *SR* poetry reviews based, and I urge those same principles on all the nation's review media. With the exception of the "notice" (which is not a review really, but simply a basic statement that the book exists, with one or two personal comments by the reviewer), I shall hope that reviews in these pages conform to the following principles. I cannot, of course, control what the reviewer writes. I can and will "kill" reviews that ignore these principles, and I can and will call more and more upon the reviewers who observe them.

1. The reader deserves an honest opinion. If he doesn't deserve it give it to him anyhow.
2. No one who offers a book for sale is sacrosanct. By the act of publication and promotion, the citizen–human-being forfeits his privileges as a noncompetitor. Having willingly subjected himself to judgment he must accept either blame or praise as it follows. If in doubt, assume that the book is signed by Anonymous.
3. Evaluation must be by stated principle. The reviewer's opinion is only as good as his methods.
4. A review without references to the text is worthless.
5. Quotation without analysis of the material quoted is suspect.
6. If you cannot document a charge, pro or con, do not make it.
7. Poetry is more important than any one poet. Serve poetry.
8. Limitations of space often make it difficult and sometimes impossible to apply these principles as carefully as one would wish. No space limitation, however, is reason enough for forgetting that these principles exist.

QUESTIONS FOR DISCUSSION

1. Look closely at the wording choices in Ciardi's original review. Could Ciardi have criticized Lindbergh's poetry without arousing his readers' hostility?
2. Ciardi defends himself by claiming that he evaluates Lindbergh's poetry according to absolute principles of poetic excellence. Can you articulate his criteria?
3. Ciardi agrees with Wagner that it is self-evidently absurd to write contradictory reviews of the same book. But is that necessarily true if these reviews are directed to quite different audiences, with different tastes and expectations?
4. Is Ciardi a bully? How does he defend his right to attack a target such as Lindbergh? Has he violated etiquette? Should etiquette be a consideration in reviewing?
5. Why does Ciardi feel compelled to stake his popularity on such an issue? What does he think would have been compromised if he had passed over the book in silence?
6. How did Ciardi miscalculate his *Saturday Review* audience in his original essay? What values did they place higher than his principles of good poetry? Do you think it likely that his defense of his review placated his critics?

SUGGESTIONS FOR WRITING

1. At the end of his defense, Ciardi articulates the eight principles that a good review should follow. Find a review of any "performance," whether book, movie, or music, and evaluate it according to Ciardi's criteria. Address your evaluation to the review's author.
2. Write your own review of any public production according to Ciardi's eight principles. Shape it for a publication that typically reviews such performances.
3. Construct a refutation of both Ciardi's original review of Lindbergh's poems and his subsequent defense. Or find a copy of *The Unicorn* and write your own review of it. You can aim at *Saturday Review*'s audience or your classmates.
4. Write two reviews of the same work for different audiences, one for an audience of local newspaper readers, the other for a special-interest audience defined by age, religion, sex, or expertise.
5. Examine all the reviews in a specific issue of a review publication (e.g., the Book Review Section of the *New York Times*), or a number of reviews appearing over a short time in the same publication (e.g., *Time* or *Newsweek*), or all the reviews of one work (consult the *Book Review Index*). What different criteria do these analogous sets of reviews observe? Address your analysis to the book review editors of the publications you have examined.
6. Using the data you assembled in suggestion 5, can you confirm or refute Ciardi's contention that reviews tend to be generally and spinelessly favorable?

— →» «← —

The Declaration of Independence

THOMAS JEFFERSON

— →» «← —

The Seneca Falls Declaration

ELIZABETH CADY STANTON

The purpose of an argument is often complex, and so is the relationship of one argument to another. The Declaration of Independence certainly looks like an argument addressed to an opposition, but we can assume that Thomas Jefferson labored under no illusion that his words would convince King George III that England had indeed exploited the colonies or that those colonies ought to be free and independent states. More realistically, the Declaration could be expected to increase solidarity among the Americans, to move some of the undecided to join the revolutionary cause, and to justify the colonies' action to the rest of the world.

One hundred years later at the Seneca Falls Convention of the women's rights movement, when Elizabeth Cady Stanton adapted Jefferson's ringing phrases to the cause of women's rights, she too could have had few illusions about the struggle she was initiating. She made a bold stroke by forcing her readers to parallel women's struggle for independence with America's, but she was at the same time warning women to expect a struggle. Even rights perceived as inalienable must be fought for.

Stanton's adoption of the words and form of the Declaration of Independence implied a criticism, even a refutation, of it: The earlier document does not mention women, and the freedom it proclaimed did not include them. The best Stanton could hope was that her manifesto would rebuke her opponents and unite women in a cause they could embrace as fully compatible with patriotism.

"The Declaration of Independence"

IN CONGRESS, JULY 4, 1776.

THE UNANIMOUS DECLARATION of the thirteen united STATES OF AMERICA.

When in the Course of human events, it becomes necessary for one people to dissolve the political bands which have connected them with another, and to assume among the powers of the earth, the separate and equal station to which the Laws of Nature and of Nature's God entitle them, a decent respect to the opinions of mankind requires that they should declare the causes which impel them to the separation.——— We hold these truths to be self-evident, that all men are created equal, that they are endowed by their Creator with certain unalienable Rights, that among these are Life, Liberty and the pursuit of Happiness.—That to secure these rights, Governments are instituted among Men, deriving their just powers from the consent of the governed.—That whenever any Form of Government becomes destructive of these ends, it is the Right of the People to alter or to abolish it, and to institute new Government, laying its foundation on such principles and organizing its powers in such form, as to them shall seem most likely to effect their Safety and Happiness. Prudence, indeed, will dictate that Governments long established should not be changed for light and transient causes;

and accordingly all experience hath shewn, that mankind are more disposed to suffer, while evils are sufferable, than to right themselves by abolishing the forms to which they are accustomed. But when a long train of abuses and usurpations, pursuing invariably the same Object evinces a design to reduce them under absolute Despotism, it is their right, it is their duty, to throw off such Government, and to provide new Guards for their future security.—Such has been the patient sufferance of these Colonies; and such is now the necessity which constrains them to alter their former Systems of Government. The history of the present King of Great Britain is a history of repeated injuries and usurpations, all having in direct object the establishment of an absolute Tyranny over these States. To prove this, let Facts be submitted to a candid world.

——He has refused his Assent to Laws, the most wholesome and necessary for the public good.——He has forbidden his Governors to pass Laws of immediate and pressing importance, unless suspended in their operation till his Assent should be obtained; and when so suspended, he has utterly neglected to attend to them.——He has refused to pass other Laws for the accommodation of large districts of people, unless those people would relinquish the right of Representation in the Legislature, a right inestimable to them and formidable to tyrants only.——He has called together legislative bodies at places unusual, uncomfortable, and distant from the depository of their public Records, for the sole purpose of fatiguing them into compliance with his measures.——He has dissolved Representative Houses repeatedly, for opposing with manly firmness his invasions on the rights of the people.

——He has refused for a long time, after such dissolutions, to cause others to be elected; whereby the Legislative powers, incapable of Annihilation, have returned to the People at large for their exercise; the State remaining in the mean time exposed to all the dangers of invasion from without, and convulsions within.——He has endeavoured to prevent the population of these States; for that purpose obstructing the Laws for Naturalization of Foreigners; refusing to pass others to encourage their migrations hither, and raising the conditions of new Appropriations of Lands.——He has obstructed the Administration of Justice, by refusing his Assent to Laws for establishing Judiciary powers.—— He has made Judges dependent on his Will alone, for the tenure of their offices, and the amount and payment of their salaries.——He has erected a multitude of New Offices, and sent hither swarms of Officers to harass our people, and eat out their substance.——He has kept among us, in times of peace, Standing Armies without the Consent of our legislatures.——He has affected to render the Military independent of and superior to the Civil power.————He has combined with others to subject us to a jurisdiction foreign to our constitution, and unacknowledged by our laws; giving his Assent to their Acts of pretended Legislation:—For Quartering large bodies of armed troops among us:—For protecting them, by a mock Trial, from punishment for any Murders which they should commit on the Inhabitants of these States:—For cutting off our Trade with all parts of the world:—For imposing Taxes on us without our Consent:—For depriving us in many cases, of the benefits of Trial by Jury:—For transporting us beyond Seas to be tried for pretended offences:—For abolishing the free System of English Laws in a neighbouring Province, establishing therein an Arbitrary government, and enlarging its Boundaries so as to render it at once an example and fit instrument for introducing the same absolute rule into these Colonies:—For taking away our Charters, abolishing our most valuable Laws, and altering fundamentally the Forms of our Governments:—For suspending our own Legislatures, and declaring themselves invested with power to legislate for us in all cases whatsoever.—He has abdicated Government here, by declaring us out of his Protection and waging War against us:—He has plundered our seas, ravaged our Coasts, burnt our towns, and destroyed the lives of our people.—He is at this time transporting large Armies of foreign Mercenaries to compleat the works of death, desolation and tyranny, already begun with circumstances of Cruelty & Perfidy scarcely paralleled in the most barbarous ages, and totally unworthy the Head of a civilized nation.—He has constrained our fellow Citizens taken Captive on the high Seas to bear Arms against their Country, to become the executioners of their friends and Brethren, or to fall themselves by their Hands.—He has excited domestic insurrections amongst us, and has endeavoured to bring on the inhabitants of our frontiers, the merciless Indian Savages, whose known rule of warfare, is an undistinguished destruction of all ages, sexes and conditions. In every stage of these Oppressions We have Petitioned for Redress in the most humble terms: Our repeated Petitions have been answered only by repeated injury. A Prince, whose character is thus marked by every act which may define a Tyrant, is unfit to be the ruler of a free people. Nor have We been wanting in attentions to our British brethren. We have warned them from time to time of attempts by their legislature to extend an unwarrantable jurisdiction over us. We have reminded them of the circumstances of our emigration and settlement here. We have appealed to their native justice and magnanimity, and we have conjured them by the ties of our common kindred to disavow these usurpations, which, would inevitably interrupt our connections and correspondence. They too have been deaf to the voice of justice and of consanguinity. We must, therefore, acquiesce in the necessity, which denounces our Separation, and hold them, as we hold the rest of mankind, Enemies in War, in Peace Friends.

WE, THEREFORE, the Representatives of the UNITED STATES OF AMERICA, in General Congress Assembled, appealing to the Supreme Judge of the world for the rectitude of our intentions, do, in the Name and by Authority of the good People of these Colonies, solemnly publish and declare, That these United Colonies are, and of Right ought to be FREE AND INDEPENDENT STATES; that they are Absolved from all Allegiance to the British Crown, and that all political connection between them and the State of Great Britain, is and ought to be totally dissolved; and that as Free and Independent States, they have full Power to levy War, conclude Peace, contract Alliances, establish Commerce, and to do all other Acts and Things which Independent States may of right do. ————And for the support of this Declaration, with a firm reliance on the protection of divine Providence, we mutually pledge to each other our Lives, our Fortunes and our sacred Honor.

"Declaration of Sentiments and Resolutions"

When, in the course of human events, it becomes necessary for one portion of the family of man to assume among the people of the earth a position different from that which they have hitherto occupied, but one to which the laws of nature and of nature's God entitle them, a decent respect to the opinions of mankind requires that they should declare the causes that impel them to such a course.

We hold these truths to be self-evident: that all men and women are created equal; that they are endowed by their Creator with certain inalienable rights; that among these are life, liberty, and the pursuit of happiness; that to secure these rights governments are instituted, deriving their just powers from the consent of the governed. Whenever any form of government becomes destructive of these ends, it is the right of those who suffer from it to refuse allegiance to it, and to insist upon the institution of a new government, laying its foundation on such principles, and organizing its powers in such form, as to them shall seem most likely to effect their safety and happiness. Prudence, indeed, will dictate that governments long established should not be changed for light and transient causes; and accordingly all experience hath shown that mankind are more disposed to suffer, while evils are sufferable, than to right themselves by abolishing the forms to which they were accustomed. But when a long train of abuses and usurpations, pursuing invariably the same object evinces a design to reduce them under absolute despotism, it is their duty to throw off such government, and to provide new guards for their future security. Such has been the patient sufferance of the women under this government, and such is now the necessity which constrains them to demand the equal station to which they are entitled.

The history of mankind is a history of repeated injuries and usurpations on the part of man toward woman, having in direct object the establishment of an absolute tyranny over her. To prove this, let facts be submitted to a candid world.

He has never permitted her to exercise her inalienable right to the elective franchise.

He has compelled her to submit to laws, in the formation of which she had no voice.

He has withheld from her rights which are given to the most ignorant and degraded men—both natives and foreigners.

Having deprived her of this first right of a citizen, the elective franchise, thereby leaving her without representation in the halls of legislation, he has oppressed her on all sides.

He has made her, if married, in the eye of the law, civilly dead.

He has taken from her all right in property, even to the wages she earns.

He has made her, morally, an irresponsible being, as she can commit many crimes with impunity, provided they be done in the presence of her husband. In the covenant of marriage, she is compelled to promise obedience to her husband, he becoming, to all intents and purposes, her master—the law giving him power to deprive her of her liberty, and to administer chastisement.

He has so framed the laws of divorce, as to what shall be the proper causes, and in case of separation, to whom the guardianship of the children shall be given, as to be wholly regardless of the happiness of women—the law, in all cases, going upon a false supposition of the supremacy of man, and giving all power into his hands.

After depriving her of all rights as a married woman, if single, and the owner of property, he has taxed her to support a government which recognizes her only when her property can be made profitable to it.

He has monopolized nearly all the profitable employments, and from those she is permitted to follow, she receives but a scanty remuneration. He closes against her all the avenues to wealth and distinction which he considers most honorable to himself. As a teacher of theology, medicine, or law, she is not known.

He has denied her the facilities for obtaining a thorough education, all colleges being closed against her.

He allows her in Church, as well as State, but a subordinate position, claiming Apostolic authority for her exclusion from the ministry, and, with some exceptions, from any public participation in the affairs of the Church.

He has created a false public sentiment by giving to the world a different code of morals for men and women, by which moral delinquencies which exclude women from society, are not only tolerated, but deemed of little account in man.

He has usurped the prerogative of Jehovah himself, claiming it as his right to assign for her a sphere of action, when that belongs to her conscience and to her God.

He has endeavored, in every way that he could, to destroy her confidence in her own powers, to lessen her self-respect, and to make her willing to lead a dependent and abject life.

Now, in view of this entire disfranchisement of one-half the people of this country, their social and religious degradation—in view of the unjust laws above mentioned, and because women do feel themselves aggrieved, oppressed, and fraudulently deprived of their most sacred rights, we insist that they have immediate admission to all the rights and privileges which belong to them as citizens of the United States.

In entering upon the great work before us, we anticipate no small amount of misconception, misrepresentation, and ridicule; but we shall use every instrumentality within our power to effect our object. We shall employ agents, circulate tracts, petition the State and National legislatures, and endeavor to enlist the pulpit and the press in our behalf. We hope this Convention will be followed by a series of Conventions embracing every part of the country.

. . .

WHEREAS, The great precept of nature is conceded to be, that "man shall pursue his own true and substantial happiness." Blackstone in his Commentaries remarks, that this law of Nature being coeval with mankind, and dictated by God himself, is of course superior in obligation to any other. It is binding over all the globe, in all countries and at all times; no human laws are of any validity if contrary to this, and such of them as are valid, derive all their force, and all their validity, and all their authority, mediately and immediately, from this original; therefore,

Resolved, That such laws as conflict, in any way, with the true and substantial happiness of woman, are contrary to the great precept of nature and of no validity, for this is "superior in obligation to any other."

Resolved, That all laws which prevent woman from occupying such a station in society as her conscience shall dictate, or which place her in a position inferior to that of man, are contrary to the great precept of nature, and therefore of no force or authority.

Resolved, That woman is man's equal—was intended to be so by the Creator, and the highest good of the race demands that she should be recognized as such.

Resolved, That the women of this country ought to be enlightened in regard to the laws under which they live, that they may no longer publish their degradation by declaring themselves satisfied with their present position, nor their ignorance, by asserting that they have all the rights they want.

Resolved, That inasmuch as man, while claiming for himself intellectual superiority, does accord to woman moral superiority, it is preeminently his duty to encourage her to speak and teach, as she has an opportunity, in all religious assemblies.

Resolved, That the same amount of virtue, delicacy, and refinement of behavior that is required of woman in the social state, should also be required of man, and the same transgressions should be visited with equal severity on both man and woman.

Resolved, That the objection of indelicacy and impropriety, which is so often brought against woman when she addresses a public audience, comes with a very ill-grace from those who encourage, by their attendance, her appearance on the stage, in the concert, or in feats of the circus.

Resolved, That woman has too long rested satisfied in the circumscribed limits which corrupt customs and a perverted application of the Scriptures have marked out for her, and that it is time she should move in the enlarged sphere which her great Creator has assigned her.

Resolved, That it is the duty of the women of this country to secure to themselves their sacred right to the elective franchise.

Resolved, That the equality of human rights results necessarily from the fact of the identity of the race in capabilities and responsibilities.

Resolved, therefore, That, being invested by the Creator with the same capabilities, and the same consciousness of responsibility for their exercise, it is demonstrably the right and duty of woman, equally with man, to promote every righteous cause by every righteous means; and especially in regard to the great subjects of morals and religion, it is self-evidently her right to participate with her brother in teaching them, both in private and in public, by writing and by speaking, by any instrumentalities proper to be used, and in any assemblies proper to be held; and this being a self-evident truth growing out of the divinely implanted principles of human nature, any custom or authority adverse to it, whether modern or wearing the hoary sanction of antiquity, is to be regarded as a self-evident falsehood, and at war with mankind.

. . .

Resolved, That the speedy success of our cause depends upon the zealous and untiring efforts of both men and women, for the overthrow of the monopoly of the pulpit, and for the securing to woman an equal participation with men in the various trades, professions, and commerce.

QUESTIONS FOR DISCUSSION

1. Why did the women of the Seneca Falls convention give their declaration almost exactly the same opening as the Declaration of Independence? Is there any difference in the principles they appeal to? What is the significance of any slight differences in wording?
2. To whom does the "he" in the two declarations refer? What is the rhetorical effect of the catalog of abuses, all beginning in the same way? What associations are added to the second by its reflection of the first?
3. How do the aims of the two declarations differ? Do the women want the dissolution of a form of government?
4. At what audience is the Seneca Falls Declaration directed? Does its audience differ from that of the Declaration of Independence? In what ways were both documents aimed at their own sponsors?
5. Why do the women not simply stop when they declare themselves free and equal to men? Why, in other words, do they not make their document absolutely symmetrical to the Declaration of Independence? Why do they go on to resolutions?
6. Can you detect any difference between the voice or style or method of argument in either declaration that would lead you to call one "male" and the other "female"?

SUGGESTIONS FOR WRITING

1. Decide to what extent the resolutions of the Seneca Falls Declaration have been accomplished and write an updated "Declaration," addressed at women of today, resolving to redress the inequities remaining.
2. Compare the goals of the women's movement today with those expressed in the Seneca Falls Declaration [1876] and characterize the difference between the two movements either for an audience of NOW members or for unaffiliated women.
3. The Declaration of Independence is obviously not written to persuade George III to change his ways toward the colonies. Try rewriting it as though your purpose were to persuade the king to treat the colonies better and to end the war that had just begun.
4. On any subject of your choice, write a "Declaration" demanding change based on a catalog of abuses. Make your language as emotional and powerful as the two declarations you just read. Like the declarations you just read, yours will be speaking to both those wronged and those who have the power to correct the wrong.
5. Both of these declarations argue from universal principles, yet it is often practical and economic factors that determine the political status of groups. Examine the economic causes or effects of the participation or exclusion of women in any particular industry, whether union dominated or not. Address your argument to the discriminating institution.